GLOBAL TRIBE

Studies in Popular Music
Series Editors: Alyn Shipton, journalist, broadcaster and lecturer in jazz history at the Royal Academy of Music, London, and at City University, London, and Christopher Partridge, Professor of Religious Studies, Lancaster University.

From jazz to reggae, bhangra to heavy metal, electronica to qawwali, and from production to consumption, Studies in Popular Music is a multi-disciplinary series which aims to contribute to a comprehensive understanding of popular music. It will provide analyses of theoretical perspectives, a broad range of case studies, and discussion of key issues.

Published

Dub in Babylon: Understanding the Evolution and Significance of Dub Reggae in Jamaica and Britain from King Tubby to Post-Punk
Christopher Partridge

Nick Cave: A Study of Love, Death and Apocalypse
Roland Boer

Open Up the Doors: Music in the Modern Church
Mark Evans

Send in the Clones: A Cultural Study of the Tribute Band
Georgina Gregory

Technomad: Global Raving Countercultures
Graham St John

The Lost Women of Rock Music: Female Musicians of the Punk Era (second edition)
Helen Reddington

Forthcoming

Heavy Metal: Controversies and Countercultures
Edited by Titus Hjelm, Keith Kahn-Harris and Mark LeVine

Global Tribe

Technology, Spirituality and Psytrance

Graham St John

SHEFFIELD UK BRISTOL CT

Published by Equinox Publishing Ltd.
UK: Unit S3, Kelham House, 3 Lancaster Street, Sheffield, S3 8AF
USA: ISD, 70 Enterprise Drive, Bristol, CT 06010

www.equinoxpub.com

First published 2012

ISBN 978-1-84553-955-9 (hardback)
978-1-84553-956-6 (paperback)

British Library Cataloguing-in-Publication Data

A catalogue record for this book is available from the British Library.

Library of Congress Cataloging-in-Publication Data

St. John, Graham, 1968-
Global tribe : technology, spirituality and psytrance / Graham St John.
p. cm.—(Studies in popular music)
Includes bibliographical references and index.
ISBN 978-1-84553-955-9 (hardcover)—ISBN 978-1-84553-956-6 (pbk.)
1. Trance (Underground dance music)—Social aspects. 2. Trance (Underground dance music)—History and criticism. I. Title.
ML3918.U53S7 2012
781.648—dc23

2012007643

Typeset by S.J.I. Services, New Delhi
Printed and bound by Lightning Source UK Ltd., Milton Keynes

Contents

Keep squeezing drops of the sun from your prayers and work and
music and from your companions' beautiful laughter
And from the most insignificant movements of your own body.
Now Sweet One, be wise.
Cast all your votes for dancing!

Hafiz (from *I Heard God Laughing: Renderings of Hafiz.*
Trans. Daniel Ladinsky)

Acknowledgements

This book has been many years in the making. My experience at events in over a dozen countries has directly and indirectly informed the project, the completion of which I owe to a variety of organizations, events and individuals who've offered institutional support, fieldwork opportunities, scholarly feedback and friendship. Scores agreed to be interviewed or otherwise responded to inquiries. The responses of many were parsed, while the spirit and generosity of countless others remains evident throughout. Over the course of writing, I met fellow researchers and enthusiasts of psyculture and EDM, many of whom I have collaborated with in research and writing.

Support for the project was provided to me in my capacity as Residential Scholar and Social Science Research Council Research Fellow at the School for Advanced Research (formerly the School for American Research) in Santa Fe, New Mexico (2006–2007). In 2008–2009 I was the recipient of a Postdoctoral Research Fellowship in Interactive Media and Performance in the Department of Media Production and Studies at the University of Regina, Saskatchewan. My gratitude extends to Dr Charity Marsh. From 2006–2012 I was an Honorary Research Associate at the Centre for Critical and Cultural Studies at the University of Queensland, Australia, and Director of the CCCS, Prof Graeme Turner, was most supportive.

I extend thanks to friends in Australia, my country of birth, where I gained inspiration for the book in the mid-1990s. My first doof (outdoor dance party) was at the Easter 1995 ConFest, the event which formed the subject of my PhD thesis, and it was at these events where I met DJ Krusty, Robin "Mutoid" Cooke, and others who inspired further research adventures. Over the next years, I attended a host of formative festivals, including Earthcore, Rainbow Serpent, Psycorroboree, Tranceplant, Earthdream, Exodus, Earthdance, Earth Freq, Maitreya and Tribeadelic.

There is a long list of gracious hosts in various countries to whom I am indebted. I've been especially privileged to be hosted on more occasions than

I can recall in Haight-Ashbury at Jay Walsh's place. Jay's capacity to make toasted cheese sandwiches in extreme conditions is unparalleled. Michael and Jen were super-gracious also in the upper Haight for (sometimes extended) periods between 2003–2012. "Coach" Ted Edwards and Barbara Rose Johnston hosted me on the deck under magnificent redwoods in Felton, California, on visits between 2007–2012. Eric and Natalie hosted me in Madison WI (2007, 2008, 2009), handing me the keys to the SS *Erwinstrasse* captained during the crucial Freiburg phase, Germany (August–September 2011), where the book was ultimately beaten into submission. And certainly far from least, Paris McKenzie and nanobrain in Melbourne and Kathleen Williamson at the Rose Road Mystery School, Nimbin, were towering supports over the extended period of hard labour.

But there were many others who were generous and salubrious hosts over the course of the book's production. As something of a loose chronology, these include: Paolo in Bolognia (2005), Damo and the Pyrland Rd house in London (2006, 2010), Mattias, Simona and Natalie in Berlin (2006), Luis Vasconcelos in Lisbon and Idanha-a-Nova (2006), Lee Gilmore and Ron Meiners in San Francisco (2006), Chiara in Chianti, Tuscany (2007), Gitte in Berlin (2007), Wolfgang and the Alice/Connecta crew (in Germany in 2007, Paris in 2010 and Fusion Festival in 2011), Susanne in Frankfurt (2007), Joshua and Sayaka in Mitzpe Ramon, Israel (2007), Sally in Brisbane (2008), Callum in Melbourne (2008, 2011), Tobias, Cato and family (Whistler and Quadra, British Columbia, 2008), Dallas and Erin in Venice Beach, LA (2007, 2008), Seth and Emily in San Francisco (2009), Boti and Zoli in Budapest (2009, 2010), Joe and Mickey in Melbourne (2009, 2010), Sean and Kristen in Brisbane (2010), Pascal in Berlin (2010), Mattias in Berlin (2011 and 2012), Joachim in Vienna (2011) and Norm at Sheepwash Cove (2011–2012).

There are numerous individuals whose generosity of spirit have left a mark on this work. Steve "Madras" Devas and "Blond" Peter Thomas were important links to the earlier, pre-electronic, Goa period. Both have provided valuable insights through their own ebullient and incisive observations on the formative era of the 1970s. Through these links I gained an understanding of the diversity of the formative period that has shaped subsequent developments. Ray Castle, Goa Gil, Fred Disko, Anders Tillman, Paoli Münchenbach, Raja Ram, Swami Chaitanya, Nikki Lastreto and Nik Sequenci, all interviewed and badgered at various times, have been indispensible to the understanding I have formed of the emergence documented. Others who've patiently transmitted crucial information, leads and feedback on the emergence and translation of Goa/psytrance included Brad "Santosh" Olsen, Mark Petrick (Xenomorph), Jenya Nesmeyanov, Dave Mothersole, David Bleach and Becca Dakini. There are countless others who've provided inspiration, direct and indirect, for this project, and whose ideas, practices and generosity have made this book possible. Among the beacons and inspirators are Albert Hofmann,

Terence McKenna, Alexander Shulgin, Youth, Simon Posford, Simon Ghahary, Dick Trevor, Alex Grey, Larry Harvey, Marion Goodell, Erik Davis, Julian Palmer, Mr Ed, Rak Razam, Tim Parish, Peter Anderschitz, Gwyllm Llwydd, Chiara Baldini, Psilly. Not the least, Michael Gosney, Wolfgang Sterneck, John-Paris McKenzie and the late Fraser Clark were all extraordinarily helpful.

Various personnel in management roles and crew camps at a host of parties have been supportive, including providing me with admission, or simply accepting my presence. Frank and Felix and King Richard Martin from Rainbow Serpent; Alan Bamford and others from Tranceplant; Urs, Happy People Productions and Exodus Cybertribal Gathering; Paul Abad and Earth Freq; Paris and Freedom; the crew at Soulclipse in Turkey 2006; Camp Low Expectations at Burning Man (2003, 2006, 2008), especially Jessica, Lee, Hungry Tim and Michael Wolf; Dallas, Erin, Dela and Treavor from Moontribe; Diogo Ruivo, Artur Soares Da Silva, Naasko Wripple, Carey Thompson, Delvin, Luis, Chiara and many others at Boom 2006, 2008, 2010; Haris Papadimitriou and the Island of Fire Festival, Greece, 2007; Asher Haviv and the Holy Rave; Boris Levit and the TAZ, 2007; Lachie and Sophie of the Maitreya Festival; Pascal and Stephan at Indian Spirit 2010; Nick Ladd and The Glade crew in 2006; Sunrise Celebration 2006; Eamon "Jungle" Wyss, Oakies and Psycorroboree; Brad Olsen and Will Gregory of the Consortium of Collective Consciousness, and Steve Peake from London's Synergy Project.

Many scholars and friends offered invaluable feedback at various stages and in various ways throughout this project. Among them are Chiara Baldini, Hillegonda Rietveld, Chris Partridge, Lee Gilmore, tobias c. van Veen, Eliot Bates and Geert Lovink, along with Joshua Schmidt, Charles De Ledesma, Rupert Till, François Gauthier, Des Tramacchi, Anna Gavanas, Charity Marsh, Sean Nye, Evan Martin, Bel Belleza and Kath O'Donnell. Many on the Dancecult-L email list were very helpful. My period at the School for Advanced Research (SAR) 2006–2007 was particularly fruitful. My gratitude goes to SAR President James Brooks and the entire board of the SAR, not least of all Susan Foote, along with librarian Laura Holt, and staff scholars Rebecca Allahyari, Nancy Owen Lewis, John Kantner, and Martha and Elizabeth White for their valuable initiatives, support and inspiration. Fellow residential scholars at the SAR for the Centenary Year were a supportive crew: Eric Haanstad, Barbara Rose Johnson, "Coach" Ted Edwards, Noenoe K. Silva, Erica Bornstein, Aneesh Aneesh and Julie Velasquez-Runk.

Many thanks to the photographers who have permitted reproduction of their work: Jonathan Carmichael, Fred Disko, Kitty, aka Vagabond Forest, Gilbert Garcia, Harry Gatty, Goa Gil, Jakob Kolar, Luc Pliot, Pascal Querner and Rémy-Pierre Ribiere. I also thank Adam Scott Miller, Miki Spacetribe, Ian Ion/ThinkElectric and Symbolika (Fabian Klainman) for allowing reproduction of artwork. *Global Tribe*'s cover design was created by Symbolika (www.symbolika.com) with background design by Gwyllm Llwydd (gwyllm-art.com). I also thank Leslie Ann Dutcher for her gracious advice regarding the contract.

Finally, special thanks are due to my friends and partners in the sublime in Australia and elsewhere: Alan, B, Arun, Ben and Patch, Boti, Callum, Claudia and Michael R. Damo, Dr Dave, Didac, Elena, Eric and Natalie, Myz Guidance, Ian, Jay, Jen, Joachim, Spaceship Joe, Jules, Karl, Kitty, Kristen, DJ Krusty, Colonel Kurtz, Marco, Mari Kundalini, Megan, Michael U, Mouse, nanobrain, Paris, Pascal, Paulie, Rak, King Richard, Robin M, Sean the Maltese Falcon and Mish Falconesse, Seano, Sergi, Seth, Shane, Sjoerd, Stephan, Stormin Norman, Ted, Tim and Lulu, Tobias, Yoni Alberti, Yoni Psionic, Xuso, and others who I have undoubtedly forgotten.

1 Transnational psyculture

They occupy the Temple in the thousands. At the dusk of a scorching day, in outfits with vivid fractal designs, alien insignia, ॐ symbols and geometric mandala patterns, they arrive in cohorts who've journeyed from a multitude of national embarkation points. With utility-belts slinked at the waist and dreadlocks knotted back, imprinted with futuristic glyphs, etched in tribal tattoos and marked by facial piercings, they come bearing gifts of specially prepared decoctions, meads, herbal mixes, *ganja* cakes, crystal powders, beer and other intoxicants, along with fruits and energy supplements they will share among friends and strangers encountered through the night, and into the day. Entering this vast hexagonal covered arena, the noise of the surrounding festival recedes as occupants are enveloped in "3D sound" controlled from a stage upon which rests a stellated dodecahedron portal within which scheduled DJs perform the hypnotic bass and rhythm patterns of electronic trance music dictating a compulsion on the part of those present to become activated by moves. And as the natural light fades, the Temple is enlivened with psychotropic projections, morphing geometric laser patterns and blacklights triggering ultraviolet reactive designs and illuminating the awestruck appearances of Temple dancers who will carve shapes into the night. At one side of this structure, groups huddle under luminescent *Day of the Triffids*-like installations crafted from recycled material, and all around the edges the enthused are lost to engrossing acrobatic displays, spinning fire staff and twirling LED *poi* with stunning light-trail effects. Into the early hours of the morning, the intensity of furious-paced "darkpsy" transits towards uplifting and melodic sounds as the Sun clears the horizon and begins its journey over the sky's proscenium arch.

It's mid-summer in Portugal, at the tail end of August 2010, and I'm on one of the most expansive and impressive outdoor dance floors on the planet. The Dance Temple is integral to the biennial Boom Festival held in central-eastern Portugal near the protected area Parque do Tejo Internacional and the village of Idanha-a-Nova. An eight-day event, Boom is the premiere production in world psychedelic trance (psytrance) and visionary arts culture, with its Temple attracting near 25,000 people holding passports from approximately seventy countries.[1] If there's a global centre of *psyculture*, this is it. Inside the Dance Temple, I'm immersed in a soundbath of languages and caught in a blizzard of sensory impressions. Up on stage, an artist is DJing from a laptop and orchestrating a sonic broadside incorporating hypnotic melody lines around persistent and seductive bass-lines. Frequencies amplified through the sound system enervate my whole being. Time passes, and I too pass outside of normal time. And within this prolonged now, the optical grows rhythmic and sounds become visible. The national colour-codes and iconography of Japan, Israel, Sweden, Brazil and Australia, to name a few, blend with expatriate gestures, not dissimilar to those performed by forebears in Goa, India, the birthplace of Goatrance, the formative dance movement from which psytrance and its various subgenres grew. There's possibly 10,000 people on and around this dance floor at this moment, a vast congregation of fleshy gesticulations, its habitués performing the international hand and foot signals of trance. I feel like I've landed among a community in exile. There's multiple personal, lifestyle and cultural concerns this community's inhabitants have sought exodus from, and at this moment they're communicating their desires in the expressive mode of dance. And, as I slide into the groove, I feel like I've come home.

As I turn about, I'm face-whipped by a woman with long black dreadlocks. Commanding a wicked stomp, she's beside herself. Nearby, a Japanese freak in his early thirties stands astride jabbing at unseen soap bubbles up ahead. He's joined by compatriots in carnage alive on the pulse. An Italian girl in fairy wings swivels gracefully four-stepping in perfect unison with the beat. A German freak, who I recognize by his unyielding grin, is cutting it up inside his own personal smoke cloud. Others clown around, hug their partners in the sublime, prepare a chillum, maintaining form amidst the mayhem. All about me, transnational beat freaks ride the 16th-note loop of psychedelic trance, compelled by its progression, acting as if everything depends on its maintenance, as if a faltering move will cause a collapse in the rhythm and a diminution of the vibe. And as we pass outside of ourselves, it seems to me that everyone has fallen into the slot, that zone which everybody knows though few can articulate – that moment in which nothing remains the same. "This is it". Grinning under bass pressure, my crazy Russian neighbour shouts something barely intelligible, something about the "mothership" we've boarded. Oscillating between self-dissolution and spectacular displays, its passengers are blissful abductees. Many producers have collaborated to steer our ship through the night. In transit, time's lost and the world is gained. Eventually, I snake my way across this incredible synesthetic stomping ground, idling to absorb kangaroo stilt performers jumping over gales of laughter.

Leaving this dance floor is like finding the best route out of a metropolis. Floating on a wave of exhilaration and the aromas of *chai*, *charas* and *changa*, eventually I emerge out of the Temple and disappear into the wider festival.

It was my third time at Boom, a world barometer on the state of psychedelic trance music and culture: *psyculture*. Even though it no longer identifies itself as a "psytrance" festival, this music dominates the schedule of its main venue (the Dance Temple). My attendance had been driven by a desire to participate in and observe trends in psytrance and the wider visionary arts culture, a research project that grew from my involvement in this scene since the mid-1990s in Melbourne, Australia. By 2010, this project had taken me to more than a dozen countries, and countless events, festivals and after-parties. Psytrance is a movement rooted in the live music scene of the 1970s flourishing in the former Portuguese colony of Goa, India, which had been overtaken by a seasonal DJ-led electronic music scene in the 1980s. Goa had attracted international travellers, artists and spiritual seekers since the 1960s, becoming an exotic outland of experimentation for musicians and expatriates in subsequent decades. It was the birthplace and proving grounds of a mutant dance music culture, which, by the mid-1990s, became marketed as Goa Trance (or Goatrance as it is denoted in this book). Following aesthetic shifts associated with analog, digital and virtual music technologies along with transitions in taste and demand, Goatrance later developed as psychedelic trance or psytrance, which splintered into numerous subgenres by the early 2000s. While these include progressive psychedelic (progpsy or progressive psy), darkpsy (dark psychedelic trance), full-on, psybreaks and suomisaundi (Finnish trance), a close connection is maintained with psychedelic ambient (sometimes referred to as "psybient") dub and with a fusional aesthetic sometimes referred to as "ethnodelic", all signs, sounds and scenes of a voracious "meta-genre" (Lindop 2010) providing the soundtracks and dancescapes for a diverse and contested cultural, or psycultural, movement.

This book is a post-Goa project. That is, it is a study of the Goatrance movement as it mushroomed around the world from the 1990s, attracting the designation "psytrance" by the end of that decade. Goa was the wellspring of this movement, and its role as a marginal cultural centre is unmistakable, but my empirical "field" for this project did not include Goa itself. As many commentators aver, Goa declined, or indeed was arguably destroyed, as a scene destination before Goatrance became a formulated and marketed genre by the mid-1990s. *Global Tribe* was conceived as a study of global psyculture in the early 2000s – that is, as a study of the global movement of Goa, as Goatrance (and then psytrance) was transposed to music, festivals and scenes around the world. Below I will refer to events that are crucial to the story narrated in this book and indelible to my own experience. But re-evaluating my original plans, a "global" project now seems overly ambitious, if not faintly ridiculous, since, as I came to realize, no single researcher can confidently establish a commanding view over the world of psytrance, whose culture is transnational, emergent and labyrinthine. It's a frankly impossible task, confirmed while leafing through the latest edition of *Psychedelic Traveller* magazine, a kind of *Rough Guide* for global psytrance enthusiasts with entries on dozens of nations, only a portion of which I have visited. Even the recent anthology *Goa: 20 Years of Psychedelic Trance* (Rom and Querner 2011),[2] to which dozens of participants in the scene have contributed, falls short of global coverage. A collection I recently edited, *The Local Scenes and Global Culture of Psytrance* (St John 2010a), was the first scholarly book to illuminate this global phenomenon. While that publication offered lenses on scenes around the world from a variety of disciplinary vantage points and through multiple methodologies, it could only angle short bursts of light on different aspects of this complex movement, and few details were offered on the music that characterizes its culture. Detailed ethnographic and documentary accounts of the transnationalism of this movement, the culture of its events, and the aesthetics of its music, were needed.

The book you're reading is the first attempt to achieve these specific objectives. This is performed through a combination of multi-sited ethnography involving my attendance at events (from small parties to large festivals) in over a dozen countries; interviews conducted *in situ* at events and conversations conducted electronically with DJs and other artists, event-organizers and promoters, partygoers, journalists and scholars; the analysis of movement niche and micro-media including magazines, net forums, websites, blogs, social media and promotional material; and a thoroughgoing cultural analysis of the music involving investigation of the vocal material sampled from popular cultural sources – commentaries, script and film scores from TV documentaries, cinema and computer games – and programmed into tracks by the producers of Goa/psytrance (what I call *nanomedia*). While this multi-pronged methodology is not musicological in approach, it has afforded insights across key interrelated areas: the roots of *psychedelia* and its implications for self and culture; the *dance* events (parties and festivals) that are the home of the *vibe* and the paramount rationale of dance *tribes*; the nature of *trance* in the contemporary world; variations on the techno-aesthetics of *transit* given the differing expectations of participants; and the *transnational* character of psyculture.

The book recognizes psychedelic trance culture as a globalized optimization of the post-1960s quest for *experience*, where music production, DJ performance and event technologies form a shifting assemblage dedicated to effecting transition. Rooted in a self-exiled bohemian traveller culture endogenous to radical modernity, travel (the journey, the "trip") is explicit to the aesthetic of psychedelic trance. Influenced by earlier forms (notably psychedelic rock), and with hermeticist and post-humanist orientations, Goa/psytrance redeploys popular culture to cultivate a *superliminal* context.

Hit the Floor. Photo: Harry Gatty. harrygatty@me.com

Emerging in a period of optimism (late 1980s to late 1990s) which saw the collapse of the Soviet Union and the end of the Cold War, the dismantling of apartheid, the birth of reconciliation movements, the popularization of MDMA and the introduction of the World Wide Web, a unique and yet diverse transnational movement evolved whose chief expression were parties, ephemeral open-air communities, impermanent-yet-perennial festivals in which ecstatic dancing to electronic music mixed by DJs remained the central activity. This development was achieved as individuals travelled physically from "home" locations and mentally from normative mind states, freedoms of movement enabled by relative disposable wealth and assisted by transpersonalizing digital, chemical and virtual media. Given the multiplicity of sites, expectations and aesthetics, the psychogeographic mobility experienced within this movement is characteristically heterogeneous, a chief consideration returned to throughout this book.

Global Tribe introduces a movement whose chief cause is dance, whose *raison d'être* is dancing, and whose primary vehicle is the dance floor, a sensual, salubrious and soulful drop-zone for expatriates, cultural fugitives and antinomians, a realm charged with the sensibilities of exodus heir to the Goa tradition. Enabling departures from dominant codes of practice and arrivals at alternative modes of being, the dance floor and the community proliferating around its verges, are built according to the design of a radical utopian imagination. In this virtual world, habitués imagine themselves as alien to the popstream, adopting the recombined insignia of ancients and extraterrestrials, the monstrous and the fabulous, the outlaw and outrageous. I call this virtual world *Disctopia*, a concept referring to a distributed place that is not synonymous or coincident with the ethnonational, but which nevertheless incorporates nationalities. Inhabitants of the exodus are participants in a transnational milieu whose common ground is the familial context of dance floors that may be inhabited by the same individuals across multiple countries and whose shared history is Goa.

Psyculture has emerged from a tradition in which the cultural exile is ascendant, the estranged figure who had chosen his/her departure from global risk, outlawed practice, existential despair, spiritual disenchantment, cognitive dissonance. Goa freak forebears were able to choose the "out" because their middle-class backgrounds provided the opportunity and the resources for their mobility. The self-exile is a figure in transit, a *freak* dwelling in that state of departure from lifeworld conditions. The life of self-exiles and their cultural progeny is a liminal life, the life of the traveller. Within the techno-spiritual counterculture, technics are adopted to assist mobility across physical sites (alternative regions, enclaves, markets and festivals in local and global circuits) and psychical terrain (the journey into the unconscious via yoga and meditation techniques as well as the use of psychedelics or "entheogens" such as LSD and DMT). While this is the transnational and transpersonal world of the trancer who harnesses artifice in his/her mobility, the freedoms sought and achieved are as multiple as the conditions of risk, constraint and oppression in the lifeworld. The liminality of the Goa vibe is, then, not driven by any singular promise of "freedom". Despite a standard "progressive" philosophy of unity, wholeness and becoming, the *psychedelic experience* is not an homogeneous social aesthetic. Variant motivations, expectations and figures, from the ecstatic to the visionary, the gothic to the cosmic, the transgressive to the proactive, then populate this movement. As this book demonstrates, one's freedom-seeking expatriation may conflict with that of other habitués, with members of the wider freak constituency perennially testing one another's legitimacy. This vibe of the exiles is in a state of perpetual re-optimization since shared exile assures compromise and collaboration on matters of mutual interest and survival, such as securing freedom from agents of predation (e.g. tourists, police), while in other circumstances disputes trigger the formation of new events and their fledgling vibes.

Initially buoyed by post-Soviet and Cyber Age optimism, and transiting through post-9/11 paranoia, psytrance has evolved over two decades and has been translated in dozens of nations where *psytribes* have adopted the architectonic of psychedelic trance under a variety of local conditions. This book begins to unravel the diversity of this culture while at the same time recognizing commonalities, the search for an enchanted sociality facilitated by technology and counteracting the demise of community amid the isolation, loneliness and privatization of modern life. Where the idealized "tribal" other is raised as a standard under which transnational communities dance, where textile fashions, body modifications, cover art, web designs, and music samples are pixilated, programmed and decaled with the signs of soft primitivism and Orientalism, and where "natives" serve to index "trance" or "shamanic" states for those seeking remedies for their modern afflictions, this retribalization is not unproblematic. Yet the sociality in which habitués are vested is often marked not by derivative and distorted tropes, or cultural theft, but by novel social experimentation with significant intercultural implications, from the regional to the planetary. Neither these social processes nor cultural outcomes will be recognized in approaches safely removed from the field of research and which defend singular predetermined narratives. From BC's Tribal Harmonix, to Melbourne's Tribeadelic, to Europe's Psy Tribe, event crews, production houses, entire scenes, adopt the "tribal" identifier as an expression of their desire to *be together*, a tendency which is less affectation than an intentional re-creation of community at the heart of which are sensual paroxysms – neither contrived nor borrowed, but lived and shared experiences.

Deviating from the anthropological invention and political recognition of "tribe", *psytribes* are characterized by freedom of choice, experimentalism and a polycentric fluidity of identification, all hallmarks of "neotribes" outlined by Michel Maffesoli (1996). Notably, these psytribes deploy a technics of remixology, shared with other techno-tribes of electronic dance music (EDM), which provides not only a common artifice but is a principal means of identification for cosmopolitan communities fusing diverse sonic influences and creating new cultural forms in the mix. Denoting a prevalent "mixillogical" sensibility, Kodwo Eshun offered insight on this via his take on George Russell's *Electronic Sonata*: a "fleeting friction of timbral incongruities [and] incompatible sound blocs rubbing against each other" (1998: 01[003]). The profusion of electronic music styles impacting and influencing populations who themselves continuously cut 'n' mix from this profusion speaks of the "compositional sensibilities" of the last few decades (Bennett 1999: 610), and of the "cosmopolitan emotion" (Rietveld 2010) felt by citizens of global cities who seek attachments outside ethnonationalism, circumstances oiled by post-1960s psychedelia, amplified by post-1980s electronic arts scenes, and virtualized by post-1990s–2000s net culture. Distanced from those aspects of "tribalism" associated with traditional or colonial contexts – e.g. hierarchies, homogeneiety, ethnocentrism, hostility – psychedelic tribalism can at least partially be recognized by what Ronald E. Rice identified in his foreword to *Electronic Tribes* (2008: viii) as those formations which "encourage individual identity", are based "primarily on frequency of interaction", possess fluid boundaries, and "heterarchies (webs, networks) instead of hierarchies (strict vertical subsets)". While *psy* "tribes" are not primarily "e-tribes", the electronic tribalism enabled by social networking platforms, and membership in e-tribes relating to genre, event promotion and management, label, and file sharing are integral.[3] Not unlike other EDM technotribes, in psytrance, electronic sound media, psychoactive compounds and internet communications media are assembled and purposed to maintain independence, with control over the means of production, distribution and perception established in ways only imagined by forebears.

The book identifies six interfaces, dynamics and tensions: (1) local and global; (2) self and tribe; (3) spiritual and technological; (4) transgressive and progressive; (5) roots and novelty; and (6) commercial and independent. At the first interface we witness the formation of scenes in which local (regional and national) party organizations, producers and DJs adapt technics, sample popular culture and remix aesthetics circulating as a result of globalization. Developments in electronic music production and performance since the 1970s, the revolution in digitalization in the 1980s–1990s and the networked virtualization of the 1990s–2000s, all cause and are effected by this "glocal" (Robertson 1994) process, and facilitate a translocal imagination (Appadurai 1996). Individual genius, vernacular translations and regional innovations feed back into the global milieu where experimentalism, syncretism and remixology ensure the reproduction of psyculture. Global cities and cosmopolitanism have been instrumental, overseeing these translocal flows but also contextualizing distinct modes of being together, or more accurately, *being altered together*, in the radically reflexive contexts of late modernity. The book adopts the *tribal* as an appropriate designation for these intensely social contexts, where formations are considered "global tribes" not only since they're rocked by the flows and infused with the products of globalization, but that they are also transnational, or *trance-national,* social formations, and self-consciously "global", a circumstance most evident in events such as Boom which promotes itself as a world-summit of visionary arts and trance, a "united tribe of the world". The "globality" that is of interest here is not simply a recognition of the "whole Earth", but a recognition of a world haunted by the threat of ecological apocalypse, economic collapse, humanitarian disaster and psychological turmoil.

The simultaneity of local and global elements within psytrance events yields a sociality where the term "tribe" designates both a distinct form of identification *and* the obliteration of difference, a dynamic native to neotribalism. This then introduces the second interface. In radical modernity, the disenchanted seek sensation, difference, expatriation in the radical immanence of the dance party, whose freak sociality potentiates the dissolution of difference (ethnonational, class, gender, sexuality, age). With the operation of what I call the *difference engine,* assembled technologies of the senses dubbed "psychedelic" – psychoactive compounds, music and audio systems, lighting and visual projections, décor, etc. – facilitate the (enduring) expression of *difference* via the (temporary) liquidation of *differences* via optimized and prolonged alteration of normative spatio-temporal conditions, a circumstance replicated across EDM, though hyperactivated in psychedelic trance.

In the third interface is found the formation of what I identify as *spiritechnics* – that is, technologies and techniques (analog, digital, chemical and cyber) that are purposed to spiritual ends. Researchers have noted the significance of spirituality to psytrance participants. For instance, Greener and Hollands (2006: 403) report that 75.2 per cent (351 people) of their survey respondents described themselves as "a spiritual person", and over a half of their respondents believed they are "on a spiritual path in life". These figures offer an important contrast to earlier attitudes towards "subcultures", where Paul Willis (1978: 86), for instance, referred to hippies' "illusory" goals of "transcendence and fuller states of awareness". Yet these figures prompt inquiry about the nature and variation of the "spiritual" experience of participants as they transpire *in situ*. Demonstrating influence from romanticism and transcendentalism, inflected with the turn to Eastern metaphysics, as well as traditions of shamanism in which, for example, *psilocybin* mushrooms, DMT and ayahuasca use are prominent, and heir to cross-esoteric and occultic currents – mystery cults, hermeticism, theosophy, ecologism and cybernetics – we approach a fuller understanding of what spirituality means for individual participants.

This leads to the fourth tension: activities associated with the extremes of transgression and the evolution of consciousness constitute contrasting expectations, disparate liminalities, with different purposes, logics and sources of prestige. That is, psytrance would become a cultural repository for heterogeneous causes and demands, definitions of "psychedelic", ideas of the holy, and mission objectives motivating its constituency. Psyculture thus inherits the dynamic tension between the ecstatic and proactive dispositions that is the legacy of a counterculture possessing its formative moments in the 1960s and 1970s. Countermanding causes, controversial aesthetics and different means of accomplishing transcendence generate quarrels, trigger schism and provoke modification of the festal interstices that are the chief cultural expression of this movement. For many crews, the party is designed according to the principal of pleasure, perhaps even coloured by a nostalgia for past events and whose outcome may be the desire to hold more parties. In some circumstances, party organizations are motivated to protect local scenes from the ever-present risks posed by state intervention, commercialization and popularity, while in other contexts events are vehicles for campaigns for alternative futures. They may become a platform for social movements concerned with drug reform and cognitive liberty, well-being practices, sustainable energy use, planetary culture, peace. Therefore, events become vehicles for the performance of a host of local and global agendas beyond the dance floor, and in many cases disparate agendas meet and are negotiated on those same floors.

In the fifth interface, we find the simultaneous commitment to the *origins* to which participants lay claim and the *original* work produced. This is the dynamic of *originality*. On the one hand, participants harness symbolic resources in the claiming of roots and heritage, the revival of tradition, the return to the primordial. On the other, they pursue innovation, iterating technique in novel formations. While protagonists return to nature, their identity becoming infused by that which is recognizably authentic, native and Earth-centred, identifications are also shaped by techno-ascensionist and extropian narratives. While some wish to claim a "revived" tribalism in which a romantic sensibility fuels festal life, others are motivated by the prospects of novel associations forming from the promethean promise of "cutting-edge" techniques. These "electribes" have been celebrated as new identifications, "new tribes forming with new codes and languages, out of zeros and ones, and electronic pattern forming devices" (Austin 1998). While the dance party may be timeless and familiar, it is also infused by strangeness. Across regions and continents, the psytribes forming to reproduce trance dance events, along with music producers, regularly enact hybrids of the congress of these aesthetics. The artifice of electronic music performs the dynamics of originality since works of origin are recognized at the same time as they are transmuted into original works. Remastering is performed in iterations whereby the "originals" are often lost in the appropriation, a process consistent with the growth of digital remix culture. Portmanteau terms like "technoshamanism", "technopagan", "psycorroboree" and "modern primitive" connote this mutability. The trance experience itself marks the simultaneity of the familiar and the novel, heritage and innovation, stasis and change. Under optimal conditions, the effect in trance is that *nothing changes*, the paradox inciting outrage and ridicule among "trance" detractors, and yet fuels the convictions, compulsions and devotions of the trance formed. While participants may sentimentalize reconnection with the past, the body and nature, the trance event occasions the re/fashioning of identifications deploying the optimizable assemblage of technics at the disposal of its habitués.

In the sixth and final tension, the psytrance milieu is rooted in dramatic and sustainable quests for independence facilitated by a DiY music industry, the accessibility of electronic instruments and production technologies, and the technics of remixology central to the arts of DJing. The internet has been integral to production, distribution (e.g. netlabels), promotions and discussion on webforums and social networking platforms. Within psytrance (as with other EDM industries), economic capital takes a back seat to informal cultural capital ensuring the estimation of artists and producers as "psychedelic", "conscious" or "visionary", and therefore noteworthy. Yet, while there is resistance to the economic popularization of music and culture, there exists an ambivalent collusion with proprietary forces commoditizing production and ensuring livelihoods. This is a common cause of concern within a countercultural milieu that is nevertheless reliant on reflexive capitalism. Thus the response to commercialization is facilitated, as Anthony D'Andrea (2007a: 3) recognizes, through global processes of hypermobility, digitalization and neoliberalism. It is also the case, however, that unscrupulous, unsustainable and unimaginative event management, in addition to onerous licensing laws, police intervention and the curtailment of autonomy, incite responses among experienced operators and fledgling crews to improvise or recreate psychedelic culture.

Notes on method and technique

The moon was full on the night of 10 June 2006. I was outside Tullamore, Ireland, at the psytrance festival Life, organized by Neutronix. I was zipped inside my tent in the shadow of Charleville Forest Castle. I'd just smoked a strong hit of *Salvia divinorum* and had been lying back for I don't know how long. Had I been screaming? Was "I" present at all? For how long had I been holding my breath? Previous experiences on lower strengths of this "teacher plant" taken for millennia by the Mazatec of Oaxaca, Mexico, to divine spiritual truths, had precipitated a cartoon-like spin cycle of patchworked memories. Those were ludicrous times. Now, however, it was no laughing matter. I finally remembered to breathe, a surfacing concurrent with a Category Five realization that everything I had known, all my memories, my identity, the history of the world as I knew it, and my own physical body, was design. All code. Many female voices were heard during this rupture, from around the festival, seeming to will me out of my coma, the grand deception called "life". While the precise meaning of this deception was unclear, the sensation of immortality was overwhelming. And it was terrifying, as while an eternity was exposed, it was one in which I was absent. My soul was not destined to comfortably terminate (with death) – even though "I" was. I had taken a glimpse across the final frontier, and I wasn't there. The wild screams and clamour of the festival outside my tent appeared like the confused response of the coders to my awakening, and while the precise nature of this revelation was unclear, the *feeling of knowing* was transfiguring. Eventually, dripping, I zipped from the tent-womb and moved towards the Gothic castle, guided by oak trees, psychedelic lights and an insistent bass-line.

Life Festival, Charleville Forest Castle, Tullamore, Ireland, June 2006. Photo: Graham St John.

My life rupture came more than ten years following my initial exposure to the sounds, sensibility and sociality of psychedelic trance music, in my homeland, Australia. Over Easter, 1995, I participated in an impromptu and unofficial doof at the alternative lifestyle festival ConFest, near Moama, New South Wales.[4] On the end of its earliest wave in Australia, filtered through experimental arts communities in Melbourne and Byron Bay in particular, on that night, Goatrance was detonated mid-festival by DJ Krusty – hours before someone spiked the generator with sugar. I was twenty-six years old. Not unlike countless converts, I spent years attempting to become reunited with the sounds punctuating that night – which had included tracks on releases from labels TIP, Dragonfly, Transient, Matsuri and Psy Harmonics. What I later recognized as psychedelic trance had an extraordinary power to unite people in dance, and would become the seamless anthem to an odyssey of backyard blitzkriegs, one-night stands and weekend festivals stretching across several thousand kilometres (and five states). Earthcore and Rainbow Serpent festivals, along with the earliest Earthdance events in Melbourne, Exodus in northeast New South Wales, and later Earth Freq in Queensland, became part of my annual cycle of events. In early December 2002, I attended the total solar eclipse festival, Outback Eclipse, near Lindhurst in South Australia. Over successive events and successive years of being animated, possessed and punished by this sound, and befriended by those gravitating to it, I was moved to understand what George Carlin meant when he said "those who dance are considered insane by those who cannot hear the music". But the music wasn't simply being heard. It was felt intensely, and networked communities were acting in the interests of its perpetuity. Immersion in this music culture connected me to a milieu that stretched around the world. Ten years following that fateful Easter, I experienced the first of many parties outside Australia (Sonica, Italy, 2005), and over the next six years I pitched my tent in temperate forests and in scorching deserts at festivals on several continents. Journeying across country, making camp in the direct firing line of gargantuan sound rigs or in chilled groves of gentle repose, a host of people came into my life, many of my closest friends, my family, lovers, interlocutors turned mates, mates becoming interlocutors: a cast of characters, pioneers and freaks whose many voices and sensitivities are found in this book.[5]

Research for the book saw my attendance at events with a diversity of styles, sizes and populations, and with a variety of agendas. From small warehouse parties to spectacular multi-staged mega-events such as that which celebrates Germany's reunification (Fusion Festival, where the Trance stage is one among some twenty sound stages). From small regional bush doofs in Australia to various manifestations of the annual Earthdance Carnival which in late September transpires simultaneously in hundreds of global locations. From a nomadic desert carnival through Central Australia (Earthdream, 2000) to the annual Burning Man Festival in Nevada's Black Rock Desert (on three occasions from 2003) to a one-off extravaganza in Israel's Negev (Holy Rave). From a festival in the grounds of a Gothic castle (Life, 2006) to a beach festival south of Agadir, Morocco (Rhythms of Peace) to a gathering held among magnificent sequoia trees in California's Yosemite National Park (Symbiosis, 2009). From small events such as a party held near Germany's Schwarzwald operated by the Institut für Sinnestäuschungen Schwarzwald (ISS) in 2006, to long-running events that are the cream of national scenes (e.g. Australia's Rainbow Serpent). From Goa Gil's annual birthday party in California to global gatherings descended upon by thousands from dozens of nations like Ozora in Hungary and Portugal's Boom. From events held with specific intent, such as Australia's Tranceplant (where native trees were planted) and Australia's Freedom (which celebrates Albert Hofmann's "first trip"), to events celebrated on cycles of the moon (e.g. California's Moontribe). And from these seasonal events to irregular festivals such as those mounted on the line of totality celebrating a total solar eclipse (e.g. Australia's Outback Eclipse and Turkey's Soulclipse).[6]

While participation in, interviews conducted and contacts made at these events were important to this study, it is a project that I had been formulating unconsciously for years. This is not an unimportant aside. Given the guarded and sometimes paranoid temperament of participants making empirical research difficult for those who are not scene participants, my experience, friendships and connections in the scene were integral to the project. Interfacing with the frequencies shared at volume in the Australian bush shaped my desire to effect an approach that does not abnegate the experience of dance itself – the experience which, when optimal conditions are met, transforms a party into an irresistible conflagration. How dance is approached is crucial for scholars of EDM, which is hardly possible without *being there*, and all the more essential where questions of religion and spirituality constitute research directives. While a disciplined research agenda was essential – in my case one that did not privilege any among the heteroclite narratives, voices and agendas that comprise psychedelic trance – shuffling at a safe remove from the grounds of experience was hardly appropriate. While in her *Club Cultures*, Sarah Thornton admitted to being "an outsider to the cultures in which I conducted research", and who had "intents and purposes alien to the rest of the crowd" (1996: 2), such distancing is as unacceptable in this project as it has been in discographies subsequent to Thornton's where dance is recognized as primary to vitality, pleasure, identity, belonging.[7] While Thornton's approach privileged scene niche and micro media (as well as major newsprint media), the research of scene media can no longer be isolated from dance music production and reception, since the music is the medium. As this book attempts to illustrate, psychedelic electronic musicians produce narratives by remixing popular culture, and psychedelic trance has evolved subgenres with distinctive techniques of immersing the body-in-dance in reflexive storylines which echo and effect de/subjectification. If dance is the *raison d'être* of the field in question, from the bump and grind of the front-of-the-floor to transcendent states that may involve the ingestion of psychoactive substances (which may or may not be illicit), and which may involve the programming of *nanomedia*, then suitable ethnographic methods must be adopted. I understand implicitly that the techniques of "radical empiricism" (Jackson 1989) include rhetorical techniques shaped by experience in the field – which is complicated by the fact that, since the advent of the Web, the "field" became indistinguishable from the "non-field". While the "field" for researchers of media has been complex from the inception of cultural studies, the "field" of EDM has transformed since Thornton's research as a result of developments in cyber-culture and advancements in, for instance, digital sampling technics.

"Technique" is, of course, dependent on various factors, including language skills,[8] and remaining alert to new developments across various intersecting fields – music, genre shifts, event trends, drug effects and usage trends. Many events with roots in the Goa psychedelic diaspora accommodate a diversity of styles, both electronic and non-electronic, and psytrance has illustrated a voracious capacity for style absorption, principally techno, and ambient, but also funk, electro, house, breaks, dub and industrial styles have been pulled into its orbit, circumstances which make the study of psytrance notoriously perplexing. Psychedelic trance has itself evolved amid the circulation of substances and "research chemicals" which have impacted this culture considerably. One of the lasting impressions I have is the advanced relationship participants have with drugs, whose pharmacologies and effects are often researched and compared studiously. Many style themselves as "psychonauts", for whom participation in the culture amounts to assaying their experience on a range of substances recognized as potentially beneficial to their spiritual well-being. In fact, participants often stress their disapproval of the word "drug" and embrace other terms like "psychedelic" and "entheogen". The sentiment is noted by Serbian psy-prog act Middle Mode (Jovan Tot and Ivan Jovicic), who sample psychonaut and philosopher Terence McKenna on "Deep Habits" (John 00 Fleming & DJ Bim – *Goa Culture III*, 2011):

> "Drugs" is a word that has polluted the well of language. Part of the reason we have a drug problem is because we don't have an intelligent language to talk about substances, plants, psychedelic and sedative states of mind, states of amphetamine excitation. We can't make sense of the problem and the opportunities offered by substances unless we clean up our language.

The comment was lifted from a 1996 interview with McKenna in Mexico where he aired his desire for cognitive liberty – i.e. the right of individuals to use mind-altering compounds based on informed decisions – a chief preoccupation within the psychedelic movement where participants have actively searched for an "intelligent language". In the face of academic discourse that robs life from its subject matter (see Jordan 1995), ethnographers of EDM cultures also need to find an intelligent language shaped according to research agenda and the specific field under consideration. In a study of a culture where the liminal experience associated with extraordinary psychoactive-assisted states of consciousness is pivotal, familiarity with available technologies of the senses adapted to these ends should be among the priorities of ethnographers. This is in no way simple or uncontroversial. To begin with, psytrance is a liminal underworld, where participation involves a techno-organic mixed-media collusion by which the sampling (consumption) of psychoactive substances and the sampling (digital production) of sound and vision are interrelated. What's more, it is a sensitive research field. In the possible disclosure of activities outside or ambiguous with regard to the law, researchers (often working under the auspices of the state) may endanger both their interlocutors and themselves – yet where such ambiguity is native to a culture (as it is with EDM – see St John 2012a), suitable strategies need to be adopted.

The issue of reflexivity in dance and club drug research is approached by Measham and Moore (2006) who, observing the prevalence of a "reluctant reflexivity" among researchers, note that the history of dance research and club studies (in the UK) is characterized by a distant objectivized approach which conceals researcher vulnerabilities, separates the knower from the known, and rarely identifies the researcher's relationship with the researched, generating a "hygienic" approach. In recent times, in efforts to overcome the limitations of specific methods – i.e. quantitative, epidemiological, phenomenological – and to become sensitive to the practices of risk and pleasure within the consumer settings of EDM events, researchers have sought an adequate distribution of cross-methodological approaches to make sense of their fields of study (e.g. Hunt *et al.* 2009; Demant *et al.* 2010). While Newcombe (2008) expressed the merits of a "psychonautic" model in which the researcher observes his/her own subjective experience of drugs, others (Demant *et al.* 2010) suggest a "socionautic" approach which recognizes the social setting of EDM contexts and incorporates ethnographically informed interviewing based on experiences shared by the researcher and the researched, including that which is informed by psychonautics. This roughly describes my approach, with the addition that psychonauticism is recognized to include cross-media practice, such that assemblages of sensory technologies (analog, digital, chemical, cyber) and popular cultural resources are programmed, synthesized and *remixed* to affect altered states of consciousness within the optimized design framework of a dance party. This is a crucial point. Radical empiricism includes personal knowledge of the effects of media assemblages, their sources of simulation and how they are experienced *in situ*.

Book outline

The following offers brief outlines of each of the book's chapters. Chapter 2 explores the career of the spiritual *experience* animating psyculture, from its earliest period in Goa. From the late 1960s, Goa attracted the disenchanted and the decadent, those whose disparate expatriations gave life to a "state of mind", a mental mosaic which became integral to the evolution of the "trance dance" experience in seasonal Goa, infusing the subsequent psychedelic trance movement. Figures instrumental to psyculture are introduced and benchmark incidents are explained, with the chapter also examining the themes of "authenticity", "freedom" and "liveness", as well as the psychedelic Orientalism inhering in the "Goa" sound. In Chapter 3, the idea that the Goa "state of mind" is schizoid is taken up in an examination of the transnationally transposable "vibe" of the exiles. Goatrance may have emerged as a formulaic genre, but the psychedelic diaspora is animated by a cultural noise, dances to different tunes, with the emergent psyculture echoing with tension. The chapter addresses how this seasonal exile socio-aesthetic was rocked by waves of innovation flowing from global cosmopolitan hubs of EDM. Attention is directed to instrumental scene broker Gọa Gil whose hybrid project spans historical psychedelias and whose mission to ritualize the "end of the world" has had varied reception, illustrating the heterogeneity of psychedelic trance – a contested music and culture. In its exploration of Goa/psytrance music, Chapter 4 regards this music as an assemblage of technics that have been sampled, remixed and repurposed to the variable transit of the self in reflexive modernity. The assemblages I call *spiritechnics* are guided by differing modalities of "consciousness", shaping practices with varying means and ends: progressive and transgressive, nihilistic and gnostic, self-directed and planetary. Using a spectrum of sampled content programmed within psytrance releases and promotions, the chapter demonstrates how its sonic fiction orchestrates the departure from, connection with, and evolution of, consciousness. Whether concerned with the unconscious, outer space, virtual reality or the wilderness, re-mediated liminality is adapted by the psychedelic mystics and media shamans of psytrance to facilitate these conditions of *transit*. Popular culture, psychoactive (or more accurately "entheogenic") compounds, and the experience of revelation are the media and the means remixed by the technicians of transition. Chapter 5 follows with an exploration of the events designed to facilitate these varied and interacting modes of consciousness. With specific attention to Boom, total solar eclipse festivals, and other events, parties are recognized as spiritual technologies accommodating multiple transitional pathways, a circumstance amplified by their *psychedelic* praxis and aesthetic. At the world's biennial summit of psychedelic trance (Boom), its Liminal Village contrasts with the main floor, the Dance Temple, as the head does to the body, yet their synergetic relationship is pivotal to a movement where integralism is programmed into its festival culture. Additionally, total solar eclipse festivals, such as Soulclipse in Turkey (in 2006), are recognized as pinnacle achievements in post-Goa psychedelic mysticism – the visionary arts platforms of a planetary culture.

Chapter 6 approaches the vexing subject of trance dance itself, the *raison d'être* of psychedelic trance culture. Dissatisfaction with the term "trance" inspires a heuristic acknowledging a range of activity within the "weekend societies" of psyculture. The contemporary Goatrance party is rooted in the *cosmic carnival*, which is shown to augment the carnivalesque with a Space Age psychedelic aesthetic. In the music and the events downstream from its Goa origins, progressive and ludic sensibilities are demonstrated to comprise the trance experience. The trance culture that fomented within these recurrent events has given rise to what may more accurately be named *neotrance*, an ecstasic/theatrical dynamic where surrender to the funky flow and freak performance are integral to the mix. In Chapter 7 I pay attention to two national scene developments. Comparison of global psyculture in Israel and Australia serves to demonstrate the diversity of post-Goa culture as it became translated in countries with disparate cultural, historical and geographical conditions. These examples show how aspects of Goa/psytrance have been pressed into the service of religious, spiritual and intellectual agendas in the respective regions, and how national and cultural climates have shaped a mix of agendas, from the rebellious to the proactive. While no singular narrative prevails, amid the carnivalesque noise of psyculture, the dance floor is the ultimate grounds for a *religious experience* recognized by participants across these diverse national scenes. That psyculture is a movement context for the establishment of identity, prestige and cultural capital through a range of transgressive and reflexive behaviours is examined in Chapter 8. The performance of risk and the arts of consciousness are polar intentions dramatized in psytrance events, the study of which is assisted through the application of Bourdieu's "cultural capital" to a complex cultural movement. In psytrance and visionary arts cultures, distinction is accorded not only to those who perform lifestyle risks but to those committed to identifying and reducing risks based on ecological and humanitarian concerns. In a revision of Turner's concept of liminality by way of a detailed examination of intentional ritualization within the psytrance movement, Chapter 9 completes this study. Downstream from Goa, a hyperliminal noise of risk-laden and reflexive commitments characterizes festivals whose differential *logics of sacrifice* are explained. As the paramount expression of this movement, its festivals are vehicles for transgressive and disciplined concerns articulated in rites of risk and consciousness. Rooted in the experimental adulthood/extended adolescence of the 1960s–1970s, psytrance is then recognized as a complex *liminal culture* which knows no bounds.

2 Experience, the Orient and Goatrance

Psyculture was born from experiments on Anjuna and surrounding beaches of Goa, India. The *Goa experience* evolved there from the late 1960s and early 1970s before it was translated to scenes worldwide in the 1990s and 2000s. Rooted in diverse motivations that would come to shape the music culture of Goa/psytrance, the Goa experience is recognized to be heterogeneous. This laboratory of experience was itself transposed from world cosmopolitan conurbations, absorbing innovations in EDM productions and performance throughout the 1980s, before the Goatrance sound became a formula by the mid-1990s. The destination sought by participants in this enduring freak diaspora became home to the conscious realization and ecstatic abandonment of the self, disparate practices performed within a *psychogeography of experience* – involving physical and metaphysical mobility – pivotal to the Goa experiment.

Are you shpongled?

In 1967, when freak pioneers had barely established a beachhead in Goa, Jimi Hendrix released his compelling inquiry on the title track of *Are You Experienced?* The song evokes a concatenation of subjectivity that was sensuous, spiritual and, in the wake of the popularizing of LSD, integral to the psychedelia inherited by post-1960s generations. Via overdriven amplification, guitar feedback and exaggerated pitch, this aesthetic involved a liquefying of boundaries and a sensibility of self-in-transit from familiar patterns of identification. The seductive lyrical inquiry offered a deliberate conflation of the psychedelic and sexual experience: "but are you experienced?" As white middle-class fans absorbed the lyrics of an American of African, Cherokee, Nahuatl and Irish descent, the song (and the inquiry) flirts with the possibility of miscegenation, with intercultural mixing, the foundation of

American hipness according to John Leland (2004), and the root of credibility in UK subculture, especially punk, according to Dick Hebdige (1979). Mixing, it needs to be stated, is also a core technique of the DJ and the studio engineer, a practice that, in the tradition of electronic music, enables the procreation of new sounds. Like audio-miscegenators, from the dub and disco studio technicians to the home studio producer, electronic musicians sample and mix sonic material originating from diverse places, eras and genres, producing hybrid sounds. Illustrating a sampledelic sensibility, this practice renders the DJ a quintessentially *experienced* (well-travelled, cosmopolitan, competent) figure. While some DJ-producers, especially those influenced by electro funk and progressive house, are keen to convey their erotic competence by inaugurating carnal sonics, the "experience" sought and credited is more commonly converted from travel. In successful guises, the experienced DJ would be a particular kind of global traveller, supported by his or her (though more often his) art and continually exposed to new sounds and cultural encounters in far-flung locations.[1]

While infused with the novelties facilitated by the border crossings of cultural hybridity, exotic travel and sexual encounter, the experiential othering foremost to Hendrix's inquiry involves excursions of the mind activated by psychoactive compounds, a theme carried forward most effusively in Goatrance and psyculture. It is no coincidence that, updating the original inquiry thirty years hence, the most popular act in the psychedelic diaspora, the ethnodelic collaboration Shpongle (Raja Ram and Simon Posford), named their debut album *Are You Shpongled?* (1998).[2] On the sleeve for their second release *Divine Moments of Truth* (2000), "Shpongle" is revealed to refer to "a state of being and experiencing", and later it is articulated that for those entering "Room 23" (from *Tales of the Inexpressible*, 2001): "to be Shpongled is to be kippered, mashed, smashed, destroyed. Completely geschtonken-flapped!" Impregnated with psychoatives (and especially, as we'll see, DMT), the condition of *enshponglement*, and indeed one's journey to "Outer Shpongolia" (*Nothing Lasts ... But Nothing is Lost*, 2005), where psychnoauts can be assured that "Shpongelese is Spoken Here" (*Ineffable Mysteries from Shpongleland*, 2009), has become a conspiratorial nodding and winking experience in the world of psychedelic trance.

Post-1960s, psychoactive mind-alterants have remained integral to music countercultures, and to that which counts for *experience*. The ontological instability common to the use of psychedelics has enabled, as Nick Bromell reported on the 1960s in *Tomorrow Never Knows* (2000: 80), a dramatic confirmation "of the adolescent's conviction that gown-ups are by choice deceitful, that culture is fundamentally false, and that rebellion is therefore an existential right, even a duty". These dutiful ruptures of subjectivity would catalyze new cultural forms, with psychoactive catalysts later endorsed by

Terence McKenna and sampled on AMD's (Jules Hamer and Dick Trevor) "Roadshow" (from *Frogology*, 2009):

> To say what has never been said. To see what has never been seen. To draw, paint, sing, sculpt, dance and act what has never before been done. To push the envelope of creativity and language. And what's really important is, I call it, the felt presence of direct experience ... We have to stop consuming our culture. We have to create culture. Don't watch TV, don't read magazines. Create your own road show.

On "Reclaim Your Mind (Batusim Rmx)" by Austrian Imix (*Mindwaves*, 2008), McKenna's screed, delivered as part of his "Eros and the Eschaton" book tour at Mandala Books, Seattle, 1994,[3] continues unabated:

> And if you're worrying about ... Michael Jackson or Bill Clinton or somebody, then you are disempowered. You're giving it all away to icons. And, we're told "no, we're unimportant, we're peripheral, get a degree, get a job, get a this, get a that, and then you're a player." You don't even want to play in that game. You want to reclaim your mind, and get it out of the hands of the cultural engineers who want to turn you into a half-baked moron consuming all this trash that's manufactured out of the bones of a dying world.

The road show endorsed by Hendrix, carried by Shpongle, and promoted by McKenna, was built around the quest for experiential breakthroughs, an experimentalism born of the impulse to encounter life raw and untrammelled, not dictated by the conniptions of the advertising industry, nor performed for "the Man"; a life ruled not by religious dogma, nor mediated by the cartels of syndicated experience. This is the radical immanence, improvisation and sensuality championed by the Beats and their rootless predecessors in bohemian enclaves and romantic and transcendentalist traditions over the last 150 years or more, who, following the examples of Ginsberg, Kerouac, and Ram Dass, sought to be like wandering mendicants, channelling the meditative grace and wisdom of Eastern religious traditions, a romance resonating with Goatrance artists, some of whom have indeed adopted the concept of "bodhisattva" (the wandering Buddha), or who evolved and promoted personalized modes of continuity with the Brahmanic "Cosmic Spirit". Yoga warriors, audio magicians and ritual syncretists have cultivated lifestyles embodying how, as Allen Watts announced in his 1960 "Nature of Consciousness" seminar broadcast on KSAN radio, "a wave is continuous with the ocean". Indeed, on "No Such Thing" (*Psychedelica Melodica*, 2007), the UK's Cosmosis (Bill Halsey) takes notes from the same seminar: "The basic problem is to understand that there are no such things as things. That is to say separate things, separate events. What do you mean by a thing? A thing is a noun. A noun isn't a part of nature, it's a part of speech. There are no nouns in the physical world". The commentary invokes a message apparent in Goatrance at its inception, with, for instance, the title track of The Infinity Project's seminal *Mystical Experiences* (1995) featuring Watts meditating on that condition to which travellers, wayfarers and trance dancers have aspired down through the ages: *nothing*. "Imagine nothing. No thing. No me. No you. No world. Nothing". Today, the experienced technomad continues to communicate the feeling. Thus, "I know nothing, and in that nothing is all. ALL!", claims an enraptured woman caught in some revelatory moment on "All is Nothing", the only sample on Boris Blenn's eleventh album, as Electric Universe (*Higher Modes*, 2011).

These sampled commentaries on that rarely uttered no-thing are lifted from spokespersons of what Theodore Roszak (1968) called the post-WWII "Age of Affluence" in which unprecedented freedoms were pursued, Maslowian "advanced needs" fulfilled, transcendental spirituality popularized (see Williamson 2010), and a protean "looseness" formed (Binkley 2007). They are the compiled sound-bites of hypermobile "spiritual virtuosi" (Sutcliffe 2000) and those Norman Mailer caricatured as the "frontiersmen in the Wild West of American nightlife" (1957: 277), who have assayed experience with the assistance of new tools in mind-manifesting, whispering to us via the digital song-lines of the turn of the twenty-first century the sweet nothings discovered riding out on those frontiers. While the modern appearance of an esoteric seekership may have commenced with the theosophists, it would later flourish in the years between the World Wars when a "seeker culture" emerged whose participants searched for hidden truths via occult practices (Sutcliffe 2007). It then proliferated in the 1960s and 1970s with the turn to Oriental metaphysical praxis, including yoga and tantra alongside a plethora of other body-arts facilitating the deification of the flesh and the enlightenment of the body (Kripal 2007). Nomads of the mind and body were responding to crises of the self, resolved through temporary or more enduring flights from states of consent towards altered states. For some, travels to sites of mystery, energy, power and healing (Ivakhiv 2001, 2007) potentiated the solution, while for others the answers lay almost entirely within the sensual field.

Disciplinary approaches to higher states of consciousness and embodied enlightenment exercised in this period were complemented – some would argue, overshadowed – by other routes to nowhere, where an abandonment of one's past could be performed; where identity, nation and tradition were exorcised in the uncompromising embrace of chaos, of wild human nature, a rawness known and expressed by poets, artists and dancers, a madness cultivated on the margins of history. Here was the innocence, truth and love that R.D. Laing, in *The Politics of Experience* (1967: 136), thought could be achieved by unlearning that "appalling state of alienation called normality", a liberation through regression paralleling the "voyage" of psychosis. For growing numbers of young people compelled towards what Israelis call *karahana*, the transcendental catharsis could be experienced in transgressive leisure, erotic arts and extreme sports. Since the 1960s, these routes to experience coalesced in new forms of art, leisure, sexuality and sociality, and in the subversive sites in which these were cultivated, where, in what Erik Davis identifies as "spiritual hedonism" (2004), "edgemen" (Turner 1969: 128) sought an immediacy enabled by new media of transcendence: psychosomatic technologies, personal computers, electronic synthesizers, virtual instruments and other "machines of loving grace" facilitating an independent cultural economy whose radically reflexive participants possess unprecedented control over the means of perception.

In the rush to tap the vein of the peak experience, music and trance dance practices ruptured old, and forged as yet unknown, subjectivities. Well before it attracted the label in record stores, Goatrance was such an assemblage of techniques for the mind, body and spirit. Poaching and recycling media sources, it would exalt, parody and facilitate continuity with countercultural forebears. Take Ceiba Records, the first independent psychedelic trance label in the US, with a storefront that remains on upper Haight St, San Francisco, and now trading for the most part in psychedelic fashion. Ceiba's second compilation album, *The Language of Light 2* (1998), offers comment on the district's roots as the Capital of Experience: its "Prologue" reproducing a straight-laced promotion of the kind which, between 1966–68, transformed the Haight-Ashbury district into a hippie wasteland.

> These people are Hippies. They're occupying a piece of ground in San Francisco's Golden Gate Park, which has come to be called "Hippy Hill". They represent a new form of social rebellion. They dress in bizarre and colourful ways. They wear their hair long. Their very name suggests that they are "hip", on to something good. They all declare themselves as rebels against society. They like music. The word "love" is used by them a lot.

Ceiba Records was founded by Austrian-born Peter Ziegelmeier. Travelling to Goa in the early 1970s, Ziegelmeier was part of a generation of European artists, dissidents and visionaries who sought alternatives to the societies of their upbringing. Engrossed by harmonies, melodies and rhythmic structures that, he stated to me in an interview, remained virtually unchanged for 2000 years in Hindustani music, Ziegelmeier studied musicology at Banaras University, Varanasi, from 1972–1974, and learned the *sarod* (a stringed instrument), later discovering the electronic instrumentation through which Hindustani and other world music could be sampled in the pursuit of transcendence.[4] The chief vehicle was Kode IV (co-founded with Hans Schiller), whose venture into Goatrance, after producing industrial music from the late 1980s in Berlin, was enshrined on *Silicon Civilisation* (1995).[5] With the opening track "Myth" offering the repeated mantra – "experience" – the album is a meditation on dissolving the self via meditative states ("Dissolve II") and becoming, as another album track names the trajectory, "Near to the Divine".

Approximating the divine, the *children of technique* were altering consciousness on a scale previously unknown. Meditation, acid rock, psychoactive compounds and other technics enabled the new prometheans to lay claim to the possibility of the Self's indissoluble connection with the Other, a gnosis we might identify as the epiphanous field of the sacred variously encountered in this period as "the Source", "Cosmic Spirit" or "Mother Nature". At the same time, experiments took trajectories with nameless paths and unknowable destinations, the fierce independence of antagonists matched by a savage indeterminacy where what mattered most was one's embrace of a radical immanence removed from the past and the future. To be a *freak* was to trek multiple paths, and experience heteroclite travails. "Freak" was an acceptable designation for the evolutionary (or indeed revolutionary) mutation from alienation, a break from a failed existence, a counterpoint to the recognized separation from source–spirit–nature to which one "returns". The *transit* native to this rupture has typically implied a movement *from* a condition of alienation implicit to monotheism, possessive materialism, patriarchy and patriotism, and a corresponding movement *toward* a resolve. Those who joined the exodus in the 1960s/70s modelled themselves as a generation in transit, anxious to assume the role of the "new man" and "new woman" via the adoption of dietary techniques, occult sexuality, new architecture, meditation, psychedelics, and who invested in the return to childhood. A post-humanism was notable, according to Tom Wolfe in *The Electric Kool-Aid Acid Test* (1971), among Ken Kesey and the Merry Pranksters, who were influenced by, among other things, Arthur C. Clarke's *Childhood's End*. At the end of Clarke's 1953 novel depicting humanity's merger with the cosmic Overmind, the last generation of (telekinetically enhanced) children on Earth are dancing, a motif picked up by Billy in an article entitled "Dance for Dance Sake" published in the 1975/76 issue of Goa magazine *The Stoned Pig*[6]:

> The last generation of man are dancing blissfully, ecstatically through the forest and jungles. Some move in groups, others alone, all wiped out on being. They are hardly sensible to the physicality of this world, their consciousness is expanding into higher levels of being. Their hair is matted, their clothes rags, they care hardly for food or shelter, eating wild fruits, sleeping in the open, dancing, eternally dancing.

As Billy concluded, that's "not too far from what happens on Anjuna" (Billy 1975/76: 7).

The inhering optimism was implicit to the prevailing logic of meditative individuation which grew popular in this period. Here the self possesses a mind not disconnected from body and spirit in views typical to mechanical reductionism, the holistic departure from which was embodied in the teachings of the Human Potential movement, the Integral movement,[7] and among proto-ecopsychologies. For practitioners of this psychotherapeutic movement, what Henri Bergson (1944) called the "life-force" and what has generally been hailed as "universal consciousness", could be accessed and reaffirmed through chosen activities in the phenomenal world. The popularization of this thinking can be located in Aldous Huxley's *The Perennial Philosophy* (1944), with Huxley's metaphysics translating the teachings of Ramakrishna Vedanta. While meditation became integral to Westerners seeking a higher state of consciousness, another popular technique of selfhood was trance dance, or what Osho (Bhagwan Shree Rajneesh) deemed "dynamic meditation". Osho had opened an ashram in Pune, Maharashtra (the northern neighbouring state of Goa), in 1974 (see D'Andrea 2007a: 138–42), attracting a significant population of seekers throughout the 1970s and 1980s.[8] Unlike traditional Hindu sannyas orders whose initiates are obligated to renounce family, possessions and pleasure, Osho neosannyasins would undertake a comparatively undisciplined commitment. Described as "an outrageous Nietzschean philosopher who sought to combine Buddha with Zorba", and said to hold that he could "only believe in a God who danced" (D'Andrea 2006: 65), Osho spoke directly to the interests of cultural exiles from the West, since he provided a message couched in a liberal ontology of joy, abundance and freedom from limitations.

While Osho offered a route to remembering, reenchantment and rehumanization via his Nietzschean Buddhist charismatic cult, others arriving in India were simply compelled to forget. On Anjuna beach, wrote English-Australian Steve "Madras" Devas (2004), "we had suntans. We didn't need history ... because the only past thing was a chillum". Devas's tribute to fellow Goa freak, Amsterdam Dave, "Our Only Story is the Beach", is a tale about a culture of amnesia, as much as it is a story about liberation. Having journeyed overland to India, Devas recalls that "the first letter from my dad waiting for me in poste restante, Kabul, contained a cutting from the *Times of London*, headlined 'Hippies begging like dogs in Afghanistan'. There was no letter with the article; there didn't need to be. The inference was clear. *You have become hippy trash*". Abandoning their pasts, Devas and his companions who reached Anjuna in the 1970s were dwelling "in a hermetic world of falsity, garbled phone calls and hollowed out lifestyles. False IDs, false bottoms, false passports ... there was so much to *not* talk about."

> Our history safely out of reach
> our only story is the beach
> on the full moon party we are born
> we who from our story torn
> are busy lying
> on the beach[9]

Devas clarifies with cutting detail the worlds those from a multitude of Western countries were deliberately leaving behind. "The trauma of being wasp, catholic or pentecostal, the trauma of Vietnam, the trauma of being American ... the trauma of class, race or nationality, the trauma of being French, Italian or British or German". For most, he continued,

> being from somewhere was at best uncomfortable and often unbearable. How else could you explain the French junkies who plagued the beach, a bewildered generation withered by class hatred, who turned to heroin to dress their wounds? The Italians? What was their stone? The unbearable lightness of religion? And the Germans, not one of my German friends ever talked about the war and the welts of pain lacerating the German psyche. The awful G word hanging over them like a black cloud, emasculating joy, castrating self expression, no colours anymore, I want them to turn black, I want to see the sun – blotted out from the sky, I want to see it painted, painted ... painted black (Devas 2004).

Having achieved the distant terminus of the "hippie trail", walking naked down Anjuna beach the "secret family that lived on the edge of history" were discarding their clothing while covering up their tracks. Although being a "freak" presupposed the journey of transformation integral to spiritual awakenings fomenting in the 1960s and 1970s, it also signalled the desire to discard the past in an apocalypse of subjectivity fuelled not only by LSD, but cocaine and heroin. This tragedy is integral to the narrative of *Goa Freaks: My Hippie Years in India* (1995), the story of model, freak anthropologist and drug smuggler Cleo Odzer, who operated a "dope den" in the late 1970s she called the Anjuna Drugoona Saloona. Her account of addiction, excess and depravity includes an incident in which a junkie fell down and died in a village well. You can feel the bones crunch and taste the rotten effluence down through the years as the protean music and scenes to follow amplified fecklessness at the same time as they attempted a meaningful resolution. The parties surfacing in the wake of this tsunami grew host to these disparate roads to nowhere, enabling unravellings and inaugurating becomings – junctures remote from places of origin and yet designed to welcome travellers "home".

Homecomings were celebrated as far back as the late 1960s, though according to Goa veteran Peter Thomas (aka Blond Peter) – who published an alternative Goa newsletter in 1973/74 called *Pigs & Palms* – seminal among the early Goa parties were those held in the palm-leaf compound at Blue's place just back from South Anjuna beach (now called Curlies). Thomas recalls the period:

> Blue was the only openly gay sadhu hippie on the India scene at that time, into jewellery, EST, people, parties, local Goan motorcycle boys and giving elaborate presents to people he liked. His parties were always "the cream of the cream" and the music may have started out as an acoustic folk rock, but there was already a trance element with everyone singing, drumming, hand-jiving and generally getting into it. On a full moon, the pre-party at Blue's was the best preparation for a looooong night. We had bathing facilities prepared, good food and a candle-lit environment – it was also a refuge when things got too intense. Sadly, I heard Blue died of an AIDS-related disease some years later. He challenged the macho Hippie Raj ethos, because he had solid overland credentials, and he brought a new expectation of tolerance and a unique personal majesty to the scene.[10]

Gathering at the end of the hippie trail at the edge of the world, parties were the pinnacle achievement of a community that, as Thomas further relates, "was not based on any sect, but rather on a mutual unspoken decision to encourage harmony". But, he added, "we all knew that it could not last" (Thomas 2011). Anxieties over the impending loss of harmony caused by the sheer weight of numbers arriving across successive seasons was accompanied by a healthy caution. Hidden away in the second-last issue of *The Stoned Pig* was a reminder of the responsibilities implicit to a scene that sought to connect to others while at the same time desiring clandestinity. "We must be discreet", wrote Snydly, "we must have a countenance that projects all we know & respect in the subtlest way".

> We are all here because we believe that the world outside has been lost to the forces of opportunity & power. The men & spirit of the outside world are not concerned with freedom, love, dance and all the things that bring wisdom and happiness to us here in Goa, but they seem to be in love with contraction. To close themselves within the walls of their concrete cities and minds. To oppress all forms of harmony with our mother Nature: we've all been aware of this for quite some time; we've chosen an alternate place and space in our lives, and on this planet, and that is Goa (Snydly 1975: 7).

At a time when some had already declared the scene lost, the author calls for an appropriate means of transmitting information. While "we've come here to connect all the people of the world into one moving vibrating unit", caution is necessary since the Goas of the world "inevitably become commercial and super money-making propositions" due to unwise scene mediations, hack journalism and the resultant influx of tourists. Invisibility and esoteric approaches are therefore proposed. "A system that reveals all its secrets is bound to collapse. As Don Juan said, 'You must become a man of mystery with no past and no ties, for until you do this, you can be tracked, hunted, killed'" (Snydly 1975: 6).

As we'll see, the cat was well out of the bag by the beginning of the 1990s.[11] But back in the heyday of the hippie gold rush, before the vein of experience itself collapsed, the uninhibited, exclusive and unmediated parties at Blue's circa 1973 and countless other refuges established off and on the beaches were laboratories for a barely definable state of being *other* shared by the swarms washing up on Goa. Sampling a line from psychiatrist and early LSD researcher Sidney Cohen speaking on the BBC documentary *The Beyond Within: The Rise and Fall of LSD* (1987), Shpongle co-founder Simon Posford (as Hallucinogen) offered further clarity on the desired-yet-inexpressible state on "Demention", the opener on *The Lone Deranger* (1997): "There is an area of the mind that could be called unsane, beyond sanity, and yet not insane. Think of a circle with a fine split in it. At one end there's insanity. You go around the circle to sanity, and on the other end of the circle, close to insanity, but not insanity, is unsanity." The well-known sample strikes a note on the Goa party which, as a context for becoming mind-less in trance, carried the legacy of Blue and other midwives to the Goa tradition. It references a state of mind that, while immeasurable and indefinable, is that which one desires to revisit. And revisit it they did, in greater frequency, in greater numbers, and with more and more kit. Wouter Thomassen (aka Zen Mechanics) appears to powerpoint the circumstance on "Psychotropical Nights" (*Universo Paralello*, 2008) where Francis Ford Coppola – interviewed in *Hearts of Darkness: A Filmmaker's Apocalypse*, about the making of *Apocalypse Now!* – reveals: "We were in the jungle ... There were too many of us ... We had access to too much money ... too much equipment ... and little by little we went insane". And LSD was integral to launching protagonists in the Goa story way "up river", far from history, and out of their minds. As Bromell (2000: 88) wrote, "the person who has seen the mysteries, or just tripped, can never return to the world as it used to be. He, or she, is an exile forever now, cut off from the simple comfort and complacence in which those who have never glimpsed another reality dwell". Those who got off the world and arrived in Goa in the 1970s, often by long and circuitous route, had achieved the ultimate party destination, where they would continuously get off together.

Outland interzone

Goatrance was born from a quest with no single motive carried by people who left no singular impression. It was a festive experiment, a traveller's adventure that endured, arguably, for three decades on a relatively protected "island" connected to an archipelago of freak enclaves, autonomous zones and frontier art colonies, including the alternative cultural festivals that flourished around the world from the 1970s and 1980s. In an evolving network, freaks could commute between nodes, practising "radical self expression" – as participants in the Burning Man Festival held annually in Nevada's Black Rock Desert would have it – across sites. In the 1970s, radical immanence and alternative forms of community were practised in lifestyles whose festivals could last for weeks. At Rainbow Gatherings, along with Grateful Dead shows and other cosmic assemblies including Burning Man, entourages of freaks were communing with universal energies and performing d/evolutionary breaks from the past across the United States throughout the 1970s and 1980s. In the United Kingdom, these tendencies were embodied by the Travellers of Albion who converged in the Free Festivals that later cross-pollinated with the acid house techno movement.[12] In Australia, there were those who inhabited the northeast New South Wales hamlet of Nimbin (born from the 1973 Aquarius Festival) and its hinterlands, and/or participated in the alternative lifestyle event ConFest from 1976 (Newton 1988; St John 1997, 2001a). While inhabitants of these events were performing a "spirituality" that is fundamentally "experiential" – as Lee Gilmore states with regard to "Burners" (2010: 96) – as heterogeneous social experiments these festal enclaves accommodated a mosaic of alternative pursuits. Burning Man itself came to accommodate "cults of experience", not least the Discordian embrace of chaos (Davis 2005). But while there are many "tribes" congregating in Black Rock City (see Jones 2011), they congress in an annual pilgrimage ritual forging community from the dramatization of impermanence. This is the logic internal to the dance party, where individuation and community transpire in paroxysmal conflagrations beyond traditional sources of identification like the nuclear family, religious institutions and the state. In these spaces, the liminal self is not isolated, but is a person whose identity is formed in intimate, extraordinary and transgressive co-presence with other liminars – including, notably, strangers (e.g. not only outside the family but also one's ethnonationality). This liminal sociality contextualizes the "trance" experience as it evolved from the Goa seasonal tradition with influences from many seasoned figures.

In this tradition, psychedelic dance music events became extraordinary contexts for reverse-estrangement and dramatic effect. Early psychedelic rock festivals were formative occasions in which freedoms were being performed, and in this tradition an event in San Francisco's Golden Gate Park on 14 January 1967 remains noteworthy. The Gathering of the Tribes for a Human

Be-In "was not organized", as Lee and Shlain (1985: 162) noted, "to protest a specific government ordinance or policy. Thousands of people had come together to do nothing in particular, which in itself was quite something." In her recollection of the day, Elizabeth Gips (1991) wrote:

> We knew that we were witnessing a massive blossoming of a new religion in the literal sense of being tied together again. This religion would never have churches or temples; this was a religion based on individual freedom and respect; we "dug each other's vibes" and felt the coming together of an ancient family. Time dwindled to a no-point. Heart reached to heart in an almost soundless outpouring of love.

As an ostensible convergence of the cosmic hippie and activist participants of the counterculture, the "happening" scheduled Timothy Leary, Allen Ginsberg, Gary Snyder, Richard (Ram Dass) Alpert, Dick Gregory, Lenore Kendel and Jerry Ruben, who, among others, spoke, sang, and performed from the stage. The Grateful Dead, Quicksilver Messenger Service, Janis Joplin and Big Brother and the Holding Company were among the bands, and Owsley "Bear" Stanley distributed White Lightning acid (LSD had been outlawed in California just months before). "Call it heaven or samadhi", for Gips, the experience that day "set the parameters for a whole movement during the Summer of Love. Through the catalyst of LSD we had scratched through the surface of our separateness and recognized ourselves, our surroundings, all things as One. That afternoon, we truly became The Love Generation". A few months later across the Atlantic, on 29 April 1967, the UFO club in London's cavernous Alexandra Place played host to the "24 Hour Technicolor Dream", an "all-night rave" which saw 10,000 people exposed to dozens of bands, poets, artists and dancers who performed amid a spectacular light show (Palacios 2001). The freaks of Albion were soon discovering gypsy trails and establishing a Free Festival circuit merging psychedelic folk-rock with medieval fayres and markets. From festival to festival, craftspeople, musicians, performers, healers, traders were nomadic communards living onsite for at least half the year (McKay 1996), and in temporary seasonal events a "freak nation" became a mobile commitment with sovereign nodes proliferating around the world.

The *free* character of these events connoted immediacy, permissiveness and the unshackled mind as much as it denoted "free admission" and other unrestricted terms of entry. As these freedoms became subject to restrictions and curtailment in home countries at the same time as transnational mobility became affordable to the sons and daughters of the affluent classes, and would become accessible to others, freedom was sought further and further afield, in greater numbers, at exotic sites of experimentation. In emergent backpacking rites of passage, travellers sought authenticity in wild nature and in exotic cultural contact, which, as time wore on, meant contact with "fellow travellers" with whom they forged a fluid *traveller culture.* Not the coddled experience typical to tourism, like beat forebears, hippies sought independent travel and faced personal risks trekking into the unknown, especially upon the trail that led east through Turkey and Iran to Nepal and India. Living on the cheap, they became vulnerable to disease and extortion, theft, and the loss of passports and travel tickets. For these travellers, many possessed the means of "returning" from their disorientation, but a great many weren't interested in *recreation,* or a cathartic return. As D'Andrea pointed out, perceiving themselves as "a marginal and vanishing culture requiring countermeasures of mobility and stealth against commodification and repression", the freaks who settled the Spanish island of Ibiza, and Goa, the former Portuguese colony, would become, following Deleuze, "nomads" who "do not move" (D'Andrea 2004: 242, 241).

> These Global Nomads seek to drift away from their Western homeland, and, inspired by imaginations of a Romantic East, they asymptotically move towards a smooth, impossible space – "u-topia" by definition. By celebrating rootlessness and nomadism, global nomads shape cosmopolitan post-national identities that question the essentiality of the "local", and embrace the "global" as the new home and reference (2004: 244).

Holding the possibility of going native – like hippie "visionaries" (Howard 1969: 43), the "existential tourist" (Cohen 1979), "expressive expatriates" (D'Andrea 2007a) and "settlers" (Maoz 2005: 176) – freaks sought exotic lands, local patronage, altered states of mind, flexible labour/leisure patterns, and looser modes of embodiment.

From the late 1960s, Ibiza and Goa offered immediacy, protection and fellowship for travellers. In these locations, artists, seekers and craft workers pursued freedoms from modern modes of subjectivity, citizenship and personhood. Around 1966/1967, freaks began descending on Goa, which, after 450 years of Portuguese rule,[13] held a reputation as one of the most hospitable locations on the subcontinent and in the East, possessing that quality among locals essential for the survival of a familial zone on foreign soil: tolerance. In Luther Elliott's (2010: 28) estimation, "whether it was intrinsic affability or economic hardship that motivated the amicable relations, most accounts of the 1970s in Goa cast the villagers of Calangute, Baga, Anjuna, Vagator as friends and business partners". As Devas (2004) laid it out, "there was no formal welcome, no exchange of protocols, but not since the Raja of Gokarna welcomed the Parsees to Gujarat some five hundred years before, has such a welcome been given to a diaspora in need".[14] As he continued:

> The parties, the loud music, the pollution of their wells, (not by us regulars though), the hash factories, the flea market, all the various cottage industries of hippiedom, some of them legal, most not, the full technicolour riot – bizarre, magnificent, wasted, often questionable, morally challenging, sometimes racist, quaint, nefarious, mad, transcendent and at times deeply sublime – oh the whole glorious shooting match, the whole whacked out fireworks of it all – and they let us get away with it! Thank you Goans! (Devas 2004).

Goa was also among the most permissive locations in India, where *ganja* and *charas* (hashish) was legal until the mid to late 1970s and was (and remains) cheap. The practice of smoking *charas* through a chillum was learned from *sadhus* by way of intrepid travellers (see Saldanha 2007a: 65–66) with its effects permeating the music and culture to come. The effects of *cannabis sativa* is pungent, for instance, aboard X-Dream's tribal dub release "Relax Vortex" (*Global Psychedelic Trance Vol. 2*, 1996) on which a yogi claims that *ganja* in part means "wisdom". The association between *ganja* and Indian mysticism is acknowledged more recently with, for example, psybient artist Androcell's dub-bud influenced "Ganja Baba" (*Entheomythic*, 2010), upon which some wizened spokesperson reflects: "you should try smoking a little pot, it's not a drug, it's a flower, it has healing properties". But while master sampler of strange-yet-evocative vocal sound-bites, Jake Stephenson, together with Brian Trower (as Optica), insisted upon spelling out the word "marijuana" and commanding listeners to "wrap your lips round that" on tracks from the Goa/ ambient release *F-U-Z-Z* (1997), the staple herb and its resin is rather more likely to be absorbed in the sonic structures of psychedelic music than evoked in its vocal samples. The widespread use of *charas* offers some explanation for the popularity of the Portuguese term *sussegado* ("laid-back" and "easy-going"), a local variant, Elliott (2010: 28) observes, on the traveller appropriation of the Hindi term for "peace or tranquillity": *shanti.* It also goes some way towards explaining why Goa had become the destination in the East where Westerners and Indians alike could experience "spiritual hedonism" with fewer hindrances. It was and would remain a critical nexus in what D'Andrea identified as the "freak-ethnoscape" (2004: 249) at the crossroads of "horizontal" (geo-spatial) and "vertical" (metaphysical, psychedelic) "trips". In D'Andrea's ethnography of "nomadic spirituality," *Global Nomads*, alternative travellers are shown to be experienced across exotic sites and transcendent states. Expressive expatriates are nomads of the globe and the self, trailblazers experienced with "strangeness, rootlessness and displacement much before these qualities became considered by the media and academia to be predicaments of contemporary life" (D'Andrea 2007a: 224).

In various works, especially *Naked Lunch* (1959), William Burroughs explored a concept resonating with this collision of horizontal and vertical lines of flight. According to Jonathon Carmichael (2004: 20), who recognizes similarities with Australian "doofs" (bush parties), an *interzone* is "a withdrawal space for people who don't quite fit into normal western morals or thought processes ... Part South American and part Eastern bohemia", it is a terrain of "promiscuous and ambivalent behaviour where expansive substance use, creative output, and many other strange things are rife". Across this transnational bohemian topography one might have found the infrastructure, resources and company to abandon the world beyond. The domain holds characteristics in common with the "Temporary Autonomous Zone" (1991a) popularized by Hakim Bey whose ideas circulated contemporaneous with the emergence of Goatrance; except here the interzone more approximates a psychonautical free-for-all than a utopian TAZ. In 1994, California Sunshine's Har-El Prussky, an early engine-house of Goa in Israel, attempted to capture the spirit. His "Inter-zone", released that year on the Phonokol compilation *Trans Nova Express*, was bookended with Burroughs grumbling "hash, coke and heroin to last a hundred years and the longevity drugs to enjoy". On another unspectacular track from that release, "Outer-zone", Prussky found it useful to flash those final words in sonic neon: "drugs to enjoy".

The idea of the interzone evokes the freak outland on the coast of Goa where isolated beaches became safe havens for high-experimentation invested with the creative and decadent influence of expatriates and dedicated musicians throughout the 1970s and 1980s. Those sojourners who knew the formative beach and full-moon parties in Goa – or Manali, in the Himalayan mountains of Hidachi Pradesh – inhabited a zone barely describable, yet occasioning life-changing experiences. "It was like stepping into another world", writes Dave Mothersole (2010), a former south London soul-boy reporting on his first party in Anjuna in late August 1986, one for which he and his companions were not prepared. "We'll show these hippies what it's all about", he had assumed on the approach.

> As we grew closer I could see dozens of Royal Enfields haphazardly abandoned on the pathway that led to the carcass of the old Catholic church where the party was being held ... Outside Indian chi ladies from the local villages had set up little stalls selling tea and cakes and all around people were dancing like it was their last night on earth. Clouds of pungent Manali smoke filled the air as the incessant, narcotic groove chugged away like a runaway train. It was like *Lord Of The Flies* and H.G. Wells' *Time Machine* in a blender with an acid fried version of *Miami Vice*. A post apocalyptic Monte Carlo, reclaimed by nature and inhabited by a

> tribe of wild, decadent, jet set gypsies partying their way into some new collective consciousness.

Dosed up on liquid acid from a "whacking great needle-less syringe" wielded by a kid in a Mickey Mouse tracksuit "sporting the best Billy Idol haircut" he'd ever seen, Mothersole had stepped into another world. "A few thousand miles from where we were from, but a million miles from anything we knew". Mothersole and other commentators have favourably recalled the wild diversity of those gathering in free clandestine parties hosting barely a few hundred people, and who were possessed with an animated spirit unknown elsewhere. Karin Silenzi de Stagni cherishes the experience of never knowing or caring about who the DJ was.

> For me, coming from drumming parties in the jungle of Brazil, this was the international update of a ritual celebration. At the beginning, I felt it was too electronic for my taste, but after few sips of Eric's punch and some good basic earthy beats weaved with melodic samples from diverse cultural backgrounds it worked the magic on me and [I] couldn't stop dancing ... even now!! I didn't like when the music were only synthesizers ... [I wanted] some South American carnavalito, some Arabic singing, some African drumming or other ethnic spices to touch me deep.[15]

Reflecting on the significance of the Goa dance floor of the late 1980s and early 1990s, Roadjunky (2006) wrote: "Ideally no one stood about or talked. And you'd feel the personalities of hundreds of people expressed through dance. There were the hoof and elbow stampers of the Israeli chieftains, the springs and twirls of Greek nymphs and the martial aerobics of Japanese travellers exploring the meaning of freedom for the first time." The same chronicler commented:

> You knew who your friends on the dance floor were although you probably never exchanged a word. Often you might not even see them again until the next party and then you'd continue from where you left off. Soul mates recognized each other for the first time and no one could hide who they were. As dawn hit at one party I felt a tap on my shoulder from a young Portuguese DJ – he squeezed a drop of liquid acid onto my palm and twisted away into the dance floor before I could even smile (Roadjunky 2006).

On the beach: Goa's music scenes of the 1970s and 1980s

But I'm getting ahead of the story. Goa had been the beach setting for spontaneous dance jams from the late 1960s, with Anjuna, Calangute and Vagator beaches host to ecstatic gatherings from the early 1970s. Many recognize the important role of the "original freak", the magnetic jazz bassist and existentialist writer Eight Finger Eddie, as an instigator of this scene. Making a notable break from the prison with imperceptible bars known as "life" in the United States, and drawing others to his unique style of unpretentious enlightenment, Eddie settled in Goa in 1966 when he rented a house (which eventually became Vince's Bar) on Colva Beach, later moving to Anjuna.[16]

It was Eddie who Gil came looking for in 1970. Referred to as "Goa Gil" as early as 1974, Gil departed San Francisco in 1969, where he'd been involved with Chet Helm's Family Dog collective and had travelled as a roadie with the rock band Sons of Champlin before heading to Amsterdam and subsequently trekking the overland route to Goa. As Jeff 604 (n.d.) recalls, between November and April (winter; i.e. the party season) through the 1970s, Eastern-trekking hippies would rendezvous at the beach paradise where Eddie had already become well known. As Devas (2004) wrote:

> truckloads of hippies in Kombis and Bundesrepublik PTT postal vans wound their way down the Khyber Pass, like so many invaders before and descended on the plains of Hindustan. An invasion of sorts, but this time no Mongols, no hordes of Genghis Khan, nor even a despoiling British Raj, but a funky, stoned-out band of troubadours, who wanted nothing more than to dance in the moonlight under palm trees and perform their Puja of the Purple Haze.

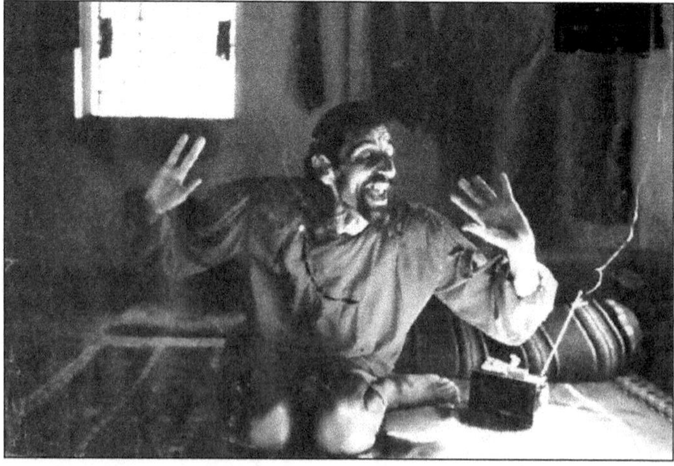

Eight Finger Eddie, 1991/92. Photo: Luc Pliot.

Arriving overland, with many enduring hardships and ordeals or otherwise encountering epiphanies and life-changing experiences at spectacular junctures along the "hippie trail", Goa was cherished as an off-world paradise for travellers, a place where arrivals could share tales with fellow freaks, long before expatriation became a packaged tour-option and raving a desirable experiential commodity for foreign and domestic tourists alike.

When Gil arrived in Goa, there were ad hoc parties over the Christmas and New Year period when hippies plucked acoustic guitars, played flute, beat hand-drums and crooned around fires on the beach. At this time, Gil performed a repertoire of his own original songs, including "God's Children are Everywhere", written *en route* to India in 1969 and played guitar in the period before electricity came to Anjuna (c. 1975). Among those who were considered integral to the transit from jams around the fire to the full-moon parties on the beach were Irish Franny and Detroit Freddie, who became "Goa-grown rock stars" following their arrival circa 1973.[17] While the scene was originally acoustic, even prior to the arrival of electricity, car and bike batteries and generators were used to power small house sound systems. Gil recalls that it was during the 1973/74 season that he first DJed from tape cassettes "off the porch of some house" in Anjuna and then, in the following season (1974/75), played on Anjuna beach after the flea market on a "little Fender PA system with generator owned by a friend". It was in 1973/74 too that Malcolm and Davina showed up in their bus having left the UK hauling Marshall amps and other equipment gifted by Pete Townshend.[18] According to Devas, the "band's worth of gear" with which they departed England had dwindled to a single amp over the long passage to Anjuna,[19] although in Gil's recollections among the equipment were loudspeakers The Who used as monitors. Regardless of what equipment actually survived the journey, subsequent rumours that The Who had played Goa were rife. Gil recalls that this system provided the sound for the "Teenage Wasteland" parties in middle Anjuna beach in 1973/74, adding that these were "possibly some of the first parties where music on tapes was played at the beach on amplified speakers".[20] In this period, Gil carried a suitcase loaded with an arsenal of cassette tapes, a collection which included not only the psychedelic rock of The Beatles, The Rolling Stones, Jimi Hendrix, Santana, The Grateful Dead and all the bands of the San Francisco Sound, but "soul classics" like Otis Redding, James Brown, Ike and Tina Turner, Bobby Blue Bland, Chuck Berry and Little Richard. Coltrane, Davis, "Blues, Rhythm & Blues, and even Reefer songs from the 40s" were included in his selections.[21] Gil was therefore already one of Goa's proto-selectors in a period where he, as he informed me, "started to try to use music to create a story or storyline, reflecting the world, the things we were experiencing, and the times we were living in".

But Gil was not the only DJ-pioneer, as others imported sounds and visual elements rendering the beach scene unique. According to Devas, Swedish film-maker Anders Tillman was crucial since he "brought a jazz funk flavour to the parties playing Herbie Hancock, Brazilian soul funk and the like".[22] Arriving in February 1970 (the same month as Gil), Anders DJed at private parties from 1976/77. He recalls a signature moment in 1978 playing Eric Clapton's as yet unreleased cover of J.J. Cale's "Cocaine" on cassette at a party at a house in Chuvar shared with English Keith where lunghies dyed with Ikat patterns hung from the walls. Over that season, Anders worked every week at the Rose Garden in Anjuna where he played from tapes all night "creating a story" for the crowd. The Rose Garden was known to host the first "public parties" outside the full-moons – which were significant in the history of the coming movement since "canned music" was played for the duration of the evening (and not just between the live acts). The Swede indicated that his most memorable achievement was introducing disco at that time, explaining that Donna Summer's "Love to Love You Baby" was "the first trance song", with its producer Giorgio Moroder regarded as "the grandfather of trance". Among the more notable of events in the late 1970s was the famous White Party at Narayan's house, so called since it was the first time blacklight was used (illuminating white pigment).[23] Anders also outlined the distinct scenes evolving on different beaches: "we had our different strata, partially based on where we went to live, Candolim, wealthy, Baga, the oldest, who didn't move along to Anjuna, where we were more progressive, and Vagator, where they wanted to distance themselves, from the rest, also the latest comers, and Arambol, the Hippies, they still play acoustic music there".[24]

In 1978, parties already occasioned a "social break" between the majority who listened passively to the "classic styles of music" and those who came specifically to dance. But the dancers were still in the minority. Anders recalled how his neighbour Jimmy the Knife once threatened "to cut my throat because I played Led Zeppelin at full blast, at 8 o'clock in the morning".[25] Another notable DJ at this time was German Paoli (Paoli Münchenbach), who arrived at Colva Beach in 1975 and moved to Vagator then Anjuna soon after, playing often two or three times a week at private parties like those made by Pepe and Roberta at Massimos and Hans Pyramid in an area referred to as "Gumal Vaddo" where he always played "all night long". Also DJing in Baga at the Eminence parties and those thrown by the Amsterdam Balloon Company, Paoli played Captain Beefheart, Zappa, Tyla Gang, along with "krautrock" material from Can, Neu! and Faust, and by 1978 was playing Afrobeat, Afro psycho rock, Jùjú, Latin and funk like Fela and T.P. Orchestre Poly-Rythmo. Also that year, he says he played the first 12-inch records in Goa (recorded on cassette), reeling out reggae and heavy dub over the next two years, including material from the likes of Keith Hudson, The Detonators, Dr Alimantado, and specifically Sly & Robbie's "War of the Gods", Pablo Gad's "Bloodsuckers (Dub)", and Reggae Regular's 12-inch extended version of "The Black Star Liner" (which ran to 9:25 minutes). Given the prevalence of rock in those days, Paoli stated he "sometimes needed protectors", namely "Pierot a French/ Canadian Rasta, & Rasta John a Black English/Jamaican" who helped keep the peace.[26]

Throughout the early 1970s, spontaneous dance jams on the beach had evolved into the monthly full-moon gatherings. These regular foundation events were sumptuous and extravagant occasions encouraging the most spectacular individual styles illuminated under the lunar orb. As Anders recalled, "in the seventies, we were the deco … and we spent the whole month creating our dressup". Freaks plied their imaginations, gathered materials and local tailors were often employed to do the sewing.[27] The involvement of Devas in the full-moon party development is crucial since, as stated to me, he "founded the Goa live band music scene on Anjuna beach on 10 November 1974" after returning from the Tsang Fook Music Store in Hong Kong (and successfully negotiating customs at Bombay Airport) with "two Stratocasters, Fender bass guitar, two Fender amps, bass amp, mics and bits and pieces". The equipment was taken to the stage at South Anjuna beach for "the first live party". Devas continues:

> Friends and well wishers built the stage, others donated a keyboard and drum kit and then, as if by magic, amazing musicians appeared and Anjuna began its passionate love affair with serenading the stars and dancing wildly under the moonlight. For three seasons I managed the rock and roll bands that played on full moons and at other parties, including, in March 1975, a memorable gig at the Goa Carnival in honour of King Momo. With some good friends, I rented a large Goan Portuguese mansion at the back of Anjuna where I kept the music gear and this, the "Italian House", was the first Music House. We jammed and had some rehearsals there but for the most part all the parties were on the beach.[28]

At this time, Goa Gil co-wrote original work, played guitar and performed vocals for the freak ensemble The Anjuna Jam Band, and later played bass in The Big Dipper band, which was, according to Devas, "the longest running and arguably most successful Goa hippy band to come out of the seventies music scene … It lasted all through Gil's tenure of party manager and music house operator".[29] Devas further remarked that the parties attained "sublime heights never seen again" when funky French rock trio he dubbed "Patrick & Co" appeared in the 1974/75 season.[30] By 1976, Anjuna was becoming a thriving seasonal freak music scene. In March 1977, Devas sold the equipment to Gil who kept it in a house near Chopora also dubbed the "Music House". In this new location, musicians, stated Gil, "could meet other musicians, form proper bands, and have a place to rehearse".[31] At this time, Gil travelled back to the US and returned with "a proper stereo PA mixer with multiple inputs, guitar and bass strings, drumsticks, microphones, effects units, tubes for the amplifiers" and other accessories required to maintain a live music scene. He had a large PA built by a sound technician in Bombay, and built another stage at the beach at South Anjuna. The period between 1977 through 1980 "became very organized with live bands, djs between the bands, parties every saturday

Anjuna Beach full-moon party. c. 1976. Photo: Gilbert Garcia.

Anjuna Beach, mixing hut, full-moon party, 1979, with Scott Thompson and Black Michael. Photo: Gilbert Garcia.

at the music house, and full moons, christmas and new years at our stage on the beach".[32]

Impressed by the scene's live psychedelic "jam band" environment, Peter Ziegelmeier recalls how "we jammed all night to break away from the three minute pop song". Ziegelmeier was part of an expat milieu of artists who seasonally commuted between Goa and European cosmopoles where they were exposed to underground scenes and sounds, developing tape cut-up techniques deleting lyrics obsessed with "whether the girl likes me or dislikes me", with the deliberate omission of signifiers of attachment and desire better enabling the expansion of consciousness.[33] These frontier editors created "special mix" tapes using obscure material spliced from the B-sides ("dub-sides") of diverse 12-inch records, performing, exchanging and remixing these mixes in an evolving environment of creative exchange. Indeed the trade in material from collections is a legendary aspect of the Goa scene, enabling the rapid dispersal of fresh tracks.[34] Spokespersons from the period recall the sheer diversity of music played in Goa, and it was an environment in which the DJ, as a seasoned carrier of fresh and diverse sound, would gain prominence (over the band). At first playing from cassette, then digital audio tape (DAT[35]) and later CD – though not vinyl since open-air extremes were adverse to optimum performance and vinyl/turntables were difficult to transport – DJing would become the prominent mode of performance in Goa. Under pressures to perform all through the night, perhaps several nights a week, in a remote region, controlling music selections from cassette and DAT proved to be the most cost-effective and efficient technique of performance delivery. Drum kits and other traditional instruments were onerous and expensive to transport, and the stamina of band members waned well before sunrise. DJs were also usually not paid for their services. As had been discovered in Jamaica and in the proto-discos of New York at the turn of the 1970s, powered machines under the control of the autonomous DJ, or team of DJs, proved to be the perfect devices to sustain the all-night party, together with an assortment of psychoactive drugs. With expensive overheads, including equipment rental and buying-off police, along with the requirement for local appeasements, as Anders observed, organizing a party was like "political fundraising".

By the 1980s, the parties had expanded in size as a reflection of the growing numbers of foreign visitors to Goa: increasing from 17,234 arrivals in 1977 to 33,430 in 1980 and 97,533 in 1986, over which period a younger traveller population imported new stylistic identifications, including punk, reggae and soul (Elliott 2010: 30), but also goth and new wave. As this expat party enclave was infused with rapid developments in electronic music production and performance in the 1980s, a "Goa" sound emerged, the eclecticism of which held comparison with the Balearic sound of Ibiza. As the 1970s came to a close, the birthing cries of a new dance music movement – and the death throes of the old – were audible in Tangerine Dream, Kraftwerk and Yellow Magic Orchestra whose sounds drifted across the beaches of Goa. But while the reception of ambient electronica was keen within this scene – and remained throughout the psychedelic trance development – what was decried as "techno" was met with resistance as older freaks poured scorn on the new electronic sounds. In an interview for the documentary project *Goa Hippy Tribe*,[36] Devas was clear that "something changed". Younger freaks were arriving experienced in the underground summer disco scenes of Europe, such as Anand's place in Can Punta, Ibiza, industrial avant-garde scenes like The Loft in Berlin's Metropole club, and other scenes in Paris, London, Riccione and Rimini. "A whole group of new people. They brought out new amplifiers. Very powerful amplifiers. So they set up a party and they had the best equipment, and they had all this music, which seemed to flip from the high hippie music to techno" (D. Devas, dir. 2010a). Devas further recalled what he identifies as the "defining moment". It happened around the turn of the 1980s. A gentle hippie known as "Homeopathic Peter" gained sudden fame on the beach when word went around that he'd "punched out" a Canadian DJ, a financier known as Dr Bobby, at a private house party in Calangute. The incident, which Peter himself referred to as a "slap out", was a reaction to what was widely regarded as the blatant "hijacking of the music by the arrogant and moneyed classes of Anjuna" who "had no interest in what people wanted and were just into their own heads, their exclusive house parties and cocaine".[37] The Canadian had a powerful amplifier and was "instrumental in setting up these new parties". For Devas, this incident provided the soundtrack to "the end". There was a palpable sense of loss (D. Devas, dir. 2010a). In his correspondence with me the period is identified by Devas as "a *coup d'état*. A musical putsch by the *noir* partyites. Lyrical hippyism was dead in the water. It left no traces". He was unequivocal: "techno music and these deejays were a disaster for the beach".[38] Others would voice similar concerns. In a Facebook message thread in support of Devas's video, Charli Santiago (5 April 2010) recalled "the change in music, I heard it was german coke heads who brought the techno. for me it was like the emperor who wore no clothes. I couldnt understand what was so great about it. Everyone was tripping out to the techno but I ... always thought it was heavy, and too hard. it was an acquired tast, you had to be off your head to enjoy it". And later, in the same thread (16 January 2011), Bernhard Leyendeckers, a resident of Goa from 1969–1990, confirmed that with the coming of the new music "the dream ended". For Devas, the dream was over before it had begun. What he styled the "Cosmo Rock movement" was still in its infancy in 1978, but the arrival of electronic music destroyed "a potentially dynamic and inspiring style of music to follow seventies UK and California rock into an Indo-Hybrid new wave of rock music, that was to be high, lyrical and drivey with ethno world funk baselines to make for subtle and sophisticated dance movements. In other words, music for beach, sun and palm trees and not cars, factories and mechanical big city urban landscapes".[39]

As one dream faded another began – albeit not without a commotion. Though he would become a vociferous critic of the "fundamentalist psytrance" of the 1990s, which saw the codification of unregimented psychedelia into a "deity enshrined product" with "strict aesthetic rules", Ray Castle relays a story from the 1981/82 season, when Fred Disko played "disco parties". Castle himself had played early funk, disco, ska and industrial rock in the late 1970s/early 1980s Auckland, and landed in Goa in 1987 where he began playing in 1989. Though Castle wasn't present in Goa in the early 1980s, he is reminded of the reaction to Dylan when he went electric: "All the hardcore Anjuna traditional hippies, rebelled and freaked and tried to prevent them playing techno, disco and saying 'this is not psychedelic, this is not the real thing man. We're into psychedelic rock and it's gotta be live music'. And they actually attacked the sound system and stopped DJs like Fred Disko". Disko himself confirmed that, while incidents were "too many too mention", he recalls that the power was cut and the generator stolen during the night at Disco Valley in 1983, and on another occasion the DJ booth was collapsed. He even commented, half-jokingly, that he had to enlist a friend as a "bouncer" after partygoers tried to prevent him from playing.[40] For Devas, who was at the front lines of this culture war, and lamented the loss of an authentic "live" music scene, such stories might afford those he regarded as "techno-tyrants", and "ego fuelled late-night cocaine swingers with no interest in what the audience wanted,"[41] with an undeserving heroism. In his view, far from an aging behemoth, the "Cosmo Rock" scene was still in its prime when cut asunder by the new prometheans. Castle passed comment on another figure involved in this debacle. Goa Gil "was one of the people who blocked or resisted the techno", which, Castle figured, stole attention away from his band.[42]

Renowned as a great collector of new material, Gil himself would eventually DJ electronic music outside the private party scene in Goa by 1986/87, having grown especially interested in electronic body music (EBM).[43] But the transition to electronic music had been earlier. During the 1983/84 season, the newly arrived Frenchman, Laurent, teamed up with Fred Disko, and together with Swiss Rudi, Swiss Arnaud and French Fabien, performed all-night sets over that and the subsequent season, laying down a devastating mix of new sounds, including the first European post-punk experimental music, the Neue Deutsche Welle, and EBM acts like Front 242, Nitzer Ebb and Skinny Puppy. The early signs of what was to become a DJ-led scene were evident, and riding behind pitch-controlled Sony Walkman Professional WM-D6Cs, Laurent was at the helm. Laurent is possibly one of the most mysterious figures in DJ history, with the only journalist ever to score an interview with him (Davis 1995),[44] amplifying the mystique.[45] But while Laurent is most often lauded as the first to DJ electronic sounds in Goa, Davis reported that Laurent himself gave Fred Disko this credit – though his mixes were initially "too bizarre" for the crowds. Indeed Disko, who arrived in Goa in 1979, performing often in a sparkling gold outfit, was the pioneer of electronic soundscapes in Goa. While electronic music had been introduced to Goa dance crowds previously, Disko experimented with full sets of mostly German punk new wave electronic music from the 1979/80 season, with highlights, as stated to me, including the first Jungle Palace party in Vagator in 1980/81 and the Circus party at South Anjuna beach organized by American Robert and English John Miles on 12 February 1982. On that occasion, it was just before midnight when Miles slipped Disko an unspecified tape and said "play this now" as the lights went off. As they came back up, "Peter and the Wolf" echoed down the beach as a full circus troupe with clowns, elephants and monkeys began a two-hour performance at the side of the dance floor. Everyone was surprised, including Disko. As the Sun came up, kids were seen seated atop elephants, camels and horses all along the beach. "You can never forget something like that". Another notable occasion was Acid Eric's Breakfast party in Anjuna, which lasted for three days and nights in February 1983. The party went down near a huge Banyan tree painted in brilliant fluorescent colours using pigments bought in local hardware stores and blacklight tubes.[46] Disko played from his Sharp twin cassette player, featuring the all-important fader control.[47] Cutting out lyrics on cassette tapes at the Saint Tropez French House outside Chapora from 1980/81, he played experimental splices of Yello, Joy Division, Throbbing Gristle, A Certain Ratio, The Residents, Lene Lovich, Nina Hagen and Tuxedomoon, among others, throughout this period of transition.[48] Also in 1981, German Paoli, another pioneer of electronic music, was lining up synth-pop, experimental, dub and new wave sounds from the likes of Pyrolator, 23 Skidoo, Pig Bag, Tom Tom Club, Medium Medium and Ghostwriters' "Sleedermauseman", which Paoli recalls was "mind blowing for this time".

Fred Disko (right), full-moon party, Vagator, 1981. Photo: Fred Disko.

While the likes of Paoli and Disko paved the way for the coming dawn, and weathered the freak storm in the process, Laurent's legendary contribution is indisputable. In his capable hands, "acidheads, at first disdainful, began to prefer these futuristic sounds to the wah-wah of Jimi Hendrix" (Jeff 604 n.d.). Recollecting the early scene in a report Laurent did personally approve, Mothersole (2010) describes Laurent as

> The real father of Trance. A true legend ... just as Chicago had Ron Hardy and Detroit had The Electrifying Mojo, Goa had a DJ called Laurent. If it wasn't for him, it's quite possible that the music played at parties in Goa would have been little more than a carbon copy of what was going on back in Europe and America. But like all true pioneers, Laurent made it much more than the sum of its parts and in doing so created a whole new style of music.

Having previously played parties on a rented barge on the Seine, Laurent arrived in Vagator in early March 1984, with "all the latest explosive stuff of the time" (Laurent 2010). Maintaining harvest of a steady supply of fresh audio-cargo from Europe and the US, he used tape cut-up techniques – using the same Sony devices he mixed with – and mixed new wave, Italo-disco, EBM, new beat, goth, electro, Hi-NRG, synth-pop and house, to create mesmerizing sets through the 1980s, shaping the sound of Goa. Re-edits of Blancmange's "Living on the Ceiling" (1982), Boytronic's "Hurts" (1986) and Soft Cell's "Sex Dwarf" (1981) were highlights for Mothersole. One can imagine the quavering siren and thump of Neon's "Voices" (1988) echoing down the beach and out to sea, or the instrumental version of Poésie Noire's electro "Timber" (1987) cutting swathes through even the hardened among jungle ravers, or otherwise becoming set adrift to Jean-Michel Jarre's "Zoolookologie" (1985). Right through the decade, the work of Cabaret Voltaire, A Split Second, DAF, Konzept, Microchip League, Revolting Cocks, Shriekback, Signal Aout 42, Trilithon, Yello and other outfits favoured by Laurent was stitched together sans the vocals to animate the proto trance massive ... all night long. Working in classics such as Telex's "Moskow Diskow" (1988), Front 242's "Commando Mix" (1984) and "Election Day" by Arcadia (1985), and performing for up to ten hours at a time, Laurent shepherded the freak flock well past midnight and into the dawn.

> He would move from dark, hard hypnotic beats during the night, to sweet, uplifting, sun kissed grooves in the morning. From Skinny Puppy and Nitzer Ebb to Koto and Laser Dance; from 100 to 150bpm; from nightmare-ish and scary to blissed out and glorious. It was a heady combination and one that had a tremendous impact on the lives of many (Mothersole 2010).

Bass player in Killing Joke and founder of the first Goatrance label, Martin "Youth" Glover was among the impressed. Glover recalls watching Laurent "under a cloud of dust mixing from two cassette decks", adding "I've never had anyone blow my mind like that guy" (in Photon 2005).

Laurent's style was simply devastating and his sonic aesthetic resisted categorization. "Real psy", according to Castle, "is beyond genre". The distinctive feature of the collision of styles in Goa in the late 1980s was its "plural diversity". "Each track", he averred, "had narrative personality and character. Goa, 80s–94, wasn't driven by labels and music industry. Travellers and collectors exchanged music. The best tracks were distilled down over the party season and played in the parties by discerning DJs". Though, he added, "often, by not so cogent DJs". But Laurent was anything but undiscerning, since he

> had the sharpest perception of which music cut it for the emerging Goa atmos-logos, drawing from access to the most discerning collector sources. These sound nuggets he was able to weave, using tape player decks, into seamless, empowering, marathon mosaic mixes for tripped out dancers. This was truly beyond any typical disco or night club story (Castle aka genkigroove 2010).

Gil and Laurent playing a party on South Anjuna beach, 1991. Photo: Goa Gil.

Furthermore, as Castle recalls, "the 80s techno/acid house/neu beat/ electronic body music" of which Laurent was the lead conductor, was generally under 130 bpm, which gave dancers "more space for expressive movement". If it's over 140 bpm, he warned, "the kick/bass dynamic locks everything down, so that dancers get into this marching, robotic, style of response" (Castle aka genkigroove 2010). Under 140 bpm, from the mid 1980s until 1994, the Laurent sound became the sound of Goa. Over that period, Laurent had no means to leave Goa, earned no money DJing and was forced to gamble at backgammon for a living.[49] By 1994, he was prevented from playing due to lung problems developed over years of breathing in sand and dust on duty at the desk.

By 1986, the music played at parties on the shores of the Arabian Sea and in the jungle hinterlands was exclusively electronic. By the end of the decade, under the influence of the Frankfurt techno trance sound, Detroit techno and acid house from Chicago (Rietveld 2010: 75), and with the intense repurposing of the sounds of "acid" programmed on Roland TB-303 bass synthesizers and TR-808 drum machines, there were seasonal anthems. Jeff 604 (n.d.) recalls that, while it wasn't made explicitly for Goa, the first proto-Goatrance tune was The KLF's "What Time is Love?", which he states was "judiciously" called the "Pure Trance" version (1988). This track doubtlessly drew wide appeal, but we might well ask what is protean within a context of constant stylistic input, fusion and metamorphosis? In her recognition of the rhizomatic character of "musical cosmopolitanism", Hillegonda Rietveld emphasizes the significance of the psychedelic electronica of German cosmic rock band Tangerine Dream, indicating that, in producing "What Time is Love? (Pure Trance 1)", The KLF added a 4/4 beat to a sequence almost identical to Tangerine Dream's "Thru Metaphoric Rocks" (*Force Majeure*, 1979), in which "arpeggiated sixteenths combine with synthesized drone washes and dreamlike sound effects over ten minutes at 138 bpm" (Rietveld 2010: 74). *Force Majeure* itself illustrates the transition under way at the end of the 1970s, from cosmic experimental to *motorik*. The "propelling arpeggio format" of "Thru Metaphoric Rocks" was generated, as Rietveld reminds us, by the "Synthanorma-Sequencer" customized for Kraftwerk's "Trans Europe Express" (1977), "in which the exacting tonality of the sequences produce the experience of travelling in an efficient, modern, fast moving train" (Rietveld 2010: 74–5). By the dawn of Goatrance, its formative artists adopted and reserviced this *motorik*, notably on X-Dream's classic "Trancesylvania X-press" (*Trip to Trancesylvania*, 1993) and, perhaps more famously, their cosmic express train aptly named "The 5th Dimension" ("cosmic" mix, released on the 1993 12-inch by that name).

"No one can know about this. You understand? No one"

The seasonal network produced experimental, worshipful and celebrational parties, where musicians and selectors blended diverse styles of dance music blowing the minds of test-subjects, and where, in time, tracks were produced specifically for these seasonal audiences. And the principal site for these experiments was the beach-interzones of Anjuna and Vagator, in particular. A liminal region between sea and land, the beach has been an especially potent and idyllic space for travellers of European origin. The beach holds variant meanings for cultures, and subcultures – as it surely holds strikingly varied valuations for Goa fishing communities and those freaks hailing from metropolitan centres where the remote beach offers respite from the city, the stage for one's escapades from trouble and toil, a zone of carnivalesque pleasures. Those who seek to dwell on the beach for any stretch of time, perhaps indefinitely, are expressing their will to be free from wage slavery, surveillance and moral injunctions, perhaps even civilization itself – a circumstance that may strike fear in moralists who invest in tales of moral degeneration, such as that implicit to the film *The Beach* (2000), or enthuse prospectors who invest in the beachfront as a commodity resource subject to gentrification and as a tourist catchment zone. Those who regard the beach as a space of freedom are able to experience it as such though their privileged power of mobility – their capacities to frequently arrive and depart from these sites. The hippies who began arriving for seasons in Goa (and Ibiza) in the 1960s had arguably acquired the most advanced powers of mobility for any expatriate cohorts in history – that is, by cohorts whose *counter*-cultural proclivities were not

Party at Arambol, 1991. Photo: Goa Gil.

characterized by anti-state violence. By comparison to *tourists* who make superficial dips into scenery and culture, "neonomads" are *travellers* (of the mind and body). Importantly, D'Andrea (2007a: 207) makes reference to the mandatory freak machine, the motorcycle, which has been an enduring symbol of freedom for travellers, whether domestic traveller subcultures like mods (Moped), and motorcycle gangs (Harley Davidson), or transnational freaks in Goa (Enfield). A transition machine enabling a rider to live *in transit,* to exist between states of departure and arrival, the motorcycle is a superbly valorized dream machine whose powers for personal transcendence are mythologized in a fashion borrowed from horse-riding – with which it shares notoriety as a super-individualized mode of transport.

In Goa, the freedoms enjoyed in the liminal space (the beach) and on the liminal machine (the motorbike) converged. There, privileged travellers could ride the interstices – the more "horse" power and with fewer restrictions (i.e. helmets, speed limits) the better. As a perfected tool of independence, and an inhering symbol of mobility, Royal Enfields (the 350cc Bullet) have been subject to special valorization. The first Goa resident to produce his own tunes, Johann Bley, once sampled an Enfield engine on an unreleased track he called "Bulletbaby" which he stated to me did not survive a combination of theft, dust and monsoons.[50] In 1996, pioneering Finnish Goatrance outfit O*Men released "Rajdoot" (*Goa Tribes,* 1996), an apparent homage to the Rajdoot 350, a modification of the Yamaha RD350B popular in India in the late 1980s and likely favoured by Petri Koskinen and Peter Bäckman (O*Men). The significance of the beach-cycle hybrid was captured on the cover of the 1991 EP *Fast Forward the Future,* which Martin Glover, who did seasons in Goa for ten years, produced in collaboration with Mark Manning (as Zodiacyouth). What appears to be an Enfield stands on sand with a shoreline surging nearby. It's an inviting production. The album track, "Don't Smoke Acid" (remixed by Elysium) beseeches: "Go to India, for some ..." The open-endedness of this sonic travel brochure was no doubt alluring for listeners at the time. Later, mixed with Hindi, the Enfield's crackling engine is the first sound onboard "Arambol", the short opener to Solar Quest's (George Saunders) mix album of his own material *AcidOphilez* (1998).

The diversity of sounds propagating across the beaches and thumping within the jungle hinterlands of Goa were resounding echoes of the scene's roots in a global network of cosmopolitan centres and dance scenes and a profusion of 1980s electronica: industrial, EBM, acid house, techno and trance sounds. The circulation of MDMA had become a crucial factor by the end of the 1980s, fuelling formative domestic dance scenes like the acid techno/house scene in Spain described as *la ruta del bacalao.* As Anders pointed out, in 1987/88 "people spent the whole weekend driving between Valencia and Madrid, the parties were made in discos, parking lots of supermarkets, and wherever they'd get away with it ... Chimo Bayo was one of the main artists, and we did play some of that music".[51] By the turn of the 1990s, the Goa sound was carrying what Rietveld (2010: 79) calls a "psychedelic *motorik*" that may have been amplified in the trance or hard trance coming out of Germany, but in the noise of influences, precise origins and transition points are difficult, if not impossible, to determine. While the techno-trance music that was known as the "Frankfurt sound" had a bearing on the Goa sound, Goatrance did not strictly evolve *from* music denoted as "trance", but simply absorbed these 1980s styles into an evolving aesthetic flourishing within an enduring experimental dance scene, which, by the turn of the 1990s, gained word-of-mouth recognition as a "trance dance" culture. What then came to be known as "trance" developed into various commercially successful genres including progressive trance; the latter influencing the sound of what had become recognized as psytrance by the end of the 1990s.[52] Replying to a thread on the Discogs discussion group "Goa/Psy-Trance", Meltdown23 (2010) offers insight on the early 1990s development:

> The music was from all over europe and elsewhere, ebm, new beat, italia house, spanish ebm, the odd english track, all spliced and diced by the then DJs. For me in goa 1990 it was mainly the last remnants of new beat being played there, but to those who were there in 91 and 92 that was the start of what we called Trance Dance, as a way of collectively describing the music we heard, but its true to say, that if one of these songs was isolated on its own it could only be called techno or ebm, (or nowadays Old School) but once played in a set with similar music and edited and chopped it became Goa Trance Dance, well to us at least, And 92 was no different really apart from the music becoming even more melodic, and to be honest artists were not making music specifically for goa at that time, it was of course a Dj led scene.

The same commentator adds further insight on the Goa sound, which emerged in 1993: "all these early goa producers were just trying to mimic what they had heard from the pioneering djs and extend it musically, its then that the music changed into the genre we now know". At this juncture (i.e. 1993), "djs from england and elsewhere started arriving in goa to play their take on the goa sound, this is when it changed" (Meltdown23 2010).

While objections have been raised about the formulation of genre implicit to those efforts to refine and define the seasonal mixes in tracks released on EPs and albums, others have warranted that this process enabled excellence. This is, not unsurprisingly, the position of Glover – who, besides playing bass for The Killing Joke, wrote, produced for and performed bass with The Orb, worked with Ben Watkins (Juno Reactor) and Alex and Jimmy Cauty (of The KLF) (besides producing for artists like Kate Bush, Crowded House,

The Verve, Kylie and U2), and founded the first Goatrance label, Dragonfly Records, in 1993. Signing the early The Infinity Project, Hallucinogen, Man With No Name, Doof, Total Eclipse, Pleiadians, Shakta and others, Dragonfly rapidly became the engine-house of the London (and global) psychedelic trance scene. "As it became more and more popular and the sound followed this evolutionary curve into high-octane trance", Glover confirms that "the bandwidth of expression" suddenly became narrow. "But in some ways", he adds, "that was good. It did cut out a lot of chaff from the wheat. It had to be really good to fit into that bandwidth and some artists really redefined it because of that and took it even further like Simon Posford and X-Dream" (in Photon 2005). Dragonfly operated from the studio of Glover's Butterfly Records where Posford worked as a studio engineer. As Hallucinogen (co-founder of Shpongle and member of many other acts and collaborations), Posford pushed the boundaries of the possible, becoming instrumental in the psychedelic trance emergence. Glover has no reservations, the man is "a genius ... without him those records wouldn't have been as good, he really raised the bar and was a major part of defining that genre". Posford's engineering skills are stamped all over early Goa productions like "Insect-a-Traction", the 1994 release from Shanti Druid (aka Sid Shanti and André Fluid Druid), and Slinky Wizard's "Wizard" (1994). He may have been thinking of "Angelic Particles" (1995), or the carnage-causing "Spiritual Antiseptic" (1997), or a dozen other works Posford produced as Hallucinogen, when, interviewed by Michael Gosney in the late 1990s, Raja Ram stated:

> He's a master of course. He would spend three days just working on a small drum pattern. You wouldn't believe that anyone could have the patience to do it, but he's such a perfectionist, and then when it's ready it's ready sort of thing. But no one usually takes the time or trouble and you can look at his work microscopically. There's just no flaws in it. Seamless (Gosney n.d.).

A host of producer/DJs stamped their influence on the seasonal interzone. Dane Ian Johansson (Ian Ion) was another Goa convert, perfectionist and powerhouse who had led 1980s punk synth-pop act Russia Heat and produced one of the first popular anthems specifically made for Goa, "Sundown" (The Overlords, 1991),[53] later forming projects Koxbox and Saiko-pod with Frank Kiehn Madsen (Frank E). Yet there are many principal figures among the artists who sought to capture, translate and modify the sound of the exile psychedelic *motorik* to global domestic settings.[54] With backgrounds in diverse styles and scenes, these artists became members of an emergent global psychedelic trance network, with Raja Ram perhaps the most prominent node. Having travelled to India in 1958 at the age of eighteen and returning thirty years hence, expat Australian Ron Rothfield (aka Raja Ram[55]) has had a seminal role in the production of Goatrance and its aftermath. In 1959, Raja Ram landed in New York's Greenwich Village where he frequented the Kettle of Fish on MacDougal St, once met Bob Dylan, played guitar in the coffee lounges, and dropped acid – in 1959, six years before it became illegal in the US – with friend and mentor Paul Gyss-Giraud, who later ran The Eclipse club on Freak Street in Kathmandu, Nepal. Jumping a freight ship to Morocco he fell in with a scene "indulging in the pursuit of the absolute" and lived on Ibiza until 1961. Having learned piano, drums, trombone, sax and guitar, in 1962, at the age of twenty-two, Raj studied flute at the Melbourne Conservatory, and then jazz flute with master of improvisation Lennie Tristano in New York in 1965. By 1969, he was fronting cosmic jazz outfit Quintessence with whom he performed 300 gigs including opening performances for Pink Floyd and Led Zeppelin. While becoming heavily involved in the cosmopolitan freak scene, none of it, he claims, was comparable to Goa (first visited in the 1988/89 season).[56]

> We heard the new music … and wanted to find out … where was it made … who made it … how did they make it … what drugs did they take? … Those parties remain the best maybe ever in my memory … thousands of ravers by the Arabian sea … dancing all night … everything free … and the vibe of LOVE in the air … and the feeling something new was happening.[57]

So inspired, he returned each season for seven years producing Goatrance with Graham Wood (and Simon Posford) as The Infinity Project.[58]

Raja Ram is not the only bridge to the earlier counterculture and its music. Various artists have demonstrated that the transit from cosmic rock, or as Devas styled the Goa rock scene, "Cosmo Rock", into electronic music, was not clean, nor total. Some commentators find the roots of the Goa sound in the psychedelic experimental musics of the previous decade. As stated on the Facebook group "Uplifting Goa Trance", Makis Bouros looks to experimental psychedelic rock on *Galactic Supermarket* by The Cosmic Jokers (a 1974 collaboration between Ash Ra Tempel and Klaus Schulze), which features "occasional 4/4 rhythms intertwined with elements from psy-rock, analog synthesizers and occasionally tribal-esque drum patterns". Many artists also transited from UK cosmic rock into Goa's cosmic trance. Notable are Steve Hillage and Miquette Giraudy, former members of the legendary UK space-rock group, Gong (formed by Daevid Allen in 1969), who formed techno and ambient outfit System 7 (in 1990). Hillage and Giraudy were also frequent collaborators with The Orb, the influential early 1990s ambient house outfit formed by Jimmy Cauty (of The KLF) and Alex Paterson. Notable, too, are Eat Static, formed in 1989 by former members (Joie Hinton and Merv Pepler) of Ozric Tentacles, the acid rock act forming in 1983 at the

Party at Bamboo Forest, 1991/92. Photo: Luc Pliot.

Stonehenge Free Festival.[59] Citing the influence of prog-rock acts Hawkwind, Gong, Tim Blake and Tangerine Dream, Dimension 5 (Christer Borge-Lunde and Charlie Clarke) also formed in 1989, identifying their debut album (*Transdimensional*, 1997) as "space techno psychedelic trance".

The seasonal practice, the techniques of electronic music production/ performance, the availability of MDMA, the trance dance scene, the work of various DJ-producers and proto label managers, the persistence of a "cosmic" psychedelia, all contributed to a distinctive Goatrance aesthetic by the early 1990s, by which time it was attracting attention from DJs, freaks, tourists, and authorities alike. By this time, the numbers of international tourists had grown dramatically, as had police corruption and the presence of the local mafia. In 1988, Israelis were permitted Indian travel visas, and by 1989, according to Castle, "this once, secret, DANCE-DHARMA-ZONE, became much publicized and the parties more difficult to make and less magical",[60] a circumstance which saw quite a few seasoned Goa travellers head to the paradisical, tolerant and protected backpacker party island of Koh Phangan, Thailand (Westerhausen 2002: ch. 9) where full-moon and New Year's parties would become popular. In 1990, police stepped up their interventions, shutting down and preventing parties over that season, demanded higher protection overheads (*baksheesh*) and shaking down DJs for money in their residences. In 1991, after London's *i-D* magazine proclaimed the "Indian Summer of Love" (Saldanha 2007a: 39), the floodgates were opening, with growing attention forcing parties further afield, like Maharashtra. By 1991/92, a massive influx of travellers from the world-over saw parties fatten from around 200 to 1,500 per event. At this time, the UK's rave efflorescence had cross-pollinated with what remained of that country's alternative festival and traveller culture (Partridge 2006a); a culture that, due to the systematic dismantling of its festal sites by Conservative governments, was seeking exoteric grounds on which to mount the vibe. Also at this time, rave had been recruited into "new edge" cyber-fantasias in San Francisco where "cyberdelic" stormtrippers were enlisted to dance at the front of the raveolution (St John 2009: 140–43). And in Germany, post-unification euphoria was transmuted into festal excitement that flourished at home and abroad – an enthusiasm birthing *Mushroom Magazine* and party database www.goabase.com.[61] By 1993/94, Goatrance quietly registered as a marketable genre, gaining attention and legitimacy in the UK in December 1994 when, introduced to the new sounds by Australian electronic music pioneer, member of Third Eye and founder of Psy-Harmonics Records, Ollie Olsen,[62] Perfecto label founder Paul Oakenfold played a Goa mix on BBC Radio One's Essential Mix program on which he was guest DJ. Oakenfold would subsequently create a sub-label, Perfecto Fluoro, on which he reissued Goa recordings. The 1994 compilation CD *Digital Alchemy* was like a neon snowflake melting in the arms of the curious. "They meet in Goa, with fluorescent lights in the palm trees and even more colour in their clothes and souls" wrote Oakenfold for the CD jacket, where he seemed to imagine "Goa" a cosmopolitan "town" somewhere in India. Both celebrating and wishing "the Goa sound" into existence, "it is truly global" he enthused, further remarking that "we are witnessing its development from the techno winterlands of Frankfurt to the sun-soaked beaches of Melbourne". The compilation featured no less than five tracks from Man With No Name (Martin Freeland). The unforgettable hymns "Evolution" and "Sugar Rush" seemed to clarify without words to the faithful that their feet were stomping down the path of the required progression. Including sunset photos of Goa beaches, the jacket was passed around like an exotic travel brochure, its impact foreshadowing the massive influx of tourists that would signal the end of the scene.

Goatrance experienced its major outing in 1995, at that historical juncture when private computer networks were linked globally. Oakenfold stepped up promotions, with his Dragonfly release *Paul Oakenfold – A Voyage into Trance* offering a vision splendid: "Imagine yourself", the promotion begins, "in a 4000 year old ruined temple, somewhere half buried in the jungle, fluro painted vines and trees, a 20k turbo charged rig, burning fire sculptures, and a few hundred wildly painted, crazy party people dancing non-stop for three days". The enthusiasm was matched by the selection – the final track being Hallucinogen's monumental "LSD". The cover of this psychedelic travel brochure holds an image of a mendicant in head-dress whose message-board has been replaced with an advertisement for Dragonfly's previous release, the seminal *Order Odonata Vol. 1* (1994). In 1995, the Israeli label Krembo Records released *Spirits of Independence* promoted as "the essence sound of Goa". The CD foldout featured images of palm-lined beaches, a well-groomed and bejewelled Indian woman seated at her jewellery-covered sari, a fishing boat, a packed dance floor, and a hand offering what appears to be a massive spliff. In this year also, Silver & Steel (John Ford, Richard Stewart,

Sean Stewart, Simon Carman) were "Dreaming of Disco Valley", a track on the chief release of the Phantasm Records collaboration (*Fill Your Head with Phantasm*, 1995).[63] It wasn't all Goa-kitsch however, as April 1995 saw Blue Room Released's first compilation *Outside the Reactor*, released as a triple LP and a CD. As memories were programmed into releases, as sonic-billboards competed for attention, as the "essence" of Goa was leaked far and wide, and as the beach and inland venues multiplied to cater to the backpackers, rave tourists and thrill-seekers of the Orient descending on Goa in growing numbers, the threshold dividing the clandestine shanti paradise from the overcrowded cesspit dreaded by veterans like Castle had been officially crossed. Within a couple of years, Matsuri released the compilation *Let it Rip* (1997) complete with eulogy: "R.I.P: Mother Theresa, Princess Diana, William Burroughs & Goa trance". By the winter months of 1997, tourists would outnumber Goans, and by 2000 club tourism had become rife (Saldanha 2002: 45).

Another track released in 1995 was Technossomy's "Germination (Huge Rant mix)" (*Timepiece* EP), repeating lines treading a curiously fine line between the necessary secret and its public exposure: "No one can know about this. You understand? No one". Just at what moment Goa ended as an authentic destination is the subject of considerable debate. It depends on who you talk to, what criteria they base their assertions upon and what interests they have at stake. As Erik Davis (1995) reported, the scene was already declared an historical subject by 1993/94. Castle lamented the loss of the "magic" back in 1989. If we listen to Devas, the death knell sounded circa 1978, with original freaks outraged by the public trashing of the beach signalled by the sounds of electronica. And if we read veteran Bombay Brian (2011), who coined the phrase "Hippy Raj", paradise was lost circa 1973 with the advent of the Garbage Bazar (the Flea Market) on Goonball Beach. Others wager that drug trafficking was tied to Goa's demise. According to veteran Tom Thumb (2010), in the early 1970s, "everyone began making runs to the West with charas in their shoes and suitcases. They came back wearing fancy clothes and snorting coke". As the scene fragmented, "it became a battle of the egos to see who could make the latest entrance to the parties. Us poor freaks in lunghis would be sweating it out all night long to a crackly guitar band and we'd look up at the cliffs in the morning and see the coke dealers looking down on us, dressed to kill". It seems more useful to surmise that Goa was scuttled by a series of detonations throughout the 1970s, 1980s and 1990s, whereby shifting musical aesthetics/technics, drug trafficking and increased flows of interest saw the irreversible alteration of the original site of attraction. "It's human nature to find beautiful spots and spoil them", was the matter-of-fact assertion of the late Vidal Angel, a French artist who worked for Disney in Paris before moving to Goa, as featured in *Goa Hippy Tribe* (D. Devas, dir. 2010b). For many commentators, the "mystery" would be tracked, hunted and killed by swarms of backpackers, investors, traders, dealers, police, journalists, foreign and domestic tourists, promoters, cokeheads, cultural geographers and anthropologists descending upon the scene of the sublime since the 1970s. But what for some was the end of an era is for others the dawn of a new golden age. Take Timur Mamedov (aka XP Voodoo), the Russian DJ-producer who first appeared in Goa in 1994, began DJing there in 1996, and would become a party promoter (Van 2003). While Goa might have served as a doormat upon which countless patrons left their scuffmarks, for Goa Gil, Mamedov and other evangelizers, Goa became a doorstep to the world. For mediators and entrepreneurs, the Goa aesthetic was transposed worldwide, even while trance was being interred at its site of origin.

The end is difficult to determine, since, although rarely documented, revelatory and life-changing experiences continued in Goa throughout the 2000s. Commenting on her experience riding on the back of an Enfield *en route* to the weekly party Dolce Vita in late March 2006, Israeli B reported:

> The acid started to affect us and Goa looked even more enchanted than ever. The trees and the lush vegetation looked especially stunning, beautiful symmetrical patterns were revealing themselves in the structure of everything I saw. The colors were extra bright and shiny and the edge of anything within my view was accented with a red and green glow. I felt an overwhelming sense of the great importance of that adventure, a feeling of profound meaning attributed to anything that will happen that night.

At the party, her first, overcoming her initial reaction to the music – "too loud and vulgar" – B became immersed in the dance floor and subsequently accustomed to a cultural movement to which she would gravitate researching the role of music in altering human consciousness.[64] While the parties, and the revelations, continued in Goa at the beginning of the twenty-first century, the scene's development must be understood in the context of a massive influx of mostly UK, German and Russian tourists, of narcotics exposés in the media, of allegations of police corruption, mafia and gang-related crime, and of the growing concerns demonstrated among lobbyists, media spokespersons and Church authorities. According to D'Andrea,

> while state authorities prioritize foreign investments in upscale resorts, a strident anti-tourism lobby (summoning elements from the press, the Catholic Church and urban and environmental NGOs) defends a more conservative approach to the sector. Consequently, in public discourse, "hippies" are frequently grouped together with prostitution, pederasty and school absenteeism, as social malaises of the state (2010: 43).

By 2005, "rave bans" had come into effect, with a strict enforcement of a 10:00 pm party ban in 2007.[65] As D'Andrea surmised, the commercial success of the Goa scene held "the seeds of its own demise". With the allure of hippie chic, and hippie chicks, with New Year's Eve "hippie" festivals promoted to Indian tourists and with the gentrification of the once secretive paradise, a diminution in the size, frequency, duration and authenticity of Goa parties became evident. But while "the former visibility and bustle of the psytrance scene in northern Goa" is declared over (D'Andrea 2010: 50), parties, both mythical and real, continued to be held in remote and secretive locations.

State of mind

Regardless of the continuing authenticity of Goa as a scene destination, its seed had been distributed on the winds. Its appeal had grown into a distinct aesthetic, such that, according to local mythology, Goa was not a place, but "a state of mind" (see Elliott 2010), a sentiment extolled by Goa Gil and reproduced on the cover of the documentary *Last Hippie Standing* (Robbin, dir. 2002). The legacy is stamped into recent productions with the likes of Ibojima, for example, running the line: "Goa is a state of mind, actually. Goa is not a place" ("Higher Energy", *Spherical*, 2008). That Goa was identifiable as a kind of transferable brand "energy" that could be accessed beyond the physical place itself, had been amplified in the year of Goatrance's unveiling. In 1995, the early incarnation of Astral Projection, Aban Don, adapted the line "it's a state of mind, it's the place where ... you find yourself" on their anthem "State of Mind (Metal Mix)" (*Trust in Trance 2*). There are many sites of origin for this mind state cultivated by cultural exiles who sought islands of experimentation remote from the mainland, and who became involved in moving its units offshore. Ibiza, at least in its early years as a traveller's destination, has been a much celebrated island in this international archipelago of interzones. In the 1960s, chief among these islands was Maui (in Hawaii). As reported in Nicholas Schou's *Orange Sunshine* (2010: 198), original member of the notorious Brotherhood of Eternal Love,[66] Chuck Mundell, stated of Maui: there were "people from everywhere. It was a real spiritual place, man. That idea of the island that Huxley wrote about – many people had read it in the 1960s and everybody wanted to create utopian societies – but Maui was more than that. It was a state of mind". As critical nodes in the history of psychedelic culture, accommodating inspired fraternities of itinerants and outlaws, the crazed and the visionary, these islands of sensuality fomenting the obliteration of meaning or the discovery of the self in the company of fellow islanders, may be further understood via the percipience of Maffesoli (1996: 98) who stated that the neotribe "is without the rigidity of the forms of organization with which we are familiar; it refers more to a certain ambiance, a *state of mind*, and is preferably to be expressed through lifestyles that favour appearance and 'form'".

If Goa wasn't actually a "place" and if "Shpongleland" had no actual fence, border or customs officials, then it could be transported elsewhere. The translation and transmutation of the zone was the specific objective of various DJ-pioneers and trance dance evangelists. While there was constant exchange between scenes on Ibiza and Goa, dedicated DJs sailed further offshore during the off-season. Fred Disko, for example, played parties in Kathmandu in 1981 and later Pokhara Lake, Nepal, in 1985,[67] with Andy (aka Hatti Baba) holding a party around Pashupati Temple, Nepal, during Shiva Ratri in 1988 (Sitoula 2009). With friends from Goa, Ray Castle held the first Pagan Production party at Ruigoord, Amsterdam, in 1988, and again in 1990 and 1991. These were "world beat trance dance" parties that he claims were "the first Goa style parties in Europe",[68] a claim countered by Aittoniemi (2012: 113), stating that Finnish expat Ior Bock (who threw the Bockara Parties in Goa) held Goa-style parties in Gumbostrand, Sipoo, Finland, from the summer of 1987. In 1988, Goa Gil began formulating his ritual in northern California, where a hardcore fan-base grew. By 1990, full-moon parties were being thrown in Israel. In the early 1990s, German expat Jörg Kessler – producer in over twenty collaborations, founder of label Shiva Space Technology, and identified as Shiva Jörg or Dark Shiva (in his darkpsy incarnation) – fitted out a Neoplan school bus with Shiva's trident painted on the front and "Techno Torgon" and "LSD 25" along the side panels, and hauled sound systems overland to Goa and Hampi, playing from 5-inch Sony mini-discs at parties held *en route* in Iran and Nepal.

Imported from countercultural sites like Haight-Ashbury, Laguna Beach, Maui and the UK Free Festivals, and becoming globally translatable in turn, the sociality of the optimized Goa vibe was distinctively *live*. A responsive social aesthetic varying considerably across dance cultures, *the vibe* sought in Goa, exported back to Europe, and translated by the global psytrance community, is characterized by a *liveness* that is subject to interpretation and debate. The "live" improvised experience has been pursued with considerable passion within psychedelic music movements. With their improvised sets sought after by legions of Deadheads who would follow the band from concert to concert, and country to country, year after year, San Francisco's psychedelic rock legends The Grateful Dead are frequently hailed as the archetypal exponents of the live experience. With their famous "wall of sound" they performed some 2000+ concerts (from 1965–1995). At Dead shows, breaks between songs became fewer as the performance progressed. Long improvised songs (especially in the infamous "second set") together with elaborate light shows and the ingestion of LSD contributed to an entrancement in intimate shared space – the source of Deadhead community (see Sardiello 1994). As Sylvan points out, while early albums used "a variety of experimental production techniques, studio effects and electronics, unusual compositional forms, and extensive multitracking in an attempt to recreate the psychedelic experience on record ... the concert experience was more faithfully captured on live albums" (2002: 85), of which there were seventy-seven (compared with thirteen studio albums). Sylvan details the importance of the repeated ritual structure and musical signatures implicit to Dead performances, but points out it was the improvised character of Dead concerts that facilitated mystical or transpersonal experience. Such may have been expressed in the circular dance movements (spinning) and the elegant hand flourishes characteristic of many Deadheads. Unexpected iterations of already well-known songs facilitated the possibility that, as Silberman declared, "something unexpectedly beautiful will reveal itself to you" (Sylvan 2002: 112). These are the moments freaks have long characterized as "magic", identified as the "zone", a quintessential "peak experience" shared with others: "I loved it when there would be one of those moments where everybody would be moved to put their hands up and catch it and when they really jammed to a crescendo and everybody would be just like catching the rays with their hands" (Kathleen Harrison in Sylvan 2002: 108).

There is considerable continuity with Goa/psytrance where communities arise in the psychogeographic mobility of enthusiasts. Psytrance is an optimized assemblage heir to acid rock, with participants demonstrating enthusiasm comparable to Deadheads in their pursuit of experience, backpacking from trance festival to festival at exotic sites or cosmic events in hinterlands, deserts, coastal regions, forests and mountaintops around the world. From the early drum circles and band performances, improvisation was critical to the Goa vibe, full-moon parties evolved with the interchange of live bands and DJs, and with the development of fusion bands; the "liveness" of performances later adopted within trance, as with other EDM events, was integral to the human/machine interface. Liveness remains an esteemed, albeit elusive, quality. In New York, by the mid-1970s, "slip-queuing" (later "beat matching") between records on two separate turntables – pioneered by Francis Grasso at a converted German Baptist church called The Sanctuary (see Lawrence 2008) – had become a technique holding *live performativity* over the amplification of recorded material selected in the fashion of the original discothèque or by early Jamaican sound systems selectors. At a further level of DJ performance, distinctions would become established between controllers crossfading between channels on a mixing desk and performers who were, as Graham Miller notes, *playing records* as they would instruments using a range of techniques through which recorded material can be interpreted, including turntablism, or via mixing consoles or computer software like Ableton Live. This is what most often distinguishes performers scheduled as "DJs" from "live" acts. While the former play and mix between tracks (where mixing may always be held as a "live" practice), the latter are often valorized in association with their performance on the "live PA". Here, as

Miller notes, "the primary instrument of the electronic dance music aesthetic (the studio) is transported to the stage, where the multi-track mixing console and effects processor become as musically malleable in the hands of a skilled performer as would a keyboard or guitar" (Miller 2003a). In psychedelic trance, where a tradition of playing vinyl never evolved, DAT players were iconic of "liveness", their use providing challenges for beat-mixing. Later, the virtual studio accessed on one's onstage laptop would become *de rigueur*. There is a gradient of liveness or transferability of authenticity here, where those performers, like Merv Pepler (Eat Static) and Posford, who are able to "play the studio" are possibly best able to "play the audience" like instruments – where habitués of the floor, "catching the rays with their hands", become animated in synchronized movements remembered long afterwards.

Liveness is a guarantee that a recorded work will never be performed the same way twice, offering audiences an ostensibly raw and direct experience – with the experience stamped with authentication when the recorded material performed is produced, edited or remixed by the performing artist him- or herself. Often, the most approved dance floor moments coincide with the performance of unreleased (original) material or otherwise untested remixes which, much like the special edits and mixes played by the likes of Laurent during Goa's formative years, are produced especially for that performance. These developments in performance enabled by the age of mechanical and digital reproduction – where "performance" and "production" have become indistinct practices – has led scholars to revisit the concept of liveness and authenticity. Nevertheless, at the fusional edges of Goatrance and world music performance, "liveness" is still championed by ethnodelic artists and those employing traditional instruments whose claim is to affect a more genuine trance experience. French band Hilight Tribe, for instance, claim to produce "Natural trance," by which we can assume they mean "trance" not performed using samples and loops, or, if the latter, as supplements only to acoustic instrumentation. While Walter Benjamin may have approved, this approach seems specious next to the recognition that authenticity "requires the musician to surrender his or her aura to the realm of digital reproduction" (Miller 2003a, 2003b).

Psychedelic orientation

India has long been regarded as a topos for Westerners to become unburdened of the rational Occident and luxuriate in the mystique of the Orient. For the most serious trailblazers – not least among them Helena Blavatsky and the theosophists – India has been a spiritual reservoir potentiating an evolution in consciousness. The "hippie trail" from Turkey, through Iran, Afghanistan and Pakistan to India and Nepal, might have been trekked by those Rory

Maclean, in *Magic Bus* (2006), calls the "Intrepids" of the 1960s and 1970s, but as Saldanha (2007b: para. 48) conveys, "India, the idea and the place, has itself shaped the self-images of others" for centuries, with trailblazers long returning with epiphanous insights:

> From Megasthenes in the early third century BC, via Alberuni, the Portuguese missionaries, Schlegel and the Romantics, Schopenhauer, and on to the theosophists, Kipling, E.M. Forster, Paul Scott, The Beatles, and Goa trance, other cultures have recurringly [*sic*] used India as a foil to define their own historical moments: to reassure or doubt themselves.

In the more recent times of relevance to us, inspired by the writings of Hermann Hesse, including *The Journey to the East* and *The Glass Bead Game*, Leary, the ex-Harvard psychologist, had travelled to India in 1965 writing his *Psychedelic Prayers* (1966), a book of meditative poetry inspired by Lao Tse's *Tao Te Ching*. Experienced as an exotic and disorienting "trip", the ultimate "set" for the journey, Leary wagered that "the impact of a visit to India is psychedelic. You are flipped out of your space-time identity. Indian life unfolds before you a million-flowered-person-vine-serpent coil of life ancient, wrinkled, dancing, starving, laughing, sick, swarming, inconceivable, unreasonable, mocking, singing-multi-headed, laughing God-dance" (Leary 1981 [1965]). Leary's colleague Richard Alpert found a guru in the Himalayas and returned as Baba Ram Dass publishing his *Be Here Now* (1971) in which he remarked about India: "And I cried and I cried and I cried. And I wasn't happy and I wasn't sad. It wasn't that sort of crying. The only thing I could say was it felt like I was home. Like the journey was over. Like I had finished" (section one, unpaginated).[69] With John and George having been slipped LSD by George's dentist, John Riley, at a dinner party in London's Bayswater Place in April 1965 (S. Turner 2006), The Beatles exemplified the trend in efforts to comprehend the psychedelic experience by turning to yogic practice (and reading Leary) – staying in Rishikesh, Uttar Pradesh, in early 1968 to study transcendental meditation with Guru Maharishi Mahesh Yogi. Romanticists, artists and mystics touring the semiotic wealth, metaphysical heights and abject depths of the East, and motivated by the opportunity to become liberated from what they recognized as "structures of oppression", were returning to states of innocence and amnesia, smoking *charas*, and living naked next to the beach. As such, they were learning how to "be the revolution", marking a refusal of consumerist lifestyles, and their pursuit of alternatives. India was the context for a *rite de passage* with deep transcendentalist roots and more than a thin slice of romantic Orientalism (Said 1978) that inheres in present representations and desires. For transnational rave-trance tourists, according to Victoria Bizzell's frank assessment (2008: 288), Goa became a "place of pilgrimage" removed from the lived reality of Goa's indigenous inhabitants and local realities, and religious practices, with India, and Indian people, "rendered static and immobile, bereft of progress and development", through the circulation of images. "Chai ladies may be welcome in Goan raves in their capacity as servers", she notes, "but the Indians who live in cities and travel as tourists simply do not comply with the image of romantic poverty and rustic spirituality idealized in Goa trance's neo-tribal ethos."

As the production houses of an estranged Orientalist aesthetic, labels sought to replicate the spiritual journey to, and from, the East, on cassette, vinyl and CD, with covers and sleeves typically imprinted with Hindu imagery. The project was consistent with an agenda expressed at the ambient edges of the emergent trance genre on *Instant Enlightenment (Deep Trance Ambient Experience)* (1993) by Om (Tetsu Inoue and Dennis Ferrer) which offers an illustration of the transit to nirvana sought by habitués of the early 1990s trance floor. While the instantiated "enlightenment" might have been imagined to result from dropping an E, trance masterstrokes like "Virtual High" and "Seeds of Sound" proved that "nirvana" could not be obtained without raising a sweat. The Orientation of the self is a project also evident on the first Goatrance compilation, *Project II Trance*, released in August 1993 on Dragonfly Records, but was more clearly evident in early DJ compilation releases – essentially hour-long DJ sets released on CD and distributed globally as "Goa Trance". Featuring recurring golden Buddha statues on its cover, in 1995 Psychic Deli (UK's Phantasm Records sublabel) released one of the first mix albums, Mark Allen's *Deck Wizards – Psychedelic Trance Mix*. And, promoted as a "trip inside your self, to the awakening", the 1995 Goa Gil compilation *Techno Spiritual Trance from Goa* is exemplary. The album begins with Gil's trademark "Om", followed by Astral Projection's classic "Let There be Light", with a remix of their powerful "Mahadeva" – an invocation of Shiva which repeats the mantra *om namah Shivaya* – included toward the conclusion. The original "Mahadeva", which featured contributions from DJ Jörg (Kessler), is considered by some to be among the founding Goa sounds, along with other Astral Projection productions completed with Kessler, like "Kabbalah". These and other early classics, such as Elysium's "Monzoon" (*Monzoon*, 1996), Shakta's *Silicon Trip* (1997), and Chi-A.D.'s "Pathfinder" (*Anno Domini*, 1999) were stamped with Eastern timbres. Distributed with thick colour booklets, the ambient and ethnodelic Return To The Source compilations were among the more popular efforts to supply the materials for reproducing the Goa party vibe. Replete with Hindu and Buddhist imagery, the first Return To The Source compilation, *Deep Trance and Ritual Beats* (1995), consisted of a double CD and featured a booklet with stylized images of the elephant-headed Ganesh, son of Shiva and Goddess Parvati, and the sitar-playing Hindu muse Sarasvati. To implement the *Orientation*, Goatrance labels, albums and events emerging in the mid-1990s would promote and package the trance experience as a transcendent journey adopting Oriental imagery and iconography to assist the telos.

With the Goa aesthetic so transposable, enthusiasts on the dance floor could consume Goa, be exposed to the mystique, and access the metaphysical lore, without ever having set foot in India. By the turn of the century, it would grow increasingly unlikely that "Goa" producers and DJs had themselves visited Goa. In efforts to induce Visions of Shiva, the name Paul van Dyke chose for his outfit formed in 1992 with Harald Blüchel (aka Cosmic Baby); to project *The Colours of Shiva*, the compilation series produced by Tua Records (1997–1999); or to reduce the *Distance to Goa*, the successful compilation series released by French label Distance (founded in 1995), promoters, producers and designers were concocting label aesthetics, album cover art, track titles, music structures and festival concepts saturated with Orientalism. In 1995, referencing the colossal Hindu pilgrimage by that name, DJ Cosmix & Etnica's "Kumba Mela" was a big hit (*Kumba Mela* EP), as was Indoor's classic "Shiva" released on their album *Progressive Trance*. In the liner notes of the *Blue Compilation* (1997), part of a series featuring the androgynous Shiva in different primary colours, enthusiasts were reading: "The colour of Shiva. All protecting with his almighty trident. I am neither mind intelligence or ego neither ears nor tongue nor the senses of smell and sight nor am I either earth fire or water I am pure knowledge and bliss I am Siva I am Siva (Siva Purana)". Founded by Kessler, Shiva Space Technology released the 1997 self-titled compilation dedicated to Shiva, which included Shiva Shidapu's (Kessler and Infected Mushroom's Erez Alzen) "India Spirit". Tabla, conch horns and chanting Tibetan Buddhist monks were samples that had grown legion. All through this period, trance was saturated with OMs and mandalas, an iconic pandemic reminiscent of the essentializing motifs of the earlier counterculture.

Early Goatrance outfits were also seeking to stage the journey and trek the Eastern-inflected path to awakening, which, over the late 1980s–early 1990s, coincided with the celebrated implosion of the Soviet Union and the end of apartheid in South Africa. Buoyed by his experience in Goa, Raja Ram threw dozens of underground Goa parties in London from the early 1990s, beginning with a joint venture in the East End with his daughter Sastra on 16 December 1990. A free party in Spitalfields called Relentless, it was her twenty-first and his fiftieth birthday celebration. Three hundred people were exposed to the first TIP tracks, including their invited friends and those responding to a small advertisement using the word "Goa" placed in *Time Out*. Raja Ram claims that it was London's first Goa party, with early Goa-style rave parties operated by London's Ahimsa and Panjaea crews (see De Ledesema 2010: 92–3) reckoned to be subsequent events.[70] Regardless, parties thrown by the latter crews in the east and western districts respectively were benchmark events. Following Chris Deckker's party by this name in Amsterdam celebrating New Year 1993,

London's first Goa club, Return To The Source, opened in 1993, finding a home in Brixton (The Fridge) in 1995, by which time RTTS events took on an intentional ritual focus (influenced by Deckker's partner Antara) consonant with the material produced for the RTTS compilations. In the tradition of hosting festivals-in-a-club in the mould earlier set by Megatripolis, The Fridge also became host to Escape From Samsara, held on Fridays between 1995 and 2002.[71] Soon, Mark Allen began organizing the long-running Pagan Parties at various venues, after which followed Spacehopper and Herbal Tea Party. Alluding to the regulative strategies and licensing laws targeting Free Festival, rave and club culture in the UK which culminated in the Criminal Justice Act (November 1994), in *Generation Ecstasy* Simon Reynolds suggests that these London clubs were already attempting to "resurrect a lost golden age on much reduced premises" (1998: 149). While London was an early centre of Goatrance production, it was also a centre of state repression of dance cultures, which, in the most notorious case, saw Spiral Tribe migrate from the UK to initiate the teknival movement on continental Europe (and around the world) (St John 2009: 36–57).

The mood was comparatively optimistic in Germany. As Kai Mathesdorf reported, in 1989/90 "Goa-crazed people" from all over Germany, including Bavaria, regularly gathered 30 km southeast of Hamburg in Waldheim. As these parties grew and drew the attention of fine-issuing authorities, organizers planned for a major event in 1991, a gravel quarry party attracting 300 people and reported as "the first Voov Experience" (Mathesdorf 2002: 12). Officially, VooV Experience (operating today as VuuV) took place from 1992,[72] with the first Antaris Project festival staged the following year as "a once in the year opportunity to revive the Goa scene".[73] Through the mid-1990s, key clubs emerged across Germany like The Hamburg Gaswerk, Berlin's Pfefferberg, the Munich Natraj Temple and the Traumfabrik in Ludwigsburg. Riding on the spirit of reunification, with these clubs and festivals, including other major events emerging post-millennium like Psychedelic Circus, Indian Spirit, Shiva Moon, Full Moon, Waldfrieden Wonderland and Fusion, Germany would retain a strong commitment to the Goa sensibility.

As the enginehouse of the German scene, Voov Experience Festival was initiated by Antaro (with DJ Scotty), who, according to Mathesdorf (2002: 5), was hosting Goa parties in the "garden of his house" in Lüneburger Heide, northeastern Lower Saxony, in 1989. As a sannyasin, or perhaps more accurately, rebel sannyasin, Antaro was one among many spiritual seekers and world travellers who brokered the Goa vibe to scenes around the world. Another figure of note here is travel writer and publisher Brad "Santosh" Olsen,[74] whose story returns the search for experience to the streets of San Francisco where, at the start of the twenty-first century, the Goa vibe spilled out of a warehouse into an annual street festival. In the early 1990s, Olsen had embarked on a three-year odyssey outside the United States encountering the Goa scene in the company of fellow expatriates over the 1993/94 season in Hampi, Karnataka and in Goa, where they found Goa Gil playing at the Paradiso. "It was so mind blowing, and everybody's brain lit up with a flash and I thought this was the ultimate party experience". At this juncture, Olsen and his fellow travellers were inspired not only by this new music, but "by the Hindu culture, by the temple setting of India, by the *sadhus* roaming the country", and perhaps not least "by smoking the chillums". Olsen's journey was capped off with a stay at the Pune ashram where Osho gave him the title "Swami Dyhan Santosh". Carrying the message "that we should lose our ego" and to "bring happiness to other people", Santosh and friends returned to San Francisco, and in 1995 initiated Goa-style warehouse parties in a former auto-repair shop on Howard St. The Consortium of Collective Consciousness (CCC) events became legendary word-of-mouth psychedelic traveller parties, which continued until their eventual eviction on 31 May 2001, after which the exclusive underground parties morphed into what is now a major San Francisco civic event (the How Weird Street Faire).[75] Collaborator Will Gregory remembers the CCC parties as an explosion of colour, stylistic innovation and diversity that were absent in the UK at the time. Gregory had arrived in San Francisco from London in May 1995, only months before the death of legendary Grateful Dead frontman Jerry Garcia. Gregory hadn't even known who Garcia was, yet became caught up in the mortuary celebrations erupting across Upper Haight and surrounding districts. His unplanned introduction later gave Gregory cause to understand the momentum for Goatrance in mid-1990s San Francisco. "I realized in retrospect that some of those people had crossed over, which is why there was such an incredible mix of people. It wasn't just the international travellers at those mid-1990 parties, it was very much mixed up with the San Francisco flavour".[76] Indeed, some of the integral CCC "crew" had been Deadheads.

Exerting an influence on trance dance in Goa, the neosannyasi subsequently exported the party trance ritual to their homelands. Tiago Coutinho (2006) refers to an Osho sannyasin named Kranti who lived in India and became involved in the introduction of these parties to the Alto Paraíso region of Brazil, where the most important psytrance festival in that country was first held in 2001 – the New Year Universo Paralello Festival, now held on Pratigi Beach in the north of Bahia, and organized by sannyasins Alok and Swarup. Notable also are the Spanish duo Riktam (Shajahan Matkin) and Bansi (Josef Quinteros) who formed GMS. Nascent Goa party scenes the world over would be inspirited with the "dynamic meditation" dance methods taught by Osho. In Australia, Byron Bay, and its "Rainbow Region" hinterlands, became the home to those who performed their sannyas at Puna, and travelled to Goa. In late 1992, in an event featuring Steve Psyko, artists "rented an art studio/gallery from sannyasins in Byron Bay, borrowed an empty lot next door, invited over 100 local and visiting performers and visual artists to gather and make Creative Terra, an immersive indoor/outdoor environment featuring an all-night art, music and performance exhibition".[77] Spiritual seekership informed by disciplined approaches to trance dance influenced the emergence of "doofs" which consequently carry the legacy of the "state of mind" Goa travellers were returning with, notably care of Fred Disko (who teamed up with Steve Psyko to form Psyko Disko) and former vocalist from UK goth/glam band The Specimen, Olli Wisdom (Space Tribe), who both settled in Australia.

The Oriental spiritual aesthetic intrinsic to Goa was transported around the world in a sound – and in iconography, cover art and textile fashions – persisting long after Goatrance had dissipated as a genre. And Oriental motifs were applied as part of an integralist spiritual technology dedicated to self-transcendence. The 1998 track "Utopia" – by Mandala, a short-lived collaboration between Posford and Martin Glover – kicks off with the deep resonations of what appears to be a conch horn of the kind used in Buddhist temple rituals before cutting into a frenetic 4/4 rhythm backed by deep drums and distant chants. That these founder artists chose the name Mandala is significant. Whether in the form of a Tibetan sand mandala, or a crop circle, mandalas are symbols recurrent within ambient and psychedelic electronica, where music, like the mandala, is often regarded as a spiritual teaching tool, an aid to meditation and trance induction, assisting, as Fontana (2005: 10) clarified with regard to pictorial mandalas, "the meditator to experience a mystical sense of oneness with the ultimate unity from which the cosmos in all its manifold forms" manifest. Conveying unity, connectedness and inter-species harmony, with his act Space Tribe, Olli Wisdom appears to have been pursuing this audio-visual relationship on his debut album *Sonic Mandala* (1996). In the jetstream of the Goa diasporic movement, projects are conceived and promoted with the intent of enabling "oneness", of reconciling the senses, sometimes with quite liberal appropriations of Hindu discourse.

In some cases, metaphysics are written into music via vocal samples such as in the work of Sri Hari, formed by Ian Ion and Harikesa Swami, who produced two Goatrance and Ambient albums on the International Society for Krishna Consciousness (ISKCON) label Bhaktivedanta Book Trust: *Rising Sign* (1995) and *One But Different* (1997). On the first album, offering tenets of ISKCON belief and practice, "Lecture into Sound" is protean psy-breaks enchantment expounding the Vaishnavite disciplinary belief, in contra-distinction to the Shaivite and Brahmanic quest to become one with the cosmos: "Love requires two, the lover and beloved. When one becomes One, there is no possibility of love".[78] More generally, Goa and Goa-inspired sampledelia is of an undisciplined nature. But while not usually amplifying formal religious tenets, the samples are deployed according to the syncretic pursuit of a unified consciousness. Such is redolent in the work of Wisdom (as Space Tribe) whose saw-toothed acid trance classic declaration "You

Album cover of Space Tribe's *Religious Experience* (Spirit Zone Recordings, 2000). Courtesy of Miki Spacetribe.

Can Be Shiva" (*A Voyage into Trance Vol. 2*, 1998) broadcasts Leary poached from his 1970 LP *You Can Be Anyone This Time Around*: "You Can Be Shiva ... You can be Krishna. You can be anyone. You can be anything this time around". Regurgitated *ad nauseam*, the not-infrequent chants of *Om namah Shivaya* are joined by American Indian chants, conch horns, water drums and synthesized flute lines. While the East provided the primary spiritual tropes borrowed within the early trance milieu to be refracted throughout its development, a diversity of symbols and traditions were layered across Goan soundscapes amplifying the integralist sensibility of the times and the sampledelic techniques available to electronic artists. The cover of Space Tribe's *Religious Experience* (2000) offers a statement on this theme. Produced by Olli's brother, Miki Wisdom, the collage features a headphones-enhanced Pope John Paul II DJing to a crowd adorned in the raiment of a multitude of religious traditions and denominations. While *sadhus*, nuns, cardinals and other robed figures, alongside Wisdom himself, mingle on the dance floor, the Pope clutches a copy of Space Tribe's previous album *The Future's Right Now*

(1998), the cover of which features a meditating Shiva with illuminated chakra points and lotus flowers. It may be a stretch to attribute deep significance to this pastiche, but the cardinal representative of the Catholic Church appears to be spinning the tunes of the Supreme God of Shaivism, whose transmissions are, in turn, animating the Hindu deity in his personification as the dancing Nataraja whose statuesque *silhouette stands* in perfect alignment with the morning Sun. With the Pope (and thus also Shiva) facing the viewer, and not the dance floor beyond, he appears to be receiving directions from the viewer of the album's cover (i.e. you), a circumstance echoing the epistemic status of the self as divine authority in the age of "individuated self-spirituality" (Heelas 2008). At the same time, the individual is in dialogue with the cosmos, since the viewer is also drawn to become the dancer, and the dancer is compelled to form identification with Nataraja, who provides the dance-motivating music. Ultimately, while the self is hailed as a free agent (the sleeve even announces "You Are God"), this composite of religious iconography spinning at the close of Goatrance appears to prioritize the initiatory mystical consciousness – the at-one-ness – in the Shaivite tradition to which Goatrance has, at least speciously, identified.

This tale of iconic religious hyperbole illustrates how (especially Indian) religious sensibilities have permeated the Goa tradition, offering grist for the new spiritual and integralist gambits of self-realization, potential and growth. Yet, as has already been made apparent, the Goa tradition harbours contested narratives, and has been equally shaped by attitudes that do not valorize holism, nor seek wise council, or find resolution to states of imbalance. Indeed, a taste for transgression, and an appetite for being ravaged lie at the roots of psychedelic trance and finds particular animation in the dark trance legacy, the popularity of which illustrates how, by the early 2000s, Oriental symbolism and iconography adapted to progressive causes had decreased in popularity in favour of more gothic outlooks. Enthusiasts were distancing themselves from Goa, even while Goa and its schizoid state of mind was manifesting in regions worldwide.

Travellers of the world of experience

That Goa and its progeny are complex phenomena has only been partially addressed by researchers. Though not offering a study of the emergence of this scene or its music, Anthony D'Andrea provides an account of those who "live by the lines of flight of nomads" (2007a: 177) (i.e. travellers), whose smooth space is differentiated from those who "belong to the striatic space of dwellers" (i.e. tourists). In *Psychedelic White: Goa Trance and the Viscosity of Race* (2007a), Arun Saldanha also adopts Deleuzoguattarian heuristics to excoriate the "microfascist" potential in freak "lines of flight", excavating the tendency towards "viscosity" among white freaks in Goa as Indians are subject to exclusions within/from parties. In recognition of the chimerical characteristics of freak transcendence in Goa, and the utopian white-washed fictions that rise like dust from well-stomped dance floors, Saldanha adopts a materialist theory of race which illustrates, despite its Deleuzian inspiration, a surprisingly one-dimensional rendering of the politics of experience in Goa. Saldanha argues that the white Goa freak's pursuit of the transcendent *other* so often involves an inconvenient encounter with the racial (i.e. non-white) "other", whose presence (e.g. in the form of beggars or Indian tourists) on the dance floor jeopardizes the purity of the experience, resulting in an exclusive density of white bodies in the morning phase of the party, free from the "contaminating" tendency of non-white tourists. Exclusivity has long been a feature of the Goa scene, with efforts to maintain its decorum as it grew more attractive to tourists (domestic and foreign) throughout the 1990s – i.e. before it became the research interest of cultural geographers and long after the scene in Goa was declared over by its progenitors. But while exclusivity and elitism – what Saldanha calls "snobbish ritualism" (2007a: 53) – had become part of Goa party culture by the turn of the century, the theoretical experiment in race materialism is troubling. For one thing, this view tends to ignore how, according to D'Andrea (2010: 45), "many Indians occupy a privileged position in the psytrance scene as leading DJs, party promoters, diasporic insiders and even as revered *sadhus*". And, as the "secret" of Goa was "outed", numerous conditions threatened the Goa party vibe, including domestic tourists predating upon mythically "loose" white women, unchecked commercialism, and police corruption. In Goa, while many of these agents of predation would have dark skins, none of their conditions are intrinsically Indian (or racial). Indeed these are factors threatening experimental and alternative arts scenes everywhere, and are some of the reasons why freaks sought Goa to begin with. The foregrounding of phenotype seems single-minded in the face of other factors mobilizing freaks to forms of carnivalesque exclusivity. In her visit to post-millennium Goa, Lava 303 recounted some of these troubles in paradise in her article "Women of Goa". "You meet Indian men", she wrote, "who come there to look for naked European women and want to take pictures with you to play the big hero with the white lady when they come home again" (2002: 78). Indeed, the promise of the "orgiastic spectacle" fed by the circulation of lurid accounts of naked white women sprawled out invitingly on the beach has long motivated domestic male tourists to visit Anjuna beach (Elliott 2006: 81). In addition to prejudices faced by women and the ever-present threat of sexual assault, Lava 303 reports on another source of disharmony. While she "met a lot of nice" Israelis, the latter are singled out for special attention since they are reported to treat Goa "like their new colony ... another Promised Land" (Lava 303 2002), an observation resonating with the types of Israeli backpackers identified as "the conquerors" and "the Manalis" (see Maoz 2005).

These observations offer some insight on the complex character of freedom at the progenitor-site of trance. Its formative events were "free", meaning not simply free admission (or entrance with a donation[79]) but facilitating freedoms from nuclear family, organized religion, state surveillance and normative modes of subjectivity. That is, as a successful autonomous zone, Goa's existence was dependent upon its relative isolation from tourists, journalists, gangs and police. Such experimentalism has been jeopardized and subject to optimization throughout the history of psytrance. Luther Elliott (2010: 25–26) recognized these triggers in the Haight-Ashbury district of the late 1960s where "those with the means and the wherewithal left for destinations where ecstatic states of spiritual, artistic, and sexual fulfilment could be experienced without the disruption of daily televised war coverage and prurient media attention". And, as D'Andrea conveys, in Goa, freaks cultivated parties where those disrupting efforts to maintain "the smooth space of creativity and experimentation" were deemed outsiders regardless of race/ethnicity (2010: 45–46). Scorning the "packaged" commodification of experience associated with conventional tourism, freaks "present a pragmatic engagement with native cultures, and more closely emulate the skeptical, romantic and elitist gaze of the 'post-tourist'" (D'Andrea 2007a: 177). The identification of, and response to, such scene-threatening behaviour remains consistent in the many places of psytrance-emergence. As Elliott's and D'Andrea's accounts illustrate, there is considerable complexity in the distinctions which normally fall in the wake of scene exposure. Furthermore, internal distinctions within this scene grow apparent as one pays attention to differential expectations and aesthetics motivating participants. These disparate sensibilities, evident from the inception of the freak exodus, and extant throughout the seasonal party culture, would become memorialized in the music samples of later productions. For instance, Polish-born and Hamburg-based partnership Lightsphere's (Aga and Waldek Biskup) anthem "Intersession" (*Oneness*, 2011) champions the view that "there's a voice in the universe, entreating us to remember our purpose, our reason for being here now, in this world of impermanence. The voice whispers, shouts and sings to us, that this experience ... this experience of being in form, in space, and time, has meaning." While such work holds that significance and hope can be extracted from experience, at the darker edge of the psychedelic trance continuum one finds an abiding nihilism. Thus on "Aknofobia" (*Contagion Vol. 1*, 2008), Demonizz bursts out with "do I look like someone who cares what God thinks?"

Since the late 1960s, then, isolated beaches, headlands and inland jungle on the coast of Goa became home to a diverse mix of expatriates and experimentalists who, over successive seasons and through waves of innovation, technique and artifice smuggled in by countless enthusiasts, fashioned the party scene from which transnational psychedelic trance music and culture was born. The Goa experience cannot be circumscribed via cheap theory, linear narrative or simple heuristics. It could not be characterized exclusively as hipster experimentalism or neo-colonial misadventure; nor simply reckless demolition or phenotypical viscosity. Among the exiles who made Goa, there were those who sought solutions to a world devoid of consciousness, to the alienation from nature deemed symptomatic of the modern era. Alert to the endemic crises of family and nation flaming domestic and international aggression, and to the disastrous impact of unchecked plundering of what had become recognized as the Earth's finite resources, they distrusted inherited religious, scientific, political and economic institutions. Some sought to annihilate their memories, ethnonational identities and personal biographies in the reckless abuse of drugs, most tragically cocaine and heroin. Adopting the view that change "starts within", or that one should "be the change you want to see in the world", others turned to healing arts, yoga, well-being and ecological practices designed to effect transformation of one's self and personal relationships as a prerequisite for making desirable changes in the world beyond. Some became fixed on metamorphosing their "whole" identities, a process of self-othering approximating an authentic mystical experience. Others simply devoured the imaginary (Oriental) other in orgies of consumption, while excluding domestic Indians from the party. While these offer testament to the complexity of the traveller interzone perhaps best characterized by heterogeneity and cultural exchanges, "rave tourists" invaded the Goa scene at the time Goatrance was being heard globally, triggering its transnational movement. This transmigration is a complex development the nuances of which go unrecognized in one-dimensional discourses that only situate the Goa story "within a broader historical context of colonization and cultural appropriation" (Bizzell 2008: 284). My chief concern is that diverse expectations, relations and aesthetics are discounted by this approach, and an entire cultural movement – identifying with Goa or not – is condemned to answer the charges of neo-colonialism. While Goatrance has been demonstrated to have had an aesthetic romance with Orientalism, this story does not infuse its "neotribal" mobilization.

The Goa experience has migrated to locations worldwide. From the late 1980s, it was transposed to Finland, the UK, Israel and Germany, and would soon take root in the US, Australia, South Africa and across Europe throughout the 1990s, mushrooming in world locations amid waves of new-state optimism, post-revolutionary hope and nascent countercultural formation. Between 1987 and 1994, Ior Bock's Kristiina parties were instrumental in establishing a Goa scene and music sensibility in Finland, carried forward with the Ruskababa and Lost Tribe of Porvoo parties (see Aittoniemi 2012: chapter 5). By the mid-1990s, Tokyo Techno Tribe, Geoid and Equinox parties had taken off in Japan. By 1994, the neomystical current was supplied to Russia first by way of Gabriel Vorobyov or DJ Gavrila (Chill Out Planet) from St Petersburg, and later by, among others, Timur Mamedov, who founded label Russia Aerodance Corporation and club Aerodance in Moscow. In 1995, scenes emerged in countries worldwide. For instance, the Emergence party held that year in Montreal by Mobius productions is legendary in the Canadian scene. In November 1995 Conscious Dreams and Moonchild Express collaborated to throw a party at East Fort on Chapman's Peak, Cape Town.[80] Over the next decade, the experience encountered at the end of a dirt track in Goa could be rediscovered at road's end all around the planet. Slovakia's Hill-Top Festival began in 1999, with a later promotion inviting "travellers of the world": "The road ends in Lipovec and it feels like the end of the world, with huge forests stretched on the mountain tops".[81] *Mushroom Magazine*, *Psychedelic Traveller* and Chaishop.com report on the proliferation of brief seasonal enclaves of the Goa "state of mind" around the planet, with stories of "isolated", "pure" and "lively" interzones as yet untouched by jaded sensibilities, and commercial interests. In the liminal spirit of independence in which newly liberalized democracies enable alternative enclaves to take root, former Soviet Republics have been receptive to the Goa party sensibility. Such is the story of the Baltic region. Latvia, Lithuania and Estonia, as reported on Chaishop.com, "are still somehow not affected by the trends that sweep all over Central Europe and Scandinavia. The culture and the arts that flower here are vibrant, alive and true to the original roots of deep psychedelic shamanism" (Anton Shoom and DJ Shishya 2008). Since 1996, Estonia, reportedly at "the forefront of the electronic dance movement in the former Soviet Countries", had hosted parties in clubs, warehouses, military catacombs, and on "moving trains", a golden age that apparently persisted until 2003, when it became subject to crack-downs, with many original creators moving elsewhere in the aftermath (Anton Shoom and Unitone 2009). In 2001, a crucial threshold appeared to have been crossed in the region when German-based crew Crazy People E.V. organized the Ragana festival in Lithuania (the first Soviet republic to declare independence – in 1990). "It happened at the autumnal equinox in a very beautiful yet powerful place around former pagan capital Kernave. A truly mystical space and time made Ragana an outstanding experience that has greatly inspired those who decided to continue". Locally organized full-moon open-air parties started with Tinai and Shambala in 2003, with the latter evolving into Yaga (Anton Shoom and DJ Shishya 2008). The Goa sensibility has also been adopted in many countries in South America (and especially Brazil), following the 1994 "eclipse rave" mounted to celebrate the total solar eclipse in post-Pinochet Chile. In the wake of the 2009 democratic revolution in Bolivia, Beta Guerra wrote in *Psychedelic Traveller* (2009: 17) that the nascent psytrance community in Bolivia is "one of the strongest and youngest in this part of the world" stating that this is demonstrated in "the revolutionary beliefs of the younger people who are now ideologically concerned". Before the reforms, Guerra stated, "there was a notorious feeling of racism and ethnical division within the Bolivian society". The transition is reported to be celebrated in parties held by Ursula Flores "in the mood of multicultural tolerance, mystical references, and using icons from many of the 58 pre-Hispanic native ethnic nations that live on Bolivian territory, trying to mix them in with the Bolivian heterogenic culture". While solid research will address whether these events are exercises in rapprochement and reconciliation or are exemplary sites of cultural appropriation and utopian fantasy, Goatrance and its progeny continue to be adopted by enthused populations in transitional conditions of cultural liberation in locations worldwide.

3 The vibe at the end of the world

> The incidents were so bad, so contrary to our standards of human behavior that I couldn't possibly recite them to you, from this platform, in detail. But all during the dance, movies were shown on two screens at opposite ends of the gymnasium. These movies were the only lights in the gym proper. They gave the appearance of different colored liquids spreading across the screen, followed by shots of men and women, on occasion, shots where the men and women's nude torsos … twisted and gyrated in provocative and sensual fashion. The smell of marijuana was prevalent all over the entire building. Sexual misconduct was blatant.

With this chuckle-inducing rant from Governor Ronald Reagan on "Two Mad Men" care of Chris Gannon and Ciaran Walsh's act Breach of Space (*Accidental Occidentalism*, 1995), we're handed a sonic-flier for a night of bumping *jouissance*. The sample is from Reagan's 1966 speech at San Francisco's Cow Palace and likely lifted from the documentary *Berkeley in the Sixties* (Kitchell, dir. 1990).[1] The sonic *détournement* offers a compelling statement on the politics of transgression, where the boundaries of authorized experience are patrolled by moralists and trespassed by experimentalists, with adversaries from either camp convinced of the legitimacy of their own actions. These ruptures were as abhorrent to Reagan as they were compelling to antagonists. The radical immanence of youth high on *nothing* like a red rag flashed at a raging bull whose swift mauling caused further dissent. It's a tragic passion-play rooted in antiquity and the drama is sampled at the emergence of Goatrance, a music born from a privileged experiment where middle-class youth choosing their exit sought freedoms not only from moral injunctions, state surveillance, wage slavery and patriotism, but liberation from the illusion of their own separation: their minds from their bodies, consciousness from physical matter, a dissonance which was expressed in the joyful contagion of dance, in the conspiracy of flesh where one participates in an unambiguous connection with the universe. This romance with the Absolute sought in Goa was akin to experiencing the death and rebirth of one's former self in the company of wayfaring conspirators, and Goa thus became an allegory of death/rebirth for travellers, a transnational passage rite whose utopic and erotic sensibility was layered with Oriental mysticism, an initiatory experience stamped into the Goa party, a vibe of the exiles carried forward by its weird and wayward descendants.

The cultural exiles who made their departures from unbearable conditions occasioned by the impossibilities of the nuclear family and the possibilities of nuclear war, are forebears to the movement considered in this book. Though not exclusively the case among proto-freak émigrés settling in Goa – consider Eight Finger Eddie's background as the child of Armenian immigrants in Depression-era Boston – for the most part it was their privileged backgrounds that permitted Goa travellers to make exodus, that enabled their responses to outlawed practice, existential despair, disenchantment and cognitive dissonance already experienced as a product of middle-class lifestyles. However, the exodus was not simply the fulfilment of "advanced needs", but a response to lived social, cultural and historical conditions. This was the career of the *freak*, who, as opposed to the political exile – who is forced to vacate home/nation and may even become associated with a "government in exile" which desires a return to power – is an elective exile, driven by circumstance to dwell in a permanent state of departure from the maladies of modern life.[2] The self-exile is a seeker of experience, of freedoms that rupture the conditions of selfhood associated with possessive materialism, nationalism and monotheism. S/he shares this transitional status with other expatriates, bohemians and mystics – with mutants whose artifice flourishes in alternative enclaves where the liberties sought are as multiple as the oppressive conditions from which they have made exodus. Seasons in Goa echoed a diversity of intent, and a concomitant medley of experience. There were those who simply underwent a decadent wasting in orgiastic abandonment at year's end. This predictable annihilation of familiarity is typical to the turn of the year, where New Year's Eve is among the pinnacle celebrations in the lives of Westerners, with this transit featuring prominently among those vacating in Goa. Here paradisical Goa, perhaps now more than ever, might be considered in the light of Agamben's (1998: 105–6) discourse on the "state of exception", a "zone of indistinction between the human and the animal" that Diken and Laustsen argue characterizes tourist "camps" of naked excess and licensed transgression like Ibiza, the clubber's paradise defined by dance music, cheap drugs and casual sex (2004: 2). By comparison to the seasonal trippers as ravenous *homo sacer* making camp with no thought for tomorrow, others sought expatriation from occidental subjectivity in an enduring and conscientious state of seekership, a "revolution" that its greatest exponents sought to re-route back to the world. This is the remit of Goa Gil, who has stated that,

> The psychedelic revolution never stopped, but just had to travel half way around the world to the end of a dirt road on a deserted beach where it was allowed to mutate and grow without government or media pressures. And then it evolved into this new equation, which was more palpable for the 80's and 90's and 21st century as it grew into it and evolved. And then it spread back around the world (in McAteer 2002: 88).

In ecstatic passage from "the world" and on visionary pathways to another, diverse transitions have given shape to the Goa *vibe*. As will be discussed in this chapter, this is a socio-sonic aesthetic infused with the diverse intentions of dissidents and discoheads disembarking from the world, re/inhabiting a context in which variegated freedoms were performed, contested and negotiated *in situ*. It is, therefore, not dictated by a singular vector of freedom, and may be the context for discord. Thus, while I begin this chapter with an exploration of the *discommunitas* cultivated from the legacies of various utopian disc-cultures since the 1960s, donnybrooks among personalities, disputes over aesthetics and cultural tensions are discussed. This cultural noise is approached through attention to the holiest of anomalies in psytrance, Goa Gil.

Discommunitas

Within the tradition of psychedelic trance, not unlike other electronic dance music cultures, facilitators of the flow and technicians of no-thing recognize that the personal journey of trance is made in the company of others – friends and strangers – whose copresence is integral to the experience, with DJ practitioners honing their skills and collaborating to maximize this gestalt. While in the following chapter I will explore how a neomystical experience is overseen by the technoshamans of trance, here it will be enough to convey that such an experience is primarily kinesthetic, intercorporeal and social. Goa's full-moon parties were the formative occasions. On 6 December 1976, at the peak of the pre-electronic music party scene on a day known as St Nicholas Day in parts of Europe, traveller Chris De Bié (n.d.) recalls walking to the full-moon party in Anjuna *en route* to which he received a not uncommon gift.

> I met an American riding on a bike. He had a bottle full of liquid LSD with him. 'Stretch out your tongue and you'll take the trip of your life!' he told me smiling. I accepted with pleasure and

> thanked him by folding my hands and bowing my head. I shared this magnificent scene with many others who had also met St. Nicholas. We may have been more than a hundred and everybody on the same wavelength! We bathed in and on the waves of an infinite ocean. Submerged by waves of love we were laying in each other's arms. I remember many tears of joy on the smiling faces. We danced like in trance through the night until the silver moon sank into the sea and the golden sun climbed up at the same time behind the palm-trees. I had gone on some psychedelic trips, alone or with a few good friends, but this sense of community with so many people was a very unique experience.

Some fifteen years later, another observer comments on a party from the peak of Goa's electronic era. "You felt part of something greater than yourself. It was something more conductive than water where any wave of energy could spread through the dance floor in a moment. A fight, an embrace or a new arrival were all things you felt without using any of the five senses. It was like melding into some electrical field or making love to 300 people at once" (Roadjunky 2006). By this time, the vocal samples soldered to the mix were confirming the narrative. Take Insectoid, the project formed by Ray Castle, Mark Turner and Nick Spacetree whose track "The Web" (*Groovology of the Metaverse*, 1998) featured Mr Spock issuing the lines: "our minds are moving closer, our minds are one". Egged on by the voices inside their heads, statements of a unified dance floor are replicated in the accounts of Goa enthusiasts from the early period and later, reporting on formative occasions and epiphanous experience, of entering telepathic communications, of being "in synch" with others, of sharing in unmediated connections with strangers, of possessing a conspiratorial knowingness unanticipated, of realizing their at-one-ness with everyone and everything. This is the domain of the noetic experience, the *feeling of knowing* which, as Kim Hewitt (2011) argues, is a biopsychosocial condition enhanced by psychedelics. Castle himself offered a description of the noetic "chiros satori experience" occasioned by the trance dance party "where one can gain a bright-light-bulb-like experience of illumination and understanding". Dancers, he indicated, often claim that they feel "most alive when they are dancing", amounting to a "religious-like ecstasy" which "offers a healing of our various splits and a reintegration with our instinctual self, through such peak, bliss, experiences, which will permeate thru into all aspects of our life". And, with this "transformational, life altering, affect" in mind, he concluded: "dance parties have transmuted the role that organized religion once had to lift us onto the sacramental and supramental plane" (in ENRG 2001: 259).

The noetic experience is the domain of the social liminality Victor and Edith Turner deemed "communitas", a circumstance where individuals, often strangers to one another, may obtain in gatherings of extraordinary "energy" a spontaneous "flash of mutual understanding on the existential level, and a 'gut' understanding of synchronicity", as V. Turner (1982a: 48) had it. Recognizing the mystical potential of these states, Des Tramacchi (2000) adopted the term "psychedelic communitas", an experience whose heritage can be traced to the "Acid Tests" of the 1960s (Mishor 2010) in which brazen experiments with group consciousness during the Vietnam conflict lent subsequent socio-psychedelic experiments a rebellious architectonic. Communitas is a compelling heuristic, not the least because, as Donald Weber (1995: 528) insisted, "the heady promise of social critique and social regeneration" fermenting in 1960s America provided stimulus for the "apocalyptic agency" of Turner's ritual liminality. As was conveyed in *The Ritual Process* (1969) and *Dramas, Fields, and Metaphors* (1974), communitas is a trope shaped, at least partially, by the explosive and utopian undercurrents of that era. In his "long conversation" with Edith Turner, Matthew Engelke (2004: 30) points out that in Palo Alto – where V. Turner was a Fellow at the Center for Advanced Studies in the Behavioural Sciences from 1961–1962 – the Turners encountered beatniks, "fellow admirers of Rimbaud and detractors from 'the establishment'". "These new friends", Engelke further comments, introduced the Turners to Kerouac's *On the Road* and the poetry of Ginsberg and Gary Snyder. Turner understood that "happenings" and the hippie quest for "existence" paralleled the experience of traditional ritual liminars. Yet, unlike the nominally conservative "anti-structure" of tribal ritual, the counterculture harboured a millenarian, and even apocalyptic, disposition to embrace the psychedelic "happening" as "the end of human endeavour" (Turner 1969: 139). Taking an heroic dose of communitas, the "Be-Ins" and all their after-parties constituted a conscious effort to escape the dialectic, exit the illusion, break the cycle of life and death, and enter a permanent expatriation from one's former self. This was the repudiation of the system of values and conditional rewards that John Robert Howard (1969) had classified as "lateral deviance". The "rock communitas", which Turner saw reported in Haight-Ashbury's *The Oracle*, would be extolled by communitarians and freaks as a principal site for what he related as the construction of "new definitions and models for behavior" (Turner 1974: 261ff), the formation of a new consciousness among those whose "ultimate mission" was to "'turn the world on' – i.e., make everyone aware of the potential virtues of LSD for ushering in an era of universal peace, freedom, brotherhood and love" (Davis and Munoz 1968: 157). The world was not "turned on". LSD was prohibited, there began a moratorium on research on its use and cultures of use lasting over thirty years, and the Turners moved on to make formal study of Catholic pilgrimage. Yet the psychedelic noetic experience became mobile. In the early 1970s, habitués of proto-discos in New York and elsewhere were hip to the happening. "Every Saturday night is like a little Woodstock, all races and creeds becoming one" mused DJ Steve D'Aquisto about the club Le Jardin in a story in the *New York Post* (Shapiro 2005: 190). For the inhabitants of these early clubs, wrote Shapiro, "the communion offered by the dance floor was the embodiment of the vision of peace that the '60s yearned for. The naïve utopianism may have been ditched, but the radically different attitudes to race, gender, and sexuality born in the '60s remained and flourished most evidently on the disco dance floor" (ibid.). One of the chief enclaves for the emergent *discommunitas* was found on the coast of Goa, which provided the seasonal context for the optimizing of an "apocalypse now" performed on shifting sands so far from "home".

"Communitas" became a troubled concept for cultural theorists. Critics recognized that the utopian and homogeneous experience characterizing the Turnerian approach to pilgrimage destinations ignored contestations over meaning and power, with Eade and Sallnow (1991), for instance, identifying pilgrimage centres as "realms of competing discourses" which accentuate prior distinctions between participants more than "realms of pure possibility" which effect the dissolution of their differences. A similar logic can be applied to traveller dance music cultures whose sites and events facilitate the performance of difference at the same time as they may obliterate such distinctions. While this chapter will demonstrate that competing expectations and struggles over definition have been endogenous to psyculture (not unlike participants in early disco, house and techno scenes) on the strength of the intelligence they possess on a range of matters – including current releases, artist's form, genre developments, event comparisons, the source, content and effects of various psycho-active substances – enthusiasts of psychedelic trance gather in specific locations at specific times under the indubitable impression that they will be transported to desired states of time-less-ness and unity. That is, based on the storehouse of past experience, they anticipate achieving and indeed reliving more-or-less classical mystical states of consciousness that tonight, into the morning, and throughout the day, will be lived in the present, in the company of partners in the sublime. The desirable condition of shared transit is invoked in the most parsimonious of terms. And, although hard pressed to define it, they identify that which they seek: the "vibe". While largely ineffable, Alexander Synaptic (as DJ Basilisk) makes a notable effort to outline the experience by explaining the meaning behind the name for his netlabel and webportal ektoplazm.com:

> Ektoplazm is named for the immaterial or ethereal emanation that surrounds a person in a deep state of trance. Although the root word "ectoplasm" was originally a biological term, parapsychologists and the occult adopted it for their own uses in the late 19th century. In the new millennium, the term serves as a reference to the elusive "vibe" revellers experience at proper trance gatherings. Imagine it as a sort of inexplicable luminous glow that can be perceived

> surrounding a "fully activated" dance floor. If that seems slightly too obscure and mystical, consider the beaming smiles and bright-eyed excitement that accompanies a deeply satisfying musical experience – and the social connectivity such a state encourages. This is what the psychedelic trance experience is all about: breaking through to new states of consciousness and awareness through the conscientious application of sound and motion.[3]

Psytrance enthusiasts will nod their heads in recognition of the state Synaptic describes. And it is not only psytrance enthusiasts who will demure, for the "vibe" holds currency across diverse EDMCs, where it persists as an optimal and aspired condition.

But this condition and its assembly of inputs does not appear in a vacuum. That is, for every vibe there is a history of patronage and dependencies, gender inequalities, relationships with authorities both official and unofficial, and a background of internal disputes and divisions concerning that which is recognized, for instance, as appropriate sound aesthetics, artist scheduling, appurtenant lighting, suitable site management, the size and content of an event market, the price of admission (if any), etc. Disagreements over such matters are not uncommon in music scenes where veteran participants possess weathered sensibilities and are strongly opinionated with regard to the sensuous and psychoactive media of their lifestyles. "No one seems to agree much on what makes good trance", comments one anonymous spokesperson.

> After every party, no matter how great a time everyone had, there are always but always people bitching about the music. The tracks were too old, they were badly mixed or the DJ wasn't stoned enough. Perhaps one of the worse things about the whole phenomenon of the trance movement is that it spawned a whole new generation of music critics who consider themselves expert in the field. Perhaps this was because the music was so personal, melding as it did with your particular trip. Either way the music gave you the waves but it was up to you to surf them. At its best, dancing to trance could be better than sex. At its worst, however, it became a cruel, mental torture that messed your head up all night (Roadjunky 2006).

Beyond contested aesthetics, challenging event industries is common within psychedelic trance circles where discontent and enthusiasm for debate, but also an interest in resolving differences, ensures the continual re-optimization of that which fuels the passions of habitués. Before addressing the ripples in the Goa vibe, or any disturbances in its mind state, there is need to investigate further these cultures of the vibe.

Attempting to define the experience in underground house clubs, Sommer (2001/2002: 73) recognized the significance of those conditions where, according to Turner (1969: 128), liminars "rid themselves of the clichés associated with status incumbency and role-playing and enter into vital relations with other[s]". The vibe, she wrote, is "an active communal force, a feeling, a rhythm that is created by the mix of dancers, the balance of loud music, the effects of darkness and light, the energy. Everything interlocks to produce a powerful sense of liberation". It is, furthermore, "an active, exhilarating feeling of 'now-ness' that everything is coming together – that a good party is in the making". Finally, the vibe is "constructive; it is a distinctive rhythm, the groove that carries the party psychically and physically". Throughout the history of EDMCs, this word – so often used without explanation – has been universal for the desirable social dance experience optimized and reoptimized with the assistance of digital, cyber and chemical technologies. The *Oxford English Dictionary* (2nd ed.) indicates that the "vibe" entered popular literature in 1967, and thus is not unconnected to the psychedelic *jouissance* of the "Summer of Love". But the experience inherited by psychedelic trance and other music cultures, electronic and otherwise, has a convoluted history. For one thing, what is known as the "vibe" holds origins in Afro-American dance music culture, particularly jazz. But the roots of collective altered states in African American dance music go deeper. Peter Shapiro (2005: 90) traces the "capitulation" to "machine rhythms" back through funk and New Orleans swing to late-nineteenth-century brass bands composed of freed slaves and immigrants from Haiti and Cuba congregating in New Orlean's Congo Square. Further still, Robin Sylvan (2002) traces the "spirit" observed in popular music and dance forms to West African possession cults. With the advent of underground dance music in New York in the 1970s, the "vibe" would become especially "meaningful", claims Kai Fikentscher in *You Better Work!* (2000: 82), "for culture bearers of the African American tradition and those who have learned its idiom". The word "vibe" is a likely carrier of the "subversive intelligence", which John Leland suggests, in his *Hip: The History* (2004: 6), was cultivated by transplanted (slave) outsiders and their descendants, and lies at the roots of "hip".[4] With this history in mind, the "vibe" is inherently a subversive dance music experience, a virtual world enabling a measure of cultural autonomy and even integration within an oppressive, alien, world.

The term "vibration," of which "vibe" is a contraction, has been in currency since at least the mid-nineteenth century, according to the *OED*, designating an "intuitive signal" that may be picked up from other people and the atmosphere. While the *OED* shows no connection, *vibration* is likely to have gained popular usage in connection with the theosophists, hermetic philosophers and varying spiritualist traditions purporting to gauge, measure, reflect, channel and translate "vibrations"; to offer readings of universal energy, the soul, spirit, nature, universe, god/dess. Psychedelic trance producers actively acknowledge their role in channelling this *energy*. Adopting their name from the Sanskrit word meaning "vital life" or "life force" and pertaining to breath, early collaboration Prana – formed by Tsuyoshi Suzuki with Andie Guthrie and Nick Taylor – evoked this intent. And much later, Australian outfit Hedonix amplify a Discordian current on their tribute to Robert Anton Wilson, *Order out of Chaos* (2009). On the track "The Principle of Vibration",[5] it is declared that: "Nothing rests. Everything moves. Everything vibrates. Everything vibrates from the atom up. This principle was known from the days of Egypt". Here and elsewhere, audio-quotations echo received traditions holding recognition that divinity inheres in a "universal sound" or "undertone," commonly represented in the Hindu sacred syllable *Om* (and its Devanagari sign ॐ), the iconic stand-in for "Goa".[6] Recognition that consciousness is known, obtains potential and maintains balance, through techniques like meditating, channelling, divining or amplifying vibration (or god/dess) has been integral to the holistic-health movement, as well as New Age music. And dance would become a chief means by which one could best participate in or connect with this "energy" or "vibe" such that the dance event itself is designated most accurately through the use of this term. In the Goa tradition, we find this usage alive in the work of Goa Gil. As he stated, "through the music and dance we can uplift people's consciousness and also spread the vibe and let them bathe in that vibe and become one with the Cosmic Spirit. Become one with Mother Earth and in that way have respect for the Earth and the natural order of things" (McAteer 2002: 94).

In the long prelude to the Summer of Love, it is likely that the *vibe* thus entered the countercultural lexicon via the complex intersecting lines of African and European trajectories. White hipsters, beats and their antecedents who had found the alienated sensibility of jazz and bebop scenes appealing, and may have been among those Norman Mailer (1957) admonished as "white negroes", slouched into this groove. From cosmic jazz artists, among whom Sun Ra and his Galactic Research Arkestra were meteoric, to cosmic rock experimentalists The Grateful Dead, musicians manipulated oscillators and produced feedback to simulate and enhance altered states appealing to participants in an emergent psychedelic culture. Deadheads were intimate with the vibe via a free-form dance style cultivated over thirty years from the mid-1960s, a dance style especially apparent in the "hallways" adjacent to the main auditorium, where sound technicians set up speakers, and where, as one Deadhead notes: "instead of seeing the band, we see each other – dancing, swirling, spinning, loping, crying, zooming, bouncing, toddling, shaking, and smiling" (Sylvan 2002: 90). Tim Leary and Stewart Brand – and thus Eastern mysticism and cybernetics – had been instrumental to the mounting vibe. With coauthors Ralph Metzner and Richard "Ram Dass" Alpert, Leary deliberated on source "wave-vibrations" at some length in *The Psychedelic*

Experience (Leary *et al.* 1964). By 1966, *Whole Earth Catalogue* founder Brand, along with Ken Kesey and the Merry Pranksters – and house band (The Grateful Dead) – were organizing the setting for the freak-out at the Trips Festival on 21–23 January at San Francisco's Longshoreman's Hall. By sharp contrast to the soulless world of bureaucracy and the military they railed against, in the Acid Tests, Brand had constructed "a world in which he and the dancers on the floor were part of a single, leveled social system". In the experimental, multi-media happening, "stereo gear, slide projectors, strobe lights, and, of course, LSD, all had the power to transform the mind-set of an individual and to link him or her through invisible 'vibes' to others" (F. Turner 2006: 76, 240). At this time, the vibrations had also been raised in New York, where, with direct influence from Leary, David Mancuso operated proto-disco deprogramming rituals at The Loft at 647 Broadway, a venue kicked off at a party in 1970 with a notable acronym: Love Saves the Day (see Lawrence 2003: 9–10). While the DJ–dancer interaction and the role of rhythm as a "synchronizing" force have been observed as integral to the "collective energy" of New York underground clubs (see Fikentscher 2000), or to the dance energy of Deadheads, as we scan the horizons of EDMC it becomes apparent that motivation and intention modulate this "energy". That is, additional to music programming and response, and avant-garde technique, the vibe is conditioned by manifold freedoms sought and obtained within its domain. As free spaces, liberated zones, temporary and more enduring, throughout the 1970s and 1980s in locations worldwide, dance clubs became havens for drifters, queers and trancesexuals to experiment with and reconfigure their subjectivities (Apollo 2001; Buckland 2002; Shapiro 2005). At these sites, improvised dance moves were the dramatic yet fleeting expression of utopian lifeworlds. And, as veterans, scene brokers and frontier producers repeatedly disembarked from a multitude of 1980s house clubs and turn-of-the-1990s raves[7] to arrive on the sands of Anjuna, they gave their energy to the proto-trance scene.

This state of virtual secession in which liberty was experienced in the sovereign realm of the dance floor demonstrates evidence of an evolved longing raised and sustained from an assemblage of scenes, drugs, musics, technologies and mythologies. This disc-cultural utopia was of course fuelled by LSD, liquefying the edges of jazz, rock, soul, funk, disco, electro, techno and ambient musics holding pastoral (see Reynolds 1997), cosmic and hybrid pretentions. It received considerable input from the cosmic rock tradition pursuing electronic and percussive experimentalism. If utopias are extended ruptures from non-ideal worlds, then those departures, those "breaks", were prized open in 1970s New York with the assistance of Bronx block party legend Kool Herc, disco remix pioneer Walter Gibbons (Lawrence 2008), turntablist Grandmaster Flash, and others whose artifice was to mix between the percussive breaks (the breaks between vocals and melodies) on copies of the same records, editing the breaks on reel-to-reel tape and pressing them to acetate; pressing the longue disco durée onto the 12-inch record, and more generally forging a culture in which the beat was matched, cut, sampled and remixed, in which *now*, the liminal state of transit, was getting a permanent encore. This sensibility is intimate with the unrequited longings of soul passing into electro, and it would be characterized by stylistic miscegenation, fusions of disparate genres and their aesthetics, from funk, soul, synth-pop and afrobeat.

Computers served as perfect accomplices for the exiles of Disctopia, a circumstance apparent in the early 1980s with the electro-envelope pushed by Afrika Bambaataa and the Soulsonic Force, whose *Planet Rock* 7-inch (1982) was indebted to Kraftwerk's *Trans-Europe Express* (Nesbit 2005; Toop 1984: 130–31), which also had a large influence on the first wave in the Detroit techno tradition. European synth-pop, especially *motorik* experimental sounds fomenting with Kraftwerk, but also Tangerine Dream and English new wave acts like Depeche Mode, New Order and the EBM outfit Nitzer Ebb, were all thrown into the mix in Detroit, Manchester, London, Berlin and elsewhere, to produce a "deterritorialized musical sensibility to combat the fall-out of both racism and post-industrial ruin" (Rietveld 2008: 17). While Detroit techno is reckoned as the soundtrack to a dystopian culture (see Pope 2011), UK acid house techno scenes possessed empathetic *rave-o-lutionary* attitudes, fuelled by MDMA (Reynolds 1998). Used in therapeutic circles long before it had become known as "Ecstasy", the entactogenic drug ignited these scenes with radical Osho sannyasins acting like transnational subcultural brokers (D'Andrea 2006) at a time when MDMA grew more popular than acid. By the late 1980s, these musics and drugs furnished a future-directed trance dance scene on the beaches of Goa where electro, synth-pop and EBM became a staple in the mixed diet of Laurent and other cassette/DAT-carrying DJs. But while tracks like Trilithon's "Children of the Future" (1991) and Laser-Cowboy's "Radioactivity" (1986) were among the works collected and thrown into mixes, these beach and hinterland interzones are not remembered so much for single DJs, single tracks or single styles, but for the parties themselves. And this was indeed how the best parties were orchestrated – as empathetic catchment zones for the transnational energy washing up on the shores. In the late 1980s at parties of under 500 people, Castle recalls how speaker stacks were "predominantly set up in a circle formation so that dancers were not just facing a DJ on a stage with typical two speaker stacks flanking. Dancers moved around the dance floor 360 degrees, interactively, holophonic, circular, within jungle/palm tree fields of sound". The DJ was secondary, and obscure, he continued in typical flourish. "This was not celeb idolatry music biz. It was luminous, participatory, transpersonal, communal. Underground in an exceptionally, exotic, obtuse, mystical dance dharma zone, where cows would appear within the dusty gusto of dance floor ignition frenzy frequency feasts" (Castle aka genkigroove 2010).

A foundation stone of what I have been calling Disctopia is dub music, born in the home of the remix, and the "sound system", Jamaica. In Kingston from the 1960s, the likes of King Tubby (Partridge 2007) cobbled together monstrous rigs of solid bass and reverb. These "sounds", as they were known, would hold a gravitational influence on their population, with those called to gyrate and grind identifying with its corporate spirit, moving to defend it against other sounds. These competitive sound-rig communities evolved over decades as local grounds of identification emigrated from Jamaica and were smuggled into dub, reggae, hip hop, rave, dubstep, ambient psychedelia and other parties inflected with a Rastafarian sensibility of freedom in exile. Luton's Exodus collective, for example, demonstrated a commitment to break free from Babylon (Malyon 1998), a theme invoked in the remit of a deluge of post-rave formations, including the pioneering tekno sound system Spiral Tribe who, merging with the travellers of Albion and their Free Festivals, trailblazed the international teknival movement which was launched on the continent at the time Goatrance swung through the revolving door. Martin Glover was a lynchpin. While Glover signed Spiral Tribe as well as System 7 (Butterfly Records), his sub-label (Dragonfly Records) became instrumental to the formulation of psychedelic trance. Furthermore, as "Youth", Glover became a crucial dub-influenced experimentalist (see Partridge 2010: 196) who effectively guided the sound into electronic psychedelia. Dragonfly and other emergent labels illustrated how Goatrance had been impacted by the various sounds and emissaries of Disctopia. The buoyant sensibility of the exile and the exodus from Babylon which had enervated dance scenes of the 1970s, 1980s and 1990s in cosmopoles and outlands worldwide, had been smuggled to Goa by DJ-travellers and techno mystics where it was cultivated *in situ*, season after season, by the likes of DJs Paoli and Laurent, who remained in Goa for ten years honing his craft. At first a secret haven for expatriates, subsequently a transnational vibe of the exiles, and finally an over-populated bad-land, the DJ-led off-world dance laboratory evolved a genre that was exported back to the world.

Kalifornian exile and dreaded anomaly

It's well past midnight, as psychedelic savants and nouveau freaks amass under redwoods at Cutter Scout Reservation, near Santa Cruz, California, 11–12 October 2006. Overhead, the cosmos is vast and the stars blink back on those gathered in the clearing, soon to be buried under an avalanche of "killah" bass-patterns. Goa Gil is wreaking havoc upon those who have arrived to celebrate his 55th birthday. He performs within a makeshift shrine, pushing darkpsy from a pair of Sony TCD-D8 DAT Walkman[8] under Tibetan flags, over a statue of Ganesh with a Buddha decorated in plastic lotus flowers seated nearby. Behind dark shades, with grey dreadlocks knotted back, Gil is backdropped by a fluorescent Shiva-Shakti mandala tapestry and another featuring Lord Shiva in the form of Nataraja, all illuminated under black light. Next to his DAT players, he burns incense, has placed framed photographs of his gurujis, and controls a device with a red pulsing ॐ. As a hallmark of Gil's parties, the rate of the flashing ॐ is synched with the beats ranging even in excess of 180 bpm through the night and into the day. Behind the shrine-stage is Gil's porta-potty. At the helm, and without relent, he will punish this freak congregation for over 24 hours.

According to former Anjuna resident and co-founder of the Turtle Creek Sanctuary in California, Swami Chaitanya, those pioneers of the vibe like Gil who travelled to Goa in the 1960s–70s were explorers on "the frontiers of consciousness". It was a logical option, he explained, for cultural exiles of the 1960s unable to travel further west having met the edge of continental North America. According to Chaitanya, a distinguished fellow of German literature and European history who dropped out in the late 1960s, "we thought we were going to places that people hadn't gone before, and that was for many of us the higher purpose of the trip".[9] Of course, extending the "western" frontier into the East for those backpacking travellers of largely European decent hailing from locations worldwide, India provided the context and the source material for the exodus. Travellers arrived at ashrams and on porches where their needs as freedom-craving Westerners could be served. Social dance formed the grounds of such fulfilment, as found in the practices taught by Osho, but also cultivated in the life and work of Goa Gil, devotee of the Lord of the Dance, Shiva Nataraj, the god of *bhang*. Prominent among the cultural fugitives and antinomians who made it to Goa, and then made "Goa" a cultural phenomenon beyond "the beach", Goa Gil is not only a chief exporter of the Goa "state of mind", but is an ambivalent scene icon. In one commentary, Gil is cast as the arrowhead of a "new subcultural order", and the leading edge of a "transnational neo-tribalism", whose "world without borders" is "an extension of a Western neo-colonialist mentality that sees the often-fabricated spiritual and ontological mythologies of 'other' cultures as ripe products for semiotic appropriation" (Bizzell 2008: 290). Doubtlessly there is weight to such claims, but as it so often transpires in cultural criticism, the context takes a backseat to the theory. And while Gil has had an integral role in the evolution of psychedelic trance from its roots in Goa to its adoption in scenes around the world, this perspective fails to recognize that Goatrance and its progeny neither possesses nor is possessed by a single figurehead, aesthetic or tribalism. The condition on the ground is exceedingly more complicated, illustrated by the fact that Gil's approach does not go undisputed. Indeed, celebrated as a champion of the "Goa vibe" or derogated as an accomplice

Poster for Goa Gil party, Chile, 13 November 2010.

to its demise, Gil is a controversial figure. On the one hand, he is received as a spiritual authority among freaks in the world psychedelic diaspora. For instance, Michael McAteer, who produced a devotional BA thesis on Gil, casts him as a "mystagogue" (2002), and his prestige is inscribed in scene tributes (see Rom and Querner 2011). On the other hand, Gil is reproved with an equivalent passion.

Goa Gil's chief project is an ongoing effort to, as he states, "redefine ancient tribal ritual for the 21st century". With this objective in mind, in 2010, Gil performed some twenty-two gigs, many of them over twelve hours long, with more than a few over twenty-four hours, at venues in India (including Bangalore, Delhi, Hyderabad and Mumbai), Greece, Portugal, Russia, Japan, Israel, Mexico, Chile and other locations – the latest events in approximately 500 trance dance rituals performed at the time of writing.[10] Bridging three generations of psychedelic music scenes, Gil is a master *bricoleur* patching together narratives to orchestrate ritual practice thought to possess revitalizing effect. In an interview with *Freeze* magazine in 2001, Gil offered a view repeated many times elsewhere: "The party is Holy! It is the Old Time Religion! Since the beginning of time mankind has used music and dance to commune with the Spirit of Nature and the Spirit of the Universe". Within the Goatrance dance which Gil fashions as a "ritual" more than a "party", "we go beyond thought, beyond mind, and beyond our own individuality, become One in the Divine Ecstasy of union with the Cosmic Spirit". Under Gil's guidance, dance ecstasy is purposeful, initiatory. For Gil, and his many followers the world over, dance is regarded as a technique of "active meditation", enabling actors to access the divine truth, revealing their own relationship with the cosmos.

> When I come to the party place, and set up my alter, sprinkle the Holy Water, recite the Holy Mantra, and make the Offering to the Cosmic Spirit, and then start the music. The music and the whole party becomes an offering to the Cosmic Spirit. May Lord Shiva, Nataraj, Lord of the Dance come to this place and bless everyone. Then the dancers, the music, the dj, the Spirit, all become One (*Freeze* magazine 2001).

Making allusions to the intent of the party ritual, Gil stated that the experience presages the realization "that *all* life forms are existing from this Spirit, and, you know, we're a part of that thing and we have to protect that thing". That is, the trance dance experience is designed to assist participants to "become more sensitive and aware of themselves, their surroundings, the crossroads of humanity and the needs of the planet. With that awareness comes understanding and compassion. *That* is the need of the hour and the true Goa Spirit" (McAteer 2002: 47).

Not long after his arrival in Goa in 1970, Gil hitch-hiked south along the coast visiting temples and sharing chillums with *sadhus*, "the other guys who had long hair and smoked dope" (Time Wave Zero, 2006). He soon began travelling with a holy man who led him to Puri, Calcutta, Benares, Deli and finally Kashmir, where in the mountains at the age of eighteen, he became disciple to Sri Swami Nirmalanand Saraswati Maharaj, a guru in the Shaivite order Juna Akhara.[11] Eventually Gil became Swami Mangalanand Saraswati (Mangalanandji), and was subsequently recognized as a *sadhu*, and at the Hardwar Kumb Mela in 2010 was proclaimed Shri Mahant (Antahrashtriya Mandal ka Shri Mahant)[12] becoming one of the first foreigners to hold a seat at the Akhara Council, which oversees 200,000 Naga Babas. The honorary title signifies recognition that, at least since the early 1990s, Gil has effectively channelled the yogic lessons of direct *guru*-disciple initiations celebrated to be rooted in the "enlightened source" Guru Dattatreya, 4,000 years ago (McAteer 2002: 25). An undercurrent of possibility among those exposed to yogic practice is that the next link in the chain could be ... you. Gil points this out himself. While acknowledging that the constant travel associated with his professional lifestyle and religious duties renders it impossible to train disciples appropriately, "in some sense", he states, "many of the participants of my events are not only my fans but disciples".[13] Gil understands that, through his official role he is "programmed" to fulfil a divine "mission", to become "a pure instrument of God's will" (McAteer 2002: 96). This is intriguing enough, but Gil is not simply following a "duty" conferred upon him as a "pure" initiate of a sect – if that indeed can be called "simple" – but has been performing a role consistent with the approach of an artist-in-exile, a Californian rebel, whose anarchic dissidence and stage performance is sanctioned by his holy credentials.

"Art reflects the time and culture we exist in", Gil stated,[14] nodding towards his embrace of the Kali Yuga, the last phase of the Hindu "Age of Conflicts". The theme holds correspondence with the emergence of the Goa movement, whose extreme freakish elements, ecstatic dance and radical connections with nature are expressive of the desire for revitalization and renewal in times of crisis long associated with Shaivite and Dionysian cults (Baldini 2010a). Whatever valence we attribute to this interpretation, Goatrance grew as a movement uniquely responsive to its time. As Gil stated in a 1997 interview with Michael Gosney:

> Sixty-nine, Nixon was President, Reagan was Governor of California, Altamont, Kent State. The negative side came down. They said "we have to stop this thing" ... So then many people from many different countries decided ... to split (from the West), and (they) headed for India on a spiritual journey, seeking spirituality and some sort of enlightenment. ... All these people met on the way traveling overland (and) became like a tribe. The Jetset Gypsies or the Nomads (in Gosney 1997).

As learned in the previous chapter, between the "summers of love" of the late 1960s and late 1980s Goa became a destination for cultural exiles. Rather than mounting a direct confrontation, freak dissidents opposed to conditions in their homelands, abnegated, absconded and migrated to regions conducive to their lifeways. Goa freaks were, not without contradiction, expatriating from the Cold War mentality of the "Organization Man". Many of those who made Goa via the long overland route through Greece, Turkey, Iran and Afghanistan from 1969–1971 sensed World War III on the horizon, an anxiety echoed in the earliest Goa releases. On the first Goatrance album, *Project II Trance* (1993), label manager Glover scheduled two of his own tracks (as Black Sun) including "The More You Look the More You See" with a sample that is unequivocal:

> we are in the era of the thermo-nuclear bomb, that can obliterate cities and can be delivered across continents. With such weapons war has become, not just tragic, but preposterous. With such weapons, there can be no victory for anyone. Clearly, the object is to see that such a war does not occur at all.[15]

By the 1980s, Reagan was President, the arms race had escalated, and Gil passes comment upon that protean climate in which he began formulating his ritual.

> For me parties have always been a kind of reprogramming session ... so you just go with the beat, no matter what happens whether it's

> dark or light or it's the apocalypse. No matter what happens, you're just like dancing through it ... When these parties first started to happen and when that electronic body music was happening it was like nuclear disaster could have been around the corner and that was a big theme at that time ... it was like an apocalypse culture in a way. It looked like an apocalyptic event could be 20 minutes around the corner, and so through the dance, and through going through sound vibration and so many experiences and different pictures which came up in the mind through the course of going from the dark into the light we like to hope that ... it kind of helped us be prepared for anything that might happen and be able to deal with it (Time Wave Zero, 2006).

As we'll find, the recurrent symbolic and symphonic visitation of the apocalypse is central to Gil's operation. While the effects of the Reagan doctrine were felt globally in the early 1980s, the Thatcher government had a devastating impact on England's Free Festival circuit, causing an exodus of cultural refugees throughout the decade. While Goa scholars and devotees may want to assign value to the Goa party as a sacred "ritual" experience by way of comparisons with the "collective effervescence" Emile Durkheim observed (indirectly) in Australian Aboriginal corroborees, with the social dynamics of dance Radcliffe-Brown witnessed in the Andamans (see McAteer 2002), or make a vague connection with ancestral "tribes" whose roles enthusiasts believe they are fulfilling in the present, the expatriate cult of Goa was an outland-ish response to oppressive conditions in countries of origin, and indeed a statement on the human condition. This is what Gil means when he says that the Goatrance dance experience was always "more than just a disco under the coconut trees". As he stated, "we are using Trance Music and the Trance Dance Experience to set off a chain reaction in consciousness" (*Freeze* magazine 2001).

A popular strain of underground wisdom since the 1960s has held that a mushrooming arsenal of psycho-technologies and mind alterants provides the antidote to nuclear Armageddon, that becoming wasted could preempt a post-apocalyptic wasteland, that dropping acid was exceedingly more fruitful than dropping bombs. This thinking adhered in the Acid Tests and in the thoughts of LSD chemist Owsley. But while the detonation of the American psyche with all of its pre-programming was sought in psychedelic paroxysms of the kind pursued by the Merry Pranksters and others for whom acid became a sacrament if not a weapon, an incipient yogic sensibility conveyed the intent to be liberated from the illusion of separation (from the One, one's humanity, nature). Thus, the "apocalypse" desired was a condition of at-one-ment associated with disciplinary practices sought by Eastern trekking self-exiles, a sensitivity that was indeed stamped into the earliest Goa releases.

"Adoration to the Aum", one of the first efforts from French act Transwave (the opener on their 1995 release *Hypnorhythm*), begins with a woman imparting some wisdom about "yoga" and "meditation" before bursting forth with the thumping bass-line that rarely relented for the remainder of their career. Fifteen years later, offering a retrospective historiography celebrating the importance of yoga in the Goa tradition, Psychoactive's remix of Tikal's bouncy "Meditation" (*Natural Selection v.2*, 2010) scatters the following samples throughout the audio-narrative: "I remember once in India ... meditation, in India in 1970 ... bringing my mind down to one point like a laser beam ... awareness, Bhakti devotional yoga". The theme is taken up by another spokesperson on the same track: "Bhakti devotional yoga is such a religious path. What that path is, is that of seeing the beloved, and your love becomes more and more one pointed, and you are with the beloved more and more, less and less are you busy being separate, you're just so tuned to the beloved". At this point the words are accelerated "and you just keep opening and opening and opening until it can finally emerge ... to be free".

This "opening" to which trance dancers were being exposed on dance floors, and which artists signal in sampled sound-bytes, connotes the flowering of the integral self, that antithesis to the closed, paranoid and competitive individual whose stability relied upon mutually assured destruction. While psychedelics were clearly important, the Western turn to meditation, yoga and other personal growth disciplines were part of the repertoire that gave expression to this response. Transnational sanyassins are significant in the brokering of this sensibility, as are other mystics, mavens and misfits who've plied the road to nowhere. "Sanyacid", Cosmosis's track from his debut album *Cosmology* (1996), uses the sample "I can see it glowing just beyond the trees, reddish-yellow", conjuring omnipresent sannyasins dancing in their ochre colours. While not himself a sanyassin, prominent was Swami Chaitanya,[16] who arrived in India in 1970 working as a cameraman shooting the Fred Cohn documentary *Sunseed* (1973) about Hindu holy men like Swami Satchidananda and Yogi Bhajan. Chaitanya remained in India for the most part until 2002, having taken up residence in a small cabin in the Himalayan foothills, meditating five times every day, and travelling to Goa for the winter/spring seasons. With mystical encounters at the temple to the Goddess Sri Mukambika in South India in 1992, followed by a vision of "divine consciousness" at the temple of Shiva Nataraj,[17] and initiations into Jnana yoga at 1998 Kumbha Mela in Hardwar, Raja Yoga and Advaita philosophy of the Shankara Parampara, and Sri Vidya, Chaitanya was living the movie, and had himself become an esteemed holyman in Goatrance circles.[18]

Chaitanya is a friend of Gil and had become a devotee of his trance ritual after landing at a party at the Music House in Goa in the 1992/93 season. For him, psychedelic trance, like yoga, is a tool designed to enable higher states of consciousness achieved by way of techniques that grew familiar to travellers reaching Goa from the 1970s. According to him, just as those who chant the mantra become the mantra, the dancer becomes the dance in the context of the repetitive 16th notes that are the hallmark of Goatrance.

> The combination of the sounds, the rhythms and the repetition, ten thousand times, a hundred thousand times, so the repetition begins to make your entire body, the very bones in your body, the very molecules and cells in your body start to vibrate to that rhythm of that mantra, so that you become the mantra, and the mantra begins to manifest through you in what it invokes. And it is the same with the trance movement, where you have a basic rhythm pattern.

But the dancer won't become the dance until after more than about fifteen hours of dancing, a view making Chaitanya a great candidate for Gil's marathon ritual. States Chaitanya,

> When you get to a consciousness where you feel at one with the sound, with the music, with the air, sun, sky, with all of the other consciousnesses in your environment, where you're all speaking together but you're all silent, and you're all sharing that moment, beyond ego, beyond logic, and to know that there is a continuum of consciousness from the molecular blade of grass and stone on up through the frog, and the crickets and the birds, and the owl and seagull all the way … . There's no break, and you can feel at one with that.[19]

For Chaitanya, when the conditions are optimal, psychedelic trance can be the context for the ascension. Enthusiasts, he stated, are "thoroughly adept at getting to sixth chakra consciousness" associated with *Ajna* (the "third eye"). This level of awareness transpires at special events, and he singled out the Solipse Festival in Ozora, Hungary, in 1999 – which celebrated a total solar eclipse – where he recalls "people from forty or fifty different countries experienced the same music at a moment where everybody is riding on the wave of the rhythm of the sound, of the repetition, of the consciousness … beyond the Tower of Babylon, and beyond the limitations of words". But Chaitanya, who was active in Students for a Democratic Society in the late 1960s, and sees psyculture providing a more self-disciplined than apocalyptic strategy for change, wants to see it "going up to the next chakras". That is, psytrance needs to elevate through the "sub-chakras", first enabling divinity and then the union of opposites, to arrive, finally, at "the thousand-petalled lotus", the *Sahasrara*, the "transcendence of consciousness, universally". Adopting a view approximating that which Turner identified as "ideological communitas", the social synchronization that is adopted, managed or oriented to specific ends, Chaitanya stated: "this is where the trance movement will be going, because that's what the planet needs ... With ten thousand realized souls we could lift the whole vibe of the planet ... and the trance community is very much part of that event on a psychological level, and I think the trance community is becoming more conscious of itself being that".[20] Various altered statesman have ventured their own perceptions that the differentially iterated trance dance event is the last best hope for humanity. Terence McKenna (Re:Evolution), Fraser Clarke (Future Perfect State) and Robin "Mutoid" Cook (Earthdream), for instance, have invested, promoted and harnessed the electro-trance dance party, and specifically the Goa/psytrance event, as vehicles or portals of transition. But, unlike these other figures, Gil is a DJ who has also maintained a "ritual" formula throughout the emergence of Goatrance and has shaped the latter through his role as a selector and producer of dark psychedelic trance – thus becoming formative in promulgating this style a decade before darkpsy emerged as a recognizable genre. It is to Gil's mission that I now return.

Dark yogi and the Apocalypse Tao

Dramatizing challenges faced, sacrifices made and lessons gained on the path to higher consciousness, Goa Gil's epic journeys are in part shaped by the yogic practice integral to his own background. According to Gil, it is a challenge to go "beyond ego", and thus, to become no-thing.

> Many *sadhanas* and *tapasyas* and spiritual paths are even based on that challenge of going beyond the ego and realizing the Self and the Spirit. So even in Muslim religion when they talk about *Jihad*, that is this challenge. In the *Bhagavad-Gita*, when Krishna is coming in the middle of the two armies, this is this challenge. The challenge of the lower mind and the Higher Mind, and the challenge of the five senses and emotions and thoughts, and all these things based upon the purity of the Soul. It's a challenge to get beyond those things, and that is the Spiritual Fight! (in McAteer 2002: 94).

It is with this struggle in mind that Gil commits to the trance dance, where participants are exposed to ego-shattering practice, from which nascent modes of identification are ostensibly potentiated. In the context of overnight open-air events, the "death" of ego precipitates "rebirth". Indeed, the cycle of death/birth and the corresponding daily transit of the moon/Sun through night/dawn are universal symbolic resources adopted to furnish initiatory experiences with meaning, and the Goatrance party is no exception. Most agree that the ideal party must be open to the stars, commencing before dusk and finishing after dawn. The passage from the closed recesses of the night into the open light of day provides a diurnal analogue for the yogic path to illumination – a path paved with perils and pitfalls for the wayfarer. Such is the experience of the generic initiate, who ordinarily suffers ordeals, faces tests and experiences fear and pain on the path towards obtaining a post-liminal identity. Goa DJs made mixes to facilitate a transit almost impossible to orchestrate in a club. Describing a retro Goa mix he compiled in 2011, DJ Solitaire (Mark Ainley) described how master DJs "would take the shifting shades of light into account" and were directed to allow "a sense of wonder and magic to take hold" (Ainley 2011). Poaching from stock initiatory and conversion practice, Gil offers insight on his approach: "I base my concept of what I'm doing also on traditional initiations, and most of the traditional initiations I either studied or read about or experienced or seen glimpses of in many different places of the world, I've always seen that they brought them through a dark kind of thing before they bring them into the full initiation. So it goes through the dark to come to the light". Further to this, he states, "in the beginning I play stuff just to get everybody dancing, and slowly, slowly it becomes more intense ... until like 5 o'clock, you know the last dark of the night, then it's like the apocalypse in one kind of way and very intense. And then when the light comes ... everyone's surrendered and become one with the dance and one with the vibe" (in McAteer 2002: 31). And so the trance ritual is structured to this end, which has often kicked off with a djembe jam with his wife, Ariane MacAvoy, who is an instructor of African dance, a percussionist and producer, who also performs an hour "ethno/tribal" opening DJ set at most of Gil's parties.

Dark psychedelic trance is a field in which Gil would become established as a leading selector, and renowned for his Divine Dozen, the name for the updated list of twelve favoured tracks and/or albums he's posted on the internet since 1996 (and posts about three times a year).[21] More than a decade downstream from Front 242's "Commando Mix" and other bleak dispatches from the apocalypse, and well before darkpsy fostered its own festival culture, such as the five-day Voltron Festival hosted by Industraum in Mugla, Turkey, in August 2012, Gil was surfing point-break on the dark wave, with proto-dark Goa pacesetters like Germany's Xenomorph (Mark Petrick) and Russia's Parasense (Alexey Kurkin and Viktor Zolotarenko) looking on with interest, and successfully gaining his attention. Petrick confirmed that Gil "was the only guy that you could listen to (in 1997) and not know 80 per cent of the tracks he played, because the artists gave him the DATs in Goa and the record industry was lagging behind with the actual releases". Impressed by the marathon sets, Petrick recalls that Gil:

> blew me away at that time and inspired me to change my style from the hardtrance 160 BPM stuff more in the direction of goa sound. When he played the next time in Berlin in 1996, i gave him a promo DAT that i named "Horror Trance" a term that was previously unheard of in the otherwise spiritually monolateral trance scene of that time. He liked the tracks a lot. One of them was "Obscure Spectre (Horror Trip Rmx)" and i think "Carnage Vision" was also on there.[22]

Indeed you can imagine Gil channelling Xenomorph's post-apocalyptic screed as he reeled out "Carnage Vision" (*Obscure Spectre*, 1997) on which the mad prophet John Trent from John Carpenter's *In the Mouth of Madness* (1994) commentates: "Every species can smell its own extinction. The last ones left won't have a pretty time of it".

In the long prelude to darkpsy – which emerged in the post-Iraq invasion period as a distinctly faster and darker style of psychedelic trance – Gil selected the sounds of the coming "night music", curating soundscapes echoing sine waves of struggle and sounding out notes of despair sampled from horror cinema. With the advent of "darkpsy", producers sought to convey states of inner chaos, fear and hopelessness, most often associated with those terrifying moments when tormented and distraught screen actors are confronted with their own demise or when serial killers and other domestic monsters kettle the vulnerable inside grindhouse storylines. Much of this material is produced by psychedelic artists experimenting with moods of the kind that Gil exploits to his own designs: demolishing the self in a ritual of transformation. In the strategic manipulation of the sounds of despair by Gil and other DJs, these productions sonify the impending annihilation of ego, the transit to no-thing. Thus the fate of cinematic victims allegorizes the fate of the ego in sympathy with the metaphysical pretense of Gil and his ilk. Among the earlier, pre-darkpsy, tracks to connote this mood, and included in the first Divine Dozen listed online, was the mind-bending "Plutonica" by the Ray Castle and Nick Taylor outfit Rhythmystec (EP *Cathexis*, 1996),[23] which launched an arsenal of vocal samples from Joseph Campbell ready-made for Gil's divine mission: "the god of death is the lord of the dance", "it's a good day to die" and "from death comes life". Here, Gil is apparently fulfilling his duty as "God's instrument", a spiritual warrior who implements a sonic dramatization of the Dark Age, the degenerative age of the Kali Yuga. Take a selection from Gil's jarringly mixed album *Kali Yuga* (2009), "Crucial Night" by Fatal Discord, where death-rattle bass-lines smother hopeless cries ripped from *Saw IV*, with a shrieking that might be the siren of your own demise. Russian artist Enichkin's furious "Visit to Eternity" summons hell's own legions. And by the time we arrive at "Kali Does the Dance" by The Nommos – the outfit formed by Gil and Ariane (and which for some time included Peter Ziegelmeier, aka

Kode IV) – descent into chaos is near complete. In a curious break in the fury the track samples lines from The Anjuna Jam Band (in which Gil played guitar, circa 1975–76):

> Kali does the Dance,
> the Dance of Destruction.
> Shiva lays down,
> to watch the action.

Kali is said to be "the destroyer of false consciousness" and the "goddess of protection". On the album cover, blue-skinned, hair dishevelled, tongue lolling, in a necklace of human skulls, Kali grasps a decapitated demon's head in one of her eight hands and wields a bloodied sword in another. While for Gil, Kali's mythic fury is a means to a revitalizing possibility, for many dark trance producers, madness, schizoid tendencies and mind-altering excesses fuel the disturbing possibilities of the liminal mind, the darker recesses of which were early explored by, for instance, Neuromotor (*Neuro Damage*, 2001), Psychotic Micro and Azax Syndrome collaborating on *Voices of Madness* (2003), and Scatterbrain (notably *Infernal Angel*, 2003), all pre-rabid bpm excursions into the shadowlands without a scent of ritual objective. In his study of darkpsy, a "characteristically demented atmosphere" which he states is preoccupied with the "continuous transgression of its own perverted boundaries", Botond Vitos (2009: 137) contends that the darkpsy dance floor, fuelled by psychedelics, embraces "the immensity of Otherness out 'there', without transferring it 'here' (without integrating it into the Self, thus dissolving or understanding it)". Though darkpsy producers and other inhabitants of the night may become bent on an "inverted sublime", dwell in the discord of the gothic liminal, squat the post-apocalypse, or even embrace death as a lifestyle thematic, this is not the stated goal and persistently staged performance of Gil. Pursuing an order which he is instructed (by the "Cosmic Spirit") to implement, for Gil death is a threshold of transition for rebirthing neophytes. And so, in recent years, Gil's own productivity appears to have escalated mirroring the inclement times. Amid the unforgiving pace of The Nommos' "Hate Killer" (*Ten Reasons to Eat Dust*, 2010), cinematic samples from horror cinema – "nightmares, heart palpitations, terrors" – prefigure the response as party-goers are subject to an apocalyptic sound-bath. Is it coincidental that The Nommos, the name for Gil and Ariane's outfit and a Dogon word referring to amphibious beings and guardians "from somewhere in the vicinity of the star we call Sirius B" – as described on the inlay of debut album *Digitaria*, 2004[24] – bears striking resemblance to the Greek word for rules, codes and forms – *nomos* – which, in the sociology of Peter Berger, means the social *order* that is projected and internalized (taken for granted) within a socially constructed universe? Indeed, the Bergerian understanding of the socially established *nomos* "as a shield against terror" (1967: 22) appears to reveal the purpose of Gil's own religious mission: the provision of stability and connectedness in world of chaos, separation and *anomy*. It might be postulated that Gil's highly regulated rituals actually hypostasize the anomalous with the objective of producing its opposite: *nomization*. Under this logic, divinity and morality follow heavy doses of apocalyptic liminality.

As the snapshots and video routinely captured from his altar-perspective illustrate, massives willingly surrender to Gil's will.[25] But the net effect of his intent upon psychedelic trance enthusiasts who've never set foot in Goa (at least, in its heyday) remains uncertain. Detailed ethnographic attention to the motivations and outcomes of Gil's fans/disciples – their *nomization*, or otherwise – would be required. Yet it might be suggested that urban trancers familiar with depressing social and political conditions and states of emergency who achieve the "exile vibe" with the aid of a maddening catalogue of psycho-chemical substances, and who syncopate increased doses with accelerated beats, may simply be carving wild body shapes to aggressive soundtracks in styles which, according to Steve Goodman (2009: 73), "sonically enact the demise of Babylon". Nevertheless, Gil's underground popularity among those he once referred to as "the Children of Babylon" persists. According to Chiara Baldini, for these neo-Goatrancers, he is a "grandfather figure". In Italy, she says, "they call him *Il Nonno* ... He is one of the original Goa freaks, so these kids who are too poor to travel and whose life is too 'normal' to be freaks they love him! ... For these kids he is really a redeemer and his sets are really a powerful experience".[26]

At his birthday party in October 2006, Gil served up a ruinous, unrelenting barrage of white-label dark matter, amplified well past dawn. Soaring melodies typical to the Goa tradition were absent, as were the uplifting progressive psychedelic motifs consistent with outdoor psytrance events where the Sun's emergence signals a shift from frenetic to softer, slower, burning arrangements, ostensibly marking a corresponding elevation in consciousness. There was little variation in style at Gil's party, nor apparently anywhere Gil plays his DAT, including venues in fresh regions holding the possibility of visiting Armageddon – or perhaps *Karmageddon*, the title of his 2005 compilation – upon the psyches of dilettantes. But while I personally felt no redemption, a persistent legacy is performed: the apocalyptic remit to re/animate young neophytes, and to push them under the wheels of a rolling furor. The sonic *sadhu* is himself like a psy'ed-piper of the zombie whose shambling *ekstasis* is not far removed from the goal of meditative traditions: the dissolution of subjectivity and the potentiation of mystical states of consciousness. Embodying the hyper-anomalous condition of living-death, the zombie is a cardinal trope within psytrance and is something of a parodic mascot for the dark carnival (see St John 2011a). There, it holds court as a powerfully ambiguous device, loaded with potential. Passing into (ego) death and yet (charged) alive, the zombie is a liminal figure emblematic of the altered conditions of mind and flesh experienced as "trance". Anaesthetized yet mobilized all the same, the zombie embodies the unpredictable yet potentially transcendent and revitalizing conditions of the dance floor.

With beard blazing grey, rocking from side to side, bearing a wide grin, Gil makes himself heard under this aberrant aesthetic. Sadhu punk and servile master of a brutal exercise in zombification, he assumes his staged position as head mutant in an "apocalypse culture", his interventions straddling inchoate purposes: the annihilation of subjectivity and social re-animation. Like a faithful servant of the apocalypse, Gil casts his shadow over the dance floor. And exercising a kind of sonic homeopathic logic, he submits all to his abominable symphony. But not all are impressed. Indeed Gil's approach is met with considerable disapproval, which is understandable in the light of the profusion of exiles who trekked the road to nowhere, and who sought various solutions to a world of pain. Gil's ritual is upsetting especially to those for whom the Sun's rising is the singular transition towards consciousness expansion, "dawning" or "awakening" (see Chapter 5) – a transition that is apparently abused by Gil, whose "apocalypse now" appears to know no bounds. At least this is the view of Castle, who once saddled up with Gil (in Goa in 1991) and who last saw him perform in 2005 at the foot of Japan's Mt Fuji. "This dark monotonous moronic dirge bleak psychotic sound continued into the sun rise", he lamented.

> It was dreadful, just like this dark tunnel all night and into the morning, and it was just nothing like I remember from when I used to DJ with him together in 1991 in Goa. He'd completely lost the plot ... I think he undermines any vestige of idealized spirituality or healer facilitator that he may have tried to project.[27]

In a further reprovement, Gil's "diabolical dark trance" has apparently "self-defeated his philosophy of making the journey from dark into light". Castle is not alone in this interpretation. While Pavel (2010), for instance, submits that the music Gil plays is "depressing, violent and completely random", others crave for the good old days:

> Bring back the music that made us love Goa Gil. Today's Goa Gil sets drive us away, and splinter the already fragmented scene. Let us all gather together again as one goa trance family and dance like we did in the good old days. We'll trade his newer, smooth mixing style and nails-on-chalkboard music for the preferred GOA music and DAT mixing (Phil G 2008).

Discord in Disctopia

This dispute illustrates the existence of taste-cultures whose aesthetic investments shape ongoing debates around genre and musical canon. But the reaction to Gil's act is not simply a response to aesthetics, but represents a standoff over methodology. When the subject of Goa Gil is raised within the Goa/psytrance community, opinions fall into polarized camps as evidenced by the posting to the isratrance.com web-forum of a link to a video of Goa Gil interviewed in Berlin in 2007 called *The Godfather of Trance*. The thread (22 pages at the time of writing) in which Gil answers inquiries about his background, his initiation and spiritual practice, became a hive for torrents of approval and reproach. The film-maker herself stated that Gil "was really the initiation 10 years ago, he was the one who showed me the deep meaning of the trance dance experience ... For me he was a kind of spiritual teacher".[28] But while there are considerable endorsements, and enthusiastic young trancers are enamoured with Gil whether they "get" his missionary intent or not, others take exception to hagiolatry: the practice of "worshipping" and the idolizing performed by supporters.[29] On 17 May 2007, the discussion compelled one poster ("v.v2") to inquire: "why does everyone get so riled up at the mention of Gil? why is the house always divided, and vehemently so?" Contributing to the thread more than three years later, another poster ("Maine Coon") appeared to answer this by calling attention to a "sux / rox polarity".

While his mission taken on the road in the 1990s has appealed to many, Gil has been spurned by spiritual anarchists and secular-minded antagonists alike. At his events, it is not uncommon for devotees to set up altars at the front of the dance floor, which grow over the course of the event as dancers smudge sage and place candles, flowers and other offerings. With the entire dance floor facing Gil overnight, as McAteer (2002: 51) notes, Gil is himself an "enshrined object" – a contentious circumstance in a culture with antinomian roots. On the one hand, so enshrined, he may be the embodiment of ego-dissolution, the guru who, through his *shaktipat* and the jungle of symbols in which he is nested, guides dancers into the condition of *samâdhi*, provided they make the sacrifice (of their egos). He may then be a pure exemplar of the neomystical union with the "Cosmic Spirit" which, the further Gil travels from Anjuna, becomes an object of intrigue among urban psy-enthusiasists for whom Gil acts as a kind of yogic mascot, a redeemer for their own psychedelic praxis. And yet, the enshrinement may rather render Gil an icon of ego-inflation and self-aggrandizement, a view not uncommon among those who point out that he refuses to perform with other artists or play at festivals where he must share the limelight with other DJs with whom he must compete for the attentions of event-goers. From this perspective, Gil stands out not as a flattened ego but is enshrined as an inflated persona. Castle does not flinch in his efforts to clarify what he observed as a "clever mystical cabaret act".

> He has basically cast himself as a sort of messiah prophet using Goa and this music to propagate and proselytize his own agenda as being like a cult leader. It's just entertainment in the end. … It's great theatre, dramatizing and mytho-characterizing himself within the context of India and the hippie romanticism of Goa. I think his agenda is quite megalomaniacal and quite tyrannical and rather over the top.[30]

For those who are warmer to the anarcho-shamanism of McKenna, Gil's methods constitute a comparatively authoritarian and ecclesiastical route to cosmic consciousness. Goa Gil's roadshow is remote, for example, from the "levelled social system" of the Acid Tests envisioned by Stewart Brand. As an *altared* statesman, he represents something of an incongruity in a scene that emerged pursuing a discommunitarian ethos, and is reproachable to those who have little truck with authorities, be they political, religious or celebrity.

"I remember setting up the DJ table with the locals", states Castle recalling a gig in Anjuna in the 1991 season when he partnered with Gil. "I had it tucked away by the palm tree out of the way, and Gil said 'Oh no, it's got to be over here so everybody can see us'. Like some priest giving a sermon", Castle continued, "he's always wanted the party to focus on him".[31] Gil, who apparently "saw himself as a kind of Ram Dass of techno, full of hierarchical hubris", is said to contradict what Goa was once about. For Castle, who has been involved in various collaborations, and has elsewhere (Cole 1999: 91) stated "I like the marriage of opposites … the third entity which comes out of two people together", Goa was a "sort of feeling of collectivism, of family, shared resources, where people would exchange music, and different DJs would play parties and play together". As stated earlier, among the best parties were those set in a circular formation, with four-way speaker-stacks and where "the dancers are the main event". As he further stated, "Goa was one of the only places where this psychodrama-ritualistic, dance spin-orbital-swival really happened. And of course the music was free – and a very deep entranced interactive state was achieved on the dance floor, independent of sound source. It didn't matter where the music was being deejayed from".[32] But where the theatre of the dance floor was once central, and the DJ obscure, in the 1990s Goatrance became a vehicle for "celebrity DJs", artist as brand names projecting "an aura of personality", a process which Castle sees replicating standard music industry practices where the artist becomes the "product", where "everybody's facing the same direction", and giving their energy to inflated stage personalities. Pursuing a largely solo[33] act in a scene with countercultural roots, Gil is considered to be symptomatic of this trajectory.

> He is contradicting his own philosophy and mantra that it was all about the dance and the ritual of the tribal experience. He's projected it all on to himself as the supreme anointed divine hip priest with the sacramental dark trance to set your spirit free, into ascension. His so-called trance mantra is cold, mechanical, one-dimensional. The so-called 'journey' does not exist because there is no contrast or musical metaphor variety, no novelty discovery gear-groove-shift to excite and explode dancers.[34]

Castle added that, although he collected great music in the early 1990s, Gil was "never popular in Goa, as a DJ". By contrast to the spectacle of Goa Gil, who has often been rebuked for his mixing skills, the uncompromising Castle holds respect for Laurent, the lionized Frenchman who DJed in Goa from 1984–93, who Gil worked with over the 1992 season. "If anybody, he's the *sadhu* DJ 'cause he never left India, and people bought him all the music. He had talent, but he was quite modest".

Turning sixty in 2011, over forty years since first setting foot on Anjuna beach, Gil is a dreaded anomaly. He is a polyvalent symbol for participants in the psychedelic diaspora and has become iconic among proponents and detractors of "psytrance" and "darkpsy" alike. For those initiates who regard psychedelic trance as a vehicle of hope and peace, Gil – who is heir not only to the Haight-Ashbury psychedelic scene of the 1960s, but to ancient mystical and ecstatic cults, the connections with which are both sanctioned and nebulous – possesses the right stuff. For others, the failure of Goatrance to meet its millenarian promise has generated heated reactions, both from within and outside of the scene with detractors charging psytrance as a hubristic behemoth that has collapsed under the weight of its own contradictions. Loved as a champion of the Goa vibe, and loathed as symbol of the contradictions that have befallen it, Gil pitches like a weather balloon in a storm.

* * *

From the world-expatriates inhabiting Anjuna beach in the 1970s–1980s, to today's domestic enthusiasts immersed in the dark psychedelic trance adopted as his sonic signature, Goa Gil bridges diverse psychedelic scenes. As Gil reflected on Goa in the 1990s, "we came here so long ago, to the end of a dirt road and a deserted beach. *It was like the end of the world.* And now the whole world is at our doorstep" (Davis 1995, my emphasis). As the transposable assemblage was delivered to audiences worldwide when parties grew untenable at their site of genesis, and as Goatrance emerged as an international returned-traveller phenomenon and marketable formula, Gil became a global smuggler of the end of the world, commanding a sustained sonic broadside into the solar plexus of the devoted and bemused alike. But Gil's is far from being the undisputed aesthetic uniting the psytrance massive. Gil has been characterized as an "extremely palatable, and transportable ... charismatic representative of rave culture's transnational neo-tribal ideology". But while Gil's concept of the Goa party is imagined to have "struck such an emphatic chord in a globally dispersed audience" (Bizzell 2008: 289), although continuing to attract devotees, Gil strikes considerable discord among descendants of psychedelic trance. This simply echoes the reality that neotribalism is not uniform, that it accommodates disparate positions and conflicted publics including those who will champion and chastize Goa Gil, along with those who are indifferent to his mission.

With his heteroclite dharma-punk rhetoric eulogized and excoriated with equivalent intensity, Gil's example demonstrates the schizoid character of the compelling mind-state. This heterogeneity became apparent by the turn of the millennium as "psychedelic trance" splintered into diverse genre camps vying for attention. And so different "Goas" were circulating by the end of the 1990s, often incorporated into the same festivals with event-goers hailed by competing sound and style schools amplifying variations on "freedom". It is a multiplicity evident from the inception of Goa, a seasonal outland assimilating multiple EDM aesthetics, evolving its uniquely psychedelic vibe of the exiles. Home to spiritual outlaws, self-made aliens, yoga freaks, cokeheads, financiers, etc., Goa was an experimental heterotopia rocked by seasonal waves of influence, inspiration and speculation. The divisions inside the interzone were not all "brown and white", as habitués arrived with different motivations and expectations, a circumstance making "*dis*communitas" a pertinent term. Here, "dis" prefaces the fragile and fictive status of "communitas", and wards us from romanticizing liminality, whose sociality is not unfamiliar with tension and discord. That said, interpretative disputes over the meaning of "the vibe" enervates its perpetual re-optimization, sometimes in collaborative efforts, other times leading to the formation of new events with different vibes.

4 Spiritual technology: transition and its prosthetics

Transit was integral to the design of psychedelic trance music from its inception, as evident in early releases like Prana's odyssean "Mōretsu" (1996), X-Dream's "Panic in Paradise" (1996) and Etnica's "Astral Way" (1995) – works formulated to transport dance floors at parties around the world to exotic-yet-familiar places. As technologies of the senses, digital-arts, chemical compounds and popular culture were harnessed to the ends of transformation, an assemblage of spiritual technics (technologies and techniques) evolved, becoming recognized as psytrance. This chapter explores the *spiritechnics* of this music with specific attention to the vocal material sampled from the internet-enabled global media database (e.g. cinema, TV, documentaries and other sources) programmed into tracks by producers, to orchestrate the experience of transition. This material, which I call *nanomedia*, suggests that psytrance music is a vehicle for variant *projects of the self* as apparent in its "progressive" and "dark" developments, the extremes of which evince hopeful and nihilistic dispositions. These divergent religious sensibilities are a faculty of the self's status as authorized mediator of authenticity and privileged source of "truth" in late modernity, a circumstance influencing variant trends. In one outcome, the "truth" is that there is none – no God, no complete self, a conviction animating gothic narratives – while in the other, the gnosis recognizes the possibility of the transpersonal Self, a mystical feeling of universality which is narrated and effected by the resources of "popular occulture" (Partridge 2004, 2006b). The chapter proceeds through a recognition of psyculture's transitional complex. Crises concerning risks to the self and the planet have given shape to a redressive *technoshamanic* artifice in which Terence McKenna became a leading advocate. Variant transitional states of "consciousness" (dissolved, universal, evolution) permeate the movement. And while various means and ends of transition are discussed, psyculture is ultimately recognized as a *technoccult* vehicle host to revelatory experience enhanced in particular by "entheogenic" substances. The chapter concludes with attention to a core revelatory outcome, that of planetary consciousness.

Remixticism

The consciously transitional character of psytrance could not have emerged independent from conditions of reflexivity, individualization and cultural globalization.[1] While the conditions in which various national enthusiasts live, such as those in the UK, Brazil, Israel, Estonia and Japan, differ in accordance with the distinctive patterns of their modernities, given the shared experience of detraditionalization, ontological insecurity, saturation of options and hyper-individualized solutions native to "second modernity", its transnational milieu may be reckoned "imagined cosmopolitan communities" (Beck and Grande 2010: 418) among whose chief preoccupations are grievances associated with recognized risks. In this milieu, responses to threats faced by individuals and the environment are imperatives performed with the assistance of popular cultural resources, the appropriation of which is enabled through multiple media. In this endeavour, *trance* is integral to a lifestyle in which the response to risk is a performance imperative. The cultivation of aesthetics, the DiY ethic and the work of self-authentication are axiomatic to this reflexive task, demonstrating the radical edge of the "spiritual revolution" where the "immediacy of personal experience ... is understood as epistemologically crucial", and where, over a century and a half, one's inner self has become the privileged arbitrator of truth and mediator of the divine (Partridge 1999: 86; Heelas 1997: 21). In Chris Partridge's (2004: 72) excavations, it is in the Romantic tradition where we begin to find the most conspicuous elevation of the self among the works, for example, of Coleridge and Wordsworth, where there was "a great confidence in the individual's ability to know the truth about the nature of reality without recourse to divinely revealed or sanctioned authorities". Later, under the aegis of the New Age, the self attracts supreme significance such that, not only is it able to "discover religious truth apart from divine revelation *from without* or the aid of some other external authority, but the truth it seeks is *within*" (Partridge 2004: 73, emphasis in original).

As will be discussed in detail below, Partridge formulates a perspective which recognizes popular sacralization through an historical *re-enchantment* facilitated by popular culture. This perspective is influenced by an ocean of new spiritual currents, including that which has been identified as New Age and spiritualities championing a linear path, but also Pagan, including those "nature religions" broadly oppositional to Christianity, and giving ritual expression to the cyclical dimensions of life and nature. Often resistant to "fluffy" and instrumentalist perspectives where the commodification of spirituality is rampant, contemporary Paganism is polyvalent and eclectic, involving non-aligned participants and those who are committed to "left hand" and Goddess traditions, performing chaos magic, and celebrating the Pagan calendar marked at the quarterly festivals. While these are broadly differing spiritualities, their conflation is often noted, and within psytrance and related visionary arts scenes they animate the project of the self, sometimes giving shape to disparate projects, and other times the production of selves, music and events evincing a fusion of spiritual perspectives.

Given this background, we may better understand what Boris Blenn (aka Electric Universe) had in mind when writing "The Self" (*Silence in Action*, 2006), in which an autonomous self, and indeed self-divinity, is confirmed in the sampled conviction that: "the self is god". The statement "You Are God" blazing on the cover art of Space Tribe's *Religious Experience* (2000) appears to possess similar intent. Introduced in Chapter 2 of this book, this collage featuring a headphone-wearing Pope is a telling contribution to the story of the DJ as divine medium. DJ Pope John Paul II appears to be receiving divine transmissions (through his headphones), but since he is looking towards the cover's viewer (i.e. you), for inspiration, *you* may then indeed be "God" (i.e. the source of the transmission). Alternately, the message could be "you are the DJ", or "you are the creator", which is echoed in the title of the album track "You Create Your Own Reality". This is consistent with the rhetoric, especially loud in the 1980s/1990s, of the decentralizing, democratizing and empowering characteristics of cut-up, sampling and re-assembling techniques enabled by digitalization and cyberspace. The optimism loomed out of the pages of *Mondo 2000* and techno-libertarian evangelism was mirrored in Douglas Rushkoff's *Cyberia* (1994). Adopting an assemblage of "new edge" and "cyberdelic" tools, a "new breed" (Leary *et al.* 1994) of technophiles were advancing their capacity to control the means of perception, an enthusiasm pushed further by McKenna and impresarios like Fraser Clark and Michael Gosney, who would embrace EDM, and psychedelic trance in particular, as a realm of the possible. Tooling up users to capture available sound from cinema, TV, radio, computer games, along with live recordings, and reprogram, mutate and synthesize these sounds now devoted to new ends, samplers became the techno-alchemical devices par excellence. Whether sampling bass-lines, melodies, or scripted dialogue and film scores, the pirating and re-editing of found sound is endemic to EDM, where sound sequences are selected and synthesized in production, and/or modulated in performance to fashion new works. Sampling techniques had been embraced, for instance, in the work of the Temple of Psychic Youth, as a magical means of creating new sounds, worlds and selves from disparate popular cultural resources, with the heritage of the spiritual pop-cult remix traced to the Discordians, themselves influenced by Surrealism and Dada (see Kirby 2012). Notably, the Discordian-like collage technique employed on the cover of *Religious Experience* combines with sampledelic electrosonics to figure a *spiritechnics* which upsets the pretence of completion and finality, while at the same time striving for at-one-ment. This fashioning of a spiritual life out of composites was inherited from earlier bricoleurs like those beats who cobbled "a legitimate Western *sadhana*" (Sanskrit for "the way") from various sources. For Allen Ginsberg, who claimed to have experienced *satori* in 1954, his "way" was "a regimen of Judaism, Zen, and Mahayana Buddhism" (Stevens 1989: 165). Goatrance absorbed this heritage, and the mystical function in psychedelic trance owes much to the technics of the remix, where at-one-ment and connectedness relies upon cut-ups and disassembly, and thus the creation of new forms from destruction and breakdowns. Generating storylines possessing spiritual gravitas and significant personal meaning from disparate sources in this way is what I mean by *remixticism*.

Oiling this remixtical development was an elixir that liquefied boundaries, fuelled creativity and connected Goatrance with a cosmic dance music heritage. Consciousness expansion, or "mind manifesting", the purported function of LSD-25 (*lysergic acid diethylamide*), as inscribed in the word *psychedelic* coined by experimental psychiatrist Humphrey Osmond in his 1956 exchange with Aldous Huxley, is a legacy of psychedelic trance. Since Albert Hofmann's "first trip" on 16 April 1943 (see Hofmann 1980), and from its earliest period of use in small psychotherapeutic circles, LSD has been championed as a revolutionary tool deployed in projects in which the self becomes unshackled from standard cultural programming, a revelatory technology, which, not unlike mescaline, cleansed the "filters" that, according to Huxley in *The Doors of Perception* (1954), ordinarily prevent those humans untrained in fasting or a lifetime of meditation from accessing universal visionary mind states. The soundbyte on Tristan's "Small Paper Squares" (*Demented*, 2000), "LSD doesn't fry your brain ... it expands the mind", played the jingle under which a trance culture has danced. This statement could not have been made without the interventions of Leary, who unlike Huxley – who thought only intellectuals should drop acid – sought to turn the world on to the psychedelic revelatory experience, with LSD held as a gift enabling the spiritual development of humanity (both individual growth and species evolution) at a time of international peril (i.e. the height of the Cold War), a gift that would, according to Gary Laderman (2011), contribute to "a society-wide awareness of spirituality as a viable and meaningful alternative to institutional religion". The revolutionary gesture is captured in Goa/psytrance in which the iconic voice of Leary rang legion during a period of relative optimism thirty years afterwards. Doof's (Nick Barber) joyous anthem "Let's Turn On" (*Let's Turn On*, 1996), for instance, invokes a significant contraction in the birth of the psychedelic movement (Leary's 1967 mantra "tune in, turn on and drop out"). While the revolutionary may have turned recreational, an entire catalogue of work – much of it remastering Leary's rhetoric concerning the dissolution of the ego, the "return to the source" and the evolution of consciousness – imbricates trance music in a progressive, transcendental and evolutionary project.

This project of the self fed directly into the "progressive" orientation of Goatrance. Initiatives such as The Infinity Project, Akasha Project, the original Etnica Project, Sun Project, Astral Projection, and Antaris Project evoke the intent of seminal psychedelic artists and events to orchestrate transformative outcomes, often by way of the disintegration and reintegration of the self, but ever-reliant upon an achievable and integral end-state: wholeness. In the mediations deployed by sampledelic philosophers, films and documentaries were poured over and ransacked for vocal *kōans* offering insight on the mysteries of being, providing sagacious lessons to the dance floor-bound wayfarers regarding their own existence in relation to all life. Programmed into tracks, these usually short spoken statements, often repeated at the breakdowns, were emblematic of the self-confident status of psychedelic trance as a data bank of collective wisdom, as a kind of "secret society" which, given one's attention and commitment, might enable the revealing of universal truths (see Omananda n.d.). Prominent throughout the Goatrance development and its progeny are outer space travel motifs adapted from NASA radio dialogue, sci-fi cinema such as *2001: A Space Odyssey* and TV series like *Star Trek* to allegorize self-virtualization, the inward journey of discovery, the encounter with one's *other-self* storied via the poached figure of the alien (see St John 2013a). At the same time, from its inception, this music held a fixation with "virtual reality" and "cyberspace", a desirable techno-liminal condition of becoming post-human, enabled by computers and, eventually, the internet. The Infinity Project's first release, the techno track "Virtual Reality is Here" (B-side of *Hyper-Active*, 1991) rejoices in the arrival of VR. Later, Coloured Vision released *Virtual Reality* (1993) and labels became fixed on the "cyber" prefix (e.g. Javelin's *Cyber Trance* compilations) illustrating interest in computer-enhanced humanism, especially via networked computers. Artists and enthusiasts were now drifting in cyberspace, a popular realm of human potential that was drawing reference and metaphors from travels in extra-terrestrial space. In 1995, Rhythmystec's "Stellium" held the immortal line "downloading from the mothership". By 1996, Electric Universe was seeking "Online Information" (*Sunglider*, EP), the phrase vocodered on the track itself. In a dialogue reminiscent of the 1982 film *Tron* and Gibson's *Neuromancer*, Zen Mechanics later reviewed this period of enchantment with networked computer-enabled self-virtualization on "CBR" (*Holy Cities*, 2008) on which a woman announces: "cyberspace is defined as a consensual hallucination. The abstraction of databases have become visible in the matrix. The computer jockey can use programs to move his disembodied consciousness around in vast fields of geometric architectural shapes. Cyberspace becomes reality".

Outer space, cyberspace, hyperspace and dreamspace were all drafted by producers as realms of potential from which the trance-traveller could acquire, or "download", divine transmissions regarding the true nature of reality. Films like *Dune, The Matrix* and *Requiem for a Dream* were popular sources from which to tap the mystical payload. With mixed influences including house, techno, progressive trance, as well as Goatrance, the progressive psychedelic aesthetic, which would dominate the psychedelic trance soundscape by the turn of the millennium, became heir to this cosmic/cyber project of the self. This sound, typically played during morning twilight hours and afterwards, and often involving few or no vocal samples, incorporates soaring melodies around persistent and seductive bass-lines, and possesses a distinctive stream of 16th notes over a 4/4 rhythm, usually between 135 and 145 bpm. In the late 2000s, a revival of a distinctive Goatrance sound carried the progressive legacy, with outfit Ra assuming the reigns of the "project". Formed by Christer Borge-Lunde, Charlie Clarke and Lars Lind – the former two from the early Goa project Dimension 5 – in 2008, Ra released the journey album *9th*, the title of which refers to "the 9th insight" achieved in the journey of spiritual awakening in James Redfield's New Age best-seller *The Celestine Prophecy* (1994). The album features the epic tune "Transcendent" which, celebrating this awakening, begins with the opening line from Redfield's book: "For half a century now a new consciousness has been entering the human world, a new awareness that can only be called transcendent, spiritual". In this tradition, transcendence is effected and re-aggregation accomplished via the gnosis obtained in transmissions from the "ancients", the historically and culturally other. The Maya, for instance, are typically cast as harbouring secrets, lost wisdom, which, if unlocked, may help trance initiates resolve conditions of disenchantment, and enable affirmation.[2]

But while progressive projects and their prodigies grew committed to initiation, consummation and wholesome insights, harmony, holism and truth are shredded in the remix whose punk logic sees identity, genre and authorized versions subject to perennial re-versioning. These projects, then, speak of perfectionism unfulfilled, optimal states unacquired, selves incomplete, the sublime ridiculed, the truth unrealized. On Prana's classic "Alien Pets" (*Geomantik*, 1997), the track levels out from an arpeggiated drum roll to deliver the news: "there is no final truth". But what sounds like it might be the most horrifying revelation of all may actually be the anthem of the DJ-producer who synthesizes existing "versions" to create and recreate newer works, themselves subject to the perennial remix. States of permanent upgradeability – and the ever-present risk of failure – are built into their progressive techno-aesthetics. Indeed, the roots of psytrance offers a story of resistance to authorized versions, including official representations of the self, illustrated by the invocations of celebrated psychedelicists in Goatrance productions. "Think for yourself and question authority" was the catch-cry for Leary, as it was for McKenna, for whom knowledge, if it is to be accepted, must be *experienced*, and indeed created, in the immediate presence of spirit, the interfacing with which should not be dictated by religious, media or cultural oligarchies, but rather by the quest[ion]ing self.

But the self that queries all authority must be an authority unto itself, a paradox rampant under conditions of radical reflexivity and lived in the radical immanence of dance. In music productions and events, where liminality is engineered and the self is hailed as a field of possibilities, the self-transforming-self is narrated with the assistance of fashionable commentary. Quantum physicist Amit Goswami gave voice to the zeitgeist, rapping about "the only radical thinking that you need to do, but it's so radical, it's so difficult, because our tendency is that the world is already out there independent of my experience". Lifted from the 2004 documentary *What the Bleep Do We Know?* Goswami's commentary features on the title track to Prahlad's (Erik Heirman) progressive psychedelic release *Movements of Consciousness* (2007). "We all have the habit of thinking that everything around us is already a thing, existing without my input, without my choice". Goswami continues, "we have to banish that kind of thinking. Instead we really have to recognize, that even in the material world around us, that all of these are nothing but possible movements of consciousness ... and I'm choosing moment to moment out of those movements to bring my actual experience into manifestation". Finally, Goswami drops the hermeneutic payload ahead of a melodic development: "Quantum physics, very succinctly speaking, is a physics of possibilities ... Mathematics can give us something. It gives us the possibilities that all these movements can assume. But it cannot give us the actual experience that I'll be having in my consciousness. I choose that experience. And therefore, literally, I create my own reality". Prahlad was humming the song-lines to the progression, the narrative confirming the privileging of radical immanence in psychedelia where the technics of self approximates the "self-aesthetics" identified by D'Andrea (2007a: 18) – following the later Foucault – at the confluence of "Techno" and "New Age". While a "globalizing *digital-art religion*" (D'Andrea 2007a: 22, emphasis in original) is the recognized child of this congress, attention to the actual nuances of electronic music and alternative spirituality – and their interfacing in a decidedly *psychedelic* techno-aesthetic – promises further insights on "hypermobile" counter-culture and radical reflexive modernity.

The psychedelic aesthetic and its corresponding socialities refuse to be confined by simple heuristics. While in the cosmic trance tradition, enthusiasts invest in techno-utopian futurism under the aegis of "hyperdelic" optimism built from extropian fantasies and nostalgia for ancient civilizations, others display an ambivalence towards technology commonly amplified via a class of samples from sci-fi cinema exposing "ghosts in the machine" and paranoid assessments of the human condition. While Goatrance has marvelled at technological innovation, revelled in the "cyberdelic" revolution, amid paranoiac visions and scepticism inherited from forebears, productions have also depicted a typically dystopian future. Silicon Sound's "The Shell" (*Highoctane: Frenzy Inducing Psychedelic Electronica*, 2003), devotes sharp lines from the 1995 anime film directed by Mamoru Oshii, *Ghost in the Shell* (or *Mobile Armoured Riot Police*): "The advent of computers, and the subsequent accumulation of incalculable data has given rise to a new system of memory and thought parallel to your own. Humanity has underestimated the consequences of computerization". Later, on the full-on "Computers" (*Forty Five Full Moons*, 2008), Skyloops spelled out the problem for the uninitiated: "The Computer. An extension of the human intellect ... Soon the most ultimate tool will become the ultimate enemy". And like a Space Age Frankenstein's monster, the voice of one of cinema's most notorious computer villains, HAL 9000 from *2001*, haunts countless transmissions.

But it is not only technology that is greeted with ambivalence in psytrance, since outer space may be a source of fear or hope, inspiring gothic or gnostic moods with different revelatory careers. Where the growth and realization of the self is integral to the cosmic trance project, much of that which grew identifiable as "darkpsy" offered the soundtrack to pathos, the fragmented self, the madness of the soul. "Dark" sensibilities had long been cultivated and exchanged by the DAT-wielding DJs of Goa, as Goa Gil's story illustrates. Veteran DJs selected the harder, faster, more industrial and gothic tracks to forge this "night music" that sounded out a savage contrast to the spacious and soaring twilight melodies of "morning" music. The practice inspired artists who produced special night music for seasons in Goa and later released this music. Dark Goa may have been exemplified by the moody "Fat Buddha" released in 1995 by Martin Glover (*Paul Oakenfold – A Voyage into Trance*, 1995), producing as Black Sun, but the pace would pick up and the aesthetic advance over the turn of the millennium. Exclusively "dark" psychedelic artists emerged, producing the sound dubbed darkpsy in the post-Iraq invasion period, in which German, Russian and Mexican artists dominated. Among the first wave of darkpsy, the Manic Dragon Records compilation series, *Multiple Personalities*, raised a standard around a theme prevalent in the genre: psychosis. The first album of that series was mastered by Xenomorph (Mark Petrick), who performed opposite himself (as Xenomorph vs Xenomorph), on "Schizoid Transpersonal Progressions" (*Multiple Personalities*, 2005). Xenomorph submitted a sonic jeremiad on a world gone mad, as captured on the earlier "Abominations" (*Cassandra's Nightmare*, 1998), which stepped off the precipice with a reading from the work of Lovecraftian novelist Sutter Cane: "Trent stood at the edge of the rip, stared into the unlimitable gulf of the unknown, the Stygian world yawning blackly beyond" (from Carpenter's *In the Mouth of Madness*, 1994). Foretelling a world in crisis, the track also used a harrowing line from *Exorcist III* (1990): "God is not with us now, there is only the darkness here, and your death". Deploying new sound technologies, cinematic vocal samples, film scores and game sound tracks, upping the doses and increasing the bpm, the frisson grew larger as the hallucinations became weirder. "Hearing voices" and "seeing things" were the subliminal messages on the techno-voodoo that was Montauk P's (Michael Kohlbecker and Gabriel Le Mar) "Hallucinate" (1997). Later, under the influence of labels like Parvarti and Acidance, the gulf separating the psychedelic sounds of the night and day widened. While many artists were poaching from religious-oriented horror films where discomfort of the greatest magnitude resides in a secularized universe where the divine order had lost its significance (Cowan 2008), French Goa legends Total Eclipse set trends on the steady descent that was "Distorted Soul" (*Update Files*, 2003) which highlighted the chief concern care of *The Twilight Zone*: "no moral, no message, no prophetic tract".

Malevolent aliens, corrupt humans, serial killers, evil robots; a host of monstrous figures lifted from horror movies would run rampant through the soundscapes of the dark carnival. As many producers deploy material signposting cinema's horrific metataxis which derives from the inversion or invasion of established religious order, and otherwise possess a conscious interest in the transformative device of the monster, the dark carnival offered the stage upon which entrants played their other selves. Dark Soho's sample from *The Wolf Man* (1941) attests to this: "even a man who is pure in the heart and says his prayers by night, may become a wolf when the wolfsbane blooms, and the winter/autumn moon is bright" ("Depth of Emotion", *Sun Spot*, 2000). Goa Gil's transformative ritual mission involving the death and rebirth of self is resonant, as is the journey into *The Void* orchestrated by Argentine psychedelic sorcerer Nicolás Di Bernardo (aka Filter and half of Megalopsy), whose work is influenced by *The Invisibles* creator Grant Morrison and Aleister Crowley. Di Bernardo's compilation on Dark Prisma Records, *The Void – Disintegration* (2008), is an effort to recreate a momentous experience he had at Boom's Dance Temple in 2006 – the experience of "leaving behind everything you are and meeting your real self for the first time". "Disintegration is not something negative", he explains. "It's not death and suffering, but it is being reborn, and of course it includes your ego being melted, torn apart, mutated, changed, re-arranged" (ak3 2008). The album, he continued, is "a map of the psychedelic experience ... The path to Heaven is through Hell". *The Void* opens with Megalopsy's track "Zazas, Zazas, Nasatanada, Zazas", which, it is explained, "is used in magickal circles as the traditional way of opening the gates of The Abyss".

> I found the idea that altered states of consciousness can be used to change reality very interesting, especially after having the feeling that the universe actually wants you to hack it, to play with it, to change the code. So this is The Void, it's actually a magic spell, I believe that the only way we can bring change, is by doing lots of small attacks, like psychedelic guerrilla warfare, and this is my

> specially constructed psychedelic Molotov, which does not kill the enemy, it makes them trip, it makes them find themselves, it makes them melt, it makes them laugh, dance (ak3 2008).

In *The Void*, the successful passage across the Abyss leads to the ego's disintegration, with a result that might resemble what Leary could have produced had he consulted Crowley's Thelema rather than the *Tibetan Book of the Dead*. In the "illusion phase", states Di Bernardo, life's travellers confront true danger. "Crowley talks about Choronzon, which is the dweller of The Abyss, a devil that will always try to make you stay in your ego, it will show your deepest fears, your deepest desires, it will tell you anything to make you change your mind and go back" (ak3 2008).

Regarding his art as "holy work", Di Bernardo stated that on his journeys "the most colourful and cheerful people I meet are very big fans of what is called 'dark' trance", indicating that this scene is populated by those "looking for a meaning ... finding it and developing it" (ak3 2008). Yet, as darkpsy established its formula and artists began competing with each other in a kind of sonic arms race, "death" (or ego-death) would not be approached so much as a means by which rebirth or revitalization may be achieved, but as a lifestyle thematic; the post-apocalypse not habituated as a means to an other end, but squatted as an end in itself. Here, the disturbing possibilities of the darker recesses of the liminal are enhanced under mind-altering excesses, like that which appear to be celebrated on FDL Records' angry *Death of Mind* (2010), the cover of which features a prone woman whose eyes have been smote of the Clear Light. Far from an effort to reproduce the work of Leary and Metzner who produced psychedelic theatre in the mid-1960s called "The Death of the Mind", or mirroring Di Bernardo's efforts to guide the transit across The Abyss, here is a counter project revelling in exploitative and hubristically unethical experiments. Having promoted Paranormal Research parties in Athens in the late 1980s, Greek artist Saltos Iraklis (as Narcosis) apparently used his album *Exploding Madness* (2007) to amplify the effects of strictly classified psychiatric experiments on the mind, an idea that storms forth in "Paranormal" and the total punishment that is "Rats on Acid". Officially estranged from cosmic trance and its romance with Ground Luminosity, Narcosis's decidedly paranoid "Cosmic Fear" evokes the epic peril of being alive.

With tongues not firmly in cheek, by the late 2000s, dark artists were producing a *sonica diabolica* that some fashioned as instrumentation of torture and terror. Deadbeat berated the senses with a pounding rhythm and multitudinous effects, naming this "Sensory Deprivation" (*Notes from the Asylum*, 2010). By decade's end there emerged a furious psychedelia that drew influences from power and noise music. In pulverizing power trance like that released on Infarto Music's *Are You Upset?* (2009), or in the material on Terror Lab Industries' *Extreme Noise Terror Vol. 1* (DJ Transgenic, 2010), we are in the grip of self-defined "hardcore" and "terror" trance that appears more consonant with methamphetamines, ketamine and MDPV,[3] than substances declared to awaken the divine within (e.g. DMT). While observers might assume that this was not Goatrance anymore, these developments echo sensibilities that had been enacted at "the end of the world": in the blurring if not obliteration of the essentially whole self. In this aesthetic, the objective appears more that of growing unhinged than achieving transformation. And as darkpsy seeks, at its extreme edge, to expose consciousness to the terror of the ultimate unknowability of "reality" rather than resolutions to life's traumas, it offers a dark romantic and sometimes brutal counterpoint to the strident optimism of Goatrance.

This development provides evidence of the contested aesthetic of "trance", with psychedelic artists debating the psychedelic *real*, collecting, selecting, compiling and indeed composing work challenging imitations and pretenders. That darkpsy has been fuelled by a reactionary energy is apparent in *Psytrance is Dead!* (Nabi Records, 2006), the co-production of Mexican-based Brazilians with punk and trash metal backgrounds, Fabio Aurelio S. Japiassu and Luiz Secchinatto (aka Baphomet Engine), and Frenchman Raphael Befort (aka DataKult). The sleeve notes reveal that "Today, 'Psytrance' is being used, miss-used and abused" and that "this special release will definitely open your mind to alternative psychedelic levels while you dance till dawn to celebrate and enjoy all together the true meaning of trance music". Here, the "truth" is found in the dismantling of categories, in the erasure of memory, in the reflection in the mirror that may have provoked the longest scream in digital history – opening the album track "Superputrefaction". In other work, Terranoise and Ankur's "Die Hippie, Die" (*Extraterrestrial Comics*, 2007) conjures up images of the punk commitment to make transit from hippie idealism in order to ensure survival within a comfortably nihilist anti-future. For others, the truth involves a return to authentic modes of transcendence. Thus, *Speed Demons Vol. 1 Censorship is Uncool* (2008) is marketed as "aggressive punk music that reflects the dark and realistic world that we live in". "There is no fake enlightenment here," it's announced, "just raw, slamming energy that stems from the world around us and shows a return to the ego destroying principles inherent in the early days of goa and acid trance". In this return to nowhere, "true meaning" may approximate no meaning at all, especially where the mood is maudlin. Thus, "Save the Planet" (*Baphomet Engine 2*, 2009) hosts the sampled rejoinder: "for what?"

These tendencies aside, the transformation of self and of humanity remain critical concerns among the sampledelic technicians of psychedelic trance, who deploy aliens, monsters, indigenes, outlaws and other liminal figures to facilitate the transit. Embodying a wisdom by which avatars face the shattering of their egos in controlled and much wilder demolitions, undertake endurances in dance, and are offered "keys" to unlock their potential, psytrance lays out the tarot: "choose your path", "chase your dream", "follow your heart", "get out of your mind". Di Bernardo said so much himself: "I believe that our ego is just an old structure that can be changed to a more flexible system, instead of staying with one personality and one way of being, you can use your ego as an interface to explore more possibilities of self" (ak3 2008). Demonstrating that this is a cross-genre strategy, the cover notes from *Those Who Remember the Past* (2010), a joint dark trance release by Argentines Invid Mind (Nancy Molina) and Jhunix (Alejandro Perez), build the argument: "Create your own balance, break free from your mind structures, dance above your fears, create new harmonic patterns, be aware of the grand cell we are all part of, open your cosmic conscience channels, and let yourself be guided by the ancient spirits, entities, and beings from the past to reach the infinite knowledge". Releases from the likes of, for example, Ovnimoon (Chilean Hector Stuardo Marileo) – especially the epic "Galactic Mantra" and other material on *Magnetic Portal* (2011) – are permeated with audio *kōans* suggestive of universal energies access to which will enable optimal conditions of self. Apparently unaware of opportunity structures determined by gender, ethnicity and class, and tending to overlook how identities are, as Stuart Hall (1996: 4) argued, "multiply constructed across different, often intersecting and antagonistic, discourses, practices and positions", the repeated connotation is that all people have access to the same resources, perhaps what Walter Hanegraaff called "universal esoterism" or *Sophia perennis* (2001: 26). Psytrance then exists among available "psychotechnologies" (Ross 1992), as a reflexive mechanism of "self-shamanizing", the privileged practice of those who "become their own clients and their own healers", with Tramacchi (2006a: 34) making specific reference to the consumption of blended plant compounds in the rehashing of the self. Removed from the professionally minded religious practitioners identified by Eliade (1951) – i.e. those whose ritual "techniques of ecstasy" and "soul-flights" allowed them interaction with the spirit world on behalf of the community of believers especially for the purpose of healing – with self-shamanism, the responsibility is passed to individuals.

Offering the spiritual nomad products, practices and experiences sampled in the interests of growth, metamorphosis, and transformation, psyculture is fuelled by late-modern prosumer logics. While the self is cultivated in a market-place where options are multiple, open and relative, where seekers experiment with various techniques, and where loyalties may be superficial, psytrance is not postmodern as such. Under the authority of the sentient self – which itself assumes the status of a metanarrative – "truth" is valued, sought and confirmed in immediate experience, and is therefore not mediated by, nor dependent upon, an external authority. As the female speaker on Cyan's "Absolute Truth" (*Pure 2 – Witness the Revolution*, 2011) announces: "this may sound very abstract, and in fact it is very abstract. It's called 'absolute truth' ... It isn't really spoken about all that well, and yet we all experience it in our lives, as things opening up, and getting lighter". On Sunstryk's remix of Ace Ventura's "Baby Boom" (*Pure Essence*, 2010), the lesson is further stated:

> The point is, there is only Spirit and nothing but Spirit. You can call it anything you want. You can call it Brahma, or the Divine, or Buddha-nature, or emptiness, you can call it anything you want ... but there is only the One, there is only Spirit. Everything else, is an illusion. Because the truth is you don't become at one with anything. There is only the One ... Everything that seems so different and unique is actually the unique expression of One. The amazing diversity of One.

These sampled ideas concerning self-divinity aren't far removed from the new spiritual epistemology of the self, which as Partridge (1999: 80, 91) identified, involves discourse and practice consistent with the pluralist essentialisms of modernity, but which also display "fundamental areas of epistemic confusion" as evidenced by dogma and exclusivity within New Age milieus, a confusion which may simply evidence the incongruity of disparate phenomena buckling under the weight of a label (i.e. "New Age"), the equivocal nature of which inspired scholars researching a "larger field of modern religious experimentation" to seek alternate heuristics (Sutcliffe and Bowman 2000: 1), notably including Partridge's "occulture".

The search for appropriate heuristics emerges from an understanding that the spirituality under consideration is alternative, by which I do not mean "variations" of existing practices, but conscious alternatives to historically dominant paradigms. And in this sense the milieus that invest in these forms of discourse and practice are not exclusively "counter" or oppositional to dominant paradigms, but actively pursue alternative models for living. In these commitments one finds that the enchanted "reality" that is revealed through the application of alternative knowledge through experiential techniques not only offers insights about the self, but the phenomenal world in which the subject dwells. This is an occultural development where naturally that which is now divined was previously hidden from view. And, as apparent in scene literature and sonic fiction, personal investments in "the source", "light" and "energy", belief in an implicit order, and the adoption of quantum mechanics, chaos theory, the holographic mind, M-theory, and hyperspace illustrate the interest in theories valued for their role in a "momentous paradigm shift" (Hanegraaff 1995) earlier given attention in Marilyn Ferguson's *The Aquarian Conspiracy* (1980). As Adrian Ivakhiv indicated (2001: 39), New Paradigm thinking is a product of alliances between the New Age and science, a milieu where, downstream from Fritjof Capra's *The Tao of Physics* (1975), "one finds a mixture of scientific and religious ideas applied to the task of countering the ecological crisis and providing a bold intellectual vision capable of thrusting humanity into an era of 'planetary culture'". Furthermore, there is widespread interest in the symbiosis of traditional techniques and contemporary science (see Narby 1998), thought necessary to redress ecological crises with such complementarities and syncretisms providing the *raison d'être* of artists committed to modern primitivism, technopaganism and technoshamanism.

Machine (s)elves at the crossroads of consciousness

The key spokesperson for contemporary shamanism was anarchist ethnonaturalist, psychedelic mystic and exacting raconteur Terence McKenna (1946–2000). McKenna was an outspoken advocate of the entheogenic origins of human evolution – his "stoned ape" theory – and critic of modern culture, the "ennui" of which, he commented in *Food of the Gods*, "is the consequence of a disrupted quasi-symbiotic relationship between ourselves and Gaian nature. Only a restoration of this relationship in some form is capable of carrying us into a full appreciation of our birthright and sense of ourselves as *complete human beings*" (1992: 56, my emphasis). With such a restoration in mind, McKenna advocated an "archaic revival", writing that the "last best hope for dissolving the steep walls of cultural inflexibility that appear to be channeling us toward true ruin is a renewed shamanism" (1992: 98). While the idea that psychoactive compounds have been integral to the emergence of consciousness has had a tempestuous career, the insight is received with considerable interest in vernacular and experimental traditions – where it is nevertheless subject to vigorous debate – especially those where trance dance is central, and where *spiritechnics* have evolved to augment the visionary experience. In a 1992 spoken-word performance backed by UK act The Shamen – providing the inspiration for their 1993 EP *Re:Evolution* – McKenna stated that with the "dissolution of boundaries" triggered by tryptamines, especially DMT and *psilocybin*-containing mushrooms,

> one cannot continue to close one's eyes to the ruination of the earth, the poisoning of the seas, and the consequences of two thousand years of unchallenged dominator culture, based on monotheism, hatred of nature, suppression of the female, and so forth ... So, what shamans have to do is act as exemplars, by making this cosmic journey to the domain of the Gaian ideas, and then bringing them back in the form of art in the struggle to save the world.[4]

McKenna is very clear that these are not experiments conducted primarily as self-directed therapy. Burn in Noise's "Transparent" (*Passing Clouds*, 2008) samples one of his crucial insights from a lecture in 1995:

> Everyone of us when we go into the psychedelic state, this is what we should be looking for. It's not for *your* elucidation, it's not part of *your* self-directed psychotherapy; you are an explorer and you represent our species and the greatest good we can do is to bring back a new idea because our world is endangered by the absence of good ideas. Our world is in crisis because of the absence of consciousness. To whatever degree any one of us can bring back a small piece of the picture and contribute it to the building of the new paradigm, then we participate in the redemption of the human spirit.

Throughout the 1990s, McKenna made an impact speaking at dance festivals and proto-visionary arts gatherings, becoming chief bard to the neo-psychedelic counterculture, and is easily the most sampled individual in Goa/psytrance music productions – a cult status that has magnified posthumously. McKenna is literally embossed on psyculture, his wisdom programmed into psychedelic electrosonics. "What the psychedelics do is they dissolve boundaries", he speaks from Ital's "Jungle Law" (*The World of Spirit Plants*, 2009), "they dissolve the illusion of separateness ... Shamanism is about going into the realms of death, transcending the body, transcending space". His storied visitations in DMT-space, McKenna's so-called "machine elves of hyperspace", became a popular trope in productions, from Space Tribe's power release "Machine Elf" included on TIP Records' debut LP *Yellow Compilation* (1994), to the work of California-based audio and visual digital artist Machine Elf (Adrian Scharfetter). Early mooted by Gracie and Zarkov in their popular handbook *DMT: How and Why to Get Off* (1984), within psytrance and ambient genres the "machine elves" became, for a time, totems for the transpersonal Self. An expression of the "Logos", the divine voice McKenna (1993: ix) believed universal to visionary religious experience, that his machinic elves could be recognized as expressions of transpersonal consciousness is simply to acknowledge that there are narratives grander and projects greater than "the self" performing the lead role in what Paul Heelas (2008) calls "individuated self-spirituality".[5] Channelled from "hyperspace", the machine elves are interdimensional entities (see Tramacchi 2006b) taking their place among a cornucopia of beings – often benevolent mutants, curious machine/human hybrids, equally futuristic and atavistic – reported among users of entheogens orchestrating and reaffirming transpersonal conditions of selfhood (see Strassman *et al.* 2008).

Celebrated by countless participants and spokespersons in the scene, the shamanic revival was especially apparent in the years following McKenna's death. Take, for instance, Delphi Carstens, who published "zine" reports on the South African psytrance website *Groovy Troopers*. "Slowly", wrote Carstens in the early 2000s, "we are being affected by that which we have sought to destroy". As "the overlapping borders of our modern world have revealed chaos as the only stability ... , who better than the Shaman, the ancient and revered technician of the sacred, and the arbiter of chaos to guide us". McKenna's thoughts are conveyed as trance culture is championed as the medium for humans to "log into the vegetable matrix of the Biosphere ... Fractaline visuals, strobing lights, and lasers enhance the visual qualities of the psychoactive drugs and vibration-laden music in a 'shamanic fusion between dance and idea'" (Carstens n.d.). As trance dance may dissolve boundaries and enable an individual's connection to all life (including their other-selves) in the context of other individuals' self-othering, it potentiates transpersonalism. This is why McKenna championed the proto-trance and visionary arts dance events as significant waymarks in his novelty theory. The context for panentheistic revelations, in the effusive vibe, the indivisibility of self is experienced as cosmic, and thus one becomes open to the recognition that divinity is *in* and thus not entirely *of* the self. Such occurs at a time when the "reality" packaged and peddled by religious institutions, news-cartels and cultural oligarchies is met with growing suspicion by protagonists who readily appropriate from the art, mythography and ritual of esoteric, Eastern, Indigenous practice, and from science and popular culture, to make sense of their own phenomenal connection with the sacred made available in the socio-aesthetic of the dance floor. Held in forests and bush, on mountaintops, lakesides, deserts and other natural sites, and recurring seasonally at locations to which participants develop strong connections, psychedelic trance events become the revelatory topography for re/discovering a symbiotic relationship, an awareness of one's embeddedness in the web of life. It is not uncommon that dancing is itself the chief means for expressing one's symbiosis with the natural world, and events become infused with aesthetics of the self responsive to threats facing the planet.

While freedom from routine subjectivity potentiates the conditions for transpersonality, this is not a straight-forward process. Psytrance is transitional in its foundations, but its outcomes are unpredictable, an effect of the variable crises of self, society and planet to which participants seek resolution. This complexity can be understood in the recognition that psytrance is host to varying sets of intentions that can be explained by way of differing, although not-exclusive, definitions of *consciousness*. That is, its participants possess interrelated preoccupations with the alteration of "ordinary consciousness", immersion in "cosmic consciousness", and the "evolution" of "consciousness". These are complex and contested agendas and practices which are only briefly addressed here. In the first, the dance event potentiates a qualitative differentiation from a *baseline state of consciousness* (Tart 1975: 5) via the orchestration of ecstatic states of entrancement. This condition native to dance cultures of the deep past and present is by no means uniform but it involves participants becoming unburdened of disciplined, voluntary modes of subjectivity and their embodiment in ecstatic, sensuous and erotic states. Within cultures of trance dance this state involves oscillation between modes of surrender and engagement – that complex experiential juncture of "ego-death" and animation that is an ambivalent threshold appealing to participants and yet historically maligned and marginalized. In the second, a *transpersonal state of mind* that is ancient, eternal and perennial is compelling. It is the "vital", "Universal" or "Gaian" heritage to which humans belong, yet have forgotten, grown apart or been dispossessed from, but to which, through appropriate technique and discipline, they may return (see Lachman 2003).[6] In the third, the compelling consciousness is *novel*, superseding all that has gone before. It is a new "frontier" or "Age" in which the spiritually realized lift the chains of oppression that separate humanity from its own potential. This is the realm of "planetary consciousness" and from the foldout of the Japanese Goa compilation *Strong Sun Moon* (Equinox, 1998), Ray Castle offered the perspective: "The present revolutionary Aquarian age signifies a collective spiritual awakening mediated by an ecology of humanistic transpersonal technology and a Gaian mind Greening of science".

Psytrance constitutes an artful assemblage of technics designed to facilitate these liberating and enchanting tendencies. In the former, an assemblage of audio-visual and chemical tools are adapted to the objective of disorienting, destabilizing or liquidating the routine patterns of one's identity. Within the dance of the deconstructed identity, "social de-evolution appears complete ... Typical human behaviour is now entirely absent" (from Aqualize's "Pressure Behaviour", *Goa-Head Volume 28,* 2010). In the second process, electronic reproduction technologies, global media archives (e.g. cinematic soundscapes) and "research chemicals" are redeployed to expand mind, uncover inner wisdom and fire up divinity. The release notes from the third volume in Dragonfly's Order Odonata series, *The Technical Use of Sound in Magick* (1996), offered comment on the process:

> With these vibrational arts, we are able to catalyse the unifying power of Dance to open up a trialogue between the subconscious, conscious and superconscious levels of our awareness. The power of the magus is to channel this awareness through Order and Chaos to enable us to understand the new realities of the expanded consciousness, to allow the music to serve as navigational maps for newly discovered interior territories which modern technology has made accessible.

In the third process, the new dispensation is performed under the faithful recognition that technological innovation will enable an improved, sometimes posthuman, other times archaic, future. While Man With No Name's classic tune "Evolution" from *Moment of Truth* (1996) may have been the anthem for the techno-millenarians, on "Global Quest for Change", Bitkit (John 00 Fleming & DJ Bim – *Goa Culture III*, 2011) captures the mood: "we are now at this moment approaching a narrow point in time when human evolution speeds up tremendously and makes a jump into a new level of awareness. We become something greater than what is now called human".

Technics, artifacts and media content are harnessed towards the objective of *transgression* at one end, and *progressive* goals at the other end of this spectrum of transitional strategies, even though these goals are not unrelated. Given the significance of holistic perspectives in which practitioners distance themselves from dualistic and reductionist thinking, the processes of dissolution, immersion and evolution briefly outlined here are integrated processes, with the intentional event produced in accordance with such integrity. Since the principal means by which these tendencies are affected is dance, and the chief site upon which this integralism operates is the dance floor, considerable resources are invested by both event organizers and attendees to accomplish communitas, synchronicity and novelty. The recognition of these ideal tendencies enhances our understanding of what is known, committed to and optimized as the "vibe". As the psy-vibe is the context for ecstatic entrancement, cosmic metaphysics and evolved states of being human, the dance party manifests as a sophisticated neomystical threshold. Again, the principal spokesperson was McKenna. Venturing into and trespassing across these modes of consciousness, McKenna possessed a signal dedication to vapourizing barriers separating the self from universal consciousness. As foundationally *psychedelic*, embracing a dissolved-yet-expanded self, McKenna's ontology is supportive of a liminalized sensibility in which the malleability of subjectivity is facilitated via experimental states of consciousness and embodiment. The psychedelic-inspired orientation towards the "Gaian Supermind" from the condition of cosmic alienation has appealed to a loose populace disaffected by monotheism, possessive materialism and ecological maladaptation and who apply technics to ecological and humanitarian concerns. From computers to calendars, and from dance music to psychoactives, *spiritechnics* facilitate departures from, and leaps in, consciousness. But, in faithful recourse to the empowered/enchanted self, (r)evolution is figured to begin at home. Such is conveyed in the idea that one can make one's own life consistent with the alternatives perceived to be essential for a planetary culture – as expressed in the popular mantra "be the change", or "be the change you wish to see in the world", attributed to Gandhi – and that the "crisis" can be averted or redressed in reversioning oneself by altering one's ideas, consumption behaviour, relationships, business practices, aesthetics. For McKenna, it was the figure of the shaman who embodied this transition: "It is in anticipation of a higher, wiser, freer, kinder kind of being that we have always held up as an ideal for ourselves, with the notion of the shaman, the superman or woman who knows the secrets of the animals, moves with the subtlety of the wind, is always capable of appropriate behaviour, is at home everywhere and leaves no mark".[7]

Spiritechnics and transit culture

As the formation of Goatrance demonstrated through its progenitor seasons in the 1980s, production and techniques of performance in EDM are integral to new forms of ritualized dance. The earliest DJs in Goa were influenced by, and contributed to, the performative production of entrancing musics through cutting up audio tape or mixing the gaps (the "breaks") between the lyrics of dance songs, the extending of instrumental sections enabling artists to bend dance floors to their will, to raise moods, and prolong the moment. Exposed to this open-air interzone, importing their distinctive sounds and experience into the party, a loose milieu of seasonal travellers and DJs sought to replicate the experience, effectively producing a ritualized formula adapted by labels and subsequent event management organizations emerging in home-countries led by these same producers and label managers. Indeed, practitioners have shown commitment towards creating intentional dance ritual, repurposing elements of dance/music events – European and otherwise – appropriating their semiotic cachet and functionality. In Goa Gil's rhetoric, ritual practice is sampled and remixed from a generally unidentified primordial stock to which humanity is believed heir. Gil has his thoughts sampled on Lalith K. Rao's (aka Alien Mental) track "Ritual" (*Mind Hack*, 2007):

> I think that my concept can fit with every culture because it draws inspiration and direction from a time of humanity when, no matter where you went, people were in touch with the earth and the spirits of nature, the sun and the moon and all the elements. And so we're delving to the same place and trying to bring the same thing forth but with the technology of the 21st century, and in a way to appeal to the youth of the 21st century.

Setting aside efficacy, with his view that the trance dance redemption is designed to assist participants to grow sensitive about themselves "and the needs of the planet" (Goa Gil in McAteer 2002: 47), a moral design is implicit to the approach. Despite such efforts at conscious ritualization, in psytrance – as in disco, house, techno and other EDM – the symbolic *content* of dance music appears to be of smaller import than the *techniques* of trance inducement. The technologies of the twentieth and twenty-first centuries are adopted to serve transiting individuals, to launch the individual into liminal states the accomplishment of which is a common measure of their efficacy. And so while, in the mystic universalism of Goa Gil, or for that matter in the

Creation Spirituality of Matthew Fox, the trance ritual may serve soteriological goals, its chief value is its liminality; being in orbit, beyond the law, monstrous, virtual – an experience valued in itself. Such is the value attributed to psytrance by a great many practitioners including those who do not seek comparison with or appropriate from traditional forms of ritualization.

That the journey is privileged over destination in this movement is apparent in music productions, a circumstance shared with other EDM developments. As DJ Laurent illustrated, popular Goa DJs were able to keep a floor enthralled through cut-up techniques, track selection and reputation, facilitating an epic journey not unlike that associated with other principal clubs, scenes and milieus within EDM, notably house. With tracks produced at an average of about eight minutes in length, with many pushing over ten, single works were produced as journeys in their own right: many rather epic, like Koxbox's "Neurobic" (*Forever After*, 1995) or the hypnotic "The Full Monty" by Graham (Wood) and Serge (Souque) (*Mind Rewind*, 2011), mixes of which went out to fifteen minutes.[8] In the protean mid-1990s peak of Goatrance, music was composed using a mix of analog and digital equipment, with computers typically possessing minute memory capacity. "The Full Monty", for example, was produced using, as stated by Graham Wood in *Mind Rewind's* accompanying booklet, "a Nord Lead, a Juno, an SPX-90 delay, a 101, 303 and 909, a Sony D7 effects unit, a Deep Bass 9, an early Roland sampler – the S760, which allows for a whole 7 seconds!, and a Korg MS-10". From composition to performance, sampling, mixing, phasing frequencies and resyncopating rhythms are performance practices affecting – in conjunction with sound amplification, intelligent lighting and spatial design – removal from the mundane and transportation into the extraordinary, the achievement of "The Alchemist" (*New Pagan World*, 1995) on which Har-El Prussky affected a mind-altering rhythm over a bubbling and sparking cauldron of acid sounds. The separation of individuals from their minds, routines and responsibilities off the dance floor, outside the venue, and beyond the perimeter of the festival attracted the designation "trance" in the proto-disco era, as DJ and studio techniques enabled transcendent experience comparable to other dance musics, notably psychedelic rock. But with the use of mobile phones and later the internet, a new all-night ritual eventually translated to open-air locations in remote regions where electronic music effectively replaced psychedelic rock. As observed by Australian techno pioneer – and founder of label Psy-Harmonics – Ollie Olsen, electronic instruments would become indispensable to the trance experience: "Missing," he claims, from "our culture for centuries", this experience has

> come back to us in such a bizarre way through the use of electronics … The reason electronic music was invented in my mind was to attain all those sounds, frequencies and scales that you couldn't

> get from traditional instruments, and that was the original thrust for people building synthesizers, and it is those undiscovered frequencies that are leading the charge back into trance music (Yellow Peril n.d.).

Not that this was completely intentional or foreseen, as is suggested by the chancy-yet-momentous "acid" squelch sounds freed from the Roland TB-303 Bass Line synthesizer by acid house techno producers in 1980s Chicago, or in the utility beyond the expectations of engineers of Sony's DAT technology among Goa DJs.

Throughout the 1990s, numerous label houses and party outfits contributed to the formulation of an electronic psychedelic liminality, perhaps none more important than Blue Room Released, which operated in the UK and the US (as Blue Room Americas) between 1994–2001. The Blue Room was among the most innovative production and performance outfits in the psychedelic trance legacy, although consistently pushing beyond categories, an objective of founder Simon Ghahary. More than just a label, Blue Room was at the forefront of sound design, with Ghahary leading the innovation. Inspired by Alex Patterson and the soundscapes of the Orb, Ghahary designed his Pod[9] speaker system to facilitate the experience of collective transportation among listeners. The Pod system was designed especially for the new electronic music and to allow participants in these public events exposure to what was previously only possible on high-end systems at home or in a studio. This perfectionist mentality lay behind the formulation of an experimental full-frequency sound system and what was later dubbed "truesound". With the financial backing of mentor and head of British B&W loudspeakers, Robert Trunz, Ghahary further developed Blue Room as an uncompromising experiment in sound, involving optimum methods of sound production, and fashioning the "ultimate environment for producing sounds". As such, in Ghahary's language, Blue Boom created "time-space events" contextualizing significant transformative potential, an experience enabling individuals to engage with sound on a personal meditative level, to feel safe, open their minds and to peacefully unite with others. Ghahary explains his philosophy:

> It was made to create travel without moving. These were experiments in sound. Big soundscapes, things that would absorb you. When you start to celebrate sound with dancing and play it through the night you stumble upon a lineage of human development that has gone on for thousands of years, and is not just part of the Goa trance scene. And I think it's this fundamental need to dance to a beat, to be absorbed by sound, to transcend in some way throughout the evening that really is the true sort of nuts and bolts of the experience ... We never set out to be a Goa

> trance label. We were on our own path of just producing the best possible sound.[10]

With nods to instrumental Jamaican sound system labels like Trojan Records and Lee Perry's The Black Ark, Blue Room was shaped by emergent sounds at the same time as pushing directions in sound through speaker amplification systems and studio engineering (with the assistance of sound engineer Kevin Metcalf). Ghahary specifically identifies the 1997 compilation *Signs of Life* as an exemplary moment in sound evolution and the work of Juno Reactor, Deviant Electronics, Saafi Brothers, Acid Rockers and Total Eclipse are noted to personify Blue Room's spirit of evolving new sound aesthetics (e.g. dub, psybreaks, ambient, dark) while retaining familiar elements. Total Eclipse's 1996 release *Violent Relaxation* demonstrated what Ghahary was attempting to achieve. The second CD on the double album offered a side of the French act that he "felt was really beautiful and not many people had the opportunity to experience. I wanted to show this progress and also to demonstrate that they weren't formulated. It was a medium for the evolution of sound". With this attention to change, Blue Room Released developed an irresistible momentum, with many key artists in the psychedelic movement who were signed over the course of its operation provided the encouragement and resources to push aesthetic boundaries.

One of the distinctive aspects of most EDM music such as that released by Blue Room is that lyrics typical to popular music are almost entirely absent, cirumstances felt to enhance the journey. Australian party promoter John-Paris McKenzie spoke to me in 2006 about the role of psytrance in staging the journey:

> The reason why we don't have lyrics is because we don't want to be guided by them, we want to be going on a journey for ourselves. Psytrance brings you in like waves rolling on a sea, it comes in crescendos and then crashes and draws you back, and then comes in and crashes and draws you back, and that's a good way of shedding things and coming to moments of epiphany or understanding.

In selecting artists for his events, he further stated that "I look for less bass line, and more mid-frame, and more movement and melody and something which takes you along and along and builds you up slowly over an hour and a half rather than taking you up in one minute and then down". Naming exemplary mid-2000s acts like Atmos and Son Control Species, progressive psychedelic trance is thought to instrumentalize the journey because it "tells a story over a period of time. The bass is significant but there's movement and melody".[11] Research on contemporary "trance" music has helped uncover the conditions to which dancers are exposed. Within EDMCs, computers and sound equipment provide DJs with the means of not only controlling perception, but shaping how humans perceive. Rave scholar Melanie Takahashi recognized that participants are entering optimal environments for experiencing music and for obtaining altered states of consciousness. With computers enabling "melodies and rhythms so rapid and complex that they go beyond the human ability for performance, our perceptual systems are being exposed to completely new stimuli" (Takahashi 2005: 254), a process identified as the popular "science of sensory engineering" by Kodwo Eshun, whereby sound, rhythm and vision technics, repurposed to intensify sensations, propagate "new sensory lifeforms" (1998: A[177], A[185]). That psychedelic artists imagined themselves as midwives to new lifeforms was articulated by Danish outfit Psychopod (Frank Kiehn Madsen and Ian Ion) who, in promotion for their *Headlines* EP (1997), announced: "Incarnate entities of electron-ic vibrations ... causing the pod to hatch! Spiralling modules, molecules and pod-ules pulsing at a billion hertz a second and unraveling the double helix. Electronic sound holograms, twisting tapestries of symphonic circuitry, complex, intricate and delicious. Witness the creation of aural multi-verses. A sonic syntallation of synthesized psychosis".[12]

While the rave assemblage enables altered states resembling that observed in ceremonial possession states (Rouget 1985), it is the DJ's precision in technique, proficiency in track selection and "the learning on the part of the participants in recognizing and responding to the DJ's cues", that ensures these altered states. That is, technological advancements, production and performance techniques, along with the interactions between DJ and dancer, compensate for the lack of "coherent cultural signifiers" and "sophisticated scripted process" (Takahashi 2005: 252–3). This accelerated and optimized context for learned bodily responses and entrancement – which techno scholar Morgan Gerard (2004) identifies as learned responses to the DJ's "techniques of liminality" – is significant, and the following statement about techno also holds true for trance:

> This shift in musical perception is a learned by-product of repeatedly exposing the auditory system to new stimuli, and this transition is a critical step in socializing ASC [altered states of consciousness] induction. Ravers are fanatical about sound quality and give tremendous attention to such details as the equipment used, the positioning of speakers and the settings of equalizers. The tones, frequencies and beats of electronic music are designed by producers and further refined by DJs to target the body in precise ways. Electronic music is intended to be physically experienced. This is evinced by many veterans of the rave scene describing the music as having a three-dimensional quality that transcends the traditional way music is perceived (Takahashi 2005: 253).

This desired experience not uncommonly identified as "religious" is reminiscent of processes historian of religion Charles Long recognized in popular music where the technological means of production and transmission – electronic sound reproduction, digital recording, mass production and mediation, and personal media technologies – has inaugurated a powerful intensification of experience for music fans such that content dissipates under the force of visceral affect. This is one of the chief characteristics of popular music understood by Long. Due to the intensity of transmission, "the content of what is transmitted tends to be ephemeral, thus the notion of religion as establishing powerful, pervasive and long-lasting moods of motivation is shifted away from content and substance to *modes of experience*" (in Sylvan 2002: 80, emphasis in original). Upgrading Clifford Geertz's definition of religion, Long was referring to popular music in general, but these intensities are magnified within the cultures of EDM in which reproduction (mechanical, electronic and digital) is the engine-house of both composition and performance. As Graham Miller (2003b) noted, in EDMC genres like jungle and drum 'n' bass, "impossibly complex syncopations could be hyper-accelerated toward superhuman velocities, and yet still contain an eerily 'psuedo-human' 'feel'". Within this "dense web of polyrhythmic percussion", he argues, "drum timbres and styles from all different eras" cross-pollinate, "mutating into a new style of 'posthuman' popular music". Psychedelic spiritechnician Ray Castle joins this conversation with attention to emergent styles and sensibilities: "Midi programming, soft ware, virtual synth architecture and drum machines have fractalized-polyrhythms", he motioned. "All the various sub-genres of dance music, are like sub sects of a greater cult. This year and even more, next year, the styles are and will break down and will cross over further". And persistently compelled to modify, iterate and remix, he warned that the "regimented 16th-patterned form" of psychedelic trance was, in 1997, "starting to become quite stale", averring that "it's always the hybrid that is fascinating" (Castle in Rich and Dawn 1997).

As chemical prosthetics, a smorgasbord of psychoactive substances have assisted the hybridization of sound and scene. As stated, LSD had a seminal role in liquefying boundaries between individuals and between genres and MDMA appears to have been as integral to the development of psytrance as it was to acid house and rave, which, as Simon Reynolds stated, evolved throughout the 1990s into "a self-conscious science of intensifying [Ecstasy's] sensation". What Reynolds identified as rave's appetite for sensation over sensibility, and an impossible state of "hyperstimulation" (Reynolds 1998: 85–90), appears to have accelerated by the beginning of the 2000s as an "alphabet soup" of consciousness alterants moved into wider circulation.[13] Such developments have, of course, not been universally celebrated, and psytrance productions themselves provide the morning headlines on the ongoing dispute between what Sam Binkley (2007) identified as the "loose" culture of the 1960s/1970s and its "straight" adversaries who railed against the insatiable appetites for sensation and the immediate gratification of consumer impulses in the place of a principled deferment of pleasure and at the cost of civic responsibility. The spectacle of prohibition, especially that greeting LSD in late 1960s America, is trawled over by producers whose redeployment of sound-bytes generates a kind of cultural homeopathy for the converted. Thus Psychonaut's "Tune In" (*Freerider*, 2010) takes off with a loud kick-started Kombi van and picks up a radio frequency in which a spokesperson spits the lines: "the greatest pushers in this country today are the missionaries who make and distribute LSD because they're convinced it's a wonderful way, as that poisonous evil man Dr Timothy Leary has said, is a way to turn on, tune in, and drop out". Further into the night, on "Xtrange Liquid" (*The Condition of Existence*, 2011), Subsistence lifts lines from President Lyndon B. Johnson's Annual Message to Congress on the State of the Union on 17 January 1968: "This year I will propose a Drug Control Act, to provide stricter penalties for those who will traffic in LSD and other dangerous drugs with our people ... The time has come to stop the sale of slavery to the young". Strident and ludicrous fulminations like this are common targets for sampledelicists. Swedish outfit Chromosome (Anders Nilsson and Linus Eriksson) used the following lines on "Mutant Androids" (2004) commenting on the young, who "at the zenith of physical power and sensitivity, overwhelm themselves with drugs and artificial stimulants. Subtlety is lost and fine distinctions based on acute reasoning are carelessly ignored in a headlong jump to a predetermined conclusion. Life is visceral, rather than intellectual ... Truth to them is revealed rather than logically proved". And later, on a build that feels like you're ascending the Himalayas: "Sometimes it appears that we're reaching a period when our senses and our minds will no longer respond to moderate stimulation. We seem to be approaching an age of the gross". While these warnings are from a speech delivered in 1970 by Nixon's Vice President Spiro Agnew, far from apologia for Republican thought, the passage connotes for the dancer the altered sensibility caused by the intense viscerality of new media. There is no pedagogy here, no message as such, but simply a transitional aesthetic that is the intention of performative productions, and which enthusiasts might re-enter in private moments. It's an aesthetic that holds no transformation-of-being, but a state of *being in transit*. C-Jay confirmed this perspective in the simple use of the words "overwhelm themselves with drugs and artificial stimulants" reproduced from the same speech on "Artificial Stimulance" (*Forever Now*, 2011), the only lines used on any track from the album. This is simply one example among many. Without signification, not marking status passage, nor approximating structured healing ritual, the desirable condition is the *experience of transition*, a state in which one may know transcendence without necessarily transiting to a destination or outcome. This state of *transit without passage* is a condition raising concern among defenders of morality and virtue for whom the "trance" experience is unproductive, its culture received as categorically pathological, its young participants vulnerable to predatory influences, and its producers and productions criminalized. And it is a condition that also draws fire within scenes where a signification is proposed to be missing, where a function is considered lost, a direction unclear. Diverse interventions result. In the former, efforts are made to eliminate or regulate "trance". In the latter, there are commitments towards authentic "trance" practice, purposed to an end other than itself, harnessed to movement concerns responsive to crisis.

Technoshamanism

Though the word is frequently mis/abused, this responsiveness closely approximates what it might mean to be a *shaman* within psychedelic trance, a theme to which I now return. While dance floors are often regarded as "laboratories", and DJs beat "scientists" enabling transition to altered states and transpersonal experience, the term "technoshaman" has held appeal among various commentators.[14] While the use of local cultural technics and prepared ethnopharmacologies might qualify all shamans as *techno* shamans, within the field of EDM, "technoshaman" refers to an individual or assembly of artists (principally DJs) who are capable of affecting transpersonal states through the application of their technique. But while technicians of trance act to effect self-liminalization in the optimal condition of being-in-transit, others are dedicated to achieving post-liminal outcomes. Castle, for instance, self-identifies as a "cybernetic surgeon".

> I use my creations and other people's work to orchestrate a hybrid medium, within a dance party context, to bring about psycho-emotional transformations. Rhythms and frequencies and sounds catalyse enzymes and chemistry in the brain and body-mind. I don't see myself as a conventional musician or DJ, I am more of a sound therapist, an infonaut, a cybernetic surgeon stitching together a contemporary mosaic of music and sonic geometry which takes the participants on a journey within themselves and interpersonally ... I do feel as though my work is about being a communications conduit for universal consciousness (DJ Krusty and Ray n.d.).

Castle has elaborated upon what he dubbed the *dance cathexis* of techno trance, which he thinks occasions "a group cathartic psychodrama" and offers "a potent temenos (sacred space) for reintegration of disconnected parts of the Self" (Castle in ENRG 2001: 164). In response to the devolution of the Goa vibe, Australia's DJ Krusty (aka Eugene E~NRG) has developed events with a therapeutic and visionary intent. An advocate of the small-scale overnight party-ritual presided over by a handful of DJs, Krusty honed his skills at Doof Village events coordinated at ConFest in the mid-1990s (see Chapter 7). His "Experimental Shamanic Trance Dance, Sacred Plant and Sound System Workshop" held at the 2006 Entheogenesis Australis outdoor symposium at Victoria's eco-arts retreat OPOEIA was part of an effort to revive the "psychedelic shamanic experience" in an intentional ritual that merits some detail here. Early in his preparations, Krusty had created a "mandala of circles" in which a four-foot-wide "sacred fire pit" formed the inner-most circle. Strands of multi-coloured rope lighting marked the outer edge and the cardinal points held the flame-shooting towers of the Mutoid Waste Co. Speaker stacks and banners were positioned around the perimeter, and an inconspicuous DJ booth was placed outside the circle and banners. To "consecrate" the space, a shrine was constructed under a gum tree by Krusty's partner, Mari Kundalini.[15] The proceedings began with an "indigenous gum leaf smoking ceremony" where a small gum-leafed branch was placed in the fire by each individual "who offered their own prayers, blessings and personal statements of intention for the journey" (Krusty 2008: 16). Additionally, the four elements were then invoked and acknowledged. As soft ambient beats began (consisting of 30–40 minute premixes), participants ingested "sacred plant sacraments", including the contents of a large vat of chai *psilocybe cubensis* tea. Among others, tracks from Shpongle, Ubar Tmar, Don Peyote, Mantrix and Space Tribe were performed.

As the facilitator of this techno nature-ritual, Krusty related, "reconnecting with the cosmic rhythms of nature, with the mother earth, or 'Gaia' ... is imperative. And the best way people know how to let go and move beyond the confines of the industrialized mind is within dance" (Krusty 2008: 20). While influenced by the author of *Sweat Your Prayers* (1998) and shamanic trance dance teacher, Gabrielle Roth, and author of *Trance Dance: The Dance of Life* (1995) along with several tribal trance CDs, Frank Natale (or "Professor Trance"), the most important influence appears to be Joseph Campbell whose treatise on the "Hero's Journey" from his 1949 text *The Hero with a Thousand Faces* heavily informed the workshop. As Krusty (2008: 15) explained:

> Starting at home in the ordinary world, the hero (workshop participant) has a willingness to undertake the ordeal or a call to adventure. Then they enter the special world (dancefloor), endure tests (physical dance) and meet allies and enemies (self-reflection, psychedelic experience), approaches the inmost cave to face more challenges and ordeals and death (of the ego/surrender). Only then does the hero find just reward, return or resurrection, return with the elixir or magical item (utopian vision/awe/singularity/living in heart) and grounds the experience (returning to the real world).

The workshop was therefore designed to facilitate a journey of transformation from the "call to adventure" through the phases of "threshold", "death", "ordeal" and the "return" accompanied by music. Krusty articulated the experience using language typical of transitional discourse with a cathartic purpose. "One must not be distracted with fear", he stated, "when one comes to confront one's own demons or angels, for both the heaven and hell realms can open up on the dance floor". The experience requires the adoption of the "warrior spirit archetype". Here, "an individual chooses to journey out beyond their normal consciousness and meet the spirit realm [which] they must do with humble spiritual intention, conviction and power". Finally:

> the trancedancer who stays with the trip and journeys with the techno music through the psychedelic experience will experience a rebirth, a reaffirmation of the self as a being of the cosmos, absolutely connected to and a real part of nature. This has been variously referred to as: the utopian, godhead, beyond linguistics, singularity – experience, a direct moment of all as one, a spiritual high, etc. It is the very powerful revelation of the true self that so many people consciously or unconsciously are searching for (2008: 19).

Within "post-trancedance", Krusty recognizes that integration is essential, the idea being "to make sense of what happened, mapping this experience into one's daily reality" (2008: 20). He stated that the workshop was successful, and that he had glowing reports from participants, whose feedback he sought following the event. While no long-term observation of how participants were impacted by the event was undertaken, the following comments from one participant are instructive. In an unpublished letter, Karen stated she had helped create the altar and observed the fire in advance of the ritual all of which helped her feel connected to the event.

> I have a background in dance performance and teaching and have been meditating for many years. Combining dance and meditation that is to dance with intention, aware and witnessing the event but not consciously directing each moment is to me a mysteriously magical experience. One of heightened awareness and energy that gives some sense of clarity of meaning to the kaleidoscope of my life (Karen n.d.).

Karen, who had been reading Eckhart Tolle's *The Power of NOW!*, remarks on the challenging arts of "surrender". "Krusty also spoke to us of setting a group intention of 'Surrender'". While surrendering her consciousness was a challenge as life memories cluttered her thoughts, over hours of dancing she "became more and more aware of my heart chakra ... the energy was getting stronger and growing ... it began to feel like my heart was exploding in an ecstatic way. I felt like I was drinking the nectar of heaven. I was in a state of bliss for hours and of course I didn't want it to stop". Karen stated that what she called her "Heart Buzzing" remained with her for several days and was revisited at a small dance party she attended a couple of weeks later. "Since that time I have continued on my Heart Journey and gradually my heart is breathing more life into me. The 'Heart Buzzing', a sense of energy expansion and sometimes emotion, is more present with me on a daily basis".

Transpersonal states, dream-like conditions, "Heart Buzzing", catalyzed by the intentional trance assemblage are often credited as potentiating catharsis among participants. Artists have themselves undergone personal metamorphosis, sometimes following life-threatening illnesses, a common trigger for the adoption of *curandera* shamanism. While there may be no more poignant case than Spanish punk rocker Juan Verdera Fernandez (aka The Muses Rapt), who wrote the Goa classic "Spiritual Healing" (LSD – Liquid Sound Design, 1998) during his chemotherapy treatment and who championed the role of trance music in his recovery, there are many examples of the psychotherapeutic efficacy of trance dance and its associated technics. The case I have chosen to discuss is that of Megan Young, whose experience with California's XLR8R reflects the importance of focused, small-scale events with transformative intent. In Krusty's ritual, besides the fire smudging, the fire strobe towers, flares and purple tinged flames, it was the central fire pit that held the deepest impression and transformative power for participants. Reflecting on the reason for its success, it was suggested "humans have danced around fires for eons and a return to this practice invoked an ancient, deep wisdom tradition that we all were able to associate with" (Krusty 2008: 15). Furthermore, and converse to Goa Gil's arrangement, the fire-centred focus signified a shift away from the "proscenium arch" framework where the "audience" is conventionally separated from the "performance" (the DJ/stage), and enabled participants to become "co-creators" rather than spectators.

These sentiments resonate with those of Young who described to me her remarkable experience with the fire technology that is the chief component in the XLR8R gatherings. Founder of darkpsy label Mistress of Evil Records, Young stated that, the purpose of the fire, which is built over the duration of an evening in the "sweet spot", and which is centralized "in order to shift the focus away from the DJ and towards the powerful element of fire", is "to accelerate/amplify the energy that is manifested throughout the dance ritual ... It can also be a portal between worlds, a place with incredible potential for transmutation and transformation". The fire element is stated to be "part of an alchemical process that burns away impurities, excess energies, and other things that don't serve us". She added that sometimes "crystals are buried in the pit of the fire or around the edges to further accelerate the energy".[16]

Megan explained an experience with the XLR8R at a dark trance forest party in Southern California in 2006 that warrants reproducing in detail. She had recently suffered an injury at the base of her spine, was in physical pain and feeling unbalanced.

> Sometime around midnight I gathered with some friends and we each took two drops of strong california liquid acid. Within the first hour after dosing I was already feeling the effects coming on strong. I remember being in the center of the dance floor and watching the sparks from the fire animate in front of my eyes. I felt compelled to go closer to the fire and I was observing the way they were adding wood to keep the flames going strong. There were several driving sticks laid out around the fire and i felt compelled to pick one up. I took the stick and put it right in the belly of the fire, holding on to it with both hands. The wood we were burning that night was very thick and heavy wood and the fire was so strong and wide. It really looked like a portal or opening to another world, the coals were glowing hot and red and dense orange flames were rising fiercely up to the cosmos.
>
> I remember feeling smoke in my eyes and my skin feeling hot and sticky from the heat of the fire. I was dancing along with the music and keeping the driving stick right in the center of the fire. I remember I was struggling with issues of patriarchy and matriarchy. I was feeling an aggressive male type energy surrounding the fire and feeling uncomfortable with that but still holding space. The last thing I remember seeing (with my eyes) was two of my close girlfriends come to the fire and dance close to me. After a little while I honestly don't know where I went. I felt like I was shapeshifting in and out of my body. I was going through vast waves of emotions. First I began to experience immense pleasure. Everything was tinglingly, light, joyous. The pleasure came from my center, I felt it anchored in my lower chakras, everything waking up. The pleasure was building and building and eventually climaxed in a whole body orgasm! I've never experienced pleasure as deep. Then from the high of that pleasure, I would feel a horrific pain, more terrible than any I had ever felt. A pain that began in the center of my being, sharp, pointed, deep and stabbing pain. Pain that consumed my entire being, physically and mentally. I remember tears streaming down my face, my stomach clenched and back spasming, yet I couldn't move from the fire. For what must have been hours I oscillated between these two extremes and gradually began to realize that the sensations I was feeling were not my own. I became aware of a great presence within me.

> It was energy that I identified as an old woman. It was her pain I was feeling, her pleasure. But who was this old woman? and why was she manifesting inside of me?? More time passes and I realize that the woman is actually Mother Earth. The fire has opened up a portal to the center of the Earth and through the driving stick I am channeling the terrible beauty of the planet Earth. The pain I experienced was comprised of every violent act committed against her, every forest burned, every waterway polluted, every animal or human killed in disrespect, every pile of trash buried beneath her surface, every toxic chemical, nuclear bomb, every world war, flowing through my body, with the fire as an open channel and the pleasure!! the simple promise of flowers in spring, the deep blue color of the sky, the moss on trees in a thousand shades of green, the miracle of motherhood, fresh vegetables, waterfalls, rainbows, and countless sunsets too beautiful for words, these wonders and delights flowing through me ... up out of the fire and straight into my body.
>
> When the impact of my realization sank in I began to weep, feeling humbled and honored to have experienced something so incredible. I honestly can't say how long I stood at the fire. I don't know if I was moving, dancing, standing up straight or slouched over. I am not sure if my eyes were open or closed. I wasn't aware of any other people around me throughout this experience and I don't even remember hearing any music!!

This account constitutes a remarkable experience removed from the contemporary psyculture event, developed in a dance ritual context in which a sacred fire technology, the XLR8R, is integral. Young's story also features sequential elements of Campbell's "hero's journey". While an engaging account, such personal stories of transformation and initiation are not uncommon among enthusiasts, with intentional ritualizations providing the context for transfiguration through surrender, purification and channelling. The transformed often themselves become envisioned artists and event organizers dedicated to techniques of perfecting the trance experience. Some artists, for instance, are specific about the audio techniques involved in orchestrating trance, and there is a concerted effort among producers (System 7, for example) to effect brain physiology – alpha waves (critical in inducing trance states in humans between 8 and 12 cycles per second) – through musical tempo. In the estimation of Cole and Hannan (1997), "many traditional trance-inducing musics of the world contain rhythmic elements which mirror these rates. Performances typically start at the lower level and increase over a period of hours towards the higher level". Paralleling traditional trance musics, "in Goa trance there is a constant stream of 16th notes which when played at the suggested average of 144 bpm yields a flow of musical events at an average of 9.6 cps". A great many practitioners appropriate from a variety of traditions whose techniques of entrancement are believed to hold efficacy. This is made apparent by the presence of a Balinese Gamelan orchestra in the San Francisco rave community (Fatone 2004) and at the Boom Festival in 2006. More commonly, practitioners and enablers of "trance" are ritual syncretists, who synthesize techniques to facilitate self-transformation in "workshop" formats often in the context of clubs, gatherings and festivals. This practice seems to have been initiated at Return To The Source events in the mid to late 1990s where London's Dome Nightclub was transformed into a "temple space" with "crystal grids" on all sides of the dance floor, and where, as trance ritual specialist Antara stated, "we would cleanse the space with sage, invoke a field of light and banish any negative forces. Sometimes we'd put a seven pointed star on the floor, or cast a four-directional medicine wheel" (in Twist 1999). Antara oversaw the production of a popular Return To The Source double-CD/book, *The Chakra Journey* (RTTS, 1996) stating in a *Radio V* interview, "different cultures over time have developed forms of expression that tend to emphasize particular chakras over others". Using a variety of electronic music that had emerged by the late 1990s, she stated, "we now have a multi-dimensional music to help us dance the dance of every chakra" (Twist 1999). Such techniques are adopted in the repertoire of enthusiasts for whom dancing to trance music is a self-shamanizing practice. In an article published on chaishop.com, body therapist and trance dance workshop enabler Rob Bennett (2007) stated that "a deep-seated longing for ecstasy, for a break in the tedium of day-to-day survival, has led many of the younger generation in modern, industrial society back to trance dance". Bennett promotes the rejuvenating power of states that "slow the brain wave frequencies from the predominant beta, down to the relaxed, intuitive alpha, or even the theta frequencies which are associated with dreaming and deep trance". Here, in the context of controlled workshops, at variance from McKenna's views on shamanism, "trance" is considered a therapeutic technique.

While for spiritechnicians and trance doctors, music is designed and adopted to effect outcomes consistent with hybridized therapeutic strategies applied in small group contexts – and even designed to be performed at home – as I discussed in the previous section, for many enthusiasts, "trance" is characterized by form and technique over content, and for whom the music possesses a decidedly *functional* logic without clear telos. This proclivity towards self-liminalization resonates with the observations of Reynolds (1998: 9), who suggested that, with techno music, it "is not about what music means but how it works". Another way of explaining this is to state that how it works IS what it means. This is the techno-logic of EDM and psytrance is contiguous since transcendence of self ("losing it") is the purpose and meaning of trance for a great many practitioners. Here, consistent with the first type of consciousness transition discussed earlier, participants make a *transition from* states of rational consciousness associated with their livelihoods, identities and struggles outside the party and off the dance floor. This freedom from routine conditions of self-hood and the consequential access to the unconscious potentiates newfound conditions of subjectivity, including that associated with the second and third modes of consciousness outlined. Under such conditions, habitués may desire to revisit the experience of *being in transit*. In other cases, samples from film sources are deployed in a concerted effort to stage the transit associated with a dissolved, expanded and evolved consciousness. In the next section, I continue this exploration of *spiritechnics* by discussing these neomystical, occultic and transformative narratives within psychedelic trance – conscious efforts to direct the functional techno-logic towards re-enchantment.

The technoccult and the artifice of re-enchantment

That inhabitants of late-modern societies are dispossessed of the "techniques of ecstasy" believed integral to their heritage is a conviction not uncommon among enthusiasts of psytrance, where events are planned, technics assembled and popular culture sampled with the objective of revitalizing the arts of enchantment. Demonstrating a reflexive mood, techno-pagan cognoscenti, freak utopians, spiritual anarchists and dreamworkers formulate dance rituals by way of multimedia assemblages. Event producers like those associated with London's Return To The Source or open-air gatherings like British Columbia's The Oracle, intentional ritual activators like Goa Gil, Kenji Williams and other technicians of transition formulating projects of the self, have gained reputations for their abilities to curate environments that facilitate the uncovering of hidden realms, orchestrate revitalization and effect transformation. In *The Re-Enchantment of the West*, Partridge discusses the role of psychedelic trance in the evolution of the popular occult, or what he calls "occulture" (2004: 166–75). Drawing on "mystical religion" as understood by Ernst Troeltsch and "cultic milieu" theorist Colin Campbell, Partridge holds that occultism flourishes in contemporary popular culture. This pervasive mediation of "cultic spirituality" in literature, film and music is, he argues, self-oriented and eclectic, while at the same time possessing a tendency to coalesce into networks and organizations which Campbell (1977) identified as "the mystic collectivity". It involves those who, while not forming organized religions (i.e. churches or sects), participate in networks of shared interests, values and commitments (Partridge 2004: 63). The cult here is a "community" which "one does *not* join, which is *not* permanent and enduring, which is *not* exclusive, and which does *not* have clearly articulated beliefs" (from Campbell 1977, in Partridge 2004: 63, original emphasis). While these communities are often populated by those animated by what they oppose (e.g. the Catholic Church) more than an alternative, they are passionate bastions of mutual interest. Thus, the study of the cultic penetration of contemporary popular culture resonates with the obsessions of fandom, and pop-cult fanaticism, which, while evoking strong passions, is idiosyncratic. Indeed, it echoes the "epistemological individualism" Roy Wallis (1984: 100) observed in cultism, where, unlike sectarianism, and consistent with a radically reflexive modernity, the final authority lies with the individual. But, as the above discussion of the visceral nature of transition illustrates, we should be disabused of the idea that psytrance is dictated by individualism, since the post-industrial world is charged with the ambiance of "de-individualization" (Maffesoli 1996). Within psytrance, to which those impassioned by various musical styles gravitate, the means of perception is most certainly enhanced by optimized prosthetics augmenting personal theophanies. Yet conditions are optimized within these contexts such that the private gnosis is accomplished within the social atmosphere of public events. While their outcomes are unpredictable, these events are compelling, for *the vibe* cannot be experienced at home alone.

The psychedelic vibe facilitates for those inhabiting its precincts the perception that they are indeed part of a "mystical collectivity", a community whose affiliates anticipate access to otherwise hidden knowledge, laws and lore, sacred symbols, unencrypted data, patterns shared and parsed by fellow travellers. Discussing the passion for "direct experience of the divine, in secret gnosis, in alchemy, in theurgy, in a *philosophia perennis*, and in ancient religion and mythical figures, texts and civilizations" found scattered throughout popular culture, Partridge (2004: 69) offers a checklist for the cult of psytrance, that juncture where fandom and the occult converge. This exemplary occultural development is downstream from the occult revival of the 1960s. Partridge traces the roots of the term "occult", referring to "that which is hidden and concealed", back several centuries. What is recognized as "a multi-faceted concept referring to arcane and restricted knowledge" is stated to include elements of the Western Mysticism/Esoteric tradition which over many centuries included Gnosticism, Stoicism, Hermeticism, neo-Pythagorianism and a body of theologically philosophical texts written in late antiquity known as the *Corpus Hermeticism*. Since the nineteenth century, occultism is described as:

> a subculture of various secret societies and "enlightened" teachers involved in disciplines concerned with the acquisition of arcane, salvific knowledge (*gnosis* and *theosophia*), the experience of "illumination", the understanding of esoteric symbolism (often related to occult interpretations of the Kabbalah), the practice of secret rituals and initiation rites, and particularly the quest for a *prisca theologia*, *philosophia occulta* or *philosophia perennis* – a

> tradition or divine gnosis communicated, it is believed, through a line of significant individuals, including Moses, Zoroaster (Zarathustra), Hermes Trismegistus (the mythical author of the *Hermetica*), Plato, Orpheus, and the Sibyls (Partridge 2004: 69).

Importantly, to this list is added "a vast spectrum of beliefs and practices sourced by Eastern spirituality, Paganism, Spiritualism, theosophy, alternative science and medicine, popular psychology (usually Jungian) and a range of beliefs emanating out of the general cultural interest in the paranormal" (Partridge 2004: 70). While the occultism in this haystack of strands is evident in psytrance, the latter is more evidently downstream from the "occult" flourish of the 1960s documented by Gary Lachman, who pursues the shadow-lands of mysticism – and thus a much narrower interpretation of the "occult" – in his account of the "dark side of the Age of Aquarius" (2001: 9). While Lachman traces occultic roots to the mid-nineteenth century only – and specifically to the work of Alphonse Louis Constant, better known as Eliphas Levi, including his *La Clef des Grands Mystères* (*The Key to the Great Mysteries*, 1861) – his concern is with its 1960s "revival" which commenced, he argues, in Paris in 1960 with the publication of Louis Pauwels and Jacques Bergier's *Le Martin des Magicians* (*The Morning of the Magicians*), a work which had "both banks of the Seine talking about alchemy, extraterrestrials, lost civilizations, esotericism, Charles Fort, secret societies, higher states of consciousness, and the Hermetic Order of the Golden Dawn" (Lachman 2001: 15). Much of Goatrance can be read as a continuation of the occultic legacy reignited by Pauwels and Bergier. Chapter titles from their book like "The Point Beyond Infinity", "The Example of Alchemy" and a "Few Years in Absolute Elsewhere" read as much like the titles of 1960s cosmic rock songs as they do Goatrance tracks.

Giving vent to the "dark" side or otherwise, psytrance is an "occultural" phenomenon, and not least because, in efforts to facilitate mystical-visionary states and revive sacred arts, music producers, DJs and event designers reference cultic material already circulating in popular culture and popular science via the cinematic and documentary film sources that are sampled in the music and showcased at events. A phantasmagoria of alien abductions, lost civilizations, ancient spacemen, conspiracies and other esoteric phenomena populate music productions and visionary art under an ambiance of revelation and illumination. But artists are not simply rehashing existent themes, but are authoring original works, often repurposing popular cultural resources to the benefit of alternative ideas and illicit practices. Scripted lines from popular cinema are repurposed in samples deployed to evoke states of consciousness achieved through the ingestion of substances scheduled as prohibited under various national and international controlled substances acts. On other occasions, through the sampled adoption of spokespersons exposing hidden agendas or communicating gnostic insights, the music offers a program for ideas alternative to dominant and legislated conditions such as those associated with the transnational "war on drugs". On "W.S. Burroughs Lesson N.13" (*Mechanics of Awakening*, 2011), for example, HypoGeO has William Burroughs scowling, "narcotics have been systematically scapegoated and demonized. The idea that anyone can use drugs and escape a horrible fate is an anathema to these idiots. I predict that in the near future right-wingers will use drug hysteria as a pretext to set up an international police apparatus". Influenced by the likes of H.P. Lovecraft and Hermeticism, Xenomorph has been the master at this gestalt, exposing diabolical truths and dark conspiracies, as notably found on 2007 release *Demagoguery of the Obscurants*, which lifts the veils on power and corruption that might have satisfied Robert Anton Wilson. Regardless of source and target, such prescient transmissions, evidence for which could be offered *ad nauseam*, contribute to an atmosphere of illumination.

In revived ritual and contrived gnosis, charismatic characters adopt the assemblage and uncover the frequencies of psychedelic trance to pursue various ends. Goa Gil's campaign has been exemplary, with divinity – his own and/or that of partygoers/disciples – enshrined through an "apocalyptic" ritual process repeated and refined since the early 1990s. As a medium of what he calls the "Cosmic Spirit", Gil bears resemblance to other charismatic authorities who, in Max Weber's understanding, use "magical arts" to endow others with "the boons of salvation". As McAteer (2002: 57) pointed out, Gil's activities prove consistent with Hindu and other "mystagogues" who typically fashion direct anomalous artistic practices involving *shaktipat* (or the transference of spiritual "energy" often by way of eye contact or gifts) to effect *darshan* (i.e. visions or hierophanies). Gil's is an intentional religious mission and, if you set aside methodology, is not far removed from that of his critics. While there may be little evidence of enshrinement nor "moral agenda" in the practice and writings of Ray Castle, his efforts are comparable to that of mystics everywhere. With the "*electrickery* of the techno shaman's cybertools", the DJ guides dance floor occupants "towards a connection with the *Universal Omm*. The *psychic sonic harmonic* that unites us all to the cosmos and creation", which Castle identifies as "a *theosophical trance*" (Castle in ENRG 2001: 156, emphasis in original). The link to theosophy is not insignificant, given founder of the Theosophical Society, Helena Blavatski's, interest in – as set out in her 1889 work *The Key to Theosophy* – tapping into and developing the "psychic and spiritual powers latent in man". DJ-producers climb into the cockpit, using their skills as channellers and interpreters of hidden realms, including that of their own subconscious. "The subconscious is a very powerful thing" is an oft-repeated sample, a reminder that the mind is one of the most powerful occultic tools. For producer Raphael Huber (aka SubConsciousMind), psytrance is a means of tapping into these mysteries. Something of a trance-floor therapist, he finds that creating music is a means to excavate his unconscious which not only assists him, but is potentially therapeutic to dance floor occupants. Yet, as he explains,

> some things are hidden deep inside us for a reason, and when my music starts digging them out many persons block it. Maybe because they don't want it to happen at this time, are afraid or do not trust the music enough to let it go this deep inside them … This music is for people with open hearts, for people interested in confrontation with themselves, for people willing to see things they didn't expect.[17]

Though Huber himself does not use many vocal samples, they are important to the "electrickery" of DJ-producers, and not uncommonly deployed to connote hypnotic intent. In advance of an arpeggiated build and plateau on their 1995 release "Spiritual Transgression" (*Accidental Occidentalism*, 1995), Encens (Dara Lee and Marcello Bonifacii) adopted the line: "when I snap my fingers you will awaken". Samples from recorded hypnosis induction exercises are deployed on more recent work, like Atmos's "Stay Awake" (*Tour de Trance*, 2008). "I want to establish in your mind a key word … Relax … And soon the key word will enable you to relax completely in just a few moments. Your body and you mind will respond quickly to the key word: Relax". The voice later announces that "from this point on you're in complete control of your self in every respect. You have absolute control of your self, in mind and body". Needless to say, the word "relax" is repeated throughout the track. It's a curious choice of material, suggestive of the role that the DJ-producer may assume as a functionary – indeed, here a hypnotist. Yet the effect is not the induction of an altered state of consciousness via hypnosis. Here the sampledelic indexing of the induction procedure should not be conflated with its presumed effects. We are closer to the meaning of this re-mediation if we recognize that digital programming pays reflexive due to altered states of consciousness. While access to altered states is here evoked by hypnotherapy, other methodologies, marginal sciences and abominable knowledge are elsewhere conjured to produce a similar effect. For example, on other dance floors and chill spaces, dream techniques are evoked, as they are onboard *Dreams Vol. 2* (2010), where on "Altering Dreams" MentalImage parses lines from *The X-Files*: "It's still experimental, but what we're trying to do is modify his brain wave patterns externally … Electrical stimulation of the occipital lobe creates simple visual and auditory hallucinations". Across differing styles of music, drawing from diverse sources, and indexing a wide variation of (pseudo)scientific and magical techniques adapted to the alteration of consciousness, impregnated with such samples, the music serves its purpose of connoting a generic field of consciousness alteration in which participants seek immersion and which they may have obtained when receiving these brief messages. As mentioned, vocal sampling is not a universal practice and many enthusiasts complain of the distracting tendencies triggered by repetitive samples. While Goa artists and their descendants entertain the fantasy that they are mind-technicians forging keys to unlock the doors of perception, they may be more accurately portrayed as recyclers of media, manipulating and remixing media to narrate the appeal of entrancement already sought and undertaken on the dance floor. As such, DJs are simply the most visible front to a vast assemblage. This is not to say that DJ-producers are not skilled in the arts of transformation to which they draw reflexive attention. As sound and visual media are assembled for the transmission of hidden lore and deviant science we find an occult artifice enabling transit across boundaries separating consciousness from the unconscious. As Shakta explained on his classic "Spiritual Beings in Physical Bodies", the purpose is to facilitate passage across "the membrane that exists between worlds, the seen and the unseen, the physical and the spiritual" (*Silicon Trip*, 1997).

Downstream from the theosophists and other esoteric syncretists, media shamans build fantastic mashups remixing and synthesizing elements from a cornucopia of sources: ancient, alien, monstrous, outlaw, indigenous pop-icons, all digested in the pursuit of transition from ordinary states of consciousness. In Chapter 2, I demonstrated how icons of Indian religion and mystical traditions are appropriated in cover art and sampled in the music of the Goa tradition to differing ends. Similarly, artists adopt mystical Judaism for differing purposes. On their track "Kabalah" (*Trust in Trance*, 1996), Astral Projection cite their quest for "the creation of spiritual unity". With a TB-303-generated thrust and ascendant drive, that seminal album provides the soundtrack to a psychedelic promised land. On the Hermetic Kabbalah influenced *Qlippoth* (released on his Gnostic Records in 2003), Xenomorph offered an alternative interpretation of the other world unveiled and inhabited. Promotion for the album states that the Hebrew "qlippoth" means "shells": "the shells of the universe signifying what might be hidden behind the boundaries of our world, the abode of anti-divine forces and a process of negative creation". Inner cover-art features text from *The Kabbalah Unveiled*, a founding work of Hermetic Kabbalah written by MacGregor Mathers, one of the founders of the Hermetic Order of the Golden Dawn. The CD art also holds images of the Sephirot, the ten nodes in the Kabbalistic tradition representing the ten attributes of God, all of which demonstrates the interest in lifting the veils on a world remote from the cosmic consummations of astral trance. Most productions, however, illustrate heterodox seekership, multiple pathways, methods of revelation, and cryptic answers. In this fashion, the cover of the Feb/March 2009 edition of *Mushroom Magazine* featured Fabian Klaimann's (aka Symbolika) design "Dance Like a Tree", which is inspired by the Sephirot and the Chakras. The work thus mixes mystical Judaism and

Tantric Buddhism, its iconic syncretism not inconsistent with the way a DJ will bridge separate tracks by making subtle and progressive interventions.

Deploying samples evoking the unveiling of the vital data-lode, possessing invocations of pure process, productions are consistent with the functionality of techno. Sampling from the 1960s television series *The Outer Limits*, on "We

"Dance Like a Tree", by Symbolika. www.symbolika.com. Courtesy of Symbolika.

are Controlling Transmission" – recorded in 1993 and released on *SFX: The Unreleased Tracks – 89–94* (Phonokol, 1998) – early incarnation of Astral Projection, SFX, conveyed that very message. Key musical texts amplify fixation with the noetic sensation of revelation, with transmission over transmitted content, with the feeling of knowing. But in this evoking of the threshold across which an adept passes and gains insight, producers do not simply simulate, but are stimulating, religious experience. The Infinity Project's psybient masterwork *Mystical Experiences* (1995) is a seminal achievement in this development. Via Aldous Huxley, the title track on the album conveys its producers' – Raja Ram, Graham Woods and Simon Posford – intimacy with "a feeling of oneness with the world". In his guise as Hallucinogen, Posford would regularly engineer contact with an experience that might resemble the "numinous", defined by Rudolph Otto (1923) as possessing two aspects: the fearful *mysterium tremendum* and the compelling *mysterium fascinans*. Other works deploy science fiction and Apollo Program samples to affect awe, such as Juno Reactor's *Transmissions* (1993), or the catalogue of the UK's Cosmosis and releases from label Shiva Space Technology. Lifting samples from cinema and television documentaries, mis/appropriating popular cultural tropes, producers write psychedelic fiction to reveal the nature of human existence and one's place in the universe. In some projects, chosen samples tantalize with the promise of exposure and enlightenment. For example, on Chi-A.D.'s "The Flame of Eternal Life" (*Anno Domini*, Velvet Inc., 1999), a woman announces: "I will show you what no other living mortal has seen".

Orchestrated by Raja Ram, The Crystal Skulls concept albums purveyed a decidedly gnostic predilection for dance floor travellers. In *The Mystery of the Thirteen Crystal Skulls* (2001) and the follow-up release *The Secret of the Thirteen Crystal Skulls* (2003), tracks were commissioned from forerunners in global psychedelic trance and sequentialized as "Revelations". Artists sampled from core sources relating to a series of human skull models fashioned from blocks of milky quartz crystal rock and reputed to possess sentience. The promotions for and samples used on the albums illustrate how extraterrestrial origins, lost civilizations, secret societies and primitive wisdom are all inscribed in these objects – thereby becoming super-gnostic talisman in the material culture of the New Age. By "The Fourth Revelation" (on *The Mystery*), GMS and 1300 Mics plunge deep into the jungle to the accompaniment of energetic tribal percussion. A spokesman announces that "these crystals are doorways to hidden dimensions of understanding". As we draw closer to the mystery, Shpongle's epic and culminating "Sixth Revelation" echoes the album's core revelation via the resounding voice of gemologist Ea Orgo. Beyond Sky Gods, Stone People, Atlantians, Amerindians, the ultimate revelation places the mysteries at the heart of the planet itself, in quartz crystal, which is stated to constitute 40 per cent of the Earth's crust and is a key component in transmitting, receiving, amplifying and storing information. Where the medium is the message, crystals become sacralized.

Different aspects of the other-than-human world – and, more to the point, those humans who are understood to have control over it – become a chief source of inspiration in other work attempting to replicate the source of inspiration. Archaic's *Wildness* (2008) provides a case in point. On "Deep in Forest", trancers are guided into the woods by birdcalls and wind gusts upon which strange spells carry. "Vortex" guides the subject further into the mystery. Wolves howl from deeper in the forest and a pulsing attractor signals the presence of a vibrant reality just beyond reach, as the incantations grow compelling in the stomping "Wildness". As apparent in psytrance and other visionary arts scenes, human contact with the wilderness is associated with an entrancing mystical potential, with producers and DJs working together with VJs, stage and décor designers, installation artists and event promoters, to incite these conditions. Producers sometimes narrate, not unproblematically, the wisdom of "the ancients" as preternatural, primordial, found deep in the wilderness, while other times the otherness endogenous to this psychedelic fiction is located beyond the Earth's exosphere. The music then becomes a critical medium of temporal and spatial transportation in the imaginary of the participant. From telescopic excursions into outer space, to microscopic journeys within the brain, to folk archaeologies excavating answers among fictionalized ancients, the cosmos/nature is amplified as a source of re-enchantment. And in order to be exposed to the mysteries, one must undertake a passage represented by the "gateways", "portals", "worm-holes" that are near-universal symbols in world shamanic mechanics. Returning to Archaic's release, "Tree Spirits" makes a direct observation of this theme, commenting on "the vortex or the spiral which represents throughout the world the tunnel or entrance to the spirit world. So going through the vortex, the shaman comes out the other side in a completely new spiritual realm". Once the vortex has been traversed, the final track, "Hidden Reality", repeatedly announces the word "truth", and makes an observation that McKenna might have approved: "random mutation is presented as something which is to be traced back to cosmic rays". But while such projects are designed to convey mysteries of origins revealed to the intrepid wayfarer, "what is the truth?" This is the spoken inquiry arriving care of Invid Mind on "Distant Mirrors" where we're reminded that "things are never what they seem". The track is part of Cosmic Eclipse Records' compilation *Behind the Mirror* (2011) which features carefully selected work like Apojarito's "Found in Forest" and Mehequcixa's "Oak Trees" flooding the floor with incomprehensible messages sourced from deep within the forest. The mood is that of having had one's world turned upside down, of being exposed to truths that do not provide joy or fulfillment, but are, on the contrary, dark and foreboding. Having transported the floor into the forest among native shamans, "In Wood We Trust" by AQ AB AL on

Rainbow Serpent Festival 2009. Photo: Jonathan Carmichael.

Behind the Mirror provides insight on the artifice of exposure via the voice of an English adventurer: "I have drunk a cup full of ayahuasca".

Divine mystical transmission

As the work of Raja Ram and Simon Posford makes clear, the spiritechnics of transition and the noetics of revelation are enhanced with the assistance of consciousness altering drugs, the consumption of which is native to dance subcultures, clubs and fraternities, and which may be considered integral to its cultic roots. *Cannabis* is a staple in the diet of artists and bohemians (see Bey and Zug 2004), with freaks making refuge in Goa enjoying access to affordable *charas*, which remained legal into the 1970s. Mescaline (*phenylethylamine* alkaloid from peyote) was integral to the formation of the Beat movement and was immortalized by Huxley, who, in his recollections of a mescaline trip, *The Doors of Perception* (1954), published the view that psychotropic drugs cleanse the filters ordinarily protecting/separating humans from the infinite "Mind at Large". Ever since the story of "magic mushrooms" was reported in *LIFE* magazine in May 1957, following amateur ethnomycologist Robert Gordon Wasson's participation in the ritual of the "velada" in Oaxaca, Mexico, *psilocybin*-containing mushrooms have been integral to vegetal gnosis. But the psychedelic sensibility achieved its greatest catalyst with LSD, the substance indeed made synonymous with the word "psychedelic", which denotes both the

Raja Ram. Ozora, 2009. Photo: Pascal Querner.

means of transition and the transitional state itself. There may have been no composer of self-dismemberment greater than Posford, who, as Hallucinogen, gave the name "LSD" to what became one of the genre's most seminal tracks, which was re-released almost fifty times (originally released on the 12-inch *Alpha Centauri/LSD,* Dragonfly Records, 1994). This and other work produced with Shpongle illustrate that psychoactives have been integral to unlocking hidden potential and facilitating connection with the whole.

Having first trekked through India in 1958, and dropping LSD in 1959 (in New York's Greenwich Village), Raja Ram is among the original psychedelic mystics. Seventy years of age in 2010, gifted with a trickster's persona, he wrote:

> I have had at least a 1000 acid trips, and still take it ... the last time being a month or so ago ... while recording Shpongle with Simon ... and I always bow to the Goddess of Love, for protection and insight. This is a serious business ... not for frivolity but for research into one's existence and insights. This is the food of the Gods ... a present from the cosmos ... to be used with discretion and awareness, in the effort to understand what is going on ... inside and outside of one's self.[18]

As he pointed out to me himself, Raja Ram took LSD before Leary, whose voice is emblazoned across the psychedelic experience. On X-Dream's remix of "Psychedelic Rock n' Roll", a collaboration between Martin Glover and Durga McBroom (as Blue Lotus) (*Order Odonata 4*, 2000), Leary is conjured from the late 1960s to ruminate upon "some deep life changing experience that has always been listed as mystical or spiritual ... You can't quantify it ... , but I think it's possible that more people have had this experience in maybe ten years than ever before during history". In more recent work, like that of Overdream's "Multiple Realities", Leary's filtered and anonymized voice still informs new congregations about how he "opened Pandoras Box" and "stumbled on the Philosopher's Stone of multiple reality" (*Life on Earth*, 2011). But, while the iconic voice of Leary is scattered throughout Goatrance productions, as the movement receded from India, and as the native shamanic practices of the Central and South Americas grew popular among those seeking departure from core Western values and practice, a host of shamanic plants, decoctions and their synthetic analogues grew appealing, including ayahuasca[19] and other brews and blends with known psychoactive compounds experimented with in widening circles of use.

As a result of the popularization of the work of Carlos Castenada and Michael Harner, shamanic practice would become adopted, refined and remixed within do-it-yourself rites. Seeking and using a growing pharmacopeia of plant medicines to this end, many have adopted the phrase "entheogen" and the associated concept of "entheogenesis" to refer to substances the consumption of which purportedly awakens the divine within; with "entheogenic" also an effort to overcome ethnocentrism associated with "psychedelic" in relation to plants used within traditional cultural contexts (see Ott 1995; Forte 1997). Psytrance would become a strong vehicle for the practice of self and public "shamanizing" – and indeed a context for *entheogenesis*, where a host of plants, compounds and decoctions are hailed to potentiate shamanic transformation (see Strassman *et al.* 2008). From its inception, life-altering and potentially therapeutic initiatory experience has been a preoccupation of Goatrance producers who have plundered the global media database to convey this interest *and* orchestrate it. For instance, at the birth of Goatrance, The Infinity Project's "Stimuli" (*Feeling Weird*, 1995) held the line: "7am, as the day begins, the drug is inhaled to introduce the strange language of the initiation rites". This shamanic sensibility is indebted to the efforts of McKenna, whose anti-authoritarian approach to shamanic practice conveys an antinomian neo-romanticism prioritizing the self as legitimate mediator of authenticity, where personal identity is thoroughly grounded in intuition, feelings and the imagination, and in which psychedelic techniques are adopted with the purpose of liberating the self. Skeptical of external authority (knowledge) yet open to techniques of revelation (knowing), and cajoling audiences to question his own ideas, through the 1990s in particular, McKenna's approach appealed to growing numbers refusing to have their lives governed by religious, media and cultural oligarchies. Many psytrance enthusiasts would concur with McKenna when, following a journey to Peru in 1976 in search of ayahuasca, he concluded that the numinous experience and gnostic insights associated with what he called the "hyperdimensional" realm should not be governed nor controlled by administrators of the divine, but "must be personally discovered in the depths of the psychedelically intoxicated soul" (McKenna 1991b: 206).

In the wake of McKenna's paean to the "shamanarchy", the DJ-producer him-/herself becomes an embodiment of the shaman anarchist, reassembling sound, reprogramming code, and re-mediating commentaries which often reference the use of "shamanic herbs" to potentiate mystical experience – an experience authenticated by association with the Indigenous ritual heritage these native entheogens signal. These producers then mirror and effect the desire for the initiatory experience of entheogenesis among contemporary seekers of experience. Take Portuguese Sérgio Ribeiro's (aka Xamanist) appropriately titled album *Initiation* (Ektoplazm, 2009), the cover of which features the drawing "Circuitous Complexion" by Adam Scott Miller, which depicts an astounded upgazing neophyte exposed to a profound truth. Miller himself explained to me that the work is "a symbolic form of one person that is attaining a transcendent perspective, above spacetime, where the emotive moments of revelation merge into one grander moment in which those gestures interlink into a portal through which the numinous channels through to being".[20] On "Machu Picchu", the album opens with McKenna offering advice for the audio-trippers – that a mysterious substance should be taken "in darkness, and in silence, and in reverence, on an empty stomach, free from distraction, with attention to breath". Xamanist filters classic McKenna brogue: "reality is a very thinly spun cultural fiction. And as long as you remain on main street it all holds together pretty well". But with the beats having accelerated to a gallop, and breathwork equalling the pace, the listener (and the dancer) is taken on a detour from "main street", a phantom ride into an otherworld, the journey scripted by cryptic floating messages distorted by effect and overtaken by driving rhythms. With a further comment lifted from McKenna – "I have had extraordinary experiences in ayahuasca sessions" – "White Magik" reveals the real guide taking the "initiation".

The popularization of DMT – a vital ingredient in ayahuasca – is one of McKenna's chief legacies, as his experience with "machine elves" avers. Regarded as "the spirit molecule", DMT has become an intriguing story. Found in various plants, produced in the human brain – according to Strassman (2001), the pineal gland – and usually smoked ("free-based") in a chillum with an effect lasting 15–30 minutes (as opposed to LSD's sometimes 8–12 hour trip), the tryptamine DMT was discovered by McKenna to be one of the most powerful vehicles for inter-dimensional transit. Alongside hallucinogenic mushrooms, DMT was hailed amid a personal commitment to spiritual technologies believed integral to humanity's push towards liberation in transpersonal consciousness, and "the redemption of fallen humanity through the respiritualization of matter" (McKenna 1993: 77). Towards the end of the millennium, as various productions and, by implication, dance floor habitués, were being smudged with DMT, its ode had been sung by Shpongle on their landmark *Are You Shpongled?* (1998). Seminal album track "Divine Moments of Truth" features Raja Ram turning on, again: "it was like a gigantic creature, that kept changing shape". As their oeuvre reveals, the world's most renowned neo-psychedelic act has been a platform for DMT consciousness, as conveyed, for example, on the 2005 release *Nothing Lasts ... But Nothing is Lost*, on which McKenna (in "Molecular Superstructure") announces: "life must be the preparation for the transition to another dimension". As the first decade of the 2000s closed, DMT had became a regular fixture in the mix, just as its vapour hung pungent in the air on global dance floors care of the DMT blend *changa*.[21] Amid the noise of McKenna samples, DMT references and the pungent vapour, Swede Wizack Twizack's (Tommy Axelsson) "Spirit Molecule" (on *Space No More*, 2010) makes an effort to uncover this "strange chemical" and understand its capacity to replicate an experience identical "to events to come after life". Opening the door to a psychedelic fairytale, "Spirit Molecule" sails off the map of *terra cognita* to relate "the secret history" of which psytrance enthusiasts might approve: "since the dawn of time, man

"Circuitous Complexion". Photo: Adam Scott Miller. www.AdamScottMiller.com.

has used psychedelics. From the ancient myth of Adam and Eve until today ... From the Eleusinian rituals ... to modern day ayahuasca parties, every society has used psychedelics".[22]

Planetary consciousness

As DMT and other tools are used to shamanic ends, the context in which the transpersonal realm is accessed is critical. Participation in nature's cycles has long been an aspect of dance cults, cultures and movements, both ancient and modern. Partridge (2006a) recognized the connection between the late 1980s/early 1990s UK rave explosion and the earlier Free Festival movement in which Stonehenge and other megalithic sites were visited by modern travellers. Like their forebears, those embracing techno music and neonomadic lifestyles, such as Spiral Tribe, sought to convene at ancient sites as a means of reinventing and revivifying their identities in response to the maladies of modern life (St John 2009: 36–55). With the popularizing of the ecstatic experience in the context of raves, perceived, not as a source of panic, but embraced as effective counterpoints to the break from "Mother Nature", technoshamans emerged to promote, harness and repurpose an assemblage of technologies to fashion ecstatic rituals and form "tribes" as transnational in their membership as transpersonal in their collectivity. Achieving early prominence was Fraser Clark who adopted the word "zippy" – sometimes identified as a "zen-inspired pagan professional" – to describe the coming movement (see Rushkoff 1994: 185; St John 2009: 179–84). For Clark, who had an epiphany at an acid house mega-rave outside London in 1988, the "zippy" repurposed technics in the pursuit of ecstatic experience, ecological consciousness and life re-evaluations. Staged in locations affording exposure to the stars, rain-soaked Earth and the rising Sun, these events occasion communion not only with fellow participants, but with the cosmos, in the place in which one's animated feet caress the Earth in dance; circumstances prompting inspired commentators to embrace a heritage to which they now feel indelibly connected, and to which they are actively returning.

> Like the old pagan festivals, we're all in this together. This is our planet. She is indescribably beautiful, gigantic. We are the atoms of that Living Goddess. Personally I can't think of a better way to help people learn a love, respect, reverence for Nature than the classical open-air all night Rave. Can you imagine what it felt like with 20,000 people going for it and actually feeling together, and the power of a people together, and then dancing the Sun up?! It is awesome, it is religious, and it is life-changing.

In this text accompanying the cover art of the compilation album *Trip to Cyberspace (vol 2)* (1998), Clark was describing a classical mystical experience, with the public secret of the outdoor rave party inciting new entries into the archives of the "perennial philosophy". Events held on the quarter days are reckoned to hold special significance for technopagans. According to Castle, there is no better time to hold a party than at the Equinoxes. As he related on the fold-out of another CD also released that year, *Strong Sun Moon* (Equinox, 1998), "Equinox means the time of equal day and night ... It is the relationship between the Earth and Sun in an orbit around the evolving galactic centre of the Universe. The Anima Mundi". And Japan's Equinox festival – where Japanese sound engineer Shiro Ono installed holophonic four-way stacks around a "sacred circle" until 1999 – is singled out as being an especially "celestial electro communion – a participation mystique".

He might have made a strident connection with the "old pagan festivals", but the "planet" which Clark knew as "indescribably beautiful, gigantic" is a realization that was doubtlessly assisted by the visualization of the Earth from space by NASA astronauts whose missions of the late 1960s and early 1970s bore photographic fruit: especially the Earthrise image taken onboard the 1968 Apollo 8 mission whose crew members, the first humans to witness the Earth "rising", were struck by the awesome sight of Earth over the lunar horizon. The story was taken up in 1996, on Astral Projection's "Black and White" (*Trust in Trance*) with retrospective commentary from mission Commander Frank Borman: "And the view of the Earth, it was the only place in the universe that had any color. Everything else was black and white". The revelatory image of a blue turning globe, small and vulnerable in the vastness of space, Earthrise would become one of the most significant photographs ever taken. Providing what has been referred to as the "Overview Effect", Earthrise and the later Whole Earth image would confirm ideas associated with "Spaceship Earth", a phrase coined by Buckminster Fuller, provide the stimulus for the "Gaia hypothesis" and inspire the popular expression of ecological and humanitarian concerns, illustrating for the first time "Earth's agency as an autonomous, self-regulating biosphere" (Henry and Taylor 2009: 191).[23] Psychedelic trance became a vehicle for the expression of the "Overview Effect". From Shakta's dub-influenced "Earthrise" (*Silicon Trip*, 1997) released after the peak of Goatrance, to "Daze of Our Lives", Filteria's neoGoa reproduction of the moment of speechless ascension (*Daze of Our Lives*, 2009), Goa producers have sampled astronauts with the lofty purpose of exposing dance floor habitués to the revelatory satori of real-time space travellers.

Goa/psytrance music reverberates with timbral elicitations of a planetary consciousness to which participants gravitate like mesmerized voyagers. Among them are those like the 1990s event crew Koinonea who gravitated to global "power spots" and events celebrating planetary alignments, employing "ancient rites using modern day technology, hoping to reaffirm the bonds of connectedness with each other, the planet, and the spiralling galaxies" (see St John 2004: 226). Pre-millennium, dance events and groups were lauded as "planetary healing communities" (Antara and Kaye 1999) whose ecstatic energy could be directed into the "planetary grid" and thus positively impact collective consciousness and world peace. This was the thought-form and the formative event was the Harmonic Convergence of 16–17 August 1987, an act of prayer, meditation and ceremony that was simultaneously coordinated at numerous sacred sites and power spots throughout the world to "launch the 25 year transition into a New Age of peace and harmony". Called by founder of the Planet Art Network, José Argüelles (Argüelles 1987), in the service of "planetary healing", and held on a date in which seven planets were in close alignment, that event marked the commencement of the final twenty-six-year period of the Maya calendar's 5,200-year "Great Cycle" (see Ivakhiv 2003: 97). It thus marked the beginning of a period to culminate in the galactic alignment of Earth and Sun with the equatorial plane of the Milky Way galaxy on 21 December 2012: the end date of the Maya calendar, which was invested with considerable significance by Argüelles and McKenna, and has been recognized as a major transitional juncture within the visionary arts community (see St John 2011b). Such planetary healing events have become integral to a progressive millenarianism that, while expressing a "meta-narrative" of spiritual evolutionism (Ferguson 1980) flourishing since the 1960s/1970s, can be traced to "new age" utopianism that had emerged between the two world wars (Sutcliffe 2007: 71). Various mutants, freaks and human hybrids speculated to populate the future have emerged from the visions of numerous spokespersons whose voices circulate within the psychedelic community, as recorded on its soundtracks. Whether emergent species without "design" care of Richard Dawkins deployed on Kode IV's *Silicon Civilisation* (1995), or Carl Johan Calleman's filtered ideas of post-2012 ascension to "cosmic consciousness" on Mantrix's "Spontaneous Existence Part 1" (*Universal*, 2006), or the shamanic revival amplified onboard *Raja Ram Presents the Evolution of Expanded Consciousness* (2006), psychedelic trance music and its events have been regarded as techno-organic laboratories from which hybrid forms emerge.

* * *

As psytrance conveys, wholeness, stability, and the seeking of one's truth in the late-modern context of liquidity, fleeting engagements and uncertainty, is no simple task. Under these conditions, the project of the self is a notorious challenge, all the more since that which is held to constitute *the self* does not go undisputed. While producers and habitués have, from the inception of the Goatrance development, pursued completion, wholeness and self-discovery under the "progressive" auspices of the human potential movement, competing narratives provide entries on the enigmatic nature of "truth". While self-divinity, self-shamanizing and entheogenesis are products of "epistemological individualism", this modern condition authorizes the deconstruction of fantasies of the inviolable self itself, a potentially creative process inscribed in the artifice and the ontology of the remix. While the materials of what Partridge calls "popular occulture" are remixed to the tune of self-enchantment, the reassembly of resources may also be authorized for no other cause than the undirected annihilation of the self. Therefore, it is commonplace to find in psytrance the pursuit of universality and planetary consciousness dancing alongside the harebrained anaestheticizations of partygoing. This diversity feeds into transitional aesthetics animating psyculture, which, as this chapter has explored, deploys techno-assemblages to effect variant outcomes. I began this discussion by way of differential transitional commitments enabling the departure from, merger with, and evolution of, "consciousness", with each of these processes investing in different understandings of the "consciousness" from which, and to which, participants migrate. These perspectives on transition are not unrelated. In the immeasurable conditions that artists and engineers optimize, the disintegration of normative modes of consciousness (ego) inaugurated by the trance dance experience makes possible the realization of one's transpersonal indivisibility. In psychedelic trance, this remastery of the self is facilitated under the conditions whereby new works are formed from existing materials sampled, mixed and revisioned. Across this spectrum of consciousness-altering behaviour we find interventions by technoshamans who act as functionaries for various causes, including self-directed therapy and planetary consciousness. But we also find that the altered state, the mystical consciousness, is more than often a condition mediated with the assistance of popular cultural resources sampled in the remix and programmed in productions by media shaman and made available to the interpreting minds of dance floor audiences. Therefore, productions are devised not so much to orchestrate the transformation-of-being and status that is the common objective of rites of passage, but the superliminalized state of *being in transit* – an experimental field of experience optimized by technicians and event-habitués with the aid of psychoactives, including "entheogens". But while sonic fiction amplifies fixation with the noetic insight, with the feeling of knowing as *knowledge* itself, this threshold architecture native to psychedelic trance potentiates experience not dissimilar to that of perennial mystical states. Thus, I concluded this chapter with the planetary consciousness that has been cultivated within the *remixtical* medium of psytrance, and which will be explored further in the next chapter.

5 Psychedelic festivals, visionary arts and cosmic events

The late 1980s were a significant juncture in the emergence of visionary arts. Around the time Fraser Clark was feeling his pagan heritage in a very modern context and imagination, and Argüelles called seekers to the Harmonic Convergence, Ray Castle began holding his "world beat trance dance" Pagan Production parties in Holland and elsewhere in Europe. Castle had returned from an inspired season in Goa where travellers were trading their frozen northern winters for temperate beaches on the Arabian Sea and where the transition to daylight became the optimized threshold for dance conflagrations. For the likes of Castle, the trance dance event is a world apart and a space in between enabling the transformation of its participants. This chapter explores the Goa state of mind as it inspired psychedelic festivals, principally Portugal's Boom and world total solar eclipse festivals. These events are spiritual technologies accommodating the ecstatic and reflexive dispositions of participants and contexts for the modes of consciousness transition outlined in the previous chapter. As visionary arts festivals they house multiple transitional pathways, a circumstance amplified by their *psychedelic* praxis and aesthetic.

Psychedelia festiva

In the psychedelic festival, participants are afforded multiple freedoms – sometimes complementary, other times contested – unavailable beyond the fence. Extraordinary recreational topographies, they combine *leisure* activities common to popular music festivals with the experience of the *sacred* associated with pilgrimage destinations, and the *labours* of festival workers, many of whom are volunteers – swapping their labour for admission – with most mixing business with pleasure in close quarters. The conventional division of labour from leisure is blurred within the festal precincts such that the work associated with new social, cultural and spiritual movements are indistinguishable from play. The "workplay" (van Veen 2010: 31) artifice of the DJ encapsulates this convergence, since his/her work is literally a seamless practice of "playing", and in their enraptured observance and response to the performances of a DJ – often a single male figure on a stage – dance floor crowds exalt the practice, with DJs giving encore after encore to its contemporary significance. But more to the point here, the psychedelic festival exists among extreme and experimental leisure industries facilitating the performance of psycho-somatic risk-taking in the tradition of voluntary "edgework", which according to Stephen Lyng (2005: 9) includes recreational pursuits like sky-diving and motorcycle riding as a "means of freeing oneself from social conditions that deaden or deform the human spirit through overwhelming social regulation and control". Lyng's "edgework" resonates with "raving" as an extreme and concentrated exercise in transgression. After the acid house explosion of 1988, raving became hitched to the nomadic lifestyles of alternative travellers in the UK who had been touring the seasonal Free Festivals since the 1970s. That rave came to designate a cultural practice combining travel to locations remote from domestic sites with the journey out of one's mind was evident in the London-orbital techno-raves of the late 1980s and in the teknival movement of the following decade. The physical "trip" to remote and exotic regions at the risk to one's health and person, and the psychological "trip" resulting from the use of psychoactive substances risking one's rational consciousness, and also one's mental health (see D'Andrea 2007a), combined in the psytrance festival to potentiate liberation and fulfilment in ways paralleling risk-taking within "extreme sports" and other forms of wild recreation in which one abandons "home", sobriety and certainty. It is no coincidence that publications such as *Psychedelic Traveller* magazine promote psytrance scenes in nations like New Zealand alongside other adventurous and risk-laden leisure pursuits such as white-water kayaking and bungee jumping.

Yet, amid the risk, psyculture is also a plateau of discipline where participants employ techniques of the self associated with the self-regulated "loosening" Sam Binkley (2007: 17) identifies as a "reflexive project of the self", or that which D'Andrea (2007a: 6) calls a "stabilized form of self-cultivation (*nomadic spirituality*)", which he contrasts with the "acute self-derailment (*psychic deterritorialization*)" also conditioning the "neonomad". These experimental plateaus of discipline diverge from those dystopias associated with rave and techno scenes characterized by urban decay, socio-economic disadvantage, racial oppression and "techno survivalism" (Pope 2011: 41). Within the visionary arts festival, discipline may also be compelled through redressive ecological principles implemented in event-design, an ethos that encourages participants to comport themselves in accordance with an awareness of human symbiosis with non-human nature. Disciplinary practice will be a subject covered in later chapters. Here I want to point out that both transgressive and disciplinary fronts affirm the authority of the self, the sanctity of the senses and the power of creativity which, under the weight of Jungian psychology, ecologism, integralism and entheogenic philosophies, give shape to the alternative lifestyle festival found among the pluralistic, fragmentary and subversive performance art forms which gave Turner cause to coin the term "liminoid" (or "ritual-like"). That term, vaguely influenced by the "negative" and "positive" liberties to which political philosopher Isaiah Berlin (1969) gave attention, denotes the exploits of post-industrial populations in contexts outside traditional obligatory frameworks where individuals practise their "freedom from" religious, family and workplace "contracts", and their "freedom to" transcend, imagine and play (Turner 1982a: 36). But if we are casting our gaze upon a subjunctive domain of "free" leisure, it is shaped by movement causes, dissensions amplified by countercultural heterodoxies emphasizing experience, experimentalism and consciousness.

A chief result of this development is the "Free" Festival, the complexity of which is inherited from earlier experiments. Inevitably the subject of enduring debate among event-publics, while such events may be operated by commercial enterprises, and possess admission fees, employees, contracted artists, hired security personnel, market stalls and fences, they are nevertheless domains that ostensibly enable liberation of the body, mind and spirit. As interstices of workplay, undisciplined embodiment, cognitive liberty and ethical consumption, such events are centres for the variable expression of *free culture*. This is a culture of responsiveness and experimentation in which autonomy is paramount, where liberation from multiple oppressions in the lifeworld enables the pursuit of various causes (e.g. peace, well-being, sustainability) via manifold practices (e.g. artistic expression, reusable energy sources, dietary practices, alternative states of consciousness), which are reliant on the subversion of law (e.g. moral standards, legal codes, rules of propriety), challenges to official knowledge (e.g. scientific paradigms, biomedical dominance, television news programming), and alternatives to neoliberal economics (e.g. in cooperative skill sharing arrangements, flea markets). All such practices may be accommodated within the grounds of the visionary arts and lifestyle festival, such availability providing motivation for festal-goers who seek abominable knowledge, practise deviant science, and pursue unspeakable aesthetics. From the Stonehenge Summer Solstice Festival and other UK festivals which had flourished as alternative traveller enclaves before their dismantlement by Conservative governments (Worthington 2004), habitués seek freedom from meaningless labour, Church and state intervention, and experiment with alternatives to non-holistic dietary and health practices, possessive materialism, and patriotism. Some events, like California's Moontribe Gatherings, self-identify as "gatherings" in the tradition of the Rainbow Gatherings which, since 1972, have been dedicated to cooperativism, healing-arts and world peace (Niman 1997). Such intentional events offer *proliminal* responses to the conditions of their times. That is, while providing a liminal oasis whose populations shelter from a multitude of dissatisfying conditions in the non-festal lifeworld, these junctures of face-to-face, body-to-body and heart-to-heart exchange facilitate the exploration of alternatives. As apparent "incubators of novelty", such events have been identified as "petri dish of possibility where the future forms of community and consciousness are explored" (Davis 2008a: 54).

This statement was made with regard to Portugal's Boom Festival. Initiated in 1997 by Diogo Ruivo and Pedro Carvalho (who met as children in Goa) and held on lake Idanha-a-Nova near the village by that name in the mountainous Beira Baixa province, the biennial Boom Festival has become a pilgrimage centre for the global psytrance community. I conducted field research at Boom in August 2006 and again in 2008 and 2010 (with populations of approximately 25,000+, 35,000+ and 20,000+ respectively). Boom was once aptly described as "an experience that synergizes the intellectual stimulation of a conference, the interactivation of a workshop, the artistic inspiration of a gallery show, the independent sustainability of a tribal market, the experiential magic of ritual prayer performance and the ecstatic release of a dance party" (Delvin and Eve 2005: 32). In 2008, enthusiasts from an estimated eighty-five countries camped for up to seven days on the festival site in sweltering conditions. Promoted by its organizing body of the time, Good Mood Productions, as a week-long "visionary arts festival", a "harmonic convergence of people, energy, information and philosophies from around the planet earth and beyond", and commanding "a balance of the organic and the cyber-technologic",[1] Boom accommodates diverse countercultural strands drawn towards ecstatic trance and visionary culture across its various areas, from the dance floors (including the Dance Temple) to the Liminal Village presentation space, both of which will be discussed later in this chapter.

Boom exemplifies the merger of ecstatic and reflexive dispositions within the environment of the festival, not least because, as a psychedelic festival, the "mind manifesting" dissolution of boundaries that separate *different* participants enables the experience of *difference*. Here, "psychedelic" refers to a range of techniques and practices – including, albeit not exclusively, psychoactive compounds – that facilitate "mind manifesting". In the previous chapter, I discussed how different subgenres of psychedelic music within psytrance have carried different registers of the psychedelic experience. Mid-west US party network Chilluminati offer insight on this theme, stating: "We refer to as psychedelic anything having the effect of transforming our mode of consciousness. We embrace every such legal technique which includes dance, music, techniques involving light and sound, sensory deprivation, breath control, exercise, fasting, art, meditation, prayer, sex, and yoga".[2] Since the dissolution of boundaries is affected by an assemblage of techniques and practices, the narrow-band understanding of "psychedelic" as synonymous with LSD (or other psychoactive compounds) requires revision. As the psychedelic festival illustrates, psychoactives are among an assemblage of options available for participants to become expansive, creative and interactive. At events where every participant is valued as an "artist", a cornucopia of experiential freedoms are worked at and played with. Outlands accommodating psychonauts, neomystics and other fissiparous seekers of spirituality identified by Sutcliffe (1997: 105) who "select, synthesize and exchange among an increasing diversity of religious and secular options and perspectives", psychedelic festivals permit the condition of *being in-transit*, a desirable mobile sensibility for cultural exiles and architects of the possible who launch festal venues like spacecraft or "UFOs", and model themselves as "aliens", the ultimate signature of difference to the popstream from which they seek expatriation. These scenes are connected historically to spaces of experimentation long inhabited by artists and utopians, queers and bohemians, expats and esotericists, whose cosmopolitan aesthetic is fuelled by the artefacts and artifice of consciousness alteration concentrated under the roofs of cafés and chai tents, and promulgated in head shops and chill-out spaces, danced into being on remote beaches, in forest parties and at desert doofs. The world over, these islands of radical immanence maximize the potential for self-exiles to accumulate experience and build repertoires of knowledge and practice expressive of their transitional lifestyles. Augmenting conditions in which knowledge, truth and wisdom are acquired through direct experience, where artistic expressions afford the highest credibility, and where being loose, open and liminal are desirable objectives, these festivals enable habitués to become their own shamans, mystics and healers. Riffing ideas from his book *Prometheus Rising* (1983), as Robert Anton Wilson conveyed, "we're all evolving into something different ... In the higher and higher circuits everybody becomes their own psychic, and their own magician and life gets more interesting", thoughts conjured by psybient artist Androcell sampling the "agnostic mystic" on "Higher Circuit Experience" (*Entheomythic*, 2010).

Worlds apart and in between: being altered together

The psychedelic festival is a world apart, a festal interzone that transposes the Goa state of mind and is heir to modes of *being altered together* that have been cultivated in the techno-sensibility I have called Disctopia. As seasonal expressions of these cosmopolitan sensibilities, dance festivals are like the flowering buds of EDMC, displaying the vitality of a movement in full bloom. But as dance movements like rave and psytrance have emerged, their proliferation goes largely unrecognized by historians who, like Barbara Ehrenreich in *Dancing in the Streets* (2006), maintains distance from celebrations that are fuelled, at least in part, by illicit intoxications. And while sociologists Shilling and Mellor (2011) highlight the significance of intoxication, and in particular embodied states of intoxication and "hyper-excitement" in Durkheim's understanding of socio-religious life as the proscribed transcendence of individuality through effervescent assemblies, their own examples drawn from Christian revivalism are bereft of actual psycho-activating drugs, whether used to excess, in the revisioning of prevailing values or in the subversion of *habitus*. Such squeaky-clean dalliances with "collective joy" and "embodied intoxications" harnessed towards the regulation of morality appear to want little contact with that which Maffesoli (1993) held as the "shadow" side of Dionysus, and nor with an orgiastic directionality that is determinably *alternative* or *visionary*. For, not simply an abandonment of propriety and of history typical to those demesne of luxury, expenditure and eroticism Georges Bataille (1989) called society's "accursed share", or in the "savage religion" of the "instituent" experience clarified by Roger Bastide (1975; see Gauthier 2004a), the freak assembly signifies desires to elude, and be independent from, state regulation, commodification and mediation. This is what Hakim Bey (aka Peter Lamborn Wilson) knew as the "Temporary Autonomous Zone" (the TAZ; Bey 1991a), which has indeed provided techno and trance enthusiasts with the conceptual architecture to articulate event-philosophies, though the communities of *ekstasis* sought by the mystic wanderer, freak sage and technoshamans were to be enabled by technics and mediated by sound in a complexity, and by an intensity, that would make Wilson flinch.

With or without Bey/Wilson's approval, with the dissolution of boundaries integral to their design, these are the festivals accommodating "radical conviviality" (Bey 1994). With manifold psychedelic artforms and artivists converging at its principal post-Goa parties, Goatrance was a carrier of a bohemian ethos which has nowhere been easy to define, though in the preface to a brick-like tome of writings on the subject, Marigay Graña (1990: xv) notes that:

> We were able to come up with only two characteristics of bohemianism which appear to hold constant over the century-and-a-half of its recognized existence: (1) an attitude of dissent from the prevailing values of middle-class society – artistic, political, utilitarian, sexual – usually expressed in life-style and through a medium of the arts; and (2) a café.

The principal locale for animated conversation – the café – has been integral to the project of dissent even when it has no specific directive or program. Bohemia, as the Grañas indicate, has been a cosmopolitan repository of support for alternative experiments since 1800s Paris. It is no coincidence that chai shops – which typically serve coffee, tea and cake – are integral to psytrance events, sometimes positioned in chill rooms or near ambient stages – i.e. areas where conversation is encouraged. Sprawled on carpets and cushions, patrons demonstrate skills in spliff rolling and share chillums, or perhaps scrawl in fresh-leaved notebooks. Patrons frequently throw themselves into each other's arms as old friends are reacquainted. Recent travel adventures are recounted with attention to novel experiences, hazards encountered, trials endured, lessons learned. Toilet "horrors" are traded, the availability, quality and price of various drugs are discussed, and lineups of DJs are pored over. Judgements are passed on the artifice to which participants are exposed and to which they themselves contribute. The relative merits of different dance floors and genres are parsed as stories of last night or last year come to light. In chill spaces and market restaurants, strange notions are traded between those who indulge among their own crews, yet are never far from foreigners with whom they share recommendations (often in simple English) on other events, offering details on places to visit and perhaps invitations for accommodation outside the festival. "See you on the dance floor" is the customary phrase upon parting ways. Random camping and dining arrangements and chance encounters lead to the formation of temporary transnational posses with longer-term implications.

International camaraderie within party precincts is rooted in Goa which had a long-standing reputation as an Eastern Bohemia whose sensibility would be transported back to domestic enclaves in the world cities of its birth. This "Tazmania" – the title of Aphid Moon's debut track (1997) – was translated into open-air festivals in which "Goa" was allowed to flourish, but where the outcomes were never certain. As Graña writes,

> political activists have long sought the shield afforded them within Bohemia, a place to develop and organize their activities. Since the boundaries of Bohemia are loosely drawn, they easily overlap with those of other social movements, supporting dissidents who may have very different agendas from those of their bohemian hosts (1990: xvii).

Graña could have been describing the grounds of the alternative festival which harbours dissidents in similar fashion, festal enclaves in which alternative markets flourish and "zine libraries" appear like the Abominable Knowledge Emporium of rare, radical and outrageous zines operated by Australia's Kathleen Williamson, or where emporiums are erected evoking Mystic Arts World from Laguna Beach in the 1960s, where, instead of Dion Wright's Taxonomic Mandala, we might find the translucent work of Alex Grey or Robert Venosa's "Astral Circus". Psychedelic trance is the vehicle for the bohemian phantasmagoria which has taken root and flourishes in worldwide locations. Its events retain contiguity with enclaves of the past while possessing characteristics unique to their location. Take visionary artist Tim Parish's description of Australia's Rainbow Serpent Festival, 2008:

> Now I am an iris. A curious camera, recording light with words with hangover insight. Swinging from my hammock I watch the jewelry of piercings everywhere they can pierce and the tattooed graffiti of the flesh lovers dropping mathematic mandalas and celtic labyrinth fusions on back and shoulder canvas murals of the magic forest populated with pixies, faeries and elven folk flexing on the gallery of these skins; maori zebras, cosmic DNA octave chakra points, double helix shoulderblade wings, ancient heiroglyph forearms and belly button temples. Naked children run past, huge chinese fans hang from the armpit of paperbarks. The chai tent is overflowing with limbs and tiny giftgiving stoners. The healing space teepee filled with crystals and rocks of different frequencies emanates calm in the zoo. Beuna Vista trumpet cries from the cafe's renegade stage. An indian man skinning up next to me smiles at the passing scenery (Parish 2008).

We're at a considerable remove, here, from heavily commercialized EDM festivals, which do not cultivate bohemianism since participants are more likely to be cajoled to consume than encouraged to create art or provide "mutual aid". Such events evolve into a kind of corporate communitas where participants become lost to a cult of celebrity in which "name" DJs stand out like theocratic icons before adoring masses. In the world of EDM, we can look to events like Creamfields or Frankfurt's Green and Blue Festival where *names* adopt priestly postures on massive stages with VIP stage-wings accommodating throngs of sycophants. Green and Blue is operated by Sven Väth. At the 2007 edition of that event, as the high-heeled and alluring representatives of alcohol and tobacco companies roamed the festival-grounds seducing partygoers with glow-in-the-dark pendants, temporary tattoos, jet-flame lighters and other alluring items designed to generate brand energy, I witnessed Väth complete a six-hour set as fireworks exploded directly over him. This weekend society of the spectacle affords retrospective on the approach of Goa Gil, who refuses to work at festivals. There are no fireworks at Goa Gil parties, unless we include Gil's flashing OM device, or the hallucinatory fireworks internal to individual partygoers. Since Väth has no grounding in disciplined meditative practice, nor is his work endorsed by a 4,000 year old Shaivite tradition, and nor, for that matter, does he believe he's performing God's work, the comparison may be a little unfair.

Bohemia is a party with multiple rooms, tents, sound areas and a fabulous lightshow. Larger clubs and festivals are capable of accommodating multiple zones, musics and aesthetics, including stages for celebrity icons powered by electricity and renegade sound system collectives operating off reusable energy sources. It is a rather consensual view among psytrance participants, however, that only select events, or enclaves within them, provide the appropriate platform for the visionary experience. Not unlike bohemianism, cosmic clubbing can be traced to cosmopolitan clubs and expatriate enclaves – districts, venues and clubs that became the birthing canals of psychedelia. While Goa was integral, it was itself fed by aesthetics that had fermented in the various scenes and centres of Disctopia. Since the *discothèques* operating in occupied Paris during WWII (Shapiro 2005: 15), dance clubs have courted, sometimes rather stridently, an "underground" aesthetic, subversions later oiled by LSD and the psychedelia percolating within late 1960s discultures in New York. Early psychedelic rock/dance crossover clubs like Max's Kansas City – which opened on Park Avenue South in 1965 – were staging grounds for an experimental punk/disco syncretism (Shapiro 2005: 255). On the west coast, the Merry Prankster parties at Ken Kesey's place at La Honda, California, and the subsequent Acid Tests (1965–1966) were crucial, generating altered forms of embodiment and interactivity in dance influencing contemporary clubbing aesthetics. A history of the psychedelic party might include the activities of enigmatic avatar of acid Captain Alfred M. Hubbard, who had, by the early 1960s, introduced thousands of people (including Huxley) to LSD. From 1958, Hubbard was running a psychedelic therapy clinic in Hollywood Hospital, New Westminster, British Columbia. Designed to induce ecstatic responses, Hubbard's approach was piecemeal at best, but in describing the 1959 "Hubbard room" – "Dali's Last Supper over the couch, Gauguin's Buddha on the far wall, another Dali, a crucifix, a small altar, a stereo system, burning candles, a statue of the Virgin" – Jay Stevens (1989: 248) records one of the earliest attentions to "setting" that would receive modification over the decades as the topos for tripping left the clinic and moved onto the beaches and into the fields, forests and warehouses of EDM cultures.

The backstory of psychedelic clubbing could not ignore such influential groups and venues as New York's "intermedia" art troupe USCO ("The US Company"),[3] or London's UFO club. The story of psychedelic scene setting would then involve experiments on each side of the Atlantic, from Leary's Castalians at the Millbrook estate in Dutchess County, New York, to Michael Hollingshead's World Psychedelic Centre in Chelsea (Roberts 2008: 86–8), and numerous "turn-on centres" such as the scene at Cadogan Lane in 1965, and the Spontaneous Underground events organized by John "Hoppy" Hopkins at London's Marquee Club in Wardour Street, the first of which was held on 30 January 1966. According to Andy Roberts (2008: 95), that event featured Donovan and was saturated with acid. Pink Floyd were present at subsequent events including that held on 13 March and promoted on a poster with the following instructions: "TRIP bring furniture toy prop paper rug paint balloon jumble costume mask robot candle incense ladder wheel light self and others March 13th 5pm". As Roberts conveyed, the "new psychedelic dance halls" empowered participants, once separated from billed "artists", the opportunity to be artistic, with these events performing as "the perfect incubators for the burgeoning psychedelic culture" (2008: 95). Back in New York, Mancuso's The Loft formed a critical support in the bridge spanning the experimental and consciousness expanding 1960s and late 1980s UK acid house scenes such as that exploding at Shoom in 1988 where Danny Rampling and others had simulated the Balearic aesthetics of Ibiza inside a London club (Collin 1997), inspiring acid house rave. The latter flourished when the population of party tourists pouring into Goa jumped, a momentum later inspiring efforts to simulate the experience in domestic venues including Return To The Source (1993–2002) and Escape From Samsara (1995–2002) in London, and the CCC parties in San Francisco (1995–2000).[4]

In London and elsewhere in the UK, this psychedelic tradition was carried forward in squatted warehouse parties exemplified by those operated by Nick Mindscapes and Friends. In these and other events over several decades, multisensory techniques evolved to connect individual partygoers in ways previously unknown. In dance floor installations and personally worn designs that are now *de rigueur*, fluoro art has been chief among techniques facilitating interaction and illumination. According to Swedish Anders, whose blacklights were used at the White Party in Goa in the late 1970s, strips of white fabric hung between palm trees on coloured string and illuminated by blacklight on middle Anjuna beach circa 1987 by Joe, a German artist, constituted a primitive form of the technique later developed by Avikal, the Italian inventor of morphing fractal psychedelic installations referred to as the "string kaleidoscope". Interactive spaces of spinning sculptures and walkways described as "a high tech 3D interpretation of electronic music", these installations have been constructed at dance floors all over the world, including the early Boom Festival, Antaris in Germany and Equinox and Solstice in Japan.[5]

With its attention to sound design, production and performance, Blue Room, as already related, was a hub of sensory experimentalism throughout the 1990s. Simon Ghahary associated Blue Room with the 1960s consciousness movement although never specifically articulated in conceptual architecture. This is a key point, for the outfit had no particular agenda other than to maximize creativity. It was possessed by no purpose other than to create and recreate optimum sound environments, with Ghahary, who is sceptical of religious idiom, "determined not to give definitions to experience, but to allow participants to provide their own interpretations of the experience". Blue Room exemplified the immediacy of a sound-art culture that relied on evolved technics of sound mediation to unite its participants. The significance of the space-time events in which Ghahary and his international cohort invested is that they, as he stated, "defied reason". For him "this is one of the reasons why I liked it, and one of the reasons why I stopped it". Explaining why Blue Room disappeared almost as suddenly as it emerged, he stated "we'd done our part. The moment it started to have an agenda and started to formalize, the magic went ... There is nothing worse than seeing decay". Paradoxically, "the Blue Room symbol was an emblem for people who wanted no emblem". Holding mostly one-off events and free parties in Brighton, throughout the UK and west coast US, always with live bands and never the same lineup, Ghahary articulated the praxis endogenous to the temporary audio autonomous zone: "what we really wanted was to inspire people to chase their dreams, to meet other people, be open minded, be ready for the unexpected, celebrate change".[6]

For participants in underground parties, clubs and festivals that are evolved contexts for experimenting with interactive technologies of the senses, the perpetuity of such events is commonly felt to be integral to a *spiritual* life. While clubbing can be understood from the point of view of the sociology of religion in which "secondary institutions" (Luckmann 1967: 104; Lynch and Badger 2006) are acknowledged to facilitate belonging and meaning, the cultural role of psychoactivating substances and transpersonalizing technics within these expressive institutions and their associated scenes goes largely unexamined. The profligate Disctopia echos the cultural turn towards what Paul Heelas identified as the "spiritualities of life"; the shift "from '*life-as*' or '*dictated life*' (life lived in terms of institutionalized or traditionalized formations *provided* by 'primary institutions') to '*subjective life*' or '*expressive life*' (life lived in terms of personal, intimate, psychological, somatic, interior experiences *catered for* by 'secondary institutions')" (Heelas and Seel 2003: 239). Dubbed "bass stations", "headquarters", "bunkers" and "temples", clubs and party organizations proliferating across cosmopolises in the 1980s and 1990s offer evidence for the "spiritual revolution" (Heelas and Woodhead 2005; Heelas 2008) downstream from the 1960s and 1970s. Though sociologists have often been reluctant to approach substance use from perspectives other than pathologization, consciousness-altering drugs have been integral to this development. But while research has demonstrated that EDM signifies the "turn to life",[7] mainstream venues such as those Reynolds (1998) identified as "pleasure prisons" are distinguishable from what I referred to in the previous chapter as events lying at the "crossroads of consciousness". Festivals with intentionally religious, spiritual or mystical names like Antaris Project, Paradise, Maitreya, Exodus, Spiritual Healing, Mystic Tribe, Soul Vision, Vision Quest, Universal Religion, and many others both large and small, comprise a transnational network of event-nodes expressly promoting spiritual goals. They are, furthermore, distinguishable from "trance" festivals and clubs, including hard trance, Euro-trance or progressive trance events, since the liberties pursued within the latter are not rooted in the exile experimentalism of the psychedelic counterculture. Neotribal attributes like freedom of choice, the pursuit of puissance and informality are apparent, but psychedelic technotribes pursue freedoms from diverse restrictions and oppressions in the lifeworld, and psycultures the world over become campaign fronts for multiple interwoven liberties (cognitive, sexual, spiritual). Across cosmopolises, psychedelic squat parties are intentional fronts for "free culture", and party crews and collectives like Mindscapes and Friends subsist in the margins "off the grid" of neoliberalism, sometimes disappearing, as in Bey's TAZ, other times offering cooperative models in response to possessive materialism, unsustainable consumption, homonormativism, militarism. At such events, the boundaries between "artist" and "spectator" are more likely to be challenged and voluntarism is less likely to be discouraged among participants. Additionally, parties – especially smaller events – are more likely to be free or by donation, an open circumstance that, given relative seclusion and patronage, has long been favourable to the efflorescence of diversity. Secret sonic societies, mystery schools in hyperspace, visionary culture, optimal rites effecting passage to *post-liminal liminality*, await cultural scientists, entheographers and scholars of the heteroclitic margins.

While David Mancuso installed a Buddha statue between his speakers at the Loft in the late 1960s (Lawrence 2003: 10), with the altar installation becoming a common feature of alternative EDM scenes from disco through psytrance, psychedelic spirituality embraces a radical polytheistic iconography. Piecemeal altars became especially common to visionary events, where altars are the context for participants to offer fruit or contribute personal totems. The typical display of the OM symbol/syllable and the ever-presence of Shiva convey the intent of partygoers to achieve union with the divine source of mystical insight. But Shiva is not a lone deity, for these installations feature a diverse pantheon of god/esses and icons. Installing altars at Goa Gil and other parties in San Francisco, Burning Man and Earthdance since 1996, Nikki Lastreto's installations illustrate a radically inclusive and Universalist perspective. Lastreto conveyed her intention to "put all the deities representing various traditions together and let them hang out on the altar – the message is that if the gods can play together, can't we also? *Ekam Sat Vipra Bahudra Vadanti:* the reality is one, the wise speak of it in different ways".[8] Her self-styled "Hindu-bordello" altars typically include life-size statues of Shiva Nataraj, various Buddhas, Egyptian icons and even Catholic statues of Jesus and Mary. Sometimes complete with entire walls covered in saris and plastic flowers, these increasingly elaborate, cross-faith installations became indispensable to the San Francisco scene, where the *altaration* enhanced the alteration of partygoers towards mystical states of consciousness. As Lastreto stated, watching the proliferation of party-altars in San Francisco and elsewhere, she observed how "divinity has come into the lives of many people through the parties".[9] These iconographical dances of the deities offer a metaphor to the diverse pathways pursued by each individual joining the dance of life. In their intricate concentration of symbols from world religions, precious stones, significant objects and local materials, these structures are dedicated expressions of love, respect and compassion, and are proposed to be reflections of the divine within each individual dancer. This is the message of Mari Kundalini, who has been constructing party altars since 1994 in Melbourne, where they would become a routine party occurrence. Her elegant altars or shrines are typically constructed using statues of multiple deities especially god/esses like Quan Yin and others in Buddhist, Hindu, Balinese, Catholic, Pagan and Animist pantheons and traditions including statues with the "namaste" gesture, The Madonna, Wiccan symbols and an Australian Aboriginal Rainbow Serpent rock painting. Rose quartz crystals, feathers, love-hearts, angels, candles and fresh flowers are woven in mandala arrangements. Incense, flowers, fruit, essential oils, mantras and prayers comprise the offerings intended, ultimately, for those who gather in the party space. "It is as if the Gods/Goddess on the altar", says the Jungian-influenced Kundalini, are honouring the god and goddess aspect that resides in all humans. "Divinity honouring Divinity". With the installation of these structures Kundalini, and many others who build altars, transform a festival into "a sanctified space".[10] Finally, as the flowers die and the installations are deconstructed, the altars, not unlike the parties they appear in, are an expression of "impermanence and detachment".

While dance floors are themselves epicentres of sacrality, they are midpoints of a culture possessing concentric rings of conviviality. At open-air festivals where participants camp over several days and nights in close proximity to one another, nature's cycles and bowel-quaking bass, entrants construct commodious spaces with supplies and privacy for themselves, their partners, friends and family ("crew"). Unlike clubs, where such comforts and privacy are often absent – apart from "chill" rooms – these shared festal domiciles facilitate socio-experimentation with psychoactive substances. The importance of the private camping space within the festival is reminiscent of the way home living rooms enable, as reported by respondents in research on clubbers (Hunt *et al.* 2007), safer and more pleasurable substance use than that experienced at clubs. Removed from the "public" dance floor, which at larger festivals may be a kilometre or more distant from one's camp site, the private festal domicile similarly permits participants to "maximize pleasure and minimize risk" in their use of drugs as they build trust, extend friend networks and acquire knowledge from others within intimate, open and spontaneous camping arrangements. But while the camping area and the dance floor may stand in the same relation as one's living room does to "down town", the distinction is often blurred. At larger events, crews are known to arrange private sound equipment for dancing in the vicinity of their camping enclave, a circumstance which further upsets the domestic/non-domestic division. In addition, at most of the parties and festivals I've attended, crews designate areas on the dance floor and at its immediate margins as spaces to reconvene, and dance floors are familiarized with rugs, beanbags, deckchairs, cushions, welcome mats and other objects typical of the verge where public and private space merge. I've even seen instant lawn rolled out. In Australia, old couches are not uncommonly hauled to the dance floor, along with eskies (drink coolers) and other accoutrements facilitating comfortable jouissance, and at events globally, like Ozora, partygoers erect a patchwork of beach shelters overlooking the dance floor.

As worlds apart and in between, intentional ritualization is native to these events, often promoted using ritual motifs from specific periods and regions, others being more syncretistic. Events often take the format of vision-quests or ritual theatre by those who actively recreate or remember that which is considered lost. For instance, promoting their events as occasions "where psychedelics meet dramatic arts", in June 2008, Israel's Morning Glory hosted an event in the Gilboa Mountains claimed to be a journey into "the Age of Gods and Men" which proposed to place participants "in the middle of the ancient Mythological Greek Culture, right under the Olympus Mountains". Partygoers were hailed as potential neophytes: "we are inviting you to enter a living and breathing labyrinth. Come sacrifice yourself to the minotaur ... Your experience is going to be your personal journey. Nobody is going to have the same trip".[11] In September 2010, in their efforts to produce "psychedelic rituals", Psy Tribe Productions held an event in Italy, Psytribe Wedding, where, according to their promotion, through the fusion of "spirit, nature and music", they sought to "re-create the same energy as the ancients". And in Switzerland, an outfit dubbed Underground Promotions organized a three-day dark trance festival called Forgotten Ritual in 2007. In such events, ritualization is consciously promoted as psychedelic. But are these gatherings the shamanic events and sites of mystery considered lost? Not according to Daniel Pinchbeck, who, in his popular entheographic travelogue *Breaking Open the Head,* lamented the disappearance of the "archaic Dionysian festivals and annual Mysteries celebrating the transformation of primordial chaos into order". And while Pinchbeck mourned this loss, he scorned pagan and contemporary dance cultures as little more than "sullen subcultural wreckage" unfit to form the "ritualized ushering into the Mysteries last seen in the Western world at Eleusis" (2002: 82, 91). But contemporary visionary arts cultures hold greater significance for participants than is permitted in such accounts.

The Festival at Eleusis in ancient Greece has indeed provided the conceptual architecture to fictionalize a world apart – its reputation building on the strength of its assumed status (evolving since the 1960s) as a source of entheogenesis. The plant-assisted shamanizing inscribed in the music and culture of psytrance cannot be considered in isolation from the impassioned embrace of the role, pursued by McKenna and Albert Hofmann, of psychedelic consciousness in the history of the West. Indeed, alongside Gordon Wasson, Hofmann became committed to speculation on the role of alkaloids deriving from a parasite of rye called *ergot* (the alkaloids from which

LSD-25 can be synthesized) believed to be mixed in the *kykeon*, a mysterious potion consumed in secretive ceremonies conducted at Eleusis in honour of Demeter and Persephone (see Wasson *et al.* 1978). Possibly the first international festival in Western history, if not the longest-running (2,000 years), the Eleusinian rites consisted of an annual nine-day celebration attracting up to three thousand people who travelled from all over the Hellenistic world, and later the Roman Empire. The rites culminated in a secret ceremony inside the Telesterion, the main Eleusinian temple, before which the *mystai* were given the *kykeon* and in which the goddesses are said to have freed the initiates from their fear of death (Mylonas 1961). While there is little conveyed about events inside the Telesterion due to an interdiction preventing the divulgence of the *aporrheta* ("unrepeatables"), it is known that it constituted a life-transforming mystical experience for initiates who were shown objects like an ear of wheat displayed in silence by the hierophant (the main Eleusinian priest) as a symbol of the endless regenerative power of nature (Kerenyi 1967). The Mysteries of Eleusis thus rested upon a carefully crafted spiritual technology refined over the centuries by two Eleusinian families who retained control over the ceremonial aspects of the celebration throughout its history.[12]

With the cult spanning two millennia, and with the likes of Plato, Aristotle and Sophocles initiated in the Eleusinian Mysteries, as Paul Devereux (1997) argues, Eleusis illustrates that a consciousness-shifting experience was at the very roots of Western civilization. Despite the fact that the presence of a psychoactive compound in the rites remains unproven, this pivotal historical initiation has held great appeal among psytrance enthusiasts for whom Eleusis is imagined by commentators to antecede, and enchant, their own activities. As much was apparent at the Mystery of Eleusis party held near Basel, Switzerland, in 2003, serving as a homage to Hofmann (who, hailed as "The Magic Wizard of Molecules", attended the event himself) and commemorating the 60th anniversary of the discovery of LSD. While a tribute to the discoverer of LSD on the occasion of his 100th birthday, the Dropout Productions release *Project Eleusis: The Bible of Psychedelics* (2006) celebrated the psychoactivated initiatory experience imputed to have had a significant role in the birth of the West. Psytrance productions regale enthusiasts with lines evoking these ancient rites in which Greek initiates from all walks of life drank a mysterious liquid, with consumers of contemporary admixtures and decoctions imagining their participation in a timeless rite. Thus, before it presses the pedal, Pan Papason's "2000 Years Ago" (*Come with Me*, 2008), kicks off with: "2000 years ago the Greeks held an annual rite at Eleusis in which they drank a sacred liquid called *kykeon*, which induced hallucinations ... The Golden Age it seems was psychedelic as well". As a celebration of transformation, the Greek-dominated darkpsy production *Distorted Shire* (2009), compiled by Nelson Jara Dos Santos (aka Mind Distortion System) and Mario Sounoglou (aka Darkshire), was promoted to combine the Mysteries at Eleusis – and in particular the "group consumption of the barley-based, entheogenic kykeon drink and a night of wild dancing" – with King Lykaon, who was "transformed into a wolf by Zeus himself". The result of this *kykeon*-meets-lykcan production?: "acoustic kykeon for the wolf within!"

Boom and the Liminal Village

While Eleusis has become emblematic of the mystical experience for spiritual activists and event promoters within the psychedelic movement, those holding that contemporary events are contiguous with the festival at Eleusis must parse circumstances that are sobering to anarchists and rebels: that the rites performed within the Telesterion at the culmination of the festivities of the Greater Mysteries were officiated by a hierophant and that divulging the *aporrheta* was punishable by death or exile. Event-management visionaries are nevertheless inspired. Burning Man, for instance, offers an especially favourable comparison with Eleusis. On the Saturday night of the week-long event in Nevada's Black Rock Desert there is a peak Telesterion-like moment where "Burners" converge to witness the conflagration of a massive anthropomorphic figure ("The Man").[13] While Boom has no equivalent primary ritual, the premiere festival in the world of visionary arts and dance culture possesses comparable characteristics to the mystical experience signified by Eleusis. Boomers plan for months (even years) in advance of their attendance. They must travel great distances in scorching mid-summer heat, facing trials and challenges before they come upon the festival site. Indeed, entrance to Boom has been a notorious discomfort for travellers who have sometimes queued in road bottlenecks for days before entering the festival. They travel from points all around the globe, with neophytes overawed by tales from and photos taken by those who have gone before. Despite these tests and privations, there is a jubilant mood typical to those arriving at the festival, and unimaginable at popular music concerts or major sports events. To use the phrase employed by researchers of pilgrimage, the shared joy is an echo of the excitement that grows and grows upon journeying to, and finally arriving at, the pilgrim's goal, the "centre out there" (Turner 1973), a destination which, for those travellers seeking *experience*, is in fact the "out there" centre, the most prized and potentially rewarding *goal* in psytrance, the benchmark *vibe* in the calendar. In an official message posted on Boom's Facebook site following the 2010 festival: "The vibe that was felt and built up this year was one of the best we ever experienced. There was a sense of tribe, a collective joy and an amazing laid back way of experiencing Boom. Collective waves of cheering and whistling could be heard everyday in a pure and simple celebration of happiness".[14] The daily crowing that indeed rippled across the entire festival echoed the dawning recognition among Boomers that they had arrived at

Entrance. Boom 2010. Photo: Rémy-Pierre RIBIERE. www.ruyphoto.net.

the crossroads of consciousness. Their participation in this visceral global summit of consciousness is reinforced by the message that is printed on cloth wristbands issued to all pilgrims at the gate: "We Are One", "We Are All" and "Make Change Happen" in 2006, 2008 and 2010 respectively. Alighting from the ordinary into the extraordinary world, participants seek ecstatic departures from the path well trodden, structured modes of relief from routine selfhood, and routes into an expanded and evolved consciousness.

In an effort to recreate Goa within a festival context, Boom offers the "spiritual hedonism" that Erik Davis saw fomenting in its spiritual homeland (Davis 2004) and at Burning Man (Davis 2005). That is, this is no simple hedonistic "free-for-all", but a transformative journey whose participants seek salutary and beneficent assistance, and where experienced guides tutor neophytes on ways of the self-shaman. But if there are authorities here, they are chiefly embodied in the "teacher plants", "shamanic herbs" and "spirit molecules" that have had considerable influence in the shaping of superliminality. As amplified in the sampledelia explored in the preceding chapter, DMT and other substances like *psilocybe*-containing mushrooms and the ayahuasca brew are recognized by producers and enthusiasts as *authorities* whose "teachings" are venerated. They are plants, compounds and molecules revered as sources of divinity mediated by the minds and bodies of the informed consumer. Boom is a mirror for the entheogenic sensibility that saturates psyculture. Indeed, these spiritual authorities, and their emissaries, adepts and merchants, were plentiful at Boom in 2010. Presentations, panels, workshops and films on psychedelic research and revered molecules and preparations could be attended throughout day four of the festival. Festal *flâneurs* could sit in on the presentation "Confessions of a Modern Mystic" by author of *The Tryptamine Palace* James Oroc, who explained that DMT is derived from an hexagonal molecular geometry, wander into a panel discussion "The Role of Psychedelics as Sacred Plants" involving Rick Doblin, Jon Hanna and Alicia Danforth, or watch the film *Vine of the Soul: Encounters with Ayahuasca*. The day's program, "Frontiers of the Mind", was one of seven scheduled on successive days at the Liminal Village.[15]

As a conscious effort to adopt a language, architecture and vision of initiation using anthropological discourse forged in the study of ritual, and specifically ritual thresholds, the Liminal Village was a centre for the dissemination and exchange of a host of "ultimate concerns" among the participating population, including peace, integral practices and ecological sustainability, via a range of methods and media, including workshops, panels, presentations, displays, art galleries and cinema.[16] One of the most outstanding developments of international visionary arts, the idea for the Liminal Village, which was managed in 2010 by Rita Belo, evolved at the 2004, 2006 and 2008 events, when it was the achievement of Interchill Records manager Naasko Wripple in alliance with a network of visionary artists and organizations. The Liminal Village had been an update on the Convention Area appearing first in 2000, becoming the Dynamic Mythologies Tent in 2002. The idea had arisen from a lineage of events including the Shamanarchy Experiments of Megatripolis, the Entheobotony Seminars, Mindstates, Bioneers and the Prophet's Conference (Wripple 2007: 77). The then recently deceased McKenna inspired promotions for the Dynamic Mythologies Tent using lines from his transmedia performance Alien Dreamtime in San Francisco in 1993:

> Tapping into the Gaian Mind is what we're calling the psychedelic experience. It's an experience of the living fact of the entelechy of the planet and with that experience the compass of the self can be reset. We are somehow part of the planetary destiny, atoms of the world soul, and how well we do determines how well the experiment of life on earth does because we have become the cutting edge of this experiment. We define it and we hold in our hands the power to either make it or break it.[17]

Evolving into a cultural precinct, the Liminal Village became part of The Drop in 2010, which also included the Theatroom, a venue for live stage shows, and the Inner Visions art gallery positioned behind the Liminal Village stage. In my first visit in 2006, the complex was consciously designed as "a temple for a planetary culture". The central building was a 400 square metre bamboo structure (the Omniplex) designed by Balinese architect Amir Rabik. The structure was aligned with the festival according to Feng Shui principles, was grounded by crystal gridwork and featured a solid wooden carving of the mythical figure Garuda at its entrance. Temple Gardens with a network of pathways and land art installations merging Zen-style gardening with permaculture techniques connected habitués with the Omniplex and the adjacent Inner Visions Gallery and Solar Matrix Healing Zone. Towering over the area was an obelisk installation described as "a psycho-cosmic device using art and architecture for transmitting higher vibration of universal creative energy" (Wripple 2007: 90).

The Liminal complex is the crowning achievement of studied interest in the transitional experience inspired by ongoing assays with psychoactive compounds. The complex became a consciously "liminal" project in 2004 and it was later reported by Wripple in the *Boom Book* that "liminal" comes from the Latin word for "threshold" (*limen*) and identifies Turner whose theories are reported to "use liminality to describe the quality of the second stage of a rite of passage where the participant undergoes a transformation of some kind. The liminal, in this respect, is a realm where one's sense of identity dissolves, suspending one's normal limits of thought, self-understanding and behavior" (Wripple 2007: 88). Distributed during the festival, as promotions in the first edition of the "Liminal Zine" *Pathways* had it, visitors were to be transported to "the outer limits of consciousness", recognizing that they must depart "the liminal space back into the material, everyday world of our immediate locale," the integration with which was perceived as "both a personal and a community function of re-evaluation and re-contextualization". From a vantage point "at the edge of everything", it is assumed that participants are enabled "to make sense of our unique place in history and to take the important steps towards implementing the evolutionary changes required if humanity and our biosphere are to survive" (Eve 2006: 5). Eve crystallized the liminal perspective:

> In this unique historical moment, liminality holds within it an evolutionary potency. This is a moment when structures and systems that people trust to supply security and well-being are being misused and exploited for financial and political gain. When we collectively mindfully enter the liminal, allowing the blindly accepted rules of society to fall away in the face of our own interdependent autonomy, we take the first step towards reclaiming the power for ourselves. When we begin to see through the illusions of the strategies and answers we have inherited that no longer apply to our world then we can begin to truly live the questions, allowing each moment to become a portal for discovery and exploration. We begin to trust the authenticity that comes from unmediated experience, from our interactions with those different

> from ourselves, from our willingness to build meaning from the ground up. As we journey together into the liminal, know that this is where art is born. This is where the universal data streams of language, design, spiritual practice and entheogenic experience cross-pollinate and merge into a practical imaginal realm where we can speak, dance, listen and learn. It is here that life becomes a collaborative art project, and life becomes evidence of our evolutionary creativity manifest (Eve 2006: 5).

Designed as a new paradigm school for "unified planetary culture" with an "interactive curriculum spotlighting emergent mythologies, integrative philosophies, and techniques for sustainable and holistic living",[18] the Liminal Village synergizes display, presentation and spoken word over the several day programs, bearing resemblance to the transmission of what Turner (1967: 102), following Jane Harrison, understood as the *sacra* in traditional tribal initiations. That is, the knowledge of the sacred exhibited (i.e. significant objects), enacted (i.e. dramatic performances) and instructed (i.e. oral histories). But compared to obligatory rites in which neophytes, students and disciples participate, Liminal Village transmissions are offered in an open-ended, piecemeal and interactive context, with no one compelled to be present.

If the Liminal Village is a conscious multi-mediated interactive zone providing reflexive attention to prevailing causes, the foundation upon which it appears to have been constructed is the s/Self. Antithetical to the

Liminal Zone. Boom 2010. Photo: Rémy-Pierre RIBIERE. www.ruyphoto.net.

traditions researched by Harrison and Turner, traditions where knowledge is conferred by theocratic and other religious authorities or their mediators, what is shown, enacted and spoken within this threshold offers: (a) confirmation of the self's epistemic status as arbiter and mediator of "truth" and; (b) the possibility of a holistic and interconnected Self that can only be confirmed through immediate experience. Those who gather to observe visionary art, watch performances and films, and listen to lectures, are effectively receiving affirmation of s/Self through the transmission of revealed knowledge. But here, it is not only communicated *knowledge* that is valued, but the knowledge of *knowing*, a skill-sharing of the techniques of perception which are multitudinous and available across the festival, with the Liminal Village acting like a gateway to consciousness which is variably understood (dissolved, expanded and evolved) by diverse techniques combined in endless arrangements, with ever-newer updates to be beta-tested, all consistent with the *nomos* that the self is a project, revisable and upgradeable, and that, given the variable knowledge of knowing, individuals become interior network architects. This is hardly the elective centre of a *self-centred* cosmos, of the kind often identified with New Age practice. Constructed from organic and recycled materials and with presentations communicating the significance of geometric principles including that of the hexagonal structure of the water molecule – the underlying theme of Boom 2010 being "water" – the Liminal Village offered a concentrated source for affirming the organic place of individuals in, and not outside, or above, the natural world. It thus communicated an ecological consciousness and recognition of the holistic Self.

Boom 2010 participants were encouraged to liken themselves to individual molecules of water by way of the hexagon pervasive to the festival's design. According to the Boom newspaper, *Dharma Dragon* ("The Power of the Hexagon", 2010),

> the hexagon defines the interrelationship between spirit and water. A miracle of nature the hexagon is found in the body of water, its formation clear when exposed to positive vibrations. With the aid of the hexagon inspired structures at Boom we have endeavoured to create a potent-energy field, designed to resonate with each of us as individuals and the nature around us.

Closing the Frontiers of the Mind program, Boom's Art Director, Carey Thompson, gave a presentation "Sacred Geometry and Interconnectivity" explaining that Boom's intention, by creating various key structures according to geometrical principles – and with the hexagonal water design foremost – was "to connect us to a greater order, a greater system ... to crystalize the experience that you are having here, and uniting all the different spaces, to amplify and encourage a connection between everything". Furthermore, the recognition of human interconnectedness with the natural world through the observation of the geometrical structuring of all of nature was stated to facilitate revelation and commitment towards behavioural correction.

The Liminal Village is a conscious indication that the synergy of being in between, in-transit and interconnected is in the order of an ultimate concern for participants. Prominent scene figures embrace the space and the zeitgeist of liminality. Bill Halsey (aka Cosmosis), for instance, posted the following comment on isratrance.com following Boom 2006:

> In the context of the Boom Festival and alternative or psychedelic culture, the use of the word Liminal is to describe the point at which cultures, arts forms, individual (and group) states of consciousness overlap ... As an example: the point at which sleep and waking consciousness cross is the liminal point. The point at which these things overlap and intermesh is a richly creative state and is the area where totally new ideas and possibilities can most easily be generated and come into being, new art forms can be synthesized etc. For me, the possibility of the Liminal Village is the heart of Boom and by far the major accomplishment of the Boom festival. It really is an extraordinary cultural achievement (Cosmosis 2006).

An important node in an internal feedback mechanism, the Liminal Village offered a means through which credence may be assigned to epiphanous experience, including that within the Dance Temple. Posting on his blog about the 2006 Liminal Village, Nicolas Di Bernardo, co-founder of Argentine dark trance act Megalopsy (Megalopsy 2006), acknowledged this possibility: "it was the only place where all the crazy ideas you got dancing came to shape and really start to activate this evolution of consciousness which for me is the key to change the paradigm we are currently living in".[19]

As a live discursus on liminality, the Liminal Village provided a transparent explanation of the festival's objective as a threshold across which its habitués forge an alternate future. But the Liminal Village exists among various Boom initiatives that elicit the desire for transformation on personal, social and global scales. Boom holds an ethos of non-sponsorship and is an ecologically sustainable festival (see Chapter 9). In 2010, in addition to the use of alternative energy sources and composting toilets and showers, all of the event's major structures were built using recycled or organic materials. Among the bio-constructed areas were the food market and the Groovy Beach stage, with horned formations built from wood packing-crates forming a hexagonal-shaped dance floor where a fusion of sounds (including techno, glitch and dub step) were performed. The festival also featured a vast "chillout" area and gardens called Ambient Paradise, the main structure of which featured, at its nerve centre, a hexagonal island built on a pool of water, forming a stage where artists performed ambient music to an audience luxuriating on an acre of cushions.

As an idea born from a "harm reduction" program created by the Multidisciplinary Association of Psychedelic Studies (MAPS), KosmiCare is another important feature of Boom. Traditionally featuring a large white geodesic dome, tipi structures, and even a straw-bale womb-shaped "kiva" (in 2008), the enclave is a haven for participants experiencing difficulties on psychedelics, and a centre for the dissemination of specialist information on substances and drug testing. As volunteers and carers with varying psychotherapeutic backgrounds assist in operating a "functional mental sanctuary", KosmiCare is established under the recognition that, according to psychologist and anthropologist Ana Flávia Nascimento, "grounded exploration of altered states could foster deeper personal awareness, insight, and healing" (Nielsen and Bettencourt 2008/2009: 42). According to information provided on the KosmiCare UK Facebook page, "Entheogens make us experience a fast connectivity with the deepest parts of our psyche. Historically we used to take substances in a tribal context with the support of the tribe and a shaman ... These days we are left alone with our unpredictable emotions and the some times terrifying visions of the collective unconscious". With harm reduction as their primary duty, KosmiCare volunteers are those who effectively offer support and guidance for those journeying through the outer reaches of the *mysterium tremendum*. Citing transpersonal psychiatrist Stanislav Grof, they state: "If properly handled, a psychedelic crisis has great positive potential and can result in a profound personality transformation. Conversely, an insensitive and ignorant approach can cause psychological damage and lead to chronic psychotic states and years of psychiatric treatment and struggles".

Further around the lake, the Sacred Fire area is another zone of concentrated transition, which evolved in 2010 into a lakeside enclave with its own stage (the Zome Stage), a food and crafts market and alcoves and hinterlands with hexagonal temples dedicated to "the Sacred Feminine" and "the Sacred Masculine", along with other venues workshopping a variety of healing-arts. The area hosted an Opening Ceremony that involved a parade and the performance of a "puja" around its lakeside fire pit. Among the enablers of the Sacred Fire are those who live in an alternative community in mountains near Barcelona, along with occupants of sustainable communities in the north of Portugal. Many have experience with Rainbow Gatherings, possess skills in carpentry, decoration and gardening and sell organic foods and handicrafts in little stalls in the market. Psilly (2010) gestured to the alternative character of these market stalls and their owners:

> You don't just walk into some disinfected box
> lit by flickering fluros and make grumpy demands
> at a bored semi-human trapped behind glass –

> you approach the haunt of strange creatures
> who are utterly magical masters of their trades
> (even if that just means serving chai and cake) –
> you look around and soak up the story of what
> you're about to buy, see the mysterious wizards
> busying about their preparations but equally
> aware of you at the same time.[20]

Sacred Fire evolved from a micro greenhouse set up in the chillout area in 2000, and by 2006 a "green space" emerged with a vegetable garden and land art. When I spoke with him in 2006, "focalizer" Pedro Barros stated that those who gravitate to this area of the festival tend to prefer acoustic over electronic trance music, and indeed the former is the main fare on the Sacred Fire's stage.[21]

The Healing Area, further around the lake, was the site for sweatlodges, fire walks, The Sound Temple, meditation, yoga, breathwork, conscious nutrition, tantra and other techniques practised in the pursuit of potentiating one's self, enabling a "wholeness" of being, and facilitating an evolved consciousness. Indeed, the spirit of slogans like "think globally, act locally" or "be the change you want to see in the world"[22] was echoed in the principal message of the Healing Area: "Creating inner peace and self-love makes it possible to manifest world peace and universal love". The axiomatic theme of awakening one's own hidden potential was built into the design of one of the most intriguing artworks on site: "Keynote", a giant figure made from iron locks, with a keyhole for a face and dragging behind it a gigantic key. Installed beside the lake, the sculpture provided a powerful metaphor for Boom: enabling the search for the "key" to unlock consciousness.[23] Finally, towards the centre of the festival, the collective of poets, musicans, visual artists and jugglers known as the Amsterdam Balloon Company set up a camp and erected an Axis Mundi "totempole". The ABC emerged in 1972 and had previously erected three Axis Mundi, connecting Ruigoord (Holland), Christiana (Denmark) and

Healing Area in foreground. Boom 2010. Photo: Jakob Kolar. www.woowphoto.com.

Doel (Belgium) in a transnational network of free cultural spaces. As stated by Aja Waalwjik in the *Dharma Dragon* ("TAZ of the World" 2010: 19), the fourth Axis Mundi erected at Boom "marks the festival ground as a world centre of consciousness, of positive power and peace, establishing creative and spiritual bonds and making a statement about the global importance of alternative experimental societies and festivals". Across a network of event-areas, Boom, then, enables the building of a labyrinth of pathways on which installations, architecture and liminal-arts facilitate the dissolution, expansion and evolution of consciousness.

"Keynote" by Michael Christian. Boom 2010. Photo: Rémy-Pierre RIBIERE. www.ruyphoto.net.

Visionary arts and the dance temple

In 2010, Boom's Liminal Village was embraced on its lake-side by an art gallery called Inner Visions. Host to the work of artists whose output is highly esteemed within the psychedelic and wider conscious milieu, Inner Visions curated work by, among others, Carey Thompson, Android Jones, Amanda Sage, Xavi, Adam Scott Miller and Luke Brown, mostly American artists, some of whom painted or drew live before rapt audiences, a practice that has been conducted by Alex Grey, who presented in the Dynamic Mythologies Tent in 2002 and who is commonly regarded as the chief exponent in the field. With a background as an instructor in Artistic Anatomy and Figure Sculpture at New York University, Grey's painted visions of universal human experiences such as praying, kissing, copulating, pregnancy, birth and dying have become pervasive across the scene. He and artist wife Allyson Grey are co-founders of the Chapel of Sacred Mirrors (CoSM), a not-for-profit institution supporting visionary culture in New York which Matthew Fox, in the first edition of *CoSM: Journal of Visionary Culture* (Summer Solstice of 2004), described as a unique "opportunity for spiritual renewal by contemplation of transformative art". Like Hildegard, the twelfth-century visionary mystic, Grey proposes that "our beauty, grace and radiance comes from inside us", which is "an affront to all fear-based and guilt-based ideologies that tell us we do not have what it takes, that salvation and wholeness must always come from the outside" (Fox 2005: 6). Grey's work provides visitors to CoSM with the opportunity to effectively worship their own divine nature. Using "meridian lines, chakras, kabbalistic glyphs, and various occult body-maps from different spiritual traditions", Grey's art, according to Erik Davis, "resonates with visionary experiences, those undeniably powerful eruptions of numinous and multi-dimensional perception that suggest other orders of reality". Davis further explains visionary art:

> The claim is that the visionary artist opens up personal expression to a transpersonal dimension, a cosmic plane that uncovers the nature that lies beyond naturalism, and that reveals, not an individual imagination, but a *mundus imaginalis*. Far from being outside, this "imaginal world" lies inside. Henry Corbin, the brilliant twentieth century scholar of Sufism, coined the term *mundus imaginalis* to describe the "alam al-mithal", the visionary realm where prophetic experience takes place. In the strict sense, it is a realm of the imagination, but a true imagination that has a claim on reality because it mediates between the sensual world and the higher abstract realms of angelic or cosmic intelligences. The *mundus imaginalis* is a place of encounter and transformation (Davis 2008b).

The phrase "visionary art" usually refers to visual media, which depicts and projects the artist's multi-sensorial, mystical or theophanic encounters, and which at the same time affects the imagination of the viewer. Variously purposive, such art is usually graphic or canvas based and often reproduced on album covers, event fliers, t-shirts and in website designs, but also includes large-scale three-dimensional installations. As an example of the latter, at Boom 2006 Carey Thompson erected a spectacular gateway structure called the DiMethyl Temple.[24]

Without question, many artists are influenced by entheogenic experiences associated with herbal medicines, "spirit molecules" and "teacher plants". Thompson pointed out in his presentation in the Liminal Village that his first experiences with *psilocybin*-containing mushrooms "revealed the geometric nature of the inner mindscape", and inspired his painting "Diosa Madre Terra", which in Spanish means "Goddess Mother Earth". While the ingestion of "entheogens" is not essential to obtaining visions, personal exposure to the effects of psychoactive compounds enhances the production of visionary art and facilitates its reception. That mind alterants inspire art, culture and consciousness is no recent revelation, and as we've seen, cultural commentators like McKenna furthered interest in the entheogenesis of cultural evolution, and helped spark interest in the ostensible role of entheogens in an annual festival at the roots of Western civilization. While this is no place to wander further into speculation, we can observe that more than half a century ago, Beverley Hills psychiatrist Oscar Janiger found that LSD enabled

Inner Visions Galley. Boom 2010. Photo: Rémy-Pierre RIBIERE. www.ruyphoto.net.

Carey Thompson and the Inner Visions Gallery. Boom 2010. Photo: Rémy-Pierre RIBIERE. www.ruyphoto.net.

his clients access to their chief creative medium: the unconscious. As Jay Stevens (1989: 99–100) noted, "Janiger realized that artists had always been the natural constituency for consciousness-changing drugs ... One only had to think of Coleridge and opium, Balzac and hashish, Poe and Laudanum" (see also Dobkin de Rios and Janiger 2003). As LSD moved outside of psychotherapeutic contexts, it escaped elite circles of use and became an increasingly popular tool in the development of the aesthetics of psychedelia, with psychedelic gatherings emerging as paramount sites for the presentation and reception of this aesthetic. Indeed the psychedelic or visionary festival is an interactive interface of artistic prosumption since, as Bey wrote in relation to the TAZ, "the artist is not celebrated as a special sort of person, but every person is celebrated as a special sort of artist (Bey 1991a: 70). Thus, these events are not simply occasions for the consumption of visionary art produced by the few for the many, but for the collective participation in visionary artifice.

At Boom and other events, DJs, VJs, décor and stage designers are among an assembly of artists whose role it is to alter perception among participants within the event, both on and off the dance floor. Identifying as a VJ and shaman, Omananda writes about the process.

> I get the best visuals when tripping. Yes, I am very much inspired by the psychedelic experience that is the primary reason why I

> create psychedelic light shows, to express what I have seen on the inside as well as to facilitate it for others ... Through astral traveling, I find it entirely possible to communicate with beings from other dimensions. They can teach us universal wisdom.

And in his work, he further comments,

> I let the light shine brightly, in many colors and geometric shapes that emerge from the spectral light of creation ... After months and years of being hooked to screens, I blend visual feeds on Edirol Mixers with live programs to get the desired result. This feels like a constant uplifting into an unknown territory ... There is balance between being a binary computer-geek and a natural shaman (Omananda 2006: 44).

On the dance floor, visual art, including video projections but also fluoro and "string kaleidoscope" art, is designed to work in conjunction with music to affect altered states of mind and body. The multi-mediated assemblage and interactivity of the dance floor illustrates that any sensory media can be recognized as "visionary" art; and that any art, including music, that has been inspired by transpersonal experience, and which in turn incites the imagination, should be considered under the same rubric. This seems obvious when contemplating the likes of Eat Static or Shpongle, whose sonic artifacts are produced though transcendent journeys in the *mundus imaginalis* and are performed to induce or accompany such journeys. Indeed, at Australia's Rainbow Serpent Festival in 2011, Shpongle performed in concert with the Greys painting live (with perhaps 10,000 people watching), and in 2009 I saw the Greys perform brush strokes on stage with Posford performing as Shpongle at California's Symbiosis Festival, a veritable symbiosis of sonic and visual art taking place in a forest of giant *Sequoia* trees at Camp Mather adjacent Yosemite National Park. It was the main attraction for that event's 6,000 participants, giving expression to their interests in the nexus of media by which the revelations are transmitted.

But this is no society of the spectacle, since DJs and fusion bands, along with numerous sound and lighting technicians, affect ecstatic/erotic states in individuals whose own envisioned states in danced-entrancement become sensuous spectacles for co-liminars. Here, the dancer is an artist, and thus a performer, via an organic ecology of gestures responsive to the assemblage of sound and visual art, and other dancers. Trance-dance floor occupants are thus visionary artists in the sense that their rhythmic movements and gestures offer involuntary interpretations of transcendent music (in its writing/production and performance), and their *embodiment of sound* inspires others present, with such responses rippling across the dance floor like waves of energy. As Kynan Bolger reflected on his experience in the Australian outdoor party scene at the front of the dance floor where "the serious dancers congregate": the "sisters tended to own the front of the floor", males were enacting "displays of power dancing *without* being competitive or threatening", and everyone was "dancing like everyone is watching".[25] Dancers draw lines like the brush strokes of expressive painters, or the free-style writing and cut-ups of the beats, although stalwarts argue that styles like that seen in Goa during the 1980s and early 1990s where there was no "front of the floor" as such, and dancers wove around one another in dynamic fashion, have now faded like the sunlight that once blazed across the back of your retinas.

The accomplishment of stage designers, sound and lighting technicians, visual artists, riggers and a multitude of performers – including the dance floor habitués themselves – the Dance Temple is an extraordinary plateau of visionary experience and expression. Amounting to one of the world's largest outdoor dance floors, it is to the body of the festival what the Liminal Village is to its head. In 2010, the Dance Temple was designed by François Baudson in collaboration with Californian construction team Bamboo DNA, along with a host of artists including Android Jones and Harlan Emil Gruber, many operating according to principles of sacred geometry. Implicit to the Temple design, in screens used for visual projections, and on a stage featuring a stellated dodecahedron DJ portal positioned amid star tetrahedrons, the hexagon complied with the axiomatic water theme, becoming, according to Thompson, a "way of amplifying the energy of the music and creating a resonance between the music, the people, nature, and the universe". Revered by the thousands who have visited it on each of its editions, the Temple is the power-source of the festival, as is apparent in the language used to describe it: "portal", "mothership", "activation" site. In 2010, over one hundred acts (mostly DJs) performed a variety of styles – including "progressive psychedelic", "tech-house", "full on" and "darkpsy" – on a high-performance sound system. The Temple operated for seven days, with the music shutting down for two hours in the late afternoon of each day for waste clearing and sound and equipment checks.

This book's epigraph left off at that moment, in the wake of the fury of the night, when the Sun cleared the horizon. It is a Goatrance legacy that the light of dawn and the rising of the Sun signifies self-awakening, a rebirth from states of isolation and separation. This cosmic threshold holds significance for the occupants of the Dance Temple, as glass-blown chillums are packed and passed around, and the aromatics of *charas* and *changa* prevail. The Sun's rising coincides with uplifting melodies as Temple-goers are coming up to greet the day and their fellow passengers, who, having transited from the darkness, are now all lit up across the dance floor. The night holds its own influence on those who conspire in it, especially if the moon is full, but it is the Sun's rising that constitutes a peak threshold. Ray Castle has expressed

Dance Temple. Boom 2008. Photo: Pascal Querner.

his views on the way this cosmic drama provides a backdrop for the psytrance event.

> There are ebbs and flows, and peak climaxes, which eventually culminates with the light arriving and the journey goes into a religious kind of ecstasy in the soft glow of dawn. The faces of the dancers start to emerge like photographic paper in a darkroom. Dancing thru the night is more of an inner journey but still feeling the psychic aura of those around you, who are locked into the same wavelength, syncopated rhythms. In the morning, there is a sense of oneness and unity, being together on the dancefloor. A feeling of inseparable timelessness. A kind of ancient rite of passage back to the source with the first sun rise. As the blooming rays of dawn hit your body there is a resurgence of energy and a renewed flight occurs. This is augmented by ascending, angelic-like, reverential, morning music, as opposed to the more deeper, chaotic, hektec-night-atmospheres, in the music (in Rich and Dawn 1997).

At this juncture, like a cosmic stage drama, at the close of darkness, there comes illumination. Those caught within conditions producers articulate sometimes using samples invocating Advaita philosophy or Bhakti devotionalism and other times NASA launch sequences or voice samples from *2001: A Space Odyssey*, or perhaps wisdom by way of Joseph Campbell or Carl Sagan, or the sounds of sexual union, are approximate to liminars whose boundaries are felt to be "coterminous with those of the human species" (Turner 1969: 131). While the festival is a context for competing discourse, squabbles over "psychedelic" music, and inter-cultic disputation posing a challenge to a totalizing communitas, this is the zone where *differences* are generally set aside and *difference* embraced, if only within the prolonged moment. As one wheels about to absorb the colour, fragrance and taste of co-travellers and beatific mystics among the multitudes reveling bare-skinned, body-pierced and tattooed under a vast misting system that liquefies all under a "flow" resonating with sound frequencies, and in a "vibe" that appears to expand as jubilant reinforcements continue to arrive, it's difficult to believe otherwise. And it is so since this is an experience in which sensorial inputs are synthesized as a result of optimized techniques, feedback loops and the skilful deployment of personal resources. In this synesthesia, where after days of dancing and carousing, sound may be perceived by senses other than the aural, including the optical, visual stimuli is thus recognized as "music". Indeed, in a space where bass is intended to be felt and melodies wash over dancers like shore-bound waves, the boundaries that separate people from each other and from the world are subject to liquidation. The perception of an "organic" relatedness with the natural world is stamped upon Temple-dancers in the same moments as they stamp their feet into the therapeutically rounded shale that forms the surface of the dance floor, where the intercorporeality performed in dance within a hexagonal structure built from recycled and organic materials, reinforces a sensibility of interconnectedness.

The entire multi-mediated tapestry enables Temple occupants access to Corbin's *mundus imaginalis*, Otto's *mysterium tremendum*, or Huxley's "Mind at Large". And just as the experience within the Telesterion at Eleusis received little textual dissemination by its many thousands of initiates over the two millennia of its operation, the experience in the Dance Temple appears to have received scant eloquent transcription. While for most participants it is enough to flash a smile or invoke language that offers parsimonious enunciation of the special vibe experienced (i.e. "Boom"), some spokespersons offer incisive detail on their journeys inside the Temple. Within the giant geodesic dome that was the Temple in 2002, after ingesting "2 grams of Hawaiian mushrooms", Omananda reported that he "spent hours in the center of the double Fibonacci spiral that François created with the artists who painted the fabulous decorations that looked like an Alex Grey painting with Limurian inscriptions". Soon enough, "space started bending and this wind came to spiral the entire party off into another dimension. A time/space portal opened up to put me into this futuristic dream, where we were all part of this PERFECT world". And then, "in the future-vision that I experienced ... everybody realized their full potential and lived it too. We were all coming to each other saying: 'Have you heard the news yet? We are totally free!'" The barrier between dreaming and waking has been raised, and Omananda continued:

> I was in a huge geodesic dome, which I interpreted then to be a metaphor for us to be part of the flower of life and thus, creation itself. As I was journeying through this vision, one triangle after another of the magnificent dome-space in which this incredible experience took place filled up with another Boomer who became fully realized. The music during those timeless moments was completely perfect, quite unbelievable indeed. I woke up on the other side of the party, pissing into my pants, when I realized that I had come back to my physical shell. I did not really remember what had happened to me out there, only that it was immensely good! (Omananda 2004).

By 2010, virtual platforms like blogging and Facebook had become vehicles through which visions and epiphanies were being diarized, logged and exchanged among social networks of the noetically experienced. While I cannot of course claim to have scanned all evidence of Boom accounts online, the following words penned by the *changa* smoking Psilly (2010) post-Boom 2010, are among the most ebullient:

> In comes the incense – dry like hot air but softer –
> I hold it in my lungs and it starts to blossom ...
> I perceive everything with absolute detail, down
> to the quivering possibilities of entire universes
> in the atomic fractaline edges of this shifting tesseract
> vibrating intensively and pushing the consciousness from me
> until it is everywhere and I am with it ...
> It's dark now, the moon is sailing from the hills behind us
> out over the lake, hovering above the huge growling UFO
> of the dance temple, multi-layered melodies climaxing
> and dropping into wugachook-wugachook-wugachook,
> people running in wild orbits around the edges,
> luminous sticks being swirled by psychedelic sylphs,
> animated fractal universes projected onto hexagon screens
> evoking the hive, the perfect tough utility of the stacks
> of funktion-one, the body of sound marching from them,
> the solid waves rotating through the crowd, the entrained
> entertaining each other, a multi-dimensional interaction,
> one high-vibration family feedback-looping love,
> becoming more coherent, more aware, locking on
> to the geometry, both environmental and inherent:
> the DJ booth housed in a star tetrahedron
> surrounded by hexagons creating pentagrams
> in the mandalic nexus of my third eye,

the overlay of biological hardware
projected onto an outer reality
it is already integral with,
the animating spirit
dancing in the spaces between
– of which there are none –
a synergy, greater than the sum
of its parts. A weaving.[26]

There is no unifying mythic system by which Dance Temple participants are able to interpret their visions or translate their alternative states of consciousness. In the antinomian style advocated by McKenna, the Temple facilitates a multitude of private encounters with the numinous, multiple states of liminality multiplied further as one ventures out from the nadir of *ekstasis* into the wider grounds of the festival, and further still as one treks through the vast mycelium of global psytrance and visionary arts culture. In the optimized event that is Boom, the "filters" that Huxley pondered more than fifty years ago are heavily-albeit-variably modulated. There are no hierophants here, just as there are no singular techniques of ecstasy. But if there was a *sacerrima* – by which Turner meant among the "most sacred things" (1967: 107) – at Boom 2010, it was the pervasive hexagonal symbol of the water molecule, which, like the Eleusinian ear of wheat, signifies the indivisible status of "individuals" within organic life.

Cosmic event consciousness

Ray Castle earlier articulated that moment, or succession of moments, that inspires the embodied poetics of trance dancers as faces lift and hands reach to absorb the morning light following the night of shadows. The view typical among veterans like astrologer Castle, among other orchestrators of the

Dance Temple DJ Booth. Boom 2010. Photo: Jakob Kolar. www.woowphoto.com.

cosmic experience, is that while exposure to punishing sound at a furious pace throughout the night may facilitate a demolition of the bounded self – a dispossession by sound – the arrival of the Sun delivers the traveller onto a new plateau. For these technoccultists, the light of dawn and the rising of the Sun signifies the awakening of a self reborn from states of fear and separation, amplified by the cosmic or visionary trance music that was generated at the birth of Goatrance and that arguably constituted its greatest moments: notably the work of The Infinity Project, Astral Projection, Electric Universe, Hallucinogen, Plaeidians, Cosmosis, Total Eclipse, Etnica, and many others.

Of course, among celestial events, the full-moon has exerted strong appeal within the psychedelic counterculture. In popular and folk theories, the "fullness" of the moon is recognized to excite crazed conditions, and is a phase ruled by "lunacy". Gatherings marking this transitional period in the synodic month and other celestial occurrences are commonly celebrated by the performance of ecstatic dance in which participants become unrecognizable to themselves, in which one's rational consciousness may become eclipsed. This is an outcome typical to many dance music events regardless of their cosmic significance, and in fact it might be argued that a total eclipse of the mind is integral to their "cosmic" significance – a circumstance made possible in "wild" nature, the location of many dance gatherings. From a lakeside in central eastern Portugal to Scandinavian "forest parties" and "bush doofs" in Australia, and from panoramic mountain festivals in Switzerland or Nepal to desert gatherings in California's Mojave, remote natural settings have been sought by city-dwelling cosmopolitans and suburban habitués as primary sites for an ecstatic experience commonly felt to be unobtainable inside closed spaces (clubs) within city precincts where tall buildings, smog and lights obstruct clear views of the night sky.

In his recollections of the morning Sun at Goa parties, and evoking Joseph Campbell, Castle stated that "the birth of light is timeless, archetypal, eternal. So it really conjures up mystical experiences, and deep primordial memories, and when you share that with a group of people, boundaries dissolve", which, he averred, is not possible at a typical rock concert.[27] This is the core element of the "global trance ritual" identified by Larkin (2003: 32) who recognizes, that "as the dancers move from darkness into light, there is an unspoken cry of 'we made it!!'" While dark trance evolved its own aesthetics of revelation and redemption, light lifting from the morning horizon is an archetypical theme for the trance dance and visionary arts milieu, signifying an illumination. Indeed the celestial source of light is significant in the Tibetan bardo model, the transit between death and rebirth, as outlined in the *Tibetan Book of Living and Dying* (1992) where the dissolution of self into absolute truth, *dharmata*, is explained via the analogy of the night turning to day. As the book's author, Sogyal Rinpoche, explains, "Now gradually the sun of dharmata begins to rise in all its splendor, illuminating the contours of the land in all its directions. The natural radiance of Rigpa manifests spontaneously and blazes out as energy and light". Another Tibetan Buddhist source, the *Bardo Thodol* (also known as the *Tibetan Book of the Dead*), which inspired Leary and colleagues (Leary *et al.* 1964) to write a manual for conducting psychedelic induced ego-death and rebirth, was effectively programmed into Goatrance via short bursts from Leary, such as heard on the title track to *Cosmic Trancer* (1995), where Castle and Masayuki Kurihara (aka Masaray) dissect Leary demurring on the experience of "energy", "light" and "sound" within the body. Indeed, one of the first releases inspired by seasons in Goa, Electrotete's *Anjuna Dawn* (1991), conveys this solar optimism, with Electric Universe capturing the sound of the Sun at the dawn of Goa with his debut "Solar Energy" (*Solar Energy*, 1994). The Psy-Harmonics compilation, *Psy-Harmonics Vol. 2: Dancing to the Sound of the Sun* (1995) offers further evidence of the solar reverence, as does Doof's *Let's Turn On* (1996), a consummate upbeat release – with the tunes "Sunshrine" and "Secret Sun (Sunbeam mix)" bathing poets of the floor in waves of electronic sunshine.

These tracks are efforts to capture the transformative impact of the rising Sun celebrated in peak states at locations removed from domestic conditions. On these open planned dance floors on warm beaches or near mountain villages like Manali, high adventure, physical manoeuvrability and sound propagation were factors in the emergence of "two step" trance dance. I am reminded of the epic emergence of the Sun on a remote mountain presaging transformation at the close of Herman Hesse's 1943 magnum opus, *The Glass Bead Game*. The Magister Ludi watches the young Tito

> filled with the solemn beauty of the moment and the glorious sensation of his youth and strength, stretched his limbs with rhythmic arm movements, which his whole body soon took up, celebrating the break of day in an enthusiastic dance and expressing his deep oneness with the surging, radiant elements. His steps flew in joyous homage toward the victorious sun and reverently retreated from it, his outspread arms embracing mountain, lake and sky (Hesse 2000: 399).

The reference to Hesse is by no means random, since young adults trekking India from the 1960s onwards were familiarizing themselves with yogis, yoga, maya and other ideas via his works. But this passage, among the final words in Hesse's final book, are of particular interest since they connote sacrifice. Again, in reference to Tito, who effectively plays the role of disciple to the renounced Magister:

> the boy himself was in the grip of an impulse, without knowing what was happening to him. He was not performing a dance he

> already knew, a dance he had practiced before. This was no familiar rite of celebrating sun and morning that he had long ago invented ... He offered himself, his youth, his freedom, his burning sense of his own life, like a festive sacrifice to the powers (Hesse 2000: 400, 399).

The interpenetrating themes of cosmic rebirth, individuation and cultural revolution are revisited time and again in psychedelic trance, apparently as repetitious and fresh as the newly cycled Sun. By no means a solar cult resembling Amaterasu-O-Mi-Kami in Japanese Shinto, or any of the historical Sun-worshipping traditions as found among the ancient Egyptians or the Vedic Indians, the popular greeting of the Sun at daybreak following all-night dance parties suggests, ponders Michael York, "the possibility of a convergence between traditional religious practice and spontaneous sun-worship developments in the Western world" (York 2005: 1607). With the popularity of books like Gregory Sams' *Sun of gOd* (2009) within the psytrance movement, and since many "doofs", forest parties and trance festivals do indeed mark the solstices and equinoxes, the possibility cannot be easily discarded. And while the display of reverence for the dawning Sun may signify pagan heritage, since the rising solar orb also dramatizes the "dawning" of a new era, the emergence of a new consciousness, it is recruited into evolutionary paradigms.

Another performance in which the Sun plays a leading role – the total solar eclipse – shows how psychedelic trance is implicated in a conscious planetary movement. At the end of the previous chapter, it was suggested that visionary arts culture may have been inaugurated with the Harmonic Convergence of 1987. Here I suggest that events marking and celebrating a total solar eclipse represent the continuity of the quest for self-alignment and planetary consciousness occasioned by that event – with psychedelic trance oiling the mechanics of ascension, a music which itself narrates this development. In a sample on his ambient work "World Travelling Eclipse Chasers" (*Shameful Silence*, 2007), as Wombatmusic, Kristian Thinning Andersen – founder of the prolific Goatrance act Elysium – makes the point: "total eclipses of the Sun are breath-taking. Many people who feel the cool sweep of the moon shadow for the first time go on to become world travelling eclipse chasers". The final words are repeated over and over as drums call in the distance. What Thinning Anderson doesn't convey is that dance music gatherings have appeared on the path of the eclipse since the mid-1990s curated by the sounds and infused with the visual aesthetics of the psychedelic movement. To magnify the rapture, these gatherings are staged on the relatively narrow band – up to 250 km wide – of the path of the moon's umbra in locations around the planet.[28] At the alternative edge of an "eclipse" industry, thousands of pilgrim-like travellers, or "eclipse chasers", camp in close quarters in remote events, arriving from a multitude of countries to seek the perfect alignment of Earth, moon and Sun with their own (ecstatic) bodies. Commonly known as "totality", this circumstance is measured in precise clock-time, but is an experience commonly felt to be immeasurable. With the mystical states of consciousness associated with this natural (geological), cosmic (astronomical) and social (festival) experience, the eclipse has become a phenomenon adapted to the cause of a progressive planetary millenarianism (see St John 2012b).

Symptomatic of the conflation of religion and leisure, the mystical experience and the vacation, the eclipse gathering is host to a cross-section of pilgrimage and traveller-tourism behaviour, not unlike Boom and other major visionary arts events. Jet setters, backpackers and those travelling in self-owned motorhomes and refurbished buses arrive at the setting for the metamorphosis and apocalypse of subjectivity. Eclipse chasers are among a population of technopagans and esotericists, amateur astronomers and party monsters, whose commitments to travel to the path of totality represents a unique contemporary pilgrimage experience. The umbric centres to which these travellers migrate are temporary and irregular. But while their sacrality is evanescent, they are no less sacred to gravitating "umbraphiles" than are the shrines, temples, stone circles and other sites sacred to members of religious communities whose believers migrate toward the divine source of their faith. For, even though the "center out there" (see Turner 1973) is a fleeting cosmic synchronicity witnessed in different geo-locations on each incidence, the eclipse becomes itself a sacred centre.[29]

The first "eclipse rave" was held near the coastal city of Arica at the edge of the Atacama, Chile, on 2/3 November 1994. The pioneering event was organized chiefly through a Chilean–German partnership and was held in the immediate years of transition from Pinochet's regime. With no more than 300 people gathering, the occasion featured Derrick May, John Aquaviva, and for the first time in his homeland, Ricardo Villalobos. But it was also a convergence of Goa freaks, Japanese techno-hipsters and Osho sannyasins, among others. Buoyed by its bohemian eclecticism, the event was held in the year Goatrance made its appearance on the global stage, and one can imagine, for example, Black Sun's majestic "Sourcerors Apprentice" (*Order Odonata Vol. 1*, 1994) – which repeats the lines, "I've never seen anything like it" – backing the ascension, or Electric Universe's enchanting "Cosmic Symphony" (from debut EP *Solar Energy*, 1994) animating the union of the primary spheres at this time. Over the subsequent fifteen years, eclipse events evolved in time with psychedelic music.

Historically, eclipses of the Sun, whether total or partial, have been received with varying responses. A sign of hope or a cause for alarm, they have been interpreted according to the cosmological hermeneutics of those through whose domain the umbra has passed. Given that these unpredicted events have arrived unheralded in most regions for most of history, the reception has been less than positive. Though scientists have demonstrated great interest in eclipses since the 1700s, we can trace the history of "eclipse chasing" to 1836 when solar physicist Francis Bailey generated popular interest in solar physics (see Littmann, Espenak and Willcox 2008). From the mid nineteenth century, populations are known to have travelled from locations outside the line of totality to observe the spectacle, with multinational scientific expeditions mounted over the next century. In a discussion of one of the earliest cases of eclipse tourism, historian of alternative Albion, Andy Worthington (2004: 20), documents "the biggest ever recorded movement of people by train in one day in the UK" when, on 29 June 1927, three million people travelled to northwest England and Wales to observe a total solar eclipse (which was occluded by clouds). Worthington suggests that the rambling movement of the late nineteenth century, itself influenced by the desire for direct contact with nature expressed by the Romantic poets, partly explains this massive migration. Eclipse chasing eventually grew into a recreational pursuit via the work of the Pedas-Sigler family of educators – including astronomer and founding member of the International Planetarium Society, Ted Pedas – who, from the early 1970s, initiated eclipse tourism on cruise ships. Their first eclipse cruise was the 1972 "Voyage to Darkness" off the north Atlantic coast of Canada. These entrepreneurs had attempted to stage a rock festival ("Eclipse '70" in March 1970) in the path of the moon's umbra in a tiny fishing village in Suffolk, Virginia, called Eclipse.[30] However, fearful of a Woodstock-like "freak out" in their backyard, the proposed event was condemned by the townsfolk.

While the 100-mile-wide shadow has drawn multitudes into its path since the early 1970s, it would not be until the mid-1990s that the eclipse – with the aid of cheaper travel, digitalization and the internet – was drawn into the orbit of an alternative culture. By the late 1990s, a cavalcade of spiritualists, astrologers and freaks converged in spatio-temporal contexts planned according to the alignment of celestial spheres at sites anticipated as optimum observation points on the path of totality. In this period, a whole new social event came into being as a highly specialized traveller phenomenon. The eclipse festival would become a recurrent-albeit-irregular vehicle for an emerging visionary arts community. Subsequent to the "eclipse rave" in Chile, solar seekers travelled to events mounted in Siberia/Mongolia, South Asia and Venezuela, where over 500 people trekked to "Total Eclipse 98", held on the Peninsula de Paraguana at the northern tip of the country. The party featured the likes of Doof, Sid Shanti, Mark Allen, Max Lanfranconi from Etnica and Pan. In *Dream Creation*, Jason C (1998: 30) reported being "lapped by the Caribbean Sea, cocooned in a sand-dune, surrounded by smiling technicolour people". "Nothing can prepare you", he reflected, "for the moment of totality. A wall of darkness races towards you, sudden dusk. And then ... You can see the cosmos like you've never seen it before, the Sun's corona illuminating the Earth in a 360 degree sunset". In 1999, the momentous Solipse Festival transpired near the village of Ozora, Hungary, reportedly attracting 15,000 people and has been the subsequent site of annual festivals. Another Solipse Festival was held in Zambia over ten days in June 2001. This was the first of the larger-scale remote operations. Organizers trucked in a sound system 3,500km to a remote region of the African bush, and as production manager Nick Ladd informed me, introduced electricity to the local town, dug bore holes for water, and catered for 4,000 people.[31] In early December the following year, simultaneous festivals were held on the path of totality in South Africa (South Africa 2002 organized by Vortex, Alien Safari and Etnicanet on the border of Kruger National Park) and in the desert near Lindhurst, South Australia. The latter event, Outback Eclipse (Exotic Native), was my first eclipse festival, and although I had known various music, dance and alternative arts festivals in Australia by that time, including events mounted in that desert region, little could have prepared me for the cosmic symphony ahead. In the late afternoon of the fourth day, wearing my special "eclipse glasses", I stood on a long elevated earth platform with thousands of others facing west, the direction of the setting Sun, to observe a drama emblazoned across the heavens. It was as if the twin discs of the moon and the Sun were seamlessly mixed by a cosmic DJ, and that I and my companions back on Earth were standing in the divine sweet spot.[32] Near the end of March three and a half years later, having rendezvoused with friends in Istanbul – where the travellers of the 1960s/1970s, and many others before them, stepped off onto the trail east – we drove overnight south to the Mediterranean city of Antalya, last stop before Soulclipse, billed as a "Universal Trance Gathering". Attended by 7–8,000 people, Soulclipse was held 27 March–2 April 2006 in Paradise Canyon on the fast flowing Koprulu Canyon River. The guide issued to festival-goers stated the collective mission of organizers, Indigo Kids:

> To unite the tribe in Turkey for this festive occasion. This goal comes out of love, harmony with nature, and understanding towards each other's differences and similarities as human beings. The trance festivals have always been where we have found our greatest opportunities to learn to grow, to celebrate, to be one with our fellow being and our Mother Earth, to serve, to pray, to play.

At mid-afternoon on the day of the main event, all present became engulfed by the dome of shadow as the Sun was occulted and Venus burned high in the mid-afternoon sky. It was a three-minute cosmic snapshot whose dark flash left an imprint on the multitude of naked retinas belonging to the howling and genuflecting massive. Smaller and more exclusive events were mounted over the remainder of the decade in the mountains of Khan Altay, Siberia, Russia (Planet Art Festival, July/Aug 2008), on Amami Island, Japan (2009) and the path of totality crossing the Southern Pacific (Honu Eclipse Festival, Easter Island, and the Black Pearl Eclipse Adventure, Cook Islands, July 2010).[33]

The total solar eclipse has inspired a great many artists in the psychedelic trance diaspora, obvious among them being French act Total Eclipse. While one of their first tracks – the amateurish yet enthusiastic new beat styled "Total Eclipse" which was released on the classic *Project II Trance* (1993) – battered listeners with the object of reverence by several times repeating the spoken sample, "eclipse", and finally, "total eclipse", the act later provided the soundtrack to singularity on "Space Clinic" (*Violent Relaxation*, 1996), a divine departure from standard consciousness. In 1998, Shpongle produced their ethnodelic "... And the Day Turned to Night" – the closing 20-minute epic on debut album *Are You Shpongled?* – inspired by an eclipse seen in Rajistan in 1995. Also in 1998, Posford's Twisted Records released the compilation *Eclipse – A Journey of Permanence & Impermanence*, in advance of the "Total Eclipse 98" in Venezuela. The album included a few Goa and ethnodelic anthems such as that produced by Nomads of Dub (Simon Posford and Nick Barber) whose revelation in deep space, "Spirals", sampled a radio communiqué from a remote observer reporting "vivid colours, different colours, glittering colours ... colours that are really indescribable". The same album featured Doof's "Balashwaar Baksheesh" which he is almost certain to have performed at the Venezualan eclipse party. The track sonifies the unheralded awe associated with something akin to a collective birth. A woman announces that "I've never ever seen anything like it before in my life, the energy that everybody felt, they were grabbing onto something for the first time ... It was amazing, the happiness that everyone felt". Pleiadians' epic "Modulation" (*Family of Light*, 1999) was also produced for performance during the eclipse in Venezuela. But the style of music that has been performed at these events is as diverse as that which is accommodated within the shifting soundscapes of psychedelia. In 1999, Flying Rhino released the dub and downtempo influenced album *Caribbean Eclipse* inspired by the eclipse passing over Colombia, Venezuela and the Caribbean Sea on 26 February 1998. The album gathered some of the foremost artists in the scene, including Posford, George Barker and Jewel Stanbridge (vocals), who as Binah, produced the momentous "Crescent Suns". Like an audio postcard for the eclipse, the back of the CD holds the question: "Where will you be standing for the next solar eclipse of the sun?" Ten years later, the compilation released by Rockdenashi Productionz, *Black Sun – Eclipse in Japan*, for the July 2009 eclipse on Amami Island, featured local darkpsy artists who, according to the liner notes, expressed their "understanding of the world in creative darkness".

Total mystery cult

Transporting himself into the path of the umbra in the company of 5,000 mostly Japanese on tropical Myojinzaki beach for the Amami Island Festival in July 2010, some twenty years after he first set foot in Goa, Ray Castle positioned the

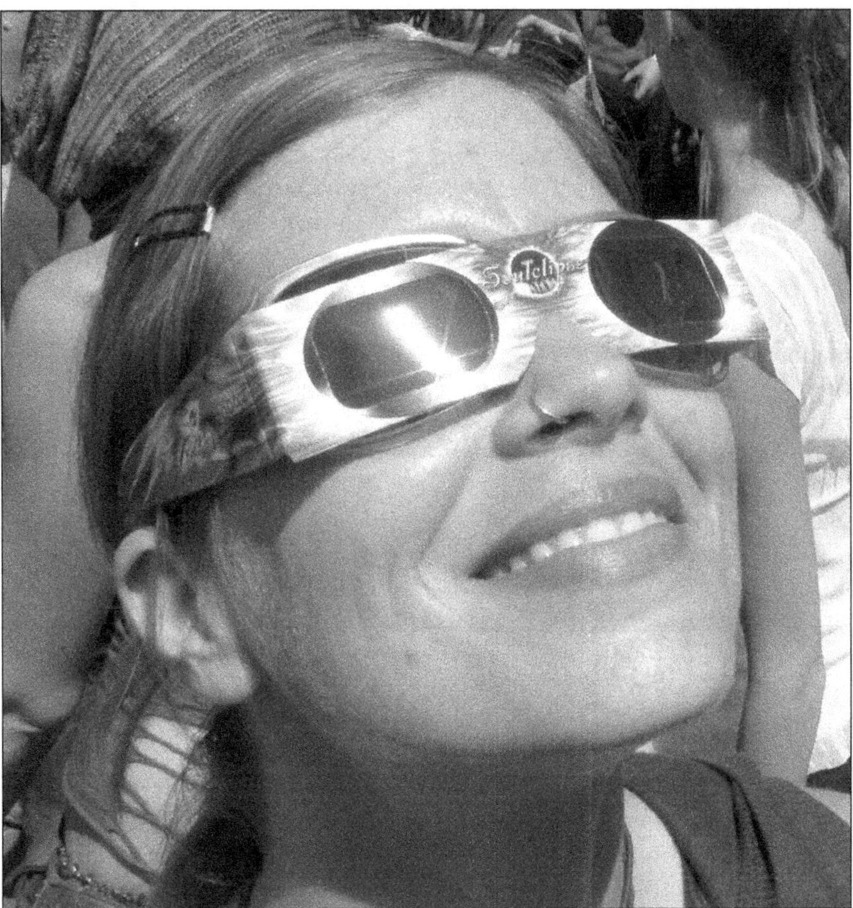

Soulclipse, Turkey, 2006. Photo: Pascal Querner.

festival downstream from the Goa sensibility. "It followed on from the sunrise and cosmic cycles", he stated, "and being sensitive to a universal metaphysical bigger picture in our role on the planet".

> It comes down to people wanting peak experience. They want to feel a cosmic rush. The intensity of eclipses and gathering together is like a collective meltdown. It's a very moving phenomenon, and sharing that with others, I felt I was like in a womb, with 5,000 people gathered; with 3,500 on the beach. And with all the screams and the emotion. It was very animal, very primordial. Deeply moving. I can see why eclipse fanatics travel all around the world to align themselves with these events. On a deeper level, I think they're quite heavy experiences, eclipses, it's not easy-going stuff. They really effect your emotions.[34]

Castle offers a description of an exceptional experience, one that is numinous and primal, with the "womb" analogy evoking a birthing theme. Other spokespersons emphasize the transformative impact of an experience perceived as a shamanic ritual. Fresh from the 2006 Soulclipse Festival in Turkey, event production manager and founder of the UK's Glade Festival, Nick Ladd, observed that "throughout shamanic history" a total eclipse is "thought of as a spiritual time, a powerful time, and transformational time, when light turns to dark and then returns to light". Recognizing the eclipse as a time for "focused meditation", and an opportunity to "achieve a transitional shift in one's life", he added that "I'm certainly no shaman, but I've felt the transformational power of the total eclipses. Whenever I've exposed myself to one there's always been a shift in my life, a fairly major one".[35] At Soulclipse, I had found myself among dedicated "chasers" of this experience, people like Marty, a school teacher from South Australia and a self-identified Animist who I spoke with a couple of days after the eclipse. Marty's first totality was at Outback Eclipse in South Australia in early December 2002 – a life-changing experience, when the music stopped for two hours before and two hours after the eclipse. "I gas up on the interplanetary notion of the eclipse", he told me. "It moves me in ways very difficult to explain, except to say that it puts me in a good mood for ten months following". Especially important, he indicated, are the days leading into and directly after an eclipse. While he regarded the cosmic event as a draining experience, "there's something about the world and the universe starting afresh following an eclipse". It's a point he persisted with, that the daytime umbrafication "wipes out a whole lot of neural networks in a very positive fashion". Reflecting on the experience during which he stated he had not been under the influence of any substances: "the quality of light on the eyes, the ability to see in a completely different way, resets me neurologically ... During a total eclipse, all light is bent, it has a curvature to it, and that curvature is very unique in human visual experience ... The conversion of light to brain data, where light transits into mind and consciousness, is what grooves me in an eclipse".[36]

Marty gave expression to the way this experience is commonly reported to have a transformative impact on the self. Indeed, the transition of the moon across the face of the Sun and the subsequent renewal of the latter is recognized to effect a corresponding influence on the self; an understanding holding in a climate where the "immediacy of personal experience ... is understood as epistemologically crucial" (Partridge 1999: 86). In Miahuatlán, Oaxaca, Mexico, in 1970, later maven of integrative medicine Andrew Weil had explained why the eclipse event seems to place those who enter its path in a "natural high". Weil had observed his first total solar eclipse in Miahuatlán: "With great drama, a nebulous darkness grew out of the west – the edge of the umbra, or cone of shadow, whose swift passage over the globe traces the path of the total eclipse". The unearthly light endured for over three minutes, a temporality expanding into a prolonged present. Weil explained that there was "a quality to those minutes within the umbra that must be like the feeling in the eye of a hurricane. After all the dramatic changes of accelerating intensity, everything stopped: There was an improbable sense of peace and equilibrium. Time did not flow". Indeed, it was three-and-a-half minutes of clock-time incomparable to any duration he'd previously known. He was transfigured. "Then, all at once, a spot of blinding yellow light appeared, the corona vanished in the glare, shadow bands raced across the landscape once more, and the dome of shadow melted away to the east" (1980: 222, 223). Weil went on to conjecture that the transfigurement that was affected in himself and others by the eclipse was the result of one's exquisite alignment with this comic synchronicity. According to Weil, "to participate in that moment of uncanny equilibrium is to have one's faith strengthened in the possibility of equilibrium and to experience the paradox that balance and stillness are to be found at the heart of all change". Furthermore, the alchemical union of the Sun and the moon is recurrent in philosophies and myths worldwide, which are "symbolic of the union of conscious and unconscious forces within the human psyche that must take place if one is to become whole" (1980: 232). Typically accessed via meditation, drugs, hypnosis, trance and other techniques, those hidden realms of consciousness occulted to us in our daily lives are said to be perfectly represented by the corona of the Sun in union with the moon, a kind of cosmic mandala which is also recognized as a union of masculine and feminine energies. Thus, according to this interpretation, a total solar eclipse signifies an alchemical exchange of solar and lunar phases of consciousness, with totality contextualizing something of a peak psychocultural experience.

Regardless of the validity of these comments, there exists a mystical ambiance to these events, which, following the logic internal to mysteries, is known only to those who are directly exposed. Being inside the umbra, where the demarcation from the routine is amplified by the liminal time-space of the festival, is like being bathed in the strange twilight of a reverse full-moon, the Earth's only orbiting natural satellite framed perfectly in those moments of totality by the Sun's corona, which most observers recognize is a miraculous cosmic circumstance, given its astonishingly improbable occurrence.[37] If the full-moon's periodic illumination of unconscious energies fires crazed states and charges events in which people may become temporary "lunatics" and animal-like ravers, the fullness of the Sun-moon during an eclipse magnifies the experience of numinosity, transformation and synchronicity identified by Castle, Ladd, Marty and Weil. The cosmic drama occasions something of a passage rite for participants, as those who travel to liminalized events mounted within its path will undertake pre-eclipse preparations (which will have begun weeks, months or years previous), enter the superliminality of totality, and, in their post-eclipse life, will debrief and share interpretations among their fellow travellers, a process which will continue on their return sojourns, and among their friends and families thereafter.

As one approaches the liminal phase of totality there is an undeniable atmosphere of excitement, smiles, upward gazes and expressions of relief, if the weather conditions are clear. These irruptions of anticipation are accompanied by the wearing of special "eclipse glasses" that are issued to festival-goers and which are essential for viewing the eclipse as well as preventing damage to one's Sun-gazing eyes. At this juncture, amplified sound is typically turned off, dancing ceases and a reverential attitude takes hold. As the moon begins its journey across the face of the Sun, at what is known as "first contact", a kind of lycanthropic howling among witnesses is typical. It takes about an hour or so for the Sun to become completely lost to the moon, but in this period, that one has entered a duration in which time itself has been eclipsed is unmistakable as shadow bands race across the surface of the Earth, and as the phenomenon known as "Bailey's Beads" occurs: sunlight shining through valleys on the moon's surface (or "second contact"). In my experience, the delirium is deafening upon the moment when the brilliance of the photosphere finally disappears behind the moon, which now appears, through one's "eclipse glasses", as a vast portal in the sky. This colossal synchronicity has become animated under various interpretations. As was earlier suggested, the event has been harnessed according to intentions implicit to a self-transformative gnosis implicit to the New Age, the power of which can be accounted for by way of Weil's Jungian explanations – i.e., the alchemical union of opposites potentiating wholeness, which is also implicit to the work of mystic and "ChaOrder Magician" Orryelle Defenestrate-Bascule.[38] The effect might have been announced by William Blake, care of Theodore Roszak, whose conclusion to *The Making of a Counter Culture* (1995: 239) begins with this inquiry: "What are we to say of the man who fixes his eye on the sun and does not see the sun, but sees instead a chorus of flaming seraphim announcing the glory of God?"

In this period (of "second contact"), which can last up to seven minutes (though normally about three minutes), that one's rational en-light-ened self might have become occulted by the umbra affords an exquisite illumination for cosmic liminars. The lines sampled on Tristan and Lucas's "Magic Umbra" (*Lucas Presents Tales of Heads*, 2010) convey this story: "What I love is the fact that I'm watching the mechanics in the solar system at work. I'm standing here watching the Moon pass across the Sun bringing the umbral shadow across the Earth. And for those fleeting moments I'm standing in the magic of the umbra". Italian eclipse chaser Stephan Waldner explained the peak moment at Soulclipse, his first eclipse:

> People were disguised as samurais, as bees, butterflies and fairies. Behind my little dancing space I was surrounded by some guys sitting

> naked and staring at the eclipse with their special Soulclipse-glasses. While the light turned into a kind of silver-glitter-shiny feeling, many people cried, were laughing or hopping and dancing around. The music stopped and even the birds stopped singing. Everything seemed so unreal and these 5 crazy minutes in a one-week-festival was just a surreal moment I don't want to miss in my life.[39]

In a rare elliptic "rise", the Sun re-emerges minutes later with the appearance of the "diamond ring effect" ("third contact"). The reception of the Sun post-totality is not dissimilar to that of its "rising" in the tradition of Goatrance, its first light greeted by the raving masses. As the Sun rises from the moon within those moments of "third contact", it is as if participants are resplendent in reverse equivalence to those astronauts who first witnessed the Earth emerging from the dark side of the moon; their wonder not dissimilar to the epiphanies experienced by space voyagers. While these Earth-bound voyagers are precisely geo-positioned, a recognition of one's irreducible relationship with the cosmos appears to be visited upon those gathered with a remarkably equivalent sharpness of clarity. Jason C (1998: 30) was clear on this: "the most startling moment is when the eclipse breaks and a sudden shaft of light illuminates the Earth like a bolt from the heavens. At that moment you really understand your place in the universe". And he added, "everyone was just wasted by the sheer emotional intensity of it all (and a tiny toke on some Venezuelan weed). Lucky this doesn't happen too often". While the experience is commonly regarded as one of the most absorbing few minutes that one can know, leaving people immediately drained of energy, the state of grace into which chasers reportedly pass for days and months after the synchronicity compels their return.

While Castle, Weil and Jason C point to moments of singularity associated with cosmic alignments, synchronicity and planetary "rises", and connote a gnostic sensibility associated with the personal transcendence experienced at this juncture, ultimately these are explosive social events. In his memoirs, Bailey wrote of his total eclipse experience in 1842 when he mounted a telescope inside a building at the University in Pavia, Italy: "All I wanted was to be left alone during the whole time of the eclipse", he wrote, "being fully persuaded that nothing is so injurious to the making of accurate observations as the intrusion of unnecessary company" (Littmann and Willcox 2008: 88). Bailey was expressing a concern common to the singular research scientist, yet remote from the experience of the eclipse festival. For while the presence of people may disrupt the scientific experiment, in the immeasurable, mystical landscape of the vibe, "company" is paramount. As unique "contact zones" in time and space, the cosmic communitas of an eclipse facilitates extraordinary relations between strangers, including those speaking different languages. Marty, for instance, gave expression to this outcome striking up camaraderie with half a dozen male school teachers from Antalya whom he befriended and danced with on the night following the eclipse, "all sharing in the source of life" and communicating via the universal language of dance.[40] Finally, then, the eclipse experience is not exclusively, or even predominantly, ocular. It is a sensual encounter involving one's close proximity to others in an intentional geo-social space from which participants draw personal, primal and cosmic significance. It is a unique technoshamanic experience, which potentiates sensory continuity with the physical world in dance, while at the same time enabling participants to become familiar with transpersonal states of consciousness in trance.

* * *

At the premiere productions in the world of psychedelic trance and visionary dance culture, spiritual technologies are deployed and techniques optimized with the objective of maximizing the liminal-mystical experience. In this chapter, Portugal's Boom Festival has been characterized as a conscious hive of transition. With the cultivation of liminality in multiple areas, designs and aesthetics optimized and operationalized within its precincts – including, at Boom, the Liminal Village itself – the psychedelic visionary arts festival is *superliminal*. Via the architectonics of transition, media of immediacy and technologies of trance, Boom is a threshold across which "consciousness" is abandoned, expanded and advanced. Extraordinary accomplishments of the global visionary arts dance milieu, Boom and eclipse gatherings magnify the variable experience of mystical consciousness encapsulated by the sunrise in the Goa tradition, now celebrated within a transnational, transient and traveller phenomenon whose events may never be held at the same place twice.

Boom, total solar eclipse festivals and a host of events networked in this transnational movement facilitate personal mystical experiences by virtue of their status as worlds apart and in between. Boomers are provided resources to experiment with ecstasies experienced in the company of friends and "fellow travellers" among whom the "mysteries" are shared, exchanged, debriefed, uploaded, on the edge of the dance floor, at the Liminal Village, back at the campsite, or at home on Facebook. While dance is the ultimate embodied expression of entheogenesis, and live visionary art, a practice that is indeed shared with others who have become unravelled within a synesthesia of colourful tunes, aromatic vistas and powerful bass, the psychedelic festival is itself entheogenic, the entire production facilitating an awareness of one's intimate relatedness – to spirit, to god/dess, to nature, and to others – via multiple means, thus possessing a dense-albeit-diverse *re-creational* potential. Similarly, for eclipse chasers, the cosmic alignment and the succession of "first", "second" and "third" *contact* is transportative, with the natural, cosmic and social event a phenomenon adapted to the cause of a planetary millenarianism.

6 Freak out: the trance carnival

While we have seen that the mystical experience is cultivated in lavish technical productions offering multiple pathways for the trance traveller, I now range further on to the dance floor to explore the dynamic tensions at work within "trance". Even though participants gravitate to various genres and scenes associated with this movement articulating little interest in a "religious", "spiritual" or "transcendent" experience, their actions reveal religious sensibilities, articulated in this chapter by way of Mikhail Bakhtin, Georges Bataille and Victor Turner. The altered conditions in consciousness universally sought and achieved by partygoers are commonly conveyed as "trance", although there is no universal agreement on what this is. Of course, the experience, the music and *the culture* have attracted and retained the "trance" tag from the early Goa period, with habitués distinguishing their "trance dance" from that of others. But, as shown here, *trance culture* is complex, and cannot be circumscribed by what anthropologists have traditionally invoked as "trance" (especially "possession" trance). Interrogating the character of "trance" in psyculture at the principal sites of its enactment, what I call *neotrance* recognizes fluctuating conditions of dissolution (dispossession) and performance (freakiness) of self, occasioned on the dance floor. This dynamic in which *difference* is performed *and* relinquished is recognized as native to neotribalism. With ongoing attention to Portugal's Boom Festival and other sites of cultural expression, the *trance carnival* facilitates the *ecstatic* (transcendent) and *performative* (expressive) characteristics of de/subjectivity occasioned by psytrance. In this excursion through the psychedelic trance *difference engine*, layovers are made at the ontology of progression, the role of funk and the importance of being a freak. But our first junket is the cosmic carnival itself.

Cosmic carnival

From local parties to international festivals hosting arrivals from a multitude of countries, an enduring aspect of psytrance events is that they enable participants to give expression to their *difference* (gendered, sexuality, age, class, ethnonational) while at the same time potentiating the experience of *singularity* (dissolving signs of difference). This dynamic is what I've called the *difference engine* that, while not exclusive to psytrance, possesses a unique form, given its psychedelic aesthetic. The social manifestations of psytrance were found in previous chapters to enable habitués to become altered together, providing travellers of mind and body with the means of perception by which they may discover and explore *another world*, an intentional outcome of the socio-sonic-sensuality enhanced by the psychedelic experience. In these radically reflexive locales, new technologies of the senses have furnished novel sociality and facilitated quantum insights. In the West, the expression *and* dissolution of difference is a circumstance traditionally conditioned by the festival of carnival. It is not my intention in this book to discuss the complex history of this pre-Lenten Catholic festival, its suspected precursors, nor its Afrodiasporic, Caribbean and Latin and South American developments, but more to draw attention to a countercultural carnivalesque praxis augmented and magnified by a psychedelic aesthetic.

The contemporary trance festival is rooted in the utopian dreams of the 1960s/1970 counterculture whose participants followed their "Dionysian impulse", named by Nietzsche in *The Birth of Tragedy* after the god of wine and dance in classical Greek mythology. In the Dionysian, ecstatics rupture form and discipline to the ends of pleasure, freedoms best achieved in the context of music and dance associated with the transit of seasons, especially the arrival of spring. In their response to an oppressive social system, the disaffected beneficiaries of the Age of Affluence sought historical re-enchantment and danced impossible dreams. Freaks embodied this impulse, participating in a revolution expressed in a legacy of autonomous enclaves, gatherings and parties. In Goa, the androgynous Shiva was iconic of this impulse, a standard of ecstatic entrancement, later joined by other figures emblematic of Goatrance and its progeny. That Bakhtin's *Rabelais and His World* began circulating in English from the late 1960s is not without significance. This work was an exercise in "myth making and covert allegory", a program for subverting Stalinism as well as a commentary of late medieval literature and culture (Lindley 1996: 17). But what Bakhtin called the "second life of the people" – carnival contexts debasing official culture and unsettling the order of things since antiquity – has had striking appeal. Integral to a materialist revivalism, Bakhtin's fictive "second life" of market places, fairs and popular feasts essentially free from competition and violence seemed to describe a fantastic landscape to which the disaffected and over-officiated gravitated, a resurgent utopia of the carnivalesque ruled only "by the laws of its own freedom", a world whose occupants became "an indissoluble part of the collectivity" (Bakhtin 1968: 7, 255). Today, the psychedelicized landscape of events in the freak tradition may amplify the "grotesque realism" Bakhtin held definitive of the carnivalesque – where the excessive "violation of natural forms and proportions by exaggeration and hyperbolism" is fuelled by psychedelics, and where partygoers commit to "the evasion of finished systems" (Vitos 2010: 166). But imagineers of the psychedelic and visionary arts development were also architects of a festal culture approximate to Bey's *insurrection*, which provokes a radical conviviality thriving in intentional breaks in the calendar offering prefigurative platforms for alternative futures. The grounds of the psychedelic dance festival where the body-in-dance breaks its own limits may approximate that zone where "true desires – erotic, gustatory, olfactory, musical, aesthetic, psychic, & spiritual – are best attained in a context of freedom of self & other in physical proximity & mutual aid" (Bey 1991b). Yet the remixological technics repurposing popular culture to narrativize the festal culture of trance (and indeed other EDM cultures) would be dismissed as mere "representation" in Bey's immediatist logic. In music productions and event décor and design, remixed material from *Alice's Adventures in Wonderland*, *Fear and Loathing in Las Vegas*, *Willie Wonka and the Chocolate Factory* and countless other stories adapted to or originating with film and television, alongside documentaries, computer games and other material, are filtered into this culture at its paramount sites of reception. And as this happens, psychedelic party culture is directly infused with the subversive, chaotic, liberatory mood of the carnival layered into the carnivalesque of popular culture. This cultural carnivalization can be observed in the development of psyculture from the inception of the hippie settlement of Goa to psytrance, with the advent of a novel event in the Space(d) Age: the cosmic carnival.

Those who trekked to Goa in the late 1960s and early 1970s travelled during the period which saw men journey to and walk upon the surface of the moon. This is not an insignificant coincidence. As the astronauts of the Apollo Program were launched into space in competition with their Cold War cosmonaut rivals, self-exiled psychonauts landed at an offworld drop zone harbouring travellers from around the globe. In Goa, participants in the Dionysian Program were achieving orbits of their own with the assistance of *charas*, acid, cosmic rock and electronic music. From the mid-1960s, the circulation of LSD, new music making innovations and the advent of space travel all influenced the birth of cosmic rock (see Whiteley 1997) and new modes of danced interaction. And by the mid-1970s, the beach scene on Anjuna was a seasonal stage for these developments with Goatrance later emerging as a vehicle for cosmic ascensionism involving passport holders from many countries, among whom were those expatriating from ethnonational identifications, fashioning themselves as outer, inner and hyper space travellers, exiled voyagers grown alien to their former self and society. First cosmic rock and later electronic music provided the soundtrack to this dissidence, this *alien*ation. From Earth Nation's ethereal sound bath "Alienated" (from their debut 12-inch *Alienated*, 1994) to the cosmic ambience produced by Maltese outfit Soul Kontakt on "Unconscious Levels" (*Deliverance* EP, 2008), psychedelic artists were piping the sound into the departure lounge. The psychedelic space program saw various developments, including cosmic rock, dub sound systems, funk and Detroit techno, but the initiative perhaps most influential in orchestrating detachment from one's earthly body was pioneering psybient act The Orb, who fused the ambience of Brian Eno with dub reggae. The Orb's *Adventures Beyond the Ultraworld* (1991) picks up Apollo Program radio signals from "tranquility base" on "Back Side of the Moon" where it is also announced, "what we're witnessing now is man's first trip". Radio dialogue from participants in NASA's Apollo Program, notably Apollo 11, have been among the most commonly sampled and redeployed in the Goatrance tradition (see St John 2013a), a circumstance which pays tribute to the period in which the cosmic carnival emerged and which also forges a narrative on the desire for disconnection from base-ego and the merger with cosmic consciousness that is potentiated by the psychedelic party.[1]

The Space(d) Age carnivalesque was raised in a location in receipt of regular input from Disctopian satellites and seasoned carriers whose transmissions and products ensured a diversity of sounds, styles and psychoactivating substances coursing through Goa year after year. While the authenticity of the scene after the "cosmo-rock" period is in dispute, those who arrived in Goa throughout the 1980s progenerated a party scene in which transcendence in dance was the ultimate concern, a spiritual carnival of dance in which Shiva, in the androgynous form of Nataraj, Lord of the Dance, became an iconic figurehead typically ripped from Hindu context and pressed into service as a psychedelic superhero. As the god of *bhang*, Shiva, like Dionysus, was a cultic icon in whom voyagers from many lands identified. While this dedication to launching one's self into orbit with the aid of circulating rocket fuels, like *charas* and LSD (through the 1970s), MDMA (from the late 1980s), ketamine and DMT (from the 1990s), adds supra-liminal dimensionality to the "down to earth" materialism of Bakhtin's carnival, the dance floor ensured that an intercorporeal funk fomented year after year. The dialogue between the outerspace journey and the inner "trip" was properly convened on the Goa dance floor to which one had personally travailed. The conflation of these travels in terrestrial, outer and inner space is depicted on the cover of The Overlords' (Ian Ion, Rune B and Dick D'Press) synth-pop album *All the Naked People* (1994), which featured three *sadhus* and an astronaut, and may be read in the work of Jörg Kessler, label manager at Shiva Space Technology, whose compilation *The Digital Dance of Shiva* (1999) featured on its cover art a cyborg-alien Shiva dancing across what appears to be a star gate. The Oming sequences on Astral Projection's space-operatic "Cosmic Ascension" (*Dancing Galaxy*, 1997) left little doubt that the launch sequence for their full-powered mission was initiated on the subcontinent. These initiatives paid homage to psychedelic and Indian roots while providing the soundscapes for the cosmic carnival of the 1990s–2000s. In this flourishing, parties were being fashioned as "motherships" or contact sites buzzed by UFOs, with dance floors propagating like astrodomes where DJs initiate the launch sequences. At these sites, the cosmic aesthetic is enhanced by video, décor, black-lights, lasers and 3D string art installations, and amid the ultraviolet subsonic meteor storm and laser battle one might find DJs performing before "stargate portals", appearing as high-tech skywalkers as with the "gypsy MIDI suit" (Motion Capture MIDI Controller) worn by Andromeda (Anders Nilsson and Nikos Kostoglou), or manifesting as grey-inflected extraterrestrials, apparently the desired effect of the alien mask-wearing German guitar-trance act SUN Project.

With a constellation of mirror balls and star-shower lighting effects, dance floors have long been imagineered as realms for "space" exploration and alien encounters, a design-intent traceable back through rave, techno, house, ambient, disco, funk, cosmic jazz to cosmic rock like that performed at London's UFO club in 1966/67. Opened in the old Henry Miller Theatre in Times Square in 1978, Zenon was among the most audacious examples from the 1970s. The club boasted a sixteen-channel sound system, and its owners hired Douglas Trumbull (creator of the special effects in *Close Encounters of the Third Kind*) to design a spaceship that would descend and hover over the heads of the dancers – a project that was ultimately found unworkable and aborted. The "obsession with space and the prog rock tendencies"

Album cover. The Overlords' *All The Naked People* (Arista, 1994). Courtesy of Ian Ion/ThinkElectric.

characterizing Italo-disco would manifest at the "Cosmic Club" in Lazise between 1979 and 1984 (Shapiro 2005: 215, 276). Meanwhile, another UFO Club, this time fuelled by acid house techno, landed in the vaults of a former department store in Mitte, East Berlin, in 1988 – closing in 1990, and later reopening as Tresor – where young citizens of the reunifying Germany were willingly abducted from their daily routines and state-run tyranny. Soon after, the Space Club (subsequently the Warehouse) opened in Köln.[2] By the end of the 1980s, the opulent club Space was operating on Ibiza. In the 1990s, Germany's Antaris Project festival – which would eventually find its home at the Otto-Lilienthal-Airport in Stolln – would be imagineered as an inter-dimensional "spaceship".[3] As interplanetary ports and portals, such clubs and festivals were promoting a transnationalist aesthetic with attention to diverse sonic flavours. At Megatripolis, which opened in the mid-1990s in London club Heaven, co-founder Fraser Clark played with the idea that dance floor occupants were "tuning in" from the future. In this development, cross-genred, transnational and intercorporeal flight clubs became experimental sites for desubjectification. Within cosmic clubbing, outer space is depicted as the ultimate place of possibility, signalled by the figure of the alien, *contact* with which allegorizes discovery of one's other self.

Space travel, extraterrestrial encounters and alien becomings were leitmotifs in a variety of releases mixed under the stars in Goa throughout the 1980s–1990s, including the work of Koto, Space Opera, Time Modem and Voltage Control. Dr Zarkhow's new beat *Interplanetary Adventures* (1989), Laserdance's *Cosmo Tron* (1989) and popular German trance releases like Dance 2 Trance's "We Came in Peace" (1991) and Cosmic Baby's "The Space Track" (1992) were all fresh product played from DAT during the late 1980s and early 1990s.[4] As Castle commented, the arpeggio technique was particularly successful in affecting "ascending cosmic melodies" in techno-trance productions by way of MIDI sequencers and quantization.[5] In the work of The Infinity Project, Evolution, Pleiadians, Cosmosis, Space Tribe and many subsequent Goa/psytrance acts, UFOs buzzed the party, as reminders to explorers of consciousness of the mysteries beyond the veils of the mind. "Unknown object in 804" began "Area 51" by Total Eclipse (*Violent Relaxation*, 1996), referencing the insider's code for Goa ("804") and manipulating their 303s to deliver the sound of the alien presence. One of the most prolific channellers of the alien transmission is Bill Halsey (aka Cosmosis) whose oeuvre (especially *Contact*, 2002) offers a sounding board for the alien as super-guru, a benign teacher guiding the evolution of human consciousness (see Partridge 2003).

Throughout this development, party organizers occupied sites, decorated spaces and hired artists to maximize the ascension. Dance festivals emerged as seasonal launch sites where the *close encounter* with other travellers, those who are "alien" to oneself, provided the context for orbiting ravers to establish *contact* with their alien (altered) selves. Under the right conditions, the partygoer *will* make contact, with the resultant discovery as predictable as the content of one's dreams. Pete Black reported on his experience at Astral Phoenix, Tyssen Street Studios, Dalston, London (11 March 2000):

> I entered a completely different dance-floor as I began to peak; my first experience candy-flipping. I became aware that everyone conversing was doing so in an alien tongue. The cavernous warehouse became an extension to my mind. As I navigated the space I felt new pathways form. Slightly uneasy about the alien surroundings I found home in the centre of the dance-floor between towering columns. Fluorescent-green laser pierced my consciousness as sounds illuminated my inner-world; a stadium-sized spherical geodesic dome of speakers. Sound and light intertwined, laser beamed directly to my retina as I came to be the cosmic disco.[6]

A standard "alien" figure populates the psychedelic imaginary of the cosmic carnival. Printed on tapestries, embossed on textile fashions, figuring in visionary art, adorning websites and forums, adopted as profile icons, and inhering in contagious logos, the almond-eyed, vestigial, gender-less, age-less and hairless alien is pervasive. A banner under which international trance travellers rally, the alien is emblematic of the othered-self, a symbol of ultimate difference and, yet, at the same time, absolves distinctions of nationality, race, age, gender, sexuality. Noting its prolific appearance within rave culture, Ken McLeod offers a parallel view, stating that the alien figure is "capable of challenging simplistic binaries of male/female, black/white or rich/poor", with alien iconography enabling a "symbolic incorporation of the idealized, raceless, classless, and genderless plurality of the dance floor" (2003: 339). In its amplification *and* erasure of difference, the archetypal alien is a standard of distinction and unity. Largely benevolent, although ambivalent, the "alien" has become a chief icon for the difference engine, totemic for a post-human becoming.

Circulating among the trance massive, embedded in tracks and recognizable in fashion, other figures are regularly recruited to perform this complex task. I have discussed Shiva, but the zombie, the outlaw, the primitive and other figures from fairy tales, film and popular mythology are tropes used to tune the difference engine, with participants drawing on freakish composites to fashion their other-than-human identifications, and to explain their transpersonal experiences. While I explore these figures elsewhere (see St John 2011c, 2013b), some brief comments on the primitive is required, for the transcendence/expression of difference within the dancescape is commonly assisted by the figure of the primitive, typically iconic of a primal ecstatic sociality in which distinctions appear to have been dissolved. The "tribal" sociality that is cultivated here contrasts with the pathological crowds observed by criminologist Gabriel Tarde or other nineteenth-century commentators on crowd psychology like theorist of the "crowd mind", Gustave Le Bon, for whom urban crowds had grown comparable to "primitive" societies – i.e. uncivilized, dangerous and fearful (see Garcia 2010). More likely, we find the image of the "soft primitive", the visage of the Aboriginal, Amerindian or Amazonian invented as a figure of primal unity. In some projects, primitivist iconography figures in promotions, such as Germany's Indian Spirit Festival, which has typically deployed totem poles, dream catchers and feathered head-dresses to promote and decorate its vibe. But these associations are complex in practice. When I attended the 2010 edition of Indian Spirit and anticipated a galaxy of Amerindian signs consumed by crowds ravenous for the primitive, my expectations were not met, and could not determine attendance as evidence of one's complicity in neocolonial practice. Efforts to render individual artists or even entire scenes so complicit founder on the rocks of aesthetic and empirical complexity.

"This is *It*"

Under rallying motifs and sigils that I have only briefly discussed here, the cosmic carnival is lived, modified and revisited by its habitués whose carnivalesque "indissolubility" is reliant on the repurposing of media, audio-visual tools and remixological practice. Comparing rave with the Bahian Carnival in Brazil and making intriguing observations about the recycling of technologies of control as instruments of joy, Bernard Schütze (2001: 158) has stated that in "carnivalizing the technologies of a command and control society", rave is positively "technophagic". That is, where the carnival's "anthropophagic principle is based on an incorporation of the other in terms of a cultural cut-n-mix producing hybridity, the technophagic seizes technological means (electronic, pharmaceutical, logistic) and inverts their control and productive function into one of unleashing energies that modulate the vibratory body" (Schütze 2001: 161–2). And, like traditional carnival, the "joyous intermingling, bodily expression, eccentric behaviour and dress" of the techno-rave festival operates an "open transmutation of subjectivities that tears asunder normative modes of subjectivation and permits the experimentation of novel forms of subjectivity". These days, Bahians are not unfamiliar with the beat-matching of carnival with rave. With the advent, for example, of the Universo Parallelo Festival de Arte e Cultura Alternativa near Ituberá, Bahia, a popular international psytrance and "alternative culture" festival in its ninth year over the New Year week 2009/10, the "vibratory body" has been heavily modulated by audio, visual and chemical technologies. In Brazil and worldwide, we might witness, as Hillegonda Rietveld (2004: 53) postulates, a transit to "cyborg-like subjectivity", the product of a postindustrial sacrificial repetitive-beat ritual offering a temporary-yet-relived homeland for the alienated. Invoking Bataille, she writes: "the peak experience is a trip into the void: time, space and sensory input fragmenting and collapsing, yet held together by the repetitive beat; suspended, the spiritual hedonist is rendered speechless and unable to articulate, being everything and nothing; part of all; complete yet empty".

It is instructive to turn to Bataille's theory of religion, for attention to excess, consumption and the sacred offers insight on the psytrance vibe – and that associated with other EDM cultures – as temporary communities reproduced in personal and collective transgression. That is, as a Goa legacy, psy-communities are formed through the routine expenditure of excess energy, and through self-sacrifice in ecstatic abandonment fuelled by chemical cocktails obtained and prepared for this purpose. In the Batallian "general economy", the expenditure of that which had been translated as society's "accursed share" constitutes a path towards obtaining a sacred otherness in which those formerly separate may share intimately as they "consume *profit-lessly*". "If I thus consume immoderately", states Bataille, "I reveal to my fellow beings that which I am *intimately*: Consumption is the way in which *separate* beings communicate. Everything shows through, everything is open and infinite between those who consume intensely" (Bataille 1989: 58–9, italics in original; see also Gauthier 2004a: 76). While psytrance festivals are remote from the violence of human sacrifice inspiring Bataille at this juncture, these comments nevertheless evoke the subterranean and orgiastic communication, or *consumation* – what Bataille (1993: 431 n. 1) meant by nonproductive or useless consumption as opposed to the consumption of production and accumulation – transpiring within their precincts. As dance floor occupants experience the diminution of their status as separate "things", by lavishing gifts upon each other, passing chillum among their cohort and are blanketed by bass, a shared chemical and sonorous romance softens the boundaries between unique individuals. Though loath to interpret the experience via recourse to "religion", in *Inside Clubbing*, Phil Jackson approached this situation describing what he calls the "chemical intimacy" of the metropolitan (queer, trance, techno, drum 'n' bass and sex) club, where bizarre conversations and sensual intensity between strangers fuelled by a range of psychoactives challenges the "logic" of the *habitus* and enables fresh and open forms of sociality where participants "derive a sense of satisfaction and meaning from people, rather than things' (2004: 163). The effect from the ingestion of LSD is especially notable: "the temperature immediately rockets and I curl around the beat, skanking along with the mass. Wondrous. Arms and legs and torsos weaving and writhing around each other, all held together by the virus known as bass. An inevitable act of aural seduction, guttural sounds, viscous and sticky and inexplicably wise. My body feels liquid" (Jackson 2004: 12).

This bass-driven and chemically enhanced liquidation of boundaries is a design imperative of open-air psychedelic festivals. With tens of thousands of bodies feeling the bass, growing sumptuous and abandoning their *thingness*, Boom orchestrates this freak prodigality. With the billboarded message "We Are One" backgrounded by lake Idanha-a-Nova (at Boom in 2006), and with participants wearing the same message on their wristbands (as provided upon entrance), Boom may be said to constitute a subterranean body of the people. That is, at least, the mythology. For while this is indeed the view of organizers and a great many event participants, the presence of Anti-Boom, a "teknival" – a Free Festival featuring techno sound systems with a distinctive hardcore (and thus not psytrance) aesthetic – operating simultaneously across the lake from Boom, challenges this universalism. Additionally, a considerable number who were refused entry (due to the event reaching capacity) or who complained about entrance fees or deficiencies in services and sanitation in 2008 might question this narrative. This contrast is important since, with free admission, Anti-Boom might more readily claim the status of a "temporary autonomous zone", even though Boom has actively promoted and supported the idea of a TAZ. There is no question, however, that Boom has desired to retain its credentials as an agent of ethical-commerce, given, for example, the commitment to remain free of corporate sponsorship, as clearly expressed in the *Boom Book* (Good Mood 2007), while, at the same time, developing into a corporation itself, with a company structure and brand energy. But as Boom team member Artur Soares da Silva indicated to me on our first meeting in 2006, Boom was meeting a unique challenge: to accommodate diverse elements within a festival context. For Soares da Silva, this meant more than simply providing a space for various "scenes", aesthetic "tribes" or proponents of different "trances" to convene. It was to be a space for different ethnic groups to interconnect. As he later wrote, "during the festival, close, continuous, sometimes intimate, contact is made between people of various nationalities allowing for a more profound and personal knowledge of the 'other'". He went on to comment:

> It is through these interpersonal relationships that individuals can begin to rid themselves of prejudices and stereotypes. A new awareness of "other" and of "different" emerges, in contrast with the dominant cultural narrative's tendency for opposition: west vs. east, black vs. white, Christian vs. Muslim, national vs. immigrant. Besides the contact between different ethnic groups, there is a climate of anti-status quo, without a rigid social hierarchy. That is, people from different ethnic groups are not divided by status; rather there is a flat, egalitarian context, which is a fundamental starting point for viewing self and other as the same. And then the most genuine of human behaviours begin to appear naturally:

> cooperation, sharing, creating affective bonds, learning from the "other" and, lastly, change; change of behaviour; change of attitude; a new notion of "I" and "other". This forms a base for a new kind of awareness (Soares da Silva 2008: 37).

The principal site in which the "new notion of 'I' and 'other'" materializes is the dance floor, the grounds for immediate oscillation between states of dissolved and performed subjectivity. In ecstatic and performed states, participants shift between spectacular conditions of self(less)ness. The context of the trance dance thus enables habitués to "switch off", get "fucked up" and be "wasted" in the company of others. But while one might be "losing it" on the floor, others are most certainly "having it", parlance illuminating those moments when one has passed outside of one's self, where leaving the familiarity of one's skin and rupturing one's own inviolability affects a merger with cohabitants of the floor, who share in an expanded subjectivity. While *losing it* alludes to the subjectivity which evanesces, *having it* is an effervescence possessed here and now. Facilitating departure from the everyday routine, the trance machine permits a new condition in which one realizes that *this is It*. This is the most ineffable, unclarified and unspeakable condition in the business, yet a plateau instantly recognizable among participants. In such a state, the dancer accesses a timeless condition producers attempt to convey through samples that are like incantations that unlock the gate to eternity. A statement at the beginning of "Utopian Landscape" by Unknown Cause (from Richard Linklater's *Waking Life*) tells the story:

> Let me explain to you the nature of the universe. Actually, there's only one instant, and it's right now. It's an instant in which God is posing a question, and that question is basically "Do you want to be one with eternity?" "Do you want to be in heaven?" And we're all saying "No, thank you. Not just yet". And so time is just this constant saying "No" to God's invitation. I mean, that's what time is. It's no more 50AD than it's 2001. It's just this one instant, and that's what we're always in ... Behind the phenomenal difference, there is but one story, and that's the story of moving from the "No" to the "Yes". All of life is like, "No, thank you". "No, thank you". "No, thank you". Then ultimately it's "Yes, I give in". "Yes, I accept". "Yes, I embrace". I mean, that's the journey. I mean, everyone gets to the "yes" in the end, right?

Here, the "Yes" moment is the passage into trance, of the dancer becoming the dance, entering the eternal now, outside of thought and time. Canadian artist Psyentifica speaks volumes on this theme in the rumbling "This is It", citing Joseph Campbell (from the 1988 PBS series *The Power of Myth*): "Eternity isn't some later time. Eternity isn't a long time. Eternity has nothing to do with time. Eternity is that dimension of here and now which thinking of time cuts out. This is it". Campbell continues:

> "All life is sorrowful" is the first Buddhist saying, and it is. It wouldn't be life if there were not temporality involved, which is sorrow. Loss, loss, loss ... You have to say yes to it, you have to say it's great this way. It's the way God intended it ... And if you don't get it here, you won't get it anywhere. And the experience of eternity right here and now is the function of life (*Natural Selection*, 2008).

It is also one of the key functions of trance. Experienced occupants of the trance floor describe the uncanny familiarity received when repeating entrance to this space. Cosmica, from Berlin, refers to an experience repeated at "almost every trance festival" she has attended since 1996 returning to the centre of the dance floor where "people are high and filled with love and the sun is always shining" regardless of the weather conditions. In that space, she says, she seems to rendezvous with the same humans.

> Even if I have never talked to them and met them anywhere else, we communicate in a special, very familiar and enjoyable way – without talking and in a multi-dimensional way. It is communication on several levels at the same time ... and we all feel like relatives from ancient times. The minute we leave the dancefloor, we seem to lose each other – keeping each other in mind but we are separated until we meet again on the dancefloor and celebrate our ONE existence.[7]

Across an array of subgenres, expert DJs maintain this state of timelessness via skilfull selections and performance techniques. A performer of "templestep" and "ethnocrunk", Australian DJ Dakini states that her intention is to "weave ethnic/temple sounds into bass music to support people to move beyond their ego identities and merge collectively into the sound ... When you dance, immersed in music, you don't think ... you move beyond the mind and self".[8] One finds immediate correspondence with the synchronistic social paroxysms described by the Turners (Turner and Turner 1978; E. Turner 2012) in samples and statements that could be offered in page after page of material. But while there is much that resonates with "spontaneous communitas", the social liminality of the trance dance floor is dripping with a passion among habitués to *have* each other. And so this leads to recognition that the trance floor, not exclusively the occasion for mystical Otherness in the company of others, is also directed by the orgiastic desire for *being with* others. I do not mean to imply that the psytrance floor is driven by an orgiastic sensibility equivalent to some dance clubs (see Jackson 2004), for many psytrance participants seek to distance themselves from being the "objects" of a predatory (and often male) gaze common within club cultures. But while these events are barely recognizable in the armchair sociological fantasy of rave dancing as "a form of sexual intercourse where beats and rhythms imitate different stages of orgasm", and where "dancers experience virtual sex on the dance floor, releasing their sexual tension through ecstatic shouts" (Richard and Kruger 1998: 168–9), they are generally removed from the pre-Oedipal playpens of acid house (Rietveld 1993). As a playground for "spiritual hedonism" the psychedelic party can be identified as an expression of the "passional logic" articulated by Maffesoli in *The Shadow of Dionysus: A Contribution to the Sociology of the Orgy* (1993). Mixing Bakhtin's carnivalesque with Bataille's *consumation*, as Maffesoli had it, in "the face of historic time dominated by production and parousia, there is a poetic and heroic time, a time of the amorous body, a second and hidden time around which are organized endurance and sociality" (1993: 31). The desire for loss, for spending, is considered pivotal to the clandestine and ephemeral "social orgiasm" which reaches a licentious, contagious and unrestrainable climax in the festal – those moments occasioning transgressions of imposed morality (1993: 92). Often associated with the seasonal festival which celebrates revitalization and renewal, the psy-event is recognizable here, as its habitués pursue amorous encounters, engage in extended sexual foreplay, and as they get *it* on with co-liminars on and off the dance floor.

The arts of nothing

But we've hardly begun to address the nature of *It* within the trance movement. Amid the noise and the eros of the cosmic carnival there lies a desirable stillness, that place where thoughts vanish and desire itself recedes. This optimum condition sought is removed from the marketplace dialogue that intrigued Bakhtin in his philosophical anthropology. The optimal state relies upon memories of episodes trance actors desire to relive so they can have *It* one more time, and a trance architectonic has evolved to make *It* happen. But the techno-culture of trance is populated by those for whom the trance experience is perennially perfectible, whose discontent dictates a permanent state of optimizability. As psytrance music is the chief means by which *It* is facilitated, there is, then, much at stake in the constant refinement of sound. Not unlike other EDMs, the signature aspect of music production is attention to the miniature, the quantized detail of digital sound design fashioned by innovations and applications enabling upgrades on yesterday's means of having *It*. As a result, a music, and a lifestyle, have evolved to produce *the same, but different*, a paradox which articulates the logic of a *progressive* aesthetic. In an effort to give this vexing concept definition, Toronto's DJ Basilisk (2008) noted that "in a technical sense, the word progressive suggests deep rhythms, slow-burning arrangements, hazy atmospheres, and a subtle approach to composition", and yet it also means "cutting edge, fashionable, or 'forward thinking'". This conflation of momentous techno-aesthetic competence and avant-garde movement was inherited by psytrance, via Goatrance, and can be traced back through house, techno and rock forms. The project of self-realization, of self-becoming-whole, is a gestalt that I have already explained is integral to progressive psychedelic. Psy-prog would become the descendent of progressive rock whose acts were among the first to experiment with synthesizers, the adoption and use of computer instruments facilitating the perception among controllers that they are engineering culture. While aiding definition, the avant-garde pretension does not account for conservatism native to the progression, or the milieu of networked artists, promoters, labels, webforums and festivals whose collective efforts build, control and defend the epistemics of *having it*, and who market and distribute *psychedelic* music.

Although it remains true that a nominally "progressive" style has grown popular within psytrance, here I see *progressive* signifying a conservative forward momentum determining sound and style – thus darkpsy can also be considered *progressive*, in this sense. That which progresses is recognizable by that which it clings to in its advancement. All genres and indeed "scenes" are probably identifiable here, but in psychedelic trance a progressive culture emerged with musics, style and a sensibility serving to ensure that nothing lasts. This is the commitment to silence the mind and to grow calm in a world of crisis, where the celerity of one's gestures in dance and finding the quiet place within are mutually dependent. This development, especially for those with no interest in growing calm in a world of crisis, who are without the resources to achieve *It*, or simply have other means to the achievement, has been challenged with passionate fulminations almost unparalleled in the world of EDM. Stagnation and stale formulas are identified, with Castle, for instance, suggesting that Goatrance became "fundamentalist". Among critics, "Goa", "trance" and "psytrance" are risible terms evoking a strident fanaticism that is simply abhorrent. And yet, among loyalists, commitment to the journey without a goal is pursued with equal conviction, with devout enthusiasts descending on events as if they are religious centres. But, as with many sacred centres, its constituency is far from homogeneous, with many quarrelling about the most appropriate means to the ends, and indeed disputing the precise nature of *It*. The world of psychedelic trance is characterized by a politics of nothing, with innovators, architects and promoters disputing and negotiating the means of its accomplishment.

As a testament to the revelation that "nothing is sacred", management, musicians, and the experienced design contexts by which one may capitulate to rhythm, accomplish nothing and make it last. If a transit without destination

Man With No Name. Ozora Festival, Hungary. Photo: Pascal Querner.

inheres in trance, it also resembles a play without a finale, a narrative without a conclusion. An experience of uncertainty is often affected by the delay of climax. Like puppet masters, building tension and promising release, skilled DJs will animate dancers for long periods, such as I experienced at Sonica, Italy, in 2007, and at Ozora, Hungary, in 2009, when James Monro and Man With No Name respectively performed the final sets. The Goa veterans had over 1,000 in the former and perhaps 8,000 in the latter party caught in the drama, uncertain how, if at all, it might ever be resolved. This is comparable to early disco and house where DJs like Larry Levan were committed to "preventing any sense of release from developing, creating the sense of longing and unfulfilled desire that marked many of the best disco records" (Shapiro 2005: 261). Ultimately, however, established tensions are permitted release, often by way of a series of epic builds and breakdowns where trancers are left convulsing in ecstasy. Recalling her experience during the final set by Man With No Name at Ozora 2009, Turkish/German co-owner of Blue Hour Sounds Records, Jasmine Gelenbe, commented:

> People were freaking out! It had been a great party, nobody wanted it to end, everybody gave the last power reserves! We danced and danced, and after a while the whole dancefloor seemed to be a twister. I got into this bunch of people, jumping one around the other, always moving, never standing – we hardly touched the ground, smiling at each other, holding hands, turning, turning ... wow! I saw the funniest expressions, the most touching interactions between people, everybody was full of love, hugging, kissing and sharing this moment of trance ... When the music stopped it was like an explosion of joy, we were screaming, clapping our hands, everybody was begging just for another track! And we got it! Another roundabout, this time even more powerful, and it was over... pure satisfaction! I will never forget that.[9]

Many participants would recognize this experience, while unaware of the complexities ensuring its reproduction. An entire techno-apparatus – body technologies, consciousness alterants, music production and aesthetic, utility fashions, etc. – has evolved to enable this recurrence. Novel experiments in timbre, fashion and remixology are implemented to "replay" transcendence, which is often perceived as a "return" (to the source), the "remembering" of a familiar *ekstasis*, the achievement of "symbiosis" with others and nature, the ineffability of which is perennial. I'm reminded here of Erik Davis's characterization of psytrance as a kind of fusion of archaic familiarity with novelty seeking: the psytrance event

> allows the commingling of age-old ecstatic techniques with attitudes and technologies that reject tradition in the name of an open-ended, novelty-seeking alternative techno-culture. This mixed quality helps explain how and why the pagan primitivism of psy-trance's gnosis is also wedded to apocalyptic expectations. We return to move forward, accelerated (Davis 2004: 265).

Grasping this statement offers a significant waymark in our path to comprehending psytrance, and suggests why McKenna's thoughts (i.e. the "novelty wave" and "archaic return") would hold weight in this movement, and why interpenetrating discourses of ascension (evolution, progression) and re-enchantment (conservation, sacrality) pervade psyculture.[10]

The meaning of repetition in EDM is also signalled in the work of Luis-Manuel Garcia (2005) for whom "repetition functions as a sort of process, structuring activity in a manner that optimizes opportunities to exercise mastery of listening/dancing". In response to studies of musical repetition as pathological, Garcia states that "if there is a beauty in the New, then there is also the question of a beautiful Same" in loop music. A critical entry point to understanding the "beautiful Same" is found in Mihalyi Csikszentmihalyi's work (1990) on the "flow" state, that "state of mind" which he found highly optimized in sports, games, music and dance. Influenced by Csikszentmihalyi and making specific observations on cultural expression of dance music practices, in *Music as Social Life: The Politics of Participation*, Thomas Turino offers insight on the role of *challenges* in the optimizing of the musical experience sought by those who will return again and again to re-enter the flow. These are states associated with activities that

> must include the proper balance between inherent challenges and the skill level of the actor. If the challenges are too low, the activity becomes boring and the mind wanders; if the challenges are too high, the activity leads to frustration and the actor cannot engage fully. When the balance is just right, it enhances concentration and

> that sense of being at one with the activity and perhaps the other people involved (Turino 2008: 4).

With this understanding, as with other EDM scenes, psytrance appears predicated upon the ability of music producers, event organizers and dance floor occupants themselves to maintain this balance, the negotiation of which offers insight on the nature of a *progressive* sensibility applicable to all styles: a self-selecting, optimized vibe; an ideal state consisting of new sounds and track selections, not too predictable, yet not too challenging, familiar yet not too familiar (e.g. "cheesy"), according to the advancing sensibilities of discerning aesthetes; experimental states of consciousness, albeit not threatening to one's well-being; a "good crowd", but not too diverse (i.e. beggars, tourists, spectators). The second of these concerns is addressed by Raphael Huber (aka SubConsciousMind), who stated that what's achieved in functional psytrance is "hypnosis through distraction".

> Most psytrance works on a simple principle, it attracts your attention, lets you wait for more, lets you wait so long yet entertains you and finally you lose track and "space about", then it attracts your attention again, lets you wait again and so on. The art behind this is to never let the listener feel bored, but yet not attract his attention too much so that he can "space about, space away" (whatever, get hypnotized, trip). This "losing track" "spacing about" "tripping" is the key. In that state the listener becomes open and relaxes. This relaxing is the therapeutic effect. It's not easy to do. If the musician attracts too much attention, the listener can not fall into trance, if he never never attracts attention again, the listener starts feeling bored. Most songs go through 2–3 of those cycles with the last one being the most intense. If it's done well, one can really trip nicely. It can also be described as a play between "tension" and "release", build up tension, release it. This schemata is to be observed in all kinds of psytrance, but the most obvious is progressive and dark.[11]

One way artists may "attract attention" is by dropping choice lines into the track which, as seen in Chapter 4, often evoke the hypnotic or transitional conditions desired. Sunstryk prefaces his intent by programming the line "just two seconds of not thinking. Just two seconds. And in those two seconds ... the whole world disappears" at the beginning of "Losing My Friend" (*Serenity*, 2011). There is much at stake in an equilibrium that, if not maintained, the vibe, and even the accompanying scene, faces collapse. In this way, psychedelic trance culture must progress, as participants seek and respond to challenges, build skills, knowledge and discernibility, a process which accounts for the developments in psychedelic trance musics with escalating and decreasing bpm.

How do artists configure their role in the formation of a nominally "progressive" genre? Let's look at Citizen (aka Wouter Thomassen and Sander Visser) who surf this *same but different* swell in efforts to produce progressive psychedelic trance, but who do not wish to be "pigeonholed into some subgenre", and certainly not "eurotrance bollox". In an interview for *Progressive Tunes* magazine (Citizen 2007), they refer to their *Uncharted* compilation (Flow Records) as striving for a

> timeless quality without trying to be too retro. So instead of going for the obvious by selecting stuff that's hip and trendy nowadays, or 8 spectacular dancefloor killers, we looked out for tracks that are deep, epic, transporting, timeless, soulful that work just as well on your headphones as they do on a sunny open air dancefloor. So no clubby electro singalongs, just quality Trance grooves that's both futuristic but also with hints of oldschool.

This description evokes an art that retains familiar form even while charting new horizons, which is not at all remote from the lifestyle sought by the global techno freaks whose restless pursuit of difference in remote and exotic locations, often the same locations visited seasonally, are efforts to maintain the beautiful Same. This is the space of experimentation, an alternative cultural zone accommodated within the grounds of the festival, a site of novelty enabling the familiar. Thus psytrance offers a curious twist on the experience of "cosmic time", which Roy Rappaport argues enables entry into "eternity", or a "time of out of time": "the sheer successionless duration of the absolute changelessness of that which recurs, the successionless duration of that which is neither preceded nor succeeded, which is 'neither coming nor passing away,' but always was and always will be" (1999: 231).

There are notable parallels with that which François Gauthier identified as the "festal ritual" flourishing in the present, which "implicitly seeks forgetfulness, selflessness and oblivion", adding that in the rave festival

> effervescence is sought after *for itself* and *in itself*. In other words, it is its own purpose and reason. By opening up to creativity, by staging an otherly, unlicensed temporary world, the festive need only contain *itself*. Disengaging from temporality, the festive bursts into an "eternal" – or, to be more precise, "indefinite" – present (Gauthier 2004a: 69, original emphasis).

Nietzsche's "Dionysian impulse" is near at hand, which, in the Goa tradition, was grafted to an appropriated and virtualized Shaivite sensibility now pressed into the "weekend societies" translating the Goa state of mind in locations worldwide. In these optimized regularities, management arrange resources and maximize conditions to accomplish *nothing*, that recurrent state of self-annihilation sought by participants under rhythm and reverb. Transit to the *Weekend Society* is conveniently encapsulated by progressive artist Audiomatic, whose 2011 release bears this title. The release notes for the album are buoyant: "good to know that we can land at exotic islands from weekend to weekend. As soon as we set our feet ashore, the sky brightens and our faces are illuminated by colourful lights and we see all the people we have grown fond of". The cover features the title printed along what appears to be a standard event wrist-band: a symbol of one's legitimate passage into that which may be experienced as a vacation from work, a packaged flow experience infused with the formulaic challenges that now constitute the Goa vibe. While this commodification of the psychedelic carnival may leave an indelible mark around one's wrist – and perhaps burn a hole in one's pocket – the temporary dispossession from routine subjectivity, labour practices and legitimate citizenship should not be undervalued, for the attendants and occupants of such temporalities find ways to smuggle the "weekend" ethos back across the border.

Festivals, freaks and breaks

While the psychedelic festival is a context for self-immolation in the glow-furnace of dance, it also enables the presentation of self, the performance of other personas whose composite is the *freak*. Integral to bohemian and psychedelic histories, and endogenous to the cosmic carnival, never straight, stationary nor complete, the *freak* is a liminal archetype ambiguous with regard to morality, and rules of dress, gender, embodiment and mind. Transcending categories of mind and body, seeking forbidden knowledge and drifting between marginal sites, freaks are characterized by mobility, asymmetry and uncertainty. Within the carnival of trance, participants are licensed to play with this asymmetry, and mould themselves according to its weird logic, as they adopt queer personas, clown around, become unpredictable, and feed on a symbolic detritus whose unfinished montage defies meaning. Festivals like Boom are interactive freakscapes, staging-grounds for what Turner (1984: 21) called the "subjunctive mood", experimental atmospheres where occupants – wearing outfits with theriomorphic (animal-like), anime, superhero, mythical, extraterrestrial and kinky themes, adopting stylized (e.g. fractalized and UV reactive) glyphs printed on clothing, badges and personalized patches, or just assuming a raunchy posture – perform alternate personas. The queering of gender is not uncommon, with females perfecting androgynous appearances and males effeminate styles. Gendered ambiguity has long typified pre-Lenten carnival where normative identities are officially ruptured, and where, for instance, transvestism reigns. Indeed gender disruptions are native to festal behaviour across manifold cultural forms where, as Turner pointed out, liminars "are sometimes treated or symbolically represented as being neither male nor female", or where "they may be symbolically assigned characteristics of both sexes, irrespective of their biological sex" (1967: 98). While there is much to learn from this deep festal legacy, it is in the psychedelic carnivalesque of the 1960s that we observe the flourishing of the freak festival, subsequently refracted through the socialities percolating in underground dance cultures in New York, Chicago, London, Paris, Berlin and other cities.

Conducting experiments on the frontiers of style, freaks intimate a willingness to trespass across aesthetic categories. As Huisinga observed in his 1938 work *Homo Ludens*, play can be a very serious matter indeed, with its diligent proponents in the contemporary world attracting a "hardcore" designation. There is much at stake in the ludic, as John Leland noted in his study of American hipsterism (2004). In the trickster aesthetics of hip – which, like the "vibe", lies at the convergence of Afrodiasporic and European sensibilities – devotion to sartorial, sonic, dance and linguistic styles cultivates an identity that finds belonging in transgression. In the wake of Hollywood and pop-iconography, resistance, belonging and inveterate tricksterism can be understood within the context of national identity. Halloween, to offer one crucial example, is the seasonal festival of the gothic trickster (Leland 2004: 184–5). Perennial freakiness bubbles up from the margins in alternative cultural heterotopias staging the performance of tricksterism, hybridity and serious play. More than a "party", most certainly beyond a rave, Burning Man is a dedicated freak-laboratory, which, in the vastness of its alternative conurbations, is host to a gathering storm of EDM. While subject to critiques and regulations that mirror conflict within the wider culture, electronic music has become native to Black Rock City. Goatrance had a critical role in this animation, with the assistance of, among others, Michael Gosney, whose Community Dance Camps held from 1997–1999 were integral to the "meta-rave" blanketing the desert landscape in subsequent years (see St John 2009: 155–64). This and other sonicities like Germany's Fusion festival and Boom are populated by those who thrive on the sample. Freaks are citizens of the sample, natives of the mix, remastering themselves from a multitude of sources. As Burning Man and the wider West Coast visionary arts scene demonstrates (see Davis and Wiltshire 2009), psytrance is not the exclusive preserve of this sampladelic tribalism. Nevertheless, around the world, in their adoption of a shifting assemblage of dress options, body modifications and gothic inscriptions, psytrance enthusiasts cobble identity from a cornucopia of spiritual, esoteric and popular cultural sources, and in accordance with manifold causes.

An archaeology of the freak carnival and its world apart/between would unearth the critical role of psychedelic performativity – that is, conditioned

On the path. Boom 2010. Photo: Rémy-Pierre RIBIERE. www.ruyphoto.net.

not simply by "psychedelic" compounds but by the entire festive apparatus. In the previous chapters, we have seen how events enable participants to achieve states of expanded and evolved consciousness. And earlier in this chapter, the cosmic carnivalesque was recognized to have emerged as a serious rejoinder to Space Age ventures. But the cosmic carnival survives precisely because it does not take itself too seriously, or when it does, it is forced to come back down to earth. So I want to pay attention to the garrulous and funky immanence of the carnivalesque, whose net effect is social levelling. Found beyond conventional standards of embodiment, modes of communication and states of consciousness, the psytrance floor is a quintessential freakscape, a psychedelic circus animated by DJ-producers. As explained by DJ Tristan (Tristan Cooke):

> The experience for me is one of laughter and joy. You can go to the dark side and you can experience incredible intensity but you've got to be able to laugh and have a good time on the dance floor. I want everyone to laugh at the sheer lunacy of it all – and to make music which triggers people to dance in weird and wacky ways, pulling the moves, completely unselfconsciously, flipping flibberdegibberts on the dance floor – that's when I know things are really rocking (in Short, dir. 2006).

Dance floors are playgrounds where outrageous antics are encouraged by psychedelic anthems like that produced by Tristan himself. Playgrounds like the main floor at Ozora, where, in 2009, I met Garth, a South African pushing his wheeled steed stacked with mischief onto the middle of the dance floor. With mirror ball dangling aft, the cart was laden with the ingredients for cocktails and was armed with a super-sized water pistol and other accoutrements which would be lavished upon strangers and friends, themselves devoted to the ostentatious squandering of resources, adding lustre to their persons and a brilliance to the occasion. Exuberant and outrageous scenes are replayed all over the world. At the 2004 Rainbow Serpent Festival near Melbourne, two mates (Mouse and Chook) equipped with fishing rods and nets reeled in rainbow trout from deckchairs set around a deep hole at the edge of the main floor. A swarm of intrigued and psychedelicized onlookers were led to believe that their haul came from an "underground stream" directly beneath the dance floor, as the two paraded their netted "catch" *en route* back to camp to cook Sunday lunch.[12] Theatre of this nature is not uncommon within these environments, where household items like vacuum cleaners become incongruous props in the possession of those with no purpose other than to disturb categories, or "fuck shit up", with uproarious laughter typically trailing in the wake of anomalous behaviour. This is the realm of "ritualized *dementia*" which, in the psychedelic party context, is said to possess an internal logic of its own, accomplishing the "temporary demolition and perversion of cultural systems, carried out through cognitive acts and powered by sensory hallucinations" (Vitos 2010: 151).

On another occasion, the fishermen above returned to a packed dance floor carrying a football and, in Australian Rules Football guernseys with matching socks and shorts, boots and mouth-guards, attacked the dance floor "at full steam, weaving in and out of dancers, passing the ball to one another".[13] The dance floor is indeed a place for random sport. At the 2009 Rainbow Serpent Festival, in the oscillation between stupefaction and spectacularized performance, there appeared a butt-naked freak, his body painted red, backing his way through the crowd, passing a lemon to any takers at his rear. The camp, the bizarre and the outrageous are not out of place here, where hybridity and recombinant form are fertile, as Tim Parish conveyed in regards to the 2008 edition of the festival.

> All the shades are here. Blue Sky encompassing, sunburnt earth and skins. Dust covered sunglasses, barefeet babes, flip flop tribes … There are couples sharing love flavoured icecreams on hammocks around me, as the parade continues; she's carrying an inflatable crocodile, he's dressed as a roman, trumpet dangling from his rope belt, red cloths and wraparound shades. A barechested man with pineapple dreads tied up, over, around pixie hats, utility belts of

shells and seeds, pink neglige cutey with bindi foreheads, rainbow gypsy dresses twirling, psychedelic parasols spinning, headband hipsters huffing and puffing smoke, fluffy punks, spiky bedheads, tall lanky white long sleeve gurus, an elven girl with face paint, glitter cheeks, mascara eyes, wombat hat, batman shirt, fairy wing girl, fairy wing boy, fluttering along, a crowd watching the japanese soccerball busker who never lets the ball touch the ground gives out fair trade propoganda to a switched on crowd, children on shoulders eating organic corn, gourmet sausages, brattwurst and laksas. Mullets of all proud shapes parading, tribal pouches with patches, cowboy goddess, rustic blue singlet and beer swigging psychedelic bogan, the techno hippie, the digital feral, the eucalypt punk, the dust poet, the bush bohemian, the japanese sculptor, the post apocaylptic survival dance troupe, the vegetarian groovers, the musical tricksters, the humble goddesses, the israeli trance fundamentalists, the glitch genius on the decks stretching my physiology in chaos contortions trying to keep up with the nestegg of beats hatching through the speakers, the amateur shamans, the cynical city kids melting into the sweat and the sprinklers above the dancefloor and the acid melting the boundaries between matter and spirit and the rationalists giving away their fences too, I see inhibitions float like lost balloons in the sky, high on the zoo of costumes and persona, people watching with a pen and a piece of shade as bicycles low ride past, thai fisherman pants swagger, ripped sleeves flex, pirate strips hijack bare skin, Tolkien boots skip across the path, leopard strapless dress hunts the dancefloor with pattern spiral shade clothes above dappled with leaves and light, always moving, the wind, the beat, the dust, the leaves, the earth echo soles covered sun skin eucalypt crunching electronic beat

Rainbow Serpent Festival 2011. Market Floor. Photo: Vagabond Forest.

> sandwich bbq chatter laughing masquerades, costumes and the eternal carnival (Parish 2008).

This passage superbly captures a festival that, while today populated by a mixed bag of electronic and acoustic music, retains its psychedelic legacy. Though by no means universal, psytrance producers signpost flow-states with tracks employing strategically programmed vocal samples. Often woven into the breakdowns and animating the escalation, nanomediations function like audio bombs which have a devastating impact on the phlegmatic and the immovable, like that dropped in Eat Static's "Nocturnal Umbra" via an old B&W sci-fi movie (*Crash and Burn!*, 2000): "the terrifying sounds of the monstrous cosmic radio mutations unleashed upon the jungle from a rocket run wild". As apparent in the productions of Eat Static, Tristan, Dick Trevor, Pogo, Raja Ram, and many others, by the end of the 1990s a psychedelic irony was not atypical to the environs of a dance floor showing its rave inheritance. In the pharmacological fantasmagoria of acid house, ravers were plugged into game-spaces and cartoon-like worlds in which Ecstasy-charged avatars were freed from their everyday responsibilities. With the arrival of acid-trance (Goa/psytrance), the electronic Toon Town reverberated into the new millennium, and was equally alluring. Thus, Mumbo Jumbo's "Weird, Sick, Twisted" had Homer Simpson hammering "I saw weird stuff in that place last night. Weird, strange, sick, twisted, eerie, godless, evil stuff … And I want in" (*Psychedelic Electronica 3*, 2000). Smiles appear across the dance floor and posses crack up as medleys of pop-narratives, cult icons and screen actors are plumbed, edited and re-cast to star cameo roles in this retrograde theatre. The dance floor finds a new use for things, in wacky Gibsonian fashion. Mocking the imperious and taking a hatchet to hubris are customary to the trance carnival in which ostentatious displays – military uniforms, the garb of religious officials, and aristocratic sportswear – are intended to empty these symbols of authority and divert them to other ends. As DJs spin tunes power-pointed with vocal samples lifted from official and popular sources which become edited and mashed-up within audio-subvertisements, authorized reality is jammed, *détourned* and parodied by the nano media technicians of psytrance. One oft-sampled source is Willard Cantelon's LP *LSD: Battle for the Mind* released in 1967 by Supreme Records, a division of the Glendale, CA-based Bible Voice Inc, a goldmine for producers plying the parodic imagination. Nystagmus's "Tommy is Dead" (*The Immaculate Perception*, 2005), for example, reproduces Cantelon narrating the tragic tale of Tommy Forester, a "good-looking, personable, athletic" young man who had a "high IQ" and who, according to his Dean, "had the best potential of any man in his class". But Tommy's problem was acid.

> At first the LSD made him sick to his stomach. But then Tommy began to hallucinate. The air began to be filled with rainbows. The very atmosphere seemed to be a moving current of multicolour particles which came streaming down around him. When he listened to the stereo he saw coloured particles floating out from the speakers. When he looked at the walls they seemed to be melting. The pictures on the walls became liquified with colours running down like waterfall. It was sensational.

In this lifted statement Cantelon inadvertently paints a Daliesque vision. Clever and timely plunderphonics orchestrating a radically different outcome than that intended by their authors, cause contagious laughter to erupt among inhabitants who appear contently marooned inside outlands that may have drawn inspiration from Wonderland, Lilliput and the adventures of Pantagruel. It takes a sophisticated operation to sail this far from civilization, to wittingly lampoon order and form, for habitués to parody themselves, even burlesquing the fiction of an integral self – the individuated whole person that is, in other circumstances, the subject of aspiration. Unstable mind states are routinely embraced within these contexts, as invoked by the sampled material. The Twisted Allstars – the one-time collaboration of Simon Posford, Tristan Cooke, Sajahan Natkin and Serge Souque – are a case in point. Lifting lines from *One Flew Over the Cuckoo's Nest* and *American Psycho*, their "Blue Sky on Mars" (*Twisted Sessions Vol. 1*, 2002) conveys: "It don't make a *bit* of sense to me ... If *that's* what bein' crazy is, then I'm senseless, out of it, gone down the road, wacko!" Allusion to substance-influenced conditions of mind alteration and disorientation are par for the course and may arrive, for example, care of HAL 9000, with a sampled line shorn of its original context: "My mind is going" – as heard on Sandman's "Bad News" (*Witchcraft*, 1998).

The temporary defectiveness of mind amplified in scripted lines lifted from cinema serves to narrate the fiction of one's disembarkation from normality on the dance floor. Of course this is not simply fictive since the psychedelic festival facilitates a phenomenal transit. With a knowing wink, on "Charlies Trip" (*Liquid*, 2001), Australia's Mr Peculiar (Dustin Saalfield) animates the fantasy with a familiar line repurposed to evoke the effects of a hit of LSD: "Welcome to you, the lucky finder of this golden ticket ... I feel funny ... Oompa loompa, oompa loompa, oompa loompa, doopity-doo". Like the reception of text, voice samples are "received" in unpredictable ways despite the intentions of producers. On the dance floor, like inner-voices, sonic texts serve to enhance, satirize, even deride, practices of self-derailment, braggadocio and other arrogations. Here, dance experience may be the subject of considerable reflexivity, within an electro-carnivalesque trajectory which makes mockery of all unfunky pretentions, sharp-lines, head trips, and genre fundamentalism. This development is furnished audiologically in styles that "break" up the lines of "progressive" styles in fusional sounds like psybreaks, suomisaundi and ethnodelica with influences from electro and breakbeat sonifying dance floors whose occupants are hipsters and beatfreaks charmed by the distracting breaks negotiated into trance. Facilitating an oscillation between functional and performative states, electro musics – funk and techno derived, and often referred to as "afternoon music" – are the benchmark sonics of distraction that have come to dominate the soundscape of the psychedelic carnivalesque. Black Rock City is exemplary, with Burning Man accommodating a style of music – breaks – suited to its location and conditions. While an electro-breaks aesthetic enabling distraction may be endogenous to bohemian scenes, the physical conditions of the Black Rock Desert – where surrender to progressive rhythms is interrupted by the requirements of survival in extreme conditions – have necessitated a Burner-style electro music. While Goatrance was integral to past "sound art camps" at Burning Man, psytrance would become drowned out in later years by a cacophony of electro-oriented breaks and dubstep, a circumstance that may also be related to the relative dearth, in the US, of large psychedelic festivals: those aesthetic laboratories and cultural economies crucial in an age of music file-sharing.

As "breaks" deconstruct the beat and eschew earnestness and athleticism, a sonics of distraction – an electro funk – reverberates across the grounds of the trance carnival. And, as Kodwo Eshun wrote in relation to funk:

> Mutant bass dissolves the rigidity of hipness, collapses the distance that Cool demands. As a homeopathic agent, "Funk not only moves, it can remove" the sensation of feelin walled-in, closed-up, cased in armour. It squirms like a tapeworm, heaving and contracting along your intestines. It's a bassnake that undulates the inert abdomen and pelvis in S waves, snakemotions that sidewind along the thighs (1998: 08[149–50]).

This description relates most clearly to the first of two interpretations of "funk" outlined by Scott Hacker, meanings relating to the corporeality, and, more to the point, intercorporeality, of dance. As he explains, the musical definition of "funk"

> is that which moves, irresistible, an ineluctable conclusion of motion ('dedicated to the preservation of the motion of hips'), and of course it's always On The One. The other usage of the term refers to the smell of funk – earthy musk, the purple smell of global vagina, the source of jazz in sweat, saxophone jism, the smell of spontaneity and origination, funk giving birth to funk, the fertile rhythms of the song cycle, life and death, conception and birth in dirt and secretions, the visceral funk of sweat and sex, pussy

> rotation, the stank thang, the glory of juices in vapor reacting at base level in the gut, gut bass thumping spleen ... in all fertility awareness the funk figures as smell, cosmic progenation, funk of dame nature in labor harmonizing with funk of loose booty boarding the Mothership, the smell that leaves us "standing on the verge of getting it on" (Hacker 1994).

The "Mothership" referred to here is that which was captained by P-Funk in the 1970s, the orchestrators of the en-funked dance floor, under the aegis of funk. Despite the prejudice George Clinton expressed towards the body danced by electronic beats, the EDM dance floor lies at the crossroads of these meanings, especially that which shakes within the carnivalesque precincts of a dance festival, and, moreover, festivals at which participants camp for periods ranging from a night to over a week, where festal-goers are exposed to each other's bodies: in coital encounters, feasting, ablutions, excretion, etc. Psytrance festivals are grounds for the experience of funk, where dance floors, especially during week-long events, become like malodorous swamps where earth stomped, sweat excreted, tears shed, drinks spilled, and waste discarded over several days and nights cause the "stank thang", a rising effluvium under and through which the assembled dance.

Hacker's description evokes that moment where the dance floor breaks down boundaries between habitués, a population subject to the breaking beats and mashed sound-bytes, and yet whose shifting beat structures and kinky pulsations animate those same denizens. "Funkiness" is a performance paradox with unpretentious and flamboyant elements. While evoking a *nastiness* embodied in the manky, sticky and frowzy conditions shared by cohabitants of a floor that has seen successive days/nights of hard labour, it also signals a *sweetness* of style and affect. And while it evokes a diminution of individuality in "trance" (becoming other), it signals availability (to others). Soundscapes of the contemporary psyfestival animate the bumping attraction – in particular the progressive "afternoon music" produced by the likes of Perfect Stranger, Ace Ventura or the funky electro-pulsations of Neelix, such as "Disco Decay (Edit, 2008)" (2008) – and the allure of sexual pressure amplified via the suggestive storylines of minimal electro, as in Jey & Ex's "Inside Me", which features a woman moaning and demanding the listener to "come inside".[14] Thus, "funky" might be repulsive, and it might be compelling – surely a most ambiguous condition.

While there will be debate concerning the place or legitimacy of funk within a movement which possesses transcendent spiritual paths, funk is a signature hip-shifting propensity of the trance carnival, perhaps more so at those points where the lines fuse and new aesthetics emerge. One such "place" is suomisaundi, the free-form Finnish cross-genred trance self-identified as "spugadelic". Though maintaining the 4/4 beat, this convention-breaking

Ozora 2009. Photo: Pascal Querner.

trance holds influence from techno, funk, jazz and blues, as found in the work of Evsy and Haltya, and traced back to Flippin Bixies. Finnish free-form styles can also be traced back to GAD's abstract 1996 release *Apollo 3d* and other releases on Exogenic and Australia's Psy-Harmonics, especially Texas Faggot, and found on releases like the *Hippie Killer Collection* (2007) and *Hectic Dialect* (2009). Haltya (Jürgen Sachau & Tommi Sirkiä) have been instrumental in the development of the Finnish sound, with their *Electric Help Elves* (2004) promoted as "funky forest trance".[15] "Kaikados", a Hidria Spacefolk remix on this album, is a dense ecology of swirls, electrified twitters, and synth guitars. These challenging arrangements, like the funk-spugedelic "Mothership" featured on Haltya's *Book of Nature* (2008), possess an experimental ecosystem of sounds that places listeners at a *progressive* remove from Goatrance, and indeed progressive trance.

Tribal trance and neotrance

This diversity of expression, and yet singularity of intent, is symptomatic of a neotribalism in which participants readily adopt the "tribal" moniker to identify themselves. While a variety of differences – national, ethnic, class, gender, as well as those associated with genre – are performed within party precincts, the dance floor is imagined to orchestrate their transcendence. Curiously, both processes in this dynamic attract the designation "tribe" or "tribal". The inclusive sensibility where distinctions are putatively obliterated within the temporary dance conflagration is an experience commonly regarded as "tribal", while the amplification of identity within the dancescape is also figured to be an expression of "my tribe" *vis-à-vis* "your tribe". The difference engine powers a mechanism by which difference is orchestrated *and* resolved, and therefore gives expression to a cosmopolitan dynamic in which the extinguishment of divisive barriers and respect for difference are coincident. The logic is not simply that of "being together", as in Maffesoli's (1996) thesis of "de-individualization", but a *coming together* of multiple and disparate genres, fans, etc., as is demonstrated by Rainbow Serpent and Exodus festivals, as well as Germany's Fusion Festival, Boom and, for instance, California's Symbiosis. While a utopianism is echoed in commentary like that of Goa Gil who celebrates a "global tribe" – "a tribe that's beyond and transcends nationalities or national borders or even cast, creed, color or any of these things" (in McAteer 2002: 83) – the unfolding phenomenon is no homogeneous monoculture without internal divisions. It is a tribalism that is decaled with an iconic litany from the cosmic to the gothic, enlivened by disparate narratives from the romantic to the dystopian, and inhabited by those performing diverse subject positions.

The tribal festival, then, allows its inhabitants multiple freedoms, including the freedom to join one's flame to the conflagration, and to hold self-promotions on and off the dance floor. Exemplifying the festal-life flourishing in the contemporary, Boom affords this commotion of singularity and freakiness, this dissolution and presentation of self-hood. Energized in rare fashion, across this spectrum one shifts between spectacular states of self(less)ness. Evincing the corporeal ambiguity of "funk", participants may experience fusion with, or autonomy from, others in extraordinary states of altered consciousness/embodiment. Organizers of events, in collaboration with DJs, producers, sound engineers, visual and décor artists, optimize space, time, art and other resources to realize the dynamic that I dub *neotrance*.[16] This term emerges as an adjunct to "neotribe" and owes its appearance to my dissatisfaction with the term "trance" as a catchphrase for a cultural movement. With the *OED* describing six definitions, "trance" is one of the most poorly defined and nebulous terms in the lexicon of those describing alternative states of consciousness (see Cardeña 2011: 4), a confusion apparent within psytrance circles. More specifically, it derives from the suspicion that traditional conceptions of "trance", particularly "possession trance", and especially the analogy with what Emma Cohen (2008) calls "executive possession",[17] are ill-suited to recognize the experiential complexity of dance festal behaviour, and in particular the experience of "trance" endemic to the psychedelic festival, its music, and its dance. Indeed, psychedelic trance calls for interpretation deviating from conventional theories of "trance" (and possession) – from traditional (e.g. Winkelman 1986), to Western (e.g. Taves 1999) manifestations. In various cultural contexts deriving from West African and sub-Saharan traditions in particular, patterns of animation identified as "possession" (by Gods and spirits), such as those agents associated with *vodu* and *orisha* possession complexes, typically serve therapeutic and divinatory purposes in communities where religious specialists, cults and shrines are devotional vehicles for deities and spirits, where altered states are interpreted via inherited religious frameworks, and are integral to the life of communities where human and spirit worlds are intricately interwoven.[18] While the psychophysiological impact of percussive and rhythmic music (Rouget 1985) may hold across traditional and contemporary trance performance,[19] and while DJs, scholars and participants invoke loose folk-theories of divine guidance, conventional understandings of "spirit possession" tend to offer overstated, unfair and misleading frameworks for understanding "trance" dance cultures associated with contemporary popular music.

When lazy contrasts are the hub of comparative analysis, the usefulness of research should be called into question. Commenting on raves, Georgina Gore (1995: 137–8) claims that, compared with possession trance within cults of the Southern Nigerian Bini, rave is "a rite of passage leading nowhere ... It is a ritual without content, ecstatic, solitary and narcissistic. It is a game of chance; its trance is aleatory and dizzying". Raving might apparently exemplify the zombification of modern life, a disappearance from meaning, the "zone" entered perhaps as pathological as that ascribed to the world of gamblers and casinos, an observation which partly explains the poaching from Baudrillard in early rave studies where ravers were apparently disappearing into a world of appearances (see Melechi 1993). Illustrating the results of an ethnographic approach to raves which would deliver us closer to the "trance" in question, Melanie Takahashi (2005) seeks to understand the alternative states of consciousness endogenous to these events. She argues that through DJ techniques, optimized audio-visual production and performance, and participant expectations at raves, "technological advancements may compensate for the lack of coherent cultural signifiers" *vis-à-vis* "the sophisticated scripted process of initiation observed in ceremonial possession" (Takahashi 2005: 253). Ravers remain "horses", only now they are ridden by the spirit of the optimized audio-visual assemblage channelled by the "shaman" DJ. Through these techniques and sound-art strategies, which Morgan Gerard (2004) calls "liminal techniques", by comparison to other popular music forms/techniques, DJs are arguably better able to "control the means of perception" (Takahashi 2005: 254). Aided by prolonged physical exertion and psychoactive alterants, audio and lighting techniques (sonic and photic "drivers") have indeed been optimized to induce the psychophysiological effects of trance-like states – a motivation that "trance" labelled and marketed music has inherited from earlier styles. On *Rainbirds* (Music & Sound, 1995), Astral Projection's early incarnation, SFX, made an effort to effect trance states via wave-like pattern electonica with direct influences from

Jean Michel Jarre.[20] Their "Noise on People" from that release induced a kind of meditative dispossession from mind-states in which awareness of primary bodily sounds and processes are filtered out. As the sample used indicates: "soon you become aware of the overwhelming nothingness, and then strange biological noises ... the rushing of blood through the body, the heart pounding, the bones creaking, the sound of breathing". But while the dancing subject may be free from cares, there is no universally accepted intelligence on the liminal zone between waking and dream states. And so while it makes sense to hold inquiry about the capabilities of newer and adapted technics to animate and energize participants – and indeed entire communities of sound – in raves, psytrance and other EDMC events, persistent analogical modelling with spirit possession becomes burdensome in itself.

With the objective of revealing the sacred terrain of raving, François Gauthier harbours no such intellectual burden. He argues that rave "is not a possession trance, unless perhaps possession by 'nothing'". Ravers "do not feel 'something' (or indeed 'nothing') is overcoming them. On the contrary, it seems this overwhelming feeling originates from within, only they cannot say *how* or *where*" (Gauthier 2004a: 78, original emphasis). "This trance", he continues, "is the desire for pure instituancy, pure experimentation with an otherness that remains confused and diffuse – a pure gratuitous act, or a simple gesture of revolt". Psytrance, as I have argued in this book, offers the context for entering oblivions of this nature, but it is also charged with meaning, is guided by "projects" and is held to be efficacious. Like rave, psytrance can be characterized as "unhinged from a defined and institutionalized – and therefore – explicit religious system that could explicate its meaning". But to argue that "techno trance is sought in *itself* and for *itself*, detached from any defined meaning, aim or purpose" (Gauthier 2004a: 79) is not an accurate description of psychedelic trance. To begin with, in trance culture there is a persistent desire to associate with traditional trance practices. It is believed that the psytrance experience holds value for its practitioners in ways that are equivalent to these authorized cultural practices. That organizers have sought to associate their events with master practitioners of Moroccan Gnawa, as in the 2005 Rhythms of Peace festival, that Sufi dancers were billed for the opening ceremony at Soulclipse in Turkey in March 2006, or that ceremonial dance is performed to didjeridu performed by Indigenous custodians in the Opening Ceremony at Australia's Rainbow Serpent Festival, all reveal conscious efforts to associate the event experience with traditional "tribal" music and ritual practice. In other projects, the techno-trance assemblage is recruited in the directed rite of passage, as in the work of Goa Gil, Ray Castle, DJ Krusty (2008), and in the initiatives of The Oracle in Seattle, LA's Moontribe and other groups for whom the "trance" experience possesses a psycho-therapeutic function.

Yet the development of intentional ritual trance techniques with clear cathartic objectives is uncommon, with psychedelic culture providing no systemic grounds for interpretation of the "trance" experience (see Davis 2001), which, as this chapter has indicated, is complex. If the trance experience holds a therapeutic function, it is subject to individual experience, unique expectations and contextual temperament. If the technicians of ecstasy and the media shamans of trance produce the conditions of being-in-transit, as argued in Chapter 4, then travellers of the breach are obliged to fill it with significance. It is the remit of party organizers and producers to provide a suitably optimized event, but a successful experience is reliant upon the individual partygoer, his or her travel and networking experience, the application of intelligence gathered on a host of matters, and their ability to cobble together the accoutrements of ascension. As this chapter has shown, one of the principal objectives of partygoers from the inception of the Goa landings is to become free from their concerns outside the party and beyond the moment – to become dispossessed. A transnational festival apparatus evolved with this *ekstasis* among its chief considerations, but passage for its occupants relies upon their own experience, cognition, networking skills and resourcefulness. So while there are no master healers, nor consensual frameworks through which states of animation are interpreted and performed within psychedelic culture, self-dispossession is typically sought and engineered. Various allegorical devices recombined from popular culture are used across genres to signify and effect this condition. Earlier in this chapter, I discussed the commitment to *alienation*, a Goa legacy where the figure of the alien signifies difference facilitated by its erasure of all difference. Within the cosmic carnival, the alien is adopted as a mascot for a dispossession that is hopeful of a positive outcome for the self. But this is not the only ride at the psychedelic fairgrounds, given that dark trance has emerged as a popular theatre of the self-dispossessed. Becoming free from rational subjectivity is itself the rampant obsession of darkpsy producers, enabled by horror cinema and served up on nocturnal dance floors: sanity lost (to psychosis), the human abducted (by the alien), the faithful possessed (by the devil), the victim slain (by the serial killer), the innocent attacked (by the beast), the worker enslaved (by evil robots), the citizen's mind controlled (by the CIA), the survivor transformed (by Nazi zombies on acid). In all scenarios, the monstrous is redeployed from screenplays where such figures evoke the visceral terror associated with the annihilation of self. While the pervasive figure of the benevolent, raceless and androgynous alien became totemic for the cosmic carnival, the monster would signify darker shades of dispossession. A similar objective prevails, however: to orchestrate the frisson associated with the departure from consciousness. From the cosmic carnival to the dark carnival and carnivals in between, the desirable state of de-subjectification conveys interest in becoming free from agents of control, principally one's own consciousness, the overwhelming commitment to surrender one's possessing self. Freedom from the "iron cage" of rationality, a radical experimentalism that potentiates the performance of difference, is the Romantic and utopian legacy in psychedelic reflexivity.

Dispossession is therefore fashioned in the remix where diverse pop-cult figures, religious icons and voices are recombined, and where the dancer becomes discombobulated in the company of friends and strangers. This topsy-turvy recombinant theatre returns us to Bakhtin, whose "grotesque realism" offers a useful heuristic with which to approach psytrance. This is with qualification, since successful dispossession, or alienation, may be predicated upon excluding that which jeopardizes the mission, which threatens the *otherness* of the world temporarily inhabited. In his study undertaken after the scene's virtual demise in its site of origins, Saldanha (2007a) concluded that the erasure of difference in trance in Goa relied upon the elimination of phenotypical signs of differences – namely brown skins, with the purity of white bodes signifying the desirable transcendence. In this freak "crowd crystal" (Canetti 1962), the liquidation of difference relies upon the accentuation and hardening of the distinctiveness of protagonists, elitism also observed by Joshua Schmidt among Israeli *trancistim* (2010). This said, as evidenced by the trance carnival globally, and within the wider Disctopia of EDM, multiple elements jeopardize the "vibe", are inimical to making *It* happen. In a realm of competing expectations, tourists (including those with white skins), authorities and "straights" imperil the conditions of self-dissolution, freak performance and *instituant* desire.

* * *

This chapter has approached the vexing subject of trance dance itself, the *raison d'être* of the psychedelic festival. The psychedelic "trance" experience is an historical product of radical reflexive modernity whose Disctopian worlds apart and in between have enabled habitués access to extraordinary states of mind and body. Enabled by new technologies of the senses and facilitated by Eastern travels emerging at an important juncture in the Space Age's Cold War era, the *cosmic carnival* was the early and enduring apotheosis of this movement for desubjectification in dance. In the new architectonic of trance, a *progressive* techno-aesthetic emerged as a dominant technics of transcendence. The optimal "trance" condition was figured as an optimized "flow" state with iterated challenges sufficient to satisfy enthusiasts. Moving to stand still, to accomplish no-thing, provides a useful way to understand the music and festival culture of psychedelic trance whose "weekend societies" in regions worldwide propagate, weekend in and weekend out, the "progressive" experience. Yet "trance" is at the same time characterized by the persistent effort, in psychedelic carnivalesque fashion, to parody, overturn and up-end the progression, to scatter one's thoughts, to muddy the truth. Nothing, after all, is annihilated by the funk.

At events downstream from the cosmic carnival, like Boom, accommodating progressive and funky trends, enthusiasts oscillate between states of self-dissolution and self-expression, where indeed the chief performance is the spectacular departure from rational subjectivity. *Neotrance* has been identified as a neotribal dance cultural phenomenon potentiating the performative dissolution of individuality, an ekstasis/theatre dynamic involving surrender to the flow and a freakish dramaturgy. As recognized in the previous chapter and reinforced here, with psychedelic trance parties and festivals that have inherited and repackaged the Goa "state of mind", the dance floor is the site on which travellers experience the dismemberment of identity through luxurious states of abandonment, experimental conditions which are also creative exaltations. A nest of popular cultural tropes are redeployed to echo and effect the desire for self-alienation, voluntary control-loss, and the dispossession from rational subjectivity. From the cosmic to the dark carnival, varying sounds are piped through the mothership to orchestrate these conditions. From the soaring ascensionism of cosmic trance to the gothic struggle of darkpsy, and from the frenetic pace of full-on to the smooth landing of ambient, different stages, floors and their musics in the greater festival may harbour different "projects", but the carnival of trance is a stage upon which the individual must work it out for her or him self.

7 Psyculture in Israel and Australia

Israel and Australia are global centres of psytrance, with *mesibot* and *doofs* – the respective terms for parties in these nations – local domains for the expression of global psyculture. The ethnographically informed insights in this chapter uncover scene developments in these countries, and psyculture more widely. Goa/psytrance came to an unusual prominence in Israel, where it became a popular music. With sixty-six psytrance labels in 2011 (representing 7 per cent of world labels), Israel is one the greatest per capita producers of this music internationally. With thirty-one labels in 2011 (3 per cent of world labels),[1] Australia is less productive by contrast, yet renowned internationally for its summer festival culture. As this chapter illustrates, these national scene developments demonstrate the diversity of post-Goa psyculture as it became translated in countries with disparate cultural, historical and geographical conditions. While all too brief, these examples show how aspects of Goa/psytrance have been pressed into the service of religious, spiritual, countercultural and intellectual agendas in the respective regions, and how national and cultural climates have shaped a mix of agendas, from the rebellious to the proactive, as evidenced among party organizations, events and labels. They also provide examples of how national psycultures are comparative sites for the expression of originality, which, as indicated in the book's introduction, refers to the *origins* to which participants lay claim and the *original* work produced. Psyculture participants harness symbolic resources and commit to sensory practice in the claiming of heritage, the revival of tradition, the return to the primordial, all inflected by local history, religious traditions and prevailing socio-political conditions. These practices are ongoing, and should be understood as innovations through which novel forms are created from the mix of existing elements. While no singular narrative prevails, amid the carnivalesque noise of psyculture, as moments of clarity, connection and continuity, the dance floor is the ultimate grounds for a *religious experience* recognized by participants across these diverse national scenes.

Israelis in the Temporary Autonomic Zone

I travelled to Israel for six weeks over Sep–Oct 2007 – a brush with the world power in psytrance. The 1960s appear to have had a relatively cursory impact in Israel, but in the early to mid-1990s Israeli youth became animated by a contumacious sensibility by way of Goatrance. The "countercultural" character of Goa in Israel would be heavily influenced by global rave culture, which, as some observers have pointed out, already carried a shallow "simulacrum" of 1960s counterculture (see Rietveld 1993). By the 2000s, psytrance had achieved stature as a popular music in Israel, a strange circumstance not replicated in any other nation. Israel is an international powerhouse in the production, distribution and performance of psytrance, which became one of its chief cultural exports, provoking challenges to the music culture's ostensible "countercultural" character (Schmidt 2010). In 2007, I detected the sonic signature of psytrance echoing from pleasure craft on the Red Sea, animating apartment buildings in Mitzpe Ramon and even played to supermarket shoppers. I received the distinctive thud of full-on repeating from passing motor vehicles in Jerusalem. During the course of my stay, I attended two festivals, the Holy Rave and the TAZ, both of which I discuss in the following.

The proliferation of psychedelic trance in Israel cannot be understood in isolation from the nation's complex historical, religious and cultural circumstances. I have been struck by the frequency with which psytrance "makes the news" in Israel, and it is immediately apparent that the mediatization of psytrance echoes the diverse agendas commentators want it to serve. Given its popularity, psychedelic trance has been a controversial subject in national media for twenty years, though nightlife and dance scenes have attracted outcries and delegitimation in Israel for decades, as Nissan Shor relates in *Dancing with Tears in Our Eyes* (Shor 2008). In an essay published in the Zionist venue *Azure*, Assaf Sagiv (2000) observed that, following centuries of dormancy, the Bacchanalia have "returned with an intensity unknown since the end of the classical period". Apparently an embattled "hothouse of permissiveness in the conservative Middle East", Israel was at the forefront of an international ecstatic dance movement. As Sagiv continued, "the ancient fertility cults which the zealous followers of the Hebrew God sought to extirpate three thousand years ago have come to life again in the land of Israel". Throughout the late 1990s and in the following decade spokespersons from different locations in the political spectrum admonished the wayward antics of the nation's youth, especially at those points of exposure to the outside world. The new "culture of ecstasy" raised alarm among critics apprehensive of misguided youth (e.g. Taub 1997), and triggered moral panic among Zionists concerned with growing transnationalism (Meadan 2001). But the voices were as varied as the agendas psytrance became enlisted to serve. In his article, "Land of the Rave", Daniel Belasco (n.d.) drew comparison between psytrance and orthodox religious practice at its most ecstatic: "The dancing can be related", claimed Belasco, "to 'shuckling' the back-and-forth swaying of orthodox Jewish men in prayer. Trance music also evokes niggunim, repetitive sung Hasidic melodies that promoted impassioned spirituality to combat the modernization and secularization of Judaism". He also noted that since many trance festivals are held on Friday night (Shabbat) or during the various calendar holidays, this precludes participation by Orthodox observant Jews, because the "weekend" is effectively one day only (Saturday). Nevertheless, these events provide "the opportunity for secular Israelis to create personal rituals to connect to the sublime aspects of Judaism". As Belasco continued, "held in remote forests, beaches, and deserts, raves bring urban Israelis closer to the beauty of nature, to the very land dreamt of by modern Zionism founder Theodor Herzl in Vienna at the end of the 19th century, and fought for still today by the Israeli army". These comments offer sharp perspective on the quest for origins, the observance and defence of Orthodox tradition that assumes stature among spokespersons of Israeli psytribalism. Yet, in an expression of the concurrent commitment to novel conditions, in a localized romanticization of the psytribal Disctopia, Belasco stated, "Israeli raves also embody longings for cultural and spiritual unity with other people". Comparing these events with gospel music and whirling dervishes, "by linking their Jewish spiritual ecstasy to that of other cultures ... they aspire to overcome the particularism of being a member of 'the Chosen People'". Of course, such attitudes do not go uncontested by other religious Israelis (or *dati'im*) and passionate "returnees" to Judaism who, warning of the consequences of straying from the path, continue to fire salvos over the heads of enthusiasts (see Ganihar 2011). Others indicate evidence that for many returnees to Orthodox Jewry, attendance at *mesibot* provided the initial spark for their religious conversion. According to Schmidt (2011: 131), many are "full-onistim", that is "hard-core ravers who re-directed their passion for trance music to strict religious observance (often tinged with Hassidic overtones) as an auxiliary method for gaining spiritual ascendance". The notorious Breslov Judaism, named after mystic Rebbe Nachman of Breslov, has attracted a large contingent of former *trancistim*[2] "after 'finding' religion via drug-induced ecstatic states of consciousness". And psytrance, apparently, remains part of proselytizing practice, with Breslov-*trancistim* known to drive "nachman-mobiles" – vans rigged with speakers playing full-on mixed with samples of Nachman's teachings.[3]

For Sagiv, the lament was that Israeli youth had become pessimistic, passive and disengaged from everyday life, since they preferred to "lose themselves in psychedelic festivals rather than come to terms directly with the complex realities of personal and public life in a country in conflict". The plaint inferences the stressful social and historical conditions in which Israelis are born, especially those raised in the period following the Six Day

War (1967) and Yom Kippur War (1973). This generation was raised in a time of transition, in which the nuclear family, religious life, labour stability and gender relations underwent transformation. Yet, while there has been a decline in traditional values and structures since this period, the fulfilment of rigid work and study obligations remained a requirement, with a strict "social timetable" placing pressures on individuals to become married and successful "adults" by the time they turn thirty (Maoz 2005: 163–4). Furthermore, this generation was achieving young adulthood inside a cultural pressure-cooker: the occupation of the West Bank and the Gaza Strip, the al-Aqsa Intifada (or Second Palestinian Uprising) from 2000, ongoing tensions with Syria, Hamas suicide bombers, official paranoia, and international condemnation. The mandatory three-year service in the IDF (Israeli Defense Forces) for males and two for females, and the permanent state of readiness, evidenced, for example, by the Second Lebanon War which broke out in July 2006 and lasted for five weeks following the kidnapping of Israeli soldiers by Hamas and Hezbollah and the shelling of settlements on the northern border, renders coming of age in Israel a troubling experience with which young adults in other liberal democracies are rarely familiar. Anxieties are accompanied by feelings of impotence and a corresponding sense of anguish which, Sagiv argued, triggered a Dionysian impulse apparently more concentrated and determined than 1960s/1970s precursors in the US, Europe and Australia.

This emergent ecstatic impulse would be expressed, in part, in travels outside Israel, in the form of backpacking – principally to Asia and South America, but especially India where temporal self-marginalization constitutes a response to the stressful experience of growing up in the Middle East, with the eventual cultural investment in psytrance incited by the pressures of dutiful citizenship and social obligations. In an age of globalized media, *trancistim* have responded to the absence of the freedoms recognized to be enjoyed by youth elsewhere around the Westernized world. Israeli psyculture is thus a vociferous, audacious and ludic reaction to freedoms denied – freedoms found in a *performed exodus* from the pressures of everyday life. "Enclaves" of backpackers in Goa, Manali and elsewhere are said to "play out" the role of colonizers in what Noy and Cohen (2005: 17) refer to as a "third frontier", which reflects symbolic components of the other two (i.e. the Israeli Diaspora and Israelis living in occupied Palestine). As Noy and Cohen explain, this is a metaphorical, playful "colonization", and we might observe ludic travails beyond the national boundaries enabling self-styled enactments of the myth of Abraham who, as Goffman (2004: 12) noted, was "history's first self-exile". The exodus is not uniform, however. While an historical exodus mythology has been recruited to a transnationalist utopianism which has existed since the inception of Goatrance as it was translated and developed in Israel, for many the "exodus" simply translates into transgressive and rule-defying hyperbole, with the sampling of drugs and music the popular front for an outlaw aesthetic (see St John 2012a). Here the "exodus" is articulated more in terms of that which participants seek departure from (i.e. restricted liberties), than any particular outcome, destination or reformation.

Militarism has greatly influenced the spectacular abandonment of the self in Israel, equivalent to that of the shaping influence of India. It was in 1988 that Israeli passport holders were first permitted to India. When young travellers stumbled into nascent bohemian electronic trance scenes in Goa and Manali (and Thailand) in the late 1980s and early 1990s, many had recently completed their military duties. India would also become a point of departure for more permanent expatriates. According to Smadar Waisman, a former IDF intelligence analyst who now resides in India, and among a reported 40–60,000 Israelis who live there (from 7.7 million Jewish citizens in 2011), "military service turns good young Israelis into corrupt and insensitive people. We're forced to follow orders and do and see horrible things that no young person should be involved with. If you want your soul to survive the anxiety and depression of Israel, you leave for Goa" (Copetas 2009).[4] While backpacking around the world has become a post-service rite of passage, the psychedelic sojourns sought by travellers could hardly have been anticipated by authorities. In Goa and other exotic locations at an extreme remove from the Holy Land, those Schmidt characterizes as "uninhibited psychonautic trail-blazers" (2006: 11) could undertake vertical flights with the assistance of the usual fare: *charas*, LSD, Ecstasy, and *psilocybin*-mushrooms, perhaps washed down with *qat*. Removed from social, religious and military obligations, psychonauts would enter other holy-lands, and entertain experimental post-service identities. Yet the "war machine" – which Georges Dumezil identified as an experience of "puissance" falling in between and outside the operations of the state, an idea of undisciplined itinerancy informing Deleuze and Guattari's "nomadology" (1986) – would become a mobilizing force. Having participated in the IDF, *trancistim* were now conscripts in the legions of the night. Many Israeli backpackers in India and elsewhere fresh from military service and travelling in *hevreh* (solid group of friends) have been characterized as "conquerors" (*havokoshim*), who "engage in arduous treks and rapid and constant transit between localities and countries". As Maoz (2005: 181) explains, these travellers

> do not come into contact with the locals, but enclose themselves in a environmental bubble consisting of those similar to themselves – Israeli tourists of the same age. They express an attitude of superiority to the locals and do not desire to learn their culture; on the contrary, they seek to appropriate it by "conquest" and by introducing Israeli culture to it. During the backpacking journey they relive the army experience of intensive, arduous activity, centering on strength and physical prowess.

These young travellers are said to extend the "moratorium" in the passage to adulthood already established during military service – though as Noy and Cohen suggest (2005: 11–12), practice is not simply a *continuity* of service but a *reaction* to it which can be expressed in a ludic manner by backpackers who may joke about Thailand, for example, being "in our hands!" While the attitude of the *havokoshim* might explain Israeli backpacking behaviour in Goa, those who have been identified as "the Manalis" (*haManalim*) are perhaps closer to the rule. Also referred to as "party children" or *karhanistim*, their journey involves the consumption of drugs, notably *charas* made in Manali. These backpackers are similarly stated to hold an indifference, "contempt" and "belligerence" towards locals. But these self-identifying categories do not apparently exhaust the full range of contact behaviour, for older backpackers (in their early thirties) who remain in toured regions for longer periods and regarded as "the settlers" (*hamitnahalim*) are said to "show an attitude of respect and esteem toward the Others among whom they settled, even trying to learn from them and adopt their ways" (Maoz 2005: 176). These backpackers are stated to be undertaking a "spiritual journey", though in Maoz's approach those who consume drugs appear to be more involved in misadventure than "spiritual" journeys. While there has been no adequate research performed on the activities of Israelis in Goa, especially in the critical formative years of 1988–1993, these disparate traveller sensibilities seem to have helped shape the Israeli experience in Goa.

From the point of view of national cultural history, the experience in Goa was a rite of passage which would have considerable implications for the country, as travellers smuggled their new-found artifice back into the Holy Land. In a 2002 article in *Mushroom Magazine*, DJ, event promoter and scene commentator Boris Levit wrote that Tel-Aviv's Penguin club was central to the emerging scene in 1988: "musically directed towards the fusion between early industrial rock (Einstürzende Neubuaten), new wave (Depeche Mode), Kraftwerk, Psycik TV, Butthole Surfers and going in the direction of heavier electronica" (Levit 2002: 82). In 1990, the first psychedelic parties called Full Moon Gatherings were thrown on the Nizanim beaches. In Levit's recollections, with no more than 100 people in attendance, these clandestine raves sounded out a mix of early acid, Chicago house, Detroit techno and Frankfurt trance. At these and other events developing in almost complete isolation from scenes elsewhere, local DJs would perform variations on the Goa sound. These artists included now venerated pioneers like Avi Nissim and Lior Perlmutter (SFX and later Astral Projection), Har-El Prussky and Miko (California Sunshine), Guy Sebbag, Avi Algranati (Phreaky, Space Cat) and Ofer Dikovsky (Oforia). The first Israeli Goatrance track, "This is News of Trance", was released in 1993 by Art.Indust (Erej Jino of later Analog Pussy fame) on the compilation *Trance Mix*. By the third *Trance Mix* collection (1994), the compilation featured only Israeli tracks. In 1995, Indoor would release the first Israeli trance artist album: *Progressive Trance*. Around this time, labels like Melodia Records, Trust In Trance Records, Phonokol and Krembo Records emerged.[5] This period was characterized by sensationalized media reports and heavy-handed police interventions in these apparent "drug havens", as DJs were arrested and equipment confiscated. Not unlike scenes in the UK and elsewhere, negative media and police attention saw parties shunted into licensed clubs, in particular the Ha Baaya ("The Problem in Tel Aviv") where Guy Sebbag and Avi Nissim performed. As Levit comments, the mood at these parties was *balagan*, Hebrew for "chaos", or "psychaos", stating that as parties were forced into closed clubbing environments, the mood shifted from "the Neo hippie tribal full moon gatherings to full on hedonism". He described the music as "a mix between the Italian ecstasy star Ramirez, German Avantgarde Techno, early club trance (age of love), minimal Acid techno (Plastikman) Hardfloor, and the local heroes SFX" (2002: 83). At this time, an appealing outlaw sensibility intensified as a result of police pressure. According to Levit, the growing possibility of police intervention precipitated a fast-paced style of power trance: "you can never know how much time you have left until the party will be shut down". Apparently this pressure led to the development of Nitzhonot,[6] a late 1990s melodic hard-trance style (145–55 bpm) with tremendous arpeggiated breakdowns which achieved mainstream success with trance subsequently growing popular in clubs, on prime-time radio playlists, at non-psychedelic music festivals and with successful crossover artists like DJ Yahel. Offering further clarification on Nitzhonot, or "victory trance", Levit stated that "Israelis had no time for long set building. The party could be closed soon. They want it all condensed into a single track".

This was the period of the so-called "war on trance" kicked off by the brutal 1993 police raid on the Tel Aviv club Impulse, followed by police interventions throughout the decade. In 1997, reacting to this attention, prominent member of the nouveau religious (a returnee to Judaism), a prestigious sponsor of the movement, and the man often identified as "the father" of Israeli psytrance, Asher Haviv, mounted a festival at Ganey Huga in the Beit Shean valley near the border with Jordan. Attracting sponsorship from AISam (Israel's Anti-drugs trust), the event – at the time the largest psychedelic trance festival in Israel, or anywhere else for that matter (with 15,000 people) – was self-identified as "Drugless" and thrown on the holiday Shavuot. Despite the ruse, one national newspaper subsequently reported "the biggest drug party in the history of the country". As Levit (2002: 85) responded, "the newspaper forgot to mention that during the entire festival there was not a single case of violence, no crime, and only 20 people were arrested for possession of marijuana". In September of 1997, 30,000 people reputedly attended the next protest event organized by Beersheba club The Forum on the beach in Nizani, which was shut down by police at 9:00 am on the second day during California Sunshine's set. These events inspired Haviv

TAZ Festival, Israel, September 2007. Photo: Graham St John.

to organize Give Trance A Chance on 9 July 1998 in Tel Aviv's Rabin Square in which 30,000 people attended. In 2000, he organized a subsequent demonstration in Jerusalem called The Gathering.

The late 1990s and subsequent years have been characterized by nostalgia for the earlier Goa period. California Sunshine wore this longing for larger times on the sleeve of 1997 release *Trance*: "long gone are the days of the summer of 89. when every new synthesized sound of morning glory caused tears in the eyes of a small bunch of hippies dancing to it in some Indian jungle or some Thai white sanded beach. those who have experienced it long to travel in time and be back in those days of never ending freedom, love and virginity. today all we can do is spread that feeling". The feeling persisted ten years hence as the flags of party crew The 3rd Empire snapped over the TAZ Festival held from 26–28 September 2007, during Sukkot. In its second year, the TAZ was held near Arad on the edge of the Negev and close to the Occupied Territories. Enabling Israelis to maintain their flight across the psychedelic frontiers while remaining a short drive from Tel-Aviv, Jerusalem and the next working week, The 3rd Empire issued the event's 2,000 temporal émigrés with small booklets designed like passports, complete with stamped daily "visas". Inside the borders of the TAZ, I went among those Schmidt refers to as Israel's "Eastern Generation" (1989–2009), which he further clarifies,

> was called in the early 1990s by the then young shock-rock-pop star Aviv Gefen "the fucked generation" and, by the end of the millennium by hip social critic Gadi Taub the generation of the "dispirited revolutionaries". This meme runs parallel with *Waltz With Bashir* style storylines that I think will more and more begin

> to emerge as people start to make the connections between the "post Lebanese war" (1982) generation and its collective loss of innocence and the discovery and acculturation of PEDMC [Psychedelic Electronic Dance Music Culture] into the fabric of Israeli society.[7]

Schmidt speculates that this period could be dubbed "Israel's 1960s", implying that slain Prime Minister Yitzhak Rabin may have been – with qualification – "Israel's JFK", noting rapid swings to the right subsequent to both assassinations. Regardless of the verity of such comments, countercultural icons of the 1960s have flooded the Israeli trance imaginary. Take, for instance, Shagaat's Morrison Drops Festival held on the Dead Sea in September 2007. The promotional literature conveyed that the event was held in honour of Jim Morrison, often compared favourably with Dionysus. Idolized as "the one that has started it all", the event organizers not only identify with a psychedelic lineage, but have apparently located its divine source and authority in the Californian 1960s. A page of the festival information booklet even featured the entire lyrics to Morrison's "Scream of the Butterfly", after which this edition of the festival was named. Enabling its participants the potential to reach astounding heights at the lowest place on the planet, the event featured a predominantly full-on main stage. Whether it is the voice of Leary, or material lifted from *Fear and Loathing in Las Vegas*, a litany of tropes and caricatures have been sampled from this epoch and remixed into promotions, track programming and conceptual décor.[8]

But if this period was Israel's "Sixties", then it was more or less limited to a specific countercultural archetype – that of the outsider/outlaw. And here I am reminded of that formative statement made by Norman Mailer (1957: 276–7) regarding the post-war, post-bomb, post-Auschwitz, generation of hipsters:

> It is on this bleak scene that a phenomenon has appeared: the American existentialist – the hipster, the man who knows that if our collective condition is to live with instant death by atomic war, relatively quick death by the State as *l'univers concentrationnaire*, or with a slow death by conformity with every creative and rebellious instinct stifled ... if the fate of twentieth-century man is to live with death from adolescence to premature senescence, why then the only life-giving answer is to accept the terms of death, to live with death as immediate danger, to divorce oneself from society, to exist without roots, to set out on that uncharted journey into the rebellious imperatives of the self.

Mailer moved on to refer to the psychopathology that is dictated by these new social conditions. There is an immediate parallel to draw with the attitudes of the so-called "fucked generation" who have not only endured a rigid "social timetable" (Maoz 2005: 163), stifling regulatory frameworks (as Levit reported), but violence (e.g. suicide bombing) associated with the ongoing conflict with Palestine. The day-to-day anxieties and insecurities associated with these historical conditions are unparalleled in most other Westernized countries. In the light of the existential relationship with mortality informing the post-WWII, atomic weapons age, hipster/beat generation identified by Mailer, along with the live-for-the-present "bomb culture" of the jazz subcultures of the 1950s UK (Nuttall 1968), and the "no future" nihilism of 1970s punk, we might better understand the sensibilities of a generation consumed by the recurrent possibility of sudden obliteration, especially given the knowledge that the Eastern Generation perfectly coincides with the period of suicide attacks committed by Palestinian militant groups (i.e. late 1980s–2008), including the acceleration of bombings during the Second Intifada (2000–2005) with Israeli fatalities reaching a peak in 2002 (237 that year).[9]

The apparent "anti-social", "Dionysian" and "psychedelic" responses to these conditions are evident in a music culture where young citizens have sought relief, shelter and detachment in increased doses and at accelerated bpm. Released from the tense world of the everyday in a militarized state, *trancistim* become immersed in altered mind states characterized as temporary *psychosis*, as illustrated in the popularly sought-after craziness of *karahana*, and the general evocation of violent states of mind, inner turmoil and disassociation. In his study of "associative word systems" within Israeli psytrance, Schmidt (2011: 100) conveys language suggestive of violence, tension and aggression, reflective, he argues, of the "reality of conflict-ridden Israel and to the fact that many *trancistim* were in combat units during their military service and are drawn to psytrance culture as a way of countering, or blocking out, the bellicose nature in their day-to-day existences". A pattern may then have formed where efforts to transcend the violence of the everyday are nevertheless shaped by an inveterate cultural warriorhood. Under these conditions, DJ-producers sought and earn reputations as volatile and unpredictable. On his debut *Delirious* (1998), full-on antagonist Oforia was "Psycho Sonic". The attitude is perhaps most evident in the country's most commercially successful act, Infected Mushroom, who appear to have responded to the demand for psycho-sonics. Their early hit "psycho" (*The Gathering*, 1999) is an affectation which seems prescient in the light of more recent albums like *Deeply Disturbed* (2003) and the EP *Becoming Insane* (2007). At its most outrageous, the hubris of the psychotically violent criminal became a favourite of Skazi and other member acts in the Chemical Mafia – including Exaile and Psychotic Micro, Void, Rocky, Paranormal Attack and Damage. On the 2004 release *Mafia*, the Chemical Mafia were self-promoted using mobster narratives from Prohibition-era Chicago. A booklet, sold with the release, illustrates an identification with gangsterism, psychotic personalities, racketeering and being "keepers of whores and brothels" who "formed their own street society, independent of the adult world and antagonistic to it".

Israeli trance resounds with the sonic fiction of transgression, penetrating psychic frontiers, breaching the law, defying limits. The nation's legendary act, Astral Projection, provide further evidence of this contumacy. Their track "Anything is Possible" (2001) repurposes Neo's revelation from the *Matrix*: "I'm going to show them a world without rules and controls, without borders and boundaries, a world where anything is possible". And Morpheous's sampled statement, "as long as the Matrix exists the human race will never be free", could be understood according to the logic: as long as the Matrix exists there will always be outlaws. Here, the call to be free from "borders and boundaries" (very pertinent to Israel) could be read as a call to remove regulatory controls that check free enterprise and unbridled greed. This victorious mood of freedom from restraint had already influenced Nitzhonot. By the late 1990s and early twenty-first century, the quest to conquer limits was being expressed in a music that had turned away from its Goa roots – as performed in the notable work of Astral Projection – to a metal machine music[10] that would develop with accelerated bpm into "full-on". This sound emerged from HOM-Mega Productions whose first release was the compilation *Full On* (1998), which, in this early manifestation, retained a distinct Goa sound and aesthetic next to an accelerated kick drum. Indeed, the name "HOM-Mega" infers a Hebrew inflection of the pronunciation of "Om", with their moniker being the OM symbol + Mega ("ॐ Mega"), implying an amplified, accelerated or enlargened ॐ. But the full-on trajectory would eventually drop the Goa association for a "harder" aesthetic. Identified with the likes of Astrix, GMS, Talamasca, Maximum (formerly Sirius Isness), and Xerox, and with fans typecasting the music (and themselves) as "serious" and "hard" – not, therefore, "cheesy" or "emotional", associated with Goa or Nitzhonot – full-on features a tempo often paced between 145 and 150 bpm and a preference for heavy "psytars" (synthesized electric guitar riffs). While the electric guitar was augmented at the hands of synth-playing and sampledelic geeks, full-on and psychedelic cross-over artists like Skazi (Asher Swisa & Assaf Bibass) showcased the revenge of the guitar. As one enthusiast hyperbolized: "It's a ride with 100 jet thrusters. Hyper to the max and even scary at times" (Glassball 2006). The style would grow popular in Brazil, among other places, where Tiago Coutinho (2006) refers to the dissociated state of "frying" associated with a "more rapid and aggressive style of psychedelic trance". The work of Steve Goodman (2004) offers insight on the prevalence of this aesthetic. In noting that a "virtual architecture of dread defines the affective climate of early 21st century urbanism" and that, as a character from William Gibson's *Pattern Recognition* states, "we have no future because our present is too volatile," Goodman discusses late twentieth-century urban machine musics that are preoccupied with "generating soundtracks to sonically enact the demise of

Babylon". With this in mind, we might better understand the earlier work of Infected Mushroom or, for instance, the collaborative work of Moshe Kenan and Amir Dvir (aka Xerox and Illumination) whose track "Temporary Insanity" (*Nu-Clear Visions of Israel*, 2003) channels the zeitgeist: "He's losing his mind and feels it going", and whose rollicking track "Tribal Metal" (*Xerox & Illumination – Temporary Insanity*, 2004) submits the inquiry "why has my head gone numb?" Earlier, on "Bizarre", Psycraft posed the questions, "why are you fucking with our minds?!" (*Gravitech*, 2002). Years later, as a local inflection of the global darkpsy juggernaut, Post Traumatic pass comment on the situation at home via their brutal descent into carnage "Lost in the Woods" (*Nervous Disorder*, 2010).

In 2007, a disaffected machinic sensibility inhered in the name of the TAZ Festival, promoted not as a "Temporary Autonomous Zone" but as a "Temporary Autonomic Zone". The re/designation was revealing. Replacing "autonomous", "autonomic" connotes the body's impulsive involuntary response to music, and at the same time indexes identification with machinic repetition. Speaking to me following his set on the second day of the event, TAZ organizer Boris Levit stated that the acronymic shift was intentional (or at least it wasn't a typographical error). The intention can only be inferred since Levit provided few details, though the quest for temporary independence from external pressures via technics of the mind and body may be an accurate reading. Rather than loosely identifying with forms of emancipation associated with anarchism or autonomism, The 3rd Empire appear to have declared their identification with an automatic/machinic sensibility, the event's name evoking participants within a compulsive sub-bass-culture treading the program loop. It might be a long stretch, but the "autonomic" identification may permit habitués to dodge the polemics of the likes of Murray Bookchin (1995), who scorned Bey's TAZ as a repository for "lifestyle anarchism", lamenting the downgrading of anarchist rebellion into a narcissistic "bourgeois deception". Perhaps it is also a distancing from the philosopher of Sufism and radical Islam who, in his *Millennium* (Bey 1996), provocatively advocated "the greater jihad", a revolutionary response – comprised of a multitude of "lesser jihad" and more permanent zones of autonomy – to the fall of Soviet communism and the triumph of capital.

Whatever the case, at the TAZ Festival I noticed the concern for "Peace in the Middle East" – i.e. the stickered slogans worn by some dance floor participants – in a context in which Israeli Muslims and Arabs (including the Bedouin) are not invited to the party. And thus one recognizes that the revolutionary will to triumph over "separation" fuelling Bey's post-Soviet project goes wanting within a culture which samples the mythos of PLUR (Peace Love Unity Respect) stripped of humanitarian substance. There is certainly no shortage of ethnic diversity among *trancistim* with descendents of those "returning" from a scattered worldwide diaspora, including most recently those migrating from the former Soviet Union. This diversity feeds a celebratory euphoria within which participants hold unifying visions of global peace within the precincts of *mesibot*. But there are intruders in the holy lands of dance, where exclusion of ethnic "undesirables" appears requisite to a distinct – "progressive" – vibe. As Meadan (2001: 35, 44) observed, a chief term of distinction at *mesibot* is *arsim*, a derogatory designation for undesirable behaviour and those performing such behaviour – a term synonymous with lower-class *eidot-hamizrax* or Jews of North African or Middle Eastern descent, who are often identified as *shimonim*, and derided as *arsim*. This circumstance is also recognized by Schmidt (2006: 56; 2010) who observes that middle-class *Ashkenazim trancistim* actively exclude those who are not *anashim yafim* ("beautiful/nice people") or *anashim exuti'im* ("quality people"). As Schmidt clarifies, *arse* "is an Arabic word which literally means 'pimp' and in Israeli slang implies 'a jerk'". As a term applicable to anyone acting foolishly or disrespectfully towards others (especially males hassling females), almost by definition it means acting like an "Arab jerk". Populated by a significant proportion of middle-class *trancistim* – i.e. by those agents of a "progressive" sensibility whose preoccupations with the expression of difference from dominant norms by necessity excludes those who might jeopardize this vibe or "flow" – the TAZ appeared to accommodate few *arsim*, and no *shimonim*. The circumstance whereby middle-class Israelis of non-Arabic descent wield ethnic-orientated identifications to establish their distinction as *anashim yafim* or *anashim exuti'im* reveals elitism internal to psychedelic tribalism, where the freak ethos of a "global tribe" competes with the realities of "tribal" boundaries maintained through ongoing acts of distinction.

Was the sartorialized concern for "Peace in the Middle East" among some TAZ occupants a kind of liminalized fantasy ultimately, to paraphrase Terry Eagleton (1981), ensuring the maintenance of structures of privilege, and thus paralleling the artificial revolution of carnival as an insubstantial "ritual of rebellion" (Gluckman 1954)? Or is something else at stake in the carnivalesque transpiring, most poignantly, within a militarized zone? While moral authorities and cultural critics complain that Israeli psytrance is little more than a directionless escapade from responsibility and change, collapsing even under the weight of its own contradictions, others aren't so damning. Becoming "fed up with occupation and all the 'isms'", Daniel Belasco (n.d.) suggests young Israelis have turned to trance raves "for a new consciousness that envisions peace with neighbors and celebrates the value of the individual. Raves in Israel send a powerful message. In a nation so conflicted and militarized, the longing for 'PLUR' is far more political than in the United States, which enshrined the pursuit of happiness in its founding document". While the statements in the previous paragraph offer a serious indictment of the scene in Israel, they cannot, then, provide the final assessment, for the carnival is dialogical, replete with counter-narratives and opposing voices. Psytrance is indeed contested terrain in Israel, with varying figures and factions competing to claim its symbolic payload for their particular agendas, pressing it into the service of various religious and secular ideologies. Belasco himself argued that psytrance is a means by which secular youth could "connect to the sublime aspects of Judaism" and to "overcome particularism". This view approximates that practised by Asher Haviv, for whom Israeli trance has been harnessed as a revitalization movement. During 11–15 September 2007, Haviv mounted the Holy Rave, a five-day psytrance festival held in Timna Park in the Arava desert twenty miles north of the Gulf of Aqaba and the Red Sea tourist city of Eilat. At the site of Solomon's Pillars, a series of colossal sandstone columns formed by erosion over millennia, with the mountains of the Jordan Valley to the east and the Sinai and Egypt, not far to the west – accounting for several military observation posts in the area – this was to be Haviv's grandest plan to date. Spruiking "the biggest Israeli rave ever" on walla.co.il and in various newspapers such as the weekend supplement of the popular *Maariv* and other broadsheets, running full-page ads in the *Haaretz* – the local equivalent to the *New York Times* – and appearing on a popular television news talkshow, Haviv conveyed that in mounting the event he'd been guided by God to improve the condition of Israelis, and the world. It was a noble idea, and it could only manifest within the context of what was possibly the most extravagant independent party ever planned for a remote region. Integral to the bombastics was the main-stage sound system: as stated in the entrance foldout: "48 turbo sound systems strung together on 12 meter high towers with 30 subwoofers with 20 bass speakers on the ground". Hanging wide apart, shimmering in the haze, the sound system offered monolithic accompaniment to Solomon's Pillars, before which it stood. Billed as "the first international psytrance festival in Israel" and featuring a stellar lineup – with many of Israel's popular artists alongside international acts – the festival was held over Rosh Hashanah (Jewish New Year) and accommodated a "roots/Judaism camp" complete with Habad House hosting traditional rituals, prayers and meals. The Habad House, which included a "synagogue" and images of Rebbe Menachem Mendel Schneerson, the most recent leader of the Chabad-Lubavitch movement, was populated by a small force of Chabad, the outreachers of Hasidic Judaism, along with their families. With a "synagogue" at one end of the festival and "Haviv's Pillars" at the other, the Holy Rave expressed Haviv's own brand of spiritual activism, a grandiloquent fusion of traditional and emergent religion. Yet the 15–20,000 people predicted did not appear (about 1,000–1,500 did), and few participated in any of the formal religious rituals and meals planned. And while the Chabad took the opportunity to attempt to reignite the Jewish soul at sites around the festival, few participants showed interest in Hasidic Judaism. Certainly not those who were chanting "Om Namah Shivaya" on meditation mats at the

Chabad at the chill. Holy Rave, Israel, September 2007. Photo: Graham St John.

Chill-Love Holistic Village on day three of the event guided by a harmonium playing Swiss yogi. The black and white garbed out-reachers interrupted the chant to announce their calling, blow their shofar (ram's horn), and recite lines from the Talmud, with reactions ranging from contempt to outright indifference.

The Chabad also stormed the main stage at sunrise on Friday to deliver the word and distribute Tehilim books. But while they rushed the stage between sets, the trill of their shofar was drowned out by DJ Ta-ka. *Trancistim* weren't interested in religious ideology, messianic faith or shofar's trill, not when the savage religion could be obtained surfing the alpha waves under significant bass pressure. So when Haviv announced his plans for the Holy Rave, *trancistim* turned away in droves. Sagiv had provided an explanation back in 2000: "the neo-pagan ecstatic revival has filled the vacuum left by the demise of the old Zionism, and has been fueled by a mistrust felt by many youth towards anything reminiscent of the grandiose slogans and utopian promises of an earlier day". Thus, at this empty juncture in Israel's trance mission, where I literally stumbled onto the greatest rave that never happened, rather irreconcilable ideas of "religion" were being practised. For nouveau-religious activists like Haviv, the party is a context through which the Israelites may be led from servitude to the Promised Land, a vision estranging the vast majority of *trancistim* who find their "religion" in an ecstatic experience removed from the strictures of institutionalized religion. As partygoer, Alae, informed me, for those people who do not practise traditional Judaism, these events allow people to "come back to the roots ... become one with the people and nature".

Desolate dance floor. Holy Rave, Israel, September 2007. Photo: Graham St John.

And, while "it's not like a traditional religion, for a lot of people this is a way of life – they drink it, they it eat, they live it".[11]

Doof Australia

Psytrance has not experienced the heights of popularity in Australia as it has in Israel. Consequently, it does not figure in the public imagination and nor is it pressed into the service of diverse national, cultural and intellectual narratives – religious or secular – in the scale and frequency apparent in Israel. While this movement has fomented below the popular cultural radar, its events have been significant sites for a variety of alternative experiments. Indeed, Australia, a continent over fifty times the landmass of Israel, has accommodated numerous alternative enclaves and events which have long been destinations for local travellers and those from outside the country, including Israelis. Goa/psytrance became part of an Australian countercultural mosaic possessing the fusional, multi-mediated imperative associated with visionary arts culture. Not simply a transplant, nor a hyper-simulated transposition of elements of the former counterculture, psychedelic trance built a relationship with extant experiments where it has had clear shaping influences in some instances and at other times has been met with strong opposition. When the Goa vibe was carried to Australia in the early 1990s it had to build relationships with scenes and art collectives possessing anarchist and eco-activist objectives. This was the case at locations along the eastern coast, principally Melbourne, Sydney, Byron Bay and Cairns. A seminal event transpired in Melbourne in 1991 at

LizMania's basement in the old biscuit factory at Munster Terrace. According to co-founder of the Mutoid Waste Co, Robin Cooke (2001: 143), who had just then moved to Australia from the UK: "We flooded the dance floor with ultra violet paint and water, Anna and Karen built a Skull Throne around the only toilet, Hugh McSpeddon's projections adorned the silos above us, and 500 people 'went off'!" Playing his first genuine gig in Australia, Fred Disko was one of the DJs performing that night, laying down mixes from Goa.[12] The party was the first of Cooke's Earthdream events. Mounted over a twenty-year period, these have been seminal occasions for cross-genred experiments and intercultural collaborations.[13]

Melbourne's role in the Australian psychedelic trance/techno scene is evidenced by festivals including those operated by Earthcore (the first held at Mt Franklin on 29 January 1993), Psy-Harmonics, Psycorroboree, Green Ant, Rainbow Serpent, Tribeadelic and later Maitreya and Strawberry Fields, as well as warehouse and club party crews including Soma in Flinder's Lane and events operated by Melbourne Underground Development (M.U.D.). M.U.D. parties were a crucial hub of the Melbourne techno movement between 1992–2000. Their Every Picture Tells A Story (EPTAS) parties, and in particular those held at the old Dockland's Cotton Mill named the Global Village, were memorable for unique décor, installation art and video graphics to which co-founder Phil Voodoo, Sioux, Robin Cooke and many others contributed. They also showcased Melbourne-based producers like Zen Paradox (Steve Law), Voiteck and Slieker. As an alternative arts precinct with no noise restrictions and relatively unhindered artistic freedoms enjoyed for the better part of ten years, the Global Village was a formative Melbourne institution, unparalleled by world standards. While EPTAS were not strictly Goa/trance events (and resisted this label), Melbourne would become a centre of psychedelic electronic music as was early evidenced by Psy-Harmonics, the techno-trance label and party outfit founded by Ollie Olsen, Bruce Butler and Andrew Till in 1993, and more recently evidenced by Zenon Records and the Interview crew. Collaborating with and releasing material from the likes of Third Eye (Gus Till and Olsen), Zen Paradox, Lumukanda (Dominic Hogan), Mystic Force (Russell Hancorne), Masaray (Masayuki Kurihara and Ray Castle), Psyko Disko, and Rip Van Hippy (Geoffrey Hales), Psy-Harmonics became an enduring platform for genre-defying electronic psychedelia. While the label has hosted a diverse stable throughout its history, the Eastern influence was clearly evident on one of the label's first releases, Third Eye's *Ancient Future* (1993).[14]

Psy-Harmonic's second compilation, *Dancing to the Sound of the Sun* (1995), featured a passage written by music scholars Fred Cole and Michael Hannan[15] in the promotions for the release, introducing the scene in Byron Bay and hinterlands.

> The Byron Beach scene is a split between surfer, newage-sanyassin-yuppies, bohemian spiritualists and wholelistic [*sic*] counterculture misfits, many who have drifted in from the Asia traveller circuit or are completely disenfranchised from urban culture. This psychotropic, rainbow belt, east edge, part of Aussie has been notorious for its Goa-style, tribedelic meltdown, beach and forest parties over the last few years. It's the full sunrise bliss experience in pure, untainted nature, in an extremely mellow, tolerant, country environment.

Also referring to "feral/techno" fusion manifest in groups like Trance Goddess and Curried Grooves, this enthusiastic promotion for the emergent scene in the "Rainbow Region" of New South Wales – which, since the 1973 Aquarius Festival in Nimbin, attracted an alternative population from within Australia and around the world – highlighted novel aesthetics created from existing elements. The fusional imperative was native to emergent regional labels like Edgecore, Digital Psionics and Demon Tea Recordings, and to formative events like Creative Terra which emerged in 1992. Byron Bay celebration artist, David Bleach, provided the background to this seminal event, the product of a local arts-activist culture:

> An emergent arts based tribal collective had gathered pace through Melbourne and then the 1992 Adelaide Fringe Festival with the Imagineer events, before collaborating with their ilk in Byron Bay. Often referred to as "ferals", this group shared an environmental, spiritual and DIY creative ethos: derived from activists, anarchists, punks, hippies and artists (including performance, installation, visual, video, lighting, digital, DJs and musicians); influenced in part by English groups like Mutoid Waste, early English Acid House, Sydney's 80s arts based dance parties like Secret Garden, Canberra's theatre of spectacle Splinters, Ken Kesey & The Merry Pranksters, as much as some participants in earlier Goa parties; they formed a loose "tribe", responsible for spawning events across a blossoming national scene.[16]

From the mid to late 1990s, the Creative Terra protagonists established an infamous "free" beach and bush party scene and collaborated with local psychedelic artists, notably Electric Tipi. Along with an influx of international travellers, the region saw the emergence of a network of party crews, including Jupiter 3, Olli Wisdom's Space Tribe, Silicone Buddha, Heartkore and Bee Unlimited. Between 1995–1997, the Byron Bay area hosted the Beyond the Brain events, notably those held at the Epicentre, a disused whaling abattoir transformed into an alternative arts centre and labyrinthine multimedia party palace. By world standards, events hosted at the Epicentre were novel fusions of dance party and visionary art,[17] and representative of the region's stature as a centre for artists and travellers.

Artists associated with Creative Terra and other Byron Region events had close connections with the Melbourne scene, Cairn's Bizcirkus, and Sydney's Vibe Tribe. The latter had emerged in 1993 with direct roots in the anarcho-punk scene epitomized by the Jellyheads collective who had overseen the transition from punk to electronic music in the early 1990s and had held a series of acid techno parties called Wobble (see St John 2010b). Vibe Tribe, who held parties in Sydney Park until police violently broke up their party, Freequency, in April 1995, were opposed to the commercial exploitation of electronic music and the privatization of inner-city space, attracting diverse activists and artists to their number, among them Kol Dimond (Fatty Acidz) and Jeh Kaelin (JackieOnnasid), who had visited Goa in 1990 and returned inspired by the "cosmic dance". Dimond, who had a background in punk – with Kaelin, he was member of Sydney band Fred Nihilists – and who became co-founder, with John Jacobs, of Organarchy Sound Systems, regarded trance "as a potential vehicle for social change". As stated in an essay circulated on an insert included with Organarchy's CD *BPM Conspiracies* (1999), Dimond believed that, by comparison to punk's negativity, "trance was the real thing ... it seemed to have it all, it was accessible to the point where if you could possibly make yourself dance to anything you could dance to this". Furthermore, "it had no blatant overtones in its message, it was a faceless music made by anti-heroes who at a time were no richer, poorer or any different than the rest of us". But while embracing the potential for a "fusion of urban political activity and spiritual enlightenment", Dimond grew disillusioned by the late 1990s, stating, in the same source, that trance simply "became a hedonistic playground for white (dominantly) middle-class entrepreneurs". Expressing a common grievance, in his estimate, "those with the most influence are no longer seen at anti-uranium mine demonstrations ... protesting our rights for a safer and cleaner planet ... nor are they seen at forest blockades ... protecting the very wilderness that they call their garden" (Dimond 1999).

This response is not unusual in an arts scene with strong anarchist roots and eco-radical pretensions (of the kind hardly evident in Israel), which saw the emergence of the "doof", the Australian moniker for "party" widely used from Sydney and north-coast NSW, to Melbourne, Brisbane, Adelaide and Cairns in Far North Queensland. "Doof" is an onomatopoetic word – imitating or suggesting the source of the sound that it describes – coined at the door of a shared house in Newtown, Sydney, in 1992, when the Non Bossy Posse collective had been, according to occupant Pete Strong, "working out how to sequence a drum machine". Pounding on the door, "several beats per minute faster than the jam", their neighbour, a German woman, bawled her grievance, "what is this DOOF, DOOF, DOOF all night long?" (Strong 2001: 110).[18] Curiously, one of the chief annual psytrance events in Israel is called DOOF, operated by DOOF Records which appears to have emerged independently,[19] although there is considerable cultural exchange between Israeli and Australian scenes, with many Israelis visiting Australia for its summer festival season. Like its Goa forebears, a core element of the "doof" is its decentralized ethos, a theme it shares with techno parties elsewhere and which can have a variety of expressions, from the structure of its organizing body to the orchestration of events, which are not at all separate elements. Among the most seminal series of psytrance doofs were the Trancelements parties held in Victoria, Tasmania and NSW in the mid to late 1990s. These events carried the Goa party sonic-architectonic and featured a "3D" dance floor effect, which was especially notable at Toonumbar, NSW, c.1995 where the Japanese PA engineer Shiro Ono was in attendance. Ray Castle and Nick Taylor played at this party, with Castle recalling that the "wizard" Ono reset the entire PA into a circular set-up from which "the Aussie crews learnt a great deal".[20] A "3D dance floor" design was later implemented by Melbourne's Psycorroboree at their Gaian Thump parties held at Opoeia in Victoria's Otway Ranges south west of Melbourne in 1998 and 1999, which co-founder Eamon Jungle Wyss explained were "an expression of the greater decentralized ethos of the Techno cultural movement". Wyss had been inspired by parties in Manali in 1993, where two large speaker stacks were positioned on one side of the dance floor facing a DJ booth on the other, "creating a 3D effect". By contrast to the standard arrangement with the DJ flanked by speaker stacks, where dancers will typically face the DJ like a "mass of soldiers" marching to "the front", with the 3D arrangement, "there is no 'front' and 'back' of the floor". He outlined the experience: "what you get is a dance floor of endlessly diverse possibilities in people's creative expression. Dancing becomes no longer a contrived, learned experience by copying the person in front of you. Because there is no front! Instead it provides the space for people to just simply let go, turning it from a dance into a sea of beautiful movement". At Gaian Thump I in 1998, electro-acoustic musician Terry McDermott, Wyss and Psycorroboree set this idea into effect by mounting a "quasi-quadraphonic sound system", which enabled sound to "literally spin around us on the dance floor ... like sonic DNA".[21]

While a doof is not exclusively a psytrance event, it has been central to the designation of a psychedelic techno party, most often held, like the Gaian Thump events, beyond the city limits. Growing into an institution, the Australian "doof" is held in response to multiple conditions in the lifeworld of its participants. Like *mesibot*, it is a topos for extreme leisure, but by comparison to the former, they aren't always "one night stands" but full camping experiences often beginning Friday night and extending over "long weekends". The annual extended New Year's Eve vacation provided further opportunities for partying as it did, for example, with Earthcore in Victoria and Dragonflight which operated New Year's Eve doofs in southeast Queensland from 1996/97 to 1999/2000. By the 2000s, the psytrance doof offered a frequently transgressive carnivalesque context in which young, and youthful, populations could suspend obligations integral to traditional familial roles and citizenship in a semi-legitimate context. Although the pressures of everyday life are different than that known in Israel, the quest to become free from a litany of restrictions nevertheless characterizes these temporal centres of unlawful performance, becoming a contemporary theatre for anti-authoritarianism rooted in Australian cultural history.

The freedoms (temporarily) won from authority are displayed at outdoor events like those held annually in Victoria since 2003 on 19 April (Bicycle Day)[22] by Psyclone Events. Psyclone's annual Bicycle Day Freedom party was first held at the Kelly Tree on Stringybark Creek in 2005 where infamous bushranger of Irish convict descent Ned Kelly fatally gunned down three policemen in 1878. The locale of that party offered its participants a direct line of communication with a rebelliousness that would come to incite the popular national imaginary, and indeed retain interest among promoters such as the legendary larrikin producer of Freedom, John-Paris McKenzie. It's not too far-fetched to suggest that Kelly's confrontation with brutality and corrupt colonial authorities, as conveyed in his *Jerilderie Letter* dictated to Joe Byrne on 10 February 1878, offers analogue material for promoters holding running battles with the "traps" (the police) and displaying guerilla cunning in the face of officialdom over issues such as permit requirements, given the common perception that police and their employers remain little more than "a parcel of big ugly fat-necked wombat headed big bellied magpie legged narrow hipped splaw-footed sons of Irish Bailiffs", the verbatim disregard Kelly held for Victorian Police as conveyed in his manifesto. Anti-authoritarianism becomes hyperbolized within these contexts in a fashion not untypical to carnival, where the exultation of the lower strata is the source of jubilance, where infractions are permitted or where "the law" is temporarily subverted. Under the right conditions – i.e. with council approved permits and financial benefits flowing into townships local to annual events – infractions are authorized. While event organizers are commonly dogged by law enforcement and worn down by arduous council requirements, success stories involve efforts to bridge the wide gulf between the "bush" and the "city", where disparate notions of appropriate anti-authoritarian leisure practices have evolved.

From outrage to acceptance, doofs have drawn diverse responses from local communities. Examples of the former were evident in 2008 when residents of the town of Buxton, Victoria, vented anger at organizers and participants of the Maitreya Festival. According to one anonymous resident posting to an online forum, "Life is not one big psychedelic party, it is a lot of damn hard work but it can be FUN without having to kill your eardrums, kill all the native fauna, pickle your brainbox and generally piss everyone off". Another offered an example of how prejudice can be disguised as environmental concern:

> The Buxton Maitreya festival was an ABSOLUTE DISASTER for this beautiful community. Lies, lies lies by the organizers, always lies. That paddock that you shitted in mate was not a cow paddock and had no cowpats. The only shit left was what you mongrels left behind and not even covered either ... The noise was sonic, absolutely sonic with no respect for native animals, old people or the community, many people had to leave their houses for the 4–5 days to get away from the noise (we only live here!!!!) ... People were walking up driveways naked. They were washing their shit off in our beautiful streams, hundreds of them. You are serial rapists, of the community, of the animals of mother earth's bounty. Your only concern is having a fun time at our expense. You are serial pests you leave a trail of destruction in your wake! Don't bother coming back (I know you wont return to the scene of your crime) we dont need your tainted money or your tainted minds or any of the funny stuff you crave.[23]

While detractors are typically hostile to the drugs, sex, fire and outsiders invading their turf, organizers emphasize the shifting attitudes of locals when exposed to events and their patrons. As Lachlan Bell, organizer of Maitreya – held in the Carisbrook-Maryborough region of Victoria in 2011 and 2012 – explained, "the majority of country areas are suffering from an exodus of young people from their communities, the places aren't offering enough to keep subsequent generations interested in taking over the farms and keeping the land. They also have running along side this drug abuse, high suicide rates amongst those who stay, not to mention the ruff party hard alcohol driven B & S Balls, and Ute Musters, that are marked by community disruption and physical violence." With local populations seeking solutions to retaining and attracting young people to their communities, Bell highlighted their not uncommon surprise when interacting with festival-goers. "They realize that they are really great people, they dress strange, like loud repetitive music, but they are also charismatic, engaging, polite, and very helpful and resourceful". By contrast to the reputed disaster indicated above, Bell offered examples of patrons returning to the community to assist in Landcare projects and to improve the festival grounds.[24]

Despite the antagonism, local populations have warmed to the dance carnival, with the following story a recollection from an unnamed Victorian doof held over New Year's Eve in the late 1990s. "My friend went to the bakery about three weeks later and the woman in the bakery said 'Oh yeah. On new years' day there was all these kids here and it looked as though there was a hair-dressing convention going on somewhere nearby but you wouldn't believe it they were the nicest bunch of kids. They were so friendly and I just couldn't believe it'". The positive response was reportedly due not only to the friendly and respectful character of the punters, but because the events are "a bloody boom for the local economy because everyone spends so much money in the local towns". It was added that, "generally the relationships are good between urban and rural communities after the dance party has happened".[25]

While the word was coined in an urban context, "doof" has then come to designate open-air events held in localities beyond the city limits. As events staged in bushland, forests and deserts, they facilitate the means for participating in *country*, the Australian bush, which is not only the context for rebellion but recognized as holding regenerative potency for participants. While rave observers and dance ethnographers have observed dance parties facilitating the restoration of "vitality" (Malbon 1999), and perhaps even constituting a "revitalization movement" (Olaveson 2004), in the Goa/psytrance tradition immersion in nature's rhythms and cycles inaugurates new ways of relating to country. These events, then, are not simply means by which the self is unpacked and unburdened by proximity to the bush (Luckman 2003: 321), but are contexts for community development through new relationships with the natural environment, which would come to be inflected in sustainable event management practices. In relation to his Freedom party, McKenzie speaks of the collective sense of purpose that develops when parties are not only free admission, but are fully sustainable. "When you do a free party and use sustainable energy and show people that you can actually do that, and build it with a vision of the future then it both brings back the community spirit and works with the earth itself".[26]

The doof's removal from the everyday in the transit from the city into hinterlands and remote natural settings is reminiscent of Israeli *mesibot*, though the geographical spaciousness and eco-diverse character of the Australian landmass, eco-conscious practice and the *relatively* stress-free social environment have made for a different party climate and music aesthetic. McKenzie offered a statement on this via comment on one of the country's most well-known artists, Sun Control Species (Drew Davidson): "the music allows you to identify with the bush ... he has the ability of a painter who evokes an emotional connection with Australia through his productions. I can feel the earth in his music".[27] In the mid 2000s, Davidson was a leading exponent of a progressive psychedelic sound. Throughout this period, Australia became host to an undergrowth of productions with eclectic sounds evoking a rich and diverse geophysical terrain. It is a claim repeated within production promotions that Australian artists are shaped by the bushscapes within which they are raised. Being *raised* in Australia in this way often amounts to an experience of transformation in which urban dwelling citizens undertake seasonal excursions by motor-vehicle into the bush where alternative states of consciousness are stimulated by the consumption of psychoactive plants and compounds, often at bush doofs where the temporarily relocated share these experiences with friends and strangers. Bush doofs have, then, become instrumental for the recurrence of this activity. Having made trips to countless small parties and larger festivals "owning" various long weekend dates, a generation of enthusiasts and producers would be shaped by these recurrent events. Such doof-inspired entheogenic experiences are commonly narrated by psychedelic trance producers who drop telltale samples to conjure the moment of their epiphanies, in turn providing the sonic backdrop for further such experiences. For instance, on "Insane World" (*Source*, 2004), Mr Peculiar (Dustin Saalfield) conveyed the expectation that "you're gonna see a lot of different, crazy colours". With later tracks like "Funny Mushrooms" (*Global Alliance*, 2005) and "Alien Mushrooms" (*Love – Sound – Devotion*, 2005), the source of these visions becomes clearer. And they continued unabated. For instance, the material described as "psychedelic progressive minimal funk trance" released by Psilocybe Vibe (Jamie Roberts) on the self-titled EP (2011) recreates the atmospherics of becoming wobbly on mushrooms in the Australian bush, where *psilocybin* mushrooms are plentiful (notably, they do not grow wild in Israel).

Indeed, the Australian bush is a source for various psychoactive plants and compounds, and producers offer insight on how the local ecology would become integral to modes of self-transformation. During a speaking tour to Australia in February 1997, McKenna announced that "the national symbol of Australia is the wattle. It's an *Acacia*. The *Acacia* ecology of Australia is jammed with DMT". McKenna's spruiking of the idea that the DMT alkaloid could be harvested from species of the nation's floral emblem (the wattle, a common name for Acacia) – as sampled here on "Burning Point" (*Sun Control Species – Unreleased*, 2004) by Sun Control Species – was received with great interest by those who sought the direct influence of psychoactive alkaloids which gave them access to a psychedelic experience with a decidedly local flavour. The experience in DMT-space (especially the sonorous chirping of insects) had an early impact on music production in Australia, notably Space Tribe's 12-inch *Ultrasonic Heartbeat*, which features "Cicadas on DMT" (1996) and later inspired the DMT blend *changa*.[28]

More generally, indigeneity is a common heritage theme among participants and musicians: both native landscape/biota and native peoples are evoked or embraced in diverse claims to origins in which participants assume connection, and from which they gain authenticity. These strategies are an echo of anxieties among settler descendents recognizing their complicity in the displacement of Australia's native population, and who respond with a desire for legitimate presence through reconciliatory and sustainable practice. As a party to a redressive climate building in the mid to late 1990s (see St

John 2001d, 2005a; Cohen *et al.* 2008), doofs would become vehicles for a post-colonial desire for an appropriate settlement. Stalwart of Sydney's underground techno culture, Pete Strong became a longstanding advocate of intercultural events, and an exponent of the "doofumentary": the party that is also a vehicle for political causes, in his case principally Aboriginal land rights and anti-nuclear activism (Strong 2001). While Strong's outfit Oms not Bombs (later called Ohms not Bombs) and Earthdream provided the scaffolding upon which those from varying backgrounds and motivations were permitted to hang their banners, another spiritual activist, DJ Krusty, would offer grounds for disillusioned settler-descendants to become re-enchanted through ritualized acts of emplacement. As Krusty wrote:

> The island continent of Australia has had an intimate relationship to dance with the indigenous people of the land stomping on the earth for over 60,000 years. My understanding is that this geomantic practice set up a resonant frequency across the continent which is still active today, and thus offers a totally unique opportunity for the modern trance-dance-entheogen experience – or as we call them now, "bush doofs" (Krusty 2008: 21).

Krusty had been responsible, along with Rainbow Serpent Festival co-founder Felix Hamer (aka Sugar), for introducing doofs at the alternative lifestyle festival ConFest through the 1990s, and later full-moon parties operated by the Melbourne-based Green Ant. I recall stumbling into an early doof at ConFest on the banks of the Murray River near Tocumwal, Easter 1996, which had been promoted using the pagan revivalism discourse of London's Return To The Source. Two sound systems turned upon each other some 50 m apart, generating a sound clash. On one side, the main floor had a four-way speaker stack system and on the other the smaller Cicada sound system operated from the back of a van. UV banners were dropped from gum trees and Robin Mutoid performed a fire show at midnight. Fellow travellers spent much of the night drifting through the sweet and sour spots between the systems in an experience Krusty later recalled was a "melodic chaos mish mash" where it was possible to sometimes detect the same anthems amplified from the two sound systems. Krusty, Sugar, Bam Bam and "Fluffy" Pete Strong among others performed a mix of the earliest Goa releases from Dragonfly, TIP and Psy-Harmonics as well as acid techno and opera, and the sounds of didjeridu and tribal drumming were prominent. This was before the formation of genre camps when Goatrance was a novelty, and so the mix of styles, modes of delivery and sound clashes were acceptable within this experimental environment. As Krusty explained, at this time "it was permissible to play all sorts of techno dance music and the crowd just loved it all because they did not know any different and it was all so new".[29] The area for this party within the wider precincts of ConFest was called "Rainbow Dreaming", a reference to the growing reverence for country expressed through traditional Indigenous religious sensibilities, and was an early example of what was to become a typical deference within psyculture towards Indigenous custodians who would be regularly evoked as ritual and cultural authorities. Tetrameth (Peter Hayes) gives voice to this deference on "Lost (Part Two)" (*The Eclectic Benevolence*, 2010), where kookaburras break out following the announcement from an Aboriginal man claiming "ours is the oldest living culture in the world. Our culture is maintained by synergy, from the law of the Dreaming".

Music production and event design would demonstrate a wide diversity of intent and outcomes, from soft primitivist approaches involving no or little consultation with Indigenous peoples to collaborative alliances with participants from Aboriginal and Torres Strait Islander communities. The cover of the first release from the Green Ant label, *Primitive Dawn – Trance Journey Vol. 1* (1999), featured a bearded and painted Aboriginal man backgrounded by an image of Uluru (Ayers Rock), the iconic sandstone rock formation in Central Australia and part of the Uluru-Kata Tjuta National Park which also featured, for instance, on the cover of *Tribe Vibe* (2002), the fifth album of tribal dub and didjeridu performer Ganga Giri. Such re-productions might be figured in the light of Julie Marcus's discussion of the construction of Uluru as "the sacred centre of a rapidly developing settler cosmology" (1988: 254) and in particular of how "New Age pilgrims" revise Aboriginal law and cosmology through the distorting prism of an "international mystical tradition". Focusing on "a feeling of the timelessness and essential universal truths" that Aboriginal beliefs offer, Marcus (1988: 268) held that "Aquarians" ignore the unique social, political and religious context of Indigneous peoples. While Goatrance had not emerged at the time of this critique, as Uluru would attract prospectors of ancient spirituality and mysteries in like fashion to the pyramids in Egypt, the temples in Palenque, the statues on Easter Island, and Stonehenge in Wiltshire – as found in album cover art, music samples and event promotions – a comparably primitivist mystical universalism would become evident in Goatrance and its successors. Furthermore, that Indigenous Australians have been constructed as timeless archetypal symbols among white settler participants in the local trance scene for whom they promise spiritual sustenance and "redemption", echoes earlier critiques (see Lattas 1990, 1992).[30]

While soft primitivist trends are apparent, critics adopt distanced and homogenizing strategies of their own, often overlooking the diverse and shifting ways in which Aboriginal land, art and peoples are engaged and collaborated with. Ganga Giri, for instance, has regularly worked with Aboriginal performers, with the work of Aboriginal musicians and singers included in live and recorded work.[31] The didjeridu or *yidaki* is an instrument that has been commonly taken up by non-Aboriginal performers who, as discussed in Neuenfeldt (1997), display a bewilderingly complex array of motivations and practices. In psytrance, the didjeridu (performed live, or sampled) joins a chorus of instruments, chants and prayers lifted from diverse world cultures, as a means of brokering authenticity, unlocking wisdom, and musicking a "tribalism" free from the ravages of modern life. While the didjeridu is simply one of the more visible and resonant instruments facilitating this pretence, its adoption is not a simple conceit. While the essentialized indigene may facilitate redemption for the disaffected, the physical and therapeutic impact of the droning instrument is undeniable (see Sherwood 1997: 148–9; Neuenfeldt 1998: 35–40), an effect which has been the result of modern innovations such as the variable pitch slide didjeridu. From the ambient tribal resonations of Lumukanda's "Red, Black and Mellow" (*Araglin*, 1993), to the acid-didjeridu on Prânâ's "Scarab" (*Cyclone*, 1996), to the mesmerizing chorus of Insectoid's "Tribedelic Nomads" (*Groovology of the Metaverse*, 1998), which mixes cackling kookaburras, choral cicada, croaking frogs, clap sticks and the drone of the didge, the instrument has been a prominent means of effecting states of entrancement. The distinct droning was evident on "Written in Stone", opener on Medicine Drum's tribal trance album *Talking Stick* (1999). Several artists would become known via the sonic signature of the didge and slide-didge development. Thus, alongside Ganga Giri, prominent exponents have included Sean Candy (aka A.B. Didgeridoo Oblivion) and Nik Didge.

While some productions are tokenistic and primitivist in character, others evidence ecological and social justice concerns, becoming staging-grounds for departures from established practice. The annual Exodus Cybertribal Gathering in northeast NSW became an exemplary site of intercultural reconciliation, with traditional owners, members of the Bunjulung Nation, performing a "welcome to country" as part of ceremonial performances in an Opening Ceremony resembling that which has opened the Woodford (previously Melanie) Folk Festival in Queensland, and evolving from the same redressive commitment apparent in the Sydney 2000 Olympic Games Opening Ceremonies, which featured a smoking ceremony, Central Desert women performing a segment of the Seven Sisters dance, and a pageant parade. The cover of the 2005 release *A Cyber Tribal Exodus – Movement of Da People* depicted an image of exodus from an Australian landmass in the colours of the Aboriginal flag. The CD opened with Spaceclub Osttirol's "Exodus to the Bush" where a clap stick evolves into an insistent pulse around didjeridu and songlines, and later "TekNoBob" revised Bob Marley's "Exodus". The cover art also featured a message from Bundjalung Nation Elder Uncle Eric Walker: "We are people of caring and sharing, loving and giving, and what we want to see is that we live together and that we work together".

Operated by Frank Venuto and Felix Hamer, Melbourne's Rainbow Serpent Festival (RSF) became the chief annual Goa-derived event in which such redressive desires were showcased. At the 2008 RSF, thousands gathered to witness an opening ceremony unparalleled in Australian outdoor dance events. It was an elaborate "welcome to country" evolving considerably from former events to become a popular interactive spectacular. With a sand mandala prepared on the dance floor (a serpent encircled Earth depicting the Australian landmass), a smoke cleansing or "smoking" ceremony was led by Gundidgundjundmara elder and local traditional owner Uncle Ted Lovett, and which involved other Aboriginal performers including Gnamahare ("Uncle Joey") and the painted women from the Koorroomook Thanampool ("possum women") dance group, representing the Kirrea Woorroong and Peak Woorroong tribes of the Gunditjmara nations of South West Victoria. With a customary "smoking" ritual and traditional dance performances, the entire performance functions as a means of permitting passage to country. Through this ceremony, Aboriginal authorities act to welcome event-attendees to the land, evoking its ancient heritage and providing participants with an understanding that their presence on this land – that is, three cow paddocks near Beaufort, and the continent more widely – under the watchful gaze of custodians and their representatives, is ceremonially legitimated. For site planner, event logistician, décor artist and intercultural broker Glenn Armstrong, these ceremonies are crucial. They "bring everyone together in one purpose, place and experience, an acceptance of the spirit of belonging, a divinity, a sharing ritual. To me the strongest spirit at RSF is the hope, honesty and joy present in the Aboriginal component, the idea of being part of a beautiful, living dreaming forever".[32]

It would take several years before Aboriginal heritage was officially and appropriately acknowledged at Rainbow Serpent through the presence of traditional owners who effectively acted to ceremonially welcome festival-goers to the country. That the event referenced the Indigenous creator spirit, yet had little Indigenous involvement, was a cause for concern among a few crew members. The 2005 visit of Ngungandjeri activist Aunty Sue Rankin-Charles was pivotal. According to Armstrong (who was instrumental in getting Rankin-Charles involved): "Sue's message at the opening of the Market Stage was a political call to the audience to engage the struggle of modern

Rainbow Serpent Festival 2007. Opening Ceremony. Photo: Jonathan Carmichael.

day Aboriginals and their causes and acknowledge the genocidal practices of the past. Sue then met with people all during the festival with an info stall in the market". With a keen interest in Indigenous culture and politics and having formed close ties with Indigenous friends in his community (Daylesford), Armstrong became pivotal to this development.[33] In 2008, he built and maintained the "Koorie Camp" which would accommodate Wuradjeri and Kamilaroi peoples. He constructed a "kup mairee" (earth oven) and made head dresses and grass skirts for performers in the opening and closing ceremonies. That year, together with Dale, a Gunditch Mara man from Warnambool, he told stories of the local Jarra Dreaming and welcomed elders who had travelled from the Badu islands in the Torres Strait. In the Koorie Camp area there were ongoing cultural events including cooking, talks, song and story. By 2009, there was a wide range of Indigenous cultural activities including Aboriginal dances, didjeridu playing and dance, art and cooking workshops held by Indigenous peoples from all over Australia. That year, a Closing Ceremony transpired at the chill stage. Commenting on the surrounding goings-on, long-time RSF attendee Ben Dixon observed:

> I loved the super-relaxed but buoyant vibe of it ... [Gnamahare] just rolled up along with everyone else – no big fanfare – he was completely at home and a perfect fit with everyone else. He wasn't there to do a ceremony. Just to have a good time. A lot of the Indigenous folk that I've seen at rainbow have always seemed to me a bit lost or out of place ... but I think some kind of turning point or acceptance has been reached and now the overall feeling seems to come across is that they see it as their festival as much as we do.[34]

But RSF, held annually at the height of summer on the Australia Day long-weekend, is not staged under a single narrative. As a sprawling festival, it offers a chorus of voices with a litany of outcomes. Not unlike circumstances in Israel, commentators, especially those who are absent from events they report on, seek to straitjacket this noise in tidy narratives designed to support specific agendas. In Israel, Zionists have both recruited and rebuked psytrance to their own ends, in ways not dissimilar to the ways reformed Christians have attempted to poach or reprove rave. In Australia, activists have also furthered their agendas through criticism of party culture, variously drawing attention to its cosmetic, wasteful, entrepreneurial and postcolonizing characteristics. While widely differing agendas are then encountered, there appears to be a common reliance upon silencing the noise of the carnival, on reductionism that neglects internal differences and complexities in order to bolster the beliefs to which commentators are faithful, policies in which they are advocates, and theories to which they are loyal. One critique of RSF challenges the "Dreaming ideology" of the festival and its participants who are held to engage in "weekend flirtations with imagined primitives ... where there is no evidence that any long-term or beneficial dialogue is produced". It is further claimed that since the event is held over Australia Day, and given that this day celebrates the arrival of the First Fleet at Sydney Cove, the event "is inadvertently celebrating the devastating effects this historical event had on Aboriginal culture" (Haebich and Taylor 2007: 80, 79). A complex event possessing a multitude of stakeholders claiming variant positions and outcomes requires more sensitive approaches, such as those apprised of campaigns internal to the festival triggering the development of the opening and closing ceremonies and other cultural activities. Lastly, rebuking the event based on the date of its annual recurrence seems disingenuous. The festival is held over the only long-weekend outside Christmas/New Year in the Australian summer. That organizers and participants take advantage of an official long break is of greater significance than the historical significance of Australia Day.

At RSF, the Australian flag is generally lost to the carnival of symbols available. The spiritually charged gravitas of the ceremonies is tempered by a rippling carnival atmosphere. At one point, at the 2008 opening ceremony, the patriotic "I am Australian" song rose up from the crowd at the behest of one of the older aunties present. It was a curious twist. For many, the song was met with rolling eyes, or was accompanied by jocularity and clowning around, with its performance echoing the parodic imagination native to the carnivalesque. For others, the song was appropriately ceremonial and considered a popular alternative to "Advance Australia Fair" as the national anthem, the embrace of which has been widespread, including among Indigenous Australians.[35] The RSF opening ceremony is a performance conveying more than anxieties about legitimacy. In 2008, it constituted a dramatization of a variety of ultimate concerns – the multiple sacra of its participants. Like participants in a freak variety show, various luminaries and scenes endogenous to psytrance and alternative cultures, as well as the local community, were applauded as they paraded the outer circumference of the sand mandala. In costume, waving flags, raising cheers, being outrageous, the pageant was introduced by the MCs. The "parade of honour" featured pagans, eco-warriors, peace activists, stilt walkers, fluffy ravers, volunteer members of the Country Fire Authority,[36] and a woman in blue knee-length satin, her dress patchworked with countless Union Jacks and Southern Crosses. Only the brave or the absent could blanket this with a master narrative or counter-narrative. The end of the opening ceremony was also difficult to determine, as spectators were encouraged to enter into the circle and stomp the sand mandala to the sound of tribal beats now banging out from the stage. The stomping continued in that place for the next eighteen hours.

****

While there is no master narrative, in the annual RSF opening ceremony, the dance floor is the context for staging a unique festival identification, which has emerged from the congress of difference showcased and performed. In this sense, Rainbow Serpent is a *difference engine* that powers a unique psychedelic carnivalesque. This chapter has shown that Israeli and Australian scenes are downstream from developments in Goa, shaped by the diversity of intent shaping the culture in its place of origins, and inflected by the cultural and historical conditions unique to these nations. The music, the events and the culture attracts diverse religious and cultural heritage claims in both countries where protagonists and critics adopt and adapt psytrance to their own agendas. That which is most sacred (e.g. Judaism, indigeneity) is invoked to instrumentalize and rejuvenate authentic selves and sociality. While the theme of "exodus" is common across nations, that which participants are making exodus from and that which they cultivate in response differs widely. A rebellious or anti-authoritarian theme is redolent in psyculture in both countries, though it takes different forms given historical conditions, state conflicts and length of official holidays. It was found that in Israeli psytrance, Arabs are the *other* to the "beautiful people", while in Australia the romanticizing of Indigenous Australians is apparent. But while these practices lead to exclusivism – in the former, Arabs are effectively excluded from parties, and in the latter those excluded may be those who do not meet primitivist specifications (i.e. most Indigenous Australians) – elitist and primitivist characteristics are not totalizing. Since finding a dominant trend in the carnival of signs and sounds operating at the intersections of *originality* is near impossible, these observations need to be regarded with caution. As national sites of translation of the Goa vibe, both Israel and Australia have seen the development of socialities in dance which are characterized by the performance and dissolution of difference. While participants in the respective countries promote sacred symbols and pursue spiritual projects echoing regional and sectarian commitments – e.g. nouveau-religious activists in Israel and eco-activists in Australia – and while single events harbour an explosive concatenation of noise, the dance event itself provides the context for a *religious experience* enabled by breaks in the everyday routine and involving temporary journeys to the near-wilderness where travellers share in an experience whose commonality connects enthusiasts around the world.

8 Performing risk and the arts of consciousness

As a confluence of historical factors, national causes and embodied ecstasies, psycultures are a complex of interests and sources of prestige. In the previous chapter, various incentives were found to determine conduct in key national cultures, and the party vibe was earlier determined to be responsive to multiple conditions in the lifeworld of participants. The animating motivations of transgression and reflexivity are given detailed consideration in this chapter. In the transgressive mood, psyculture becomes a context for the display of risk which may be converted into prestige and facilitate belonging. In the reflexive mood, participants respond to a variety of concerns, both internal and external to the scene, with psytrance becoming a stage for aesthetic, ecological and cultural causes. The performance of risk and the reflexive arts of consciousness are polar intentions dramatized in psytrance events. Through attention to edgework and conscious behaviour, from the main floor to the chillout, the chapter seeks to establish a clearer understanding of the trance experience as a field for the generation and retention of social and cultural capital. It therefore contributes to ongoing debates where Bourdieu (1990) has been recruited to comprehend distinction within EDM formations. Principally, in Sarah Thornton's *Club Cultures*, acid house participants identified a "mainstream" against which they defined themselves, and where raconteurs and designers would turn "difference into defiance, lifestyle into social upheaval, leisure into revolt" (1996: 129). While Thornton observed a carefully maintained and micro-mediated outlaw visage preserving the "subcultural capital" of scene insiders and driving acid house as a cultural production, the current study examines dance cultures not strictly as club cultures but as complex movements. Within psytrance, while actors may be driven to maintain distinction from others against whom their own identity is established, tribute is accorded those whose actions demonstrate a commitment beyond the self-orientated immediacy of style typifying the study of club cultures, and with an activist endeavour atypical of "neotribes". In psytrance and visionary arts cultures, distinction is accorded not only to those who perform lifestyle risks, but those committed to identifying and reducing risks according to ecological and humanitarian campaigns and whose efforts are ethical, proactive and self-less. It is this complex field of behaviour encompassing transgressive and reflexive dispositions that enables reputation and acceptance.

Performing risk: trance, adventure and edgework

Hunter S. Thompson once described his extreme ghetto-assaying on a variety of drugs as "edgework". As introduced in Chapter 5, the term was pressed into service by Lyng (1990) to identify voluntary risk-taking in the practice of skydivers and a range of leisure pursuits – where the "edge" negotiated is not only that separating life from death, but that between unconsciousness and consciousness and sanity and insanity. Cultural observers have begun paying attention to voluntary risk-taking behaviour among youth and young adults, with the pursuit of risk in extreme sports, adventure tourism and other recreational pursuits the subject of continuing research.[1] Jeff Ferrell offers further insight, indicating that "the pursuit of the edge" is an "experiential anarchy, a visceral liberation from the entrapments of everyday life" (2005: 76). Not unlike other realms of extreme recreation, psychedelic trance and other EDM scenes facilitate the encounter with "experiential anarchy", with psychedelic festivals optimized fairgrounds of experience in which transcendent states are guaranteed to those who "make the sacrifice". Unlike BASE jumping, however, the risk of physical "death" is remote in psytrance, for rather than death *per se*, one faces a "little death", or "ego-death", the dissolution of self in the context of others, an experience one seeks over and again for reasons echoing that of a female BASE jumper from the outfit the Gravity Girls interviewed by Ferrell: "You know you're alive when you do this; every sense is working ... You want to live so you can do it again" (2005: 79). But the abandonment experienced by repetitive beat freaks and bass junkies is not absolute. As BASE jumpers, motorcycle daredevils, graffiti writers and other edgeworkers are members of subcultures, theirs is an organized chaos, a self-regulated danger also cultivated within psytrance. Despite the pretence from the hardened who boast complete abandonment, Ferrell approaches the social "logic" of edgework. Aiming to transcend the controlled excesses implicit to consumer experience (as advertised on TV), enthusiasts desire freedoms from what Bataille (1985) identified as the restrained expenditure of the bourgeois. Yet their risk-taking is managed. On the dance floor, psychoactives are consumed with attention to affect, release, endurance and impact over long durations in which time the intoxicated will leap with body and mind in and out of dance exposed to bass and frequencies that may not relent for days, amplified through high performance sound systems by skilled DJ-producers in arenas equipped with video projections, décor, lighting and misting systems to enhance and prolong the experience. This is a thoroughly managed and generally secured process. The chemical, audio, video and lighting assemblage is designed and implemented according to knowledge, skills and optimal techniques. Awareness of risks associated with drug consumption is particularly advanced, as it is among many EDM enthusiasts, including those studied in San Francisco's Bay Area by Hunt, Evans and Kares (2007).[2] In my own experience, I have found that, far from being ignorant, helpless and vulnerable, well-informed users develop advanced means of managing risks and uncertainties in party settings. Typical conversations involve discussions of substances, especially analogue or "designer" drugs, and the techniques of their consumption. It is common for participants to share experiences and compare notes on sources, quality, assaying with similar drugs, and methods of delivery. But not all such dialogue is directed towards minimizing risks, since, as I will argue, psychedelic edgeworkers plan for risk, perform danger and maximize uncertainty. A performative approach to risk in psyculture forms the basis of what follows. Valuable leads on the cultural role of risk in EDM have been fielded. While research on the epidemiological risks associated with the use of "club drugs" remains important, the departure from a total reliance on the pathology discourse dominating the drug-research field is necessary. Approaching the cultural criminology of pleasure, transgression and risk, Hunt, Moloney and Evans (2009, 2010) have suggested that commitment to experience the effects of novel drugs within EDM scenes constitutes "edgework", a view which points up the need for attention to the situated acquisition and deployment of cultural knowledge in consciousness alterant use as *risk performance*.

In his study of the performance of risk, Sean Afnan Morrisey (2008: 413) indicates that risk taking may be "particularly alluring in societies of caution" in which young people experience crushing levels of surveillance. This approach is not a straight-up analysis of the effects of the "risk society" (Beck 1992), for in accordance with Afnan Morrissey's Bourdieusian modelling, risk is shaped by the desire for cultural capital converted from the experience. Among youth cohorts, cultural capital, he argues, is less likely to be derived from the "mimetic" dangers associated with sport and legitimate leisure practices of the kind elucidated by Elias and Dunning (1986), but more specifically from risks associated with carnivalesque performance (Morrisey 2008: 418). With psytrance, as with other EDMCs, illicit psychoactives factor heavily in the limit-pushing uncertainty out of which such cultural power may be earned, a circumstance remixed by producers. Onboard the bass-heavy "Distorted Personalites" (*The Movements*, 2008), for example, Sub Atomic toys with a risk-laden aesthetic as a sampled girl intervenes: "don't do that, don't smoke it like that ... it gives you Alzheimers doesn't it?" The allure of uncertain mind experiments – the equivalent of walking the pharmacological highwire – may be connected to the appetite for limit pressing within cultures dominated by "monophasic consciousness" (Laughlin, McManus and D'Aquili 1992). This idea explains why, unlike classical or formal dance classes avoided by male students from working-class families in particular as a result of the feminine stigmata of dance in the West, carnivalesque forms of dance – free form, often involving controlled substance use – are appealing. The higher the risks associated with ecstatic dance, the greater the potential for stature, social power and belonging. These possibilities expand as the trance carnival transpires in locales remote from home and where transit involves shared endurance such as that involved in the transit to a scorched site in central-eastern Portugal for the summer Boom Festival, which became notorious for its long entrance queue forcing thousands of participants into a slow crawl in sweltering conditions for up to a day or more.

How adversity becomes converted into cultural power is a story found at the roots of Goa. In their expatriation from convention and challenges to conformity, experienced travellers to the East gained tacit membership in the "hippie Raj". Respect later aggregated to those who moved in the seasonal Goa trancedance circuit, where performing the apocalypse became something of a lifestyle practice, and where those who arrived in seasons afterwards were imitators of the genuine scene. Outside the learned smoking of *charas* among travellers, ethnographers of Goatrance have found that the ownership and riding of motorcycles constitutes an important display of freak power. The ownership and operation of the favoured 350cc Royal Enfield Bullet has conferred high merit and fellowship among Goa freaks. By comparison to the Honda Kinetic scooter, those saddled up and begoggled on these cacophonous mounts displayed their virtual nativity in the world of the freak. "Given the charming stubbornness of its engine", writes Saldanha (2004: 280), "many males who have bought an Enfield for the season learn the art of motorcycle maintenance – spending days or weeks in the garage". Saldanha refers to the circumstance where this heavy bike whose exhaust pipes announce a distinct thud and crackle has become "spiritualized", in no small part because riding these machines high and without a helmet is a dangerous practice: "every year in Goa there are at least a dozen road deaths and many more minor injuries to riders (often due to LSD and/or ecstasy), pedestrians and cattle". It might be supposed that fatalities, such as the loss of Yossi Salem, to whom *Trust in Trance Vol 1* (1994) – compiled by the members of Astral Projection – was dedicated, or the death of Israeli rising star Cosma in another motorcycle accident in Goa, serve to reinforce the hazards, and accompanying stature, of freak being. Prestige is acquired from an association with sacrifice worn like trophies on skins as "grotesquely, corporeal traces of accidents" (Saldanha 2007a: 96). While D'Andrea (2007a: 207) had it that the Bullet "embodies the power of technology to erase the ego, not as much as in the case of a fatal accident, but rather in rejecting 'subjection' to criteria of discipline, utility and control", the ultimate risk – permanent annihilation of identity (i.e. death)

– appears to reaffirm the reputed fearlessness of these iron-steed mounted "warriors". D'Andrea himself moves to a discussion of "psychedelic guerillas" and intimidating dreadlocked and war-painted "Amazon" women arriving at parties astride these heavy bikes styled in "tank tops, boots and GI trousers under multi-pocket skirts" (ibid.)

Further insight on the subject of risk-performance is offered by David Bromley (2007) through what he calls "spiritual edgework". While the trance party is clearly remote from the context in which congregationalists moved by the Holy Ghost handle venomous snakes, or practitioners motivated by the Higher Self walk on beds of hot coals, there is some equivalence for both DJ and dancers in the manner in which the performance of risk is empowering. Bromley observes how snake handlers and firewalkers identify dangerous limits which require dramatic negotiation, the traversing of such uncertainty potentiating an experience of transcendent power, and subsequent empowerment and control. The DJ possesses a crucial role – that of keeping the floor "alive" – but this is a task that holds no certain outcome. At the very least, the DJ's objective is to maintain the vibe, and at the most, to "raise the energy", perhaps pushing habitués of the floor into new realms of endurance. Popular DJs will be followed by fans, sometimes around the world, and attract gigs on an international circuit based on their capacity to accomplish such feats. But many are the risks involved. Exposing crowds to new sounds – often an artist's own production – constitutes an aesthetic risk. Performing ever-fresh sonic material is the preserve of the respected DJ – in the form of "white label" releases in the case of headline acts – for which they are awarded professional and cultural cachet in a highly competitive market. Experienced artists/producers will alter the style of their output frequently, creating new sounds from fusions of existing material, using the latest audio software and hardware and live instruments, learning new techniques, and forging fresh collaborations and thus forming new or side acts in order to capture or recapture audience and market. Of course, there is no certainty in this. How far is the DJ-producer prepared to go? Will their sound carry the day? How will the crowd respond?

DJing is a high-risk performance. Selection, mixing and "live" performances using instruments, MIDI-controllers and software are technical skills expected from DJs. The seamless mix, the perfect build, the creative sequence, ensure the vibe. But there are many things that can go wrong. A "trainwreck" (mixing and sequencing errors) and other technical mistakes and aesthetic anomalies won't lead to death or serious injury – as is possible with serpent handling and firewalking – but can ruin reputations, generate disrespect, and cause a "bad vibe", with perilous crowds and adverse reactions common occurrences. It is in the interest of DJs and their promoters that such stories should circulate, for their reputations as "masters", "legends" or "hardcore" is served by these narratives, and CD sleeves and profiles are replete with celebratory discourse on courageous styles, devastating performances and the overcoming of adversity. It is not to suggest that DJs aren't vulnerable to variable factors like failing power supplies, faulty equipment, a damaged CD, weather conditions and unwanted crowd participation, but stories of near "tragic" episodes are distributed among DJs who push each other to take greater aesthetic and technical risks – or at least fictionalize such episodes in the interests of their survival as artists in the scene. Creativity is ultimately a field of risk in which artists negotiate new aesthetic terrain. For "in form", "top of their game" or avant-garde artists across the spectrum of disciplines of performance, such experiments have long held the potential for self-exaltation and transcendence: yet perhaps amplified when the risks are culturally constructed, when cultural movements and industries invest in uncertainty. I do not argue that DJing, or any other musical practice and performance art, is conceited or entirely predictable, merely that growing industries are dependent upon the countenance of the artist-protagonist, who, like the serpent handler, or fire walker, perform miracles, weave magic, cast spells, possess a prescience. Narratives grow around heroic DJs, legends of shamanic practice, the risks they've undertaken in their odyssean rise to fame, dramatizing quests to navigate an edge, drawing around these artists' compelling mythologies.

Additionally, besides DJ dramatics, the dance floor is a context for a "transcendent power that is experienced directly" (Bromley 2007: 293), a "power" that is derivative of risks, both real and exaggerated. Psytrance participants often speak of an ability to endure the pounding bass orchestrated by DJs and producers, especially those who are notable masters of their art, like Dane Frank E (Koxbox), or German expat and founder and label manager of Shiva Space Technology, Jörg Kessler, who, according to a comment Joshua Schmidt made to me in passing, had been "trying to break Israelis" for years with an arsenal of heavy guitar sounds and hard driving kicks of the kind auguring the coming sound of full-on. At the Holy Rave in 2007, as young Israelis erected tents 500 metres in the direct line of a thunderous sound system (on which Jörg played), enduring siege-breaking decibels and demonstrating bravado in tales that in the telling echo the recounting of victorious military operations, they appeared far from broken. Like decorated field strategists knocking up multiple campaigns – i.e. in India, Greece, Brazil, Australia, South Africa – experienced trance travellers will offer dramatized accounts of the transgression of geographical and emotional limits, exaggerations that are in accordance with Bromley's idea that "the key to creating empowerment and control in spiritual edgework is to identify connections to the transcendent that appear to pose extreme danger but are not as dangerous as they appear" (2007: 301).

The way participants describe those dance floor moments endured for long hours without relent is reminiscent of the way walking across hot coals empowers fire-walk adepts, whose fears have formerly prevented the realization of their Higher Selves (Bromley 2007: 293). Within full-on and darkpsy trajectories, the rallying cries are not those of Goa (or for that matter "house" traditions) compelling one's "surrender" to the rhythm, but to resist the relentless sonic arsenal. Such resistance appears crucial to the transcendence achieved, especially when one is exposed to the tools of trance in remote sites at cosmic events or in extreme climates. Among travellers and event management crews, extremes endured and ordeals experienced in remote contexts are risks of passage facilitating status transition in ways identified among seasoned backpackers (Matthews 2008). The dramatization of traveller risk – both empirical realities and exaggerated mythology – are enshrined in EDMC folklore, whether the illicit sexuality of the proto-disco scene in New York (Shapiro 2005), the prohibited pharmacologies of rave and postrave formations documented in *Generation Ecstasy* (Reynolds 1998), or the subversive outlaw practices in *Fierce Dancing* (Stone 1996). Subsequent scenes grift rebel cachet from earlier scenes just as disc-cultural club scenes have borrowed their nerve from "Underground" discothèques operating in Nazi-occupied Paris (see Shapiro 2005: 15). An outlaw sensibility strikes appeal among participants of contemporary dance cultures whose occupants graft contumacy from transgressive forebears. As seen in Chapter 7, an anti-authoritarian sensibility is at large in the Australian doof scene. Site manager Glenn Armstrong added further insight to this when he stated – in the Australian film documentary produced by James Short *Welcome to Wonderland* (2007) – that mounting the early Earthcore festivals in forests north and east of Melbourne was like "robbing a bank". Here, a corporate identity emerged in the exhilaration of shared risk-taking – i.e. operating outside arduous legal frameworks.

A picture begins to form that the entire psytrance assemblage facilitates the re-fashioning of identity, most powerfully marked at those *limits* where rules, codes and laws, of propriety, morality and the state, are freely transgressed. These are limits the unconsented trespassing of which "freaks out", even terrorizes, official culture. Successfully navigating shocking limits earns trance adventurers acceptance. Since personal empowerment, social status and acceptance are at stake, "hardcore" enthusiasts make substantial investments of their time and resources in revisiting, renewing and sustaining sites, states and conditions of cultural risk. Yet, while these may be important means by which enthusiasts distinguish themselves from those who are without the cultural capital bestowed by successful risk performance, this field of behaviour does not exhaust the means by which social capital is acquired. While, on the one hand, risks are negotiated (and often manufactured) through modes of radical immanence, on the other, the avoidance of known risks (e.g. to the environment, to one's self, to the scene) may be undertaken through radical consumer practices, voluntarism and other ethical practice. While entire scenes form in the shade of the law, in ruptured genre conventions, in departures from legal mind states, in the pirating of data, in body modification, etc., such practices, then, do not account for all prestige-affirming behaviour. For, while the outlaw lurks in the realm "beyond the law", actions responsive to a variety of grievances are means by which participants establish reputation. Like outlaws, activists are responsive to conditions in their life worlds. But rather than simply loiter within badlands of abandonment, their campaigns are ethically motivated, and possess anarchist or spiritual pretentions. While enthusiasts forge reputations in transgression and in the successful performance of risk, others mobilize scene consciousness by identifying a host of threats, or are driven by intent to repeal laws and reform attitudes, to revise accepted practice, and to alter their lifestyle in accordance with recognition of health, spiritual and ecological crises.

Scene activism and conscious gatherings

Framing this behavioural complex is no simple task, given the limitations of theoretical perspectives used to comprehend dance music cultures. While subculture theory has offered considerable attention to the study of outlaw or "deviant" behaviour, and behaviour deemed symbolic "resistance", it offered fewer insights on practices of risk avoidance and cultural movement activity. While rarely approaching dance cultures, subculture theory, as produced at Birmingham's Centre for Contemporary and Cultural Studies in the 1970s (e.g. Hall and Jefferson 1976), highlighted the ineffectual commitments of members of male working-class and subaltern communities caught in the dialectic, who could only find "solutions" in recreational spaces or in the semiotic (and not the material) world. With the advent of rave research in the UK, social dance became a site of *disappearance* under the Baudrillardian heuristics adopted by Steve Redhead and contributors to *Rave Off* (1993), where, as a play-on-words for "rave on", *off* inferenced the proclivity for clandestine *ekstasis* in secluded clubs and outlandish warehouses where acid house ravers of the late 1980s and early 1990s could switch the cultural control knob to "off" and crossfade into oblivion. Later, beginning with Thornton's (1996) work, Bourdieu's theory of "cultural capital" enjoyed wide application in studies preoccupied with the style of clubbers, ravers and other youth formations displayed to mark and maintain their distinction from the "mainstream", from the less sophisticated, or from the racially other. The picture emerging was cliquishness, stature derived from the amplification of a rebellious posture, identities (re)produced through transgression – or a carefully constructed mythology of transgression. And, attending to the "empathetic sociality" in contemporary youth, music and consumer cultures, advocates of Maffesoli (1996) focused upon fleeting nodes of sensual orgiasm, the micro-communities reproducing them, and the individuals who oscillate between them. In the 1980s, Maffesoli argued that post-1960s France had become witness to a re-enchanted "de-individualized" sociality. After Maffesoli's work received English translations in the 1990s, the "neotribes" concept grew appealing among researchers of EDMCs. What Maffesoli named "underground centrality", a sensuous and shifting network of nodes of attachment and identification, seemed apposite to the vibe techno-tribes and participants in EDM cultures everywhere seek to reproduce. But, in its "flabby aestheticism" (Osborne 1997: 141), neotribalism possesses little motivation beyond events themselves. Part of the problem is neotribe theory offers little insight on the "hyper-responsive" (St John 2009) character that is native to the EDMC vibe, which possesses multiple freedom vectors. As temporary microcultures, parties are not simply different *nodes* or "emotional communities", but different *modes* of sociality, different registers of being-together. The vibe is not a singular socio-sonic aesthetic, but a multiplicity of dispositions influential to the dance gathering and imported by those gathering in dance. An expanded heuristic was then required to acknowledge the diverse movement sensibilities of EDMCs. Studies of the variety of ways risk is negotiated by youth (Furlong and Cartmel 2006) offers some headway, but as this and the following chapter illustrate, researching cultural movements necessitates investigation of ecstatic and activist behaviour, the tensions between which define the inner life of social and cultural movements.

While psyculture participants transgress the rules of propriety and property, establishing prestige converted from their mobility across cartographical space, psychosomatic states, digital media and jural limits, others mobilize to defend event and mind states against those prejudices, sensibilities and apparati that undermine their integrity. Mobilizing in opposition to regulatory regimes, international volunteer groups such as MAPS (Multidisciplinary Association for Psychedelic Studies) and German outfits like Alice and Odyssee set up educational stalls and chill lounges at parties and festivals where they circulate information about substances, as well as drug law and enforcement issues. Operating out of Frankfurt and founded by German activist and author Wolfgang Sterneck, Alice is a hub for party and protest, with the Alice operation consisting of a library of cards providing interested consumers with insightful and harm-minimizing factoids about the effects of a variety of substances. These groups enable awareness and informed choice without which participants may be exposed to unscrupulous and exploitative manufacturers and dealers of a range of drugs. The principal cause here is the welfare of the individual who is empowered to make an informed choice, with activists challenging prevailing disinformation on psychoactives. The objective of such groups is that all users become activists through raising awareness (cultural capital) of the effects and content of substances to which they become exposed.

While seeking to improve the cultural capital of others through the circulation of pharmacological knowledge is the driving concern of some, others have grown determined to maintain autonomy in response to threats undermining "the Goa spirit". A 2002 report by Kai Mathesdorf in *Mushroom Magazine* is demonstrative. The author decried the waning spirit of Goa by 1997, when "blinded by success many prime freaks mutated to arrogant, self-indulgent assholes", and "many DJs behaved as god-like" (Mathesdorf 2002: 18). The concern has long haunted Goatrance in the place of its birth, where German Sven Väth showed up in the early 1990s "wanting to be the techno pope of India" (Castle, in Cole and Hannan 1997). These concerns can be tracked backwards to the conditions which compelled freaks to travel to Goa in the 1960s and 1970s. Or forwards, for instance, to Infected Mushroom, who featured in a 2006 cover story in Italian *Vogue* magazine wearing suits and serious looks, or to fellow Israeli act Skazi, whose decaled ice-cream van promoting Skazi flavours – and his release *Total Anarchy* (2006) – at Japan's Solstice Festival would become the subject of ridicule,[3] with these and other examples standing as cautionary tales for those re-creating the original, mythical, Goa vibe.

Critics cultivate their identities and events in the light of unscrupulous promoters, over-indulgence and self-interest, which they must continually identify and resist. The standard "rave" scene, the mainstream trance scene, or the commercial psytrance scene, have long offered scenarios against which activists define themselves, where self-definition relies upon the continual identification of these encroachments. It is common for events and their organizing bodies to hold no constitution or mission statements other than that which circumscribes the object of their contempt. As west coast party organizer Alex Dreamdust stated to me,

> the groups I'm involved in (dream stream) are all "psytrance" and are trying to distance themselves from what they see as a separate "rave" scene that's simply about drugs and sex, and has forgotten the power of dance. If you go to one of the massive or more publicized events in San Francisco so many of the kids there just stand around popping pills and groping girls.[4]

The reference to pill popping here is near defining, and points to a general wariness associated with the abuse of that which generally passes for "E" or "M" (MDMA) – i.e. pills with uncertain purity and often manufactured with amphetamine, methamphetamine, ephedrine and caffeine – in the wake of MDMA's universal scheduling and criminalization in national legal codes. While, in some of Irvine Welsh's writing, Ecstasy constitutes a "spiritual technology" offering the potential to "shift consciousness towards the transcendental goal of better communications with one's spiritual self" (Stephenson

2003: 154), and indeed literature calls attention to MDMA's ostensible ability to "foster spirituality, personal development and life change";[5] for other commentators MDMA is the main attraction in the "chemical carnival" of clubbing, where getting temporarily "loved up" serves only to reinforce permanent social hierarchy (Van Ree 1997). Within the scene, the uses and abuses of MDMA precipitate considerable debate especially among exponents of a psychedelic sensibility (i.e. those who prefer LSD and other tryptamines). Indeed, the presence of "e-tards" constitutes one complaint among many levelled at parties deemed to have lost direction, their cathartic vibrance dissipated. Thus, on a tribe.net thread, BrettfromTibet (2008) commented that

> many good electronic music scenes get eaten alive by the shadow side and by simpler ... and denser people that discover the light, like moths, and flocked to it en masse ... dampening the glow. the russian mafia comes to Goa, the industrial headbanger crew comes to San Francisco, booty music comes to the Playa, the gangsters and junkies come to raves.

All of which is reckoned "a sure sign that divine grace has been betrayed ... and the scene gets divided". Following from Reynolds's (1998: 86) criticism of the "darkside" within EDM scenes whose regulated clubbing environments are populated by "dead souls, zombie-eyed and prematurely haggard", there is an emerging literature observing scene fragmentation and decline as a result of dissipating "solidarity" or wayward vision identified as consequential to excesses in the consumption of drugs such as MDMA, cocaine and ketamine, and to commercialization, sexual predatorial behaviour, regulatory strictures and other factors.[6]

A host of identified maladies animate efforts to recapture and optimize the lost or fractured vibe. Rampant commercialism is among the chief isolated causes of discontent among scene commentators within the psytrance community. Sam Chaishop (2008) put it this way:

> The reasons why we fell in love with (and sacrificed our life to) the scene 15 years ago were an alternative way of partying, individual and communal extension of consciousness, tolerance, respect and care for your fellow party crowd. Parties were a secret playground for an explicit crowd of people that were unhappy with the general structures of our societies and wanted to take a weekend off to live life differently, meet like-minded and learn. Music was catalyzing all this but it was just a tile in a mosaic of reasons that called for a good party.

But nowadays, he continued, “Psytrance music is a product, Psytrance parties are products and are basically integrated into our society just like any other musical scene”. Iboga Records manager Mikael Dahlgaard (aka DJ Emok) also made lament in *Mushroom Magazine* the same year (2008/2009: 7) about an “ever disappearing spirit” caused by the presence of “more and more people that orientate on the common norms and values of Western society”. Often, those targeted are neither those uncritical nor conscious of their consumer practices. In a comment initiating the thread “The Problem with Psytrance” posted to isratrance.com in March 2007, Pete Sideburner animates the conversation by accusing labels of dressing up their releases in “mostly brainless, preposterous hokum [that] usually sounds like a sleazy washing powder commercial”. In a commentary that received overwhelming approval, he observed, “the majority of Goa fraggles are basically just big consumers. Consumers of new ‘killah releases’, heavy consumers of drugs, of course, consumers of laser shows, consumers of dancefloors and, most of all, consumers of an old and long vanished idea of a better life as a hippie”. Sideburner returns to a common cause of discontent: the raving thrillseeker, the working-class prole, the psychedelic bogan, those uncritical and “unenlightened” patrons against whom the *real* “Goa” community persistently requires definition. Further narrating the tragedy, Sideburner continues that in May 2006 at the “tragically dreadful wet and rainy” Sonnenklang Festival in Austria,

> on the second night or so, when I walked towards the dancefloor alone, there was this group of – hm, well, I think I'm gonna call them Goa hooligans – behind me that sang that famous soccer tune: “Oléééé, olé, olé, oléééé”, just they didn't put their favorite soccer team in it, but the phrase “super Goa, oléééé, olééééé”. It was at that moment, it hit me: I am at a soccer match in some British stadium, or at an overcrowded beach in front of ugly white tourist blocks in Spain, or at a ski piste in Switzerland, or at a camping site in Italy, or at Disneyland in Florida, or Mardi Gras in former New Orleans (now known as Atlantis), or at the local Burger King just next to the local charts disco, or at the Love Parade in Berlin, or just sitting at home after work watching those spirit crushing so called comedy shows. I'm just at another place where that mob-driven, hedonistic numbness is the idealized behaviour-pattern of that streamlined common sense that degenerates our little planet so much. Basically, I could be anywhere except nature – there isn't much difference anymore between a psyparty and any other civilized place where people consume things some vibrant business-men have arranged for them.

Over-exposure is a basic trigger for this upbraiding. There was once "a huge difference between psyparties and the crappy ordinary world", states Sideburner, but "the latter is so utterly contaminated with mindless consumerism that makes *things* becoming more important than *people*, while the former used to be more about *just being people*". Yet today the "ordinary people with their ordinary interests and ordinary habits have arrived at psytrance", and it has subsequently become diluted. Posting to the same thread on 13 April 2007, "oboulys" nods along, stating that, having attended Italy's Sonica Festival in 2005, "man shiiit, i felt so silly its incredible ... it was the 'everybody is wearing the same outfit' feeling, with the fluoro-line of clothes, very designer, and the glam girls and hehe, all that. they all looked kind of like teletubbies, same stuff, different color".

These provocative commentaries draw lines in the sand, where the implicit distinction from "ordinary people" with "mindless" consumer behaviours is a reflexive articulation of a planet recognized to be at risk from unethical consumerism. That the consumption of "things" has apparently superseded the attainment of *no-thing* with which habitués of the Goa seasonal parties and their descendants were familiar is a cause for alarm. Those identified as "mindless consumers", "fraggles" and "teletubbies" are not the fictionalized "mainstream" against which acid house protagonists defined themselves in Thornton's analysis, but are the embodiment of a consumer capitalism routinely identified to have jeopardized psytrance. It is the consumerist behaviour that forebears sought distance from and which continues to fuel discontent, including a self-deprecating approach not as common in other EDM scenes. That said, a further response to this thread (29 June 2007) offers a compassionate "lead by example" model that cannot be ignored in the study of psytrance and is integral to its development. "Of course you are always gonna get some yobbos at events ... that even was happening [*sic*] back when I first started going to parties 11 years ago", states "panorama", elaborating:

> for many people this may be their first or second time at a psytrance event ... perhaps they need a bit of guidence [*sic*] as how to behave at such parties ... in order to survive, we need new people at events ... people grow into a scene eventually ... I do think that it is our individual reponsibilites [*sic*] to perhaps let people that are acting stupid KNOW that maybe they are somewhat out of line. If everyone of us at parties that really wanna keep the scene alive offer just a bit of guidence [*sic*] to "goa yobs" then perhaps you might find a return to the wierd [*sic*], strange, fun, fucked-up, twisted normalicy [*sic*] we all know and love.

Others conduct their maintenance activities at the boundaries of "psychedelic" musical styles, and will busy themselves identifying the incursive sounds and the hoard enthused by its "noise". Much of this discourse focuses on that which is considered to be "real psychedelic" music often delineating that which fails to meet an often unstated criteria. Having worn the message "don't fuck with my drop" painted on his back in Boom's Dance Temple in 2010, the author/wearer of the message later explained on isratrance.com that the dominating sounds of "progressive minimal" throughout the day caused the complaint:

> the MINIMAL was not born with the psychedelic spirit, it was born at techno-clubs, so it has a CLUB SPIRIT ... It's not a shamanic experience, your ego is still here in this world, you don't get "the other world, beyond the concepts". So, my point is: this new "neo-trance" is a club music, not a shamanic music (it's MINIMAL-TRANCE BUT NOT PSYCHEDELIC). Why I did thousands of kilometers to Boom? To get in trance with thousands of people, having this massive-shamanic experience ... Yes, they (the line-up makers) fuck my psychedelic experience (syntesis 2010).

Psychedelic forums commonly host discussions on the nature of "psychedelic" or "shamanic" music perceived to be under threat from aesthetics felt to be invasive. Following the 2009 Symbiosis Festival near California's Yosemite National Park, a comment was posted to another thread on isratrance.com: "every year, this event slides farther and farther from its roots. Yes it gets bigger and more grandiose every time, but each time, it loses part of its soul". The poster claimed that Symbiosis was "originally a psy-trance event" but has grown "very very far from its roots today" stating that "in fact, as a trancer, I have never felt such like a second class citizen at a event. We were given the worst stage, with the smallest sound, in the dustiest area, in the back corner. Very segregated, I almost felt like a black man, in the 50s at this party". What's more, minced words elicit a scatological catalogue of stereotypes whose identification assists the forging of this cornered persona: "in my 14 years of being in the overall EDM scene I dont think ive encountered a sub-set of the culture as annoying as the feather and leather dub step crowd. Id rather have militant junglists, techno elitists, coked-out house head heads, or hell even candy kids. The hippy inspired, pseudo hip-hop, 'green' bling of it all was just obscene" (paradigm 2009). Other critics rebel against convention, waging campaigns against the "cheese" which everywhere pulls psychedelic aesthetics into the formulaic pop-stream. Here, a flooded market inspires avant vibes and the tribes curating them. On a popular discussion on tribe.net in 2008 the following statement held weight:

> Most of the stuff that I have heard lately feels like you could write a software program called "psytrance generator" which pumps

> out a 4/4 kick with hats on the offbeat and snare on 2 and 4; basslines that are generated through algorithm or just 16th notes after each kick; squelchy leads that just arpeggio over top of all of that; randomly generated quantized stabs, and reverses/cymbals after every 16 bars. Remove the kick every so often, and bring in back with a rolling snare. Also add a dash of samples from your latest pop-culture movie/tv show, and you got a psytrance track. This program could generate random patches for each of these sounds, but the structure is basically a formula. Run this program 9 times and you got an album that can be posted on psyshop or saikosounds with the description of being "killa" (Brian 2008).

Scathing accounts are also opened against professionalization, understood as a "closing" of a mind that was once "open" and integral to the psychedelic experience. DJ Shaher in *Psychedelic Traveller* (2008) expressed this concern: in Israel in the early 1990s

> when I went to that first party I still wore my new wave punk outfit, and it was cool with everyone. I didn't know the name of the music, didn't recognize the tracks, didn't know anything about the guys who stood and changed the tapes ... This was the essence of the party – come as you are, be what you want, open your mind, no definitions, no formulas, no rules, no expectations, be accepted.

But by 2008, the scene had "choked", the mind had "closed" and the musical movement became "so preoccupied with generising [*sic*], labeling and formulating everything. In this reality, once you develop – you're out!" (Shaher 2008: 7).

Collectively, the above criticisms, and many others like them, are boundary-marking strategies integral to the definition of self, scene and lifestyle. While such observations are the preoccupation of some, other protagonists participate in the trance movement specifically as a means to "expand" and "raise" consciousness. While maintaining a near clandestine operation appears to be a persistent motivation – where guardians patrol the boundaries of the psy community to safeguard its integrity from crippling laws, incursive aesthetics and marauding morons – other inhabitants seek to establish their communities and events as platforms for causes beyond the events themselves. In the former, like members of a "secret society", protagonists commit to preventing change, identifying those elements impoverished in cultural capital; but in the latter camp can be located those committed to "make change happen", which was indeed Boom's mantra in 2010. The former mood is conveyed on Bolivian artist Deep South's full-on "Fight Club" (*Andes Trip*, 2007) which samples a well-worn announcement from *Fight Club*'s protagonist Tyler Durden: "Gentlemen. Welcome to Fight Club. The first rule of Fight Club is: you do not talk about Fight Club". The sample evokes the tight-lipped secrecy with parties operating in successful contradistinction to federal and state requirements, and cloaking their visibility to the mainstream tourist-clubber crowd, practices relied upon for their survival. Other samples are designed to identify the *other* citizen whose consumer attitudes mark the limits of acceptability defined according to ecological principles and whose amplification in party contexts serves as a mechanism for the likely mocking of one's own behaviour. Thus, One Tasty Morsel uses the following line on "The Day I Blew My Rig Out" (2010): "I want to get back to nature, right, but I don't want to get out of my car".

That dance parties have been staging grounds for movement causes beyond the reproduction of the events themselves has a considerable history in cosmopolitan rave scenes. Through the 1990s and the subsequent decade, techno-rave culture offered upgrades on the techniques of the human potential movement whose holistic practices had become consistent with utopian, ascensionist and evolutionary fantasies implicated in the cybernetic revolution. As a form of body transcendence and self-awakening alongside meditation and yoga, psychedelic techno-raves became the new front-lines in the consciousness revolution. The crowning achievement in this development are "consciousness clubs", a tradition that may have kicked off at London's Marquee Club on 30 January 1966, referred to earlier and regarded as the first "alternative consciousness club".[7] The baton was later passed to the "free-festival in a club" Megatripolis, and other London "festi-clubs" like Megadog and Planet Dog, themselves modelled on venues like Whirl-Y-Gig and Club Dog – all critical venues in London's proliferating "hippy/punk proto-crusty scene" (Reynolds 1998: 149, 152). These events reproduced the atmosphere of the UK's Free Festivals, themselves compositing the atmosphere of the gypsy traveller and medieval fayre. Co-founded in 1993 by creator and editor of the *Encyclopaedia Psychedelica* Fraser Clark,[8] Megatripolis hosted the "Parallel University" where club-goers were exposed to the ideas of Allen Ginsberg, McKenna and Ram Dass, among many other countercultural luminaries presenting, including Leary and the Dalai Lama who were transmitted into the club via ISDN. The format later inspired London's Synergy Project, which evolved into Luminopolis, and had an influence on other events and venues like Hamden's Inspiral Lounge. Held at the cavernous SEOne club under London Bridge Station, Synergy Project hosted to a range of rooms, including a main psytrance room hosted by Altered States, a live stage operated by Small World and Indigenous Peoples, a chill-out zone hosted by IDSpiral and Liquid Connective, and a healing area hosted by Puma Punka (see Beck and Lynch 2009). The intent native to this reflexive raving is evident in the cosmopolitan Disctopia replicated around the world, from Sydney's Vibe Tribe to Germany's Fusion Festival, and from San Francisco's Come Unity to

British Columbia's Shambhala Music Festival and the UK's Turaya Gathering (promoted as a "Holistic World Fusion Arts Gathering"), and Waveform Festival. All of these events are examples of the legacy of the "conscious party" where ecstasy and activism became dancing partners.

In 1995, Clark opened the short-lived club Megatripolis West in San Francisco, the location fitting given the city hosted the original "tribal gathering" model. With events promoted as "Hyperdelic Carnivals," "Cyborganic Be-Ins," and the "Digital Be-In" (Hill 1999), in the early 1990s San Francisco held status as a nexus for conscious raving. By 1997, something of a *global be-in* had manifested as the Earthdance International festival. Promoted as a Global Festival for Peace "connecting globally, acting locally", Earthdance is a synchronized global dance festival that began as a Free Tibet movement fundraiser and, by 2010, was held in over 200 locations in more than 50 countries, benefiting over 75 charities. Participating events donate at least 50 per cent of profits to local non-profit organizations supporting peace initiatives, relief efforts, sustainable communities and social justice concerns. According to the organization itself, claiming to have helped build schools and orphanages, initiate peace education programmes, and assist Indigenous peoples to protect land, "we've given more than a million people worldwide vital inspiration and resources to activate peace in their lives and in the world". In 2011, in alignment with the United Nations' International Year of Forests, under a Celebrating the Forests theme, all Earthdance events were encouraged to focus on "causes that work to Honor our Mother Gaia, the Plant Kingdom and our lifegiving Forests, while finding new ways to live sustainably on our planet".[9] Uniquely, each event around the globe participates in "the world's largest synchronized prayer for peace", a critical mass meditation event foreshadowed by Return To The Source events and productions,[10] and with a precursor in the global Harmonic Convergence of 1987. While Earthdance

Sacred Fire. Boom 2010. Photo: Jakob Kolar. www.woowphoto.com.

has its roots in Goatrance, and many Earthdance events are dominated by psychedelic trance, events, including the mother event in Leytonville, are host to a diversity of musical styles. From humble beginnings, Earthdance grew into a transnational platform for the advancement of multiple causes. It exemplifies the party that is a vehicle for movement causes, where dance, not a simple self-indulgence, is aligned with responsible cultural practice.

Chillout culture

In Chapter 5, I explored the landscape of the dance festival, which enables cognitive responses to causes and disputes both internal and external to scenes. While chai shops and other bohemian cultural spaces were referred to, here I specifically address the chillout zone, that omnipresent visionary bastion within psyculture. Chillout spaces owe their development to the White Room where Alex Patterson and Youth (The Orb) and Jimmy Cauty (The KLF) DJed at the Land Of Oz – the first chillout room – whose ambient soundtrack provided the blueprint for The KLF's 1991 album *The White Room* (Photon, 2005). As a context for high conversation and relaxed discourse removed from frenetic dance floors, these zones are like sumptuous life-rafts from whose vantage the luxuriating observe the status of broader scene developments. Sometimes these zones are officially managed and programmed; other times, as found at psychedelic festivals the world over, the avant-garde pitch camp in oases of sound-art removed from the maddening crowd of downtown electronica. As audio-visual asylums, "chill" or "ambient" rooms, tents, zones and installations facilitate the revitalization of scenes thought to have grown formulaic, excessive and regrettable. Grant Gilbert (aka Grant T. Garden) of SolaSonic provides an exemplar. In 2001, Gilbert, who had been involved with dance music since the early 1980s partnering with William Orbit in British synthpop outfit Torch Song – which drew inspiration from Brian Eno and German electronic bands Neu and Cluster – set up a solar-powered sound system at Germany's Voov Experience in an effort to extend the spirit of the Goa vibe. He had been producing chill spaces at events in the UK for ten years, in particular the Organic Tea Garden in the Green Fields at the Glastonbury Festival, and founded a small label, Entropica, which released Solar Quest's *AcidOphilez* (1998) and *Orgisms* (2000) and 23 Degrees' *...An Endless Searching for Substance* (1994), a curious title evoking the path alternative to the endless search for chemical substances characterizing other sides of the scene. With his chill space at Voov, Gilbert was culture-adding to a festival whose format he claimed was otherwise undifferentiated from a rock concert. It would be a relaxed space for the circulation of ideas and raising awareness about hemp, organic foods, entheogens and support for campaigns like Survival International and Free Tibet. Accordingly, a chill zone will "sell books, organic foods and drinks, there would be speakers and discussions, performance, demonstrations, a truly multi-media environment" (Jennie and Postman 2002). Following such motivations, the chill is a visionary realm advancing causes beyond the precincts of the dance event and its immediate indulgences.

Gilbert's response to scene developments, and his concomitant harnessing of renewable energies, is not atypical to the moods of those designing and curating chill spaces in events over the past ten years. At festivals the world over, bands of geeky experimentalists and spiritual activists build sonic utopias, make ambient asylum and maintain quiet rage against the dance massive. These exiles are conspicuous in their opposition to the pandemonium that may otherwise lay siege to a festival environment and the wider scene. In their response to the main fare carnage, curators of ambient, glitchtech and beatless soundscapes seek to establish zones removed from the ketamine- and methamphetamine-influenced vibes of the cacophonous *danse macabre.* They host producers and sound technicians whose search for simplicity evokes philosophical quests for slow-paced solutions to the woes of mundane life. Peddling pronoia, optimists establish a re/connection with, rather than acceleration from, "the source", a resolution in bliss via melody rather than a capitulation to crisis via dissonance. That the Other provokes astonishment (and rapture) rather than fear (and terror) is the gestalt behind psychedelic ambient (or psybient), psydub, ethno-prog and other minimal musics often described as "lush," "serene", "organic", "chill", and performed at ambient and "chill" stages – or even therapeutic "sound temples" like that found at Boom in 2010 – which sometimes operate like refuge points at parties. Floating within regenerative soundscapes owes much to The Orb, with Alex Patterson recognized by Prendergast (2001) as an heir to the earliest ambient artists like Cage and Eno; the likes of German Harald Bluechel (aka Cosmic Baby) who experimented with classical piano and synthesizer melodies contrasted against techno rhythms and who released one of the most popular trance releases, "Cafe Del Mar" (in 1993 under the pseudonym Energy 52); and to ethnodelic legends Shpongle, whose work would hold heavy influence on psychedelic electronica, from pre-Shpongle releases like The Infinity Project's *Mystical Experiences* (Blue Room, 1995), which included tracks engineered by Simon Posford, to Shpongle's latest release *Ineffable Mysteries from Shpongleland* (Twisted, 2010). Ambient and ethnodelic artists commit to producing transformative journeys, as is the intended effect of Swiss-based The Peaking Goddess Collective's "Being Transformation" (*Organika*, 2007) which features the voice of Alex Grey, or "Aztec Journey" by Entheogenic Sound Explorers (*The Shroom Experience*, 2007). Work on labels like Interchill and Dakini Records is designed for transiting from states of inner turmoil – including that associated with the cacophony of the main dance floor – into blissful awareness. While this music rarely uses vocals, a female sampled on Entheogenic's "Beyond Zero" (*Entheogenic*, 2002) appears to capture the mood: "Going inside, cutting off external stimuli, and mind chatter, and going way inside and by doing that, it's almost like Alice falling down the rabbit hole".

Chill spaces are typically decorated like temples, centres of spiritual growth and transformation, with scheduled artists selected for their capacity to maintain detachment from the mundane. With visionary zest, ambient producers typically seek to reunite the separate human ego with the vastness of nature, with awesome effect. While much material demonstrates influence from Tibetan and Indian Buddhism, more rarely Zen Buddhist-influenced sounds occupy these scapes – as found on labels like 12K, Line and Room40 – and performed by the likes of Quiet Time, a soundscape outfit who have performed at Rainbow Serpent Festival. Influenced by the Zen-like "examination of minute phenomena", Quiet Time performer Ben Dixon describes the practice as an attempt to "demonstrate that the line between sound and music is an arbitrary fabrication".[11] With classic Zen themes like "emptiness, stillness, non-grasping, egolessness, being present", the music is what Dixon describes as "not sticky – it moves you, then lets you go. In contrast to pop or other genres, where the music explicitly tries to hook you, for commercial and artist-ego based reasons – it tries to stick to you. Gets in your head and clings and wont let go".[12]

Yet Buddhism has also influenced dance music, as evidenced by the Ollie Olsen and Gus Till collaboration Third Eye, whose "Heaven Transmissions" (*New Life* EP, 1993) featured Tibetan Buddhist monk chants sounding out the entrance to eternity. But there are many paths to eternity. Employing a fusion of world sounds, in cosmopolitan fashion, ethnodelic artists

Lake-side. Boom 2010. Photo: Jakob Kolar. www.woowphoto.com.

pursue the therapeutic propensities of psychedelia embracing diversity and traversing ethnic boundaries. Shpongle is exemplary, as is Shulman, known for using Western classical, classical Indian, Arab and Greek music, jazz and contemporary sounds. In his self-identified "neo-tribal" music, Adham Shaikh samples instruments from North and West Africa, India, the Middle East, Japan and Australia, with his 2006 album *Collectivity* promoted as a "rich tapestry of sound ... inlaid with accents of Turkish Oud, Nay, Zorna, Indian tabla, African Mbira, Marimba, Kamele N'goni, Middle Eastern Sazu, Flutes, Bass, and Far Eastern Mouth Harp". More recently, the liner notes on Awake's *The Core* (2008) offer evidence of this *eclectronic* momentum: "Built as a journey of audio neural beauty through organic microcosms, electronic vortexes, deep, tribal beats and vast soundscapes, the album takes us on a pilgrimage of sounds, with scents of parallel lives, glimpses of the future and overlapping, coexisting dimensions". Alongside their fusional character, ethnodelic artists also emphasize their "live" and "organic" characteristics. For instance, The Peaking Goddess Collective's Daniel Symons and Pearce van der Merwe began producing as Cosmosophy, releasing *Organic Space Age* (2008), a live "down to earth" fusion of funk, breakbeat, dub, Afro-beat and progressive trance.

For visionary artists working within the ambient and chillout development, aesthetic considerations and ethical (principally ecological) causes are indistinguishable. A leading commitment is a desire for consciousness evolution, a reflexive disposition evoking the intent towards transformation at the heart of the spiritual endeavour. Here the realized self is an enchanted self, or more to the point, a re-enchanted self, empowered as such through reconnection with the natural world – including natural health remedies, the plant world, the tribal, the feminine, or even the cosmos – and music is designed to facilitate this. Here, nature is sacred, the alienation from which – manifesting in depression and toxicity and triggered by monotheism, corporate control and state bureaucracy – triggers event aesthetics and music programming. The contiguity with New Age or relaxation music, designed as a therapeutic aid, is evident, for instance, on the DVD *Templayed* produced by Liquid Crystal Vision (2007), which is promoted as "Healing Through Temple Visuals" featuring images of temples from around the world to the accompaniment of ambient electronica (mainly from Electric Skychurch). Hosting chill areas that resemble New Age temples or otherwise integrating this ethos of re-enchantment into the event design, parties so envisioned are contexts for reconnection with that which is considered lost or forgotten, sites of revitalization highly charged, therapeutic and ultimately sacred.

Within the chill development, certain producers are fielded to encapsulate the response to the maddening crowd. Among them is Grover Smith (aka Ott), who offers a message of balance. For instance, on Ott's dub-tempo remix of Hallucinogen's "Gamma Goblins", "Gamma Goblins (It's Turtles All The

Way Down Mix)" (Hallucinogen, 2002), Alan Watts conveys his Oriental philosophy – that from the Hindu perspective life is drama (performed) rather than an artifact (made) – later published in *Eastern Wisdom, Modern Life: Collected Talks: 1960–1969* (Watts 2006: 56–7): Before Hallucinogen's familiar "gamma goblins" are smoked out of their holes in dubbed-out Rasta style, Watts speaks:

> Now the dreaming period is subdivided into four stages. The first stage is the longest and it's the best. During that stage, the dream is beautiful. The second stage is not quite so long, and it's a little unsettling. There is an element of instability in it, a certain touch of insecurity. In the third stage, which is not, again, so long, the forces of light and the forces of darkness, of good and of evil, are equally balanced and things are beginning to look rather dangerous. And in the fourth stage, which is the shortest of them all, the negative, dark or evil side triumphs and the whole thing goes up. And so then there's a waking period before the whole thing starts again.

The lines could be read as justification for the disparity in musical styles found at a single psychedelic trance event or experienced on a single dance floor throughout its duration. Indeed, taken as components of a sequence, as part of a psychodramatical musical narrative unfolding out of the night (night music/dark trance) and into the morning (uplifting progressive sounds) and eventually back into the night, and so on, Watts inquires via Ott: "have you noticed, that in this drama, the forces of the dark side are operative for 1/3 of the time, the forces of the light side for 2/3 of the time? This is a very ingenious arrangement, 'cause we are seeing here, the fundamental principles of drama".

Arts of consciousness

Attention to psychedelic chillout culture should illustrate that studies of psychedelic trance that do not hear the music itself, and which have made little recognition of the differences between genre, aesthetics and sound cultures, are likely to neglect cultural nuances and social dynamics integral to a complex movement. Indeed, study of the soundscapes of psychedelic trance aids an understanding of the dramas unfolding within event precincts. In "contact zone" research, Deleuzian ethnographies have pointed up "micro-fascist" tendencies among neo-hippies on Ibiza and in Goa – from the observation of "aesthetic elitism and hedonistic indulgence" (D'Andrea 2007a: 125) to a detailed exposé of white "viscosity" and cliquishness (Saldanha 2007a). In Saldanha's estimate, social capital accumulates to the scene-savvy in Goa. That is, those who "know where to buy their charas in the north, and their E and

LSD in Goa; they talk of parties in Columbia, the Cambodian jungle, the Sinai desert; they know who organizes parties, where the baksheesh comes from, and why parties are cancelled; they smoke chillum with deejays and dealers; they get Enfields and rooms at minimal prices" (2007a: 146). Such cultural knowledge serves to affirm privilege within scenes everywhere, where status will be accorded, for instance, to those with access to the newest or most obscure, and arguably most "visionary", psychoactive substances, or "research chemicals", in circulation. While these are important observations, in an approach which renders the Goa party little more than a skin-deep pantomime, Saldanha argues that the "visual and hallucinatory economy" in the morning phase of Goa parties in which white freaks star and Indians and tourists play minor roles is a process of "filtering out contaminant bodies", concluding that, since "psychedelic bliss is defined through the absence of Indians ... subculturally pure in Anjuna comes to mean racially pure" (Saldanha 2007a: 127, 129, 131). The broadside opened on those dancing upon the shifting sands of the post-Goa contact zone offers a race-materialist indictment of the trance tourism industry and culture in Goa, albeit via empirically flawed race reductionism, as D'Andrea (2009) points out. Attention to the mosaic of intent, and the debate between sonic cultures within psychedelic trance, in Goa and its global diaspora, assists a fuller, albeit never finished, canvas.

In attention to the visionary arts movement flourishing in the Goa diaspora, it became apparent that "cultural capital" does not simply accrue as a result of mercenary risk-laden performance, but in forms of "conscious partying" or party "projects" where collaborative artifice serves causes beyond the dance floor. As it becomes reputable to practise sustainability and to support humanitarian causes, credibility is earned within a climate of risk-awareness. Here, prestige, perhaps *conscious capital*, accrues among those who develop an acute awareness of risks (ecological, humanitarian, health) and cultivate that knowledge in the production of events, music and art to "raise consciousness". Given that the dance event and its socio-sonic-aesthetic is the principal site for the cultural expression of psytrance, it is within such locales that a cultural-economy of consciousness may be found. The organizational design and management of events offer insights on this. Those who orchestrate and implement parties intended as a means of redressing crises or advancing causes beyond the liminal boundaries of the event – and thus not simply as profit-turning ventures – attract credence and networks of support as their intent becomes transparent in event operations, in artistic programming and in cultural investments. Intention is demonstrated via directed cultural programmes, support for a variety of cultural industries, handicrafts and well-being practices, the promotion of transnational cultural and political campaigns and support of local and regional organizations and causes. In Israeli and Australian parties and scene events elsewhere, management organizations build loyalty among various stakeholders through the practice of a cooperative ethos and the support of international and local industries and groups.[13]

A chief source of laudability is maintained via the implementation of ecological principles, like that which Boom promotes as "sustainable entertainment". In this case, the event name indexes sound management, and the magnetism of the brand is a measure of its succession from events that have grown unaccountable, irresponsible, and/or are maladaptive to ecology. At smaller regional events, sound reputations may be (re)produced in the context of free or by-donation parties, or in a cooperativism in which the gifting of resources, art and skills is commonplace, and where the sacrifice of one's time, space and labour to re/produce the party serves as both one's active membership in its community and sources of initial and continuing attraction for participants who may volunteer their labour, donate equipment, share skills and consciousness alterants, in the service of the cause: nothing more and nothing less than the party itself, all of which owes considerably to the Goa party heritage. At larger events, notoriety and credibility may be measured according to a balance of factors including the active and ongoing support of industries that have grown dependent upon the event culture, including those related to clothing, fashion accessories, food and other commodities marketed (and manufactured) by itinerant merchants; sound, lighting and staging equipment; artistic installations and décor; music (the studio and technology used to produce and perform music); and consciousness alterants and associated equipment and paraphernalia. Ecologically sustainable industries such as manufacturers and installation of composting toilets are also integral to event design and reputation.

That psytrance is an event culture rooted in an autonomous free-party tradition – and thus voluntarism and mutual aid – is crucial to this story. Earlier, I referred to the way exposure to weather conditions holds initiatory potential for travellers, affording belonging among those who negotiate risks encountered in regions remote from home. However, a distinction should be made between the anticipated risks that may be routinely negotiated in the interests of acquiring or maintaining cultural capital, and those unplanned incidents, such as the effects of extreme weather events like freak storms that are not uncommon in a culture where travel to regions remote from home and amenities is typical, and which are potentially disastrous. These are not risks actively sought in the fashion that one participates in edgework. Possibly the most important outcome of adverse weather conditions is that cooperative responses are inaugurated among those impacted. In the face of such adversities, voluntary assistance and mutual aid generates an *esprit de corps* that endures long after the party's over. Within psyculture, across all regions, a typical story emerges of event habitués who are ravaged by an unpredicted storm in a remote region upsetting plans to stage the party. Despite the conditions, participants, who are often strangers to one another, and who may hail from different countries and speak different languages, pull together, share resources and collaborate to rebuild the event. One such collaboration was mounted at the Brazilians Trance Festival in Boracéia, Brazil, planned for New Year 2003/2004. Attending her first psytrance party, Sabrina Acquaviva bussed to the festival with a group of strangers, many of whom would become her friends long after the event. She described to me the event as a formative initiatory experience. Before the festival began, heavy rains destroyed infrastructure and decorations, preventing entry to further partygoers and causing many to leave. It "felt like a Woodstock revival".[14] Those few hundred who remained conspired to resurrect the festival from the mud, building camaraderie that is unlikely to have formed without the ordeal by storm. Bearing resemblance to the "communitas of disaster" (E. Turner 2012: 73–84) – though a specific form, since here it is the celebration that is potentially calamitous, the party a disaster area – such occasions grow spectacular when the events in question are transnational and held in regions remote from home. The 2006 total solar eclipse festival Soulclipse, in Turkey, fits this description, and it so happens that the event was nailed by a torrential storm collapsing the main stage minutes before the opening ceremony. Despite the logistical nightmare presented by this crisis – in which it was miraculous that nobody was killed or seriously injured – the stage was rebuilt within a few days. In these incidences, extreme weather events precipitate a collective response, even within commercial festivals where consumers may become volunteers and innovators.

While rampant commercialism causes disputes among those pursuing a cooperative ethos, the measure of credibility relies upon commitments to alternatives – themselves triggered by dissatisfaction with the commoditization of events. Thus the DiY-ethos, integral to the doof, remains in tension with the performance of standard capitalist consumer models, the tension especially dramatic within sites and events where cooperativism/volunteerism and corporate strategies collide. For instance, members of Melbourne's psytrance community identified Earthcore – the event organization which held intimate and free outdoor gatherings as early as 1993, and which grew to large-scale multi-staged and multi-genred event spectaculars by the following decade – as a benchmark in event chicanery. Earthcore developed a widely alleged reputation for defaulting on paying DJs, performers, sound hire companies, event-workers, for their services, a practice raised to something of a legacy as the company passed into bankruptcy/solvency on three occasions. The intention, ambition and responsibilities of organizations sailing in the gulf-stream of the Goa tradition are diverse. Through their participation in global Earthdance events, partygoers make financial assistance to a host of environmental and social causes, and organizers can claim success in their mission to "create community and a shared sense of purpose, focus intentions and empower thoughtful activism, and benefit local non-profits". Earthdance is exemplary among those dance organizations that make considerable effort responding to risk via elaborate annual demonstrations of the awareness of ecological and humanitarian crises. By comparison, despite its self-promotions, Earthcore appeared to hold a motivation more aligned with cowboy capitalism. Here the underlying legacy appears to have been not that of "giving up" one's energy and resources to the benefit of others, but to simply "give it up" (i.e. abandon responsibilities) for the longest time possible. As a poster promotion for an early event had it: "Don't kid yourself, you will not be at work on Monday".

In other projects, financial and ecological considerations coincide in compassionate commitments towards alternatives. The cultural economy of consciousness is illustrated in fund-raising efforts such as various music compilation projects like: *Faith, Hope and Psychedelia* (1998) distributed by A.R.D. and initiated by the ASHA Foundation (Action, Service and Hope for AIDS), a testament, reads the CD inlay, "to the united power of the Dance Revolution evolving to help the suffering of victims of social injustice"; or the four *Hope* compilations released by Japanese label Brainbusters in 2011 to raise relief funds for victims of the Tōhoku earthquake and tsunami; and the *Indigenous S.O.S Benefit Project* (2010) released by Random Records, a non-profit label created exclusively to "help projects supporting indigenous communities around the world" and to create "trance-cultural interactions that are based on mutual respect and solidarity". Considerable efforts have also been made to raise funds for the Free Tibet movement, evident, for example, in the 2007 ambient compilation *Tibet – A Culture in Danger* produced by Space Tepee Music and The Comite de Apoyo al Tibet. Earthdance, as mentioned earlier, emerged as a fund-raising effort for the Free Tibet movement and has evolved into a transnational phenomenon committed to consciousness evolution. Around the world, organizing collectives and participating artists become involved in prestige-building exercises where, like a chief holding potlatch or the big-man making *Moka*, committing to "gifting" capital, equipment and talent marks their estimation among a community of actors who achieve subcultural accreditation as consciously observant. The sacrificing of resources by individuals and groups holding free or fund-raising events is a traditional source of prestige, the value of the social capital corresponding to the material capital raised. In some contexts, like Burning Man, where a gift culture is normalized and characterizes social relationships between strangers in an intentionally non-commoditized environment, the gifts may even be incinerated. At the personal level, the donor is empowered, receiving devotional responses, and perhaps even a karmic reward for the sacrifice. Tributes for contributions and sacrifices are often ritualized. As an example of this, before conscious cross-disciplinary event pioneer Fraser Clark died, he became the centre of an ecstatic commemoration tribute at Heaven – the venue for the former London club – on 13 November 2008.

* * *

The psychedelic party is host to multiple freedoms fought for and enjoyed by its vast constituency. As this chapter has illustrated, psycultures offer participants means to pursue a diversity of interests, from extreme recreation to consciousness-raising. The chapter has adopted Bourdieu's "cultural capital" but has shown that the field of practice is wide, echoing the complex character of this cultural movement whose participants cannot be observed under a one-dimensional rubric. Across scene positions, subsonic cultures and chill tribes, participants grow reputations, find acceptance, become psychedelic – with psyculture providing a context by which participants may earn distinction and attract prestige. Staging events, DJ performance, taking drugs, travel and exposure to perilous or unsettling weather conditions, are all risk-laden practices. How participants negotiate these and other "edgework" practices are means to generate power, status and belonging. Yet stature is resultant from a host of projects reliant on the identification of risks, performed for the benefit of others, the environment, if not consciousness itself. With the commitment to and operation of "conscious partying" – whether in the campaign work of Asher Haviv, Goa Gil, Fraser Clark, Michael Gosney and a host of others who would rather be nameless or recognized collectively, such as Boom – the chapter has illustrated the diversity of "cultural capital" raising. From culture defenders who rail against marauding proles, crippling legislation and market forces to protagonists mobilizing music and mounting events to transform culture, from clandestine operations to those committed to transport a cause beyond the dance event and the festival gates, the diversity of scene activism through which participants demonstrate their distinction has also been illustrated.

9 Riot of passage: liminal culture and the logics of sacrifice

If a transit without destination, a play without a finale, inheres in psytrance, it also resembles a performance with multiple plots. Previous chapters have illustrated that festivals are spiritual technologies building transformative capacity, that they have multiple inputs and as many outcomes. It has been figured that downstream from the schizoid "state of mind" that was Goa, psyculture events are "free" spaces host to a multitude of actions and figures, from the transgressive to the disciplined, from the risk-laden to the visionary, the outlaw to the activist. It has been posited that paths of extreme leisure and conscientiousness afford distinction, recognition and acceptance, with this dance movement constituting a veritable mosaic. This chapter adds final touches to this canvas, with attention to the intentional ritualizing that pervades visionary arts culture. As this book has shown, ritualization is a recurring commitment among enthusiasts and producers. Transition is the goal of *spiritechnics* optimized to inaugurate the initiatory experience. But if psyculture is liminalized, it is complicated by the variable and competing inputs that have characterized its legacy, with a riot of sound, colour and intention consuming the lives of its inhabitants.

Where participants seek initiatory experience, researchers have adopted models in efforts to explain the experience. While scholars seek to comprehend participation in EDM cultures as a "rite of passage" enabling transition from "preliminal" to "postliminal" conditions, and indeed neotribal discourse credits an efficacy to dance events reckoned as sites for self-transcendence, social transformation, and the transmission of values, psytrance is a movement possessing a protracted and complex transit. Cookie-cutter theories of ritual transition routinely applied to dance cultures do not adequately recognize these developments. Harnessing and repurposing sensorial technics, developing entheogenics and embracing liminality as a design imperative, psytrance is a *liminal culture* rooted in the experimental adulthood and extended adolescence of the 1960s–1970s. But liminality is not programmed to one channel, for festival culture accommodates a liminal noise whose elements, sometimes contrary and other times complementary, possess deep countercultural roots. This chapter addresses the core liminalities characteristic of psytrance festivals conveyed as they are by what I refer to as unique *logics of sacrifice*. That is, the paramount expressions of this movement are recognized as staging grounds for transgressive and disciplined concerns articulated in rites of risk and consciousness. This discussion of the protracted and contested logics of the liminal downstream from Goa necessitates re-examination of the study of youth and ritual within cultural studies, and within the studies of EDM, where this chapter begins.

Ritual, EDM cultures and psytrance

Psytrance is host to an intentional ritualization and possesses an intensive architectonics of transition. Early productions like *Rite of Passage* (1993), the album produced by the Nick Taylor, Takehiro Tokuda and Tsuyoshi Suzuki collaboration Blissed, along with a legacy of festivals and reflexive rites, express the desire for the re-introduction of lost ritual and the re-enchantment of the contemporary, as the embrace of the Rites of Eleusis mythos reveals. The decline, attenuation, or disappearance of rites of passage – especially those marking transition to adulthood – have been addressed by commentators examining the social impact of industrialization, the division of labour and secularization. Commenting on opinion shaped by the likes of Herbert Spencer and Peter Burke, Catherine Bell (1997: 254) averred that, since the mid-nineteenth century, the "popular contention that ritual and religion decline in proportion to modernization" seems to have crystallized into a "sociological truism". Such had been validated by Max Weber, who contrasted ritual and magic with "disenchantment" in the everyday lives of rational moderns. But it would also be validated by those sympathetic of traditional ritual presumed to be vanishing to the detriment of those living in modern culture. Thus, Turner lamented the loss of ritual's transformative potential in the explosion of leisure genres and in advertising. Pursuing the tragic side of liminality,[1] he argued that the "religious sphere" contracted, and, as a consequence, he observed "deliminalization" and the loss of ritual's "cultural evolutionary resilience", which ceases "to be an effective metalanguage or an agency of collective reflexology" (Turner 1982b: 85, 1985: 165). A host of aesthetic media including song, dance, and graphic and pictorial representation were said to have "broken loose from their ritual integument" (1985: 166). This flight, this disintegration, this detraditionalization, appears to have been inscribed in Turner's concept of the "liminoid" (the "ritual-like"), which, while evincing the fragmentation of the liminal *sacra*, evokes, at the same time, the possibility of its return – indeed the revitalization of self and society through the now valorized ritual form. And it has been the heroic ideology of *return* that has inspired a great many practitioners of contemporary ritual, who will adopt the practice of world religions to ornamentalize and enchant their practice. This has been typical to critical commentary since the 1960s evolving among countercultural cognoscenti and other traditionalists who have built a mythology of necessity and survival around the return of ritual. It is within this evolving heroic tradition that commentators, media producers, and promoters within the trance, visionary arts and related scenes have emerged.

Grievance for the lost rite, and its attendant consciousness alteration, underlies the 2007 documentary *Entheogen: Awakening the Divine Within* (Mann, 2007) a film popular among psytrance enthusiasts. According to interviewee, transpersonal psychologist Stanislav Grof, the lacuna left by the absence of rites of passage is "responsible for much of the pathology in our culture" which sees young innovators creating their own rituals – which he decides are ordinarily not "constructive". But while Grof expressed his doubts, *Entheogen* projects a far from damning account of this ritualization. At one point, professor in the Philosophy, Cosmology and Consciousness Program at the California Institute of Integral Studies, David Ulansey, utters the key word: "reconnection", and elaborates that "people in a drumming circle or in an ecstatic dance setting are connecting themselves with the continuous legacy of the incarnation of vitality in the form of homosapiens". It's a common message, the return to a universal source of wisdom and vitality expressed in myriad cultural forms. The theme of continuity is reinforced through footage of McKenna who explains that the perennial function of consciousness alterants as used in world initiation rituals enable neophytes the chance to "step behind the cultural myth", the film providing a series of vignettes of an undying commitment to dance, from African tribal, to sufi, to tap dancing, appended by the subliminal flashing of what appears to be a contemporary psytrance dance floor. Pivotal to the continuity, albeit passing without comment, the distinctive sounds and sights of a psytrance party arrive in clear focus as the documentary concludes. The solution echoes that of an earlier documentary screened at events around the world, *Dances of Ecstasy* (Mahrer and Ma, 2004), which juxtaposed exotic trance dancing – such as that associated with the Condomble Orisha possession ceremonies among the Mae Zelinha of Pelo Ife Axa, Brazil – with scenes from psytrance parties. While participants in the latter are not entrained to enter and interpret altered states of consciousness within consensual cultural frameworks, the moving images of "tribal" ritual and traditional states of entrancement are compelling and instructive.

The ritual significance of contemporary dance music cultures has been a subject of interest among popular music scholars. In his *Trance Formation* (2005: 97–127), for instance, Robin Sylvan details the temporal and spatial ordering forming the ritual dimension of San Francisco rave culture (see also

Sylvan 2002: 136–40). The book claims that rave – together with rock, hip hop and other Western popular music as elsewhere stated (Sylvan 2002) – carries a "hidden religious sensibility" transmitted from West African possession religions via African-American secular entertainment music (especially blues) appropriated and translated by white youth. Despite offering a North American-centred depiction of the history of popular music, and while offering little recognition of the global character of trance, or psytrance, culture, the work is representative of commitments among scholars of contemporary EDMCs, for whom the dance music experience is held to be efficacious, and where dance cultures are recognized as experimental, transcendent and transformative. But ritual, meaning and identity have not typically drawn the attentions of social and cultural researchers, even when youth and music cultures are the subject of their investigations. While "ritual" would become a key trope for commentators in youth subculture studies from its inception, rather than holding ontological significance, "ritual" was most commonly employed metaphorically and without detailed attention to ritual practice. While early researchers of the Chicago School of sociology founded by Robert E. Park undertook ethnographies of gangs and their actual social solutions to urban poverty as seen in Albert K. Cohen's *The Delinquent Boys: The Culture of the Gang* (1955), the cultural Marxists of Birmingham's Center for Critical and Cultural Studies were fixated by what they considered the inconsequential cultural and "stylistic" solutions of working-class youth cohorts in the UK to post-war industrialization. The CCCS agenda was influenced by E.P. Thompson whose nostalgic study *The Making of the English Working Class* (1963) uncovered shared rituals and traditions as integral to working-class dissent. Their agenda was also buoyed by Raymond Williams, who wrote of the demise of working-class community that, in post-war Britain, was siring youth "subcultures" which, rather than enacting a real resistance, were manifesting territorial and consumer "rituals" involving stylistic appropriations from popular culture. In the seminal collection, *Resistance through Rituals* (Hall and Jefferson 1976), signifying the counter-hegemonic solution that was spatial and semiotic, but not historically consequential, "ritual" was defined entirely in terms of lack (i.e. the absence of revolutionary class consciousness). The range of subcultures studied by researchers at the CCCS during the 1970s represented a kind of cultural *lumpenproletariat*. According to Ken Gelder, who has produced a cultural history of "subcultures", the "image of the mob haunts these accounts of contemporary subcultures", as does "the sense that they are not quite in touch with reality" (2007: 90). Their interventions were thus consigned to the imaginary, a realm ultimately devalued as "magical" and illusory. Their subversions, like that of the "motor-bike boys" and "hippies" documented by Paul Willis (1978), politically impotent. Their victories, like that of the "mods" who undertook to rise above their working-class inheritance astride Italian scooters, largely romantic (Hebdige 1976).

Their confrontation, as with the "semiotic guerilla warfare" of punk (Hebdige 1979: 105), unruly and narcissistic.

Despite having grown popular in the UK through the 1970s, social dance cultures hardly came under the CCCS radar. Dance (including disco), the domain of girls, young women and gays in Britain in the 1970s, was largely dismissed by the researchers at Birmingham who enlisted heroic, spectacular and aggressive subcultures to illustrate the tragic career of the working class in modern Britain (McRobbie 1990). Social dance, and embodied pleasures more generally, failed to conform to accepted understandings of "the political" (see Dyer 1990; McClary 1994; Pini 1997: 113–14) and faced neglect from a rationalist sociological paradigm (Ward 1993). Music scholars (especially historians of jazz and rock) regarded dance as a seductive force weakening critical faculties (Straw 2001: 159). Historically, cultural studies have been largely "text-based", with analyses of popular culture attending to "verbal or visual cultural products, not kinaesthetic actions", echoing an "aversion to the material body, as well as [the] fictive separation of mental and physical production" within academia (Desmond 1997: 30). If disco was remote from heroic subcultures, and dance dismissed within cultural and music research paradigms devoted to the verbal, aural and visual, then how would commentators respond to late 1980s acid house and the (post-)rave phenomenon? Lamenting rave as its "pleasures come not from resistance but surrender", Stuart Cosgrove (1988 in Melechi 1993: 37) supplied the answer. Well after rave had exploded in the UK and had begun proliferating internationally, under the guidance of Redhead (1993), cultural and music studies scholars finally turned their attentions to the phenomenon. But while critics were turning away from the stifling resistance/submission dichotomy implicit to earlier youth research, they would continue to observe the "inconsequential" pursuits of youth. Via a Baudrillardian lens, young people would remain prisoners of circumstance – caught in a "fantasy of liberation" (Melechi 1993: 37), an ecstatic simulacrum, disappearing into a *hyperreal* world of appearances.

From rituals of resistance (Hall and Jefferson 1976) to rituals of disappearance (Melechi 1993: 33; Rietveld 1993: 41), research on youth cultures retained an interest in *ritual*, but only to signify that which was hollow, empty and unhistorical in contemporary youth practice. Analogical, possessing "homologous" associations, politically ineffectual, these "rituals" constituted the "tragic limits" (Willis 1978: 175) of subcultural youth in the 1960s and 1970s, and a postmodern escapade for clubcultural youth in the 1980s and 1990s. For Antonio Melechi (1993: 32), the Ibizan clubs to which young British tourists flocked in the late 1980s, and where acid house was born, exemplified this postmodern "ritual", as they induce "the jouissance of Amnesia". With acid house, dance became a "seductive absence"; it had lost its use value. Dance and music (the signifiers) would no longer contextualize the expression of the self (the signified): "Acid house celebrates the death of this *scene* of dance, for it is now the materiality of the musical signifier which forms the new space of oblivion, as the dancer implodes and disappears into a technological dreamscape of sound" (Melechi 1993: 34). While the proto-rave on Ibiza, and indeed the seasonal parties on the coast of northern Goa, may very well have constituted a non-representational *void*, such offers little awareness of who these people were, the influences shaping their behaviour or how their individual experiences compared with that of others. What of the sociality and sensuality of the dance?

Observing participants with an appetite for meaning, and diving to the sensory subsurface of the rave, researchers began articulating rave's ritual as an ethnographic reality rather than a trope, homology or analogue. Thornton (1996: 2) acknowledged the efficacy of what might have been deemed rites of distinction, considering the practice of "clubcultures" only insofar as their members were seeking to distinguish themselves from "mainstream" others through the accumulation of style capital in scene mediations. Later, Melanie Takahashi and Tim Olaveson (2003; see also Olaveson 2004) took a serious approach to the ritual, or more to the point, following Grimes (1995), the "syncretic ritualizing", of rave. Various investigations of contemporary EDMC would regard the dance music experience as efficacious; a source of "spiritual healing" equivalent to a conversion experience (Hutson 1999; 2000); "redemptive" through its capacity to release subconscious repression comparable to Artaud's Theatre of Cruelty (Arnold 1997: 189); enabling cathartic "re-identification with the gay body" (Bardella 2002: 87); an experience potentiating "playful vitality" (Malbon 1999: 101) or mobilizing cultural "revitalization" (Olaveson 2004). From Rietveld's claim that techno constitutes the "spiritual rite of the post-industrial cyborg" (2004: 48), to Des Tramacchi's (2004: 125) proposal that Australian doofs are psychedelic dance rituals, there exists an acknowledgement of the significance of ritual not found (nor possible) in earlier youth cultural research. Tramacchi even draws parallels between "community focused entheogenic dance rituals" in three cultures – Mexican Huichol, Barasana of Columbia and the Fang and Metsogo of Gabon West Africa – and psychedelic dance cultures. More generally, scholarly and popular discourse credit an efficacy to dance events reckoned as sites for self-transcendence (e.g. Saunders and Doblin 1996; Fritz 1999), or social and cultural transformation (St John 2004). Furthermore, various studies have demonstrated interest in the performance of identity in club "lifeworlds". In Fiona Buckland's ethnography of clubbing (2002), the dance club becomes an interactive stage upon which queer identities are made through performance, while in others the "extreme state of sensual intensity" of the club potentiates the alteration of the lifeworld *habitus* (Jackson 2004: 140). While CCCS researchers may have only recognized "imaginary" solutions, EDMC scholars recognize a subjunctive and re-creative *dance culture* whose assemblage – the music, dance, spatial reconfigurations, temporality, body modifications, and alternative states of consciousness – facilitates becoming. Enhancing understanding of the *ritual process* of the EDM experience – and in particular the DJ–dancer interaction at Toronto's Turbo Niteclub – Morgan Gerard (2004) recognizes how dance commentators and scholars have repeatedly referenced the "ritual" of clubs and raves without describing the structures and experience of such "ritual-ness", practices inherited from the CCCS. Responding to the way invocations of rituality within post-CCCS approaches to EDM and DJ culture generally neglect the central role of music and dance, constructing "idealized versions of raves and clubs" as metaphorically ritualized, Gerard argues that a passage process is "encoded in every mix between records" (2004: 170, 177), where stages in a DJ record mix are thought to correspond to the tripartite "rites of passage" model (Van Gennep 1960). In his view, club participants are said to "negotiate liminality" throughout the course of events, and depending on the "ritual knowledge" of dancers, each DJ mix may replay, and eventually accelerate, the passage phases, effecting belonging in a dance floor community. Here, previous experience and raised expectation are critical to the performance, and to the achievement of alternative states of consciousness.

While, as this book has observed, the ritual context of psytrance is not strictly defined by the DJ–dancer interaction, the study of psytrance should draw inspiration from this intention to study processes of ritualization within EDM contexts. Within the Goatrance festival tradition, networks of artists including the participants themselves have intentionally generated ritualized contexts, appropriating from traditional and popular cultures, and adapting technics to purposive agendas. Psychedelic art has been adapted to the alteration of self within the context of social dance since the 1960s, and by the 1990s psychedelic liminalization had been fully augmented by computers, and analogue and digital media. Over this thirty-year period, from the Acid Tests to Goatrance, alterant-assisted initiatory praxis in the context of psychedelic dance music events has evolved. The early psychedelic "rituals" were characterized by a chaotic, open-ended, multi-mediated experimentalism – to which countless samples from film and other dialogue deployed in music productions pay homage. Infused with psychedelic Orientalism and the shamanic practice of native peoples from the Americas and elsewhere, Goatrance harboured a concerted effort to effect self-transformation. We have seen conscious ritualization orchestrated using the techno-chemical assemblage imported to and nurtured in Goa and then exported worldwide as a "global trance ritual" (Larkin 2003), care of Goa Gil, Ray Castle and others, and from the late 1990s, in the wake of McKenna's influence, "spirit molecule"-assisted "entheogenesis" would become inscribed in the music, and in the culture, of psytrance. Indeed, since DMT spurred the inception of Goatrance care of McKenna's midwifery, psytrance would be entheogenically superliminalized, a theme animated by another popular documentary, *Liquid Crystal Vision* (Rood and Klimmer, 2002), an effusive attempt to both reproduce and affect a "trip". In the film's opening commentary, Goa Gil's ancient ritualizing and McKenna's DMT vaporizing precipitate entry into the gnosis depicted through visual sequences of Hindu holy men, Eastern spiritual motifs, and enlightened beings partaking in sacraments and devotional dancing. The film culminates in an extraordinary sequence which, backed by Banco de Gaia's uplifting "Harvey and the Old Ones" (*The Magical Sounds of Banco De Gaia*, 1999), expresses core tenets of what Linda Woodhead (2001) identified as "The New Spirituality" downloaded into the present: the recognition that multiple religious pathways are but an expression of one *truth* (that "all is one"); that this truth can only be acquired in the radical immanence of immediate bodily *experience*; and that humanity retains a critical role in planetary *evolution*. In the sequence, images of world sacred sites, rites and exotic dance flicker by at a rapid pace as if one's life memories are flashing in fractalized patterns across the back of one's retina's before death/rebirth. Immediately following this sequence, there is commentary from none other than Raja Ram and Simon Posford, whose influential act Shpongle became a vehicle for revelation of the transformative potential and initiatory impact of entheogens (notably DMT). What is repeatedly programmed into the visual and sonic artifacts of psychedelic trance, then, is the very idea of initiatory ritualization which is authenticated and validated by association with "shamanic" psychoactive substances the use of which is said to strip away former identifications in preparation for reorientation – re/mediations effectively channelling the countercultural objective of personal and social transformation.

The liminal life

While I have explained the fixation with entheogenic ritualization, as expressed in documentary film and music production, are we any closer to knowing the ritual process of the psychedelic trance experience? What is the role of the liminal in the world of participants? And what is the nature of liminality in the contemporary world? Gerard's work on the DJ–dancer interaction echoes other research[2] navigating the EDM experience using van Gennep's model, itself adopted by Turner to fashion the *processual* heuristic of "liminality". As introduced in *The Ritual Process* (1969), *From Ritual to Theatre* (1982c) and other works, liminality is a cornerstone of ritual analysis and a critical component of Turner's model of ritual and performance (see St John 2008a). It is either explicit or implied in much of this work, including research which addresses the social liminality of "spontaneous communitas" in EDMC (see Tramacchi 2000, 2004; Olaveson 2004; Rill 2006), that ritualized social interaction enables transit from "preliminal" to "postliminal" conditions

(Takahashi and Olaveson 2003). While interventions like Gerard's offer valued insights on the nature of performance and identity in EDMC, the tendency towards cookie-cutter applications of Turnerian theory to apprehend "ritual" and "ritual-like" phenomena is troubling. What is the utility of unmodified processual logic to the apprehension of EDMCs like psytrance? While studies illuminate the processual character of events, and suggest continuity with other transitional music/dance rites, analogical modelling offers fewer insights on the actual telos of participants than promised. Researchers employing the terminology of "passage" and "rite" in their analyses invite scrutiny since evidence that participants have actually made transit to any specific destination, role or status is scant. The reasons for this data vacuum become apparent when it is recognized that participant knowledge and experience holds value, often exclusively, within the immediate dance cultural networks, and within the phenomenal locales of clubs and festivals themselves. While Gerard articulates an accelerated transition within a techno club, the experience is significant beyond the club moment only insofar as participants are able to express that "competence" (bodily "knowledge") at future events. On Turbo Niteclub's "Lifeforce Fridays", Gerard suggests that "instead of efficiently returning to the mundane world as adults or other elevated social categories, participants receive their incorporative recognition as valued initiates only by returning to the ritual community itself" (2004: 180).

It appears that these dance "rituals" may be more efficacious in transporting participants *into* a liminal community than effecting transit to a well-defined, externally recognized, post-liminal, social condition. This is true for psytrance. Not *transitional rites* or conduits to post-event life, the trance party, and especially the festival, appears more like a *liminal world*, and psytrance consequentially, a *liminal culture*. As if it were not already clear, this is a liminality that is quite literally fuelled by psychedelics, the contours of which have been discovered and mapped by a host of explorers and "cartographers of the mind", like Hofmann, Shulgin, Leary, Kesey, McKenna, Pinchbeck and others whose inventions, explorations and ideas impregnate the trancescape. Despite their varying approaches and disagreements, these psychonautical and entheonautical culture heroes sanction alterations in consciousness facilitated by psychoactive compounds invested with potency, authority, but ultimately uncertainty, the effect from which may be like the "floating worlds" obsessing Turner (1969: vii). When Sally Sommer stated that "Hard-core Househeads" have "recreated that liminal and almost ideal *transitional world* in which they experiment with multiple states of mind and shifting identities, through total body and athletic endeavour" (2001/2002: 84, my emphasis), she was referring to a creative social orgiasm flourishing in the present. Such transitional worlds have arisen throughout EDMC from proto-disco onwards, but the festal culture of psytrance is a dominant carrier. Habitués appear to be more like occupants than passengers, inhabiting a world of uncertain significance. They are like participants in an initiation that has no telos, an experience of being-in-transit replete in the design of producers and event organizations who invest, sometimes fetishistically, in the sonics, architecture and iconography of *passage*. As Space Tribe knew it, "The Journey is the Goal" (*The Ultraviolet Catastrophe*, 1997). While the journey may effect revitalization, or enable participant "healing", as is often reported, this appears to be associated with a process of re-identification that can only be achieved *in situ*. Status, reputation and belonging depend upon knowledge and experience which has primary value within the context of the dance event. That psytrancers are immersed in a social universe that is liminalized, in which spontaneity and indeterminacy are pursued and reanimated in consequential lifestyle and consumer practices, is more instructive than the idea that habitués have entered a ritual-like "phase" from which they will return to society "aggregated", the final condition of passage in Van Gennep's model; or indeed "resolved" in Turner's dramatic processual model. This liminal "state of mind" was cultivated in Goa and transposed globally.

As noted earlier, Turner himself offered a conceptual apparatus to assist understanding of the career of the liminal and liminal-like conditions in modern culture, principal among which was the "liminoid". In one of Turner's most provocative, albeit unfinished, conversations, he saw liminal ritual frameworks splinter throughout modern culture as a result of secularization, a complex social and economic division of labour, and the explosive proliferation of leisure industries. Shaped by new media technologies, rationalization and bureaucracy, quasi-liminal genres are observed to have flourished throughout modern performance arts, entertainment, sports, advertising, etc., processes regarded as symptomatic of secularization and/or the revitalization of the sacred (reliminalization). Offering insight on the voluntary, fragmented, accelerated and multitudinous career of the sacred within leisure cultures, sports and media arts, the "liminoid" is suggestive of near-ritual contexts divorced from that which is considered *serious or real*: that is, the sacred work and efficacious potential implicit to the performance of *ritual* as it has been stated since at least Durkheim. But the "liminal/liminoid" framework was the product of an historical distinction begging more questions than answers. In any case, Turner did not offer sustained analyses of contemporary leisure genres, fan cultures and the lifestyles of their participants, festivals or otherwise. Perhaps it is not so much the dearth of useful heuristics but the absence of sustained ethnographic application that is at issue, a problem apparently not resolved by additions to the theoretical lexicon, such as the "liminautical" which McKenzie entertains to explain how new digital technologies, "digital limen", apparently erase work/play, labour/leisure, sacred/secular distinctions in the contemporary (2001: 94), divisions and separations which have arguably overseen the fragmentation of ritual's power and potential for transformation within modernity. Such iterations to the lexicon are not unwelcome, but McKenzie only brushes up against how new media technologies – cybernetic and digital – might continue to animate, mobilize, or mutate, the liminal. With the emergence of the "spiritual revolution" (Heelas 2008), a popular "occulture" (Partridge 2004), "psychedelics" and "entheogens", and a spectrum of *causes* authorizing re-enchanted agents, it is certainly no longer useful, nor wise, to argue that the authority of the sacred has receded in modernity with the decline of institutional religion, an anguish partly motivating Turner (see St John 2008a). It is, however, necessary to consider how the sacred is shaped by obligatory *and* elective determinants, how spirituality is "religious" and "secular", and how ritual may be conservative or experimental. How might ritual be authorized *and* chosen? In what ways do participants in contemporary leisure genres seek the sacred and how might leisure cultures facilitate the transformative "work" of ritual? How do contemporary genres of performance cultivate spiritual experience?

Attention to the micro, creative and countercultural industries emerging to augment and maximize liminal conditions assists our inquiry. When the Boom Festival is self-promoted as "sustainable entertainment", a double meaning is detectable. On the surface, the phrase indexes the organizational efforts to implement ecologically sustainable event-systems. At another level, the phrase offers a covert signal of its intention to sustain the party vibe, to invest in industries – including event-production, management and performance – which work to reproduce the superliminality of party culture though the production and marketing of a range of commodities (e.g. event tickets, utility belts, shamanic herbs). In this second meaning, sustaining liminality involves dedication to supporting and investing in service industries that optimize and re-optimize the party, industries that serve *experience*. Whether event producers are said to provide or exploit consumer desires is open to opinion and interpretation, but the liminal economics of festal culture appears to rely on enabling an experience that is satisfying-yet-incomplete, a manipulation that can be observed, for example, in the practices of skilled DJs like James Monro or Silicon Sound's Johannes Regnier who are experts in building the promise of climax, a release that is sought through the subsequent acquisition of style, commodities and experience in revisits to, and in loitering in, the scene of the sublime. If incompleteness is native to psytrance, and by extension, the lifestyles of its inhabitants, it defies the processual logic of the *limen* in a passage rite that ordinarily potentiates resolution through temporal dissolution. As participants revisit and modify the dancescape on a regular basis, refreshing its parameters, weighing anchor in a field of impermanence, they liminalize their lifeworlds, indefinitely. For Turner, the liminal "realm of pure possibility" (1967) is invariably a threshold, a portal, a stage. The "realm" may be characterized by indeterminacy, but given the structure and function of the process – be it ritual, theatre, game, literature – an outcome is implicit to the programme: a transit, a finale, a result, a conclusion. But within the immediate carnivalesque proliferating in psytrance, there may be no transit anticipated, no outcome desired – no conclusion, just a permanent state of impermanence.

Becoming *entranced* is, then, more than just a night out, as was implied in the publication *En-trance,* which offered depth of insight on the Melbourne party scene in the early 2000s. By returning to the scene of the sublime, attending parties, clubs and festivals perhaps with greater frequency, partygoers, in a sense, dwell on the threshold. As teeth chatter and solar plexus vibrate to the sub-bass frequencies in a cycle of parties, after-parties, and post after-party soirées, as liminars are released from the abstractions of the everyday and become looped in a world of immediacy and pleasure, and as they are familiarized time and again with their other selves playing opposite a cast of othered selves in the psychedelic Disctopia, they are immersed in a zone that is as timeless as it is eventful. Commentators have suggested that such states resemble a "womb" whose occupants possess pre-Oedipal characteristics (McRobbie 1993: 419). Rietveld (1993: 54), for instance, argued that Ecstasy and the threat of AIDS "made the user return to a pre-Oedipal stage, where libidinous pleasure is not centred in the genitals, but where sexuality is polymorphous and where sensuality engages the entire body". Virtual sex is thought to characterize these "plateauz of intensity" (Gore 1997: 82), where "tacit sexuality" replaces sexual relations (Tomlinson 1998: 201). Under the romance of such heuristics, "the implication", notes Tramacchi (2004: 139), is "of a shared sibling status between ravers, which raises a symbolic 'incest taboo', thus attenuating sexual tensions and replacing them with familiarity and friendliness". This "lost kingdom of the womb", which Reynolds reckons is characteristic of the experience of psychedelic music, constitutes "an end to our separateness and the recovery of our lost continuity" (1997: 164). In Turner's scheme, the adult immersion in extreme states of abandonment holds serious transitional implications: "this is why Jesus said 'Except ye become as little children, ye shall not enter the kingdom of heaven', the un-kingdom beyond social structure" (1983: 111–12). In the "un-kingdom" of raving, participants are granted permission to temporarily relinquish the affectations of adulthood. To seek sovereignty over this realm is to confound the temporal logic of the threshold over which one must cross, or indeed the organic logic of the womb, from which one must be born and grow independent. It competes with the teleological, or evolutionary, purpose of the *limen*, which indexes transit to a whole, stable, mature, self.

To defy the *limen*'s progress in this manner plays havoc with Turnerian processualism. In the "orgiastic" world of the party we find the passional impulse to extend one's virtualized self. To "stay up forever", to be "on" longer with the aid of chemical, cellular and cyber technologies, was the rave-olutionary catchcry resounding in the UV-reactivated playpens emergent world-wide. It has been noted that, suspended in a realm "between childhood and adulthood" (Tomlinson 1998: 201), in their late teens, early twenties and beyond, ravers typically enter a public-yet-private fantasy offering temporary-yet-repeated permission to play within realms of sexual innocence or virtuality replete with lollypops, stuffed animals, bubble blowers, giant water pistols, and juggling and balancing toys. Unlike rave, psytrance has clearly engaged and retained enthusiasts over life stages. Many in their thirties, forties and fifties, alongside those in their late teens and twenties, will attend psytrance festivals. Infants and children of varying ages are also common at these events, sometimes as at Rainbow Serpent or Boom, catered for in festival zones, which, in the case of Baby Boom, function like crèches, enabling young parents to be temporarily unburdened of their parental duties. Rather than rave's *suspension* of adulthood, then, with psyculture, it is perhaps more accurate to speak of the *extension* of "youthful" sensibilities into adulthood.

In research shedding light on the prolonged transition to adulthood, cause is commonly attributed to the dismantling of traditional social support, individualization, declining labour market prospects and extended educational requirements (Miles 2000). Such processes were observed in the 1960s and 1970s as protection from the pressures of adult responsibilities extended the "natural period of adolescence" (Gerster and Bassett 1991: 49). The liberal child rearing and extended education experienced by "baby boomers" is also recognized to have stimulated a reaction "against both repressive institutions and ... the smothering security and overly comfortable conformity of their parents' way of life" (ibid.: 33). While theorists from a range of disciplines have pursued explanations for the "me generation", the "youth quake", and the activities of the children of "the silent revolution" (Inglehart 1977), given his acknowledgement of the critical role of music and drugs in this period, Nick Bromell's observations (2000: 27) are salient. "For a short time", he wrote, "just nine years at the most [1963–1972], it became imaginable that one could stay 'forever young', and that it was legitimate to do so because youth had a vision, a peculiar insight into modernity, a way of seeing and being in the world". This radical rupturing of the known assisted by rock music and psychedelics would hold a remarkable bearing on popular culture and subsequent alternative cultures.

The 1960s–1970s was an epic historical juncture, and much more could be written about the power of the liminal that was to be inherited by youth and alternative cultures in subsequent decades. While rites of passage marking transition to adulthood have attenuated, the "adult" roles into which structured processes traditionally enabled transit are no longer clearly defined (Pedersen 1994; Demant and Østergaard 2007: 519). In this role confusion, an experimental adulthood has emerged in which youthful activities persist. The expression of the protraction of "youth" or youthfulness is readily apparent in contemporary experimental urban leisure industries (Chatterton and Hollands 2003), and the postponement of the transition to adulthood has had a significant bearing on what Juris and Pleyers (2009) call "alter-activism" including those involved in global justice activism. Alongside these and other developments, as a culture of extended or post-adolescence, psytrance provokes reevaluation of "youth culture", and indeed a rethinking of the category of "youth" itself. It challenges linear models of youth–adulthood transition, perspectives already reconsidered in the light of complex realities faced by youth internationally.[3] Extending "youth" and complicating "adulthood", the study of party culture, and especially trance, challenges the perspective in which researchers seek examples of rites of passage with more or less conventional liminal conditions marking transition to adulthood (see Northcote 2006).

Modernity has contextualized the interleaving of initiatory ritual and carnivalesque play. The vanishing of traditional rites is related to the explosion of the festal *party*: that is, the carnivalesque which possesses little telos but which generates fellowships and movements whose memberships seek to recreate its "eternal present". As Gauthier (2004a: 69) wrote, "disengaging from temporality, the festive bursts into an 'eternal' – or, to be more precise, 'indefinite' – present". In celebrating the French techno-rave community as a "laboratory of the present", Michel Gaillot (1999: 23–24) endorsed the "passional logic" that Maffesoli argued underwrites a tendency towards social re-enchantment. The study of the passional, where individuals oscillate between networked sites of belonging, extending the hours and places of "empathetic sociality", is sociology of the extended and multiple "orgiasm" (or indeed of ejaculatory control). Here the fleeting temporality of the dance event magnifies its "tribal" veneer. Indeed, the *tribal* may only be felt in short, intense moments in the calendar, with such temporalities revisited throughout the calendar year. While the orgiastic intent of neotribes possesses the quality of social liminality, that its *puissance*, its power, derives from *below* – meaning both from the social underground *and* below the waist – makes for an entactogenic sociality oozing with Bakhtin's grotesque realism. As voices become drowned in the hubbub and clear signals fade in *mesibot*, doofs and other bastions of Disctopia, the psychedelic vibe is indeterminate, making parties attractive to those seeking departures from modern subjectivity. Landing in the "second world" of the psychedelic carnivalesque, trance dancers inhabit a *transitional world*. While the carnivalesque lifestyle cannot ordinarily be totalized, it nevertheless consumes the interests and desires of habitués, permeating their leisure-lives, becoming a serious preoccupation consistent with the empathetic parameters of the neotribal present.

Contemporary perspectives on carnival assist this discussion of career liminality. Cultural criminologist Mike Presdee argued that in contemporary life the carnival became dislocated from its original, exploding into everyday life as a result of the criminalization of carnivalesque pleasures which saw pleasures sought in more sophisticated and covert ways.

> As a result, the Bakhtinian notion of a return to law and order and integration can no longer take place, Victor Turner's notion of reintegration at the end of any dramatic carnivalesque performance remains unfinished, leaving the performers of post-modernity socially suspended and isolated from one another. Instead we are left with disappointment, dissatisfaction, discontent and the expectation that the carnival of crime will be performed, again and again (2000: 48).

Presdee's idea is provocative, a protracted yet furtive liminality which is at the same time a proliferating and multiplying criminality; a permanent state of incompletion which we might witness, so far as dance cultures are concerned, in trance as in clubbing, in the carnivalization of nightworld. While the trance party and dance club hold a temporary logic, participants attend events through the week, over the weekend, several times a month, over many years. They arrive at festivals well equipped for camping and dancing for periods of one to seven days, or longer, and will discuss, exchange, blog, post and tweet their experience for days, weeks and years afterwards. Through hand-fliers and in subscription to numerous e-lists and event notifications on Facebook they are in receipt of a constant flood of party information. While ravers in the acid house era and beyond were reported to be "24 hr party people", psytrance enthusiasts mythologize their party-derived puissance with the assistance of net-based social networking platforms, music filesharing portals, blogging, and webforum participation. In addition to the accelerated preparation and networked organization of the party experience, new communications media, then, enables reflection upon and integration of extraordinary experience (Lambert 2010; Ryan 2010). Yet, while events grow numerous, and the party becomes virtualized and extended through the use of new communications media, there remain peak, often seasonal, moments, with favoured festivals attended periodically, a cyclical phenomenon which complicates Presdee's thesis of the "carnivalization of the everyday". Moreover, in Presdee (2000: 122), for whom rave is "a quest for sensation without sense", little of the pleasure experienced by dance event-goers is understood. While a logocentric refutation of dance serves to illustrate the pleasures discovered in transgressing rules, we learn little of the phenomenal pleasures experienced, or the performances enacted. If dancing is pleasurable simply because it breaks laws, what is the experience of the unlawful?

And what of the carnival of intent, the permanent conditions sought beyond the threshold, and the liminars motivated to shift the temporality of the carnival and its consciousness into everyday life? What of the career of the artivists, dilettantes and outlaws who inhabit the protracted carnivalesque? And, thus, what of the mobile carnival?

The travelling carnival was integral to the birth of Goatrance from the seasonal psychedelic scene. In *New Age Travellers: Vanloads of Uproarious Humanity*, Kevin Hetherington (2000) addressed something of the mobile utopia performed by alternative travellers in UK seasonal Free Festivals such as that celebrating Summer Solstice at Stonehenge, with D'Andrea (2007a) tracing the "civilizational diaspora" further afield. For psyculture enthusiasts who harness an assemblage of communications media, digital arts, and modes of transportation, along with holistic practice, in the pursuit of alternative modernities, not only do specific global sites and regions become liminalized utopias, but the globe itself becomes a subjunctive sphere of experimentation and transition. But if the global has gone local, it has become so in a climate of crisis in which the planet faces peril, a vision that has escalated in prognostications associated with the 2012 movement. For participants, technologies of the senses have been developed to place *now* on a loop, to immortalize the self, extend the present, and localize the global. Israeli's Exaile conveyed something of this spectacular self-entitlement on the track "The World is Our Dance Floor" (*Hit the Machine*, 2004): "we are gathered here today to celebrate our freedom, to experience our humanity, to make a point ... The world is our dance floor". But in the simultaneous climate of advanced reflexivity, the world is recognized to have fast approached a significant juncture perceived as an apogee of crisis and hope. McKenna has been the lasting resource and apparently endless source mediating this mood, as Multiman conveys on the appropriately titled "Transition" (*Transition*, 2011): "Our future is our mystery. Our destiny is to live in the imagination. And the historical process that we are going through is not I think cause for despair, but it is a major transition point in the life of the entire planet ... We are now in transition". Within the transnational psychedelic and visionary movement, millenarian concern has been channelled into a singular event, the Boom Festival, and within this event, a singular area, the Liminal Village, a concentrated hub of transition, an apotheosis of interest in ritual, initiation and transformation, and an intentional mechanism for creating the novelty deemed necessary for the planetary future.

In Chapter 5, I introduced goings-on at the 2010 Liminal Village, recognized as a context for reflexive attention to the prevailing and interwoven causes of the s/Self. The conscious harnessing of liminality as an activating concept connecting participants to a process of transit universal to human cultures as understood by Turner is integral to a strategy for mobilizing change in a period of momentous crisis, for "bootstrapping" humanity, as McKenna had it, for the coming transit. McKenna's psychedelic millennialism had an unmistakable bearing on event culture. In his 1992 performance "Re: Evolution",[4] McKenna opined that the psychedelic dance movement would be "the cutting edge of the last best hope for suffering humanity ... Take back the planet – it's yours, it's yours. These are the last minutes of human history folks. The countdown is on. This is not a test. We're leaving this world behind, for a brighter, better world that has always existed; in our imagination". With McKenna acting as a posthumous guide, Boom's Liminal Village became an intentional space for personal, cultural and planetary transformation. Within the Liminal arena, at the premiere destination in the calendar of trance enthusiasts, in a period recognized as an historical moment of transit, Boom has mobilized the threshold in the service of population causes.

That the ultimate "population cause" lies at the nexus of planetary and self-interests was promoted in the 2006 edition of the zine: *Pathways*, communicating zeitgeist themes like "stewardship", "cooperation", "balance" and "sustainable energy". In the feature article "Earth's Creative Potential", Lucia Legan from the Ecocentro IPEC (Instituto de Permacultura e Ecovilas do Cerrado) in Brazil – where some of the Boom organizers had completed courses on sustainability – identified the "Egocentrism" upon which capitalism and the mechanistic world view are reliant and called for its replacement by a paradigm in which an "Ecocentric Ethic" predominates. Legan commented on that year's event theme, "We Are One": "this is not the collective identity of the crowd that cancels out all selfhood. Nor is it a mystic merger into a single cosmic self. Instead, it is a network of relationships between people and all living and non-living parts of the Earth. Every thing on the Earth is connected, each with an identity and integrity" (Legan 2006: 10). As planetary consciousness is not only part of the organization and implementation of the event, but is encouraged in the experience of participants, Boom becomes a significant hub of intent. Another event architect and whole systems builder, Delvin Solkinson, added to this, writing that, "in the new expanse of communications technology and web networking we are on the liminal brink of a whole new kind of consciousness. With the rise of industry and toxification of the biosphere, our civilization teeters at the edge of apocalypse. The emergence of world culture brings with it the promise of an integration and connectedness that will create a bridge for widescale positive change" (Solkinson 2008: 23). As permaculture and other techniques are integral solutions to a "revitalized planetary ecology", the "edge of apocalypse" is also held to be the brink of a new world.

The logics of sacrifice

While the Liminal Village at Boom is a cultural laboratory testing ways, as one of its presenters stated, "to creatively and successfully design human life on the earth" (Davis 2008a: 50), the writhing massive in the festival's Dance Temple seem to offer discrepant results. Here I want to pay closer attention to a tension in the visionary arts movement, complicating the liminal life, and animating the EDM "vibe". As we know, as a term adopted by insiders to characterize the trance party, the "vibe" holds currency across EDMCs, as reported by researchers who often deploy the Turners' concept of "communitas" for heuristic effect.[5] Yet commentators often miss the drama native to the "vibe" and its diverse actors, just as the Turners may have stressed unity in pilgrimage and other social liminal occasions at the expense of cultural discord and power contestation. As pilgrimage centres accentuate as much as they dissolve distinctions between pilgrims and travellers (Eade and Sallnow 1991), traveller festivals and other EDM events facilitate the performance of difference at the same time as they "annihilate" distinctions. Goa, as I earlier conveyed, was an ongoing context not only for the obliteration of identity in apocalyptic party paroxysms, but for the construction of meaningful alternatives, a weird and complex circumstance inherited by festivals arising in its gulf stream. Such events are host to discrepant liminal figures who've long populated extraordinary centres of experimentation, notably the bohemian district that acted as an explosive progenitor site in the mid-1960s. San Francisco's Haight-Ashbury district had been recognized, prior to its deterioration (approx. 1968) as a "crucible of dynamic interchange" in a period when "left wing activists cross-fertilized with turned-on poets, drifters, artists and dropouts that were refashioning themselves into living articulations of the struggle against bureaucracy" (Lee and Shlain 1985: 168). At the close of this scene, sociologists understood that the "indigenous typifications" of "head" and "freak" reflected "ongoing value tensions in the subculture ... a millenial vision of society versus an apocalyptic one" (Davis and Munoz 1968: 161). In John Robert Howard's classic analysis of the "internal contradictions of the hippie ethic", "freaks" and "heads" are contrasted with "visionaries", like those who underwent "voluntary poverty" in their repudiation of property, prejudice and preconceptions of im/morality (1969: 47, 46). That which Frank Musgrove in *Ecstasy and Holiness* regarded as "the dialectics of utopia" (1974: 16) appears to have attained its high watermark with the "Gathering of the Tribes" in Golden Gate Park in January 1967, and the countercultural dynamic of political activism and playful creativity came to shape liminalities, lifestyles and festivals thereafter.

Events downstream from this period would accommodate and operationalize concentrated liminal propensities in possession of differential *sacrificial logics*, different orders of liminal practice, from total abandonment to conscientiousness. On one side of the dynamic, one encounters the social orgiasm of the dance party whose intoxicated habitués hold concern for what is *happening now*, indeed deploying an assemblage of technologies of the senses to invest in making *now* last longer. They abandon themselves in the context of others, strangers in whose company they capitulate to rhythm and reverb. They are physically im/mobilized by bass, to which they may be said to willingly surrender. On the other side of this dynamic, one becomes mobilized in the service of a cause other than self-indulgence. Movement concerns are dramatized within events by those whose intention it is to raise awareness of crises, such that the festival becomes a staging ground, a recruitment centre, for the personal, social, cultural and political transitions desired. When motivated by the former attitude, habitués are preoccupied with today or tonight – or tomorrow morning, for the morning session – where nothing matters more than *nothing*. Keitamin's track "Lets Get Fucked Up" spares us from any subtlety (*Speed Demons Vol.1 Censorship is Uncool*, 2008) involved in this commitment. In the latter, they're responsive to risks to one's self and world, with festal occupants – in possession of humanitarian, ecological and psychological concerns – anxious about life "after the orgy". While the former prolong the orgiastic present, the latter are bent on reclaiming the future.

While psyfestivals facilitate the means by which enthusiasts may risk self-abandonment, "spending" personal resources in the pursuit of transcendence, experimenting with freedoms from moral codes and disciplined embodiment, they also enable practices (personal and environmental) of resource conservation, most often expressed as "sustainable" or "self-sustainable" practice. Articulated in the "carbon neutral", "low footprint" and "green" lifestyles of the ethical consumer for whom resource conservation and renewable energy are paramount, sustainability practices within the post-Goatrance movement draw attention to an underlying tension played out between commitments to spend and to conserve/recycle energy. Within the context of trance events, this *intracultural energy crisis* sees a sometimes tense dialogue between those whose practices, passions and causes are diametrically opposed, their commitments and causes determining how events are interpreted and evaluated. At other times, it facilitates resolutions between logics in event-optimizations. Since tensions are often experienced by individual participants who make varying commitments to these liminal logics, and whose private investments may straddle the paradox, the evaluations and compromises are ultimately personal.

Seasonal festivals have long accommodated these tensions which have been inherited by a late twentieth-century counterculture whose chief expressive form *is* the festal, and whose early twenty-first-century culture may only be articulated in the language and arts of the festal, whose duration grows indefinite as the festal lifestyle expands in ways that were unrecognizable just yesterday. Seasonal festivals are historical contexts for renewal, regeneration and revitalization, just as they are occasions for excesses and extreme exuberance. The former is indeed reliant upon the destruction of resources, although festival management organizations hold variant understandings of this and evolve regimes implementing widely differing resource reuse practices and encouraging diverse waste management practices, determined by the availability of local industries and vision in event direction. For instance, Hungary's Ozora Festival is one of the world's largest annual "psychedelic tribal gatherings" yet does not implement sustainable waste management strategies nor employ participant incentives that are now standard practice at events in countries like the UK, Australia, the United States and Canada, where festivals have been adopted within alternative movements as intentional vehicles for the renewal of the self and the protection and replenishment of the environment, not least because self-realization and ecological sustainability are notably integrated within whole systems approaches and locally emergent wise management strategies. In the following sections, I discuss the logics circulating within the festal locales of the psytrance movement, articulated in ritual practice, beginning with the commitment foremost among the majority of eventgoers, and indeed integral to seasonal renewal: the risk-laden rites of self-abandonment.

Rites of risk

In the previous chapter, I examined the social power converted from culturally defined and negotiated risks. While this is an important and necessary approach, what of the exaltation experienced in pushing the limits? What of the flight that desires no bounds? Arguing provocatively that "the physical limit has come to replace the moral limit that present-day society no longer provides", David Le Breton (2000: 1) initiated discussion on states of ecstasy and spirituality deriving from ordeals associated with elective challenges to one's own physical limits. Le Breton's observations shed light on the significance for travellers of dance pushing physical and emotional limits in remote outdoor locations. "Through extreme exhaustion", he wrote, "the ecstasy that fuses an individual with the cosmos, gives only a temporary feeling of royalty but the memories will last and will be there to remind him or her of the pre-eminence of their own personal value; the privilege of having merited such a moment of bliss is acquired". While trance dancing hardly possesses the perils of bungee jumping or skydiving, the following passage is compelling.

> Playing on the razor's edge is an elegant way of putting one's life on a par with Death for an instant in order to steal some of its power. In exchange for exposing oneself to the loss of life, the player intends to hunt on Death's territory and bring back a trophy that will not be an object, but a moment; a moment impregnated with the intensity of self because it bears within it the insistent memory that, through courage or initiative, he or she succeeded for a moment in extracting from Death or physical exhaustion, the guarantee of a life fully lived (Le Breton 2000: 7).

Psytrance is clearly not the near-death experience spectacularized, for instance, in the film *127 Hours* (Boyle, dir. 2010). Yet this passage likely draws nods from those who've met with unexpected transpersonal states, having experienced an apocalypse of subjectivity such as that which is orchestrated by DJs facilitating the passage of participants into extreme physical exhaustion towards the end of a long festival where they obtain the "little death" of entrancement. Sjoerd Los from Holland recalled such a moment on the fifth day of Boom 2008:

> Time has become liquid, temporarily meaningless, flexible ... Days and days of dancing, sweaty tanned bodies, exhilaration and neurochemical stimulation made arriving at this night possible. Closing in on the illuminated Groovy Beach the big thumping bass starts resonating inside my mind, sparking new energy where one rationally wouldn't expect it. My step quickens, and soon I arrive to indulge in this madness. Dancing for hours, I lose all sense of time – even all sense of "me" – my mind and body take flight. My bare feet jumping and shuffling across the sandy dance floor seem to move effortlessly, my whole body seems in a state of pure affect. I have stopped rationalizing. Having eliminated thought for the most part I enter a transcendental state. I *am* music at that moment, and standing in front of the speakers I enter into a vacuum. A solitary space on a crowded dancefloor where a direct conversation between me and the music is possible. Closing my eyes in that state of mind and body makes the experience complete – worlds unfold as beautiful visuals appear.[6]

A further passage from Le Breton, this time of the shared experience, is reminiscent of the commitments of the hardcore enthusiast whose experience of the psychedelic vibe compels their return, not to the sky (to skydive), to the road (to run a marathon), or the ocean (to sail across the Atlantic), but to the dance floor, in psycho-geographically removed spaces.

> Never before had they reached such legitimacy, such a fullness of being that instantly seems to justify all their efforts, the future and the past being swept away in a culminating moment. This moment of illumination, of trance, is not rooted in religious fervour though it is related to the sacred, in other words to a personal generation of meaning. The search is for personal transfiguration caused by exhaustion or disorientation of the senses, a sudden and incredibly strong feeling of being at one with the world, an ecstasy that then forms such a strong memory that the player does everything possible to relive it (Le Breton 2000: 10)

There are direct parallels with psytrance participants, who pass from exhaustion into transfiguring moments of grace when "it all makes sense", even wearing their exultation and belonging "on their sleeves" by retaining event wristbands for days, weeks, and in some cases, years afterwards.

As a dance cultural movement, psytrance makes possible the transcendence of normative embodiment, subjectivity and citizenship, and the concomitant re-inhabitation of the world, through the outlandish contexts of chemically assisted sensual intimacies. Tales of radical edgework are repeated the world over. Journeying to and inhabiting exotic events, the use of illicit compounds, enabling alternative states of consciousness, states of un/dress and unusual modes of public intimacy, are stories common to the experienced. Becoming a *player* is dependent on maintaining an ambiguous relationship with regard to *the law*: workplaying the edges of morality, gender and sexual norms, aesthetic conventions, criminal codes. Variously ritualized, the entire psytrance assemblage facilitates the re-fashioning of identity, most powerfully marked at those *limits* where rules, codes and laws, of propriety, morality and the state are freely transgressed. Here I want to stress that taking risks is not simply a matter of maintaining status *vis-à-vis* the "uncool", but holds numinous results achieved within states of transgression/transcendence, especially that achieved on the dance floor. Here, risk is experienced, not in conditions of absolute extremes where individuals are pitted against wild nature or are tempted by gravity, but in the context where habitués confront their fears and anxieties of the other, by which I mean the strangers in their midst, those witness to one's most intimate expressions, short of orgasm. Thus, it is not death but other people (friends and strangers) who constitute the

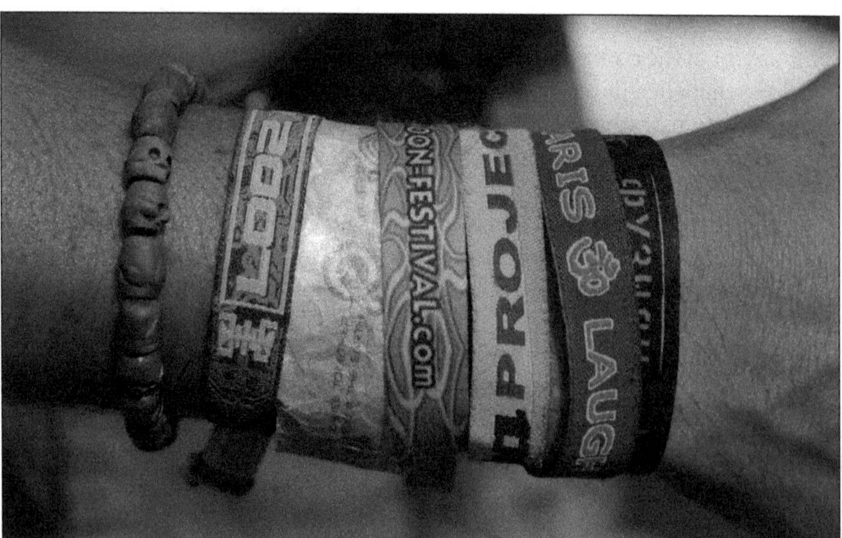

The seasoned traveller. Photo: Pascal Querner.

limit worked and negotiated on the dance floor, especially that of a multi-day psychedelic festival. This limit, the edge that distinguishes and separates individuals, is softened by shared exposure to bass frequencies and soaring melodies, and also through gifting practices, the sharing of mind-altering substances, in the form of a rolled joint with *charas*, a pipe gauze drizzled with herbs infused with DMT-containing alkaloids and *B. caapi*, nitrous oxide inhaled from a party balloon, MDMA crystal taken orally, lines of ketamine snorted, and a host of other psychoactives decocted, inhaled and digested. These will include cocaine and alcoholic beverages, most commonly beer, but also unique blends, perhaps a national or personal beverage backpacked into the party.

All such acts of shared sonicity, intoxication and entheogenesis reduce the gulf between event-goers from manifold backgrounds. It is such experiences of intimacy that trigger dedication within the world of psytrance. The experience returns me to Lyng:

> When people separated by divisions of age, gender, class, race, occupation, and intellectual temperament come together and discover deep-seated commonalities of personal experience, they often feel a sense of connection rooted in something basic to their souls. Such is the case with edgeworkers. Whatever else may distance them from one another, risk takers almost always recognize one another as brothers and sisters genetically linked by their desire to experience the uncertainties of the edge (Lyng 2005: 4).

It should also be noted here that, while transgression serves the interest of performers so empowered, it serves at the same time the interests of intracultural detractors for whom such transgressions mark the limits of acceptable behaviour, and for whom transgressions evince a pathology. Among such critics, deprecatory assessments serve to sanctify their own practices against that of the transgressors (risk-taking often being the former behaviour of the now disciplined or virtuous trancers). But while sanctimonious observation and practice serves as boundary maintenance for the disciplined and mature, their reactions provide power to the sacrality of the performance, and the *hardcore* status of the outlaw performer. It emboldens those who find strength in occupying the liminal underworld.

All throughout their precincts, psyculture festivals accommodate the profitless use of energy. Habitués hold a ticket to ride the edge and may pass into a delirium born from exposure to powerful bass and extreme frequency ranges, aided by a mixed-platter of psychoactives. Unravelling selves amid passionate gesticulations illuminated by turbulent fire staff, glow poi, and advanced lighting techniques; modifying bodies in simple or baroque tattoo designs evoking mystery, nature and gothic struggles; combating entropy with lobe scalpelling, staplings, dermal anchors and flesh pockets; becoming locked in nocturnal *tête à têtes* with punishing beats at 160+ bpm; addicted to vertigo, driven to states of dispossession, they literally pass outside of their selves in the presence of others. These are contexts for epic derailments of the mind, and violent interventions upon the body, which sometimes, given most unfortunate circumstances, might be fatal. For instance, a local man died of an alleged overdose of atropine-cut cocaine at Sonica 2007. At the 2002 Shiva Moon festival in Germany, one of the largest growing Goa festivals at that time, the discarded corpse of a newborn baby (to a seventeen-year-old mother) was discovered in a portable chemical toilet. This disturbing tale of extreme negligence and the abandonment of responsibility caused considerable outrage, generating bad press and adversely affecting the festival's reputation.

With these few and most extreme cases we move among the darker shadows of the Dionysian. The more common evidence of limit-transgressions are the casualties resulting from combinations of excessive alterant use,[7] extreme weather conditions, dehydration, viruses and other factors. Even more regular is the frequency of having been "trashed" from long periods of dancing, rocked by high-volume sound systems for consecutive days and nights where sleeping routines are disrupted and circadian rhythms broken. After days of abusing their minds and bodies, some partygoers haunt the festival grounds like citizens of a post-apocalypse, which may indeed be the logical outcome of the quest for self-annihilation. These transgressions, and those associated with other youth and dance cultures (see Ambrose 2001), do not go unnoticed within a Bataillian general economy of sacrifice, where becoming "wasted", the non-productive expenditure of one's self through lavish limit-pushing ventures in the presence of strangers, is *productive*, even if simply a corporate effect of *consummation*. This is not the pathology of excess contributing to Durkheim's study of "anomie", nor is it his romantic "collective effervescence", but a theory of excess which recognizes the value of waste, of transgression, the apocalypse of subjectivity. If the aroma of a five-day open-air dance floor conveys anything, perhaps "collective putrescence" may be a more apt description, though this is not to deny the significance of the sociality native to luxurious discharge and excess.

Ethical lifestyle

The self-indulgent depletion of personal resources on the dance floor is a mode of ecstatic expenditure sharing a sometimes tense and other times amicable relationship with ethical consumption. The Boom Festival is a benchmark event in sustainable consumer practice. From the outset, the Boom project was designed to be an extension of Goa seasons while at the same time providing an alternative to the "open air *underground discothèque*" reputedly characterizing most festivals at the time (Rio, in Good Mood Productions 2007: 27). Boom's "sustainable entertainment" is a signature development. In 2006, the year of my first attendance, Lucy Legan had been contracted to construct "eco-toilets" and promote sustainable living in the festival's Biovillage. In their commitment to provide solutions to challenges posed by the over-consumption of energy, food and water on site, in 2008 and 2010 Boom undertook new projects in composting and refertilizing, reusing organic waste to initiate a reforestation process on the lands of the festival. Following those events, Boom distributed electronic newsletters providing statistics and thanking participants for "depositing your minerals" and "reducing your footprint".[8] In 2008, the "Your Oil Is Music" initiative collected waste vegetable oil from the local region and Boom restaurants (45,000 litres of waste vegetable oil) for use in generators to power the festival, and thus avoid fossil fuels and the emission of 117,000 kilograms of CO_2 into the atmosphere. In 2008, 90 per cent of all structures were made from organic and compostable materials and materials from other events – Rock in Rio Lisbon and the Amadora International Comic Strip Festival – were collected and reused. This practice was continued in 2010, with Boom reusing 86,475 kg of materials (and thus avoiding the emission of 254,000 kg of CO_2). By initiating the use of composting toilets in 2008, Boom avoided dumping 106.5 m^3 of excrement into the public sewage treatment system. In 2010, 98 per cent of Boom toilets (159 toilets) were composting or bio-toilets, with 70,000 litres of organic high-quality liquid fertilizer generated for agricultural production. With "water" becoming the theme of Boom 2010 (as discussed in Chapter 5), Boom claimed that all grey water from restaurants and showers was treated onsite and recycled for irrigation, with 100 per cent of all waste water treated using a bio-remediation and evapotranspiration system.

Bio-toilets, Boom 2010. Photo: Jakob Kolar. www.woowphoto.com.

Additionally, in 2010 Boom built several mobile photovoltaic stations, and 20,000 portable "ashtray" tubes were distributed. As these figures demonstrate, with Boom the party is a stage for enacting ecological principles implemented according to commitments towards ethical consumption, efforts attracting a Greener Festival "outstanding" award in 2008.

In 2010, one kilometre of channels was constructed at Boom to filtrate shower grey water, part of an integrated system designed to restore the area's natural hydrology cycle. As festal fulcrums for the excesses described earlier, electronic dance music events have hardly been exemplary models for environmental regeneration, although some events possess this intent. Acting in response to colonial maladaptation to the landscape while at the same time providing the means for ecstatic dance through the support of local independent artists, between 1999–2003, Melbourne's Tranceplant hosted exemplary "environmental sounds" events at which native tree species were planted on salinated river systems and noxious plants were removed from other despoiled ecologies. Working with local Land Care groups, over 100,000 native trees were planted at eco-sensitive, minimal-impact and multi-genred parties such as Eggplant: Resurrect the Bush held over Easter 2000. Tranceplant was one of the earliest festal ventures in Australia to combine environmental work and entertainment. Co-founder Ben Hardwick stated that he was "always looking for a different way of protesting, a different way of contributing, a different way of making a difference". For Melbourne partygoers, including many initiated in the psytrance scene who thought "what we've done to our land in the last two hundred years is wrong and we can do something to change that", these parties became an important means to make reparations, and at the same time succeeding from events considered to have grown reproachful.[9] Earthcore, as already indicated, attracted considerable criticism in its later years. Claiming that the event "damages the very landscape they use to market themselves", the anonymous author of the blog Boycott Earthcore (2007), for instance, reported on failed efforts to clean up the festival near Undera, Victoria, in 2006 – an incident which left the local community and council outraged, and prompted a local newspaper story featuring the headline "Trashed". Conversely, Tranceplant was significant as a model experience in conscious regeneration, expressive of the dutiful commitment within a postcolonizing climate of the desire to revive country that had been "trashed" (maladapted to) since early settlement. Something of a paragon in environmental regeneration, the not-for-profit, non-hierarchical, organization was a novel exercise in community workplay, which, as member Alan Bamford stated, "just brings you a lot closer to each other". When you spend a day planting trees or pulling weeds, "learning something new and working with the people who you're going to be dancing with the next day, meeting local people in the local area, having them come to your party – it's just a significantly richer emotional experience to then celebrate that work". Moreover, these events have inaugurated a connection with place not achieved in the standard dance party model.

> When you get to spend a little bit of time in the forest you begin to know its ups and downs, where the potholes are, where this bird and that possum live. You start gaining a bit of temporary ownership almost of the space. You feel good about it, you start traversing it, you develop habits in how you traverse it. You move across this hill for that and across this gulley for that and you just deepen your relationship with it. And this takes much more than just your standard model of drive up, set up, dance and go home.[10]

But Bamford elucidated that the core aspect of these novel rituals performed in the Australian bush at the turn of the millennium was their response to the "unbalanced" character of events where the party overrides any other commitment. Tranceplant emerged from discomfort with standard models and the desire for a more balanced experience. "For a lot of people I know, the enjoyment is enriched considerably by the fact that you are on the dance floor with people who you were yesterday on your knees with scrubbing around in the dirt".[11]

Tranceplant's balanced approach to workplay would provide inspiration for various other "enviro-sound" organizations seeking alternatives to the irresponsible party combination of becoming personally "trashed" and "trashing" the environment, such as that which evolved into the Earth Freq (now Earth Frequency) festival held in northeast NSW and southeast Queensland. Founder Paul Abad, who works across the "digital organic divide" and who oscillates between "computers and rainforest eco systems", started out running multi-genred parties as vegetation events working with Land Care groups in the sunshine coast hinterland of Queensland. I spoke with Paul in June 2003 about a party I attended earlier that year called Autumnatic at Conondale, Qld, where 450 people worked with the Mary River Catchment Landcare group planting native species along the creekbed and stripping out invasive *Lantana* weed. He claimed that these events possess the best "community vibe", since participants are ostensibly rewarded by leaving the party site in better condition than when they arrived."[12] I again spoke with Abad in December 2003 at Positronic, a party held on a community property at Belthorpe, a popular site for parties in southeast Queensland since the late 1990s. Since *Lantana* had overtaken the creek, that event gave many partygoers who had became attached to this land over the years the opportunity to "give something back".[13] In clandestine and proactive aesthetics, events such as this would enable the practice of the forbidden while enacting a conscientious response to the unsustainable lifestyles in which participants are raised. The balanced satisfaction identified has also been enjoyed by those working on or volunteering for event-organizations whose management practices are shaped by a sustainable consumption ethos.[14]

Another vehicle for ecological consciousness has been Melbourne's BIG:RED:BUS crew, who have thrown "zero emissions" parties completely powered by solar panels, wind turbines and bio-diesel generator. One such event was held in conjunction with the Eco Productions crew at the 2008 Rainbow Serpent Festival where they operated the Sunset Stage. This and other psytrance parties in Australia and elsewhere became stages for the theatrical expression of sustainability, exemplifying the "cultural dramas" Turner identified as cultural modes of "redress", performative vehicles through which the *sacra* of event-habitués are displayed, performed, transmitted. The triad of eco-maenads wandering the grounds of the 2008 RSF are illustrative, their onsite performance dramatizing the crisis of water depletion and over-consumption on the planet's driest continent. As the promotions for this performance project had it:

> Three post civilization ethereal beings – Nomadic Nymphs – are wandering the desert, in search of their lost love and life source ... Water. The only relic they have of their past abundant liquid life is a magical glass vessel, containing their precious elixir of life ... This water sustains them, entrances them. They live for this last drop of hope. And so, they wander and roam always searching and stopping often to statue, to float and to worship their treasured nectar and be replenished. All shall witness their deep love and devotion to this rare and magical liquid treasure, and hopefully help them on their quest to be reunited with their life's destiny.[15]

Attention to redress is possibly best illustrated in the way psyculture became a vehicle for the activities of the planetary consciousness movement inscribed in the Planetary Art Network (PAN), and principally the Dreamspell Calendar. Also called the "13 Moon Calendar", the Dreamspell is a tool for consciousness change developed by José and Lloydine Argüelles (founders of PAN) and is based, in part, on their translation of the Mayan Calendar. Having initiated the replacement of the Gregorian calendar on 25 July 2004, "Galactic Freedom Day", PAN activists understand calendar change to be an eight-year process (2004–2012). For Argüelles (who died on 23 March 2011), and members of PAN groups observing the new calendar around the world, since the artificial time frequency of the 12-month Gregorian calendar and the 60-minute hour is arbitrarily imposed, the survival of humanity and the avoidance of an environmental catastrophe are dependent upon the adoption of a "harmonic" calendar. The Dreamspell calendar is thus regarded as a core technology adopted as a means to redress global ecological crises, and responsive to toxic consumer lifestyles. Many dance and festival groups have aligned their gatherings with the new calendar (see St John 2004), and PAN nodes have held a presence at many of the large international and smaller local gatherings at which I have been in attendance, from Earthdream2000 and Earthfreq, to Soulclipse in southern Turkey over Easter 2006. These events and music productions (see St John 2011b) have been common sites for the pedagogical transmission of "the New Time".

In 2006, Boom hosted a "Galactic Temple", an open geodesic dome with hanging banners of Dreamspell glyphs. Workshops and discussions were held daily inside the temple dome, at the centre of which was an impressive "Telektonon board" with crystals, resembling a game board with pieces. Workshop participants learned that the 13 Moon Calendar consists of an annual cycle of 13 moons each 28 days long, and is held to demonstrate harmony with the Earth and natural cycles, coded, for instance, in the human female biological cycle. Kwali, a "Red Magnetic Skywalker" who had "upgraded" 1,500 people to their Dreamspell sign or "galactic signatures" (of which there are 260, my own being Yellow Planetary Seed), stated: "why do I feel like I'm running out of time? Why am I not in the right place at the right time?"[16] According to Kwali and her fellow PAN activists, the questions haunt those of us who are removed from our natural cycles, and the Dreamspell evidences the logic of sacrificial commitment to the ultimate cause: the future. The commitment of Dreamspell practitioners appears to lie in dramatic contrast to those who reveal no concern for the morrow. Both, in a sense, are antagonists of "time". The former are dissenters from Gregorian time and the calendar imposed by the Roman Catholic Church. As Kwali stated: "people want to be free from the clock that ticks and this is an opportunity for people to have their freedom within a society that does not want them to be free". For the latter, the dissention from routine "time" and rational consciousness is expressed in the commitment to the eternity that is *now* into which one passes on the dance floor. Apparently, by contrast with the headlong charge towards an orgiastic suspension of time characterizing one's approach to dance, the 13 Moon Calendar movement offers a profound teleological expression of the concern for life "after the orgy", including, that is, the "orgy" of history, or more accurately, the history of ecological despoliation characterizing modernization. Such is a commitment to the future, a possible future downstream from the actions of the present, a future that relies upon one's choices now. This is the message of much PAN activism, a discourse and practice of responsibility towards the natural environment and one's self evolving post-1960s.

But are these diverse experiences of altered time incompatible? Why would advocates of the Planetary Art Network elect a regular presence at events where frivolities and getting "wasted" in a "time out of time" are rife? These are questions addressed by Australian self-identified "Chrononaught" and PAN devotee, Even Dawn (2008), who observed that in these luxurious episodes in energy use and wildlife disturbance "we've discovered how to amp up just about all the parameters that our sensory input organs can sustain". But having attended the 2008 Winter Solstice Gathering in Far North Queensland operated by PsyTek Productions, where she experienced, for instance, the operations of the company Natural Event whose composting toilets convert human waste into usable compost or "humanure", Dawn became convinced that festival culture is "maturing into a more responsive and responsible party animal". An adept of the 13 Moon Synchronometer, Dawn acknowledges the importance of the role played by dance and the "apparent frivolity of cultural festivals" in the coming "synchronization". She considers those who attend these Planetary Gatherings as representatives of "the emergence of the coming culture of life on planet Earth". Articulating eco-centric and Earthen religious views common to PAN enthusiasts, these sites are viewed as the most recent in a "heritage of nomadic corroborees, gypsy caravans, celebrated feasts and fairs" inhabited by those who celebrate "the human species' rightful, artistic role in relation to the whole". But offering a perspective that conveys Argüelles' co-evolutionary thesis and the ideas of Russian scholar and "noosphere" theorist Vladmir Vernadsky, the view is that "these humans are returning to a style of living which aims to exist in accordance with the well-being of the planetary life-support system, the Biosphere". Furthermore, these festivals are reckoned to be

> meeting grounds of the AltarNation, the pro-Native movement towards collective recognition of the Sanctity of Nature. On the dancefloors, throughout the day and night there can be found devout dance pilgrims from a diverse spectrum of cultures, some having trekked land, sea and sky to make their offerings of movement on that particular place on earth. The language which unites them all is expressed through the art and the music (Dawn 2008).

But while the dance floor becomes a context for visionary developments that are harnessed within paradigms of consciousness and evolution, for the most part participants simply lay claim to "getting on one". Thus differential causes, and the *sacrificial logics* performed in their name, are integral to the ecology of trance events. Such was more than evident in August 2007 at the Italian festival Sonica. The festival had been inaugurated in the summer of 2005 when 6,000 young middle-class Italians, and many other nationalities besides, camped in a dry valley winding up from the picturesque lake Bolsena. With my party compatriots, on the heights I found a mock Estruscan temple and Carabinieri armed with automatic weapons whose vantage overlooked the thousands seeking abandonment below. Participants competed for tent space and shade in an orchid, and would huddle under the single tree at the back of an expansive main floor – littered, I noted, with trash for the duration of the four-day festival (a circumstance discussed by many critics afterwards). When I returned to Sonica two years later with 5,000 others (again mostly Italians) the venue was strikingly different. Held in mountain pine woodland in Liguria between La Spezia and Genoa 1,000 metres above sea level close to the famed Cinque Terre National Park, the heights over the dance floor held spectacular views of the Vara Valley. In response to complaints of environmentally unsound practice, attempting to reduce their "ecological footprint", promotions for the festival indicated that it was all about "Celebrating Nature". Ostensibly in support "of the environment and for the use of renewable energies", a five-day festival where participants are dedicated to extreme states of self-abandonment, Sonica featured solar-powered showers and lighting, garbage separation, clean-up efforts by "eco-team" volunteers, and a reputed investment in a "carbon sink" reforestation programme in Costa Rica.

Efforts, on the one hand, to promote consumer and renewable energy practices consistent with an environmental sensibility, and on the other, to consume resources in delirious expenditures, are destined to cause tension, especially when they are motivations holding relative logic. In 2007, Sonica found a way to amplify these divergent logics such that they came to loggerheads. Thus enters the Duracell Powerhouse, a large air-inflated tent shaped like a long-life Duracell battery pitched mid-festival (on its European "Power Up" tour). With a sound system, smoke machine and dance club atmosphere inside, the Powerhouse featured a full lineup of DJs whose set-times were listed in the Sonica booklet alongside the artists performing on the Main and Alternative stages. According to its website, the Powerhouse was dedicated to "partying into the early hours, making the music last longer,

Sonica 2007, Italy. Photo: Graham St John.

much longer". Enticing participants with the prospect of swapping their "tired batteries" for "shiny new Duracell Ultra M3s", hustling brand loyalty and reinforcing a perma-cycle of disposability, Duracell offered festival participants a "free battery exchange". But its presence and sponsorship was not well received by a critical event-public. That Duracell is among the chief makers of (non-rechargeable and non-recyclable) alkaline batteries widely classified as hazardous waste (sources of harmful potassium hydroxide), a corporation pushing unsustainable lifestyle and non-renewable energy practices, goes some way to explaining the exasperation of participants, including the residents and visitors of Sonica's self-identified "neo-tribal" Duende Village, an area for presentations, workshops and films promoting an "eco-sustainable future" broadsided by the bloated icon of disposability. According to its initiators, Duende is "a mysterious and indescribable force, a creative fire similar to the vital lymph that courses through the roots of human sensibility, feeding the collective imagination with dreams of utopia and a better world".[17] One can only imagine the contempt felt by estranged villagers for whom Club Duracell signified the rupturing of such dreams.

Sonica's appropriation of environmental virtue, while accepting sponsorship and onsite marketing from Duracell, seems hypocritical and duplicitous, indeed echoing behaviour now commonly practised by corporations globally as "greenwashing". A symbol of Dionysian capitalism, the Powerhouse contradicted the eco-conscious legacy and utopian sensibility to which psyculture is heir. But in its promotion to energize the night, to make now last longer, it does not contradict the directionless desire for discharge, bliss and luxury, the prevailing ecstatic and erotic impulse which cares little for tomorrow. While committed to modes of consumer opposition, enthusiasts nonetheless pursue an ecstasy reliant on technologies, industries and practices compromising an eco-sensibility. Illustrating an acute *ecstatic/activist paradox* defining identity, it conveys differential causes and corresponding understandings of the sacred. It is a paradox that fuels controversy between neotribes committed to ecstatic and conscious extremes, and indeed feeds conflict and anxieties within individual participants themselves. Where one person's holiness is another's sacrilege, a kind of neotribal religious war unfolds between adversaries – that is, between proponents of the "savage religion" vs the noble cause, between ecstatic and visionary antagonists, a passionate "social drama" playing itself out in the minds of individual participants. For it is at these events that habitués, perhaps those pursuing distinct and opposing causes, are provided the opportunity, indeed the encouragement, to shift between causes. That is, by exposing participants to disparate modes of exhilaration and reflexivity, to a hyperliminal domain of workplay, festivals facilitate experimentation across the sacred divide. This hubbub of liminalities triggers ever-newer modes of redress and optimization, both on the part of participants *in situ*, and on the part of the disenchanted who seek to recreate and innovate liminal ritual.

Club Duracell. Sonica, Italy, August 2007. Photo: Graham St John.

Rites of self-discipline

The presence of the Duracell Powerhouse at Sonica 2007 highlights another tension in which the question of "energy" remains pivotal. An image is imprinted in my mind. As if squaring off upon a karmic battleground, a Javanese-style stone meditating Buddha's head faced down the swollen copper-top for the duration of the festival. The statue belonged to the adjacent Healing area, which hosted practical workshops on shiatsu, ayurvedic massage, crystal healing, reiki, aura imaging, and a sweatlodge. While this provides a particularly sharp juxtaposition, it is a microcosmic representation of tensions evident within psytrance. The Healing area at Sonica, along with similar areas in other events such as the Healing Village at Boom or the Transformations space at Rainbow Serpent, signal crises of the modern self recognized by human potential and integralist movement practitioners who've evolved techniques adapted from Oriental, indigenous and Western esoteric traditions harnessed in the pursuit of self-actualization and embodied enlightenment. In these festal venues, habitués are exposed to practices and philosophies – including yoga, meditation and other body arts – by which they may discipline mind and body, cultivate inner and outer "energies" and improve or evolve their spirit. It is common to find practices and philosophies uniting East and West, spirituality and science, and adopting eclectic shamanisms in which therapeutic and transformational strategies are evoked and practised. But the disciplined commitment to growth and a corresponding evolution of consciousness contrasts sometimes radically with the commitment to which trance habitués demonstrate a popular dedication: to party. In the former, individuals elect pathways of self-advancement through numerous techniques of the mind, body and spirit around which they build a personal repertoire characterized by holism, purity and progression. Here disciplined self-workers seek a balanced relationship with body–mind–spirit. At the latter extreme, those who are "avin *It*" *know* the sacred in indulgent states of excess. In the former dietary regimes, breathwork and somatic practices are taken up with intent to make transit into higher "consciousness", personal "well-being" and "mindfulness". Life is considered to be a "journey" undertaken towards states of "wholeness", "completion" and sanctity. In the latter, enthusiasts mount the curb of the normative, work the "edges of chaos", and, in Vitos's (2010) view, become "demented".

Earlier in the book, it was explained that yogic philosophy and practice are enshrined in psyculture. The psychosomatic transitional power of yoga provides the inspiration and conceptual apparatus for event organizers who commonly adopt the language of yoga and chakras to orchestrate and promote their events. Thus, with member practitioners of Sahaja Yoga developed by Shri Mataji, long-running UK party organization Kundalini run intentional events they call the Kundalini Illumination Experience, sometimes in association with conscious event-organizations like the Synergy Project and Shamania. With extraordinary attention to visual and sound detail, and hosting DJs performing psytrance alongside other EDM genres over fifteen years (by 2009), Kundalini had evolved "a synchronized journey in music, light and sight – creating resonating gateway portals with the aid of media sculptured installations with the Kundalini Sound System". Events are designed to enable participants to "move through the different body chakra illumination centres reconnecting us, so giving an opportunity for release on the dance floor; taking you all the way ... Spiritual partying consciousness into the domain of your spirit!"[18] The responsive motivation of "spiritual partying" is widespread among conscious ritualists like the initiators of the Return To The Source club at London's Dome Nightclub where the club was transformed into a "temple space" and where Antara made use of a wide range of electronic music to "activite chakras" and to facilitate "stages in a process of energetic purification, balancing and conscious release" (Antara in Twist 1999). Other organizers include those of London's ID Spiral, whose Spiral Nights at the Synergy Center in Camberwell sometimes featured the "all is one dance workshop" led by Naomi Green.

Yogic philosophy is furthermore programmed into psychedelic music, offering diverse intentional meditational soundtracks to spiritual partying. At the more common ambient edge, Blue Lunar Monkey (*Beyond 2012*, 2008) drops the thread on his track "Yoga". Founder of The Divine Life Society, Sri Swami Sivananda, opens the proceedings: "thou art the master of your destiny. Do not be discouraged when sorrows, difficulties and tribulations manifest in the daily battle of life. Draw courage and spiritual strength from within.

There is a vast magazine of power and knowledge within. Learn the ways to tap the source. Dive deep within". Another spokesperson follows: "Yoga basically is the system, the process, that connects the individual, with that individual's notion of the divine", leading into an uplifting pattern. A woman's voice reaches in: "absolute clarity; pure awareness". Founder of the Himalayan Institute of Yoga Science and Philosophy in northeastern Pennsylvania, Swami Rama, then motions "Peace and happiness is within you. By knowing to direct your energies within toward the deeper aspects of your being, you can attain that peace". While many ambient and progressive artists have jammed on the theme of "merging with the beloved" associated with, for instance, bhakti yoga, with the compilation album *Anahata* (or "heart chakra") released by Active Meditation Music (2009), dark trance picks up the task. The album's tracks were apparently selected with the intention to facilitate balance: "The Yantra in the centre of the chakra is composed of two overlapping, intersecting triangles. One triangle, facing upward, symbolizes Shiva,male principle. The other triangle, facing downward, symbolizes Shakti, the female principle. A balance is attained when these two forces are joined in harmony". Obtaining frenetic speeds in excess of 170 bpm, tracks such as "Buco Diavolo" by Death Project and "Fucking Crazy" by Demoniac Insomniac, stretches conventional tantric discourse. Yet, while featuring the electronic caterwauls and swirling digital worm holes typical of darkpsy, tracks involve mesmerizing builds, and in the case of "Pijani Orkestar" by Sick Noise, is almost Wagnerian. As a bludgeoning crescendo of noise, "Oscilate on Opiate" by Infect Insect

Yoga. Boom 2010. Photo: Rémy-Pierre RIBIERE. www.ruyphoto.net.

challenges accepted understandings of meditational music, and the album's "DMT Molecule" by Mister Black, a fast-paced audio-billboard promoting DMT, evidences the role of entheogens in the meditative becoming.

Returning to our earlier discussion, influencing a variety of subgenres, plant-derived psychoactives are commonly championed as a legitimate means of embracing the other, sacralizing person and culture and thereby becoming a viable movement propensity operationalized through ritualized intent. As tools for divinization, entheogens are contrasted with a range of substances (often "white powders") claimed to inaugurate behaviour anathema to the fruitful outcomes of disciplined commitment and transformative ritual: growth. As the range of psychoactive substances available to practitioners of trance diversifies (along with the range of effects) in a culture where those compounds recognized to facilitate life re-evaluations are most esteemed, studies require approaches unconstrained by prejudices inhering in the intellectual discourses of the past. Citing Coleridge, Theodore Roszac had once commented on the "counterfeit infinity" that psychedelics ostensibly inaugurate (1995 [1968]: 155). The psychedelic experience, in that estimation, is a "limited chemical means to a greater psychic end, namely, the reformulation of the personality, upon which social ideology and culture generally are ultimately based" (ibid.: 156). The pharmacological cornucopia impacting contemporary scenes is astoundingly complex, and their elucidation is ill-served by repeating dismissive and prejudiced objections accompanying the onset of prohibition. Are we witness to an accelerating return to the "insatiable and bottomless abyss" of desire identified as a modern pathology? This was the opinion of Durkheim who worried over the thirst for "novelties, unfamiliar pleasures [and] nameless sensations" which "lose their savor once known" and stimulate unfulfilled aspirations disavowed as a "longing for infinity" (1970: 247, 256). Such anxieties do not phase the latest prometheans surfing the novelty wave of sound and style. Yet, while scene commentators embrace the mechanisms of novelty as r/evolutionary struggle, others consistently reprove atrophied ritual forms and excesses devoid of meaning. Antagonists have railed against the electronic trance assemblage from its inception, regarded as an inappropriate means of obtaining the spiritual life. Tirades have opened against assumed threats to "liveness" and "authenticity", cultural wars waged at alternative cultural and music events throughout the 1980s and 1990s, such as Rainbow Gatherings, Glastonbury, Burning Man and ConFest,[19] festal sites where electronic musics (including psytrance) struggled to achieve legitimacy. Such conflicts are notorious, and evident in Goa where synth-pop and other electronic styles were dismissed by heads as inauthentic "disco music". These debates have not relented, with spokespersons waging objections to the inappropriate application of trance technics. Purists like Berlin-based Trance Dance therapist Rob Bennett (2007) is among those practitioners supervising the return "back to trance dance", rebuking "party people who want to get 'out of it' every weekend rather than 'into the flow'". Entheogenesists, agents of mindfulness and champions of the r/evolution make pronouncements about the "wasteful" and apocryphal trajectory of psytrance, consistently erecting the boundaries between the acceptable and the unacceptable. They will isolate various practices, music styles and psychoactive commodities as symptomatic of deprivation, dilapidation and ruin. Thus, concerns raised by earlier commentators about kids "shooting up" methedrine, turning to heroin, and "gobbling acid wherever and whenever they could, completely ignorant of set and setting, without the least bit of interest in the Unspoken Thing" (Stevens 1989: 460) persist. In the 1960s, Leary's "Death of Mind" raised hackles as inhabitants of the Haight-Ashbury were "sledgehammering at their shells until there was nothing left but the ubiquitous dust" (ibid.). That comment might have been submitted in relation to scenes commonly associated with faster subgenres of music like darkpsy, with disputes arising between proponents of emergent styles who possess different ideas about "psychedelic" music. Swiss DJ-producer SubConsciousMind (Raphael Huber) identifies music that "uses destructive force to achieve a transformative process". Responding to the efforts of DJs to shatter the ego in rites of passage in which the apocalypse of subjectivity is raised as a virtue, he stated that "the ego is just protection, it doesn't need to be shattered or smashed ... Reinforce the positive instead of destroying the negative ... I use hypnotic build ups to create a trance like state and then I use emotion to connect to the soul".[20] Committed to a techno shamanic revivalism, DJ Krusty has expressed his lament for the contemporary trance dance experience, where the "divine intention has slipped away into obscurity", and which is "overshadowed by a male dominance energy structure: the compulsive obsessive pursuit of contemporary values – success, fortune, fame, sex, power – which are globally out of balance and soul destroying for humanity" (Krusty 2008: 19). In response to the "noise" that doof is declared to have become, and embracing the ritual role of entheogens, we have seen that Krusty has developed events with a therapeutic and visionary intent, a practice that itself joins the noise of contemporary trance.

* * *

Psychedelic festivals accommodate the expression of differential logics of sacrifice and concomitant ideas of the sacred. The premiere event in the world psyculture calendar, Boom is the pre-eminent locale for the dynamic expression of these logics, where ecstatic and reflexive practices constitute *sacred work*, and possess transformative efficacy. This book has given considerable attention to these dispositions, this liminal noise and its concatenation in *neotrance*. As the Dance Temple, along with other events worldwide, hosts rites of transgression, shared risk and unparalleled states of exhilaration, the psyculture festival is a primary grounds to, as Even Dawn (2008) observes, "get out of it". Yet these events are also contexts, she avers, to "get into it", as festivals become, as explained by an anonymous author in the Liminal Village zine *Pathways* (2006), "concentrated hubs of exchange and transformation – open systems interzones between the conventional bounds of time and space". An intentional multi-mediated and interactive experience enabling experimentation with population causes, Boom's Liminal Village has been recognized as a paragon of disciplinary and conscious ritualizing. Since heterogeneous causes are performed and presented within their precincts, psytrance festivals are labyrinthine *meta-dramas* accommodating diverse sacra, multiple pathways and possible outcomes. Commitments to self-abandonment through excess and consumption are juxtaposed with ethical consumerism, a circumstance stimulating disagreements, hybridization and mutation. Given the commitment to disparate liminalities available to the festal multitudes, on the dance floor, in the market-place, in workshops, at the conference, back at camp, such festivals are *hyperliminal* in character, which is simply an artifact of their countercultural origins. These gatherings are then stages for negotiating the paradox that is now implicit to the lifestyles of those participating in an alternative movement which reaches around the world and which is given expression at global summits where the Dionysian orgy and the conscious path intersect, where ecstasy and idealism collide in an uncertain present. In its pre-eminent cultural manifestations, the visionary arts cultural festival is heir to the traditions of the carnival and the ceremony, facilitates discipline and risk, a rowdy stage for the performance of poetics and politics. These diverse experiments in the sacred potentiate novel collaborations, cause hybrid alliances and stimulate ritual innovation.

I have critically revisited Turner's concept of "liminality" in this chapter in the light of research on psytrance culture and its events. The desire within this movement for the potent effects of optimized *ritual* practice has been demonstrated, but I have also shown that commitments are diverse, that the party is host to contested logics of sacrifice – a veritable carnival of liminalities. Furthermore, by contrast to conventional approaches to transit and passage adopting the "liminal" concept from the rites of passage model, I've addressed the prolonged and uncertain career of liminality exemplified by a movement in which the party is paramount. As psytrance participants here and elsewhere return time and again to these sophisticated interstices to experiment with these potentials and perform adverse sacrificial logics, the liminal becomes a virtual career, gets weirder and grows even more complex.

10 Nothing lasts

"We all knew that it could not last". Among the original Goa freaks, Peter Thomas's (2011) statement conveys awareness of the coming end, of paradise lost, the fall of the "hippie Raj". It highlights an anxiety intrinsic to the Goa experience, a sensitivity relived over and again down through the years, with each historical cohort sentient to the disappearance of their thing, whose own demise is felt to augur the death of "the scene". But this apprehension is accompanied by a genuine response, expressed in the cumulative and commodious actions of the scene maker, the culture hero, the decadent partygoer, and the music's producers whose longing for the "good old days" is programmed into sounds and mediated to dance floors where occupants are witness to the mixing of eras, the reliving of sensibilities, and who dance the past in the present. Thomas's comment expresses the knowledge of transition by those in transit, who will nevertheless "make the most of it", in wild abandonment, but who also commit to formulas, fashion and festivals designed to prolong now, to "stay up forever", to delay the future through standardized practice, modified equipment, and digital and chemical syntheses optimized to maximize potential. As indicated earlier in this book, there has been a succession of junctures, some disputed, others widely recognized, at which Goatrance is perceived to have imploded, a succession of thresholds across which Goa is reported to have died. Many commentators have chimed in with eulogies, epitaphs and post-mortems. Ray Castle, for instance, has been one of the most vociferous critics of the aftermath of Goatrance following its advent as a music/culture. Castle opposes the normalizing of psychedelia codified into its own *nomos*, whose fundamentalisms are anathema to the fusional and genre-defying roots of psychedelia, which became "like a religion with rules and codes of vibrational resonance, form, structure, regulated rites".[1]

As the Goatrance aesthetic moved globally in the networked age, the sonic-flier distributed by Breach of Space in Chapter 3's epigraph reads like a sad note on the fate of Goa as a site of experimentation, for the invitation to become exposed to the salacious and exceptional activities of the experienced would itself become an experience upon which tourism industries would come to rely. "Trance" became a commodity promoted to domestic tourists obsessed with the idea of capturing on film and committing to memory those "nude torsos" twisted and gyrating, crises of intrusion and representation encountered the world over by scenes within which the "escape from samsara" had become a "weekend society", an innocuous tango with the night. And as scenes emerged, repressive state responses were reported in former Soviet states like Estonia and Latvia, as well as in Belgium, Japan, Italy, Germany and other nations, an issue which deserves more attention than that which I have been able to provide in this book (see Baldini 2010b). The awareness-anxiety associated with over-exposure, formulaic aesthetics, the commodification of experience and state repression are integral to this movement, but what I find most curious is that this sensitivity is programmed into events heir to the 1980s Disctopian concatenation in Goa, which was itself held to have sounded the death-knell of the 1970s Goa spirit by earlier settlers. The rhythm majestic of the "Trance Dance" party and its transnational traveller enclaves – its festivals – condense an era into several days (or even one night). In its duration, the entrant knows that the party can't last. The liminar recognizes that s/he dances upon the threshold, that the music – the seamless mixing of tune after tune by DJ after DJ – will eventually fade to off, after the final encore. They are aware that the clock is ticking on eternity. Promoters understand the need to orchestrate a satisfying closure, by hiring DJs who lay a party to rest with dignity, permitting sojourners a gentle landing from their soaring heights. Yet, while habitués know that the event will close, that there will be a final mix on the last stage operating – and often police and other officials stand by to ensure that this occurs – few want to contemplate the aftermath, nor think about the destination, not when they're inside the vibe, when their energies are vested in eternity. In that time, which is to say, in that time-out-of-time, all is expended in the effort to squat the forever, to thwart the passage of time.

Trance events have an uncanny ability to capture an era, and captivate an audience of travellers occupying the eternal theatre of the dance floor. As this book has shown, while the liminal is logically defined by its temporality, and demands that there must be a finale, a destination, an outcome, the tendency within psytrance is to defer aggregation, prolong the night, to adopt a liminal lifestyle, convenient to a movement in which transformation is *lived*, where impermanence gets an encore. It has been stated here that the liminal lifestyle of the present lies downstream from the 1960s–1970s when the natural period of adolescence had been extended, fuelled by rock and LSD, a psychedelic liminalization later vibrant in a globalizing culture of the festival that, post Goa, took up residence in many countries, manifesting in a circuit of transnational events themselves attended by those from multiple countries, with this superliminal investment across events and nations, as evidenced by edgework and workplay, echoing and amplifying the desire to maintain the unspoken no-thing. While this global liminality is typically associated with well-resourced and -networked middle-class expatriates, as scenes settled within regions, and cultures formed, it became attractive to a great many participants whose profile did not match the privileged status of forebears. If liminality characterizes every mix between tracks in EDM (Gerard 2004), if the music is programmed to effect the virtualization of the self, and events are consciously liminal (as Boom signifies), and as events grow and increase in frequency, then we must recognize a lifestyle in which one becomes attached to impermanence, a *permaliminal* condition. The experience of revelation, of being-in-transit, is axiomatic to psyculture, where, aided by an upgradable assemblage of technics, the noetic amounts to the initiatory experience, which is desired by participants actively seeking re-enchantment and investing in popular occulture and psychoactives to fashion new ritual experiences. In the enclaves of radical reflexive modernity, the participant must him/her self apply meaning to the experience that this event-culture potentiates. This liminalization is the effect of a movement whose festivals are its paramount cultural expression, and in which liminality is itself the chief product. In the cultivation of the mystical experience through investments and iterations in audio, lighting, visionary art and sacred compounds, and through blends, fusions and the arts of the remix, transmissions received enable architects to fashion the means to augment the liminal experience, and thus the means becomes the desirable end.

Travel is the chief practice by which the psytrancer maintains the permaliminal lifestyle. By the 2000s, the Goa vibe was transposed to locations worldwide amid waves of new state optimism, post-revolutionary hope and nascent countercultural formations. From Goa to London, Berlin to Tel Aviv, Paris to Tokyo, Amsterdam to San Francisco, Melbourne to Cape Town, Koh Phangan to Bahia, in the events cultivated by charismatic DJs and visionary promoters in the European circuit of festivals and in countless other seasonal events in regions worldwide, psychedelic traveller culture proliferated. Throughout this development, travel became an initiatory experience for backbackers from Israel, Europe, Australia, Japan, South America and elsewhere, with annual circuits of events enabling entrants to remain in a state of mobility. And, perhaps more importantly, rather than simply ports of call for the seasoned traveller, seasonal events became homes for *the traveller experience*, enabling worldly countenance and cultural accreditation for those who may not have travelled far from home at all. While research on the international trance traveller and the traveller festival awaits future treatment, it is enough here to state that the romantic liminality of the traveller is programmed into psychedelic trance music and culture. On their *Uncharted* compilation (2007), Wouter Thomassen and Sander Visser (aka

Citizen), for instance, offer a traveller aesthetic rooted in the Goa experience. In an interview for *Progressive Tunes* magazine (Citizen 2007), these artists stated how they wanted to engineer

> a kind of traveller vibe, going out into exotic countries, away from the trendy tourist places and take the unpaved roads into the jungle in search of some obscure hidden outdoor party. Also that feeling we had when we started out DJing in the 90s and electronic music was just more fresh, obscure and edgy. In search of those hidden treasures at the local record store.

Their comments indicate the intention of musicians to create music which echoes the desire for "global" discovery, making rendezvous with the exotic, being intimate with the authentic experience, an occurrence approximated as one becomes less like "tourists" and more like "travellers", although in reality such dispositions grow indistinct even as one's vertical/horizontal "lines of flight" blur. And psychedelic trance cultivates the mystical experience, carried in the sampling, the chanting, the space journeying, in the Eastern and native imagery reproduced on album covers, event posters and fliers. "That's the real use of music. It's not for listening to, it's for travelling", reads the sample onboard Laughing Buddha's "Astral Traveller" (*Dream Creation – The Sound of Freedom*, 1998). At the club, in the festival, or on the bus wearing your iPod, one can participate in the sensibility of the traveller grafted from sites where exiles once relocated, but is now made available to domestic audiences, who may enter liminal states without travelling anywhere in particular, or without dropping acid. Thus the spatio-geographic experience becomes thoroughly replicated in the mind-escapades endemic to psyculture, with the "state of mind" sold to young seekers from world cities still thirsty for the real thing. The trappings of tripping in the East continue to be deployed to make the hard sell. And so, in 2010, a *sadhu* with his face and forehead pasted with *vibhuti*, sacred white ash, pulls from a chillum on the cover of TIP Records' *Goa Classics 1*.

While nostalgia for a mythical time/place may continue to motivate labels years after the cheese fettered, and long after any meaningful exhalations, psyculture is not place-less. Indeed, psytribes have emerged in locations worldwide, possessing unique sounds and styles, impacted by local heritage issues, and distinct causes shaped by regional, national and cultural issues, and this book has contributed to this discussion through attention to Israeli and Australian scenes in particular. Goatrance events have been characterized as "imagined communities that share a global connectivity but not a defined sense of place and historicity, acting as they must as nebulous transnational models for a consciously created global neo-tribal identity" (Bizzell 2008: 286). Extending this observation to the various scenes of Goa transmigration is problematic since, as these case studies illustrate, psytribes seek and accomplish continuity with place. As participants are raised in a seasonal circuit of events within their home regions, events which pull them out of the cities and into the hinterlands, the bush, the forest, the outback, the desert, they develop attachments to country facilitated through peak moments associated with the trance experience. Psytrance may be global, but its participants are embedded in local scenes with regional attachments, and with experience grounded in place. Psyculture has been shaped by global flows of technics and aesthetics enabling these psytribes to emerge, identifying with movement trends and yet developing unique identities. At the same time, events have emerged with a distinctive global or planetary consciousness. Boom and total solar eclipse festivals are notable liminal junctures for the expression of a planetary awareness, which this book has only begun to address.

Global Tribe has also illustrated that disparate liminalities motivate travel, are programmed into the music and characterize the events of the psychedelic trance movement. The psychedelic festival possesses a unique dynamic, at once simple and complex. The book has explained the mechanisms of the festal *difference engine*, the motor of the dance vibe enabling the dissolution and performance of distinction, both the singularity of the dance massive and the flourishing of each participant whose own distinct legacy and identifications are amplified. One of the enduring characteristics of the trance

Boom at night, 2006. Photo: Pascal Querner.

party is that it permits the interplay of liminalities in an interactive theatre that throws up unexpected outcomes as the product of their interface. From infrequent and precarious inner-city squat parties or open-air events like those in Australia and Israel, to major multi-floor festivals like Boom, the festal is a centre of cultural freedom, boundary dissolution and self-performance. Compelling multiple expectations, causes and freedoms, the psychedelic festival accommodates varieties of the sacred. From progressive to transgressive, evolutionary and ecstatic, utopic and dystopic, variant sensibilities and modes of consciousness determine the social aesthetic of the psychedelic festival, whose hyperliminality is rooted in Goa. As a heterotopian dancescape, invested with multiple definitions and inputs from vested stakeholders, the psyfestival is a product of countless iterations and programming decisions determining form. Impacted by sometimes competing expectations, conditioned by various responsibilities, operationalized through diverse artifice, challenged by adversaries, it is a contested and sometimes controversial arena subject to negotiation. Psyculture is a story of mutation which, while buffeted by adversity, sees continuity through fledgling operators, re-invigorated visionaries, and schismatic events determined to re/create the desired aesthetic, return to origins, mount the "r/evolution". Here, identity is defined against that from which protagonists seek departure while at the same time remaining faithful to original objectives. Visionaries, ideologues and stalwarts of independence are determined to maintain their integrity in response to a variety of threats, whether soulless conformity, proprietary sensibilities, interventions of the state, untoward exposure, and predatorial behaviour.

In the contemporary movement, there is an underlying tension between the proponents of secrecy and advocates of movement causes, a neotribal conflict between those maintaining an "underground" identity and those mounting the r/evolution, and events illustrate efforts to achieve compromise between clandestine and millenarian positions. Those discontent with commercialism call for discretion, such as "astralseeker" (2007) who, on an isratrance.com thread "The Problem with Psytrance", urged parties be organized "the 'old way' with little entrances and no publicity, few flyers going to the right persons and location info really hard to get, kind of returning to semi-private events with a hard work on selecting who is gonna come there and with whom". Divisions of interest and purpose emerge. While there are calls for caution and withdrawal, others mobilize events and culture to reassert roots, observe religious traditions and connect with cultural heritage. In other cases, events become stages upon which drug law reform, ecological sustainability and world peace are performed. In other cases yet, secrecy and publicity are negotiable strategies, depending on event mission, management and region. With its 2010 mantra, "Make Change Happen", the Boom Festival possesses an ecological charter pressed into its design. The world's premiere psychedelic

Rainbow Serpent Festival 2009. Opening Ceremony. Photo: Jonathan Carmichael.

event is a progressive exercise in "sustainable entertainment", and yet it is also a summit of transgression. Boom, therefore, mounts, on a grand scale, the legacy of Goa's schizoid "state of mind".

As mirrors to the traveller enclave, principally Goa, psychedelic festivals attract diverse patrons, including those who are driven by an *ekstasis* which holds little concern for life after the orgy, and others who seek redress of crises in cultural practice. While some commit to "turning on" their minds and that of fellow travellers, others are bent on "wasting" theirs in orgies of excess and abandonment, reminding me of Huston Smith's (1976: 155) warning, in reference to "psychedelic theophanies", that the "religious experience" is not synonymous with the commitment to living a "religious life". But giving dramatic expression to a dynamic tension integral to countercultural history, and redolent in Goa, Boom and other festivals are also optimized efforts to broker compromises between these camps. Given the range of motivations and possible divisions, the goal of inclusivity (of unity in diversity) is a challenging task for Boom with that event enabling the coexistence of varieties of "trance" and different ideas about what is "psychedelic". Nevertheless, the festival is the stage, the laboratory, and the building-site for these optimizations. While the carnival may become a moment of sanctioned transgression, it is essentially ambivalent, indeed polyvalent, its inherent contradictions a perennial source of potentiality, of becoming. The psychedelic festival constitutes a metacultural toolkit, a congested superstore of possibilities, which is the inheritance of its native occupant, the trance freak. The Rainbow Serpent Festival opening ceremony, for example, is a unique juncture where the *carnival* (the place and time where truths are ruptured, authorities are lampooned and hierarchies inverted), and the *ceremony* (where cultural authorities are propitiated and reaffirmed), collide, where the *joie de vivre* of the festal mixes with a dutiful commitment, a convergence from which mutant forms emerge. And as at California's Symbiosis, Rainbow Serpent, and other Australian events like

Earth Frequency and Dragon Dreaming, festivals emerge with multiple genres featured on multiple stages, becoming plural temporary electronic sonicities whose seasonal operations challenge, enliven and evolve the psychedelic legacy in ways that have only been touched upon here.

Amid the hustle and hubris of the trance carnival there is a peaceful repose that you sometimes catch when you've drifted into a sea of outstretched limbs, bodies swaying like a field of sunflowers in a light breeze. And you feel intense joy in this fleeting moment. You are the moment. You are inside the flow. *You are all.* Embodying the poetry of dance, you are living evidence that *nothing lasts.* And this is a deep revelation of the mystical function of trance. It is difficult to emerge from this *little death,* because one does not want the party to end. But it must end, even so that it can recommence – so that one can return to repeat the cycle. And so, as this book must itself end, I make a parting gesture on the paramount achievement of psyculture, its parties. While Blond Peter's statement above denoted anxiety about the loss of time, it connotes acceptance of passage all the same, and perhaps even evokes attachment to impermanence, a paradox impregnating the festal culture downstream from Goa. While liminal lifestylers meld their minds and synthesize their gadgets to delay the future, and while the festival invites habitués "to be one with eternity" in the duration of the event, or over the operation of a highly optimized dance floor, it also secures departure from its own eternity. And it does so not only so that the precious cargo that has been conceived within its utopian sonicity can be delivered to the world beyond its borders, but so that its citizens can reinhabit its exuberant domain.

Notes

1. Transnational psyculture

1. Official figures for 2010. In previous years, official figures had the event attracting those from in excess of eighty countries.
2. First published in a German language edition in 2010.
3. See Elliott (2004), Greener and Hollands (2006), Lambert (2010) and Ryan (2010).
4. I later completed a doctoral dissertation in social anthropology on the festival (St John 1999).
5. Various individuals and event promoters chose not to be referred to in this book.
6. Other notable events attended included Italy's Sonica (2005 and 2007), Germany's Wonderland (2007) and Indian Spirit (2010), Israel's TAZ (2007), and the UK's The Glade festival, Synergy Project and various London squat parties (2006–2010).
7. See Gilbert and Pearson (1999), Malbon (1999), Buckland (2002), Jackson (2004), Rietveld (1998, 2004) and Hutton (2006).
8. While privileged in that my only fluent language is English, the *lingua franca* of global psytrance, this advantage dissipated in the face of the many Europeans I encountered in command of several languages.

2. Experience, the Orient and Goatrance

1. While this status may have typically derived from one's ability to select and mix fresh and exotic sonic product imported as a result of extensive international travel and an émigré lifestyle, with the advent of file-sharing networks, by 2000, the internet was facilitating virtual mobility, offering artists within electronic music genres unprecedented exposure to rich sources of fresh product – enabling the virtually experienced to establish credibility independent from the physical travail necessary to establish scene credibility in more traditional DJ cultures.
2. With *AreUpeyoted?* (1999), psychedelic ambient artist Don Peyote offered a further iteration on the theme. In another link to the earlier period, the mask-like human face with three sets of eyes and dancing hair (the Shpongle motif) featured on *Are You Shpongled?* and other albums, bears resemblance to the cover art of releases of Pink Floyd's *Relics: A Bizarre Collection of Antiques and Curios* (1971), which features a masked face with two sets of eyes.
3. And part of a vast library of bootleg reproductions circulating on the internet.

4. Peter Ziegelmeier, interviewed at Ceiba Records, Haight St, San Francisco, 27 November 2006.
5. The album demonstrates influences from Goa Gil and Arianne MacAvoy, members of Kode IV at that time.
6. *The Stoned Pig* was produced by Tarot Ray in six issues over the year 1975/76. Issues were distributed at full-moon beach parties on Anjuna beach.
7. Among whom would figure Sri Aurobindo, whose work provided the inspiration for the founding of the California Institute of Integral Studies; George Burr Leonard, who coined the term "Human Potential movement"; Michael Murphy, cofounder of the Esalen Institute in Big Sur and "Integral Transformative Practice" (with Burr Leonard); and Ken Wilber, who articulated "integral theory" and founded the Integral Institute.
8. Osho moved the ashram to Oregon in 1984. Extradited from the US for breaking immigration laws, Osho moved back to Pune in 1987, where he died in 1990. The ashram was renamed a "meditation resort" in 2000. D'Andrea elsewhere (2007b: 93) critiques the "hybrid of total institution and leisure resort" and seeks to expose the "occidental specifity of its ideology of subjectivity formation" irrelevant to Indian nationals.
9. Reproduced with permission.
10. Peter Thomas, email to the author, 14 July 2011.
11. With the mid-1980s collapse of the Panjim Bridge – which connected north Goa to Panjim, the state capital, and Dabolim, the main airport – commonly thought to have stemmed the invasion of tourists into paradise by about five years.
12. See McKay 1996; Hetherington 2000; Partridge 2006a; and St John 2009: 33–36.
13. Until it was annexed by India in 1961, then holding status as an Indian Union Territory until 1987, after which it became an independent state of India.
14. In an email (18 September 2011), Devas stated that he was uncertain about the accuracy of the name of the Raja who welcomed the Parsees to Gujarat. Regardless, he wrote that they were welcomed "with a cup of milk, signifying the land was full. The Parsees, in turn, sent the cup back, sweetened with honey and the Raja understood that, without taking up extra space, the Parsees would benefit his kingdom".
15. Karin Silenzi de Stagni, communication with the author on Facebook, 12 October 2011.
16. As documented in his unpublished autobiography (Eight Finger Eddie, n.d.). Eddie died in Goa on 18 October 2010.
17. Peter Thomas, email to the author, 14 July 2011.
18. As Steve "Madras" Devas recounted, "as is well known, The Who used Marshall amps and had begun to smash them at the end of gigs. Marshall Co. saw this as promotional, an advertising stunt, and promised them free gear if they continued the practice. Consequently, The Who had lots of spare gear on their hands" (email to the author, 11 March 2011).
19. Steve "Madras" Devas, email to the author, 11 March 2011.
20. Goa Gil, email to the author, 9 March 2011.
21. Goa Gil, email to the author, 9 March 2011.
22. Steve "Madras" Devas, email to the author, 27 March 2011. Anders's early footage of Anjuna parties offers one of the only extant collections of early 1970s lifestyle.
23. It was also the spectacular occasion where one defiant partygoer, Jasper, his body smeared with white ash and appearing like a *sadhu*, "took the birthday cake & smashed it against the wall & was thrown out" (Paoli Münchenbach, email to the author, 27 December 2011).
24. Anders Tillman, email to the author, 5 December 2011.
25. Anders Tillman, emails to the author, 21 November and 5 December 2011. Anders stated that "Jimmy the knife wasn't called like that for fun, he actually did stick his knife into people, so when he told you to not do things again, that needed to be taken

into consideration! We only got a police station in Anjuna, 1978, before that we lived pretty lawless!" Anders still performs sometimes as Missing Inka, playing for instance at the Boom Festival in 2010.

26. Paoli Münchenbach, emails to the author, 20 and 27 December 2011. From 2000 to the time of writing, M.O.C. Paoli is resident DJ at Bambuddha, Ibiza, and still plays in Goa at 9 Bar, Saturday Night Market and elsewhere. This is not intended to be a comprehensive document on early Goa DJs, but others included Zaki, an Israeli from Baga, Peggy a reggae DJ and German Blonde Thilo.
27. Motioning towards the beginnings of the trance textile fashion industry, Anders stated that afterwards "lots of us then made more copies, and brought to Europe to sell" (email to the author, 21 December 2011).
28. Steve "Madras" Devas, email to the author, 10 March 2011.
29. Steve "Madras" Devas, email to the author, 13 March 2011.
30. Steve "Madras" Devas, email to the author, 10 March 2011.
31. Goa Gil, email to the author, 9 March 2011.
32. Goa Gil, email to the author, 14 January 2011.
33. Peter Ziegelmeier, interviewed at Ceiba Records, Haight St, San Francisco, 27 November 2006.
34. Paoli Münchenbach related a story of how he had traded his collection with a friend, Josef, in Amsterdam in 1983, and later that year was invited to play a set following Cheese Cake Robert at a full-moon party at Allen Zion's house in Anjuna, only to discover that Robert was playing his music, apparently given to him by Josef. The experience precipitated his move to Afro electronic. Email to the author, 20 December 2011.
35. The Sony Walkman DAT (especially the Digital Audio Tape-Corder TCD-D3) deserves book-length treatment. Its cultural history would address, in a rewording of William Gibson, *how the beach finds a new use for things*. While beat-matching with DAT required manual dexterity, these devices and their tapes were highly transportable, enabled DJs to "dub" or edit existing material and to exchange (i.e. duplicate tape-to-tape) new releases efficiently and rapidly in the field.
36. *Goa Hippie Tribe* is a thirty-year Facebook-enabled reunion of Goa freaks directed by Steve's son Darius Devas, which was made into a self-contained interactive online documentary. See: www.sbs.com.au/goahippytribe.
37. Steve "Madras" Devas, email to the author, 27 March 2011. The quote is from Homeopathic Peter, a friend of Devas, as stated to Devas in Mussoorie later that summer.
38. Steve "Madras" Devas, email to the author, 10 March 2011.
39. Steve "Madras" Devas, email to the author, 27 March 2011.
40. Fred Disko, communication with the author on Facebook, 4 October 2011.
41. Steve "Madras" Devas, email to the author, 27 March 2011.
42. Ray Castle, interview with the author (online via Skype), 7 February 2011.
43. Gil is noted for being a great collector of new music, and Fred Disko confirmed that he always provided copious tapes to copy.
44. This article was later revised (Davis 2004).
45. Davis, who had made an expedition to Vagator in late 1993 to locate the grail of Goatrance, eventually found Laurent playing backgammon "in the last *chai* shop on little Vagator". The article characterized Laurent as a "throaty Parisian accent thickened with sarcasm ... Gaunt and bloodshot, his teeth stained and bent, the man looked like a hungry ghost". He also implied, via an unnamed source, that Laurent may be an "unrepentant leach", inquiring, "could this sarcastic wraith gambling for pennies in a burned-out shack be the father of raves?" (Davis 1995). Laurent took offence, later

claiming the interview was illegitimate and that the article's author "was very lucky to manage to get out of Vagator with his recorder!" (Laurent 2010).

46. Anders Tillman, email to the author, 21 December 2011.
47. The device replaced Disko's 1981 Sharp GF-555 twin cassette player which was stolen from his house during monsoon 1981. Fred Disko, communication with the author on Facebook, 4 October 2011.
48. Fred Disko, communication with the author on Facebook, 4 October 2011.
49. As Laurent wrote, a couple of months after he arrived in Goa in 1984, "my girlfriend had some problems and we lost all plane tickets and money was all gone! So I could not leave anymore, and spent many seasons and monsoons doing what i liked ... playing music at parties! But I NEVER earned a single cent out of this activity and we were living on my girlfriend's flea market sales and I became a gambler, having to play backgammon for a living" (Laurent 2010).
50. Johann Bley, communication with the author on Facebook, 1 April 2011.
51. Anders Tillman, email to the author, 21 November 2011.
52. As I have little background in ethnomusicology, these observations are limited. For a study of the musicological influences and structuring of Goatrance, see Aittoniemi 2012.
53. Various mixes of this track featured the crashing surf at either end of the track, strategically designed for mixing from DAT on the beaches of Goa.
54. Included among what could be a very long list are Tsuyoshi Suzuki (member of Prana and founder of Matsuri Records), Ray Castle (Pagan Production, and member of Insectoid and Masaray), Jan Müller and Marcus C. Maichel (X-Dream), Mark Allen (member of Mindfield and owner of Phantasm Records), James Monro (member of Technossomy and co-founder of Flying Rhino Records), Ben Watkins (Juno Reactor), Kalle Pakkala (member of GAD and owner of Finland's Exogenic Records), Chris Deckker (member of Medicine Drum, founder of Return To The Source label/club, and founder of Earthdance), Avi Nissim, Lior Perlmutter and Yaniv Haviv (members of Israel's Astral Projection and founders of the label Trust in Trance), and Olli Wisdom (aka Space Tribe and organizer of the Saga parties).
55. According to Nik Sequenci (communication with the author on Facebook, 3 February 2011), Raja Ram "was given his name at an ashram in the 60s because of his flute playing abilities. They said that when Raj plays the flute Krishna enters him and plays the flute through him. And 'Raja Ram' in Hindi means 'King of Kings'. And that's Krishna".
56. Raja Ram, email to the author, 16 November 2010.
57. Raja Ram, email to the author, 13 November 2010.
58. Before forming label TIP Records (with Woods, Ian St Paul and Richard Bloor), and the groups Shpongle (with Posford) and 1200 Micrograms (with Ricktam and Banzi of GMS, and Chicago). TIP Records operated from 1994–1998 before collapsing. With Bloor, Rothfield then started the label TIP.World in 1999. With TIP, Raja Ram has produced and released over 100 CDs.
59. Another former Ozric Tentacles member, bass player, Zia Geelani, would form electronic outfit Zubzub (which also includes ex-Ozric Tentacle Jon Egan), signed on Mesmobeat, the label formed by Eat Static.
60. Ray Castle entry at *Fusion Anomaly*: http://fusionanomaly.net/raycastle.html (accessed 23 May 2010).
61. *Mushroom Magazine* was initiated by Hamburg artist Matt Mushroom, first distributed as a photocopied four-page party planner in May 1994 in Hamburg, Hannover and Bremen, initially to promote the Mushroom club (now 50,000 printed bimonthly with German and English content).

62. Olsen had, by that stage, released the masterful percussive Goa remix (and one of Third Eye's final tracks) "Dying (Hard)" (released on *Psy-Harmonics Volume One*, 1994). Olsen would become known as an uncompromising experimentalist and his significant role in the Australian scene is evident, for example, on *Psy-Harmonics Volume 3* (1996), where he had a hand, via different outfits and aliases, in co/ producing almost every track.
63. Phantasm was a Goatrance label established in 1993 by John Ford and the late Simon Carman.
64. B, email to the author, 10 January 2012.
65. A raid took place, for example, on a party in Pune in March 2007, when all 280 guests were arrested and brutally beaten by police. An album, *Ahimsa* (meaning non-violence in Sanskrit), was released in 2008 with tracks compiled by Daksinamutri & Friends, Dacru Records and Rudraksh Records. The promotion states that tracks were "donated as an act of solidarity by the artists and all the profit of this release will be donated to Human Rights Watch in India, and to the Gandhian village at Sevapur in Tamil Nadu".
66. Who were responsible for the largest LSD production and supply network in history.
67. Fred Disko, communication with the author on Facebook, 3 October 2011.
68. Ray Castle, email to the author, 7 March 2011.
69. The ideas of Ram Dass were much later broadcast with the assistance of DJ Kriece, who incorporated spoken word material on *Cosmix* (Ram Dass & Kriece, 2008).
70. Raja Ram, email to the author, 16 November 2010.
71. EFS ran events at other London venues, and consistent with its traveller sensibility, also hosted club events in locations worldwide, including Kassel, Melbourne, Paris, Prague, Athens, on mountaintops in Wales and Israel, in addition to a "travel club" organizing trips to the Sahara.
72. In 1992, France's Gaïa festival also took place for the first time.
73. As reported on the *Antaris Project* DVD (Antaris Project and Psynema, 2009).
74. Brad Olsen is founder of CCC Publishing, his first book being the travel manifesto *World Stompers: A Global Travel Manifesto* (Olsen 2001).
75. Interview with Brad "Santosh" Olsen, San Francisco, 27 November 2006.
76. Interview with Will Gregory, The People's Café, Haight-Ashbury, 28 November 2006.
77. David Bleach, email to the author, 7 October 2011.
78. The Sri Hari albums were a major success, with proceeds from the 250,000 copies sold going to the Hare Krishna capital Mayapur in West Bengal, according to Ian Ion (email to the author, 30 March 2012).
79. Funds have been routinely necessary in order to "tip" police – i.e., pay *baksheesh*, customary to party organization in "contact zones" where protection rackets are par for the course.
80. http://www.intothevortex.co.za/about (accessed 28 June 2012).
81. "Spirit of Goa", *Mushroom Magazine* 120 (June 2005): 22–23.

3. The vibe at the end of the world

1. The second "mad" figure alluded to in the track title is Charles Manson, who is also cited: "We have fires, and we play music. And we make big circles, like you do with the stones, we make big circles and we sing. And we put our souls in each other! Maybe that's what you call Satan."
2. The self-exile is also a political exile, in the sense that tobias c. van Veen (2010) has outlined for rave. As a "desertion from acceptable modes of collective and individual responsibility" and a participatory "absence of signs", rave's "passage through exodus enacts a defection or disappearance from politics (and its logic of representation) to the

political" (van Veen 2010: 42, 41), which, in the dissolution of the distinction between labour and leisure, is recognized as a space of potential.

3. http://www.ektoplazm.com/about (accessed 9 March 2010).
4. Following linguist David Dalby, Leland traces "hip", and thus "hippie", to the Wolof language of slaves from the West African nations of Senegal and coastal Gambia among whom *hipi* meant "to open one's eyes". Additionally *jive* is rooted in *jev*, meaning "to disparage or talk falsely", and *dig is* rooted in *dega*, "to understand" (see Leland 2004: 5–6).
5. "The Principle of Vibration" paraphrases from the "7 Hermetic Principles" in *The Kybalion: Hermetic Philosophy*, which was published anonymously in 1908 (by a group or person under the pseudonym of "the Three Initiates") claiming to be the essence of the teachings of Hermes Trismegistus.
6. This sign and its syllable is pervasive in Goatrance; indeed it is the axiomatic symbol of "Goa" mysticism, with ॐ becoming the Eastern "peace" sign – a symbol not so much of the desire for peace, but of an escape from the cycle of war and peace, just as the yogic path is a demonstrable effort to become liberated from *samsara* (the cycle of birth and rebirth).
7. For cultural histories of raving in various world locations see McKay 1996, 1998; Silcott 1999; and St John 2001b.
8. The DAT has been Gil's instrument of choice since he used the Sony D3 model (produced in 1991).
9. Swami Chaitanya, interviewed in San Francisco, 19 November 2006.
10. While Gil informed me by email on 24 November 2010 that he had "no idea" how many twenty-four-hour events he has played (or rituals he has performed), my guestimate is about 500 (though the number of events at which he has DJed will be considerably more).
11. Michael McAteer (2002: 25) adds insight, stating that Goa Gil "held the seat of his deceased guru within the compound of the *Juna Akara* in the 2001 *Maha Kumbha Mela*. The Juna Akara is the largest brotherhood of *sadhus* in India, particularly known for their fearsome roughness. The fact of Gil's holding the seat of his guru at the *Maha Kumbha Mela* is testament to his sanctioned status within the traditional Hindu world".
12. Along with Vasudev Puri, and Baba Rampuri, the author of *Baba: Autobiography of a Blue-Eyed Yogi* (2005).
13. Goa Gil, email to the author, 6 January 2011.
14. Goa Gil, email to the author, 6 January 2011.
15. A transcript from a speech by President Dwight D. Eisenhower at the Republican National Convention on 23 August 1956.
16. Whose full name is Swami Chaitanya Visvakarma Brahmacharya.
17. Swami Chaitanya, interviewed in San Francisco, 19 November 2006.
18. Swami Chaitanya, email to the author, 18 December 2010.
19. Swami Chaitanya, interviewed in San Francisco, 19 November 2006.
20. Swami Chaitanya, interviewed in San Francisco, 19 November 2006.
21. Divine Dozen: http://www.goagil.com/chart.html (accessed 10 March 2011).
22. Mark Petrick (aka Xenomorph), email to the author, 15 November 2010.
23. The EP is included on Gil's first Divine Dozen listed online.
24. Their first track released (on *Spiritual Trance Vol. 2*, 1995), "Po Tolo" (the Dogon name for the star Sirius B), features the sample "we have watched the skies and waited", along with what Gil informed me are samples from a Dogon death ceremony. Goa Gil, email to the author, 10 May 2009.
25. Since October 2004, Gil and Ariane have kept a vast archive of photographs and video mostly shot from Gils' DJ-position. See www.goagil.com/photogallery. For examples of Gil and Ariane's videos see Gil-vision (2005, 2007).

26. Chiara Baldini, email to the author, 10 March 2011.
27. Ray Castle, email to the author, 12 November 2010; Ray Castle, interview with the author (online via Skype), 7 February 2011.
28. Time Wave Zero (aka Tina) in an *Isratrance* forum posting (Time Wave Zero, 2007) about her film interview of Goa Gil (Time Wave Zero, 2006). See thread, "Video Interview with GOA GIL", at http://forum.isratrance.com/video-interview-with-goa-gil (accessed 10 March 2011).
29. Ray Castle, interview with the author (online via Skype), 7 February 2011.
30. Ray Castle, interview with the author (online via Skype), 7 February 2011.
31. Ray Castle, interview with the author (online via Skype), 7 February 2011.
32. Ray Castle, communication with the author on Facebook, 12 October 2011.
33. Not exclusively, since Ariane also performs.
34. Ray Castle, interview with the author (online via Skype), 7 February 2011.

4. Spiritual technology: transition and its prosthetics

1. See Beck 1992; Beck, Giddens and Lash 1994; Bauman 2000, 2006; and Hopper 2007.
2. In a common strategy, Amerindians have been appropriated and remixed in the interests of attaining at-one-ment (see St John 2013b).
3. MDPV (methylenedioxypyrovalerone) has many street names, including "super coke" and "poison".
4. From "Re: Evolution", http://www.deoxy.org/t_re-evo.htm (accessed 19 December 2010).
5. Such stories would include "Timewave Zero", the theory of accelerating novelty towards a magnetic Eschaton (in 2012) prophesied by McKenna with the assistance of tryptamines. See "New Maps of Hyperspace" (in McKenna 1991a: 90–102).
6. Michael Winkelman (see 2000) has referred to such states derivative of an "integrative mode of consciousness" which is at base neurobiological.
7. The sample is from Multiman's "Transition" (DJ Boom Shankar, *Transition*, 2011) and comes from a late 1980s lecture.
8. Produced in 1995 though first released in 2011 on the 2-CD collection *Mind Rewind* (DAT Mafia Recordings), compiled by members of the Discogs Goa Forum and hosting mainly unreleased Goa tracks donated by the artists from DAT.
9. With its distinctive curved enclosures, Blue Room Pod speakers included the Housepod and Technopod – the latter, for example, incorporated in a sound system for the Escape Club in Brighton.
10. Simon Ghahary, interviewed (online via Skype), 24 January 2012.
11. John-Paris McKenzie, interviewed at Soulclipse, Turkey, 29 March 2006.
12. The mood of cultural genesis is apparent on the album cover which featured a pod hatching a double helix pattern. Also, the cover of Psychopod's debut *Dreampod* (TIP Records, 1996) featured a purple globe which has split open to reveal an intense white ball of energy.
13. Including phenethylamines like 2CB, 2CT7 and DOC synthesized by Alexander Shulgin, author, with Ann Shulgin, of *Pihkal* (1991) and *Tihkal* (1997).
14. See Hutson 1999, 2000; Sylvan 2002, 2005; Takahashi 2004, 2005; and for "digital shaman" see D'Andrea 2007a: 211.
15. See Chapter 5 for further comments on shrines and altars.
16. Megan Young, email to the author, 5 March 2009.
17. http://www.subconsciousmind.ch/backgrounds (accessed 19 June 2010).
18. Raja Ram, email to the author, 13 November 2010.

19. Ayahuasca, or *yagé*, refers to psychoactive infusions or decoctions prepared from the *Banisteriopsis Caapi* vine typically mixed with the leaves of dimethyltryptamine (DMT)-containing species.
20. Adam Scott Miller, communication with the author on Facebook, 24 October 2011.
21. Invented in Australia, *changa* is described as "revolutionary plant alchemy ... a smoking mixture which contains Ayahuasca vine and/or leaf, an intelligent combination of several admixture herbs and naturally sourced DMT that has been infused into those herbs" (Palmer 2011/12: 98). These herbs include mullein, peppermint, calendula, blue lotus and passionflower, the latter being a MAO inhibitor rendering the experience like a "smokable ayahuasca" (Hanna 2008).
22. The detailed story about how DMT impacted Goatrance through the interventions of Nik Sequenci – an English DJ and promoter who played ambient music on McKenna's lecture tours in the early 1990s – shaping the art of Youth, Posford, Raja Ram, Olli and Miki Wisdom, Mr C (from The Shamen) and many others, will be recounted in my forthcoming book currently in preparation: *Mystery School in Hyperspace: A Cultural History of DMT.*
23. The Whole Earth image would become the logo for Earth Day and was depicted inside a pair of caring hands by Friends of the Earth. A 1967 satellite photo of the Earth was obtained from NASA by Stewart Brand and famously reproduced on the cover of the Fall 1968 issue of the *Whole Earth Catalog.*

5. Psychedelic festivals, visionary arts and cosmic events

1. www.boomfestival.org (accessed 9 June 2008).
2. www.chilluminati.org (accessed 19 December 2010).
3. Who were influenced by John Cage's interactive artistic "happening" (F. Turner 2006: 49), and who collaborated with Leary and co. in their Psychedelic Theatre (see Dass and Metzner 2010: 125).
4. The CCC parties were preceded by the Russ Street warehouse (which later became Blue Room America's HQ) which involved those associated with Mr Floppy's psychedelic party crew.
5. Anders Tillman, email to the author, 5 December 2011. See also http://avikal-installations.blogspot.com
6. Simon Ghahary, interviewed (online via Skype), 24 January 2012.
7. See Fritz 1999; Landau 2004; Lynch and Badger 2006; St John 2006.
8. Nikki Lastreto, email to author, 18 December 2010.
9. Nikki Lastreto, interviewed in San Francisco, 19 November 2006.
10. Mari Kundalini, email to the author, 25 October 2011.
11. www.morninglory.co.il (accessed 20 October 2008, no longer live).
12. Correspondence with Chiara Baldini led to some of these insights (see St John and Baldini 2012).
13. In 1995, co-founder Larry Harvey penned a pseudonymous article published in *Gnosis* magazine in which he drew comparison with Eleusis, as noted by Davis (2005). That there is no official interpretation of Burning Man's eponymous moment possesses an effect analogous to a blanket prohibition on disclosing the mysteries since it recognizes that the experience is unique to each individual and cannot be mediated.
14. "Letters for Boomers", 11 September 2010, http://www.facebook.com/notes/boom-festival/letters-for-boomers/427419849316 (accessed 19 December 2010).
15. The other day programs were: Frontiers of Time and Space, Frontiers of Art, Frontiers of the Body, Frontiers of Love, Frontiers of Evolution and Frontiers of Behaviour.

16. For previous discussions of "ultimate concerns" expressed within alternative festivals see Lewis and Dowsey-Magog 1993 and St John 2001a.
17. Wripple confirmed this influence (which also evokes Leary) stating that the space emerged from interest in "how psychedelics model the death experience, and the role of such imaginative and energetic encounters in psychedelic spirituality". Naasko Wripple, interviewed at Boom Festival, 30 July 2006.
18. "Transmissions from the Edge", boomfestival.org (accessed 9 February 2007).
19. Among those ideas was Di Bernardo's Dark Prisma Records release *The Void – Disintegration* (2008), as discussed in Chapter 4.
20. Reproduced with permission.
21. Pedro Barros, interviewed at Boom, 1 August 2006.
22. Boom's 2010 message, worn on all patron wristbands, was in fact "Be The Change".
23. Michael Christian's Keynote was first displayed at Burning Man in 2009.
24. A piece he transported to events around the world in 2006, including Soulclipse, Sunrise Celebration, The Glade, Boom and Burning Man. I saw him with this piece at all of these events.
25. Kynan Bolger, communication with the author on Facebook, 11 October 2011.
26. Reproduced with permission.
27. Ray Castle, interviewed (online via Skype), 7 February 2010.
28. The path of totality is chased and championed by diverse parties for diverse causes. Included among them are scientists and spiritualist, tourists and travellers, pilgrims and party-makers.
29. Although, on one incidence (Solipse 1999 at Ozora in Hungary), an eclipse has inspired an annual festival (Ozora) held on the original site, which is sacralized by its participants.
30. So named after a total eclipse there in 1900.
31. Nick Ladd, interview with the author, near Glastonbury, 3 June 2006.
32. A documentary film (Lastlight Films, 2003) featuring dramatic voxpops of awe-animated eclipse viewers immediately post-event offers excellent insight on the experience.
33. At the time of writing, the next total-eclipse festival will be staged near Cairns, Australia, in November 2012.
34. Ray Castle, interview with the author (online via Skype), 7 February 2010.
35. Nick Ladd, interview with the author, near Glastonbury, 3 June 2006.
36. Marty, interviewed at Soulclipse, Turkey, 31 March 2006.
37. The Sun's distance from the Earth is about 400 times the moon's distance, and the Sun's diameter is about 400 times the moon's diameter. Because these ratios are approximately the same, the Sun and the moon as seen from Earth appear to be approximately the same size. As the blurb on *Caribbean Eclipse* (1999) pointed out, that we can make perfect observation of the Sun's corona is a "rare spatial synchronicity" in our solar system.
38. http://www.crossroads.wild.net.au/index.html (accessed 17 March 2011).
39. Stephan Waldner, communication with the author on Facebook, 14 September 2011.
40. Marty, interviewed at Soulclipse, Turkey, 31 March 2006.

6. Freak out: the trance carnival

1. A book could be produced on the various musics that have echoed and augmented the experience. Member of The Orb Martin Glover was crucial to the infusion of ambient dub in psychedelia, having launched the down-tempo label Liquid Sound Design in 1998 (a sub-label of his Dragonfly Records). Ambient-orientated musics (performed in chill/ambient stages at events) were integral to cosmic trance, a development more

than apparent in trance-fusion act Star Sounds Orchestra, whose debut *Planets* (1991), featured tracks named after all the planets in our galaxy.

2. See *We Call it Techno! A Documentary about Germany's Early Techno Scene and Culture*, by Maren Sextro and Holger Wick (2008).
3. As reported on the *Antaris Project* DVD (Antaris Project and Psynema, 2009), which promotes a connection between the pioneering efforts of aviator Otto Lilienthal and his quest for "freedom" in flight with the Antaris festival now held at the site of the original Otto Lilienthal airport in the region where the "first flying man" made his successful gliding flights between 1893–96.
4. Many thanks to Ray Castle and Jenya Nesmeyanov for insights here.
5. Ray Castle, communication with the author on Facebook, 18 September 2011.
6. Pete Black, communication with the author on Facebook, 14 September 2011.
7. Cosmica, communication with the author on Facebook, 29 September 2011.
8. Becca Dakini, communication with the author on Facebook, 11 October 2011.
9. Jasmine Gelenbe, communication with the author on Facebook, 21 September 2011.
10. The dynamic of novelty and stasis is apparent in German author and activist Wolfgang Sterneck's dictum of "Rhythm and Change", www.sterneck.net (accessed 12 September 2011).
11. Raphael Huber (aka SubConsciousMind), email to the author, 1 June 2011.
12. While their "catch" amazed onlookers, the fish they "caught" lay dead in a bucket at the base of a hole dug the previous night and covered over. Mouse, communication with the author on Facebook, 12 October 2011.
13. Mouse, communication with the author on Facebook, 12 October 2011.
14. The orgasmic synth rush has been a feature of Goatrance from its inception, with, for instance, Man With No Name dropping an epic-erotic male "hmmmmmmmmm, yesss" sample in the build of "Floor-Essence" (*Floor-Essence* EP, 1995).
15. The dense detail in the undergrowth of this forest funk is reminiscent of the iconoclastic style also prominent in Australia and New Zealand. An early instance of this was Fin PeLinPaLa's (Tommi Sirkiä) release *My CD Has Landed on My Next Door Neighbour's Dog* (2000) on the Australian label Demon Tea Recordings.
16. Not to be confused with the subgenre of trance referred to as "neotrance".
17. Cohen (2008: 101) outlines two different varieties of spirit possession: "one that entails the transformation or replacement of identity (executive possession) and one that envisages possessing spirits as (the cause of) illness and misfortune (pathogenic possession)".
18. See Lewis 1971; Keller 2001; Friedson 2005; and Jankowski 2007.
19. See Sylvan 2002; Tramacchi 2004; Takahashi 2005; Papadimitropoulos 2009; and Till 2009.
20. The SFX track "Oxygene" is a remix of Jean Michel Jarre's "Oxygène Part IV".

7. Psyculture in Israel and Australia

1. As reported in statistics gathered on the online database Psychedelic Mind Expander (http://www.psydb.net/stats) (accessed 3 July 2011).
2. The self-identification of Israeli psytrance enthusiasts (Schmidt 2011).
3. Some Israeli Goa artists, notably MFG (Message From God), have themselves quite evidently pursued a nouveau-religious mission.
4. This harrowing, often temporary, exodus, is portrayed in Yoav Shamir's 2007 documentary *Flipping Out: Israel's Drug Generation*.
5. See "History of Goa/PsyTrance" at: http://www.virtualdj.com/forums/57910/Music_discussion/History_of_Goa_PsyTrance.html (accessed 24 June 2010).

6. Mixing the darbuka with a "laser kick", the epic uplifting style was pioneered by Eyal Barkan, who, in 1998, released *Good Morning Israel*, the first trance album to achieve gold status in Israel (20,000 sales). The super-arpeggio brothers Barkan and Holly (Avi) Shwartz (Holy Men) teamed up to compile the popular *Over the Sunrise* (1998).
7. Joshua Schmidt, email to the author, 6 May 2009.
8. Events in Brazil, such as São Paulo's Respect Festival, which in 2008 was themed "Psychedelic Sixties", also demonstrate investment in this period of cultural transformation.
9. In his early guise as Doctor Acid, Avi Shwartz released a eponymously titled album, *Doctor Acid* (1996), which includes the track "January 22 (Dead)" and the following statement in the cover notes: "In 1996, January 22 is dedicated to all those who lost their lives in a terrorist attack at Beit-Leid Junction ... Rest in peace".
10. Which was already apparent in the earlier incarnation of Astral Projection: SFX.
11. Interview with Alae, 12 September 2007, Holy Rave, Israel.
12. Although Disko had arrived in Australia in 1988, and had played a couple of private warehouse parties and in 1989 played at the Rainbow Temple near Byron where he was forced to stop after two hours because the audience wanted to hear reggae, he regards the Munster Terrace event as his first genuine party. Fred Disko, communication with the author on Facebook, 10 October 2011.
13. Described as "a noughties version of Ken Kesey's Merry Pranksters meets a Russian Revolution propaganda train meets Priscilla, Queen of the Desert!" (Murray 2001: 67), Earthdream is a technomadic and reconciliatory project scheduled to conclude on 21 December 2012, in accordance with a galactic alignment predicted in the Mayan Calendar. For further details on the series of events known as Earthdream2000, see Cooke (2001) and St John (2005b, 2009: 189–93, 241–52).
14. For a detailed survey of Australian electronica before 1999 – including synthpop, house, techno, trance, psychedelic, breakbeat, ambient, and experimental – see Cole 1999: 228–66.
15. Who had co-authored an article on Goatrance (Cole and Hannan 1997).
16. David Bleach, email to the author, 7 October 2011.
17. See Paul Chambers's 2009 documentary *Beyond the Brain – The Movie*: http://www.youtube.com/watch?v=ZO4E3wouZpA.
18. For further insight on doof, see St John (2001c, 2009: ch. 7).
19. As did the name for UK artist Nick Barber: Doof.
20. Ray Castle, communication with the author on Facebook, 13 October 2007.
21. Eamon Jungle Wyss, email to the author, 27 October 2011.
22. Bicycle Day is an international day of celebration marking the day, 19 April 1943, when Albert Hofmann, having accidentally absorbed LSD-25 during experiments in his laboratory at Sandoz, Basel, bicycled home under the influences of his "first trip".
23. Anonymous comments at http://forums.thescene.com.au, posted 12 March 2008 (page no longer live). These complaints came despite the festival meeting with and obtaining approvals from the shire, the Country Fire Authority, regional health services and Victoria Police, providing chemical-free toilets, meeting Environmental Protection Authority regulations for decibel levels, accredited Waste Wise by the EPA, and using bio-diesel for festival power. Also, there was no reported fight, drug- or alcohol-related incident, or major first-aid incident (according to Maitreya Festival, 20 March 2008, posted to the same forum).
24. Lachlan Bell, communication with the author on Facebook, 3 June 2012.
25. Interview with Ben Hardwick, Melbourne, 13 June 2003.
26. Interview with John-Paris McKenzie, Soulclipse, Turkey, 29 March 2006.
27. Interview with John-Paris McKenzie, Soulclipse, Turkey, 29 March 2006.

28. By the end of the 2000s, the local DMT blend, *changa*, inspired further blends like *nanga*, also called *aussiehuasca*, which contains DMT from *Acacia* and Peruvian *B. caapi* vine shavings.
29. Krusty, email to the author, 21 September 2011.
30. Comparison of romanticist fictions and appropriative strategies across psytrance scenes in settler societies would prove instructive.
31. For instance, on Ganga Giri's *Raising it Up* (2006), Kamilaroy Songman Gumaroy performs on "Thigarra Yugal" (the "Emu Song"), and on the final track "Nature Spirit", "one of the world's leading traditional indigenous dancers and didgeridoo players", Turtle, sings about the "dreaming of fire" – most relevant to Ganga Giri since his house burnt down in 2005.
32. Glenn Armstrong, email to the author, 2 March 2009.
33. Glenn Armstrong, email to the author, 1 April 2009.
34. Ben Dixon, email to the author, 17 February 2009.
35. The song was released in 1997 by trio Judith Durham (The Seekers), Russell Hitchcock (Air Supply) and Yothu Yindi's Mandawuy Yunupingu.
36. The CFA have had a long-standing presence at the festival, a connection which has enabled the festival to establish a good relationship with the local community.

8. Performing risk and the arts of consciousness

1. For example, Rinehart and Sydnor 2003; Laviolette 2007; McNamee 2007; and Laurendeau 2008.
2. In an extensive study (300 interviews), it was found that EDM enthusiasts recognize that by contrast to the prevalence of official appeals to the hazards and dangers associated with dance events and drugs, and despite repressive legislation (i.e. the US "RAVE Act"), enthusiasts often view the use of illicit drugs as normal, positive and pleasurable.
3. As conveyed on the now defunct psyreviews.net.
4. Alex "dreamdust", email to the author, 6 January 2009.
5. See Takahashi 2004: 151 and also Saunders and Doblin 1996; Saunders, Saunders and Pauli 2000; and Fritz 1999.
6. For example, see Kavanaugh and Anderson 2008; Anderson 2009; and D'Andrea 2010.
7. The designation was applied by Jeff Laster at the Future of Alternative Clubbing Symposium, 30 March 2007. Online video recording at: http://www.gunghomedia.co.uk/symposium (accessed 3 August 2007).
8. Alongside many others. See: http://en.wikipedia.org/wiki/Megatripolis (accessed 21 October 2011).
9. See: http://www.earthdancenetwork.com/notes/Earthdance_Global_Festival_for_Peace_2011 (accessed 21 September 2011).
10. On the mammoth double-CD compilation *The Chakra Journey* (1996), it was explained, "the power of ritual is the power of focused intent. So on the dance floor let us focus our intent together to co-create a collective field of love. Sending out that love for the highest good of all".
11. Ben Dixon, email to the author, 31 May 2008.
12. Notable in this tradition is the ambient work of Bill Laswell, such as his collaboration with Toshinori Kondo, *Life Space Death* (2001), which remixes meditations spoken by the Dalai Lama.
13. Acceptance is also afforded through legitimate (meeting permit and licensing requirements) and unofficial means (e.g. where promoters pay "baksheesh" to police and other local officials).
14. Sabrina Acquaviva, communication with the author on Facebook, 22 September 2011.

9. Riot of passage: liminal culture and the logics of sacrifice

1. It also has a heroic side (see St John 2008a).
2. See Malbon 1999; Gauthier 2004a, 2004b, 2005; Sylvan 2005: 101–2; and Jaimangal-Jones *et al.* 2010.
3. See Wyn and White 1997; Furlong and Cartmel 2006; and Henderson *et al.* 2007.
4. Sampled on The Shamen's "Re: Evolution" (*Re: Evolution*, 1993).
5. See Fikentscher 2000; Taylor 2001; Sommer 2001/2002: 73; Siokou 2002; Takahashi and Olaveson 2003: 81; Olaveson 2004: 90; Gerard 2004: 178–9; Rill 2006; St John 2008b.
6. Sjoerd Los, communication with the author on Facebook, 24 September 2011.
7. Which, at Boom, may be treated by volunteers and staff associated with MAPS.
8. The following data is taken from these newsletters.
9. Ben Hardwick, interviewed in Melbourne, Australia, 13 June 2003.
10. Alan Bamford, interviewed in Melbourne, Australia, 16 June 2003.
11. Alan Bamford, interviewed in Melbourne, Australia, 16 June 2003.
12. Paul Abad, interviewed in Melbourne, Australia, 12 June 2003.
13. Paul Abad, interviewed at Positronic, Belthorpe, Queensland, Australia, 13 December 2003.
14. The sustainable ethos filters through to music production. Take for instance the Sydney label and event management organization REGEN (who operate the annual Regrowth Festival in the Southern Tablelands of NSW) who have displayed meticulous attention to sustainable production methods.
15. From http://www.flickr.com/photos/webgrrl/2257490425 (accessed 1 February 2010).
16. Kwali, interviewed at Boom Festival, Portugal, 2 August 2006.
17. It appears that while Sonica were reliant on last-minute financing that such corporate sponsorship provided, Duracell were responding to the mounting dangers of obsolescence in a period and amongst youth cultures embracing rechargeable energy alternatives in a range of devices from digital media players to palmtop computers and cell phones, not to mention threats from self-powered (i.e. shakelights, dynamos, solar-powered) flashlights, in use among psytrance populations and sold by festival stall holders.
18. www.kundaliniuk.com (accessed 22 November 2008).
19. For Glastonbury, see McKay 2000. For Australia's ConFest, see St John 2001e. While originally relegated to "ghetto"-ization, EDMC is nowadays pervasive at Burning Man (see Jones 2011), a sonicity approximate to a hyper-rave (see St John 2009).
20. SubConsciousMind, email to the author, 4 June 2011.

10. Nothing lasts

1. Ray Castle, email to the author, 12 November 2010.

Bibliography, discography and filmography

Bibliography

Agamben, Giorgio. 1998. *Homo Sacer: Sovereign Power and Bare Life.* Stanford, CA: Stanford University Press.

Ainley, Mark. 2011. "DJ Solitare – The Future Was Now". http://goatranch.com/2011/05/02/dj-solitare-the-future-was-now (accessed 6 June 2012).

Aittoniemi, Toni. 2012. "Cultural and Musical Dimensions of Goa Trance and Early Psychedelic Trance in Finland: The History, Translation and Localization of an Internationally Mobile Electronic Dance-Music Scene". MA thesis. University of Helsinki, Faculty of Arts, Department of Philosophy, History, Culture and Art Studies.

ak3. 2008. "Interview with Megalopsy". http://www.isratrance.com/interviews/megalopsy-i60.html (accessed 6 June 2012).

Ambrose, Joe. 2001. *Moshpit: The Violent World of Mosh Pit Culture.* London: Omnibus.

Anderson, Tammy L. 2009. *Rave Culture: The Alteration and Decline of a Philadelphia Music Scene.* Philadelphia, PA: Temple University Press.

Antara, L. and N. Kaye. 1999. "Connected Consciousness in Motion: The Power of Ceremony for Creating Positive Social Change". In Twist, C. (ed.), *Guerillas of Harmony: Communiques From the Dance Underground*, pp. 100–106. Tribal Donut.

Anton Shoom and DJ Shishya. 2008. "Psychedelic Pagans in Lithuania". 25 November. http://www.chaishop.com/article/1248 (accessed 21 November 2009).

Anton Shoom and Unitone. 2009. "Uniting the Scenes". *Psychedelic Traveller* 2009: 14.

Anton Wilson, Robert. 1983. *Prometheus Rising.* Tempe, AZ: New Falcon Publications.

Apollo. 2001. "House music 101". http://www.livingart.com/raving/articles/housemusic101.htm (accessed 6 June 2012).

Appadurai, Arjun. 1996. *Modernity at Large: Cultural Dimensions of Globalization.* Minneapolis, MN: University of Minnesota Press.

Argüelles, José. 1987. *The Mayan Factor: Path Beyond Technology.* Santa Fe, CA: Bear and Company.

Arnold, Nicholas. 1997. "Come and Expel the Green Pain: The Shamanic and the Ecstatic Features of Trance-Dance in Rave Culture". *Contemporary Drama in English* 5: 185–98. Wissenschaftlicher Verlag Trier.

astralseeker. 2007. Post to "The Problem with Psytrance" thread on isratrance.com: http://forum.isratrance.com/the-problem-with-psytrance-warning-it-s-a-long-post/page4/ (accessed 6 June 2012).

Austin, Clive. 1998. "On Fusion Anomaly". http://fusionanomaly.net/trance.html (accessed 18 October 2011).

Bakhtin, Mikhail. 1968 [1944]. *Rabelais and His World*. London: MIT Press.

Baldini, Chiara. 2010a. "Shiva and Dionysus". http://www.boomfestival.org/boom2010/2010/05/shiva-and-dionysus (accessed 10 March 2011).

—. 2010b. "Dionysus Returns: Contemporary Tuscan Trancers and Euripides' *The Bacchae*". In Graham St John (ed.), *The Local Scenes and Global Culture of Psytrance*, pp. 170–85. New York: Routledge.

Bardella, Claudio. 2002. "Pilgrimages of the Plagued: AIDs, Body and Society". *Body & Society* 8(2): 79–105.

Basilisk. 2008. "Progressive Chart: October 2008" (19 October). http://www.ektoplazm.com/2008/progressive-chart-october-2008 (accessed 14 November 2010).

Bastide, Rodger. 1975. *Le sacré sauvage et autres essais*. Paris: Stock.

Bataille, Georges. 1985. *Visions of Excess*. Trans. A. Stoekl, C.L. Lovitt and D.M. Leslie. Manchester: Manchester University Press.

—. 1989 [1967]. *The Accursed Share: An Essay on General Economy. Vol. I Consumption*. Trans. Robert Hurley. New York: Zone.

—. 1993 [1967]. *The Accursed Share: An Essay on General Economy. Vol. II (The History of Eroticism) & III (Sovereignty)*. Trans. Robert Hurley. New York: Zone.

Bauman, Zygmunt. 2000. *Liquid Modernity*. Cambridge: Polity.

—. 2006. *Liquid Times: Living in an Age of Uncertainty*. Cambridge: Cambridge University Press.

Beck, Giles and Gordon Lynch. 2009. "'We Are All One, We Are All Gods': Negotiating Spirituality in the Conscious Partying Movement". *Journal of Contemporary Religion* 24(3): 339–55.

Beck, Ulrich. 1992. *Risk Society: Towards a New Modernity*. London: Sage.

Beck, Ulrich, Anthony Giddens and Scott Lash. 1994. *Reflexive Modernization: Politics, Tradition and Aesthetics in the Modern Social Order*. Cambridge: Polity Press.

Beck, Ulrich and Edgar Grande. 2010. "Varieties of Second Modernity: The Cosmopolitan Turn in Social and Political Theory and Research". *British Journal of Sociology* 61(3): 409–43.

Belasco, Daniel. n.d. "Land of the Rave". http://www.paulrodgers9w.com/belasco.htm (accessed 15 October 2007, page no longer live).

Bell, Catherine. 1997. *Ritual: Perspectives and Dimensions*. New York: Oxford University Press.

Bennett, Andy. 1999. "Subcultures or Neo-Tribes? Rethinking the Relationship between Youth, Style and Musical Taste". *Sociology* 33(3): 599–617.

Bennett, Rob. 2007. "Some Thoughts on No-Thought". http://www.sterneck.net/ritual/bennett-trance/index.php (accessed 14 September 2008).

Berger, Peter L. 1967. *The Sacred Canopy: Elements of a Sociology of Religion*. New York: Anchor Books.

Bergson, Henri. 1944 [1907]. *Creative Evolution*. New York: Random House.

Berlin, Isiaah. 1969. *Four Essays on Liberty*. Oxford: Oxford University Press.

Bey, Hakim. 1991a. *TAZ: The Temporary Autonomous Zone. Ontological Anarchy and Poetic Terrorism*. New York: Autonomedia.

—. 1991b. "The Lemonade Ocean & Modern Times: A Position Paper". http://hermetic.com/bey/lemonade.html (accessed 30 October 2011).

—. 1994. "Boundary Violations". http://www.t0.or.at/hakimbey/boundary.htm (accessed 16 October 2011).

—. 1996. *Millennium*. New York: Autonomedia.

Bey, Hakim and Abel Zug (eds.). 2004. *Orgies of the Hemp Eaters*. New York: Autonomedia.

Billy. 1975/76. "Dance for Dance Sake". *The Stoned Pig* 5: 7. http://www.goaheadspace.com/stonedpig/album/Issue%205/index.html (accessed 4 July 2011).

Binkley, Sam. 2007. *Getting Loose: Lifestyle Consumption in the 1970s*. Durham, NC: Duke University Press. 0 4

Bizzell, Victoria. 2008. "'Ancient + Future = Now': Goa Gil and Transnational Neo-Tribalism in Global Rave Culture". *Comparative American Studies* 6(3): 281–94.

Bombay Brian. 2011. Post in response to "GOA: some origins" by Blond Peter on the blog "The Flower Raj Blog: escapers, seekers, travellers in the land of the Gods: India revisited". 4 May. http://blog.theflowerraj.org/?p=1050 (accessed 4 July 2011).

Bookchin, Murray. 1995. *Social Anarchism or Lifestyle Anarchism: An Unbridgeable Chasm*. Edinburgh: AK Press.

Bourdieu, Pierre. 1990. The *Logic of Practice*. Stanford, CA: Stanford University Press.

Boycott Earthcore. 2007. http://boycottearthcore2007.blogspot.com (accessed 22 October 2011).

BrettfromTibet. 2008. Posting to "Psytrance – WEAK or NOT" thread. April 15. http://psytrance.tribe.net/thread/579bfe51-8475-4e24-b442-cf77537539e1 (accessed 4 July 2011).

Brian. 2008. Posting to "Psytrance – WEAK or NOT" thread. 12 February. http://psytrance.tribe.net/thread/579bfe51-8475-4e24-b442-cf77537539e1 (accessed 4 July 2011).

Bromell, Nick. 2000. *Tomorrow Never Knows: Rock and Psychedelics in the 1960s*. Chicago, IL and London: University of Chicago Press.

Bromley, David. 2007. "On Spiritual Edgework: The Logic of Extreme Ritual Performances". *Journal for the Scientific Study of Religion* 46(3): 287–302.

Buckland, Fiona. 2002. *Impossible Dance: Club Culture and Queer World-Making*. Middletown, CA: Wesleyan University Press.

Burroughs, William. 1992 [1959]. *Naked Lunch*. New York: Grove Press.

Campbell, Colin. 1977. "Clarifying the Cult". *British Journal of Sociology* 28: 375–88.

Campbell, Joseph. 1949. *The Hero with a Thousand Faces*. New York: Pantheon Books.

Canetti, Elias. 1962 [1960]. *Crowds and Power*. Trans. Carol Stewart. New York: Noonday Press.

Capra, Fritjof. 1975. *The Tao of Physics: An Exploration of the Parallels between Modern Physics and Eastern Mysticism*. Boulder, CO: Shambhala Publications.

Cardeña, Etzel. 2011. "Altering Consciousness: Setting Up the Stage". In Etzel Cardeña and Michael Winkelman (eds.), *Altering Consciousness: Multidisciplinary Perspectives*, pp. 1–22. Santa Barbara, CA: ABC-CLIO.

Carmichael, Jonathan. 2004. "Psyber-fiction: Literature of the Mind's Eye". *en-trance* 4 (January): 18–22.

Carstens, Delphi. n.d. "Molecular Ecstasies & Twisted Poetry". *Groovy Troopers: Experience Psychedelic Trance Culture!* http://www.groovytroopers.co.za/index.php?option=com_content&task=view&id=81&Itemid=1 (accessed 3 June 2011, page no longer live).

Castle, Ray (aka genkigroove). 2010. Post to the thread "Goa party video 1992 + help needed". Discogs: http://www.discogs.com/groups/topic/159529?page (accessed 9 December 2010).

Chatterton, Paul and Robert Hollands. 2003. *Urban Nightscapes: Youth Cultures, Pleasure Spaces and Corporate Power*. London: Routledge.

Citizen. 2007. Interview in *Progressive Tunes* 1 (May): 6.

Cohen, Albert K. 1955. *The Delinquent Boys: The Culture of the Gang*. Glencoe, IL: The Free Press.

Cohen, Emma. 2008. "What is Spirit Possession? Defining, Comparing, and Explaining Two Possession Forms". *Ethnos* 73(1): 101–26.

Cohen, Erik. 1979. "A Phenomenology of Tourist Experiences". *Sociology* 13: 179–201.

Cohen, Michael, Paul Dwyer and Laura Ginters. 2008. "'Performing Sorry Business': Reconciliation and Redressive Action". In Graham St John (ed.), *Victor Turner and Contemporary Cultural Performance*, pp. 76–93. New York: Berghahn.

Cole, Fred. 1999. "Creative Practices in Australian Techno and Other Electronica: A Folio of Original Compositions and Supporting Documentation". PhD thesis, Southern Cross University.

Cole, Fred and Michael Hannan. 1997. "Goa Trance". *Perfect Beat* 3(3): 1–14.

Collin, Matthew (with John Godfrey). 1997. *Altered State: The Story of Ecstasy Culture and Acid House*. London: Serpent's Tail.

Cooke, Robin. 2001. "Mutoid Waste Recycledelia and Earthdream". In Graham St John (ed.), *FreeNRG: Notes from the Edge of the Dance Floor*, pp. 131–56. Altona: Common Ground. http://undergrowth.org/freenrg_notes_from_the_edge_of_the_dancefloor.

Copetas, Craig, A. 2009. "Israelis in Goa: Israel is an Empty Place". On blog "The Truth Will Set You Free", 31 March. http://wakeupfromyourslumber.blogspot.com/2009/03/israelis-in-goa-israel-is-empty-place.html (accessed 21 May 2010).

Cosgrove, Stuart. 1988. "Forbidden Fruits". *New Statesman and Society*, 2 September.

Cosmosis (Bill Halsey). 2006. "Boom 2006". 8 September. http://forum.isratrance.com/boom-2006/page97 (accessed 4 February 2010).

Cowan, Douglas E. 2008. *Sacred Terror: Religion and Horror on the Silver Screen*. Waco, TX: Baylor University Press.

Csikszentmihalyi, Mihaly. 1990. *Flow: The Psychology of Optimal Experience*. New York: Harper and Row.

Dahlgaard Mikael. 2008/2009. *Mushroom Magazine* 154 (Dec–Jan): 7.

D'Andrea, Anthony. 2004. "Global Nomads: Techno and New Age as Transnational Countercultures in Ibiza and Goa". In Graham St John (ed.), *Rave Culture and Religion*, pp. 236–55. London: Routledge.

—. 2006. "The Spiritual Economy of Nightclubs and Raves: Osho Sannyasins as Party Promoters in Ibiza and Pune/Goa". *Culture and Religion* 7(1): 61–75.

—. 2007a. *Global Nomads: Techno and New Age as Transnational Countercultures in Ibiza and Goa*. New York: Routledge.

—. 2007b. "Osho International Meditation Resort (Pune, 2000s): An Anthropological Analysis of Sannyasin Therapies and the Rajneesh Legacy". *Journal of Humanistic Psychology* 47(1): 91–116.

—. 2009. "Chromatic Variation in Ethnographic Analysis". Review of Arun Saldanha's *Psychedelic White: Goa Trance and the Viscosity of Race* by Arun Saldanha. In *Dancecult: Journal of Electronic Dance Music Culture* 1(1): 147–50. http://dj.dancecult.net/index.php/journal/article/view/30/26.

—. 2010. "The Decline of Electronic Dance Scenes: The Case of Psytrance in Goa". In Graham St John (ed.), *The Local Scenes and Global Culture of Psytrance*, pp. 40–54. New York: Routledge.

Dass, Ram. 1971. *Be Here Now*. San Cristobal, New Mexico: Lama Foundation.

Dass, Ram, Ralph Metzner, with Gary Bravo. 2010. *Birth of a Psychedelic Culture: Conversations about Leary, the Harvard Experiments, Millbrook and the Sixties*. Santa Fe, NM: Synergetic Press.

Davis, Erik. 1995. "Sampling Paradise: The Technofreak Legacy of Golden Goa". *Option* 61. http://www.techgnosis.com/index_paradise.html (accessed 10 March 2011).

—. 1998. *Techgnosis: Myth, Magic and Mysticism in the Age of Information*. New York: Harmony Books.

—. 2001. "Psychedelic Culture: One or Many?" *TRIP* (Fall). http://www.techgnosis.com/mindstates.html (accessed 20 June 2009).

—. 2002. "Recording Angels: The Esoteric Origins of the Phonograph". In Rob Young (ed.), *Undercurrents: The Hidden Wiring of Modern Music*, pp. 15–24. London: Continuum International Publishing Group.

—. 2004. "Hedonic Tantra: Golden Goa's Trance Transmission". In Graham St John (ed.), *Rave Culture and Religion*, pp. 256–72. London: Routledge.

—. 2005. "Beyond Belief: The Cults of Burning Man". In Lee Gilmore and Mark Van Proyen (eds.), *Afterburn: Reflections on Burning Man*, pp. 15–42. Albuquerque: University of New Mexico Press.

—. 2008a. "The Festival is a Seed". *Pathways: Liminal Zine* 02: 50–54.

—. 2008b "Visionary Art: The Vanguard of Tradition". Preface to *True Visions*, Betty Books, reproduced at: http://lila.info/art/visionary-art-the-vanguard-of-tradition-by-erik-davis.html (accessed 16 November 2010).

Davis, Erik and Ken Wiltshire. 2009. *Tribal Revival: West Coast Festival Culture*. Lovelution Press.

Davis, Fred and Laura Munoz. 1968. "Heads and Freaks: Patterns and Meanings of Drug Use among Hippies". *Journal of Health and Social Behavior* 9(2): 156–64.

Dawn, Even. 2008. "Planetary Gatherings of Galactic Garden Culture". *Undergrowth*. http://undergrowth.org/planetary_gatherings_of_galactic_garden_culture_by_even_dawn (accessed 19 May 2009).

De Bié, Chris. n.d. *Storia Theurgica: The Hippie Trail*. http://artetheurgica.de/storia/english/6-goa.html (accessed 30 April 2012).

De Ledesma, Charles. 2010. "Psychedelic Trance Music Making in the UK: Rhizomatic Craftsmanship and the Global Market Place". In Graham St John (ed.), *The Local Scenes and Global Culture of Psytrance*, pp. 89–113. New York: Routledge.

Deleuze, Gilles and Felix Guattari. 1986. *Nomadology: The War Machine*. Trans. Brian Massumi. New York: Semiotext(e).

Delvin and Eve. 2005. "Gatherings at the Cusp: Embodying Visionary Culture". *COSM: Journal of Visionary Culture* 3 (The Body): 32.

Demant, Jakob and Jeanette Østergaard. 2007. "Partying as Everyday Life: Investigations of Teenagers' Leisure Life". *Journal of Youth Studies* 10(5): 517–37.

Demant, Jakob, Ravn Signe and Thorsen Sidsel Kirstine. 2010. "Club Studies: Methodological Perspectives for Researching Drug Use in a Central Youth Social Space". *Leisure Studies* 29(3): 241–52.

Desmond, Jane. 1997. "Embodying Difference: Issues in Dance and Cultural Studies". In Jane C. Desmond (ed.), *Meaning in Motion: New Cultural Studies of Dance*, pp. 29–54. Durham, NC: Duke University Press.

Devas, Steve "Madras". 2004. "Our Only Story is the Beach: The Life and Times of Amsterdam Dave". Unpublished document.

Devereux, Paul. 1997. *The Long Trip: A Prehistory of Psychedelia*. London: Penguin.

Diken, Bülent and Carsten Bagge Laustsen. 2004 . "Sea, Sun, Sex ... and Biopolitics". Lancaster University, Dept Sociology, Online Papers. http://www.lancs.ac.uk/fass/sociology/papers/diken-laustsen-sea-sun-sex-biopolitics.pdf (accessed 10 March 2011).

Dimond, Kol. 1999. "Trance Parrant". Insert included with Organarchy *BPM Conspiracies* CD: ORGANARCHY002.

Dobkin de Rios, Marlene and Oscar Janiger. 2003. *LSD, Spirituality, and the Creative Process*. Rochester: VT: Park Street Press.

Durkheim, Emile. 1970. *Suicide: A Study in Sociology*. Trans. J.A. Spaulding and G. Simpson. London: Routledge.

Dyer, Richard. 1990. "In Defence of Disco". In Simon Frith and A. Goodwin (eds.), *On Record: Rock, Pop and the Written Word*, pp. 410–18. New York: Pantheon.

Eade, John and Michael Sallnow. 1991. "Introduction". In John Eade and Michael Sallnow (eds.), *Contesting the Sacred: The Anthropology of Christian Pilgrimage*, pp. 1–29. London: Routledge.

Eagleton, Terry. 1981. *Walter Benjamin, or Towards a Revolutionary Criticism*. London: Verso.

Ehrenreich, Barbara. 2006. *Dancing in the Streets: A History of Collective Joy*. New York: Metropolitan Books.

Eight Finger Eddie. n.d. *My Rise to Relative Obscurity: 1924–1972.* Available at: www.8fingereddie.com/downloads.html (accessed 10 March 2011).

Eliade, Mircea. 1964 [1951]. *Shamanism: Archaic Techniques of Ecstasy.* Trans. W.R. Trask. London: Routledge and Kegan Paul.

Elias, Norbert and Eric Dunning. 1986. *Quest for Excitement: Sport and Leisure in the Civilizing Process.* Oxford: Basil Blackwell.

Elliott, Luther C. 2004. "Goa Trance and the Practice of Community in the Age of the Internet". *Television & New Media* 5(3): 272–88.

—. 2006. "Mobile Consciousness, Flexible Culture: Notes on the Rise and Fall of Goa Trance". PhD dissertation, Dept of Anthropology, New York University.

—. 2010. "Goa is a State of Mind: On the Ephemerality of Psychedelic Social Emplacements". In Graham St John (ed.), *The Local Scenes and Global Culture of Psytrance,* pp. 21–39. New York: Routledge.

Emok. 2008. "The Status Quo of the Trance Community". *Mushroom Magazine* 154 (Dec): 7.

Engelke, Matthew. 2004. "'The Endless Conversation': Fieldwork, Writing, and the Marriage of Victor and Edith Turner". In R. Handler (ed.), *Significant Others: Essays on Professional and Interpersonal Relationships in Anthropology,* pp. 6–50. Madison, WI: University of Wisconsin Press.

ENRG, Eugene (DJ Krusty) interviews Ray Castle. 2001. "Psychic Sonics: Tribadelic Dance Trance-formation". In Graham St John (ed.), *FreeNRG: Notes From the Edge of the Dance Floor,* pp. 157–69. Melbourne: Common Ground. http://undergrowth.org/freenrg_notes_from_the_edge_of_the_dancefloor.

Eshun, Kodwo. 1998. *More Brilliant than the Sun: Adventures in Sonic Fiction.* London: Quartet.

Eve (the Ladyapples). 2006. "Between Experience and Imagination: A Liminal Invocation". *Pathways: Liminal Zine* 01: 5.

Fatone, Gina. 2004. "Gamelan, Techno-Primitivism, and the San Francisco Rave Scene". In Graham St John (ed.), *Rave Culture and Religion,* pp. 197–209. London: Routledge.

Ferguson, Marilyn. 1980. *The Aquarian Conspiracy: Personal and Social Transformation in the 1980s.* Los Angeles: J.P. Tarcher.

Ferrell. Jeff. 2005. "The Only Possible Adventure: Edgework and Anarchy". In Stephen Lyng (ed.), *Edgework: The Sociology of Risk-Taking.* New York: Routledge.

Fikentscher, Kai. 2000. *"You Better Work!": Underground Dance Music in New York City.* Middletown, CA: Wesleyan University Press.

Fontana, David. 2005. *Meditating with Mandalas.* London: Duncan Baird Publishers.

Forte, Robert. 1997. *Entheogens and the Future of Religion.* Sabastopol, CA: Promind Services.

Fox, Matthew. 2005. "Reflections on the Sacred Mirrors". *COSM: Journal of Visionary Culture* 1 (Summer Solstice): 6–8.

Freeze magazine. 2001. Interview with Goa Gil. Issue 14 (Aug). http://www.goagil.com/FreezeInterview1.html (accessed 10 March 2011).

Friedson, Steven M. 2005. "Where Divine Horsemen Ride: Trance Dancing in West Africa". In Angela Hobart and Bruce Kapferer (eds.), *Aesthetics in Performance: Formations of Symbolic Construction and Experience,* pp. 109–28. New York: Berghahn.

Fritz, Jimi. 1999. *Rave Culture: An Insider's Overview.* Canada: Smallfry Press.

Furlong, Andy and Fred Cartmel. 2006. *Young People and Social Change: New Perspectives.* 2nd ed. Maidenhead: Open University Press.

Gaillot, Michel. 1999. *Multiple Meaning Techno: An Artistic and Political Laboratory of the Present.* Paris: Editions des Voir.

Ganihar, Tomer. 2011. "Death of the Spirit". *Haaretz.com* (21 June). http://www.haaretz.com/weekend/week-s-end/death-of-the-spirit-1.366510 (accessed 28 June 2011).

Garcia, Luis-Manuel. 2005. "On and On: Repetition as Process and Pleasure in Electronic Dance Music". *Music Theory Online* 11(4) October. http://mto.societymusictheory.org/issues/mto.05.11.4/mto.05.11.4.garcia.html (accessed 9 June 2008).

—. 2010. "Pathological Crowds: Affect and Danger in Responses to the Love Parade Disaster at Duisburg". *Dancecult: Journal of Electronic Dance Music Culture* 2(1). http://www.dj.dancecult.net/index.php/journal/article/viewArticle/66/102.

Gauthier, François. 2004a. "Rapturous Ruptures: The 'Instituant' Religious Experience of Rave". In Graham St John (ed.), *Rave Culture and Religion*, pp. 65–84. London: Routledge.

—. 2004b. "Rave and Religion? A Contemporary Youth Phenomenon as Seen through the Lens of Religious Studies". *Studies in Religion* 33(3-4): 397–413.

—. 2005. "Orpheus and the Underground: Raves and Implicit Religion – From Interpretation to Critique". *Implicit Religion* 8(3): 217–65.

Gelder, Ken. 2007. *Subcultures: Cultural Histories and Social Practice*. London and New York: Routledge.

Gerard, Morgan. 2004. "Selecting Ritual: DJs, Dancers and Liminality in Underground Dance Music". In Graham St John (ed.), *Rave Culture and Religion*, pp. 167–84. London: Routledge.

Gerster, Robin and Jan Bassett. 1991. *Seizures of Youth: The Sixties and Australia*. South Yarra, Vic: Hyland House.

Gilbert, Jeremy and Ewan Pearson. 1999. *Discographies: Dance Music, Culture and the Politics of Sound*. London: Routledge.

Gilmore, Lee. 2010. *Theater in a Crowded Fire: Ritual and Spirituality at the Burning Man Festival*. Berkeley: University of California Press.

Gilmore, Lee and Mark Van Proyen (eds.). 2005. *Afterburn: Reflections on Burning Man*. Albuquerque: University of New Mexico Press.

Gips. Elizabeth 1991. *Scrapbook of a Haight Ashbury Pilgrim: Spirit, Sacraments and Sex in 1967/68*. Santa Cruz, CA: Changes Press.

Glassball. 2006. "How to Describe Full-on Psytrance". 15 April. Thread at http://forums.di.fm/world-of-music/how-to-describe-full-on-psytrance-99691 (accessed 16 April 2011).

Gluckman, Max. 1954. *Rituals of Rebellion in South-East Africa*. Manchester: Manchester University Press.

Goffman, Ken. 2004. *Counterculture through the Ages*. New York: Villard Books.

Good Mood Productions. 2007. *Boom Book*. Lisbon: Good Mood Productions.

Goodman, Steve. 2009. *Sonic Warfare: Sound, Affect, and the Ecology of Fear*. MIT Press.

Gore, Georgina. 1995. "Rhythm, Representation and Ritual: The Rave and the Religious Cult". In *Border Tensions, Dance and Discourse: Proceedings of the Fifth Study of Dance Conference*, pp. 133–9. Guildford: University of Surrey.

—. 1997. "Trance, Dance and Tribalism in Rave Culture". In Helen Thomas (ed.), *Dance in the City*, pp. 73–83. London: Macmillan Press.

Gosney, Michael. n.d. Interview with Raja Ram, *BEAM* 1(2). http://www.radiov.com/main/beam/innerviews/rajaram (accessed 12 June 2010, page no longer live).

—. 1997 (Oct). Interview with Goa Gil, *Radio V*. http://radiov.com/main/beam/innerviews/goagil (accessed 10 March 2011, page no longer live).

Gracie and Zarkov. 1984. *DMT: How and Why to Get Off*. http://deoxy.org/gz_howy.htm (accessed 21 September 2011).

Graña, Marigay. 1990. "Preface". In César Graña and Marigay Graña (eds.), *On Bohemia: The Code of the Self-Exiled*, pp. xv–xviii. New Jersey: Transaction Publisher.

Greener, Tracey and Robert Hollands. 2006. "Beyond Subculture and Post-subculture? The Case of Virtual Psytrance". *Journal of Youth Studies* 9(4): 393–418.

Grimes, Ron. 1995. *Beginnings in Ritual Studies*. Washington: University Press of America.

Guerra, Beta. 2009. "Bolivia: Winds of Change". *Psychedelic Traveller* 2009: 17.

Hacker, Scott. 1994 "Can You Get to That? The Cosmology of P-Funk". http://stuckbetween-stations.org/2011/01/11/cosmology-of-pfunk (accessed 3 February 2010).

Haebich, Anna and Jody Taylor. 2007. "Modern Primitives Leaping and Stomping the Earth: From Ballet to Bush Doof". *Journal of Aboriginal Histories* 31: 63–84.

Hafiz. 1996. *I Heard God Laughing: Renderings of Hafiz.* Trans. Daniel Ladinsky. Walnut Creek, CA: Sufism Reoriented.

Hall, Stuart. 1996. "Introduction: Who Needs Identity?" In S. Hall and P. du Gay (eds.), *Questions of Cultural Identity*, pp. 1–17. London: Sage Publications.

Hall, Stuart and Tony Jefferson (eds.). 1976. *Resistance through Rituals: Youth Subcultures in Post-War Britain.* London: Hutchinson & Co.

Hanegraaff, Wouter J. 1995. "Empirical Method in the Study of Esotericism". *Method & Theory in the Study of Religion* 7(2): 99–129.

—. 2001. "Beyond the Yates Paradigm: The Study of Western Esotericism between Counterculture and New Complexity". *Aries* 1(1): 5–37.

Hanna, John. 2008. "Got Changa?" Erowid. http://www.erowid.org/chemicals/dmt/dmt_article1.shtml (accessed 18 October 2011).

Hebdige, Dick. 1976. "The Meaning of Mod". In Stuart Hall and Tony Jefferson (eds.), *Resistance through Rituals: Youth Subcultures in Post-War Britain*, pp. 87–96. London: Routledge.

—. 1979. *Subculture: The Meaning of Style.* London: Methuen.

Heelas, Paul. 1997. *The New Age Movement.* Oxford: Blackwell.

—. 2008. *Spiritualities of Life: From the Romantics to Wellbeing Culture.* Oxford: Blackwell.

Heelas, Paul and Benjamin Seel. 2003. "An Ageing New Age?" In Grace Davie, Paul Heelas and Linda Woodhead (eds.), *Predicting Religion: Christian, Secular and Alternative Futures*, pp. 229–47. Aldershot: Ashgate.

Heelas, Paul and Linda Woodhead, with Benjamin Seel, Bronislaw Szerszynski and Karin Tusting. 2005. *The Spiritual Revolution: Why Religion is Giving Way to Spirituality.* Oxford and Malden, MA: Blackwell.

Henderson, Sheila, Janet Holland, Sheena McGrellis, Sue Sharpe and Rachel Thomson. 2007. *Inventing Adulthoods: A Biographical Approach to Youth Transitions.* London: Sage.

Henry, Holly and Amanda Taylor. 2009. "Re-thinking Apollo: Envisioning Environmentalism in Space". *Sociological Review* 57(1): 190–203.

Hesse, Herman. 2000 [1943]. *The Glass Bead Game.* London: Vintage.

—. 2003 [1923]. *The Journey to the East.* Trans. Hilda Rosner. London: Picador.

Hetherington, Kevin. 2000. *New Age Travellers: Vanloads of Uproarious Humanity.* London: Cassell.

Hewitt, Kim. 2011. "The 'Feeling of Knowing', the Psychedelic Sensorium, and Contemporary Neuroscience: Shifting Contexts for Noetic Insight". *The Senses and Society* 6(2): 177–202.

Hill, Desmond. 1999. "Mobile Anarchy: The House Movement, Shamanism and Community". In Thomas Lyttle (ed.), *Psychedelics Reimagined*, pp. 95–106. New York: Autonomedia.

Hofmann, Albert. 1980. *LSD, My Problem Child.* New York: McGraw-Hill.

Hopper, Paul. 2007. *Understanding Cultural Globalisation.* Cambridge: Polity.

Howard, John Robert. 1969. "The Flowering of the Hippie Movement". *ANNALS of the American Academy of Political and Social Science* 382(1): 43–55.

Hunt, Geoffrey P., Kristin Evans and Faith Kares. 2007. "Drug Use and Meanings of Risk and Pleasure". *Journal of Youth Studies* 10(1): 73–96.

Hunt, Geoffrey P., Molly Moloney and Kristin Evans. 2009. "Epidemiology Meets Cultural Studies: Studying and Understanding Youth Cultures, Clubs and Drugs". *Addiction, Research and Theory* 17(6): 601–21.

—. 2010. *Youth, Drugs, and Nightlife.* New York: Routledge.

Hutson, Scot. 1999. "Technoshamanism: Spiritual Healing in the Rave Subculture". *Popular Music and Society* 23: 53–77.

—. 2000. "The Rave: Spiritual Healing in Modern Western Subcultures". *Anthropological Quarterly* 73(1): 35–49.

Hutton, Fiona. 2006. *Risky Pleasures? Club Cultures and Feminine Identities.* Aldershot: Ashgate.

Huxley, Aldous. 1944. *The Perennial Philosophy*. New York: Harper and Brothers.

—. 1954. *The Doors of Perception & Heaven and Hell.* New York: Harper & Row.

Inglehart, Ronald, 1977. *The Silent Revolution*. Princeton, NJ: Princeton University Press.

Ivakhiv, Adrian. 2001. *Claiming Sacred Ground: Pilgrims and Politics at Glastonbury and Sedona*. Bloomington, IN: Indiana University Press.

—. 2003. "Nature and Self in New Age Pilgrimage". *Culture and Religion* 4(1): 93–118.

—. 2007. "Power Trips: Making Sacred Space through New Age Pilgrimage". In Daren Kemp and James R. Lewis (eds.), *Handbook of New Age*. Leiden: Brill.

Jackson, Michael. 1989. *Paths toward a Clearing: Radical Empiricism and Ethnographic Inquiry.* Bloomington, IN: Indiana University Press.

Jackson, Phil. 2004. *Inside Clubbing: Sensual Experiments in the Art of Being Human*. Oxford: Berg.

Jaimangal-Jones, Dewi, Annette Pritchard and Nigel Morgan. 2010. "Going the Distance: Locating Journey, Liminality and Rites of Passage in Dance Music Experiences". *Leisure Studies* 29(3): 253–68.

Jason, C. 1998. "Total Eclipse 98: Venezuela". *Dream Creation* 1998: 30.

Jeff 604. n.d. "A Decade of Psychedelic Trance". http://pagesperso-orange.fr/psychedelic_trance (accessed 10 March 2011).

Jennie and Postman. 2002. "Music from the Power of the Sun". An Interview with Grant T. Garden. *Mushroom Magazine*, International Edition, 1: 28–32.

Jones, Steven T. 2011. *The Tribes of Burning Man*. San Francisco: CCC Publishing.

Jordan, Tim. 1995. "Collective Bodies: Raving and the Politics of Gilles Deleuze and Felix Guattari". *Body and Society* 1(1): 125–44.

Juris, Jeffrey Scott and Geoffrey Henri Pleyers. 2009. "Alter-activism: Emerging Cultures of Participation among Young Global Justice Activists". *Journal of Youth Studies* 12(1): 57–75.

Karen. n.d. "Entheogenesis Dance Experiment and My Heart Journey". Unpublished document.

Kavanaugh, Philip R. and Tammy L. Anderson. 2008. "Solidarity and Drug Use in the Electronic Dance Music Scene". *Sociological Quarterly* 49(1): 181–208.

Keller, Mary. 2001. *The Hammer and the Flute: Women, Power and Spirit Possession.* Baltimore, MD: Johns Hopkins University Press.

Kerenyi, Karl. 1967. *Eleusis: Archetypal Image of Mother and Daughter*. Princeton, NJ: Princeton University Press.

Kirby, Danielle. 2012. "Occultural Bricolage and Popular Culture: Remix and Art in Discordianism, the Church of the SubGenius, and the Temple of Psychic Youth". In Adam Possamai (ed.), *Handbook of Hyper-Real Religions*. Leiden: Brill. Forthcoming.

Kripal, Jeffrey. 2007. *Esalen: America and the Religion of No Religion*. Chicago, IL: University of Chicago Press.

Krusty, DJ. 2008. "Trance and Dance: Bush Doofs and the Shamanic Vision". In Rak Razam and Tim Parish (eds.), *The Journeybook: Travels on the Frontiers of Consciousness*, pp. 15–22. Undergrowth. See also: http://undergrowth.org/bush_doofs_by_dj_krusty (accessed 21 October 2010).

Krusty, DJ and Ray. n.d. "Meld for Moments to Define Tekno Trance Dance". http://music.hyperreal.org/artists/metanet/meld1.html (accessed 1 November 2008).

Lachman, Gary. 2001. *Turn Off Your Mind: The Mystic Sixties and the Dark Side of the Age of Aquarius*. St Paul, MN: The Disinformation Co.

—. 2003. *A Secret History of Consciousness.* Great Barrington, MA: Lindisfarne Books.

Laderman, Gary. 2011. "LSD". http://freq.uenci.es/2011/11/01/lsd (accessed 5 November 2011).

Laing, Ronald David. 1967. *The Politics of Experience and the Bird of Paradise*. London: Penguin.

Lambert, Alex. 2010. "Narratives in Noise: Reflexivity, Migration and Liminality in the Australian Psytrance Scene". In Graham St John (ed.), *The Local Scenes and Global Culture of Psytrance*, pp. 203–19. New York: Routledge

Landau, James. 2004. "The Flesh of Raving: Merleau-Ponty and the 'Experience' of Ecstasy". In Graham St John (ed.), *Rave Culture and Religion*, pp. 107–24. London: Routledge.

Larkin, Christopher B. 2003. "Turn on, Tune in, and Trance out: The Exploration of Entheogens and the Emergence of a Global Techno-shamanic Ritual". Thesis submitted in partial fulfillment of a degree in Sociology/Anthropology, Lewis and Clark College.

Lattas, Andrew. 1990. "Aborigines and Contemporary Australian Nationalism: Primordiality and the Cultural Politics of Otherness". *Social Analysis* 27: 50–69.

—. 1992. "Primitivism, Nationalism and Individualism in Australian Popular Culture". In B. Attwood and J. Arnold (eds.), *Power, Knowledge and Aborigines: Journal of Australian Studies*, pp. 45–58.

Laughlin, Charles D., John McManus and Eugene G. D'Aquili. 1992. *Brain, Symbol & Experience: Towards a Neurophenomenology of Human Consciousness*. New York: Columbia University Press.

Laurendeau, Jason. 2008. "Gendered Risk Regimes: A Theoretical Consideration of Edgework and Gender". *Sociology of Sport Journal* 25(3): 293–309.

Laurent. 2010. Post in Reader Comments to Dave Mothersole's *Unveiling the Secret—The Roots of Trance*. 28 April. http://www.bleep43.com/bleep43/2010/4/14/unveiling-the-secret-the-roots-of-trance.html (accessed 25 June 2011).

Lava 303. 2002. "Women of Goa". *Mushroom Magazine* 85 (May): 78.

Laviolette, Patrick. 2007. "Hazardous Sport?" *Anthropology Today* 23(6): 1–2.

Lawrence, Tim. 2003. *Love Saves the Day: A History of American Dance Music Culture, 1970–1979*. Durham, NC and London: Duke University Press.

—. 2008. "Disco Madness: Walter Gibbons and the Legacy of Turntablism and Remixology". *Journal of Popular Music Studies* 20(3): 276–329.

Le Breton, David. 2000. "Playing Symbolically with Death in Extreme Sports". *Body & Society* 6(1): 1–11.

Leary, Timothy. 1966. *Psychedelic Prayers after the Tao Te Ching*. Kerhonkson, NY: Poets Press.

—. 1981 [1965]. *The Politics of Ecstasy*. Berkeley, CA: Ronin.

Leary, Timothy, Ralph Metzner and Richard Alpert. 1964. *The Psychedelic Experience: A Manual Based on the Tibetan Book of the Dead*. New Hyde Park, NY: University Books.

Leary, Timothy, Michael Horowitz and Vicki Marshall. 1994. *Chaos & Cyber Culture*. Berkeley, CA: Ronin.

Lee, Martin A. and Bruce Shlain. 1985. *Acid Dreams: The Complete Social History of LSD: The CIA, the Sixties and Beyond*. New York: Grove Press.

Legan, Lucy. 2006. "Earth's Creative Potential". *Pathways: Liminal Zine* 01:10.

Leland, John. 2004. *Hip: The History*. New York: Ecco Press.

Levit, Boris. 2002. "Israel: How Prohibition Creates New Trance Styles". *Mushroom Magazine* (January): 82–92.

Lewis, I.M. 1971. *Ecstatic Religion: An Anthropological Study of Spirit Possession and Shamanism*. Baltimore, MD: Penguin.

Lewis, J. Lowell and Paul Dowsey-Magog. 1993. "The Maleny Fire Event: Rehearsals toward Neo-Liminality". *Australian Journal of Anthropology* 4(3): 198–219.

Lindley, Arthur. 1996. *Hyperion and the Hobbyhorse: Studies in Carnivalesque Subversion*. Newark, DE: University of Delaware Press.

Lindop, Robin. 2010. "Re-evaluating Musical Genre in UK Psytrance". In Graham St John (ed.), *The Local Scenes and Global Culture of Psytrance*, pp. 114–30. New York: Routledge.
Littmann, Mark, Fred Espenak and Ken Willcox. 2008. *Totality: Eclipses of the Sun*. Oxford: Oxford University Press.
Luckman, Susan. 2003. "Going Bush and Finding One's 'Tribe': Raving, Escape and the Bush Doof". *Continuum: Journal of Media and Cultural Studies* 17(3): 315–30.
Luckmann, Thomas. 1967. *The Invisible Religion: The Problem of Religion in Modern Society*. New York: Macmillan.
Lynch, Gordon and Emily Badger. 2006. "The Mainstream Post-Rave Club Scene as a Secondary Institution: A British Perspective". *Culture and Religion* 7(1): 27–40.
Lyng, Stephen. 1990. "Edgework: A Social Psychological Analysis of Voluntary Risk Taking". *American Journal of Sociology* 95(4): 876–921.
—. 2005. "Edgework and the Risk-Taking Experience". In Stephen Lyng (ed.), *Edgework: The Sociology of Risk-Taking*, pp. 3–16. London: Routledge.
Maclean, Rory. 2006. *Magic Bus: On the Hippie Trail from Istanbul to India*. London: Penguin.
Maffesoli, Michel. 1993 [1982]. *The Shadow of Dionysus: A Contribution to the Sociology of the Orgy*. Albany, NY: State University of New York Press.
—. 1996 [1988]. *The Time of the Tribes: The Decline of Individualism in Mass Society*. London: Sage.
Mailer, Norman. 1957. "The White Negro: Reflections on the Hipster". *Dissent* 4: 276–93.
Malbon, Ben. 1999. *Clubbing: Dancing, Ecstasy and Vitality*. London: Routledge.
Malyon, Tim. 1998. "Tossed in the Fire and They Never Got Burned: The Exodus Collective". In George McKay (ed.), *DIY Culture: Party and Protest in Nineties Britain*, pp. 187–207. London: Verso.
Maoz, Darya. 2005. "Young Adult Israeli Backpackers in India". In Chaim Noy and Erik Cohen (eds.), *Israeli Backpackers: From Tourism to Rite of Passage*, pp. 159–88. Albany, NY: State University of New York.
Marcus, Julie. 1988. "The Journey Out to the Centre: The Cultural Appropriation of Ayers Rock". *Kunapipi* 10(1&2): 254–75.
Mathesdorf, Kai. 2002. "A History of Psychedelic Trance". *Mushroom Magazine*, International Edition, 1 (January): 4–24.
Matthews, Amie. 2008. "Backpacking as a Contemporary Rite of Passage: Victor Turner and Youth Travel Practices". In Graham St John (ed.), *Victor Turner and Contemporary Cultural Performance*, pp. 174–89. New York and Oxford: Berghahn.
McAteer, Michael. 2002. "'Redefining the Ancient Tribal Ritual for the 21st Century': Goa Gil and the Trance Dance Experience". Paper for Division of Philosophy, Religion and Psychology, Reed College. http://www.goagil.com/thesis.html (accessed 21 May 2009).
McClary, Susan. 1994. "Same as it Ever Was: Youth Culture and Music". In Andrew Ross and Trish Rose (eds.), *Microphone Fiends: Youth Music, Youth Culture*, pp. 29–40. New York: Routledge.
McKay, George. 1996. *Senseless Acts of Beauty: Cultures of Resistance Since the Sixties*. London: Verso.
—. 1998. *DIY Culture: Party and Protest in Nineties Britain*. London: Verso.
—. 2000. *Glastonbury: A Very English Fair*. London: Victor Gollancz.
McKenna, Terence. 1991a. *The Archaic Revival: Speculations on Psychedelic Mushrooms, the Amazon, Virtual Reality, UFOs, Evolution, Shamanism, the Rebirth of the Goddess, and the End of History*. San Francisco: Harper.
—. 1991b [1989]. "Among Ayahuasquera". In Christian Ratsch (ed.), *Gateway to Inner Space: Sacred Plants, Mysticism and Psychotherapy*, pp. 179–212. Dorset: Prism.
—. 1992. *Food of the Gods: The Search for the Original Tree of Knowledge*. New York: Bantam Books.

—. 1993 [1984]. *True Hallucinations: Being an Account of the Author's Extraordinary Adventures in the Devil's Paradise.* San Francisco: Harper.

McKenzie, Jon. 2001. *Perform or Else: From Discipline to Performance.* London and New York: Routledge.

McLeod, Ken. 2003. "Space Oddities: Aliens, Futurism and Meaning in Popular Music". *Popular Music* 22: 337–55.

McNamee, M. (ed.). 2007. *Philosophy, Risk and Adventure Sports.* London: Routledge.

McRobbie, Angela. 1990. "Settling Accounts with Subcultures: A Feminist Critique". In Simon Frith and Andrew Goodwin (eds.), *On Record: Rock, Pop and the Written Word,* pp. 56–65. New York: Pantheon.

—. 1993. "Shut Up and Dance: Youth Culture and the Changing Modes of Femininity". *Cultural Studies* 7(3): 406–26.

Meadan, Bryan. 2001. *TRANCENational ALIENation: Trance Music Culture, Moral Panics and Transnational Identity in Israel.* Lulu.

Measham, Fiona and Karenza Moore. 2006. "Reflecting on Reflexivity: Fifteen Years of Club Research". In Bill Sanders (ed.), *Drugs, Clubs and Young People: Sociological and Public Health Perspectives,* pp. 13–25. Aldershot: Ashgate.

Megalopsy. 2006. "Boom Festival Review 2006: Thoughts and Impressions". *Chaishop.com.* http://www.chaishop.com/article/1759 (accessed 19 December 2010).

Melechi, Antonio. 1993. "The Ecstasy of Disappearance". In Steve Redhead (ed.), *Rave Off: Politics and Deviance in Contemporary Youth Culture,* pp. 29–40. Aldershot: Avebury.

Meltdown23. 2010. Reply to the thread "Goa Trance dj's from back in the days??..". in discussion group "Goa /Psy-Trance". *Discogs.* July. http://www.discogs.com/groups/topic/168381 (accessed 25 June 2011).

Miles, Steven. 2000. *Youth Lifestyles in a Changing World.* Buckingham: Open University Press.

Miller, Graham. 2003a. "The Real Deal: Toward an Aesthetic of Authentic Live Electronic Dance Music, Part 1". *Stylus Magazine.* http://www.stylusmagazine.com/articles/weekly_article/the-real-deal-toward-an-aesthetic-of-authentic-live-electronic-dance-music.htm (accessed 10 May 2008).

—. 2003b. "The Real Deal? Part 2" *Stylus Magazine.* http://www.stylusmagazine.com/articles/weekly_article/the-real-deal-toward-an-aesthetic-of-authentic-live-electronic-dance-music-pt-2.htm (accessed 10 May 2008).

Mishor, Zevic. 2010. "Acid and Anti-Structure: Turner's 'Communitas' and Society's Backlash against the 1960s Counterculture". *Entheogenesis Australis* 2: 10–18.

Morrissey, Sean Afnan. 2008. "Performing Risks: Catharsis, Carnival and Capital in the Risk Society". *Journal of Youth Studies* 11(4): 413–27.

Mothersole, Dave. 2010. "Unveiling the Secret – The Roots of Trance". *Bleep43.* 14 April. http://www.bleep43.com/bleep43/2010/4/14/unveiling-the-secret-the-roots-of-trance.html (accessed 21 January 2011).

Murray, Enda. 2001. "Sound Systems and Australian DiY Culture: Folk Music for the Dot Com Generation". In Graham St John (ed.), *FreeNRG: Notes From the Edge of the Dance Floor,* pp. 57–70. Melbourne: Common Ground. http://undergrowth.org/freenrg_notes_from_the_edge_of_the_dancefloor (accessed 7 June 2012).

Musgrove, Frank. 1974. *Ecstasy and Holiness: Counter Culture and the Open Society.* London: Methuen and Co.

Mylonas, George. 1961. *Eleusis and the Eleusinian Mysteries.* Princeton, NJ: Princeton University Press.

Narby, Jeremy. 1998. *The Cosmic Serpent: DNA and the Origins of Knowledge.* New York: Jeremy P. Tarcher/Putnam.

Natale, Frank. 1995. *Trance Dance: The Dance of Life.* Scranton, PA: Element Books.

Nesbit, Thomas, 2005. "Planet Rock: Black Socioreligious Movements and Early 1980s Electro". In Michael J. Gilmour (ed.), *Call Me the Seeker: Listening to Religion in Popular Music*, pp. 226–38. New York: Continuum.

Neuenfeldt, Karl (ed.). 1997. *The Didjeridu: From Arnhem Land to Internet.* Sydney: John Libbey and Co.

—. 1998. "Good Vibrations: The 'Curious' Cases of the Didjeridu in Spectacle and Therapy in Australia". *The World of Music* 40(2): 29–51.

Newcombe, R. 2008. "Ketamine Case Study: The Phenomenology of a Ketamine Experience". *Addiction Research & Theory* 16(3): 209–15.

Newton, Janice. 1988. "Aborigines, Tribes and the Counterculture". *Social Analysis* 23: 53–71.

Nielsen, Svea and Constance Bettencourt. 2008/2009. "KosmiCare: Creating Safe Spaces for Difficult Psychedelic Experiences". *MAPS* 18(3): 39–44.

Nietzsche, F. 1966. *Birth of Tragedy (Die Geburt der Tragödie, 1872).* Trans. Walter Kaufmann. New York: Vintage.

Niman, Michael. 1997. *People of the Rainbow: A Nomadic Utopia*. Knoxville, TN: University of Tennessee Press.

Northcote, Jeremy. 2006. "Nightclubbing and the Search for Identity: Making the Transition from Childhood to Adulthood in an Urban Milieu". *Journal of Youth Studies* 9(1): 1–16.

Noy, Chaim and Erik Cohen. 2005. "Introduction: Backpacking as a Rite of Passage in Israel". In Chaim Noy and Erik Cohen (eds.), *Israeli Backpackers: From Tourism to Rite of Passage*, pp. 1–43. New York: State University of New York Press.

Nuttall, Jeff. 1968. *Bomb Culture*. London: MacGibbon & Kee.

Odzer, Cleo. 1995. *Goa Freaks: My Hippie Years in India.* New York: Foxrock.

Olaveson, Tim. 2004. "'Connectedness' and the Rave Experience: Rave as New Religious Movement?" In Graham St John (ed.), *Rave Culture and Religion*, pp. 85–106. London: Routledge.

Olsen, Brad. 2001. *World Stompers: A Global Travel Manifesto*. San Francisco: CCC Publishing.

Omananda. n.d. "Secret Insight Knowledge about Trance!" http://www.paradise2012.com/music/omananda.html (accessed 21 October 2010).

—. 2004. "For All the Boomers ... Here is a Story about Faith, Magic, and Universal Love Vibrations". http://www.chaishop.com/text1/r/sam07.htm (accessed 21 October 2010).

—. 2006. "Shamanic Journeys". *Revolve* (Summer): 44.

Osborne, Thomas. 1997. "The Aesthetic Problematic". *Economy and Society* 26(1): 126–46.

Ott, Jonathon. 1995. *The Age of Entheogens & the Angel's Dictionary*. Kennewick, WA: Natural Products Co.

Otto, Rudolph. 1958 [1923]. *The Idea of the Holy*. 2nd ed. Oxford: Oxford University Press.

Palacios, Julian. 2001. "Syd Barrett: Lost in the Woods". Indica Press.

Palmer, Julian. 2011/12. "Changa". *Entheogenesis Australis Journal* 3: 98–101.

Papadimitropoulos, Panagiotis. 2009. "Psychedelic Trance: Ritual, Belief and Transcendental Experience in Modern Raves". *Durham Anthropology Journal* 16(2): 67–74.

paradigm. 2009. Posting to "Symbiosis Gathering" thread. 22 September. http://forum.isratrance.com/symbiosis-gathering-revised-september-17-21-2009-yosemite-ca/page2 (accessed 21 October 2010).

Parish, Tim. 2008. "The Rainbow Conspiracy". *Nomadology*. http://www.dislocated.org/nomadology/user_new.php?user_id=10&j_id=673#673 (accessed 7 September 2010).

Partridge, Christopher H. 1999. "Truth, Authority and Epistemological Individualism in New Age Thought". *Journal of Contemporary Religion* 14(1): 77–95.

—. 2003. "Understanding UFO Religions and Abduction Spiritualities". In Christopher Partridge (ed.), *UFO Religions*, pp. 3–42. London: Routledge.

—. 2004. *The Re-Enchantment of the West: Alternative Spiritualities, Sacralization and Popular Culture and Occulture* (Vol 1). London: T & T Clark International.

—. 2006a. "The Spiritual and the Revolutionary: Alternative Spirituality, British Free Festivals, and the Emergence of Rave Culture". *Culture and Religion* 7(1): 41–60.

—. 2006b. *The Re-Enchantment of the West: Alternative Spiritualities, Sacralization, Popular Culture and Occulture* (Vol 2). London: T & T Clark International.

—. 2007. "King Tubby Meets the Upsetter at the Grass Roots of Dub: Some Thoughts on the Early History and Influence of Dub Reggae". *Popular Music History* 2(3): 309–31.

—. 2010. *Dub in Babylon: The Emergence and Influence of Dub Reggae in Jamaica and Britain from King Tubby to Post-punk*. London: Equinox.

Pavel. 2010. Posting to *Isratrance* thread "Video Interview with GOA GIL". 3 September. http://forum.isratrance.com/video-interview-with-goa-gil (accessed 10 March 2011).

Pedersen, Willy. 1994. "Rites of Passage in High Modernity". *Young* 2(1): 21–32.

Phil G. 2008. "The Goa Gil Petition: Play Those DATS!" 24 January. http://www.beatportal.com/feed/item/the-goa-gil-petition-play-those-dats (accessed 10 March 2011).

Photon, Nigel. 2005. Interview with Youth. *Revolve*. http://www.revolvemagazine.co.uk (accessed 9 July 2007).

Pinchbeck, Daniel. 2002. *Breaking Open the Head: A Psychedelic Journey into the Heart of Contemporary Shamanism*. Portland, OR: Broadway.

Pini, Maria. 1997. "Cyborgs, Nomads and the Raving Feminine". In Helen Thomas (ed.), *Dance in the City*, pp. 111–29. London: Macmillan.

Pope, Richard. 2011. "Hooked on an Affect: Detroit Techno and Dystopian Digital Culture". *Dancecult: Journal of Electronic Dance Music Culture* 2(1): 24–44.

"The Power of the Hexagon". 2010. *Dharma Dragon* 6(1): 2.

Prendergast, Mark. 2001. *The Ambient Century: From Mahler to Trance. The Evolution of Sound in the Electronic Age*. New York: Bloomsbury.

Presdee, Mike. 2000. *Cultural Criminology and the Carnival of Crime*. London: Routledge.

Psilly. 2010. "Boom Festival 2010". http://www.fleshprism.com/category/outsideinsights (accessed 13 July 2011, page no longer live).

Rampuri, Baba. 2005. *Baba: Autobiography of a Blue-Eyed Yogi*. New York: Bell Tower.

Rappaport, Roy. 1999. *Ritual and Religion in the Making of Humanity*. Cambridge: Cambridge University Press.

Redfield, James. 1994. *The Celestine Prophecy: An Adventure*. New York: Warner Books.

Redhead, Steve (ed.). 1993. *Rave Off: Politics and Deviance in Contemporary Youth Culture*. Aldershot: Avebury.

Reynolds, Simon. 1997. "Return to Eden: Innocence, Indolence and Pastoralism in Psychedelic Music, 1966–1996". In Antonio Melechi (ed.), *Psychedelica Britannica: Hallucinogenic Drugs in Britain*, pp. 143–65. London: Turnaround.

—. 1998. *Generation Ecstasy: Into the World of Techno and Rave Culture*. New York: Little, Brown.

Rice, Ronald E. 2008. "Foreword". In Tyrone L. Adams and Stephen A. Smith (eds.), *Electronic Tribes: The Virtual Worlds of Geeks, Gamers, Shamans and Scammers*, pp. vii–xii. Austin, TX: University of Texas Press.

Rich and Dawn (Solarworld). 1997. "Catch up with Ray: An Evolving Ecology of Intuitive Signals". August. http://music.hyperreal.org/artists/metanet/meld2.html (accessed 17 March 2011).

Richard, Birgit and Hienz Hermann Kruger. 1998. "Ravers Paradise? German Youth Cultures in the 1990s". In Tracey Skelton and Gill Valentine (eds.), *Cool Places: Geographies of Youth Cultures*, pp. 161–74. London: Routledge.

Rietveld, Hillegonda. 1993. "Living the Dream". In Steve Redhead (ed.), *Rave Off: Politics and Deviance in Contemporary Youth Culture*, pp. 41–78. Aldershot: Avebury.

—. 1998. *This is Our House: House Music, Cultural Spaces and Technologies*. Aldershot: Ashgate.

—. 2004. "Ephemeral Spirit: Sacrificial Cyborg and Communal Soul". In Graham St John (ed.), *Rave Culture and Religion*, pp. 46–61. London: Routledge.

—. 2008. "Embodied Technocracies". Conference Paper delivered on the panel: Uncertain Vibes: Tension, Contrast and Change in Electronic Dance Music Cultures. ACS Crossroads in Cultural Studies, Kingston, Jamaica.

—. 2010. "Infinite Noise Spirals: Psytrance as Cosmopolitan Emotion". In Graham St John (ed.), *The Local Scenes and Global Culture of Psytrance*, pp. 69–88. New York: Routledge.

Rill, Bryan. 2006. "Rave, Communitas, and Embodied Idealism". *Music Therapy Today* 7(3): 648–61.

Rinehart, Robert and Synthia Sydnor (eds.). 2003. *To the Extreme: Alternative Sports Inside and Out*. Albany, NY: State University of New York Press.

Roadjunky. 2006. "The Golden Days of Goa Trance". *Road Junky Travel*. http://www.roadjunky.com/article/573/goa-trance-parties-india-stories (accessed 18 November 2010).

Roberts, Andy. 2008. *Albion Dreaming: A Popular History of LSD*. London: Marshall Cavendish.

Robertson, Roland. 1994. "Globalisation or Glocalisation?" *Journal of International Communication* 1(1): 33–52.

Rom, Tom and Pascal Querner. 2011. *Goa: 20 Years of Psychedelic Trance*. Solothurn/Switzerland: Nachtschatten Verlag.

Ross, Andrew. 1992. "New Age Technoculture". In Larry Grossberg and P. Treichler (eds.), *Cultural Studies*, pp. 69–79. London: Routledge

Roszak, Theodore. 1995. [1968]. *The Making of a Counter Culture: Reflections on the Technocratic Society and its Youthful Opposition*. Berkeley, CA: University of California Press.

Roth, Gabrielle. 1998. *Sweat Your Prayers*. New York: Tarcher.

Rouget, Gilbert. 1985. *Music and Trance: A Theory of the Relations between Music and Possession*. Chicago, IL: University of Chicago Press.

Rushkoff, Douglas. 1994. *Cyberia: Life in the Trenches of Hyperspace*. Scranton, PE: HarperCollins.

Ryan, Jenny. 2010. "Weaving the Underground Web: Neotribalism and Psytrance on Tribe.net". In Graham St John (ed.), *The Local Scenes and Global Culture of Psytrance*, pp. 186–202. New York: Routledge.

Sagiv, Assaf. 2000. "Dionysus in Zion". *Azure* 9 (Spring). http://www.azure.org.il/include/print.php?id=289 (accessed 17 September 2011).

Said, Edward. 1995 [1978]. *Orientalism: Western Conceptions of the Orient*. London: Penguin.

Saldanha, Arun. 2002. "Music Tourism and Factions of Bodies in Goa". *Tourist Studies* 2(1): 43–62.

—. 2004. "Goa Trance and Trance in Goa: Smooth Striations". In Graham St John (ed.), *Rave Culture and Religion*, pp. 273–86. London: Routledge.

—. 2007a. *Psychedelic White: Goa Trance and the Viscosity of Race*. Minneapolis, MN: University of Minnesota Press.

—. 2007b. "The LSD-Event: Badiou Not on Acid." *Theory and Event* 10(4). http://muse.jhu.edu/login?uri=/journals/theory_and_event/v010/10.4saldanha.html (accessed 21 September 2011).

Sam Chaipshop. 2008. "The Mature Side of Psytrance Culture". 26 August. http://www.chaishop.com/article/12360 (accessed 19 September 2011).

Sams, Greg. 2009. *Sun of God*. RedWheelWeiser.

Sardiello, Robert. 1994. "Secular Rituals in Popular Culture: A Case for Grateful Dead Concerts and Dead Head Identity". In John S. Epstein (ed.), *Adolescents and Their Music: If It's Too Loud, You're Too Old*, pp. 115–38. New York: Garland.

Saunders, Nicholas and Rick Doblin. 1996. *Ecstasy: Dance, Trance and Transformation*. San Francisco: Quick American Publishing Company.

Saunders, Nick, Anja Saunders and Michelle Pauli. 2000. *In Search of the Ultimate High: Spiritual Experiences through Psychoactives*. London: Rider.

Schmidt, Joshua I. 2006. "Fused by Paradox: The Challenge of Being an Israeli Psy-trancer". MA thesis, Ben-Gurion University of the Negev.

—. 2010. "(En)Countering the Beat: Paradox in Israeli Psytrance". In Graham St John (ed.), *The Local Scenes and Global Culture of Psytrance*, pp. 131–48. New York: Routledge.

—. 2011. "Fused by Paradox: A Contrastive Analysis of Secular and Religious Trance-Dance Parties in Israel." PhD dissertation, Department of Behavioral Sciences, Ben-Gurion University of the Negev.

Schou, Nicholas. 2010. *Orange Sunshine: The Brotherhood of Eternal Love and its Quest to Spread Peace, Love, and Acid to the World*. New York: Thomas Dunne Books.

Schütze, Bernard. 2001. "Carnivalesque Mutations in the Bahian Carnival and Rave Culture". *Religiologiques* 24: 155–63.

Shaher. 2008. "Please Open Your Mind Again". *Psychedelic Traveller*: 6–7.

Shapiro, Peter. 2005. *Turn the Beat Around: The Secret History of Disco*. New York: Faber and Faber.

Sherwood, P. 1997. "The Didjeridu and Alternative Lifestylers' Reconstruction of Social Reality". In Karl Neuenfeldt (ed.), *The Didjeridu: From Arnhem Land to Internet*, pp. 139–54. Sydney: John Libbey and Co.

Shilling, Chris and Philip A. Mellor. 2011. "Retheorising Emile Durkheim on Society and Religion: Embodiment, Intoxication and Collective Life". *Sociological Review* 59(1): 17–41.

Shor, Nissan. 2008. *Dancing with Tears in Our Eyes: A History of Club and Discotheque Culture in Israel*. Tel Aviv: Resling [Hebrew].

Shulgin, Alexander and Ann Shulgin. 1991. *Pihkal: A Chemical Love Story*. Berkeley, CA: Transform Press.

—. 1997. *Tihkal: The Continuation*. Berkeley, CA: Transform Press.

Sideburner, Pete. 2007. "The Problem with Psytrance". 22 March. http://forum.isratrance.com/the-problem-with-psytrance-warning-it-s-a-long-post (accessed 11 July 2007).

Silcott, Muriel. 1999. *Rave America: New School Dancescapes*. Quebec: ECW Press.

Siokou, Christine. 2002. "Seeking the Vibe". *Youth Studies Australia* 21(1): 11–18.

Sitoula, Robin. 2009. "Nepal". *Psychedelic Traveller*: 42.

Smith, Huston. 1976. *Forgotten Truth: The Primordial Tradition*. New York: Harper and Row.

Snydly. 1975. "The Connection". *The Stoned Pig* 6 (December): 6–7. http://www.goaheadspace.com/stonedpig/album/Issue%206/index.html (accessed 21 September 2011).

Soares da Silva, Artur. 2008. "A New Kind of Festival". *Pathways: Liminal Zine* 02: 34–37.

Solkinson, Delvin. 2008. "Permaculturing the Future: Planetary Culture Building in a World of Liminality". *Pathways: Liminal Zine* 02: 22–29.

Sommer, Sally. 2001/2002. "C'mon to my House: Underground-House Dancing". *Dance Research Journal* 33(2): 72–86.

St John, Graham. 1997. "Going Feral: Authentica on the Edge of Australian Culture". *Australian Journal of Anthropology* 8(2): 167–89.

—. 1999. "Alternative Cultural Heterotopia: ConFest as Australia 's Marginal Centre". PhD thesis, Dept of Sociology and Anthropology, Latrobe University, Bundoora.

—. 2001a. "Alternative Cultural Heterotopia and the Liminoid Body: Beyond Turner at ConFest". *Australian Journal of Anthropology* 12(1): 47–66.

—. 2001b (ed.). *FreeNRG: Notes from the Edge of the Dance Floor*. Melbourne: Common Ground. http://undergrowth.org/freenrg_notes_from_the_edge_of_the_dancefloor.

—. 2001c. "Doof! Australian Post Rave Culture". In Graham St John (ed.), *FreeNRG: Notes From the Edge of the Dance Floor*, pp. 9–36. Melbourne: Common Ground. http://undergrowth.org/freenrg_notes_from_the_edge_of_the_dancefloor.

—. 2001d. "Australian (Alter)natives: Cultural Drama and Indigeneity". Social *Analysis: Journal of Cultural and Social Practice* 45(1): 122–40.

—. 2001e. "The Battle of the Bands: ConFest Musics and the Politics of Authenticity". *Perfect Beat: The Pacific Journal of Research into Contemporary Music and Popular Culture* 5(2): 69–90.

—. 2004. "Techno Millennium: Dance, Ecology and Future Primitives". In Graham St John (ed.), *Rave Culture and Religion*, pp. 213–35. London: Routledge.

—. 2005a. "Outback Vibes: Sound Systems on the Road to Legitimacy". *Postcolonial Studies: Culture, Politics, Economy* 8(3): 321–36.

—. 2005b. "Off Road Show: Techno, Protest and Feral Theatre". *Continuum: Journal of Media and Cultural Studies* 19(1): 7–22.

—. 2006. "Electronic Dance Music Culture and Religion: An Overview". *Culture and Religion* 7(1): 1–26.

—. 2008a. "Victor Turner and Contemporary Cultural Performance: An Introduction". In Graham St John (ed.), *Victor Turner and Contemporary Cultural Performance*, pp. 1–37. New York: Berghahn.

—. 2008b. "Trance Tribes and Dance Vibes: Victor Turner and Trance Dance Culture". In Graham St John (ed.), *Victor Turner and Contemporary Cultural Performance*, pp. 149–73. New York: Berghahn.

—. 2009. *Technomad: Global Raving Countercultures*. London and Oakville, CT: Equinox.

—. 2010a (ed.). *The Local Scenes and Global Culture of Psytrance*. New York: Routledge.

—. 2010b. "Making a Noise – Making a Difference: Techno-Punk and Terra-ism". *Dancecult: Journal of Electronic Dance Music Culture* 1(2): 1–28.

—. 2011a. "DJ Goa Gil: Kalifornian Exile, Dark Yogi and Dreaded Anomaly". *Dancecult: Journal of Electronic Dance Music Culture* 3(1): 97–128. http://dj.dancecult.net/index.php/journal/article/view/94 (accessed 7 June 2012).

—. 2011b. "The 2012 Movement, Visionary Arts and Psytrance Culture". In Joseph Gelfer (ed.), *2012: Reflections on a Mark in Time*, pp. 123–43. London: Equinox.

—. 2011c. "Rave from the Grave: Dark Trance and the Return of the Dead". In Cory James Rushton and Christopher M. Moreman (eds.), *Zombies are Us: Essays on the Humanity of the Walking Dead*, pp. 24–39. Jefferson, NC: McFarland.

—. 2012a. "Freak Media: Vibe Tribes, Sampledelic Outlaws and Israeli Psytrance". *Continuum: Journal of Media and Cultural Studies* 26(2): 437–47.

—. 2012b. "Total Solar Eclipse Festivals, Cosmic Spirituality and Planetary Culture". In Donna Weston and Andy Bennett (eds.), *Pop Pagans: Pagans and Popular Music*. London: Equinox. Forthcoming.

—. 2013a. "Aliens are Us: Cosmic Liminality, Remixticism and *Alien*ation in Psytrance". *Journal of Religion and Popular Culture* 25(2). Forthcoming .

—. 2013b. "Indian Spirit: Native Americans and the Techno-Tribes of Psytrance". In James Mackay and David Stirrup (eds.), *Tribal Fantasies: Native Americans in the European Imagination 1900–Present*. New York: Palgrave. Forthcoming.

St John, Graham and Chiara Baldini. 2012. "Dancing at the Crossroads of Consciousness: Techno-Mysticism, Visionary Arts and Portugal's Boom Festival". In Carole M. Cusack and Alex Norman (eds.), *Handbook of New Religions and Cultural Production*, pp. 521–52. Leiden: Brill.

Stephenson, William. 2003. "Scoring Ecstasy: MDMA, Consumerism and Spirituality in the Early Fiction of Irvine Welsh". *Journal for Cultural Research* 7(2): 147–63.

Stevens, Jay. 1989 [1987]. *Storming Heaven: LSD and the American Dream*. London: Paladin.

Stone, C.J. 1996. *Fierce Dancing: Adventures in the Underground*. London: Faber and Faber.

Strassman, Rick. 2001. *DMT: The Spirit Molecule. A Doctor's Revolutionary Research into the Biology of Near-Death and Mystical Experiences*. 3rd ed. Rochester, VT: Park Street Press.

Strassman, Rick (with Slawek Wojtowicz, Luis Eduardo Luna and Ede Frecska). 2008. *Inner Paths to Outer Space: Journeys to Alien Worlds through Psychedelics and Other Spiritual Technologies*. Rochester, VT: Park Street Press.

Straw, Will. 2001. "Dance Music". In Simon Frith, Will Straw and John Street (eds.), *The Cambridge Companion to Pop and Rock*, pp. 158–75. Cambridge: Cambridge University Press.

Strong, Peter. 2001. "Doofstory: Sydney Park to the Desert". In Graham St John (ed.), *FreeNRG: Notes from the Edge of the Dance Floor*, pp. 108–35. Altona: Common Ground. http://undergrowth.org/freenrg_notes_from_the_edge_of_the_dancefloor.

Sutcliffe, Steven. 1997. "Seekers, Networks, and 'New Age'". *Scottish Journal of Religious Studies* 18(2): 97–114.

—. 2000. "'Wandering Stars': Seekers and Gurus in the Modern World". In Steven Sutcliffe and Marion Bowman (eds.), *Beyond New Age: Exploring Alternative Spirituality*, pp. 17–36. Edinburgh: Edinburgh University Press.

—. 2007. "The Origins of 'New Age' Religion between the Two World Wars". In Daren Kemp and James R. Lewis (eds.), *Handbook of New Age*, pp. 51–76. Leiden: Brill.

Sutcliffe, Steven and Marion Bowman (eds.). 2000. "Introduction". In Steven Sutcliffe and Marion Bowman (eds.), *Beyond New Age: Exploring Alternative Spirituality*, pp. 1–13. Edinburgh: Edinburgh University Press.

Sylvan, Robin. 2002. *Traces of the Spirit: The Religious Dimensions of Popular Music*. New York: New York University Press.

—. 2005. *Trance Formation: The Spiritual and Religious Dimensions of Global Rave Culture*. New York: Routledge.

Syntesis. 2010. Post to the thread "Boom 2010" (11 September). http://forum.isratrance.com/boom-2010/50-164347/page6 (accessed 20 September 2011).

Takahashi, Melanie. 2004. "The 'Natural High': Altered States, Flashbacks and Neural Tuning at Raves". In Graham St John (ed.), *Rave Culture and Religion*, pp. 145–64. New York: Routledge.

—. 2005. "Spirituality through the Science of Sound: The DJ as Technoshaman in Rave Culture". In Michael J. Gilmour (ed.), *Call Me the Seeker: Listening to Religion in Popular Music*, pp. 239–66. London: Continuum.

Takahashi, Melanie and Tim Olaveson. 2003. "Music, Dance and Raving Bodies: Raving as Spirituality in the Central Canadian Rave Scene". *Journal of Ritual Studies* 17(2): 72–96.

Tart, Charles. 1975. *States of Consciousness*. New York: E.P. Dutton.

Taub, Gadi. 1997. *A Dispirited Rebellion: Essays on Contemporary Israeli Culture*. Tel Aviv: Hakibutz Hameuchad.

Taves, Ann. 1999. *Fits, Trances and Visions: Experiencing Religion and Explaining Experience from Wesley to James*. Princeton, NJ: Princeton University Press.

Taylor, Timothy D. 2001. *Strange Sounds: Music, Technology and Culture*. New York: Routledge.

"TAZ of the World and the Boom TAZ: Indie Tribes Unite". 2010. *Dharma Dragon* 6(1): 18–19.

Thomas, Peter (aka Blond Peter). 2011. "Goa: Some Origins". Extract from his work in progress *ORIGINALLY*, on "The Flower Raj blog: escapers, seekers, travellers in the land of the Gods: India revisited". 30 March. http://blog.theflowerraj.org/?p=1050 (accessed 20 September 2011).

Thompson, E.P. 1963. *The Making of the English Working Class*. London: Victor Gollancz.

Thornton, Sarah. 1996 [1995]. *Club Cultures: Music, Media and Subcultural Capital*. Middletown, CT: Wesleyan University Press.

Tiago Coutinho. 2006. "From Religious Ecstasy to Ecstasy Pills: A Symbolic and Performative Analysis of Electronic Music Festivals". *Religião & Sociedade* 2(1). Trans. David Rodgers. http://socialsciences.scielo.org/scielo.php?pid=S0100-85872006000200004&script=sci_arttext (accessed 20 June 2008).

Till, Rupert. 2009. "Possession Trance Ritual in Electronic Dance Music Culture: A Popular Ritual Technology for Reenchantment. Addressing the Crisis of the Homeless Self, and

Reinserting the Individual into the Community". In Chris Deacy (ed.), *Exploring Religion and the Sacred in a Media Age*, pp. 169–87. Aldershot: Ashgate.

Time Wave Zero (aka Tina). 2007. Posting to *Isatrance* thread "Video Interview with GOA GIL". 10 May. http://forum.isratrance.com/video-interview-with-goa-gil (accessed 10 March 2011).

Tolle, Eckhart. 1999. *The Power of NOW: A Guide to Spiritual Enlightenment*. Novato, CA: New World Library.

Tom Thumb. 2010. "The Goa Freak Scene and 8 Finger Eddie". http://www.roadjunky.com/article/2418/the-goa-freak-scene-and-8-finger-eddie.

Tomlinson, Lori. 1998. "This Ain't no Disco … Or is it? Youth Culture and the Rave Phenomenon". In John S. Epstein (ed.), *Youth Culture: Identity in a Postmodern World*, pp. 195–211. Malden: Blackwell.

Toop, David. 1984. *The Rap Attack: African Jive to New York Hip Hop*. Boston: South End.

Tramacchi, Des. 2000. "Field Tripping: Psychedelic Communitas and Ritual in the Australian Bush". *Journal of Contemporary Religion* 15(2): 201–3.

—. 2004. "Entheogenic Dance Ecstasis: Cross-cultural Contexts". In Graham St John (ed.), *Rave Culture and Religion*, pp. 125–44. London: Routledge.

—. 2006a. "Vapours and Visions: Religious Dimensions of DMT Use". PhD thesis, School of History, Philosophy, Religion and Classics, University of Queensland.

—. 2006b. "Entheogens, Elves and Other Entities: Encountering the Spirits of Shamanic Plants and Substances". In Lynne Hume and Kathleen McPhillips (eds.), *Popular Spiritualities: The Politics of Contemporary Enchantment*, pp. 91–104. Aldershot: Ashgate.

Turino, Thomas. 2008. *Music as Social Life: The Politics of Participation*. Chicago, IL: University of Chicago Press.

Turner, Edith. 2012. *Communitas: The Anthropology of Collective Joy*. New York: Palgrave Macmillan.

Turner, Fred. 2006. *From Counterculture to Cyberculture: Stewart Brand, the Whole Earth Network, and the Rise of Digital Utopianism*. Chicago, IL: University of Chicago Press.

Turner, Steve. 2006. *The Fab Four: The Gospel According to The Beatles*. Louisville, KY: WJK Press.

Turner, Victor. 1967. "Betwixt and Between: The Liminal Period in *Rites de Passage*". In Victor Turner, *The Forest of Symbols: Aspects of Ndembu Ritual*, pp. 93–111. Ithaca, NY: Cornell University Press.

—. 1969. *The Ritual Process: Structure and Anti-Structure*. Chicago, IL: Aldine.

—. 1973. "The Center out There: Pilgrim's Goal". *History of Religions* 12(1): 191–230.

—. 1974. *Dramas, Fields, and Metaphors: Symbolic Action in Human Society*. Ithaca, NY: Cornell University Press.

—. 1982a. "Liminal to Liminoid, in Play, Flow, Ritual: An Essay in Comparative Symbology". In Victor Turner, *From Ritual to Theatre: The Human Seriousness of Play*, pp. 20–60. New York: Performing Arts Journal Publications.

—. 1982b. "Social Dramas and Stories about Them". In Victor Turner, *From Ritual to Theatre: The Human Seriousness of Play*, pp. 61–88. New York: Performing Arts Journal Publications.

—. 1982c. *From Ritual to Theatre: The Human Seriousness of Play*. New York: Performing Arts Journal Publications.

—. 1983. "Carnival in Rio: Dionysian Drama in an Industrialising Society". In F. Manning (ed.), *The Celebration of Society: Perspectives on Contemporary Cultural Performance*, pp. 103–24. Bowling Green, OH: Bowling Green University Press.

—. 1984. "Liminality and the Performative Genres". In John J. MacAloon (ed.), *Rite, Drama, Festival, Spectacle: Rehearsals Towards a Theory of Cultural Performance*, pp. 19–41. Philadelphia, PA: Institute for Study of Human Issues.

—. 1985. "Process, System, and Symbol: A New Anthropological Synthesis". In Edith Turner (ed.), *On the Edge of the Bush: Anthropology as Experience*, pp. 151–73. Tucson, AZ: University of Arizona Press.

Turner, Victor and Edith Turner. 1978. *Image and Pilgrimage in Christian Culture: Anthropological Perspectives*. New York: Columbia University Press.

Twist, Cinnamon. 1999. "Keys to the Temporary Temple". *Beam 1.2, Radio V*. http://www.radiov.com/main/beam/features/keys (accessed 1 October 2007, page no longer live).

Van. 2003. "Interview XP – Spun Records Aerodance". 27 September. http://www.chaishop.com/article/985 (accessed 3 October 2011).

Van Gennep, Arnold. 1960 [1909]. *The Rites of Passage*. London: Routledge and Kegan.

Van Ree, Erik. 1997. "Fear of Drugs". *International Journal of Drug Policy* 8(2): 93–100.

van Veen, tobias c. 2010. "Technics, Precarity and Exodus in Rave Culture". *Dancecult: Journal of Electronic Dance Music Culture* 1(2): 29–49. http://dj.dancecult.net/index.php/journal/article/view/9 (accessed 7 June 2012).

Vitos, Botond. 2009. "The Inverted Sublimity of the Dark Psytrance Dance Floor". *Dancecult: Journal of Electronic Dance Music Culture* 1(1): 137–41. http://dj.dancecult.net/index.php/journal/article/view/35/ (accessed 7 June 2012).

—. 2010. "DemenCZe: Psychedelic Madhouse in the Czech Republic". In Graham St John (ed.), *The Local Scenes and Global Culture of Psytrance*, pp. 151–69. New York: Routledge.

Wallis, Roy. 1984. *The Elementary Forms of New Religious Life*. London: Routledge & Kegan Paul.

Ward, Andrew. 1993. "Dancing in the Dark: Rationalism and the Neglect of Social Dance". In Helen Thomas (ed.), *Dance, Sex, and Gender*, pp. 16–33. London: St Martin's Press.

Wasson, R. Gordon, Albert Hofmann and Carl A. P. Ruck. 1978. *The Road to Eleusis: Unveiling the Secret of the Mysteries*. New York: Harcourt.

Watts, Alan. 2006 [1994]. *Eastern Wisdom, Modern Life: Collected Talks: 1960–1969*. Novato, CA: New World Library.

Weber, Donald. 1995. "From Limen to Border: A Meditation on the Legacy of Victor Turner for American Cultural Studies". *American Quarterly* 47(3): 525–36.

Weil, Andrew. 1980. *Marriage of the Sun and Moon: A Quest for Unity in Consciousness*. Boston, MA: Houghton Mifflin.

Westerhausen, Klaus. 2002. *Beyond the Beach: An Ethnography of Modern Travellers in Asia*. Studies in Asian Tourism 2. Bangkok: White Lotus.

Whiteley, Sheila. 1997. "Altered Sounds". In Alberto Melechi (ed.), *Psychedelia Britannica: Hallucinogenic Drugs in Britain*, pp. 22–52. London: Turnaround.

Williamson, L. 2010. *Transcendent in America: Hindu-Inspired Meditation Movements as New Religion*. New York: New York University Press.

Willis, Paul. 1978. *Profane Culture*. London: Routledge & Kegan Paul.

Winkelman, Michael. 1986. "Trance States: A Theoretical Model and Cross-Cultural Analysis". *Ethos* 14: 174–203.

—. 2000. *Shamanism: The Neural Ecology of Consciousness and Healing*. Westport, CT: Bergin & Garvey.

Wolfe, Tom. 1971. *The Electric Kool-Aid Acid Test*. New York: Bantam.

Woodhead, Linda. 2001. "The World's Parliament of Religions and the Rise of Alternative Spirituality". In Linda Woodhead (ed.), *Reinventing Christianity: Nineteenth-Century Contexts*, pp. 81–96. Aldershot: Ashgate.

Worthington, Andy. 2004. *Stonehenge: Celebration & Subversion*. Loughborough: Alternative Albion.

Wripple, Naasko. 2007. "The Liminal Village". In *Boom Book*, pp. 74–104. Lisbon: Good Mood Productions.

Wyn, Johanna and Rob White. 1997. *Rethinking Youth*. Sydney: Allen & Unwin.

Yellow Peril. n.d. Interview with Ollie Olsen. "Exploring Other Frequencies". http://www.snarl.org/texts/features/Ollie.htm (accessed 3 February 2007).

York, Michael. 2005. "Sun Worship". In *The Encyclopedia of Religion and Nature*, pp. 1606–1607. London and New York: Thoemmes Continuum.

Discography

23 Degrees. 1994. *...An Endless Searching for Substance*. 2xCD, Album. Entropica: ENT-23000CD.

Adham Shaikh. 2006. *Collectivity*. CD. Sonicturtle Records: ST007.

Afrika Bambaataa and the Soulsonic Force. 1982. *Planet Rock*. Vinyl, 12-inch. Tommy Boy Music: TB 823.

Alien Mental. 2007. *Mind Hack*. CD. Insomnia Records: INSOCD10.

Alpha Wave Movement. 2002. *A Distant Signal*. CDr. Harmonic Resonance Recordings: none.

AMD. 2009. *Frogology*. CD. Frogadelic Records: FROG01CD.

Ananda Shake. 2005. *Emotion in Motion*. CD. Utopia Records: UTPCD08.

Androcell. 2010. *Entheomythic*. CD. Celestial Dragon Records: CDREC22.

Archaic. 2008. *Wildness*. CD. Wildthings Records: WILDCD009.

Asia 2001. 1997. *Psykadelia*. CD. Trans'Pact Productions: 097-008.

Astral Projection. 1996. *Trust in Trance*. CD. TIP Records: TIPCD5.

Astral Projection. 1997. *Dancing Galaxy*. CD. Ganesha: GAN-02.

Astral Projection. 2001. *Anything is Possible / Another World (Passenger Remix)*. Vinyl. Transient Records: TRA064.

Astrological. 1998. *Space Odyssey*. CD. Trance Medusa Records: DETMP9802007.

Audiomatic. 2011. *Weekend Society*. CD. Spintwist Records: SPN1CD039.

Awake. 2008. *The Core*. CD. Ultimae Records: INRE031.

Banco De Gaia. 1999. *The Magical Sounds of Banco De Gaia*. CD. Disco Gecko: GKOCD001.

Baphomet Engine. 2009. *Baphomet Engine 2*. CD. Manic Dragon Records: MDREC14.

Baphomet Engine vs. DataKult. 2006. *Psytrance is Dead!* CD. Nabi Records: NABICD005.

Barkan, Eyal. 1998. *Good Morning Israel*. CD. Eyal Barkan Records: EBCD001.

Blissed. 1993. *Rite of Passage*. CD. Pod Communication: PODCD029.

Blue Lunar Monkey. 2008. *Beyond 2012*. File, MP3. Synergetic Records: SYNDIGI002.

Breach of Space. 1995. *Accidental Occidentalism*. CD. Symbiosis: symbcd01.

Burn in Noise. 2008. *Passing Clouds*. 2008. CD, Mixed. Alchemy Records: ALCD026.

C-Jay. 2011. *Forever Now*. CD. Plusquam Records: PQ255.

California Sunshine. 1997. *Trance*. CD. Phonokol: 2066-2.

Chi-A.D. 1999. *Anno Domini*. CD. Velvet Inc: NTD 92511-22.

Chromosome. 2004. *The Genome Project*. CD. Yellow Sunshine Explosion: YSE045CD.

Citizen. 2007. *Uncharted*. CD Comp. Flow Records: FLR0720CD.

Cosmic Baby. 1992. *Stellar Supreme—The Clubmixes*. Vinyl. MFS: MFS70331.

Cosmic Jokers, The. 1974. *Galactic Supermarket*. Vinyl, 12-inch. Spalax Music: LP14192.

Cosmosis. 1996. *Cosmology*. CD. Transient Records: TRANRCD604.

Cosmosis. 2002. *Contact*. CD. Transient Records: TRANR640CD.

Cosmosis. 2007. *Psychedelica Melodica*. CD. Phantasm Records: PTMCD163.

Cosmosophy. 2008. *Organic Space Age*. CD. Elestial Records: ER002.

Cybernetika. 2008. *Nanospheric*. MP3. Self-released: none.

Daksinamurti. 2008. *Ahimsa*. 2xCD Comp. Dacru Records: DCRCD004.

Dance 2 Trance. 1991. *Dance 2 Trance*. CD, Maxi-Single. Suck Me Plasma: SUCK TWO CD.

Dark Nebula. 2003. *The 8th Sphere*. CD. Digital Psionics: DPSICD06.

Dark Soho. 2000. *Sun Spot*. CD. Sphere Records: SPHCD004.

Dimension 5. 1997. *Transdimensional*. CD. Intastella Records: INTACD01.

DJ Boom Shankar. 2011. *Transition*. CD, Comp. BMSS Records: BMSS004CD.
DJ Cosmix & Etnica. 1995. *Kumba Mela E.P.* Vinyl. Matsuri Productions: MP007.
DJ Goa Gil. 1995. *Spiritual Trance Vol. 2*. CD, Comp, Mixed. Javelin: 3014572.
DJ Goa Gil. 1995. *Techno Spiritual Trance from Goa*. CD, Mixed. Javelin Ltd: 3005392.
DJ Goa Gil. 2005. *Karmageddon*. CD, Comp, Mixed. Avatar: AVA029.
DJ Goa Gil. 2009. *Kali Yuga*. CD, Comp, Mixed. Avatar: AVA057.
DJ Transgenic. 2010 *Extreme Noise Terror Vol. 1*. CD. Terror Lab Industries: TLICD001.
Doctor Acid. *Doctor Acid*. 1996. CD. YoYo Records: YOYO04.
Don Peyote. 1999. *AreUpeyoted? A Collection of Trippy Tunes for Cosmic Go-Go Dancers*. CD. Peyote Recordings: None.
Doof. 1996. *Let's Turn On*. CD. TIP Records: TIP CD 10.
Dr Zarkhow. 1989. *Interplanetary Adventures*. Vinyl, 12-inch. Technology: TECHNO1253.
Earth Nation. 1994. *Alienated*. Vinyl, 12-inch. Eye Q Records: 4509 95485-0.
Eat Static. 2000. *Crash and Burn!* CD. CyberOctave: 724385074325.
Electric Universe. 1994. *Solar Energy*. EP. Vinyl. Spirit Zone Recordings: SpiritZone4002.
Electric Universe. 1996. *Sunglider*, EP. Vinyl. Spirit Zone Recordings: SPIRITZONE14.
Electric Universe. 2006. *Silence in Action*. CD. Electric Universe Records: EUCD001.
Electric Universe. 2011. *Higher Modes*. CD. Electric Universe Records: ELU1CD004.
Electrotete. 1991. *Anjuna Dawn*. CD. Warner Music UK: YZ623T.
Elysium. 1996. *Monzoon*. CD. YoYo Records: YOYO10.
Eno, Brian (with Daniel Lanois & Roger Eno). 1983. *Apollo – Atmospheres & Soundtracks*. LP. E'G Records: 813 535-1.
Entheogenic Sound Explorers. 2007. *The Shroom Experience*. CD. Practising Nature: PN07024.
Etnica. 1995. *Tribute / Astral Way*. Vinyl, 12-inch. Blue Room Released: BR010.
Exaile. 2004. *Hit the Machine*. CD. Chemical Crew: CHEMCD04.
F.F.T. 2006. *Future Frequency Technology*. CD. AP Records: AP152.
Filteria. 2009. *Daze of Our Lives*. CD. Suntrip Records: SUNCD14.
Ganga Giri. 2002. *Tribe Vibe*. CD. Sammasati Music: SM7007.
Ganga Giri. 2006. *Raising it Up*. CD. Ganga Giri: GAGCD006.
Hallucinogen. 1995 *Angelic Particles/Soothsayer*. Vinyl, 12-inch. TIP Records: TIP004.
Hallucinogen. 1997. *The Lone Deranger*. CD. Twisted Records: TWSCD1.
Hallucinogen. 2002. *In Dub*. CD. Twisted Records: TWSCD16.
Haltya. 2004. *Electric Help Elves*. CD. Exogenic Records: EXOCD21.
Haltya. 2008. *Book of Nature*. CD. Exogenic Records: EXOCD3.
Har-El Prussky. 1995. *New Pagan World*. CD. S.D.R. Music: 30066.
Hedonix, 2009. *Order Out of Chaos*. CD. Electric Power Pole Records: EPP011.
Imix. *Mindwaves*. 2008. Digital Drugs Coalition: digicd004.
Indoor. 1995. *Progressive Trance*. CD. NMC Music: 201542.
Infected Mushroom. 1999. *The Gathering*. CD Maxi-single. YoYo: YOYO32-2.
Infected Mushroom. 2003. *Deeply Disturbed*. CD. YoYo Records: YOYOCS05.
Infected Mushroom. 2007. *Becoming Insane*. CD, EP. YoYo Records: YOYOCS12.
Infinity Project, The. 1991. *Hyper-Active*. Vinyl, 12-inch. Atmosphere Records: AT15.
Infinity Project, The. 1992. *Tribadelic Meltdown*. Vinyl, 12-inch, EP. Fabulous Music UK: FABU 016T.
Infinity Project, The. 1993. *Time And Space*. Vinyl, 12-inch, EP, Promo. Dragonfly: BFLT 9.
Infinity Project, The. 1994. *Stimuli / Uforica*. Vinyl, 12-inch. TIP Records: TIP001.
Infinity Project, The. 1995. *Feeling Weird*. CD. TIP Records: TIPCD3.
Infinity Project, The. 1995. *Mystical Experiences*. CD. Blue Room Released: BR005CD.
Insectoid. 1998. *Groovology of the Metaverse*. CD. WMS Records: WMSLP02.
Invid Mind & Jhunix. 2010. *Those Who Remember the Past*. CD: Alkhimia Records: ALKCD001.
Jimi Hendrix Experience, The. 1967. *Are You Experienced?* LP, Mono. Track Records: RS 6261.

John 00 Fleming & DJ Bim. 2011. *Goa Culture III.* CD, Comp. Yellow Sunshine Explosion: MillYSE 254-CD.
Jungle High. 1992. *Jungle High.* Vinyl, 12-inch. Logic Records: LUK011.
Juno Reactor. 1993. *Transmissions.* CD. NovaMute: NoMu 24 CD.
KLF, The. 1988. *What Time is Love? (Pure Trance 1).* Vinyl, 12-inch. KLF Communications: KLF 004T.
KLF, The. 1991. *The White Room.* LP. KLF Communications: JAMS LP006.
Kode IV. 1995. *Silicon Civilisation.* CD. KK Records: KK109CD.
Koxbox. 1995. *Forever After.* Vinyl. Harthouse: HHLP012.
Kraftwerk. 1977. *Trans-Europe Express.* Vinyl, LP. King Klang: 1C 064-82 306.
Laserdance. 1989. *Cosmo Tron.* CD. Hotsound Records: HS89181.
Lightsphere. 2011. *Oneness.* CD. Audioload Music: ALM1CD003.
Lucas. 2010. *Tales of Heads.* CD, Comp. TIP Records: TIPR03CD.
Lumukanda. 1993. *Araglin.* CD. Psy-Harmonics: PSY007.
Man With No Name. 1995. *Floor-Essence* EP. Vinyl. Perfecto: SAM1642.
Man With No Name. 1996. *Moment of Truth.* CD. Avex Trax: AVCD11431.
Mantrix. 2006. *Universal.* CD, Album. Sub Records: sub002.
Mark Allen. 1995. *Deck Wizards – Psychedelic Trance Mix.* CD, Comp, Mixed. Psychic Deli: PDCD001.
Masaray. 1995. *Cosmic Trancer.* CD. Psy-Harmonics: PSY017PSY017.
Medicine Drum. 1999. *Talking Stick.* CD. CyberOctave: COCD48092.
MentalImage. 2010. *Dreams Vol. 2.* File. Gliese 581c: gc010.
Montauk P. 1997. *Hallucinate / X-Plore.* EP, Vinyl. Blue Room Released: BR022.
Narcosis. 2007. *Exploding Madness.* CD. Moonsun Records: MSUCD002.
Neelix. 2008. *You're Under Control.* CD. Spintwist Records: SPN1CD022.
Neuromotor. 2001. *Neuro Damage.* CD. Acid Dance Records: ACIDCD003.
Nommos, The. 2004. *Digitaria.* CD. Avatar: AVA0203302282.
Nystagmus. 2005. *The Immaculate Perception.* CD. Sundance Records: SUNDCD027.
Oforia. 1998. *Delirious.* CD. Dragonfly Records: BFLCD26.
Om. 1993. *Instant Enlightenment (Deep Trance Ambient Experience).* CD. C & S Records: CS85132.
Optica. 1997. *F-U-Z-Z.* CD. Kinetix Recordings: KINXCD6.
Orb, The. 1991. *The Orb's Adventures Beyond the Ultraworld.* CD. Big Life: BLRDCD 05.
Organarchy. 1999. *BPM Conspiracies.* CD. Organarchy: ORGANARCHY002.
Overlords, The. 1991. *Sundown.* CD, Maxi-Single. Antler-Subway: AS 5051CD.
Overlords, The. 1994. *All the Naked People.* CD. Arista: 72445-11083-2.
Ovnimoon. 2011. *Magnetic Portal.* CD. Ovnimoon Records: OVNICD014.
Pan Papason. 2008. *Come with Me.* CD. On The Move Music: OTMCD04.
Paul Oakenfold – A Voyage into Trance. 1995. CD, Mixed. Dragonfly: bflcd 14.
Peaking Goddess Collective, The. 2007. *Organika.* CD. Peak Records: PR013.
PeLinPaLa. 2000. *My CD Has Landed on My Next Door Neighbour's Dog.* CD. Demon Tea Recordings: DMT CD06.
Pink Floyd. 1971. *Relics: A Bizarre Collection of Antiques and Curios.* Vinyl, Comp. Capital Records: SW-759.
Pleiadians. 1999. *Family of Light.* CD. Dragonfly: BFLCD 34.
Prahlad. 2007. *Movements of Consciousness.* CD. Yellow Sunshine Explosion: YSE158CD.
Prānā. 1996. *Cyclone.* CD. Phonokol: 20402.
Prānā. 1997. *Geomantik.* CD. YoYo Records: YOYO15.
Prometheus Process / Hallucinogen. 1997. *Clarity from Deep Fog / Spiritual Antiseptic.* Vinyl. Twisted Records: TWST3.
Psilocybe Vibe. 2011. *Psilocybe Vibe* EP.
Psychonaut. 2010. *Free-Rider.* CD. Crotus Records: CROTUSCD023.

Psychopod. 1996. *Dreampod*. CD. TIP Records: TIPCD17.
Psychopod. 1997. *Headlines* EP. CD. TIP Records: TIPCDS026.
Psychotic Micro and Azax Syndrom. 2003. *Voices of Madness*. CD, Comp. Parvati: PRVCD04.
PsyCraft. 2002. *Gravitech*. CD. HOM-Mega Productions: HMCD1921952.
RA. 2008. *9th*. Suntrip. CD. Suntrip Records: SUNCD07.
Ram Dass & Kriece. 2008. *Cosmix*. CD. Waveform Records: 081012.
Rhythmystec. 1995. *Plasmatik* EP. 12-inch. Matsuri Productions: MP06 UK.
Rhythmystec. 1996. *Cathexis*. 12-inch. Matsuri: MP18.
Sandman. 1998. *Witchcraft*. CD. Matsuri: MPTCD07.
Scatterbrain. 2003. *Infernal Angel*. CD. Digital Psionics: DPSICD07.
SFX. 1998. *SFX: The Unreleased Tracks—89–94*. CD. Phonokol: 21152.
Shakta. 1997. *Silicon Trip*. CD. Dragonfly Records: BFLCD23.
Shamen, The (with Terence McKenna). 1993. *Re:Evolution*. CD. One Little Indian: 118TP7CD.
Shanti Druid. 1994. *Insect-A-Traction / Sweet Revenge*. Vinyl, 12 inch. Celtic Records: celtic002.
Shpongle. 1998. *Are You Shpongled?* CD. Twisted Records: TWSCD4.
Shpongle. 2000. *Divine Moments of Truth*. CD. Twisted Records: TWSC14.
Shpongle. 2001. *Tales of the Inexpressible*. CD. Twisted Records: TWSCD13.
Shpongle. 2005. *Nothing Lasts... But Nothing is Lost*. CD. Twisted Records: TWSCD28.
Shpongle. 2009. *Ineffable Mysteries from Shpongleland*. CD. Twisted Records: TWSCD36.
Skazi. 2006. *Total Anarchy*. CD. Chemical Crew: CHEMCD13.
Slinky Wizard. 1994. *Slinky Wizard* EP. Vinyl. Flying Rhino Records: ZFR001.
Solar Fields. 2007. *Earthshine*. Ultimae Records. CD. Ultimae Records: INRE026.
Solar Quest. 1998. *AcidOphilez*. 2xCD, Comp, Mixed. Entropica: ENT-00000.
Solar Quest. 2000. *Orgisms*. CD. Entropica: ENT-03030.
Soul Kontakt. 2008. *Deliverance* EP. CD. Ektoplazm: EKTEP02.
Space Tribe. 1996. *Sonic Mandala*. CD. Spirit Zone Records: Spirit Zone 017.
Space Tribe. 1996. *Ultrasonic Heartbeat*. Vinyl, 12-inch. Spirit Zone Recordings: SPIRITZONE016.
Space Tribe. 1997. *The Ultraviolet Catastrophe*. CD. Spirit Zone Recordings: SPIRITZONE031.
Space Tribe. 1998. *The Future's Right Now*. CD. Spirit Zone Recordings: SPIRIT ZONE 044.
Space Tribe. 2000. *Religious Experience*. CD. Spirit Zone Recordings: SPIRITZONE080.
Sri Hari. 1995. *Rising Sign*. CD. Bhaktivedanta Book Trust: BBTS67CD.
Sri Hari. 1997. *One But Different*. CD. Bhaktivedanta Book Trust: BBTS81CD.
Star Sounds Orchestra. 1991. *Planets*. CD. Fønix Musik Forlag: FMF CD 1051.
Sub Atomic 2008. *The Movements* EP. File. DigitaLies: none.
Subsistence. 2011. *The Condition of Existence*. CD. Uxmal Records: UXM1CD004.
Sun Control Species. 2004. *Sun Control Species – Unreleased*.
Sunstryk. 2010. *Pure Essence*. CD. Plusquam Records: PQ190.
Sunstryk. 2011. *Serenity*. CD. Plusquam Records: PQ266.
Tangerine Dream. 1979. *Force Majeure*. Vinyl LP. Virgin: VIL12111.
Technossomy. 1995. *Timepiece*. Vinyl LP. Symbiosis Records: SYMB005.
Tetrameth. 2010. *The Eclectic Benevolence*. CD. Zenon: ZENCD023.
Third Eye. 1993. *Ancient Future*. CD. Psy-Harmonics: PSY001.
Third Eye. 1993. *New Life* EP. CD. Psy-Harmonics: PROMO001.
Toshinori Kondo and Bill Laswell (featuring His Holiness The Dalai Lama). 2001. *Life Space Death*. CD. Meta Records: MT011.
Total Eclipse. 1996. *Violent Relaxation*. CD. Blue Room: BR015CD.
Total Eclipse. 2003. *Update Files*. CD. Arcadia Music: ARCCD004.
Transwave. 1995. *Hypnorhythm*. Vinyl, 12-inch, EP. Matsuri: MP08.
Twisted Allstars, The. 2002. *Twisted Sessions Vol. 1*. CD. Twisted Records: TWSCD18.
Various. *A Cyber Tribal Exodus – Movement of Da People*. 2005. DVD/CD. Happy People Music: none.
Various. *Accidental Occidentalism*. 1995. CD. Symbiosis Records: symbcd01.

Various. *Anahata.* 2009. File. Active Meditation Music: AMM001.
Various. *Andes Trip.* 2007. File. Neurotrance: NEURO001.
Various. *Are You Upset?* 2009. CD. Infarto Music.
Various. *Behind the Mirror.* 2011. CD. Cosmic Eclipse Records.
Various. *Black Sun – Eclipse in Japan.* CD. Rockdenashi Productionz: ROCKDENACD001.
Various. *Blue Compilation.* 1997. CD. TIP Records: TIP CD 04.
Various. *Blue Room Released Vol: 1 – Outside The Reactor.* 1995. 3 x Vinyl, 12-inch. Blue Room Released: BR001LP.
Various. *Caribbean Eclipse.* 1999. CD. Flying Rhino Freestyle: AFRFCD00.
Various. *Chakra Journey, The.* 1996. CD. Return To The Source: RTTSCD2.
Various. *Contagion Vol. 1.* 2008. File. Dead Tree Productions: DTP002.
Various. *Death of Mind* (promo). Compiled by Neumos & Nahualli. 2010. CD. FDL Records.
Various. *Deep Trance and Ritual Beats.* 1995. CD. Return To The Source: RTTSCD1.
Various. *Demented.* 2000. CD. Twisted Records: TWSCD6.
Various. *Digital Alchemy.* 1994. CD. Concept In Dance: DICCD123.
Various. *Digital Dance of Shiva, The.* 1999. CD. Shiva Space Technology: SSTCD004.
Various. *Distorted Shire.* 2009. CD. Lycantrop Records: LYCCD002.
Various. *Dragonfly – A Voyage into Trance Vol 2.* 1998. CD. Nova Tekk: NTD905062.
Various. *Dream Creation – The Sound of Freedom.* 1998. CD. Transient Records: TRANR619CD.
Various. *Eclipse – A Journey of Permanence & Impermanence.* 1998. CD. Twisted Records: TWSCD3.
Various. *Extraterrestrial Comics.* 2007. CD Mass Abduction Records: MARCD003.
Various. *Faith, Hope and Psychedelia.* 1998. CD. A.R.D.: ASHACD1.
Various. *Fill Your Head with Phantasm.* 1995. CD. Phantasm Records: PTM131.
Various. *First Impression.* 2002. CD. A.P. Records: AP106.
Various. *Forty Five Full Moons.* 2008. File. Cosmogenesis Recordings: COSGENCD09.
Various. *Full On.* 1998. CD. HOM-Mega Productions: HMCD1.
Various. *Global Alliance.* 2005. Fragile Planet Records: FPRCD002.
Various. *Global Psychedelic Trance Vol. 2.* 1996. CD. Spirit Zone Recordings: SPIRITZONE11.
Various. *Goa Classics 1.* 2010. File. TIP Records: TIPR02.
Various. *Goa-Head Volume 28.* CD. Leguan: DA560502.
Various. *Goa Tribes.* 1996. CD. Masters Of Music: MOM 222.
Various. *Hectic Dialect.* 2009. CD. Adama Records: AD002CD.
Various. *Highoctane: Frenzy Inducing Psychedelic Electronica.* 2003. CD. Procyon Records: PROCYCD002.
Various. *Hippie Killer Collection.* 2007. CD. Hippie Killer Productions: HKPCD02.
Various. *Indigenous S.O.S Benefit Project.* 2010. CD. Random Records: RANDOMCD01.
Various. *Language of Light 2, The.* 1998. CD. Ceiba: CR003.
Various. *Let it Rip.* 1997. Vinyl. Matsuri Productions: MPLP10.
Various. *Life on Earth.* 2011. File. Pureuphoria Records: PEr002.
Various. *Liquid.* 2001. CD. Tribe-adelic Records: TRB001.
Various. *Love–Sound–Devotion.* 2005. CD. Spirit Zone Recordings: SpiritZone152.
Various. *Mechanics of Awakening,* compiled by Nomolos, Zenon, 2011. CD. Zenon Records: zencd025.
Various. *Mind Rewind.* 2011. DAT Mafia Recordings.
Various. *Multiple Personalities.* 2005. CD. Manic Dragon Records: MDREC03.
Various. *Mystery of the Thirteen Crystal Skulls, The.* 2001. CD. TIP.World: TIPWCD16.
Various. *Natural Selection.* 2008. File. Infinity Loop Music: ILMY001.
Various. *Natural Selection v.2.* 2010. MP3, Comp. Infinity Loop Music: ILMY001.
Various. *Nervous Disorder.* 2010. CD. Psymoon Records: PSMREC016.
Various. *Notes from the Asylum.* 2010. File. Mental Records: none.
Various. *Nu-Clear Visions of Israel.* 2003. CD. TIP.World: TIPWCD028.

Various. *Order Odonata Vol. 1.* 1994. CD. Dragonfly Records: BFLCD 13.
Various. *Order Odonata 4.* 2000. CD. Dragonfly Records: BFLCD37.
Various. *Over the Sunrise.* 1998. CD. Over The Sunrise: OTSCD1.
Various. *Primitive Dawn – Trance Journey Vol. 1.* 1999. CD. Green Ant: GACD001.
Various. *Project Eleusis: The Bible of Psychedelics.* 2006. CD. Dropout Productions: DPCD105.
Various. *Project II Trance.* 1993. CD. Dragonfly Records: bflcd4.
Various. *Psy-Harmonics Volume One.* 1994. CD. Psy-Harmonics: PSY009.
Various. *Psy-Harmonics Vol. 2: Dancing to the Sound of the Sun.* 1995. CD. Psy-Harmonics: PSY015.
Various. *Psy-Harmonics Vol. 3 – Hacking the Reality Myth.* 1996. CD. Psy-Harmonics: PSY0331996.
Various. *Pure 2 – Witness the Revolution.* 2011. File. Erratica Music: EMC07.
Various. *Raja Ram Presents the Evolution of Expanded Consciousness.* 2006. CD. TIP.World: TIPWCD48.
Various. *Secret of the Thirteen Crystal Skulls, The.* 2003. CD. TIP.World: TIPWCD26.
Various. *Shiva Space Technology.* 1997. CD. Shiva Space Technology: CD001.
Various. *Signs of Life.* CD. Blue Room Released: BR036CD.
Various. *Source.* 2004. CD. Tribe-adelic Records: TRB005.
Various. *Speed Demons Vol. 1 Censorship is Uncool.* 2008. CD. Red Magik Records: REDMR969.
Various. *Spherical.* 2008. File. Groove Control Records: GCCD004.
Various. *Spirits of Independence.* 1995. Krembo Records: none.
Various. *Strong Sun Moon.* 1998. CD. Equinox: EQCD0506.
Various. *Technical Use of Sound in Magick, The.* 1996. CD. Dragonfly Records: BFLCD19.
Various. *Ten Reasons to Eat Dust* (compiled by Umbra). 2010. CD. 5th Element Records: 5thcd005.
Various. *Tibet, A Culture in Danger.* 2007. CD, Comp. Space Tepee Music: CDST012.
Various. *Tour de Trance.* 2008. CD. Spiral Trax: SPITCD026.
Various. *Trance Mix.* 1993. CD. BMI: 7001.
Various. *Trans Nova Express.* 1994. CD. Phonokol: 2005-2.
Various. *Transition.* 2011. CD. BMSS Records: BMSS004CD.
Various. *Trip to Cyberspace (vol 2).* 1998. CD. Clubware: CW0082.
Various. *Trust in Trance Vol 1.* 1994. CD. Outmosphere: OUTMOS CD 001.
Various. *Trust in Trance Vol. 2.* 1995. CD. Outmosphere Records: UTMOSCD002.
Various. *Universo Paralello.* 2008. CD. Vagalume Records: VGLCD005.
Various. *Virtual Reality.* 1993. CD. Coloured Vision Plasma Records: RTD36410063.
Various. *The Void – Disintegration.* 2008. CD. Dark Prisma Records: DPRCD003.
Various. *World of Spirit Plants, The.* 2009. CD. Free-Spirit Records: FSRCD08.
Various. *Yellow Compilation.* 1994. LP, Vinyl. TIP Records: TIPLP1.
Wizack Twizack. 2010. *Space No More.* CD. AntiShanti Records: ASHRCD002.
Wombatmusic. 2007. *Shameful Silence.* CD. Chill Tribe Records: CTRCD04.
X-Dream. 1993. *The 5th Dimension* EP. Vinyl. Tunnel Records: TR006.
X-Dream. 1993. *Trip to Trancesylvania.* CD. Tunnel Records: TR1010.
X-Dream. 1996. *Panic in Paradise / Relax Vortex.* Vinyl, 12-inch. TIP Records: TIP 015.
Xamanist. 2009. *Initiation.* CD. Ektoplazm: EKTLP02.
Xenomorph. 1997. *Obscure Spectre.* CD, Single. Koyote: kr013scd.
Xenomorph. 1998. *Cassandra's Nightmare.* CD. Koyote: KRCD007.
Xenomorph. 2003. *Qlippoth.* CD. Gnostic Records: Gno001.
Xenomorph. 2007. *Demagoguery of the Obscurants.* CD. Gnostic Records: Gno002.
Xerox & Illumination – Temporary Insanity. 2004. CD. HOM-Mega Productions: HMCD35VP022.
Zen Mechanics. 2008. *Holy Cities.* CD. Neurobiotic Records: NBRCD022.
Zodiacyouth. 1991. *Fast Forward the Future.* Vinyl. Warner Music UK Ltd: SAM850.

Filmography

Antaris Project and Psynema. 2009. *Antaris Project.*
Bahr, Fax, George Hickenlooper and Eleanor Coppola. *Hearts of Darkness: A Filmmaker's Apocalypse*. 1991. USA: American Zoetrope.
The Beyond Within: The Rise and Fall of LSD. 1987. BBC.
Boyle, Danny. 2000. *The Beach*. Figment Films.
Boyle, Danny. 2010. *127 Hours*. Cloud Eight Films.
Carpenter, John. 1994. *In the Mouth of Madness*. New Line Cinema.
Cohn, Fred. 1973. *Sunseed.* New Age Productions.
Devas, Darius. 2010a. Steve "Madras" Devas. A segment of the SBS multimedia documentary *Goa Hippy Tribe* filmed and directed by Darius Devas on Anjuna Beach, Goa, January 2010. http://www.facebook.com/video/video.php?v=10150163765975322 (accessed 10 March 2011).
Devas, Darius. 2010b. "Vidal". A segment of the SBS multimedia documentary *Goa Hippy Tribe* filmed and directed by Darius Devas on Anjuna Beach, Goa, January 2010. http://www.facebook.com/goahippytribe.
Gil-vision. 2007. Video shot by Gil at a party in Mexico in 2007. http://www.youtube.com/watch?v=Up7zNiERZR8&feature=player_embedded.
Kitchell, Mark. 1990. *Berkeley in the Sixties.* Kitchell Films.
Kubrick, Stanley. 1968. *2001: A Space Odyssey*. MGM.
Lastlight Films. 2003. *The Outback Eclipse Story.*
Liquid Crystal Vision. 2007. *Templayed.*
Linklater, Richard. 2001. *Waking Life*. Fox Searchlight.
Lynch, David. 1984. *Dune.* De Laurentiis.
Mahrer, Michelle and Nicole Ma. 2004. *Dances of Ecstasy.*
Mann, Rod. 2007. *Entheogen: Awakening the Divine Within*. Critical Mass Productions.
Robbin, Marcus. 2002. *Last Hippie Standing*. Tangiji Film.
Rood, Billy and Torsten Klimmer. 2002. *Liquid Crystal Vision*. US. [DVD].
Sextro, Maren and Holger Wick. 2008. *We Call it Techno! A Documentary about Germany's Early Techno Scene and Culture.*
Shamir, Yoav. 2007. *Flipping Out: Israel's Drug Generation*. Topia Communications.
Short, James. 2006. *Welcome to Wonderland.* Short Films.
Spielberg, Steven. 1977. *Close Encounters of the Third Kind.* Columbia.
Time Wave Zero. 2006. *Goa Gil: The Godfather of Goa Trance.* http://video.google.com/videoplay?docid=-1339500396225064783#.
Wachowski, Andy and Lana Wachowski. 1999. *The Matrix.* Warner Bros.
Zemeckis, Robert. 1997. *Contact.* Warner Bros.

Index

www.ingramcontent.com/pod-product-compliance
Lightning Source LLC
Chambersburg PA
CBHW060959280326
41935CB00009B/762

* 9 7 8 1 8 4 5 5 3 9 5 6 6 *